Additional Praise for *Christianity Is Not Great*

"*Christianity Is Not Great* shows that Christianity, even at its best, has severe problems and a sorry history that must be honestly addressed. At its worst, it is a threat to this republic, and to the health and safety of future human inhabitants of this planet."

—ABBY HAFER, senior lecturer in biology, Curry College

"Rich food for thought, not only for evangelical apologists and conservative believers, but also for those for whom faith is failing or has already failed."

—GRAHAM OPPY, professor of philosophy,
Monash University, author of *Arguing about Gods*

"Loftus's latest is a compendium of the world's most iconic freethinkers and science writers at their finest. This may very well be his most celebrated work—which is saying a great deal indeed."

—DAVID MILLS, author of *Atheist Universe*

"'By their fruits shall ye know them.' So says the Good Book. This good book, brought together by the indefatigable John Loftus, assays the fruits of Christianity, from ancient times to the present day, and documents persuasively how they are the produce of a poisonous tree. Christian apologists are quick to credit Christianity for the march of science, morality, democracy, and human rights, but the cold light of historical facts and present realities, marshaled in these pages, suggests otherwise. Overall, this fantastic collection makes a good case for religion in general being an artifact of the childhood of civilization—and a childish thing that we would do very well to put away."

—REBECCA BRADLEY,
author of *The Lateral Truth* on the Skeptic Ink Network

Published 2014 by Prometheus Books

Cover design by Nicole Sommer-Lecht

Inquiries should be addressed to
Prometheus Books
59 John Glenn Drive
Amherst, New York 14228
VOICE: 716–691–0133 • FAX: 716–691–0137
WWW.PROMETHEUSBOOKS.COM

18 17 16 15 14   5 4 3 2 1

Library of Congress Cataloging-in-Publication Data

Christianity is not great: how faith fails / edited by John W. Loftus.
        pages cm
    Includes bibliographical references and index.
    ISBN 978-1-61614-956-7 (pbk.)—ISBN 978-1-61614-957-4 (ebook)
    1. Christianity—Controversial literature. I. Loftus, John W., editor.

BL2710.C47 2014
230—dc23

                                                                2014015841

Printed in the United States of America

CHRISTIANITY IS NOT GREAT

How Faith Fails

EDITED BY

JOHN W. LOFTUS

Foreword by Hector Avalos

Prometheus Books

59 John Glenn Drive
Amherst, New York 14228

CHRISTIANITY IS NOT GREAT

Dedicated to the memory of
Christopher Hitchens (1949–2011),
journalist, author, polemicist, debater, and the quintessential curmudgeon. Hitchens
was a person of candor and integrity, who thought false claims
of any sort were not entitled to immunity from criticism.
The essays in this book reflect his commitment to
unsparing examination of religious beliefs.

"One must state it plainly. Religion comes from the period of human prehistory where nobody had the smallest idea what was going on. It comes from the bawling and fearful infancy of our species, and is a babyish attempt to meet our inescapable demand for knowledge."

—Christopher Hitchens

CONTENTS

Foreword
Hector Avalos   13

Introduction   15

1. Religious Violence and the Harms of Christianity
   John W. Loftus   21

Part One: How Faith Fails

2. The Failure of the Church and the Triumph of Reason
   Robert G. Ingersoll   43

3. The Folly of Faith: The Incompatibility
   of Science and Christianity
   Victor J. Stenger   57

4. Faith, Epistemology, and Answering
   Socrates' Question by Translation
   Peter Boghossian   75

Part Two: Political/Institutional Harms

5. Love Your Enemy, Kill Your Enemy: Crusades, Inquisitions,
   and Centuries of Christian Violence
   David Eller   87

6. Thou Shalt Not Suffer a Witch to Live:
   The Wicked Christian Witch Hunts
   John W. Loftus   108

7. They Will Make Good Slaves and Christians: Christianity,
   Colonialism, and the Destruction of Indigenous People
   David Eller   133

8. The Slave Is the Owner's Property: Christianity and the
   Savagery of Slavery
   John W. Loftus   158

9. Christianity and the Rise of American Democracy
   Richard Carrier   180

Part Three: Scientific Harms

10. The Dark Ages
    Richard Carrier   209

11. The Christian Abuse of the Sanctity of Life
    Ronald A. Lindsay   222

12. The Gender Binary and LGBTI People:
    Religious Myth and Medical Malpractice
    Veronica Drantz   242

13. Christianity Can Be Hazardous to Your Health
    Harriet Hall, MD   264

14. Christianity and the Environment
    William R. Patterson   286

15. Doth God Take Care for Oxen?:
    Christianity's Acrimony against Animals
    John W. Loftus   303

Part Four: Social and Moral Harms

16. The Christian Right and the Culture Wars
    Ed Brayton   323

17. Woman, What Have I to Do with Thee?:
    Christianity's War against Women
        Annie Laurie Gaylor   343

18. Secular Sexuality: A Direct Challenge to Christianity
        Darrel W. Ray   360

19. The Crazy-Making in Christianity:
    A Look at Real Psychological Harm
        Marlene Winell and Valerie Tarico   376

20. Abusive Pastors and Churches
        Nathan Phelps   402

Part Five: Morality, Atheism, and a Good Life

21. "Tu Quoque, Atheism?"—Our Right to Judge
        Jonathan MS Pearce   421

22. Only Humans Can Solve the Problems of the World
        James A. Lindsay   445

23. Living without God
        Russell Blackford   462

Notes   485

About the Contributors   551

FOREWORD

Anthologies are not easy to organize. Contributors have to be recruited, and they may not all be available at the time you need them. Scholars have to respect you enough as an editor to join your project if they are available.

Over the past few years, John Loftus has demonstrated his ability to recruit the best scholars and scientists to his anthologies, including *The Christian Delusion: Why Faith Fails* (2010) and *The End of Christianity* (2011), both published by Prometheus Books.

The present anthology, *Christianity Is Not Great*, is no exception. Scholars representing fields as varied as physics and anthropology are here. Unfortunately, illness and previous commitments kept me from contributing to this one. One reason I have contributed in the past is that he will allow me, as a scholar, to be as technical and as detailed as I need to be to make my arguments.

Consequently, these anthologies are some of the most substantive collections of rebuttals to theistic arguments, and specifically to Christian theistic arguments, in existence. They signal a new era insofar as atheists are organizing coherent and scholarly responses that are wide-ranging in scope, instead of just focusing on a few traditional issues (e.g., philosophical arguments against theism or creationism). These anthologies touch on, among many subjects, history, sociology, psychology, and biblical studies.

Christianity Is Not Great swiftly demolishes one of the greatest and subtlest myths promoted by believers. The demolished myth is that Christianity, even if it cannot be proved to be true, has at least been good for the world. It has supposedly freed slaves and fostered science.

On the contrary, *Christianity Is Not Great* shows that Christianity has been bad for the world precisely because its ungrounded beliefs interfere with a realistic view of our world. Unrealistic views of the world cause unnecessary pain and suffering, and those views should be rejected. Furthermore, it is simply not true that Christianity deserves credit for freeing slaves, fostering science, and other positive developments that believers usually ascribe to this religion.

Aside from the wonderful contributions, this volume is an indirect tribute to Loftus himself. John Loftus is an indefatigable laborer for atheism. He represents one of those voices who still has not received the honor he deserves. Yet few modern atheists have provided as much useful service to educating the masses about atheism as he has done.

Just think of all he does. He manages a biblioblog. He organizes anthologies. He writes his own books. He speaks around the country. He works hard to remain current about religious issues, and he is generally well read. And he does it all while holding a regular job. Yes, indefatigable would be what he is.

Each of those activities on behalf of atheism is serious and substantial in both scope and quality. For example, he presides over a biblioblog, *Debunking Christianity*, that is consistently ranked at or near the top in a world where most biblioblogs are managed by people with religious affiliations. Yet this blog has become a major showcase for some of the best atheist scholarship today.

Christianity Is Not Great reflects the comprehensive and substantive manner in which Loftus aims to promote atheism. He knows that you cannot just say that Christianity is flawed, or that religion is flawed. You have to engage in the laborious scholarship that shows that to be the case.

His past anthologies have addressed the problems and flaws in Christianity's arguments. This volume, while not neglecting those problems and flaws, concentrates on how Christianity harms some of our basic human institutions, such as politics, science, and our moral system.

The anthologies John Loftus organizes show the vitality and comprehensive intellectual approach to atheism as a way of life. That comprehensive critique of religion, and defense of the atheist worldview, is one of the hallmarks of what is called the New Atheism.

Christianity Is Not Great is summarized by its very title and substantiated by the excellent collection of essays within. And it owes its existence to the indefatigable John Loftus.

—Dr. Hector Avalos,
Professor of Religious Studies,
Iowa State University

INTRODUCTION

Like Christopher Hitchens's *God Is Not Great: How Religion Poisons Everything*, this anthology addresses the harms of Christian faith that best explain why atheists argue against it. It contains new substantive essays written by superior authors on many of the most important issues relevant to this theme. I am honored and very grateful to have such well-qualified authors agree to write chapters for it, as with the previous ones I've produced, which, like this one, used titles that were inspired by the works of other so-called New Atheists. Together with other contributors I edited *The Christian Delusion: Why Faith Fails*, titled after Richard Dawkins's *The God Delusion*, and another one, *The End of Christianity*, titled after Sam Harris's *The End of Faith*.

To include separate chapters on all the important issues relating to the theme of this book would have made it encyclopedic. So I have written the first chapter, which by itself covers seven of these issues. In it I answer such questions as:

Is religious violence worse than other kinds of violence?
Is Christianity beneficial or harmful to society?
Does Christianity cause more harm than good overall?

The last question is "What does this book attempt to show?" In answer I argue that the Christian faith "can be empirically tested by the amount of harm it has done and continues to do in our world. Jesus reportedly said, 'By their fruits ye shall know them' (Matthew 7:20). When we evaluate the fruits of Christianity the result is that it fails miserably."

This book is divided into five parts. I've placed each chapter under the heading that best suits it, although many of them are related in some way to other headings, and in a few cases they overlap each other. In part 1, "How Faith Fails," the authors cut to the chase at the outset by arguing that faith has not, and does not, help us. Faith, as a method, is notoriously unreliable, especially when compared to reason and science. That's why the Christian faith causes so much harm. For chapter 2 I've chosen to reproduce what Robert Ingersoll said at a Thanksgiving Day lecture. As America's "Great Agnostic" of the nineteenth century, he asked over and over what the church has done in comparison to what the worldly have done to make our world a better place. This selected piece is a classic, recounting the failures of the Christian church down through the centuries and the triumph of reason. He asks ,"Who are we to thank?" The answer is obvious. In chapter 3, Victor Stenger adds to Ingersoll's case from a modern perspective while arguing that "science and religion are fundamentally incompatible because of their unequivocally opposed epistemologies." For detractors who don't think religious faith is an epistemology, in chapter 4 Peter Boghossian argues both that it is, and that it "assigns a higher confidence value to a belief than is warranted by the evidence." Setting the stage for the rest of the chapters to follow, Boghossian rhetorically asks whether people should live their lives based on faith.

In part 2, "Political/Institutional Harms," the authors focus on the harms that Christian faith caused when it had absolute political power to enforce its agenda. Horrendous violence has been done by the church and justified by Christianity on massive numbers of helpless victims. Consider the chapters in this part to be historical lessons in the dangers of faith. Not only is faith a notoriously unreliable method for gaining knowledge about the universe, but it can destroy lives and the values of a free democratic society. These lessons are relevant for seeing faith for what it can do. Reading David Eller's chapters 5 and 7, on the Crusades, the Inquisition, and the destruction of indigenous people, should horrify us all. I'll bet that most Christians don't know the story of how Christianity colonized and evangelized large parts of the world. My two chapters in this part (chapters 6 and 8) shine a spotlight on the horrific Christian witch hunts as well as on the issue of slavery. These chapters, taken together, represent a full frontal attack on Christianity itself, not just on the church of the past. In chapter 9 Richard Carrier closes this part of the book by showing that Christianity was not responsible for the origins of American democracy, as many Christians argue. In fact, if we take the Bible seriously, we are forced to conclude that it is against freedom of expression, freedom of religion, and civil rights for all, something the other chapters in this part argue for at length.

In part 3, "Scientific Harms," the authors focus on the harms that Christianity causes when valuing faith above reason and science. In chapter 10

Richard Carrier argues that, contrary to all denials, the period between the fifth and the tenth century CE is best described as the Dark Ages, a period during which "almost all the best values, technologies, knowledge, and achievements of the Greco-Roman era were forgotten or abandoned, and had to be relearned and reinvented all over again many centuries later." He goes on to argue that it was a slow crawl out of it for the next five centuries and that Christians, and Christianity, were to blame. Ronald Lindsay argues in chapter 11 that the sanctity-of-life principle, as traditionally interpreted by Christians, becomes problematic "if considered a moral absolute." He concludes that "life is too valuable to be left in the hands of the theologians." Veronica Drantz in chapter 12 refutes the "binary view of sexuality," which holds that "there are only two sexes (male, female), that sex and gender are the same (female = woman, male = man), and that there is only one kind of sexual attraction (heterosexual)." She goes on to highlight the "medical atrocities imposed on gay people in an attempt to make them straight." I consider her contribution to this anthology to be the most powerful chapter on the subject. In chapter 13 Harriet Hall argues that there is "no credible evidence from scientific studies that religion improves health, but there is clear evidence that it can harm." After citing numerous cases, she concludes, "Christianity has done (and is still doing) more harm than good to individual and public health because of religious beliefs that are based on faith, not reality." In chapter 14 William Patterson argues that human-caused climate change "represents one of the greatest challenges currently faced by human beings." He effectively refutes antiscience global-warming deniers. He shows us how Christians in America, especially evangelicals, who form a powerful voting bloc, along with certain Christians in Congress, have so far successfully "impeded an effective response to this global problem." I close this part of the book by demonstrating how Christians in the Western world have, at best, not cared much about animals, and, at worst, perpetrated a great deal of needless abuse on them. I argue that this is due to the Bible's almost total lack of concern for animals and animal rights.

In part 4, "Social/Moral Harms," the authors focus on some important issues that highlight the harms Christian faith causes to our culture and to individuals within it. In chapter 16 Ed Brayton argues against the Christian right in America, contending that "conservative Christianity has been the primary impediment to social progress in the United States from its very origins." The chapter by Annie Laurie Gaylor, who has been on the forefront of arguing for the equal status of women, has a subtitle that says it all: "Christianity's War against Women." It's one of the best chapters on the subject I've read. Darrel Ray, in the anthology's eighteenth chapter, asks the reader to "Imagine no religion—in your sex life." It's a wonderful question! He first argues against the shame and guilt that Christianity produces, which results in us denying who we are as sexual beings. Then he makes a sustained case that liberating our sex lives from religion means that questions about sex should "center on the idea of consenting adults." In chapter 19 Marlene Winell and Valerie Tarico argue, in a pioneering work, for something called *Religious Trauma Syndrome* (a term coined by Winell). It's a name given to "a recognizable set of symptoms experienced as a result of prolonged exposure to a toxic religious environment and/or the trauma of leaving the religion." Winell and Tarico argue that Christian beliefs and Christian living, especially of the conservative kind, can trap people "in a cycle of self-doubt, self-criticism, and self-punishment that can drive vulnerable children and adults to mental illness or suicide." They also show us how former believers can reclaim their lives and health. Nathan Phelps closes this part of the book by providing some clear examples of what Winell and Tarico have argued. Recounting the Catholic Church's child-molestation scandals and their subsequent cover-ups, Phelps concludes there is no justification for the continued existence of that church. As the son of Fred Phelps, the excommunicated and deceased pastor of the Westboro Baptist—"God Hates Fags"—Church, Nathan has an inside scoop on what Religious Trauma Syndrome is all about, and he argues that his father's church is not the exception.

In part 5, "Morality, Atheism, and a Good Life," the authors close this anthology by dealing with three of the most common Christian objections to our case. In chapter 21 Jonathan Pearce effectively counters the objection that, as atheists, we don't have a right to judge the harms of Christianity because we supposedly don't have an objective moral standard to do so. However, we do indeed have that right, if for no other reason than that other Christians acknowledge the same harms we do. Furthermore, all of the various ethical theories used to justify actions also judge the things we consider to be harmful about Christianity. Pearce goes farther by arguing that morality presupposes atheism, something you just have to read to appreciate! In chapter 22 James

Lindsay counters the objection that we need God to solve the problems of this world. He shows why there aren't any good reasons to think God exists, though there are plenty of strong reasons to think he/she/it does not. So he argues that Christianity cannot solve the problems we face. This leads to secular humanism's conclusion that "only we, humans, can solve the problems of the world." Russell Blackford, in this anthology's twenty-third and final chapter, counters the objection that atheists cannot live a good life without God. If you want to know how atheists can live moral, meaningful, purposeful lives without a comprehensive worldview or religious belief system, then this is essential reading. What I found very interesting is that Blackford's chapter can be agreed upon by both cultural relativists and atheists who argue that science can provide us with some ethical content.

Finally, I want to thank Richard Carrier, Russell Blackford, Valerie Tarico, Ronald Lindsay, and Annie Laurie Gaylor for their valuable help on this book.

—John W. Loftus

1

RELIGIOUS VIOLENCE AND THE HARMS OF CHRISTIANITY

John W. Loftus

Even in as big a book as this one is, we could not have chapters on all the harms of Christianity. Nor could we include chapters on many of the other relevant issues having to do with the topic of this book. So in what follows I'll briefly address seven of these important issues. I'll do so by using a question-and-answer format leading up to the biggest question readers of this book will want answered: What do we hope to show by publishing it?

(1) What is it about religion that instigates violence like nothing else?

Jack David Eller has created what I consider essential reading when it comes to religion and violence in his book *Cruel Creeds, Virtuous Violence: Religious Violence across Culture and History*.[1] He presents six levels (or degrees) of violent-prone conditions that make it increasingly possible for human beings to commit acts of violence against others, irrespective of religion. They are all described with words that begin with the capital letter *I*. The first level is one's individual nature or *Instincts*. At this level human beings are prone to violence, just like the animal predecessors we evolved from. Much of nature is red in tooth and claw. Human beings are a mixture of both violent and nonviolent behavior, depending on our nature and environment. The second level is *Integration* into groups. "If humans have violent potential as individuals, that potential is multiplied in groups. . . . Groups seem to have their own dynamics, which increases violence exponentially."[2] The third level is our *Identity* as members of a particular group. Membership has its privileges, and with it comes the responsibility to support and defend the group, especially by keeping insiders in and outsiders out. The fourth level is *Institutions*. Says Eller: "What is important about institutions is that they embody the beliefs and values of the group or society and that they regularize the behavior of members of the group or society."[3] The fifth level is *Interests*, which sums up Eller's first five levels like this: "Individually, humans have a capacity for violence. Groups unleash or exacerbate that capacity, and institutions regularize and legitimize it. But interests are what largely motivate it. . . . At any rate when interests enter the picture, the cleavages between groups become more concrete and sometimes more intractable. The out-group is not just different, not just strange, but now 'in our way.'"[4] The sixth level is *Ideology*, which is "simply the 'contents' of a worldview or belief system, the ideas and beliefs and values shared by a group or movement."[5] "Certain kinds of ideologies," Eller writes, "are more prone to violence than others."[6] Those that allow people to think of themselves as being under threat, or to see the world as a battleground, or to desire a perfect world devoid of any trace of evil can instill violence.

Eller argues that these six independent conditions for violence against the out-group "converge on a single point." Increasingly they provide the grounds for the lack of empathy toward other people. Empathy, or feeling the pain of others, is "a powerful restraint against violence." But when it is not there "one of the most powerful restraints against violence has been withdrawn." And "evidence suggests that a lack of empathy is a highly dangerous thing."[7]

> A person does not have to be a sociopath to feel good about causing harm and suffering—or to feel little or nothing at all about it. Rather what we have discovered is that a human needs only a belief system that teaches that he or she is acting for a good reason (even a "higher cause"), under someone else's authority, as a member of a (threatened) group, in pursuit of interests. Along the way, if the individual can learn, by way of gradual escalation, to commit violence against someone who is worth less—or completely worthless, less than a human being—then violence becomes not only possible but likely, if not certain."[8]

Although political movements can satisfy all six of these conditions, when it comes to religion, or a certain kind of religion, Eller claims that "no other form of human organization and mobilization is so shaped by its ideology."[9] In fact, he argues, "religion may be the ultimate ideology, since its framework is so totally external (i.e., supernaturally ordained or given), its rules and standards so obligatory, its bonds unbreakable, and its legitimization so absolute . . . no other social force observed in human history can meet those conditions as well as religion."[10] Religion, then, "can actually be the *reason* and the *justification* for actions that, without the religion, people would either condemn or would never contemplate in the first place" [Eller's emphasis]. Continuing, Eller says, "In situations of authority, especially 'ultimate' authority like divine command, the normal human empathetic responses that prevent us from perpetrating injury are overridden. Individuals may not even 'want' to commit crimes and abuses, but they are commanded, and religious orders tend to trump individual objections."[11] While Eller candidly admits "not all religions are equally violent, and not all violent ones are violent in identical ways . . . without the religious ideology, some forms of violence and crime would be not only undoable but also unthinkable."[12]

(2) Is religious violence worse than other kinds of violence?

Hector Avalos has also written what I consider essential reading about religious violence, using examples from the three Abrahamic monotheisms—Christianity, Judaism, and Islam. In his book *Fighting Words: The Origins of Religious Violence* he doesn't claim religion is the root of all violence, since people, for religious motives or not, fight over what they consider scarce resources. They fight over many things other than religion, like food, shelter, money, and property. It's just that religion manufactures scarce resources to fight over (such as divine salvation) that are not really scarce, since they don't exist. His thesis is that religions are "prone to violence" because "unlike many non-religious sources of conflict, religious conflict relies solely on resources whose scarcity is wholly manufactured by, or reliant on, unverifiable premises."[13] His argument is this:

(1) Most violence is due to scare resources, real or perceived. Whenever people perceive that there is not enough of something they value, conflict may ensue to maintain or acquire that resource. This can range from love in a family to oil on a global scale.

(2) When religion causes violence, it often does so because it has *created new scarce resources*.[14]

Avalos has discovered from a careful analysis of the fundamental texts of the three Abrahamic religions how four "scarce" resources have figured repeatedly in creating religious violence among them: sacred space (churches, temples, holy cities), the creation of holy scriptures (exclusive revelations), group privilege (chosen people, the predestined select few), and salvation (only our faith saves us). Since there is no verifiable sacred space, or holy scriptures, or group privileges, or exclusive salvation, believers in the three Abrahamic religions have been killing each other for nothing. We fight over everything it seems, but by taking these religions out of the mix we would have fewer things to fight about.

If you want to see Avalos's thesis illustrated in the City of Jerusalem you need only look as far as Simon Sebag Montefiore's book *Jerusalem: The Biography*.[15] One reviewer on Amazon.com wrote of his book:

> The amount of murder, massacre, etc. for 2,000 years is appalling. Religious madness is the theme. Christians murdering Jews and being murdered and both murdering Muslims and being murdered in their turn. WHY? Because Christ was crucified here, Abraham was willing to sacrifice Isaac here, and Mohammed rode a horse with a human face aerially around the city, receiving insights as he went. So the murders and massacres are about the places where religious events are believed to have taken place.[16]

This leads to Avalos's main argument. In his words:

> Although we focus on how scarce resources cause religious violence, an overarching theme of our thesis is that the lack of verifiability in religious belief differentiates ethically the violence attributed to religion from the violence attributed to non-religious factors. This distinction will lead to our main argument, which is that religious violence is always ethically reprehensible, while the same cannot be said of nonreligious violence. . . . We argue that the quality of the scarcity created by religion is fundamentally different: If any acts of violence caused by actual scarcities are judged as immoral, then acts of violence caused by resources that are not actually scare should be judged as even more immoral. We further develop the argument that any

act of violence predicated on the acquisition or loss of a non-existent entity is always immoral and needless because bodily well-being or life is being traded for a nonexistent gain.[17]

Atheist author Greta Christina is a great writer. She has encapsulated for many of us why we argue against the Christian faith in her book *Why Are You Atheists So Angry? 99 Things That Piss Off the Godless*.[18] Maybe *angry* is too strong a word for some of us, but most of us are appalled, disgusted, dismayed, sickened, and even horrified by what we have seen in the world, especially coming from the Christian religious right. In an online essay Christina discusses the problem of religious faith, which amplifies what both Eller and Avalos have argued:

Why is religion special—and specially troubling? What makes religion different from any other ideology, community, system of morality, hypothesis about how the world works? And why does that difference makes it uniquely prone to cause damage?

I'm realizing that everything I've ever written about religion's harm boils down to one thing. It's this: Religion is ultimately dependent on belief in invisible beings, inaudible voices, intangible entities, undetectable forces, and events and judgments that happen after we die.

It therefore has no reality check.

And it is therefore uniquely armored against criticism, questioning, and self- correction. It is uniquely armored against anything that might stop it from spinning into extreme absurdity, extreme denial of reality . . . and extreme, grotesque immorality.

The thing that uniquely defines religion, the thing that sets it apart from every other ideology or hypothesis or social network, is the belief in unverifiable supernatural entities. Of course it has other elements—community, charity, philosophy, inspiration for art, etc. But those things exist in the secular world, too. They're not specific to religion. The thing that uniquely defines religion is belief in supernatural entities. Without that belief, it's not religion.

And with that belief, the capacity for religion to do harm gets cranked up to an alarmingly high level—because there's no reality check.

Any other ideology or philosophy or hypothesis about the world is eventually expected to pony up. It's expected to prove itself true and/or useful, or else correct itself, or else fall by the wayside. With religion, that is emphatically not the case. Because religion is a belief in the invisible and unknowable—and it's therefore never expected to prove that it's right, or even show good evidence for why it's right—its capacity to do harm can spin into the stratosphere.[19]

(3) What other factors lead to religious violence?

Charles Kimball, a liberal Christian scholar, argues in his book *When Religion Becomes Evil* that there are five tendencies within religion that cause evil.[20] First, religion becomes evil whenever it requires uniform assent to rigid, absolute doctrinal truths. In a different context he illustrates this, saying, "I've always been puzzled and saddened by people who make clear that they couldn't be very happy in heaven unless hell was full to overflowing with people who disagree."[21] Second, religion becomes evil when it requires believers to blindly obey the authority of a church or a charismatic leader's teachings. Third, religion becomes evil whenever it attempts to establish the ideal society, a theocracy. Fourth, religion becomes evil whenever it uses any means possible to justify the ends of defending its group identity, institutions, and sacred spaces from outsiders. Fifth, religion becomes evil when it views its wars as holy wars in support of divine causes. Kimball writes that

> more wars have been waged, more people killed, and more evil perpetrated in the name of religion than by any other institutional force in human history. The sad truth continues in our present day. In somewhat different ways, leaders and combatants continue to depict their war as a holy cause. . . . Declaring war "holy" is a sure sign of a corrupt religion.[22]

Retired bishop John Shelby Spong additionally contends in his book *The Sins of Scripture* that "the moment any religious tradition claims certainty, it turns demonic."[23] More specifically, "when certainty combines with zeal in religious matters, horror always results."[24] Spong echoes Kimball, saying:

> Embarrassing as it may be to those of us who call ourselves Christians, the fact is that more people have been killed in the history of the world in con-

flicts over and about religion than over any other single factor. Religion has so often been the source of the cruelest evil. Its darkest and most brutal side becomes visible at the moment when the adherents of any religious system identify their *understanding* of God with God.[25]

Bertrand Russell, probably the premier atheist of the last century, previously wrote about the evils of certainty, saying, "one of the most interesting and harmful delusions to which men and nations can be subjected is that of imagining themselves special instruments of the Divine Will." And he gave some examples: "Cromwell was persuaded that he was the Divinely appointed instrument of justice for suppressing Catholics and malignants. Andrew Jackson was the agent of *Manifest Destiny* in freeing North America from the incubus of Sabbath-breaking Spaniards." Such a political program "assumes a knowledge of the Divine purposes to which no rational man can lay claim, and that in the execution of them it justifies a ruthless cruelty which would be condemned if our program had a merely mundane origin. It is good to know that God is on our side, but a little confusing when you find the enemy equally convinced of the opposite." He concludes, "Most of the greatest evils that man has afflicted upon man have come through people feeling quite certain about something which, in fact, was false."[26]

Peter Boghossian in our own day wrote of the evils of certainty as well, saying, "The moment we're unshakably convinced we possess immutable truth, we become our own enemy. . . . Few things are more dangerous than people who think they're in possession of absolute truth. Honest inquiry with sincere questions and an open mind rarely contribute to the misery of the world."[27]

If nothing else then, in light of Christianity's past and present, Christians should not consider the values they have to be ultimate ones. They shouldn't blindly obey absolute truth claims with the certainty of faith. But most all of them do. They are certain they have the truth, the whole truth, and nothing but the truth. For them it's an oxymoron to have a tentative faith. A tentative faith injects doubt into the believer's prayers to their all-knowing God who desires absolute faith. We're simply much better off without blind obedience to absolute commands made by preachers and bishops who claim certain knowledge of God's will.

(4) Is Christianity beneficial or harmful to society?

To answer this question I'll deal first with the supposed societal benefits of the Christian faith and later with its societal harms. Whatever benefits we think the Christian faith has depend at least in part on which society we're talking about. When it comes to non-Christian societies or cultures, Christianity has proven itself extremely harmful, as several chapters in this book show. That should be the end of the story.

Nonetheless, in Dinesh D'Souza's book *What's So Great about Christianity*,[28] the author argues that Christianity is great because most people in Western culture are Christians, Christianity is growing in the world, and Christianity is unique. Of course, these claims are all true. Tell us something we don't know next time. That doesn't make Christianity great. It only reaffirms that more people in the Western world are Christians, that Christianity is growing, and that it is, in fact, unique. By the same standards Islam meets two of these criteria, making it great, too. And there is nothing about a majority that proves Christianity is true, especially since there is no such thing as Christianity, only Christianities, as David Eller has argued,[29] which are reflected in polls.[30] D'Souza also claims that Christianity is beneficial, although in the process he paints an unbalanced and sometimes ignorantly rosy picture of it, especially when it comes to his claims that it is the basis for morality and the origin of democracy and science.[31] It is not true that Christianity can take credit for all that's good in our society. And it is not true that Christianity causes no serious harms within it either.

Morality and politics are human inventions that have evolved over time. Religions are also human inventions. And they, too, evolve. They are inextricably linked with their given cultures. So it stands to reason that any given religion is at least somewhat beneficial to its particular culture because, as a human invention, it helped to make that culture in the first place. Each religion must therefore be beneficial to its given culture to some degree, otherwise no one would ever embrace it. We would expect this. Just ask Amish people if their religion has social benefits, or Buddhists in Thailand, or Shintoists in Japan, or Muslims in the Middle East and elsewhere. They will all affirm their religion and likely add that their cultures are better than ours, and that this, too, shows that their religions are true. Furthermore, as a given culture evolves so also does its religion, such that the religion of yesterday was beneficial to the culture of yesterday, just as the religion of tomorrow will be beneficial to the culture of tomorrow. So even if many of D'Souza's beneficial arguments are valid ones, they prove nothing more than that a Christian religious culture is beneficial to a Christian religious culture, which is a tautology and therefore trivially true. What we wouldn't expect is for a religion to cause as much harm as Christianity does, which is the major point of this book.

The fact is that several non-Christian cultures were great by the standards of their day, and even by our current standards to some degree, most notably the cultures of ancient Greece during the golden age, the Roman Empire in its early stages, several of the dynasties in ancient China, and the Empire of Islam under Muhammad—none of which were Christian ones. So there is no evidence we even need Christianity to have a good society. Even largely atheist societies have been shown to be good ones by Phil Zuckerman.[32] Therefore, if having a good society proves the dominant religious or non-religious viewpoint is true, then atheism is true by that same standard.

D'Souza and others will go on to tell us Christianity is great because it was the main motivator in starting most early American universities, most of our hospitals, and most food kitchens. But these things would have been started anyway, if for no reason other than necessity. Other non-Christian cultures have them. It just happened that Christianity has been the dominant religion in America for several centuries, that's all. Besides, these things were started by Christians who were motivated to some degree by the desire to convert people. After all, who are most vulnerable to the Christian message? They are the sick (hospitals), the poor (food kitchens), and young people leaving home for the first time to enter colleges or universities, which were mostly started to train preachers.

Turning next to the societal harms of Christian faith, it depends this time on which type of Christianity we're talking about. The more that Christians embrace reason and science, the less they cause harm. The less that Christians embrace reason and science, the more they cause harm. I very much doubt, for instance, that the Christianity embraced by John Shelby Spong would cause much harm. He has argued in a number of books against conservative evangelicalism. In his book *The Sins of Scripture* he agrees with many of the conclusions drawn by the authors in the present anthology. In *The Sins of Scripture* he embraces environmental concerns and homosexuality while condemning both sexism and anti-Semitism. However, when it comes to the fundamentalist, conservative, or evangelical wing of Christianity, one anonymous person said it this way:

> Not only is fundamentalist Christianity the greatest threat in the United States to science, tolerance, and social progress, but it is also the most prevalent form of Protestant Christianity to be found in our nation, whether you like it or not. It is the fundamentalist religious right that holds the reigns of the Republican Party (which currently controls the nation, in case you didn't realize), and it is this same fundamentalist religious right that lobbies for the teaching of lies in public school and fights against funding for embryonic research that could potentially save the lives of millions. Whether you like it or not, it is this flavor of Christianity that makes the loudest, most obnoxious, most dangerous impact on the world today, giving us plenty of good reason to direct the brunt of our attacks in its vicinity.[33]

When it comes to the political, scientific, social, and moral spheres, the ones we focus on in this book, Christianity—especially the conservative or evangelical type—has caused and still causes a great deal of harm. To the degree that various kinds of Christianities have done good in the political, scientific, social, and moral spheres, it is not because of believers' faith. Instead, the good done has followed from reasoning about how to solve real human problems and service real human needs. And while their faith might have motivated them to do good in these spheres, good intentions of Christians are simply not enough, as the chapters in this anthology show. Even with the best of intentions, there are always some bad unintended consequences that result when starting with harmful beliefs and attitudes.

(5) Is Christianity beneficial or harmful to individual believers?

As before, the individual benefits or harms of Christian faith depend on the type of Christianity we're talking about. They also depend, at least in part, on the particular culture Christians live in. Christians living inside a Christian culture will find more benefits from believing than those who live in a Muslim or Hindu culture, and vice versa.

Within a Christian religious culture the Christian faith does indeed benefit individual believers. There is no doubt in my mind about this, having been a former preacher. When Christians have faith in their God they find hope, encouragement, strength, and confidence to meet the challenges of their lives in a community of like-minded believers. I've seen Christians with faith overcome insurmountable obstacles, in part because of the support of their Christian communities. They will ask for prayers for financial assistance, and then a Christian within the community, or their church as a whole, subsequently provides them the needed help. Even apart from their Christian communities, faith helps individual Christians as well. Faith helps Christians because faith is just like a placebo prescribed by a doctor, the intent of which is to deceive patients into thinking it will solve their ills. Doctors will prescribe these sugar pills if they conclude the ills are psychosomatic ones. If patients believe the prescribed pills will heal them, then they do. The healing is therefore self-caused. Faith helps people through the difficulties of life just like a placebo helps in the healing of people with psychosomatic illnesses.[34]

So what can be harmful about this? There are several things. Let me just mention three of them. First, faith is just a placebo. It helps believers only by providing them with a false hope, a false comfort, and a self-induced illusionary strength to live their lives. It provides them with an artificial and unnecessary motivation to do good to their neighbors, providing they are actually doing good deeds. Since faith in a placebo heals believers rather than the placebo itself, the object of one's faith doesn't do any healing. So any placebo will do. If the doctor prescribed eating unleavened bread, or a certain diet, or drinking a small cup of wine, or not eating fish on Friday, it would work just as well. It could be wearing a certain type of hat, magic underwear, or a medallion or moonstone hung around one's neck. It could be performing different kinds of rituals, like genuflecting, lighting candles, or kissing statues. It could be praying with a rosary in hand, or facing toward Mecca five times a day, or in front of the Wailing Wall in Jerusalem. It could be almost anything.

The problem is that we cannot easily separate individual benefits and harms from societal ones, since what causes individual harm also causes societal harm to some degree, and vice versa. So because believers mistakenly perceive their placebos as having been helpful, they will take the perceived healing effects of their placebos as evidence that their particular religious faith is the one true cure for what ails people. And they will act accordingly in various ways, like donating to their religious causes, and voting for politicians who will support them locally and globally with potentially dire consequences for society and the world at large.

This leads to a second reason why faith can be harmful. A misdiagnosis where the placebo of faith is prescribed rather than the correct drug prescription or a needed surgery can kill people. Since having faith in faith is living one's life in a make-believe fantasy world divorced from reality, it can lead to dangerous consequences. This is the force of Harriet Hall's chapter in this book, along with other chapters that use issues other than health. Faith doesn't help to heal us when there are real physical illnesses. Faith cannot cause a loved one to come back from the dead, nor can it heal an amputee. Faith is completely ineffectual when it comes to physical problems unrelated to mental activity alone. Faith all by itself is therefore ineffectual, irrelevant, unnecessary, and can be dangerous to human flourishing. Furthermore, so long as believers think faith actually does something to help them, they remain vulnerable to any absurd possibility, scam artist, or TV preacher. It will also cause people of faith to deny or discredit science to that same degree. It can be dangerous whenever believers opt out of reality in favor of faith in faith.

Take for instance the 1995 movie *Toy Story*, produced by Pixar Animation Studios. The storyline follows a group of children's toys who pretend to be lifeless when humans are present but come to life whenever they are absent. The relationship between Woody, a pull-string cowboy doll (with the voice of Tom Hanks) and Buzz Lightyear, an astronaut action figure (with the voice of Tim Allen), was the focus. At the beginning of the movie Buzz Lightyear had the utmost confidence that he could fly and had the power to do most anything. Then Woody told him he couldn't fly, that he was merely bouncing off things into the air. Recognizing the truth, Buzz Lightyear became depressed and even refused to help in a crisis because of it. But after he embraced the truth he learned he could still do something, and he eventually helped save the day. He learned how to live life without believing in his nonexistent magical powers.

After watching that movie I thought about it quite a bit because I was questioning my faith at the time. Was Buzz Lightyear better off for knowing the truth, or was he better off before? Did the truth help him? In a like manner, would I prefer to remain blissfully ignorant or to know the truth and learn how to live without faith in a nonexistent magical, all-powerful, perfectly good God? The answer was clear. Buzz Lightyear could have been killed by thinking he could fly. He could have failed to bounce off the right spoon, instead falling to his death. So I, too, chose to live my life based on reality. Living a reality-based life, rather than a fantasy-based life, is what reasonable people should do. Choosing not to do so is irrational and can get us and others killed.

A third reason why one's faith can be harmful is that faith is of no help to us in arriving at truth. Faith stunts one's intellectual growth. Faith forever produces immature people. We must learn instead how to think exclusively in terms of the probabilities based on the available evidence. Faith doesn't add to the probabilities, so faith should be rejected by all reasonable, thinking, emotionally healthy adults,[35] including Christians like Charles Kimball and John Shelby Spong. Human beings have a very strong tendency to believe what we prefer to believe. We seek out confirming evidence rather than disconfirming evidence. That's why reasonable people must instead seek evidence, disconfirming evidence, sufficient objective evidence for what we think. We must learn to question everything if we want to know that which is true, as Guy Harrison has argued.[36]

In order to combat this faith-based mentality Peter Boghossian is trying to change how we view faith. He defines faith as "pretending to know things you don't know." He says that when we hear the word *faith* we should think of that definition. Why? Because that's what believers are doing. They're playing a childish but also potentially dangerous game of make believe without sufficient evidence, and they are in denial by arguing the evidence is sufficient to believe. So Boghossian talks in terms of the medical and/or psychological professions. Believers are infected with a faith virus. The believer is the host of this virus. And we are in the midst of a faith-virus pandemic. Boghossian says: "The pretending-to-know-things-you-don't-know pandemic hurts us all. Believing things on the basis of something other than evidence and reason causes people to misconstrue what's good for them and for their communities."[37]

All reasonable, thinking, emotionally healthy adults should acknowledge that we alone are responsible for our lives. Christians should trust in their own abilities rather than their religious faith. Many of us do just fine without faith in magical, invisible, supernatural beings and/or forces to help us, and in many cases we do much better without it.

Having said all this, I admit that many people are incapable of trusting in their own abilities due to poor upbringing, a series of failures in life, or a catastrophic event that took place. Such things as these have crippled them with self-doubt. They may need the placebo of faith just like patients may need the placebos prescribed by their doctors. But the question of whether people can handle life without the placebo of religious faith is purely an academic one. For if they are unable or unwilling to do this, it doesn't change the facts. Religious faith is still a placebo. It's a problem we need to overcome, not a problem we should ever embrace. Why would any physician or psychiatrist not want to wean patients off placebos? Those of us who argue against faith should continue doing what we're doing and let religious people decide for themselves. Our arguments can be seen as administering small dosages of reality to people of faith. This present anthology is a clarion call to get rid of the addiction to the placebo of faith as best as possible.

(6) Does Christianity cause more harm than good overall!?

In this book we are not arguing that Christianity causes more harm than good. Harriet Hall argues it does more harm than good in the one specific area of health, but that is only one factor in the harm/good equation. We do think that atheism, along with the further commitment to secular humanism, would be better for us and the world.[38] I don't think we need to say religion is always bad for people anyway, or even that it is more harmful than good for believers. To argue Christianity causes more harm than good is a larger claim to make and therefore harder to defend, even if I think it's probably the case. So this isn't our claim, nor does it need to be. For even if the Christian faith has been better overall for the world, the harm it causes still needs to be explained rather than explained away. For example, we wouldn't consider someone to be a good person if after saving a child from a burning vehicle he subsequently kicked that child in the teeth. Saving the child's life would be considered the greater deed and better for the child overall. But that good deed would never exonerate such a person from the crime of kicking the child in the teeth afterward. We would still demand an explanation for why he kicked the child in the teeth.

(7) What does this book attempt to show?

The harms of Christian faith demand a good explanation. This is especially the case if there is a perfectly loving, omnipotent, and omniscient God who invented it. The chapters in this book clearly show such a God is not the author of the Christian faith, which is based in the Bible with its terrible track record in history. The Christian faith can be empirically tested by the amount of harm it has done and continues to do in our world. Jesus reportedly said: "By their fruits ye shall know them" (Matthew 7:20). When we evaluate the fruits of Christianity, the result is that it fails miserably.

The Christian faith is the only one that claims God, the Holy Spirit, somehow mysteriously takes up "residence" in the lives of believers, illuminating them, inspiring them, teaching them, and leading them. Therefore we should see some evidence of this, especially in the recognized leaders of the church. But we don't. What we see instead is a manmade religion that has evolved with the times exactly as we would expect of any other religion that has had such a long history. The history of the church makes it look indistinguishable from a manmade religion without any divine inspiration at all. Then, too, the so-called revelation we find in the Bible looks exactly like it was written by men of their times. The God who is supposedly the greatest of all communicators, with a foreknowledge that far exceeds anything human beings could ever have, could not foresee how his so-called revelation would be discredited by its "cultured despisers" as century followed upon century. He didn't know it would be so culturally tied to the ancient superstitious world, so barbaric, so prescientific, that modern people could not believe because of it. Or, did he know this and didn't care that millions of people would die torturous deaths because of it, and that billions of people would go to hell because of how incompetent he had been and continues to be?

What does this do to liberal Christianity like that represented by Kimball and Spong? After all, their faith is more benign, more reasonable, less certain, and less harmful. Kimball (a Baptist) and Spong (an Episcopalian), attack fundamentalist or evangelical Christianity as having evil tendencies. They believe their liberalized version of faith is the true one. Their modern Protestant faith is an inclusive one that embraces religious diversity in an ecumenical, questioning interfaith dialogue. So what's the problem? It concerns the truth of the Christian faith itself. If the roots of their tree of faith are evil by their own standards, as they admit, then why do they still nest in that same tree? Continuing to do so is unreasonable, just like trying to incrementally reform the Ku Klux Clan from within. No, given the history of Christianity, even their own particular Christian faith should be rejected, plain and simple.

With hindsight, liberal believers reinvent their theology based on the lessons of history instead of abandoning it. They need to take seriously that theirs is an evolved faith that began with religious violence and has been sustained by violence for at least eighteen hundred years. As David Eller shows conclusively in his two chapters in this anthology, Christianity is red with blood in tooth and in claw. Throughout most of its history violence was its theme, its program, and its method for converting people and keeping believers in the fold. Its history is a history of violence. There is no escaping this.

The Anabaptist tradition, represented in today's world by the Amish, Mennonite, and Brethren churches, must honestly face the violence of the faith they inherited, even though they now reject the use of violence. The faith they now embrace is still dependent on this violent tradition, for much of it took place before their denominations originated. Some of it determined the very doctrines they now believe.

Let me just remind them of the few centuries after Constantine became the emperor of Rome. Constantine won the Battle of the Milvian Bridge and defeated Maxentius in the year 312 to take the Roman throne. Then in 313 he decided to solidify his rule under one religion, the Christian one represented by the cross he "saw" in the sky prior to the battle. So he insisted that the church come to an agreement about doctrine. The one doctrine the church wrestled with the most was that of the nature of Jesus. The Council of Chalcedon in the year 451 finally decided the orthodox doctrine of the incarnation. The problem is that the council didn't actually define that relationship. It merely asserted Jesus was "truly God and truly man." It said the divine and human natures coexisted in Jesus "without confusion, without change, without division, without separation," which didn't solve anything. Many attempts before and after Chalcedon were made, but none of them were accepted by the church, from Docetism, Adoptionism, Apollinarianism, Nestorianism, Arianism, and Monophysitism.

Richard Rubenstein shows in his book *When Jesus Became God* that this dispute over the nature of Jesus among Christians "had become as intense as the centuries-old conflict between Christians and pagans."[39] He explains:

> Athanasius, a future saint and uninhibited faction fighter, had his opponents excommunicated and anathematized, beaten and intimidated, kidnapped, imprisoned, and exiled to distant provinces. His adversaries, no less implacable, charged him with an assortment of crimes, including bribery, theft, extortion, sacrilege, treason, and murder. At their instigation, Athanasius was condemned by Church councils and exiled from Alexandria no less than five times, pursued on several occasions by troops dispatched by a Christian emperor to secure his arrest.[40]

But this fourth-century church conflict was only the beginning, as Phillip Jenkins tells us in *The Jesus Wars: How Four Patriarchs, Three Queens, and Two Emperors Decided What Christians Would Believe for the Next 1500 Years*. According to Jenkins,

> Horror stories about Christian violence abound in other eras, with the Crusades and Inquisition as prime exhibits; but the intra-Christian violence of the fifth- and sixth-century debates was on a far larger and more systematic scale than anything produced by the Inquisition and occurred at a much earlier stage of the church history . . . vicious civil wars still reverberated two hundred years after Chalcedon.[41]

The winners of these wars decided orthodox doctrine for the next fifteen hundred years, including the beliefs of people in the Anabaptist tradition:

> When we look at what became the church's orthodoxy, so many of those core beliefs gained the status they did as a result of what appears to be historical accident, of the workings of raw chance. . . . This was not the case of one side producing better arguments in its cause. . . . What mattered were the interests and obsessions of rival emperors and queens, the role of competing ecclesiastical princes and their churches, and the empire's military successes or failures against particular barbarian nations.[42]

When Protestants rejected the religion of the Roman Catholic Church, there was even more religious violence beginning in the sixteenth century. In France (1562–1598) there were a series of eight wars between Roman Catholics and Protestants (primarily Calvinist Huguenots), known as the French Wars of Religion. The infamous St. Bartholomew's Day Massacre took place during one of them. It started on the eve of the feast of Bartholomew, August 23, 1572, when a group of Huguenot leaders were slaughtered by Catholics. Lasting several weeks, the massacre extended across the countryside, where up to ten thousand Protestants were slaughtered.[43]

The Thirty Years' War (1618–1648) was one of the most destructive wars in European history. It pitted Christians against each other. This war was fought primarily in Germany, but other countries got involved as well. Roman Catholicism and Protestant Calvinism figured prominently in the opposing sides of this conflict. So great was the loss of life from this war that estimates show one-third of the entire population of Germany was killed. Württemberg lost three-quarters of its population. Brandenburg suffered the loss of half of its population, as did Marburg and Augsburg, while Magdeburg was reduced to rubble. Outside Germany, nearly one-third of the Czech population died as well.[44] Christian apologist Paul Copan admits that "denominational differences were a matter of life and death."[45] That's a gross understatement. We're talking about a bloodbath between what most Christians today would call their brothers and sisters in Christ.[46]

This bloodbath was largely over the authority of the Catholic Church, the means of salvation, the priesthood of all believers, the nature of the Eucharist, and the proper candidates for and mode of baptism. It was for nothing though, unlike the wars in the centuries following Constantine, which actually settled church doctrine, for while God was able to settle church doctrine through the earlier wars, he lacked the ability to do it again.

Kimball and Spong both acknowledge this violence, but they don't take it seriously. Kimball wrote, "A strong case can be made that the history of Christianity contains considerably more violence and destruction than that of most other major religions."[47] The problem is that neither he nor Spong arrive at the correct conclusion because they are blinded by their faith. I've written a lot about how believers can honestly examine their faith with no double standards or special pleading, especially in my book *The Outsider Test for Faith: How to*

Know Which Religion Is True. All that believers must do is test their religious faith from the perspective of an outsider, a nonbeliever, with the same level of reasonable skepticism they already use when examining the other religious faiths they reject. With regard to Christianity, believers just need to honestly ask themselves if they would accept any other religion that had such a terrible track record. If they wouldn't, then they should not continue identifying as Christians. It's that simple.

Part One

HOW FAITH FAILS

2

THE FAILURE OF THE CHURCH AND THE TRIUMPH OF REASON

Robert G. Ingersoll[1]

Many ages ago our fathers were living in dens and caves. Their bodies, their low foreheads, were covered with hair. They were eating berries, roots, bark and vermin. They were fond of snakes and raw fish. They discovered fire and, probably by accident, learned how to cause it by friction. They found how to warm themselves—to fight the frost and storm. They fashioned clubs and rude weapons of stone with which they killed the larger beasts and now and then each other. Slowly, painfully, almost imperceptibly they advanced. They crawled and stumbled, staggered and struggled toward the light. To them the world was unknown. On every hand was the mysterious, the sinister, the hurtful. The forests were filled with monsters, and the darkness was crowded with ghosts, devils, and fiendish gods.

These poor wretches were the slaves of fear, the sport of dreams.

Now and then, one rose a little above his fellows—used his senses—the little reason that he had—found something new—some better way. Then the people killed him and afterward knelt with reverence at his grave. Then another thinker gave his thought—was murdered—another tomb became sacred—another step was taken in advance. And so through countless years of ignorance and cruelty—of thought and crime—of murder and worship, of heroism, suffering, and self-denial, the race has reached the heights where now we stand.

Looking back over the long and devious roads that lie between the barbarism of the past and the civilization of to-day, thinking of the centuries that rolled like waves between these distant shores, we can form some idea of what our fathers suffered—of the mistakes they made—some idea of their ignorance, their stupidity—and some idea of their sense, their goodness, their heroism.

It is a long road from the savage to the scientist—from a den to a mansion—from leaves to clothes—from a flickering rush to the arc-light—from a hammer of stone to the modern mill—a long distance from the pipe of Pan to the violin—to the orchestra—from a floating log to the steamship—from a sickle to a reaper—from a flail to a threshing machine—from a crooked stick to a plow—from a spinning wheel to a spinning jenny—from a hand loom to a Jacquard—a Jacquard that weaves fair forms and wondrous flowers beyond Arachne's utmost dream—from a few hieroglyphics on the skins of beasts—on bricks of clay—to a printing press, to a library—a long distance from the messenger, traveling on foot, to the electric spark—from knives and tools of stone to those of steel—a long distance from sand to telescopes—from echo to the phonograph, the phonograph that buries in indented lines and dots the sounds of living speech, and then gives back to life the very words and voices of the dead—a long way from the trumpet to the telephone, the telephone that transports speech as swift as thought and drops the words, perfect as minted coins, in listening ears—a long way from a fallen tree to the suspension bridge—from the dried sinews of beasts to the cables of steel—from the oar to the propeller—from the sling to the rifle—from the catapult to the cannon—a long distance from revenge to law—from the club to the Legislature—from slavery to freedom—from appearance to fact—from fear to reason.

And yet the distance has been traveled by the human race. Countless obstructions have been overcome—numberless enemies have been conquered—thousands and thousands of victories have been won for the right, and millions have lived, labored and died for their fellow-men.

For the blessings we enjoy—for the happiness that is ours, we ought to be grateful. Our hearts should blossom with thankfulness.

Whom, what, should we thank?

Should we thank the church?

Christianity has controlled Christendom for at least fifteen hundred years.

During these centuries what good has the church done?

Did Christ or any of his apostles add to the sum of useful knowledge? Did they say one word in favor of any science, of any art? Did they teach their fellow-men how to make a living, how to overcome the obstructions of nature, how to prevent sickness—how to protect themselves from pain, from famine, from misery and rags?

Did they explain any of the phenomena of nature? Any of the facts that affect the life of man? Did they say anything in favor of investigation—of study—of thought? Did they teach the gospel of self-reliance, of industry—of honest effort? Can any farmer, mechanic, or scientist find in the New Testament one useful fact? Is there anything in the sacred book that can help the geologist, the astronomer, the biologist, the physician, the inventor—the manufacturer of any useful thing?

What has the church done?

From the very first it taught the vanity—the worthlessness of all earthly things. It taught the wickedness of wealth, the blessedness of poverty. It taught that the business of this life was to prepare for death. It insisted that a certain belief was necessary to ensure salvation, and that all who failed to believe, or doubted in the least would suffer eternal pain. According to the church the natural desires, ambitions and passions of man were all wicked and depraved.

To love God, to practice self-denial, to overcome desire, to despise wealth, to hate prosperity, to desert wife and children, to live on roots and berries, to repeat prayers, to wear rags, to live in filth, and drive love from the heart— these, for centuries, were the highest and most perfect virtues, and those who practiced them were saints.

What has the church done?

It has denounced pride and luxury—all things that adorn and enrich life—all the pleasures of sense—the ecstasies of love—the happiness of the hearth—the clasp and kiss of wife and child.

And the church has done this because it regarded this life as a period of probation—a time to prepare—to become spiritual—to overcome the natural— to fix the affections on the invisible—to become passionless—to subdue the flesh—to congeal the blood—to fold the wings of fancy—to become dead to the world—so that when you appeared before God you would be the exact opposite of what he made you.

What has the church done?

It pretended to have a revelation from God. It knew the road to eternal joy, the way to death. It preached salvation by faith, and declared that only orthodox believers could become angels, and all doubters would be damned. It knew this, and so knowing it became the enemy of discussion, of investigation, of thought. Why investigate, why discuss, why think when you know?

It sought to enslave the world. It appealed to force. It unsheathed the sword, lighted the fagot, forged the chain, built the dungeon, erected the scaffold, invented and used the instruments of torture. It branded, maimed and mutilated—it imprisoned and tortured—it blinded and burned, hanged and crucified, and utterly destroyed millions and millions of human beings. It touched every nerve of the body—produced every pain that can be felt, every agony that can be endured.

What has the church done?

There have been thousands of councils and synods—thousands and thousands of occasions when the clergy have met and discussed and quarreled—when pope and cardinals, bishops and priests have added to or explained their creeds—and denied the rights of others. What useful truth did they discover? What fact did they find? Did they add to the intellectual wealth of the world? Did they increase the sum of knowledge?

Did they find the medicinal virtue that dwells in any weed or flower? Did they teach us the mysteries of the metals and how to purify the ores in furnace flames? Did they show us how to improve our condition in this world? Did they give us even a hint as to any useful thing? Did they discover or show us how to produce anything for food? Did they produce anything to satisfy the hunger of man? Did they tell us anything about chemistry—how to combine and separate substances—how to subtract the hurtful—how to produce the useful?

What has the church done?

For centuries it kept the earth flat, for centuries it made all the hosts of heaven travel around this world—for centuries it clung to "sacred" knowledge, and fought facts with the ferocity of a fiend. For centuries it hated the useful. It was the deadly enemy of medicine. Disease was produced by devils and could be cured only by priests, decaying bones, and holy water. Doctors were the rivals of priests. They diverted the revenues.

The church opposed the study of anatomy—was against the dissection of the dead. Man had no right to cure disease—God would do that through his priests. Man had no right to prevent disease—diseases were sent by God as judgments. The church opposed inoculation—vaccination, and the use of chloroform and ether. It was declared to be a sin, a crime for a woman to lessen the pangs of motherhood. The church declared that woman must bear the curse of the merciful Jehovah.

What has the church done?

It taught that the insane were inhabited by devils. Insanity was not a disease. It was produced by demons. It could be cured by prayers—gifts, amulets and charms. All these had to be paid for. This enriched the church. These ideas were honestly entertained by Protestants as well as Catholics—by Luther, Calvin, Knox and Wesley.

What has the church done?

It taught the awful doctrine of witchcraft. It filled the darkness with demons— the air with devils, and the world with grief and shame. It charged men, women and children with being in league with Satan to injure their fellows. Old women were convicted for causing storms at sea—for preventing rain and for bringing frost. Girls were convicted for having changed themselves into wolves, snakes and toads. These witches were burned for causing diseases—for selling their souls and for souring beer. All these things were done with the aid of the Devil who sought to persecute the faithful, the lambs of God.

What has the church done?

It made the wife a slave—the property of the husband, and it placed the husband as much above the wife as Christ was above the husband. It taught that a nun is purer, nobler than a mother. It induced millions of pure and con- scientious girls to renounce the joys of life—to take the veil woven of night and death, to wear the habiliments of the dead—made them believe that they were the brides of Christ.

Priests, theologians, have taken advantage of women—of their gentle- ness—their love of approbation. They have lived upon their hopes and fears. Like vampires, they have sucked their blood. They have made them respon- sible for the sins of the world. They have taught them the slave virtues—meek- ness, humility—implicit obedience. They have fed their minds with mistakes, mysteries and absurdities.

What has the church done?

It was the enemy of commerce—of business. It denounced the taking of interest for money. Without taking interest for money, progress is impossible. The steamships, the great factories, the railroads have all been built with bor- rowed money, money on which interest was promised and for the most part paid.

The church was opposed to fire insurance—to life insurance. It denounced insurance in any form as gambling, as immoral. To insure your life was to declare that you had no confidence in God—that you relied on a corporation instead of divine providence. It was declared that God would provide for your widow and your fatherless children. To insure your life was to insult heaven.

What has the church done?

The church regarded epidemics as the messengers of the good God. The "Black Death" was sent by the eternal Father, whose mercy spared some and whose justice murdered the rest. To stop the scourge, they tried to soften the heart of God by kneelings and prostrations—by processions and prayers—by burning incense and by making vows. They did not try to remove the cause. The cause was God. They did not ask for pure water, but for holy water. Faith and filth lived or rather died together. Religion and rags, piety and pollution kept company. Sanctity kept its odor.

What has the church done?

It was the enemy of art and literature. It destroyed the marbles of Greece and Rome. Beauty was Pagan. It destroyed so far as it could the best literature of the world. It feared thought—but it preserved the Scriptures, the ravings of insane saints, the falsehoods of the Fathers, the bulls of popes, the accounts of miracles performed by shrines, by dried blood and faded hair, by pieces of bones and wood, by rusty nails and thorns, by handkerchiefs and rags, by water and beads and by a finger of the Holy Ghost.

What has the church done?

Christianity claims, with great pride, that it established asylums for the insane. Yes, it did. But the insane were treated as criminals. They were regarded as the homes—as the tenement houses of devils. They were persecuted and tormented. They were chained and flogged, starved and killed. The asylums were prisons, dungeons, the insane were victims and the keepers were ignorant, conscientious, pious fiends. They were not trying to help men, they were fighting devils—destroying demons. They were not actuated by love—but by hate and fear.

What has the church done?

It founded schools where facts were denied, where science was denounced and philosophy despised. Schools, where priests were made—where they were taught to hate reason and to look upon doubts as the suggestions of the Devil. Schools where the heart was hardened and the brain shriveled. Schools in which lies were sacred and truths profane. Schools for the more general diffusion of ignorance—schools to prevent thought—to suppress knowledge. Schools for the purpose of enslaving the world.

What has the church done?

It has tried to protect the people from the malice of the Devil—from ghosts and spooks, from witches and wizards and all the leering fiends that seek to poison the souls of men. It has endeavored to protect the sheep of God from the wolves of science—from the wild beasts of doubt and investigation. It has tried to wean the lambs of the Lord from the delights, the pleasures, the joys, of life. According to the philosophy of the church, the virtuous weep and suffer, the vicious laugh and thrive, the good carry a cross, and the wicked fly. But in the next life this will be reversed. Then the good will be happy, and the bad will be damned.

It gave us fiends and imps with wings like bats. It gave us ghosts and goblins, spooks and sprites, and little devils that swarmed in the bodies of men, and it gave us hell where the souls of men will roast in eternal flames. Shall we thank the church? Shall we thank them for the hell they made here? Shall we thank them for the hell of the future?

Let me be understood. I do not say and I do not think that the church was dishonest, that the clergy were insincere. I admit that all religions, all creeds, all priests, have been naturally produced. I admit, and cheerfully admit, that the believers in the supernatural have done some good—not because they believed in gods and devils—but in spite of it. I know that thousands and thousands of clergymen are honest, self-denying and humane—that they are doing what they believe to be their duty—doing what they can to induce men and women to live pure and noble lives. This is not the result of their creeds—it is because they are human.

Shall we thank the church's God? Shall we thank Nature? If we thank God or Nature for the sunshine and rain, for health and happiness, whom shall we curse for famine and pestilence, for earthquake and cyclone—for disease and death? If we cannot thank the orthodox churches—if we cannot thank the unknown, the incomprehensible, the supernatural—if we cannot thank Nature—if we cannot kneel to a Guess, or prostrate ourselves before a Perhaps—whom shall we thank?

What have the worldly done?

It is well to know that the seeds of thought were sown in our minds by the Greeks and Romans, and that our literature came from those seeds. The great literature of our language is Pagan in its thought—Pagan in its beauty—Pagan in its perfection. It is well to know that when Mohammedans were the friends of science, Christians were its enemies. How consoling it is to think that the friends of science—the men who educated their fellows—are now in hell, and that the men who persecuted and killed philosophers are now in heaven! Such is the justice of God.

The Christians of the Middle Ages, the men who were filled with the Holy Ghost, knew all about the worlds beyond the grave, but nothing about the world in which they lived. They thought the earth was flat—a little dishing if anything—that it was about five thousand years old, and that the stars were little sparkles made to beautify the night.

The fact is that Christianity was in existence for fifteen hundred years before there was an astronomer in Christendom. No follower of Christ knew the shape of the earth. The earth was demonstrated to be a globe, not by a pope or cardinal—not by a collection of clergymen—not by the "called" or the "set apart," but by a sailor. Magellan left Seville, Spain, August 10th, 1519, sailed west and kept sailing west, and the ship reached Seville, the port it left, on Sept. 7th, 1522. The world had been circumnavigated. The earth was known to be round. There had been a dispute between the Scriptures and a sailor. The fact took the sailor's side.

In 1543 Copernicus published his book, "On the Revolutions of the Heavenly Bodies." He had some idea of the vastness of the stars—of the astronomical spaces—of the insignificance of this world. In 1608, Lippersheim, a Hollander, so arranged lenses that objects were exaggerated. He invented the telescope. He gave countless worlds to our eyes, and made us citizens of the Universe. In 1610, on the night of January 7th, Galileo demonstrated the truth of the Copernican system, and in 1632, published his work on "The System of the World." In 1609, Kepler published his book "Motions of the Planet Mars." He, too, knew of the attraction of gravitation and that it acted in proportion to mass and distance. Kepler announced his Three Laws. He found and mathematically expressed the relation of distance, mass, and motion. Nothing greater has been accomplished by the human mind.

Then came Newton, Herschel and Laplace. The astronomy of Joshua and Elijah faded from the minds of intelligent men, and Jehovah became an ignorant tribal god. Men began to see that the operations of Nature were not subject to interference. That eclipses were not caused by the wrath of God— that comets had nothing to do with the destruction of empires or the death of kings, that the stars wheeled in their orbits without regard to the actions of men. In the sacred East the dawn appeared.

What have the worldly done?

A few years ago a few men became wicked enough to use their senses. They began to look and listen. They began to really see and then they began to reason. They forgot heaven and hell long enough to take some interest in this world. They began to examine soils and rocks. They noticed what had been done by rivers and seas. They found out something about the crust of the earth. They found that most of the rocks had been deposited and stratified in the water—rocks 70,000 feet in thickness. They found that the coal was once vegetable matter. They made the best calculations they could of the time required to make the coal, and concluded that it must have taken at least six or seven millions of years. They examined the chalk cliffs, found that they were composed of the microscopic shells of minute organisms, that is to say, the dust of these shells. This dust settled over areas as large as Europe and in some places the chalk is a mile in depth. This must have required many millions of years.

Lyell, the highest authority on the subject, says that it must have required, to cause the changes that we know, at least two hundred million years. Think of these vast deposits caused by the slow falling of infinitesimal atoms of impalpable dust through the silent depths of ancient seas! Think of the microscopical forms of life, constructing their minute houses of lime, giving life to others, leaving their mansions beneath the waves, and so through countless generations building the foundations of continents and islands.

At last we know that the story of creation, of the beginning of things, as told in the "sacred book," is not only untrue, but utterly absurd and idiotic. Now we know that the inspired writers did not know and that the God who inspired them did not know. We are no longer misled by myths and legends. We rely upon facts. The world is our witness and the stars testify for us.

What have the worldly done?

They have investigated the religions of the world—have read the sacred books, the prophecies, the commandments, the rules of conduct. They have studied the symbols, the ceremonies, the prayers and sacrifices. And they have shown that all religions are substantially the same—produced by the same causes—that all rest on a misconception of the facts in nature—that all are founded on ignorance and fear, on mistake and mystery.

They have found that Christianity is like the rest—that it was not a revelation, but a natural growth—that its gods and devils, its heavens and hells, were borrowed—that its ceremonies and sacraments were souvenirs of other religions—that no part of it came from heaven, but that it was all made by savage man. They found that Jehovah was a tribal god and that his ancestors had lived on the banks of the Euphrates, the Tigris, the Ganges and the Nile, and these ancestors were traced back to still more savage forms. They found that all the sacred books were filled with inspired mistake and sacred absurdity.

What have the worldly done?

They have investigated the phenomena of nature. They have invented ways to use the forces of the world, the weight of falling water—of moving air. They have changed water to steam, invented engines—the tireless giants that work for man. They have made lightning a messenger and slave. They invented movable type, taught us the art of printing and made it possible to save and transmit the intellectual wealth of the world. They connected continents with cables, cities and towns with the telegraph—brought the world into one family—made intelligence independent of distance. They taught us how to build homes, to obtain food, to weave cloth. They covered the seas with iron ships and the land with roads and steeds of steel. They gave us the tools of all the trades—the implements of labor. They chiseled statues, painted pictures and "witched the world" with form and color. They have found the cause of and the cure for many maladies that afflict the flesh and minds of men. They have given us the instruments of music and the great composers and performers have changed the common air to tones and harmonies that intoxicate, exalt and purify the soul.

They have rescued us from the prisons of fear, and snatched our souls from the fangs and claws of superstition's loathsome, crawling, flying beasts. They have given us the liberty to think and the courage to express our thoughts. They have changed the frightened, the enslaved, the kneeling, the prostrate into men and women—clothed them in their right minds and made them truly free. They have uncrowned the phantoms, wrested the scepters from the ghosts and given this world to the children of men. They have driven from the heart the fiends of fear and extinguished the flames of hell.

They have read a few leaves of the great volume—deciphered some of the records written on stone by the tireless hands of time in the dim past. They have told us something of what has been done by wind and wave, by fire and frost, by life and death, the ceaseless workers, the pauseless forces of the world. They have enlarged the horizon of the known, changed the glittering specks that shine above us to wheeling worlds, and filled all space with countless suns.

They have found the qualities of substances, the nature of things—how to analyze, separate and combine, and have enabled us to use the good and avoid the hurtful. They have given us mathematics in the higher forms, by means of which we measure the astronomical spaces, the distances to stars, the velocity at which the heavenly bodies move, their density and weight, and by which the mariner navigates the waste and trackless seas. They have given us all we have of knowledge, of literature and art. They have made life worth living. They have filled the world with conveniences, comforts and luxuries.

All this has been done by the worldly—by those, who were not "called" or "set apart" or filled with the Holy Ghost or had the slightest claim to "apostolic succession." The men who accomplished these things were not "inspired." They had no revelation—no supernatural aid. They were not clad in sacred vestments, and tiaras were not upon their brows. They were not even ordained. They used their senses, observed and recorded facts. They had confidence in reason. They were patient searchers for the truth. They turned their attention to the affairs of this world. They were not saints. They were sensible men. They worked for themselves, for wife and child and for the benefit of all.

To these men we are indebted for all we are, for all we know, for all we have. They were the creators of civilization—the founders of free states—the saviors of liberty—the destroyers of superstition and the great captains in the army of progress.

WHOM shall we thank? Standing here at the close of the 19th century—amid the trophies of thought—the triumphs of genius—here under the flag of the Great Republic—knowing something of the history of man—here on this day that has been set apart for thanksgiving, I most reverently thank the good men, the good women of the past. I thank those who cultivated the ground and changed the forests into farms—those who built rude homes and watched the faces of their happy children in the glow of fireside flames—those who domesticated horses, cattle and sheep—those who invented wheels and looms and taught us to spin and weave—those who by cultivation changed wild grasses into wheat and corn, changed bitter things to fruit, and worthless weeds to flowers, that sowed within our souls the seeds of art. I thank the artists who chiseled forms in stone and wrought with light and shade the face of man. I thank the philosophers, the thinkers, who taught us how to use our minds in the great search for truth. I thank the astronomers who explored the heavens, told us the secrets of the stars, the glories of the constellations—the geologists who found the story of the world in fossil forms, in memoranda kept in ancient rocks, in lines written by waves, by frost and fire—the anatomists who sought in muscle, nerve and bone for all the mysteries of life—the chemists who unraveled Nature's work that they might learn her art—the physicians who have laid the hand of science on the brow of pain, the hand whose magic touch restores—the surgeons who have defeated Nature's self and forced her to preserve the lives of those she labored to destroy.

I thank the great inventors—those who gave us movable type and the press, by means of which great thoughts and all discovered facts are made immortal—the inventors of engines, of the great ships, of the railways, the cables and telegraphs. I thank the great mechanics, the workers in iron and steel, in wood and stone. I thank the inventors and makers of the numberless things of use and luxury. I thank the industrious men, the loving mothers, the useful women. They are the benefactors of our race.

The inventor of pins did a thousand times more good than all the popes and cardinals, the bishops and priests—than all the clergymen and parsons, exhorters and theologians that ever lived. The inventor of matches did more for the comfort and convenience of mankind than all the founders of religions and the makers of all creeds—than all malicious monks and selfish saints.

I thank the honest men and women who have expressed their sincere thoughts, who have been true to themselves and have preserved the veracity of their souls. I thank the thinkers of Greece and Rome, Zeno and Epicurus, Cicero and Lucretius. I thank Bruno, the bravest, and Spinoza, the subtlest of men. I thank Voltaire, whose thought lighted a flame in the brain of man, unlocked the doors of superstition's cells and gave liberty to many millions of his fellow-men. Voltaire—a name that sheds light. Voltaire—a star that super-stition's darkness cannot quench.

I thank the great poets—the dramatists. I thank Homer and Aeschylus, and I thank Shakespeare above them all. I thank Burns for the heart-throbs he changed into songs, for his lyrics of flame. I thank Shelley for his Skylark, Keats for his Grecian Urn and Byron for his Prisoner of Chillon. I thank the great novelists. I thank the great sculptors. I thank the unknown man who molded and chiseled the Venus de Milo. I thank the great painters. I thank Rembrandt and Corot. I thank all who have adorned, enriched and ennobled life—all who have created the great, the noble, the heroic and artistic ideals.

I thank the statesmen who have preserved the rights of man. I thank Paine whose genius sowed the seeds of independence in the hearts of '76. I thank Jefferson whose mighty words for liberty have made the circuit of the globe. I thank the founders, the defenders, the saviors of the Republic. I thank Ericsson, the greatest mechanic of his century, for the monitor. I thank Lincoln for the Proclamation. I thank Grant for his victories and the vast host that fought for the right,—for the freedom of man. I thank them all—the living and the dead.

I thank the great scientists—those who have reached the foundation, the bed-rock—who have built upon facts—the great scientists, in whose presence theologians look silly and feel malicious. The scientists never persecuted, never imprisoned their fellow-men. They forged no chains, built no dungeons, erected no scaffolds—tore no flesh with red hot pincers—dislocated no joints on racks—crushed no bones in iron boots—extinguished no eyes—tore out no tongues and lighted no fagots. They did not pretend to be inspired—did not claim to be prophets or saints or to have been born again. They were only intelligent and honest men. They did not appeal to force or fear. They did not regard men as slaves to be ruled by torture, by lash and chain, nor as children to be cheated with illusions, rocked in the cradle of an idiot creed and soothed by a lullaby of lies.

I thank Humboldt and Helmholtz and Haeckel and Büchner. I thank Lamarck and Darwin—Darwin who revolutionized the thought of the intel-lectual world. I thank Huxley and Spencer. I thank the scientists one and all. I thank the heroes, the destroyers of prejudice and fear—the dethroners of savage gods—the extinguishers of hate's eternal fire—the heroes, the breakers of chains—the founders of free states—the makers of just laws—the heroes who fought and fell on countless fields—the heroes whose dungeons became shrines—the heroes whose blood made scaffolds sacred—the heroes, the apostles of reason, the disciples of truth, the soldiers of freedom—the heroes who held high the holy torch and filled the world with light.

With all my heart I thank them all.

3

THE FOLLY OF FAITH

The Incompatibility of Science and Christianity

Victor J. Stenger

Science and Faith

Faith is belief in the absence of supportive evidence and even in the light of contrary evidence. No one disputes that religion is based on faith. Some theologians, Christian apologists, and even a few secular scholars claim that science is also based on faith. They argue that science takes it on faith that the world is rational and that nature can be ordered in an intelligible way.

However, science makes no such assumption on faith. It analyzes observations by applying certain methodological rules and formulates models to describe those observations. It justifies that process by its practical success, not by any logical deduction derived from dubious metaphysical assumptions. We must distinguish faith from *trust*. Science has earned our trust by its proven success. Religion has destroyed our trust by its repeated failure.

Using the empirical method, science has eliminated smallpox, flown men to the moon, and discovered DNA. If science did not work, we wouldn't do it. Relying on faith, religion has brought us inquisitions, holy wars, intolerance, and antiscience. Religion does not work, but we still do it.

Science and religion are fundamentally incompatible because of their unequivocally opposed epistemologies—the contrary assumptions they make concerning what we can know about the world. Every human alive is aware of a world that seems to exist outside the body, the world of sensory experience we call the *natural*. Science is the systematic study of the observations made of the natural world with our senses and scientific instruments, and the application to human needs of the knowledge obtained.

By contrast, all major religions teach that humans possess an additional "inner" sense that allows us to access a realm lying beyond the natural world—a divine, transcendent reality we call the *supernatural*. If it does not involve the transcendent, it is not religion. Religion is a set of practices intended to communicate with that invisible world and entreat it to affect things here in the natural world.

The working hypothesis of science is that careful observation is our only reliable source of knowledge about the world. *Natural theology* accepts empirical science but views it as a means to learn about God's creation. And so, religion in general goes much further than science in giving credence to additional sources of knowledge such as scriptures, revelation, and spiritual experiences that are not based on verifiable empirical evidence. This credence is never tested. Believing "on faith" is considered a virtue rather than the delusion it really is.

No doubt science has its limits. It is hard to imagine using science to distinguish between what expert critics decide is good or bad art, poetry, or music; but religion doesn't do any better. The fact that science is limited doesn't mean that religion or any alternative system of thought can or does provide insight into what lies beyond those limits. For example, science cannot yet show precisely how the universe and life originated naturally, although many plausible scenarios exist. But this does not mean that ancient creation myths, such as those in Genesis, have any substance—any chance of eventually being verified.

Science and the Supernatural

The scientific community in general goes along with the notion that science has nothing to say about the supernatural because the methods of science, as they are currently practiced, exclude supernatural causes. However, if we truly possess an inner sense telling us about an unobservable reality that matters to us and influences our lives, then we should be able to observe the effects of that reality by scientific means. If someone's inner sense were to warn of an impending earthquake unpredicted by science, which then occurred on schedule, we would have evidence for this extrasensory source of knowledge.

So far we see no proof that the feelings people experience when they perceive themselves to be in touch with the supernatural correspond to anything outside their heads. It follows that we have no reason to rely on those feelings when they occur. Nevertheless, if such evidence or reason should show up, then scientists will have to consider it whether they like it or not.

We cannot sweep under the rug the many serious problems brought about by the scientific revolution and the exponential burst in humanity's ability to exploit Earth's resources, which is made possible by the technology that results from scientific advances. There would be no problems with overpopulation, pollution, global warming, or the threat of nuclear holocaust if science had not made these problems possible.

But does anyone want to return to the prescientific age when human life was nasty, brutish, and short? Even fire was once a new technology, and a very dangerous one that still takes great effort to control.

We can solve the problems brought about by the misuse of science only by better use of science and more rational behavior on the part of scientists, politicians, corporations, and citizens in all walks of life. And religion, as it is currently practiced, with its continued focus on closed thinking and ancient mythology, is not doing much to support the goal of a better, safer world. In fact, religion hinders our attempts to attain that goal when many believers put their faith in God rather than science.

Irreconcilable Differences

Irreconcilable differences arising from the differing viewpoints and methodology of science and religion include the origin of the universe and its physical parameters, the origin of complexity, the concepts of holism versus reductionism, the nature of mind and consciousness, and the source of morality. Some authors have ignored or distorted science in an attempt to justify their unquestioned premise of a divine reality. But the folly of faith is even deeper than its history of factual errors and misrepresentation.

Religions are characterized by hardened beliefs that when changed result in a new spinoff sect while the old one continues with perhaps depleted membership. By contrast, from the beginning science has been one continuous, if not always smooth, flow of new knowledge and progress as old ideas are cast off and new ones take their place.

Today science and religion find themselves in serious conflict. Even moderate Christians do not fully accept Darwinian evolution. Although they claim to see no conflict between their faith and evolution, they insist that God still controlled the development of life so humans would evolve. This is not at all what Darwin's theory of evolution says. It's intelligent design. There's no role for God in evolution.

In another example, greedy corporate interests and unscrupulous politicians are exploiting the antiscience attitudes embedded in popular religion to suppress scientific results on issues of global importance, such as the overpopulation and environmental degradation that threaten the generations of humanity that will follow ours.

Those who rely on observation and reason to provide an understanding of the world must stop viewing as harmless those who rely instead on superstition and the mythologies in ancient texts passed down from the childhood of our species. For the sake of the future of humanity, we must fight to expunge the fantasies of faith from human thinking.

NOMA

In his 1999 book, *Rocks of Ages*, the late renowned paleontologist Stephen Jay Gould proposed that science and religion are "non-overlapping magisteria" (NOMA).[1] He argued that the two knowledge systems deal with different aspects of life. Science, Gould wrote, is concerned with describing the "outer" world of our senses, while religion deals with the "inner" world of morality and meaning.

NOMA recalls the position enunciated by Galileo when he ran into trouble with the Church for teaching that Earth goes around the sun. He is often quoted as saying, "The Holy Spirit's intention is to teach how one goes to heaven, not how the heavens go," although it is generally assumed that he was in turn quoting Cardinal Cesare Baronius.

Many scientists—believers and nonbelievers—have adopted the NOMA position. Believing scientists compartmentalize their thinking by not incorporating into their religious thinking the *doubt-everything* position they were trained to take in their professions. A prime example is geneticist Francis Collins, who directed the Human Genome Project and at this writing directs the National Institutes of Health. His 2006 book *The Language of God: A Scientist Presents Evidence for Belief*[2] was a bestseller. However, his so-called evidence was not, as you might have thought from the title, based on his deep knowledge of DNA. Rather it was based on his own inner feeling that the world is a moral place and only God could have made it that way. Nowhere does Collins come close to applying to religion the critical skills he exhibited in his outstanding scientific career.

The founders of the scientific revolution, notably Descartes, Newton, and Kepler, freely mixed science and religion. But as science came to contradict more and more religious teachings, scientists compartmentalized their beliefs. Modern-day believing scientists, such as Collins, do not incorporate God into their science. This even includes those scientists who happen to also be members of holy orders, such as the Belgian Catholic priest Georges-Henri Lemaître who proposed the big bang in 1927 but urged Pope Pius XII not to claim it as infallible proof that God exists.

Most nonbelieving scientists want to just do their research and stay out of any fights over religion. That makes the NOMA approach appealing because it allows them to not have to think about what religion is or how it affects our social and political world. In my view, these scientists are shirking their responsibility by conceding the realms of morality and public policy to the irrationality and brutality of faith.

The US National Academy of Sciences, along with several scientific societies and proscience organizations such as the National Center for Science Education, have compromised their principles in order to stay on good terms with religion. Even the prestigious science magazine *Nature* has adopted Gould's NOMA, editorializing that problems arise between science and religion only when they "stray onto each other's territories and stir up trouble."[3]

However, Gould's proposal and these views from the top tiers of science do not describe the true roles science and religion play in society. Traditional religions are based on the belief in divinely inspired scriptures and other revelations, and they *do* try to tell us what "is" based on those beliefs. In doing so, they have proved to be almost universally incorrect.

Now, clever theologians will say that I am using science as my standard of what is correct and incorrect. Of course, scriptures could be correct, but then we have to believe (as many fundamentalists do) that God is pulling the wool over our eyes, planting phony evidence for carbon-dated fossils, geological formations, and redshifts from galaxies that imply they are far older than the six thousand years of existence accounted for by biblical creation.

The scientific descriptions of the world we observe with our senses and instruments aren't necessarily correct just because they are science. They simply work better than those found in scriptures. And if religion doesn't work in the sphere of nature, why should we expect it to work in the moral or other spheres?

Nothing prevents science from concerning itself with issues of morality and purpose. If these questions involve observable phenomena, such as human behavior, they can be analyzed with the rational methods of science. Science is more than making measurements with billion-dollar instruments and formulating models using highly sophisticated mathematics. It is about applying empirical reasoning to every aspect of life.

In *Science and Spirituality: Making Room for Faith in the Age of Science*, philosopher Michael Ruse argued that "the basic, most important claims of the Christian religion lie beyond the scope of science. They do not and could not conflict with science for they live in realms where science does not go."[4] But the fact that science cannot reject all conceivable worlds cannot be used to argue for their existence. Furthermore, many fundamental Christian claims do not lie beyond the scope of science: they conflict with it. The virgin birth, miracles, prophecies, revelations, and the resurrection are just a few of these.

Christianity and the Scientific Revolution

There can be no dispute that the scientific revolution in the seventeenth century occurred in an atmosphere in which religious and scientific ideas were deeply intertwined. But religion still held the upper hand. Historian Charles Webster writes, "No direction or energy toward science [in the seventeenth century] was undertaken without the assurance of Christian conscience, and no conceptual move was risked without confidence in its consistency with the Protestant idea of providence."[5]

It is difficult to extract precise causes of the scientific revolution from the complex history of seventeenth-century Europe except to say that it happened there and no place else. China had made significant advances in technology, but the Chinese failed to develop science. And while science and learning flourished for a time in the Islamic world, there, too, a culture of scientific development failed to endure.

Christian apologist Ian Barbour argues that the decline in science in the Islamic world was the result of the tight control of higher education by religious authorities.[6] Although Barbour doesn't admit it, the same can be said of Christendom until the Renaissance and Reformation. Similarly, government authorities controlled education in China.

Europe would not have been closed to independent thinking in the first place except for the Catholic Church. Science had flourished in polytheistic Greece and Rome, and, as mentioned, in medieval Islam. When the Roman Empire fell, the Catholic Church was there to pick up the pieces, producing an authoritarian society that brutally suppressed the slightest traces of freethinking for a thousand years.

Surely it is no coincidence that the onset of the Dark Ages coincided with the rise of Christianity. It was only with the revolts against established ecclesiastic authorities in the Renaissance and Reformation that new avenues of thought were finally opened up allowing science to flourish.

New Avenues of Thought

And these new avenues of thought are what we want to explore. Artistic and social activities with no significant political ramifications are far less important in comprehending the incompatibility of science and religion than are intellectual matters. Scientific thinking is not dissonant with Church art, music, and charitable work, or with the Church's function of providing a structure that enables people to meet, enjoy one another's company, and help each other. However, as Sam Harris says, "Science and religion—being antithetical ways of thinking about the same reality—will never come to terms."[7] And when religious notions dominate the political scene, as they do in Muslim countries and to a growing extent in America today, the world is in big trouble.

In the Dark Ages, much of Greek and Roman science and philosophy was lost in Europe but preserved and developed to new heights in the Islamic empire. However, gradually scholarship crept back into Europe as theologians such as Augustine of Hippo and Thomas Aquinas developed rational theologies that incorporated the philosophies and logic of Plato and Aristotle and translated texts became available. However, God and revelation remained the unquestioned principles upon which reason was applied.

When the Roman Catholic Church founded the first universities in Europe, Aristotle became the prime authority. Scholars used his logic, science, and philosophy to forge an amalgam of Greek and Christian thought that became known as *scholasticism*. While the value of reason and observation was recognized, these were generally viewed as inferior to revelation, since they were the products of imperfect human activity whereas revelation came directly from God.

But then the Renaissance and Reformation defied the authority of the Church, and a new science blossomed in which revelation and authority were replaced as the final arbiters of truth by observation and measurement. Significantly, the scientific revolution occurred *outside* the church-dominated universities, which remained steeped in Aristotelian scholasticism. Today, our secular universities lead the way in science while students at many church-connected universities and colleges are being taught creationism and other pseudosciences, along with mind-numbing biblical apologetics.

Nevertheless, a clean break between science and religion did not take place immediately at the start of the scientific revolution. All of the great pioneers of science—Copernicus, Galileo, Kepler, and Newton—were believers, although they hardly had a choice in the matter. Open nonbelief was nonexistent at that time. Except for Galileo, these greats incorporated their beliefs into their science. Galileo was the only one of the founders of the new science who tried to separate science from religion.

In the brief period in the eighteenth century called the Enlightenment, thinkers in Europe and America began to distinguish science and philosophy from theology. Deism flourished and atheism became intellectually respectable, at least in France.

The great bulk of humanity did not go along with atheism, however. Christianity found a way to incorporate science within its own system with the notion of *natural theology*. In natural theology, human scientific observations and theories are seen as a way to learn more about the majesty of the creator who had made the natural world and its laws in the first place.

This was quite a reasonable position at the time. After all, prior to the mid-nineteenth century science had no natural explanation for the complexity we see around us, especially in living things. When geologists showed that Earth was much older than implied in the Bible, and Darwin provided both the evidence and the theory for how life evolved without the need for God, the foundations of religious belief began to crumble.

This resulted in a very specific conflict between science and religion that has lasted to the current day, with the most recent battles being over the intelligent-design brand of creationism. While the Catholic Church and moderate Christians have claimed to have no problem with evolution, their own words demonstrate that they do not accept unguided Darwinian evolution. Instead, they subscribe to a form of God-guided evolution that is just another form of intelligent design.

The New Physics

The new physics of the twentieth century—relativity, quantum mechanics, and relativistic quantum field theory—has not struck many nerves with everyday religious believers because these ideas are comprehended by only a tiny fraction of the public. In fact, the theories of modern physics and the data that support them are monumentally misunderstood, misrepresented, and misused by many who naïvely write on these subjects without the years of study necessary to have any depth of knowledge.[8]

This is especially the case with quantum mechanics, which has been made to look mysterious and weird, even by physicists who know better but think they can spark student and public interest, and sell their popular-level books with overblown rhetoric.

While not technically theistic, modern quantum spiritualists and pseudo-scientists should be included as part of the antiscience movement that is associated with religion and the transcendental worldview. Many members of this community assert that quantum mechanics tells us we can make our own reality just by thinking we can, and that it puts our minds in tune with a cosmic consciousness that pervades the universe.[9]

This claim results from a total misunderstanding of the so-called wave-particle duality of quantum mechanics. You often hear, "An object is a particle or a wave depending on what you decide to measure." This is wrong. No one has ever measured a wavelike property associated with a single particle. Interference and diffraction effects are only observed for beams of particles, and only particles are detected, even when you are trying to measure a wavelength. The statistical behavior of these ensembles of particles is described mathematically using equations that sometimes, but not always, resemble the equations for waves.

The other, more forgivable misuse of quantum mechanics is that made by science-respecting theologians who look for a way for God to act in the universe without violating the laws of physics. They think they can do this by appealing to the Heisenberg uncertainty principle of quantum mechanics that puts limits on what you can measure with precision. They imagine God poking his finger into matter, making particles change their motion without any physicist noticing.[10]

Sure, God can do that, but he then would be breaking a law of physics, which theologians say they are trying to avoid. And think of all the poking he would have to do at the atomic level to affect the behavior of a macroscopic object such as a tennis ball.

Holism and Emergence

Theists and quantum spiritualists claim that modern physics has replaced *reductionism*, which has marked physics and indeed all science from the time of Democritus, with a new *holism* in which a system cannot be understood by simply considering the interactions of its parts but must include additional principles of the whole.[11] In fact the opposite is true. By the late seventies physics had returned to an even deeper reductionism than before with the *standard model of particles and forces*. The whole is still equal to the sum of its parts, and those parts are elementary particles—just as the Greek atomists said in the fourth century BCE.[12] This is another place where scientific and religious thinking profoundly disagree.

Once again, some scientists and science writers who should know better have been roped into joining with theologians to announce a grand new scientific principle called *emergence.* They point to the fact that nature has a hierarchy of levels of complexity ranging from elementary particles to human society. At each level we find a new scientific discipline—from physics to chemistry to biology and so on up to sociology and political science. The scholars at each level do not derive their models from particle physics but develop models for each discipline by applying their own unique methods. However, at least at the physics and chemistry level, the principles they uncover can be seen to "emerge" from the level below by what is called "bottom-up causality."

No one should expect particle physicists to answer every question. However, speculations are being widely bandied about that some emergent principles have the power to control entities at lower levels by way of "top-down" causality. At the very top of the pyramid, of course, is God up in heaven acting down on us particles below. Emergence by bottom-up causality is trivial.[13] Emergence by top-down causality is world shaking. But like so many imaginative proposals that would shake the world if true, top-down causality has exactly zero empirical support.

Twentieth-century cosmology has also been distorted by theists as constituting evidence for a creation of the universe when, in fact, modern cosmology points in quite the opposite direction. Some previous gaps in our understanding of the physics of the cosmos provided some temporary comfort to those seeking evidence for a creator. However, these gaps were decisively plugged with astronomical discoveries as the century progressed.

The Uncreated Universe

Today cosmologists can provide a variety of plausible, mathematically precise scenarios for an uncreated universe that violates no known laws of physics.[14] Furthermore, we have every indication that, despite the well-confirmed big bang, the universe, defined as all there is, had no beginning and thus no creator.[15]

Combining a naïve understanding of physics and cosmology with their preformed unscientific beliefs, many theist authors have trumpeted that the constants of physics are so delicately balanced that any deviation would make life impossible. From this they conclude that the physical constants could only have been fine-tuned by God.[16]

However, in fact there is no evidence that the universe is fine-tuned for life, and all we have here is yet another argument from ignorance.[17]

Besides, surely any God worthy of the name would not have been so incompetent as to build a vast, out-of-tune universe and then have to delicately twiddle all these knobs so that a single planet would be capable of producing sentient beings.

The Absent Spirit

The fundamental religious tenet is that a transcendent reality beyond matter exists. Evidence for this reality is supposed to be found in human experiences termed mystical or spiritual. Specifically, a large amount of data has been accumulated over the years, and published in journals and books, on near-death experiences (NDEs). These occur in about 20 percent of people resuscitated from clinical death, or something close to it. They return with a memory of light at the end of a tunnel that they are convinced was a glimpse of heaven. (Few ever glimpse hell).

However, NDE researchers have not been able to find any empirical evidence demonstrating that the experience is not all in the head. Furthermore, experiments that have attempted to independently verify the events reported by subjects, such as floating above the operating table and reading a series of numbers sitting on a high shelf not visible from the table, have uniformly failed.[18]

At the current stage of scientific development we can confidently say that no empirical or theoretical basis exists for assuming anything other than that we inhabit a universe made entirely of matter (and energy into which matter can be transformed, and vice versa). Please understand that this is not a dogmatic position. Of course we don't know everything, and we never will. The essential point is that within our existing knowledge we do not have a credible reason for requiring anything transcendent to explain anything we experience or observe. All science is provisional, and if sufficient evidence that meets all the most rigorous scientific tests were to come along to demonstrate the existence of a world beyond matter and energy, then nonbelieving scientists will change their minds.

Other metaphors for the "stuff" of the universe such as information do not diminish the need for, and primacy of, matter.

Until recent times it has been widely assumed that the human being possesses an immaterial "spirit" or "soul" that is responsible for thoughts, emotions, and conscious will. However, the evidence has become overwhelming that these all result from purely physical processes within the brain. While we still do not have a complete theory of what we call "mind," we have no empirical reason to assume that it will require any immaterial elements.

Morality

Another important issue where fundamental disagreement between science and religion exists concerns the source and nature of morality. Believers cannot see how our notions of good and evil can come from anyplace other than God. They are joined by many nonbelievers who think science has no right to say anything on the question. But scientists are investigating morality anyway and coming up with discoveries that few believers will like. While a primitive morality can be found in animals and early humans that evolved *biologically*, our modern ideas of morality more likely evolved *socially* as humans found ways to overcome some of their animal instincts by force of intellect.[19] Not only did these developments allow people to live together in some semblance of order, they also allowed us to use the ability to act cooperatively to obtain resources from the environment, to protect ourselves from predators, and so on. The incompatibility between science and religion becomes especially striking on the question of the origin of morality and ethical behavior.

Theocracy in America

The incompatibility of science and religion is more than just an intellectual debate among scholars. Faith is a folly. It requires belief in a world beyond the senses with no basis in evidence for such a world and no reason to believe in it other than the vain hope that something else is out there. However, while a false belief may be comforting or even temporarily useful, it is a dubious guide to personal life or the foundation of a successful society.

While not all believers have an uncompromising faith, and most recognize the power and value of science, an influential minority of American Christians see that materialist science needs to be "renewed" so that God is restored to his rightful place in the scheme of things.[20]

If the conflict between science and religion were just a matter of intellectual debate, a battle between (scrambled) eggheads in theology and (hard-boiled) eggheads in science and philosophy, the stakes would not be very high. But the role of religion in today's political and social scene is ubiquitous, from Islamic terrorism to attempts by the Christian right in America to replace democracy with *theocracy*.

A theocracy? In America? Most of my scientific colleagues in the comfort of their cluttered campus offices would scoff at the notion. But they need to be good scientists and look at the data. Religion has been injected into the political dialogue as never before, with politicians even claiming divine guidance. Many see no need for science or, in fact, view it with suspicion. And they are cutting back research funding drastically, which you would think should worry my colleagues just a bit.

Christian fundamentalism has been playing an increasing role in American political life. In his 2006 book *American Theocracy*, former Republican strategist and bestselling author Kevin Phillips wrote, "The rapture, end-times, and Armageddon hucksters in the United States rank with any Shiite ayatollahs, and the last two presidential elections [2000 and 2004] mark the transformation of the GOP into the first religious party in U.S. history."[21]

In her 2006 bestseller *Kingdom Coming: The Rise of Christian Nationalism*, journalist Michelle Goldberg chronicled the takeover of America by rightwing Christians.[22] In the same year Damon Linker, former editor of the Catholic magazine *First Things*, told how in over three decades a few determined men have succeeded in injecting their radical religious ideas into the nation's politics.[23]

Also in 2006, in *American Fascists: The Christian Right and the War on America*, Pulitzer-Prize-winning author and theist Chris Hedges noted:

> Democratic and Christian [values] are being dismantled, often with stealth, by
> a radical Christian movement known as dominionism, which seeks to cloak

itself in the mantle of Christian faith and American patriotism. Dominionism takes its name from Genesis 1:26–31, in which God gives human beings "dominion" over creation. This movement, small in number but influential, departs from traditional evangelicalism. Dominionists now control at least six national television networks, each reaching tens of millions of homes, and virtually all of the nation's more than 2,000 religious radio stations, as well as denominations such as the Southern Baptist Convention. Dominionism seeks to redefine traditional democratic and Christian terms and concepts to fit an ideology that calls on the radical church to take political power.[24]

More recently, Hedges has written about the role of Dominionism and the related Christian Reconstructionism in the thinking of Texas Republican senator Ted Cruz, who has assumed the mantle of leadership of the extreme conservative movement. Here's how Hedges describes it:

> This ideology calls on anointed "Christian" leaders to take over the state and make the goals and laws of the nation "biblical." It seeks to reduce government to organizing little more than defense, internal security and the protection of property rights. It fuses with the Christian religion the iconography and language of American imperialism and nationalism, along with the cruelest aspects of corporate capitalism.[25]

In *The Family: The Secret Fundamentalism at the Heart of American Power*, published in 2009, journalist Jeff Sharlet revealed how small, secretive group of extremely conservative Christians called "The Family" have wielded increasing national and international political power. They organize the yearly Washington Prayer Breakfasts attended by presidents and foreign diplomats, provide prayerful retreats for congressmen, senators, and Supreme Court justices, and preach a gospel of biblical capitalism, military might, and American empire.[26] In a follow-up volume published in 2010, *C Street: The Fundamentalist Threat to American Democracy*, Sharlet told how The Family also aided several prominent senators and congressmen in covering up their extramarital affairs.[27]

In a 2011 essay in *Religion Dispatches*, Peter Montgomery summarized how "religious right leaders and activists have spent decades creating fertile soil for anti-union campaigns through the promotion of 'biblical capitalism.'"[28] They have proclaimed that Jesus and the Bible oppose progressive taxes, capital gains taxes, estate taxes, and minimum wage laws. They also enlist Jesus in a war against unions, which they regard as unbiblical.

The founder of The Family was a Norwegian immigrant, Abraham Vereide. According to Sharlet, also writing in *Religion Dispatches*:

> In 1942 [Vereide] moved to the capital where the National Association of Manufacturers staked him to a meeting of congressmen who would become students of his spiritual politics, among them Virginia senator Absalom Willis Robertson—Pat Robertson's father. Vereide returned the manufacturers' favor by telling his new congressional followers that God wanted them to break the spine of organized labor. They did.[29]

Montgomery writes that the 1990 Christian Coalition Leadership Manual coauthored by Coalition founder Ralph Reed cites four biblical passages instructing slaves to be obedient to their masters. For example,

> Slaves, submit yourselves to your masters with all respect, not only to those who are good and considerate, but also to those who are harsh. For it is commendable if a man bears up under the pain of unjust suffering because he is conscious of God. (1 Peter 2:18–19)

Reed interprets this to mean, "Christians have a responsibility to submit to the authority of their employers, since they are designated as part of God's plan for the exercise of authority on earth by man."[30] We see here the same argument that has been used for millennia to justify the right of monarchs, no matter how incompetent or brutal, to rule over everyone else: God put them there, so it must be his will.

In 2005, journalist Chris Mooney documented how the antiscience attitudes of the George W. Bush administration, motivated in part by the heavy representation of Catholics and evangelical Christians in virtually all federal offices from the president on down and dominating most advisory panels, suppressed reports by government scientists on issues such as birth control, global warming, and stem-cell research.[31]

Antiscience is implicit or even explicit throughout this movement. Scientists have to stop just sitting back and avoiding challenging religion. The welfare and, indeed, the survival of our species are at stake.

The Republican Party today is completely dominated by the Christian right while the Democrats at least exhibit some cautious independence from Christian ideology. Here's a typical example of religious intrusion in American politics. In 2011 Senator Jim DeMint (then Republican from South Carolina and currently president of the right-wing Heritage Foundation) appeared on the Family Research Council's weekly radio show and said:

> Some are trying to separate the social, cultural issues from fiscal issues, but you really can't do that. America works, freedom works, when people have that internal gyroscope that comes from a belief in God and biblical faith. Once we push that out, you no longer have the capacity to live as a free person without the external controls of an authoritarian government. I've said it often and I believe it—the bigger government gets, the smaller God gets, as people become more dependent on government and less dependent on God.[32]

He then added:

> We've found we can't set up free societies around the world because they don't have the moral underpinnings that come from biblical faith. I don't think Christians should cower from this debate, should be told that their views and their values should be separate from government policies, because America doesn't work without the faith that created it.

Consider the recent phenomenon called the Tea Party. A 2011 poll from the Pew Forum showed a strong religious right influence on the Tea Party.[33] Among registered voters, 69 percent of those who agreed with the religious right said they also agreed with the Tea Party. Only 4 percent disagreed. Tea Party members support the social agenda of religious conservatives by large fractions: 64 percent oppose same-sex marriage; 59 percent say abortion should be illegal in most or all cases.

The religious beliefs of Americans who consider themselves part of the Tea Party were reported in a survey by Robert P. Jones and Daniel Cox as part of the Third Biennial American Values Survey.[34] They found that 47 percent believe that the Bible is the literal word of God compared to one-third of the general population and 64 percent of white evangelicals.

The Fall of Foolish Faith

Religious faith would not be such a negative force in society if it were just about religion. However, the magical thinking that becomes deeply ingrained whenever faith rules over facts warps all areas of life. It produces a frame of mind in which concepts are formulated with deep passion but without the slightest attention paid to the evidence that bears on the concept. Nowhere is this more evident than in America today where the large majority of the public hold on to a whole set of beliefs despite the total lack of evidence to support these beliefs and, indeed, strong evidence that denies them. These beliefs are not just limited to religion, but extend to the occult (often condemned by churches), economics, politics, and health.

It is not that the public lacks information. In fact, today we are all inundated with information, especially on the Internet. However, much of that information is untrustworthy and it takes a trained thinker to filter out the good from the bad. Magical thinking and blind faith are the worst mental system we can apply under these circumstances. They allow the most outrageous lies to be accepted as facts.

From its very beginning, religion has been a tool used by those in power to retain that power and keep the masses in line. This continues today as religious groups are manipulated to work against believers' own often unrecognized best interests in health and economic well-being in order to cast doubt on well-established scientific findings. This would not be possible except for the diametrically opposed worldviews of science and religion. Science is not going to change its commitment to the truth. We can only hope religion will change its commitment to nonsense.

I have an urgent plea to scientists and all thinking people. We need to focus our attention on one goal, which will not be reached in the lifetime of the youngest among us but has to be achieved someday if humanity is to survive. That goal is the replacement of foolish faith and its vanities with something more sublime—knowledge and understanding that is securely based on observable reality.[35]

4

FAITH, EPISTEMOLOGY, AND ANSWERING SOCRATES' QUESTION BY TRANSLATION

Peter Boghossian

Two Realizations

Two moments in my life indelibly changed how I understand faith.

The first was when I was in sixth grade. The last day before Christmas break the teacher started talking about Santa. A Jewish girl in class leaned into me and whispered, "My dad told me not to tell anyone there's no Santa. He said Christian kids would get upset."

I was stunned. A grand—perhaps *the* grand—conspiracy had just accidentally been revealed to me. I paused to take it in, but not for too long; I wanted her to know that I knew there was no Santa, and I needed to know if she knew of any lesser conspiracies. I stated, "Of course I know that." And I waited to see if more information was forthcoming. It wasn't, so I lied, "I know a lot of other secrets, too." She quickly replied, "You mean that Jesus isn't the Son of God?"

Shock. Dead silence. Despair.

I wasn't raised in a religious household and was never religious, but in the back of my mind I always took it for granted that there was a man named Jesus who was the Son of God. It never occurred to me not only that this wasn't true, but that there was also a vast conspiracy keeping this information secret.

I rushed home and tried to play it coy, but failed. I immediately and excitedly blurted out to my mother what my friend told me, "There is no Santa and Jesus isn't the Son of God!" She calmly responded that my friend is Jewish and they have different beliefs. I asked (in language I'm sure wasn't as well articulated as my recollection), "Doesn't it have to be the case that he either was or wasn't the Son of God? How could someone's beliefs determine what's true?" My mother calmly responded with a nonresponse—she told me that there are many different religions whose adherents have many different beliefs. She proceeded to tell me about Buddhists, who have yet another, different set of propositions they hold as true.

Thus my first insight about different faith traditions was that they make competing claims—Jesus was and was not the Son of God—and those claims cannot all be correct.

The second moment that forever changed my understanding of faith came approximately twenty years later. I was leading a discussion about the role of evidence in belief formation during a critical-thinking class at a local university. One question led to another, and a student in class told me he agreed with me in general, but that evidence needn't play a "definitive role" in religious beliefs. I wasn't sure what he meant by "definitive role," so I asked him for an example. He talked about evolution (or "Darwinism," as he termed it) and biblical passages that contradicted basic tenets of evolutionary biology.

Being the product of ten years of Catholic education, I was quite comfortable discussing scripture, so I asked for scriptural support for his assertion. When it wasn't forthcoming, I pressed him and told him either to acknowledge that his claim did not have biblical support or to repudiate it and consequently change his mind. He told me matter-of-factly that it was his faith and thus did not require definitive evidential support or argument. I brought the discussion back to epistemology (how we know what we know) and asked him—again—how he knew the claims of evolutionary biology were false and what passages in the Bible lend support to this claim. He replied, "I just told you, it's my faith. I know it because of my faith. And you don't seem to get that. It's my faith."

He was right. I didn't get it and I hadn't gotten it for decades. In spite of ten years of Jesuit education, teaching critical thinking, ethics, and rationality to thousands of students, advanced degrees in philosophy and education, and a publication record in reasoning, Socratic pedagogy, and critical thinking—I didn't get it—until that instant.

That second moment awoke me from my dogmatic slumber. It was the first moment I realized the role that faith plays in religious beliefs. Faith is an epistemology—it's a method of coming to knowledge (or of claiming it)—and conclusions that result from this epistemology are knowledge claims.[1]

In graduate school I had of course studied Søren Kierkegaard, William James, Alvin Plantinga, and various versions of fideism, but I always took these as abstract intellectual exercises—these were the sorts of positions one studies to earn a doctorate in philosophy.[2] (Of course this might mean that I never understood fideism very well.) It never occurred to me that there were actual fideists. Interestingly, it was likely my Jesuit education—which frowned upon fideism in any form and instead sought a synthesis of faith and reason—that sheltered me from this realization. Without it, I couldn't see that faith serves as an epistemological tool for religious believers.

Three Facts

Ultimately, there is no way around the following three facts: (1) faith is an epistemology; (2) in religious contexts, the term faith is used when one assigns a higher confidence value to a belief than is warranted by the evidence;[3] (3) some people live their lives (make decisions, inform actions, etc.) based upon their faith-based beliefs. For the remainder of this chapter I'll flesh out the first two of these facts and show how they relate to the third fact. First, I'll discuss knowledge, justification, and faith as an epistemology. Second, I'll discuss Sophisticated Theologians™, confidence values, and attempts to obscure facts one and two.[4] Next, I'll briefly issue a call for honesty. Finally, I'll attempt to answer one of Socrates' moral questions through word substitution of a single sentence based upon the analyses in this chapter.

Fact One: Knowledge, Justification, and Faith as Epistemology

Epistemology is a branch of philosophy focusing on how one comes to knowledge, which processes of knowing can be relied upon to lead one to truth, and what knowledge is. In *A Manual for Creating Atheists*, I unpack the statement, "faith is an epistemology" as follows:

Conclusions one comes to as the result of an epistemological process are knowledge claims. A knowledge claim is an assertion of truth. . . . For example, "I have faith Jesus Christ will heal my sickness because it says so in Luke" is a knowledge claim. The utterer of this statement is asserting Jesus will heal her. Those who make faith claims are professing *to know* something about the external world . . . when someone says, "Jesus walked on water" (Matthew 14:22–33), that person is claiming *to know* there was an historical figure named Jesus and that he, unaided by technology, literally walked across the surface of the water. "Jesus walked on water" is a knowledge claim—an objective statement of fact.[5]

Dating back to Plato's *Theaetetus*, Knowledge has been understood as Justified True Belief.[6] That is, to say one knows P (a proposition), P needs to be justified (one needs sufficient evidence to warrant belief), true (P must lawfully correspond to reality), and believed (one's verbal behavior needs to comport with one's internal state in that one needs to believe what one claims to believe).[7] Faith is an epistemology because faith is *used* as a substitute for justification (J). Faith is a process many people use to come to (or to claim to come to) knowledge.

However, Sophisticated Theologians™ and apologists, unlike rank-and-file believers, understand that conclusions resulting from a faith-based epistemology are inherently suspect; intellectually they understand that faith is a process that produces arbitrary conclusions that cannot be considered knowledge. Consequently, they obfuscate the fact that faith is an epistemology and instead claim that Christ, or "the witness of the Holy Spirit," is living within them; they claim to have faith that their feelings stand in lawful correspondence to external reality (thus, they assert the True part of Justified True Belief). To Sophisticated Theologians™, faith is unshakable confidence that their perceptions and feeling states (Plantinga terms these "properly basic") accurately map onto the terrain of objective reality.[8]

However, all this epistemological rebranding does is move faith one link further down the epistemic chain. In other words, instead of faith being an epistemology, the perception believed to be the Holy Spirit becomes the epistemological bedrock, with knowledge claims emerging from this foundation.[9]

Sophisticated Theologians™

Sophisticated Theologians™ and seasoned apologists attempt to obfuscate facts one (faith is an epistemology) and two (in religious contexts, the term *faith* is used when one assigns a higher confidence value to a belief than is warranted by the evidence), and trumpet fact three (some people live their lives based upon their faith-based beliefs as a moral virtue). These individuals—who are usually intelligent and thus more adept at rationalizing conclusions—assert that they have evidence for propositions in their faith tradition, and furthermore, that these propositions are supported by abundant historical grounding sufficient to warrant belief. In the context of Christianity, the faithful will cite a long line of ancient and contemporary Christians who share their lack of evidence but affirm their conviction: Augustine, Aquinas, Alvin Plantinga, Alister McGrath, Kerby Anderson, William Alston, Robert Audi, and so on, and those are just a few names beginning with the letter *A* (either the first or last).

The arguments of Sophisticated Theologians™ take many forms, but the basic thrust is that there is adequate historical evidence and/or argument to warrant belief in propositions within their faith tradition. Sometimes Sophisticated Theologians™ invoke prophecy; for example, contemporary Christian apologists will cite "evidence" that before the birth of Jesus there were signs that a messiah would be born (G. K. Beale, Michael Brown, Walter C. Kaiser Jr., Josh McDowell). Other times they will invoke a history of "scholarship" surrounding Christ's alleged empty tomb (William Lane Craig, Gary Habermas), or assert Christ's alleged miracles (Norman Geisler, R. Douglas Geivett, J. P. Moreland), or barrage interlocutors with biblical exegesis (N. T. Wright, Paul Copan, Ben Worthington III), or profess the accuracy and reliability of the Bible (Gleason Archer, Craig L. Blomberg, D. A. Carson), or lay out a principles of "cold case" investigations to examine the reliability of the alleged eyewitness accounts in the gospels and of the resurrection (Michael Licona, J. Warner Wallace, Richard Bauckham).

The most sophisticated of all Sophisticated Theologians™ (William Lane Craig, Alvin Plantinga, Richard Swinburne, Nicholas Wolterstorff) grasp the problem with faith-based epistemologies and understand the role of evidence in conveying warrant upon beliefs. These individuals generally eschew discussions of physical evidence and instead present complex, abstract *arguments* like the Kalām cosmological argument, or Aquinas' third argument for the existence of God, or Anselm's ontological argument, or they devise their own epistemology to validate their intuitions.

Fact Two: Assigning Higher Confidence Values to Beliefs than Are Warranted

Implicitly or explicitly, we assign confidence values to our beliefs. For example, I assign a very high confidence value to the proposition "The world existed before I was born," whereas I assign a lower confidence value to "My given name is Peter Boghossian" (however unlikely it may be, I could have been switched at birth). An even lower confidence value is assigned to propositions such as "My shoes were not made by child laborers" and "The red snapper I thought I ate for dinner tonight was actually tilapia."[10]

When the word *faith* is used in a religious context, the confidence value assigned to a belief is higher than what's warranted by the evidence. That is, faith is how believers pick up that slack—it's the difference between what the confidence value in a proposition should be (based upon the best available evidence) and what the confidence value in a proposition actually is.

Let's use the proposition, P, "Jesus walked on water," as an example. Without delving into historical esoterica, or examining whether or not the Bible constitutes sufficient evidence to warrant belief, or being bogged down by methods of evaluating historical evidence, let's accept by fiat that the confidence value a hypothetical person, S, could place in P, is a number between .000000001 and 99.[11] Now let us suppose that S, after a sincere and rigorous examination of the evidence, comes to the conclusion that P is 60 percent likely to be true. If S is asked how certain she is that Jesus walked on water, and she responds with any number higher than 60 percent—that's faith.

Fact two, then, is that one uses the word *faith* when the confidence value in a proposition is elevated above the confidence value warranted by the evidence.

Sophisticated Theologians™:
Faith, Obfuscation, and Fallacies

There's a long history of Christian "scholarship" by Sophisticated Theologians™ that is, frankly, too tedious, too disingenuous, and too corrupted by confirmation bias to deserve serious intellectual consideration.[12] These are historical attempts to either rationalize or obfuscate facts one and two and the deductive inference that follows from them: *faith* is the word one invokes when there's not enough justification (J) to warrant belief in a proposition, but when one decides to believe anyway.[13]

By sidestepping the entire corpus of Christian literature, which gives it the consideration it is due, one can examine what people mean when they use the word *faith* in a religious context and focus on truth claims as they relate to faith and faith-based epistemologies.[14] Moreover, by bypassing historical sophistry and specious attempts to legitimize faith, we can avoid the well-rehearsed responses of Sophisticated Theologians.™ For example, they say brilliant historical and contemporary figures had faith (Descartes, Newton, Kepler, Francis Collins). No matter what definition we analyze we've missed a nuance, we don't understand the contextual grounding of faith, our understanding needs much further study, or to understand faith one needs to possess it, and we've offended the faithful by disrespecting sacred ideas, and so on.

These responses have become so stale there are fallacies named after them: Courtier's Reply, Appeal to Righteous Indignation, and Appeal to Sanctity.[15] These objections have no place in a serious discussion and distract from the substance of the argument.

Being told by Sophisticated Theologians™ that one is unqualified or unsuited to discuss an argument because one is unfamiliar with the history of Christian scholarship is akin to one being told, "That's not how Spock used that word in *Star Trek* episode #10, 'The Corbomite Maneuver,' and episode #52, 'The Omega Glory'. Clearly, you've not read the surrounding literature in Whitman Books, Wanderer Books, Archway Paperback, etc. And if you had read Shatner's *Dark Victory* then you'd never have that interpretation.[16] You need to deepen your understanding before you can speak meaningfully about such issues."

The problem with these statements is that they assume further study is needed before one can come to the conclusion that people don't fly around in warp-capable starships or beam across large distances. These are also an attempt to evade substantive criticism of an argument by making one's interlocutor appear ignorant of exogenous minutiae that have no bearing on the fundamental arguments.[17] These attempts at obfuscation presuppose that whatever point of reference Sophisticated Theologians™ are using must be *the* groundwork by which faith needs to be understood.[18]

Honesty

Sophisticated Theologians™ verbally dance around fact one, that faith is an epistemology, and cloud fact two, that the word *faith* is used (in religious contexts) when higher confidence values are assigned to propositions than the evidence warrants, yet proudly proclaim fact three, that people should live their lives based upon their faith-based beliefs.

Instead of obfuscation, rationalization, insincerity, and perhaps even outright dishonesty, I will now issue a call to all Sophisticated Theologians™. Before engaging in a serious discussion about faith or epistemology, the following statement should be made at the start of the conversation: "There is insufficient evidence to warrant my confidence in a set of propositions—most of which are knowledge claims—but I've decided to lend my belief to them in spite of this." This sort of blunt, honest, forthright statement would be clearer and more sincere than the history of obfuscation that has mired and continues to obscure faith and its trappings.

The other benefit of making this candid admission is that—finally and permanently—debates over the definition of faith as "belief without sufficient evidence" can be put to rest. The conversation could then shift either to what I've termed the "benefits argument," that is, whether or not having faith is beneficial for individuals or communities, or to the moral argument, that is, whether or not one can ever be morally justified in using or propagating a faulty epistemology.

Answering Socrates' Question by Translation

I started this chapter with my two seminal realizations: (1) different faith traditions make competing claims that cannot all be correct, and (2) faith is an epistemology. These observations set me on an unexpected path of trying to understand faith.

One conclusion I came to was that the word *faith* needs to be analyzed by how it's used in a religious context and not by how its use has been rationalized for centuries. When one engages in this linguistic analysis, one is led to the inescapable conclusion I labeled fact two: the term *faith* is used when one assigns a higher confidence value to a belief than is warranted by the evidence.

Now that these terms have been clarified and relevant issues have been framed epistemologically, we can finally turn our attention to fact three—some people live their lives based upon their faith-based beliefs.

One of Socrates' well-known moral questions is: "What sort of life ought one to lead?" By making word substitutions we are now better positioned to answer Socrates' question as it relates to fact three. "Some people live their lives (make decisions, inform actions, etc.) based upon their faith-based beliefs." Formulated as a question this becomes, "Should some people live their lives based upon their faith-based beliefs?"

Let's keep the first sentence intact and change "their faith-based beliefs," in the second one to "an epistemology that assigns higher confidence values to propositions than is warranted by the evidence." Fully translated, Socrates' question as it bears on fact three thus reads, "Should some people live their lives (make decisions, inform actions, etc.) based upon an epistemology in which one assigns a higher confidence value to a belief than is warranted by the evidence?"[19] (Many of the chapters that follow answer this question by detailing the harms that result when people act on the failed epistemology that is called Christian faith.)

Rendering the question this way is more honest and more blunt than historical and contemporary attempts by Sophisticated Theologians™ to obfuscate basic facts about the use of the term *faith* and what role it should play in one's life.

Socratic Optimism: Leaving the World of Shadows

Finally, there's a wondrous optimism and happiness in Socrates' question: How should we live our lives? Our approaches to this question will at least partially determine the lives we lead. And developing the disposition to engage the question honestly and sincerely will give us an ability to discern what is likely to be true from what we want to believe.

The Socratic project of asking questions is a way to approach an authentic life. We can begin this journey by assigning confidence values to beliefs based upon the best available evidence. Once we've done this, we'll increase the likelihood that our beliefs will align with reality—only then can we create conditions outside of ourselves that enable us to flourish.

Reason, rationality, honesty, authenticity, epistemic humility, and assigning confidence values in direct proportion to evidence take us toward the good life. They're ways to escape from the cave.

Part Two

POLITICAL/INSTITUTIONAL HARMS

5

LOVE YOUR ENEMY, KILL YOUR ENEMY

Crusades, Inquisitions, and Centuries of Christian Violence

David Eller

Christians like to tout the exceptionalism of their religion. They are correct in one regard: Christianity is exceptional among the major religions for beginning with a killing and for keeping killing central to the faith ever since. No other religion, for instance, dangles a dead man from the necks of believers.

Christians claim that theirs is a religion of peace, and there are peaceful injunctions in their faith, like the fundamental commandment not to kill. Such values make the long history of Christian violence all the more perverse, but of course Christianity is utterly unexceptional in its inconsistency (for instance, Exodus 15:3 states that "The Lord is a man of war" who, according to Psalm 18:34 "teaches my hands to war") and in the failure of its followers to live up to its ideals.

This chapter will focus on two episodes of Christian violence, violence that was not only protracted but officially authorized and highly institutionalized—namely, the Crusades and the Inquisition. However, these two phenomena are not isolated from each other or from wider Christian history; indeed, we will argue here that the Inquisition was a continuation of the crusading spirit long after the war with Muslims was lost, since the Crusades themselves were not "an organized campaign under unopposed military or ecclesiastical leadership but a movement, supported by individuals whose motivations for taking the cross were as varied as their social and ethnic ties"[1] (and as varied and con- tradictory as Christianity's own opinions on war). Finally, both the Crusades and the Inquisition follow a long history of Christian justification for violence, justification that, as historian Jonathan Phillips put it, "continues to resonate in modern politics" and "shows no sign of diminishing."[2]

War and Peace (but Mostly War) in the Formation of Christianity

Christianity's attitudes toward systematic violence are by no means unique to it; like most of the rest of the religion, its thoughts and practices originated in its two main sources, Judaism and the Roman Empire. Ancient Israelite religion never pretended to be peaceful; it was rather a code of tribal law that recognized a concept of *milhemet mitzvah* or "commanded war." Milhemet mitzvah, ordered by their god, was obligatory (shirking the command could incur divine wrath) and included not only self-defense but also acquisition of territory and obliteration of an enemy. Accordingly, much of the national history in Exodus and Deuteronomy is a chronicle and guide to war, such as when the great war chief Joshua reduced the cities of Lachish, Eglon, Hebron, and Debir; he

> smote them with the edge of the sword, and utterly destroyed all the souls that were therein; he left none remaining. . . . So Joshua smote all the country of the hills, and of the south, and of the vale, and of the springs, and all their kings he left none remaining, but utterly destroyed all that breathed, *as the Lord God of Israel commanded* (Joshua 10:40, emphasis added).

Numbers 31 likewise recounts how the Hebrews warred against the Midianites, pitilessly slaying every male including children, as well as any nonvirgin women (how Moses's troops made that determination is not specified), but keeping the virgins and girls and cattle and property for themselves.

Meanwhile, the Greeks and Romans were developing a theory of "just war," with rules for initiating conflict (the *jus ad bellum*) and for executing conflict (the *jus in bellum*). The Hebrews were not particularly concerned about "just war," since war was justified by their god's command. Equally warlike, the Greeks placed limitations on weapons and tactics, declarations and combatants. But it was the Roman statesman Cicero (106-43 BCE) who gave the most articulate statement on just war. To be justified, a war had to be authorized by a proper governmental authority, formally declared, executed so as to distinguish between the innocent and the guilty, and ultimately in service of justice; the "only excuse" for war, he wrote in *De Officiis*, was "that we may live in peace unharmed."

In its early decades, Christianity was hardly in a position to make war. Indeed, Christians suffered some persecution for their beliefs but, according to Notre Dame historian of Christianity Candida Moss, not nearly as much as they like to remember; rather, all their talk of martyrdom allowed them to play the victim and emulate their dead leader.[3] At this stage, most of Christianity's thirst for destruction was turned upon itself: Church father Tertullian (160–225 CE) strongly urged believers to seek martyrdom, since the Christian's own blood was his or her only key to the gates of heaven. Tertullian's contemporary Origen (184–253 CE), in his aptly titled *Exhortation to Martyrdom*, also insisted paradoxically that the only way for a Christian to save his/her life was to lose it through martyrdom.

As for committing violence, early Christians shrank from it in horror. Blessed are the peacemakers who turn the other cheek, after all, their savior taught them. Roland Bainton found no sources before the era of Constantine, the first Roman emperor to adopt Christianity in 313, that "countenanced Christian participation in warfare."[4] For instance, no Christians served in the Roman army until 173 CE, and Tertullian wrote sternly against military service. Obeying their savior, Christian thinkers like Athenagoras and Justin Martyr recommended not resisting evil, not defending oneself, not even notifying the police if one was robbed, and happily dying for Christ instead of killing for him.

How times have changed! Christian pacifism proved to be more a virtue of the weak (causing no harm when one is too weak to cause harm) than a truly principled stance. Almost as soon as the Church stopped being persecuted, it began persecuting, now with the machinery of state on its side. Official orthodoxy branded all other interpretations unorthodoxy and heresy, and already in 385 Priscillian, the bishop of Spain, and six others were tortured and killed. The religion of peace and love had turned deadly.

You Always Hurt the Ones You Love

Despite having attained political power by the fourth century CE, "Christian rulers lacked a moral theory on war that would reconcile their beliefs as Christians with their responsibilities as statesmen."[5] But the Roman Empire (or the United States, for that matter) would quickly succumb to its rivals without a handy legitimation for worldly violence. Fortunately, one of the great minds of Christendom would provide it for them.

Augustine of Hippo (354–430) watched from his bishopric in North Africa as the Goths conquered the eternal city of Rome in 410. A fairly recent convert to Christianity himself, Augustine was well acquainted with Cicero's writing and used it to construct his own version of Christian just war. The biggest problem for Augustine and other Christians was reconciling the Christian virtue of love with the carnage of war, and he found a convenient solution. While the Christian "law of love" forbids them to harm or kill even in self-defense, "the law of love itself obliges Christians to come to the aid of others and so justifies the use of force that inflicts harm on malefactors"; happily for Christians, "'the injustice of the opposing side . . . lays on the wise man the duty of waging wars.' In carrying out such a duty, however, Christian statesmen and warriors should love the enemy they forcibly oppose."[6] In Augustine's own words, "Love does not preclude a benevolent severity, nor that correction which compassion itself dictates. . . . The love of enemies admits of no dispensation, but love does not exclude wars of mercy waged by the good."[7] Thus, to the classical pre-Christian theory of just war he added two characteristically Christian dictums: "that love should be the motive in war, and that justice should lie on one side only."[8]

With Augustine, Christianity had the permission it needed to evolve from a pacifist to a militarist religion. But the condoning of violence went much further in his and the Church's thought. Augustine was also a champion of religious persecution, specifically against heretics whose beliefs diverged from Church orthodoxy. He reasoned that crime is crime, and spiritual crime is graver than property or violent crime, and since death was the penalty for some secular offenses, for dissidents and schismatics pain, torture, and death were not unjustified. Indeed, by this logic, since the heretic was committing a spiritual crime, and doing harm to the Church, physical pain (Augustine preferred whipping and exile over execution when possible) was not persecution at all but rather punishment, *because the heretic was the guilty party*. In his mind, "There is an unjust persecution which the wicked inflict on the Church of Christ, and there is a just persecution which the Church of Christ inflicts on the wicked."[9]

Even more than criminal justice, Augustine promoted persecution as instruction and correction of error. Like a caring parent, the persecutor uses pain "to heal by love, not to injure by hatred" so that the victim "may learn not to blaspheme."[10] In the long run (if not during the torture or execution), the victim would hopefully come to appreciate and thank the persecutor: "It has been a blessing to many to be driven first by fear of bodily pain, in order afterwards to be instructed."[11] Either way, though, it was doing the heretic a favor by coercing "those who carried the standard of Christ against Christ to return to Catholic unity, under stress of fear and compulsion, rather than merely . . . leave them free to go astray and be lost."[12] In fact, Michael Gaddis, in his aptly titled *There Is No Crime in Christ*, posits that Augustine and his successors viewed persecution precisely as religious (and beneficial) coercion, which "justified itself through a disciplinary discourse: it employed calibrated violence not to destroy its target[s] but to chastise, reform, even educate them."[13]

Christianity found its doctrine of justified and loving violence in the nick of time, for the centuries after Augustine were to be particularly tumultuous ones. The year 476 is commonly given as the official fall of the Roman Empire, although Rome continued to be a significant power center, and the eastern empire based in Constantinople survived for another millennium. The so-called Dark Ages ensued, with tribal wars and petty squabbles. Meanwhile, Muhammad began receiving his revelations from Allah (merely the Arabic *al-Lah* for "God") in 610, achieving political power in the town of Medina in 622, which represents the start of the Muslim era. Within a few years of his death, a confident Islam conquered the easternmost and southernmost reaches of the old Roman Empire, taking Syria in 638 and Egypt in 641; the city of Jerusalem, sacred to Muslims as well as to Jews and Christians, surrendered to Muhammad's successor Umar in 637. By 711 Muslims sweeping across North Africa entered Spain and were only repelled from Western Europe by the Frankish warlord Charles Martel in 732.

At the same time, from the north came the threat of the Vikings. By the late

700s Norsemen were raiding from Britain to Russia, penetrating deep into Europe along the rivers and actually sailing through the Mediterranean. Many historians mark the end of the Viking era only at 1066 with their failed invasion of England. But the pagan Norse were hardly the only nearby enemies, as Christians of the new Holy Roman Empire fought wars against non-Christian European neighbors.

Inside the house of Christendom, all was not well either. The bishop of Rome (known today as the Pope) continued to declare his authority over all Christians, even after the displacement of imperial power from Rome to Constantinople, which was renamed Byzantium. Almost as the Viking threat was subsiding, the eastern and western branches of Christianity finally formally separated in 1054 over doctrinal and power disputes; known as the Great Schism, the break left Christianity permanently divided into a supposedly global Catholic Church and an assortment of national Orthodox Churches.

The Crusades against the Muslims

The first decades of the second Christian millennium were thus trying times. The apocalypse had not arrived in the year 1000, although the Viking assaults seemed like the end of the world to some. Christendom itself was rent by divisions between its two great imperial seats, and Islam ruled the western end of Europe, even as a new threat from the East arose. In 1071 the Turks handed Christians a significant defeat at the Battle of Manzikert, capturing Jerusalem from its previous Muslim overlords in the same year. In 1081 a Turkish kingdom was established at the famous Christian site of Nicaea. While Christianity as a religion was in turmoil and decline, the various national states of Europe were in their early formative stages. England, France, and central Europe were free from invaders for the first time in two centuries and eager to exhibit their national prowess.

What has come to be called the Crusades must be understood within this troubled historical context. Most importantly, as Geoffrey Hindley reminds us, the eye of western Christians was not exclusively or primarily on Jerusalem or the Muslims; after all, one Muslim ruler or another had occupied the holy city for four hundred years by the late eleventh century. In fact, Hindley contends that Pope Gregory VII (reigned 1073–85) "had envisaged a military campaign with himself as 'general and pope,' to establish papal primatial authority in Constantinople."[14] In other words, the immediate prize for the Catholic Church was not Jerusalem but the Eastern Church.

The precarious circumstances of the Eastern Roman or Byzantine Empire presented the jealous Westerners exactly the opportunity that Gregory had desired. In 1095 at the Council of Piacenza, Byzantine emperor Alexius Comnenus (sometimes spelled Alexios Komnenos) petitioned for Western aid against Turks looming on his borders; at the time, says Hindley, "there was no talk by these envoys of the Eastern Emperor liberating Jerusalem."[15] The author of the Crusades, Pope Urban II (reigned 1088–99), seized the crisis in eastern Christendom as his chance to fulfill Gregory's wish, calling upon Christians to rise to the holy cause of resisting the Turks; at the Council of Clermont, which convened on November 18, 1095, Urban "preached a sermon on the suffering of the Christians in the East and concluded with a passionate appeal for volunteers to enlist under the sign of the Cross of Christ."[16] But Michael Köhler insists too that "the conquest of the Holy Places was seemingly not a primary objective" of the Pope, and the War of the Cross as a program to take Jerusalem "was not presented to the Crusaders from the outset"; indeed, for many of the combatants, military action was "little more than an extensive conquering expedition" dressed up in Christian garb.[17]

Make no mistake, whatever its original mixed motivations, the Crusades were sponsored by the Church (recall, in order to be a just war, it had to be declared by a rightful authority) and thoroughly painted in religious terms. Crusaders frequently swore a vow to the Pope's plan, and they had crosses sewn on their clothing. Crusading was construed as an opportunity to do penance and earn a spiritual indulgence or remission from sin (the sort of spiritual horse-trading that incensed Martin Luther centuries later). In fact, the whole endeavor was not referred to as a "crusade" at all at the time but was rather understood in terms of the Christian concept of penance and pilgrimage: "men spoke of a 'general passage" (*passagium generale*), a 'journey' (*iter*), an 'expedition of the Cross' (*expeditio crucis*), or quite simply a 'pilgrimage' (Latin, *peregrinatio*), while the crusaders were commonly known as '*cruces-ignati*,' 'marked with the sign of the Cross.'"[18] Yet not all Church officials approved of the concept of crusading, including the famous Anselm of Canterbury (1033–1109).

So when the Christian militants marched eastward, their understanding and goal "had little in common with Urban's intentions and nothing at all with that of the Byzantine emperor,"[19] and quite predictably "the Crusaders who arrived in Constantinople were considerably different from the soldiers whom Alexius awaited."[20] This is especially and painfully true for the first enthusiasts to arrive, the so-called People's Crusade, led by a figure known as Peter the Hermit. Roaming from village to village encouraging the common folk to defend their religion, Peter stirred up a mob of fifteen thousand, which even the Catholic New Advent online encyclopedia characterizes as "disorganized, undisciplined, penniless hordes, almost destitute of equipment, who, surging eastward through the valley of the Danube, plundered as they went along and murdered the Jews in German cities."[21] Of various peasant armies, Peter's was the only one to reach Byzantium, where several thousand of its numbers were killed by Christian officials out of fear for the threat they posed. The survivors trekked on to Turkish territory, where they "pillaged the Turkish countryside, killed and tortured even the Christian inhabitants,"[22] and were wiped out by a Turkish army at a "battle" at Nicaea on October 21, 1096.

While that pathetic nonsense was transpiring, the official First Crusade stepped off in August 1096, passing through German lands where some Jews were forcibly converted and others slain. Perhaps one hundred thousand soldiers and camp followers reached Byzantium and then marched on to confront the Turks. After several stunning victories, the crusaders commenced their siege of Jerusalem on July 14, 1097, which was not actually controlled by the Turks but by other Muslim rivals, the Fatimids. But such distinctions were insignificant to the Christian soldiers, as were distinctions between Muslim, Christian, and Jew inside the city. Once the walls were breached,

> blood-crazed crusaders were streaming over the walls and through the streets of the northern part of the city slaughtering every living thing that crossed their path. No banner was going to save lives in this shambles, while the Jewish population of the city were cut down—man, woman, and child— where they stood hoping for sanctuary in their chief synagogue. . . .
>
> It is doubtful whether any other of the inhabitants of Jerusalem on the dreadful day survived. The native Christians had been expelled from the city before the siege began; they were lucky, for in the mayhem of sacking they too no doubt would have perished. The slaughter lasted the best part of two days.[23]

Thrilled with their accomplishment, the rapturous Christians reportedly "all flung themselves prostrate, their arms outstretched in the form of the Cross. 'Each man thought he could still see before him the crucified body of Jesus Christ. And it seemed to them that they were at the gates of Heaven.'"[24]

For many pilgrims, their task was complete, and they returned to Europe. A small contingent of Westerners remained in the East, where, if their presence "did not constitute a project of colonization," then "the most important princes of the crusading army used the opportunity for the establishment of lordships and social climbing."[25] In other words, the just and holy war rapidly morphed into a mundane territorial conquest and political occupation. Still more ignobly, Western business interests saw the opening of the East as a money-making occasion, and Hindley reckons that a Western merchant "would help a Muslim sooner than his Christian competitor."[26] Ironically, between political necessity and economic opportunism, religious enemies in the war regularly became partners and allies in the peace. Christians not only made trade deals with their former Muslim adversaries but also literally forged alliances with Fatimid Muslims against their common Turkish rival.

Köhler concludes that "an abundance of relations through treaties, alliances, and perhaps even suzerainties arose already during the First Crusade,"[27] proving that the Christians were neither too pious nor too outraged to cooperate with Muslims. Even so, the small contingent of Westerners could not hope to hold cities deep inside Muslim territory, so in response to losses to Muslim armies, Pope Eugenius III (reigned 1145–53) ordered up a Second Crusade in late 1145. The mobilization began as the first had begun, with pogroms against local Jews. Eventually two Christian militias, one German and one French, arrived to fight the Turks, but the Germans were summarily crushed in 1147, and the French briefly besieged Damascus in 1148 before retreating in humiliation.

As the Christians were fading in power, a Muslim general, Salah-ed-Din or Saladin, was rising. Between the late 1160s and late 1180s, he grew from the ruler of Egypt to the head of a resurgent Islam, reconquering Jerusalem in 1187; impressively, unlike the good Christian soldiers, he did not slaughter the city's inhabitants but actually protected local Christians from harm. But this mercy did not prevent Christian pique from demanding a Third Crusade, proclaimed by Pope Gregory VIII on October 29, 1187. Mighty Western kings like Frederick Barbarossa of the Holy Roman Empire, Louis Augustus of France, and Richard I "the Lionhearted" of England answered the call. When Barbarossa died accidentally, "many Germans thought that God has turned against their cause. We are told that some killed themselves in despair while others renounced the Christian faith and converted to the heathen."[28] Louis and Richard handed Salah-ed-Din a defeat, and Richard executed 2,700 Turkish captives after accepting a ransom payment for them, but they retreated before capturing Jerusalem, essentially achieving nothing other than confirming Salah-ed-Din's image of Christians as untrustworthy barbarians.

Rounding out a century of crusading, Pope Innocent III dialed up a Fourth Crusade in 1198, but few kings and knights heeded the call this time. The Fourth Crusade was to be the most ignominious expedition so far, finally realizing the dreams of Gregory VII and Urban II. On June 24, 1203, Western Catholic forces descended on the imperial city of Constantinople/Byzantium, where Christianity had first been adopted by Constantine nearly nine hundred years earlier. After months of siege, the city fell to the Western Christians in April, 1204: "It was subjected to three days' pillage and brutal massacre. . . . The rank and file ran amok, but knights and men at arms, abbots and monks waded into the mayhem to plunder their full share."[29] Even the Catholic New Advent online encyclopedia confesses that there was "ruthless plundering of its churches and palaces. . . . The masterpieces of antiquity, piled up in public places and in the Hippodrome, were utterly destroyed. Clerics and knights, in their eagerness to acquire famous and priceless relics, took part in the sack of the churches."[30] Some of that plunder still adorns Western sites, like the celebrated horse sculptures on display in Venice. Triumphantly, a Western/Latin/Catholic regime was installed in the East, but it collapsed within a couple of generations.

Innocent III succeeded where the Muslims had failed and would continue to fail until 1453, humbling the eastern outpost of Christianity, but this was not his only dubious feat. He inspired five crusades in all, including one in Spain in 1212 against the Islamic Almohad Empire that ruled the southern half of Spain. The official Fifth Crusade was actually a succession of invading waves between 1213 and 1221 with little to show for their effort. But the most foolish moment came in 1212, when a French peasant boy inspired the so-called Children's Crusade. Although it was not authorized by the Pope, it stimulated popular zeal and received the support of local priests; full of crusading spirit, an untold mob of peasants and children marched south and east, where some settled or were enslaved in Italy and the rest were sent home.

Despite the fact that the Crusades accomplished nothing in the long run, other than alienating Muslims, their champion, the Catholic Church, continues to praise them to this day. The aforementioned Catholic encyclopedia speaks approvingly: "If, indeed, the Christian civilization of Europe has become universal culture, in the highest sense, the glory redounds, in no small measure, to the Crusades."

Crusading against the Enemy at Home

Jonathan Phillips is totally correct that "crusading was not a static concept,"[31] nor was it pure in motive or consistent in practice. In that way, crusading, like everything else that humans do—including religion—was messy, mutable, and deeply flawed. Nevertheless, fighting by Christians and even fighting in the name of Christianity, a habit inconceivable to and incompatible with the formative years of the religion, "was too deeply established within Catholic Europe to disappear after the loss of the Holy Land."[32] Fortunately there were plenty of enemies closer at hand. In order to accommodate all of these diverse enemies of Christ, the concept of the crusade or the just war or the holy war necessarily "widened to include heretics and schismatics deemed to threaten the authority of the Church, while more than once rival popes declared crusades against one another's supporters."[33]

Even before the generally recognized Crusades were finished, popes were sending righteous armies northward against the pagans of northern Europe. As early as 1147, Christian troops brought the true religion at the point of a sword to the Wends, Sorbs, and Obotrites of Central Europe, and the Finns were attacked in 1154. Pope Celestine III announced a crusade in the Baltic region against the Livonians (Latvia today) in 1195; after various setbacks and rebellions, the Livonians were largely converted to Christianity by force around 1212. The campaign to impose faith continued against the Latgallians, Selonians, and Estonians between 1208 and 1224; war against particular Baltic peoples persisted through the century, until the Saarema (1261) and the Curonians and Semigallians (1290) were finally subdued and "saved."

The Holy Church did not have to look to the fringes of the continent to find non-Christians and anti-Christians. Prussia, the heartland of modern Germany, was still pagan in the early 1200s, attracting crusaders like Duke Konrad of Poland and his Order of Dobrzyn; the knights of the Teutonic Order joined the fray in 1226. Still greater glory awaited in Russia, where the hated Eastern Orthodox Christians dominated, but the Teutonic Knights and the Swedish army could not conquer Russia, losing the Battle of the Ice in 1242. Speaking of the Swedes, they launched a series of crusades of their own from 1150, invading Finland three times over a hundred and fifty years.

If non-Christians were an affront to religious sensibilities, Christian heretics were an abomination. It will be recalled that Augustine centuries before had advocated punishment, torture, and even death for those who twisted faith. The 1179 Council of the Lateran equated heresy with banditry, and in 1208 Pope Innocent III declared that heresy was more dangerous than Islam, since it lurked in Christianity's back yard. One of the first groups to feel the sting of what we might call "internal crusade" was the Waldensians. Followers of Peter Waldo, the Waldensians promoted a life of extreme poverty, partly in protest against the corruption and luxury of the official Church. Waldo's teachings were condemned by the Church in 1179, but when the movement did not abate, King Pedro II of Aragon (a region in present-day Spain) expelled Waldensians and set a date after which all remaining heretics would be burnt to death. Elsewhere, eighty heretics including Waldensians were burned at the stake at Strasbourg in 1212.

Within a century the Waldensian heresy was suppressed, but a more stubborn and consequential one had already broken out in the Languedoc region of France. In the town of Albi, an intensely dualistic version of Christianity emerged, which believed that the material world was wholly evil, indeed had been created by Satan; as such, Jesus could not have been a material being but was instead perfect spirit, never having incarnated, never having died or resurrected. The leaders of these Albigensians, the "Perfect Men" or "Good Men," practiced celibacy, asceticism, and poverty. The Council of Tours in 1163 authorized local rulers to combat the Albigensians, also known as the Cathars, but some princes and even priests joined them. Pope Innocent took matters into his own hands, sending his representatives to the region to root out the heresy; in exchange for their faithful service, Rome "offered the same 'remission of sins' as those fighting for the Holy Land,"[34] illustrating that this too was a crusade. Sixty Cathars were burned at Les Casses and four hundred more at Lavaur; mass executions were also reported at Moissac in 1234 and Montsegur in 1244. Within a century, this heresy too was stamped out.

Finally, the failure of the official Fifth Crusade and the unofficial Children's Crusade did not exhaust the crusading energy against the Muslims. French and English noblemen led armies to the East between 1239 and 1241, and Louis IX of France took up the crusading cause in 1244. Pope Urban IV even considered calling another crusade in 1263, and in 1290 an Italian army described as "bands of disorderly crusaders spoiling for a fight" invaded the Middle East.[35] Pope Clement V (reigned 1264–1314) was among the last to entertain the notion of a crusade against the Muslims, but by this time something much more sinister and destructive had been unleashed on Europe itself.

The Inquisition: Justice of the Cross

In the midst of the Waldensian and Albigensian crises, the Church felt the need to establish some institutional measures to deal with heresy. One method was the employment of "inquisitors" to serve as investigators and judges for the Church: teams of papal inquisitors would travel to trouble spots to uncover heretics and correct them if possible, punish them if necessary. The year 1215 is sometimes given as the launch of the Inquisition, but it really coalesced gradually from decisions and legislation both before and after that date. Another important date is 1233, when Pope Gregory IX assigned the duties of inquiry to the Dominicans, charging them thus:

> When you arrive in a city, summon the bishops, clergy, and people, and preach a solemn sermon on faith; then select certain men of good repute to help you in trying the heretics and suspects brought before your tribunal. All who, on examination, are found guilty or suspected of heresy must promise complete obedience to the commands of the Church; if they refuse, you must prosecute them according to the statutes that we have already promulgated.[36]

The first inquisitors arrived in Languedoc to investigate the Cathars in 1233. Based on the Roman legal concept of *inquisitor* or inquiry, suspected heretics were brought before one or more inquisitors, who called witnesses and conducted cross-examinations. These agents were detectives, judges, and juries in one, ordained "to find out whether the accused was or was not guilty of a certain sin, the sin of heresy and rebellion against God's truth."[37] During the early stages of a proceeding, the accused was allowed to express repentance and to vow to obey the Church. In this sense, the Inquisition "was first and foremost a penitential and proselytizing office, not a penal tribunal";[38] all it really sought was contrition and conformity. However, if defendants refused to confess and/or repent, the full weight of Augustine's love fell upon them.

After (and sometimes before) the initial interview, the suspected heretic was jailed, often for an extended period, until a full trial was conducted; in fact, imprisonment alone was frequently sufficient to extract the all-important confession and oath of obedience. When a confession was not forthcoming, torture could be applied. Religious torture used exactly the same techniques as secular/legal/criminal torture, including the rack as a tool to stretch and break the body. The *strappado*, another torture device, was a rope-and-pulley system with which the victim was lifted off the ground by his or her wrists, bound behind the back, typically resulting in dislocated shoulders; weights were attached to the feet as necessary to increase the suffering. Water torture involved pouring copious amounts of liquid down the victim's throat or placing a wet cloth in the victim's mouth, preventing breathing and swallowing; readers may recognize recent American waterboarding in this procedure.

When "interrogation" had achieved its ultimate end—either a full confession or an adamant denial of guilt—the penalty phase began. Penalties ranged from minor to capital and always, from the Church's perspective, bore a penitential quality. At the milder end were penances like wearing one or more crosses on one's clothing or making a mandatory pilgrimage. Some guilty or obstinate defendants lost their homes and property. Many were held in jail, where it was believed they would enjoy the opportunity for spiritual rehabilitation. At the extreme, the accused was put to death, generally by burning at the stake, a public spectacle called the *auto-da-fé* or "act of faith." It is important to understand that most suspects did not receive this highest punishment; for example, records from Toulouse for the years 1307 to 1323 indicate nine hundred thirty penalties, of which forty-two were death by fire while one hundred forty-three were ordered to wear crosses, three hundred seven imprisoned, twenty-two sentenced to have their homes destroyed, nine sent on pilgrimages, one exiled, and many others released without further suffering.

As John Loftus explains (this volume, chapter 9), heretics were not the only victims of Church inquisitions. In 1320, Pope John XXII authorized the Inquisition to expand its mission into investigations of witchcraft and sorcery, and theologians at the University of Paris in 1398 pronounced witchcraft and other forms of magic to be a type of heresy. Of course, this reasoning is entirely consistent with the scriptures, particularly Exodus 22:18, which stipulates, "Thou shalt not suffer a witch [or in some translations a sorceress] to live." The papal bull Summis Desiderantes of 1484 instructed the Inquisition "to proceed to the correction, imprisonment, and punishment" of witches, and within two years the infamous guidebook for the identification, interrogation, and elimination of witches, the *Malleus Maleficarum* or "Hammer of Witches" was published.

Around the same time, a new and virulent manifestation of Church paranoia and Christian violence emerged in Spain. One limitation of the older Inquisition was that its victims were and only could be Christians; the Church claimed no authority over non-Christians, and non-Christians could not rightly be accused of heresy. In 1478, in the midst of the ongoing Spanish Catholic wars against the occupying Muslims or Moors, the crusading Catholic King Ferdinand and Queen Isabella received permission from Pope Sixtus IX to operate an independent inquisition against Jews. Specifically, the target of this Spanish Inquisition was Jews who had, under the duress of continuous discrimination and violence, converted to Christianity. By 1415 as many as half of all Spanish Jews had become *conversos* or Christian converts. While this conversion ideally bought them peace from persecution, it unfortunately brought the force of the Church upon them. The conversos were widely suspected of being insincere Christians; it was feared that they practiced their old religion in secret and even seduced other Jews away from the true faith, while a few actually did deconvert and resume their ancestral religion.

In 1482, the notorious Tomas de Torquemada was appointed Grand Inquisitor of Spain; his inquisitorial courts scoured the kingdom for apostates and heretics and killed more than two thousand people by the year 1500. The threats of the Spanish Inquisition were those of the previous version, varying from fasting and pilgrimage to confiscation of property, whipping, imprisonment (sometimes disguised as temporary monasticism), forced labor, exile, and of course public execution by *auto-da-fé*. Few defendants escaped punishment: documents from Toledo show that, between 1484 and 1531, only eighty-eight people were acquitted, or just two per year.[39]

In the early 1500s, after the successful reconquest of Spain (see below), Muslims were also ordered to convert to Christianity, and those who did so were dubbed *Moriscos*. These new Christians were suspected of duplicity like their Jewish counterparts and subjected to Inquisitorial discipline. There were only fourteen documented Morisco executions, but many more had their culture and language banned and their wealth seized. With the outbreak of Protestantism soon thereafter (see below), the Inquisition had yet more work to do, rooting out those heretics. By the mid-1700s, the Spanish Inquisition had spent most of its energy, although it was not formally ended until 1834—but not before this "daughter of faith and fanaticism"[40] had accumulated forty-nine thousand arrests and as many as ten thousands deaths.[41]

The Inquisition may seem like a sadistic aberration to us today, but it is essential to appreciate that it was fully authorized and fully institutionalized by the Church of the time. Indeed, as Maycock judged it, the Inquisition was, in its intentions and in its forms, precisely "an *ecclesiastical court* and a *weapon of internal* Church discipline" (emphasis in the original).[42] That is, as Augustine had imagined centuries before, heretics were criminals, torture and punishment and execution were exercises in criminal justice, and the Inquisition was the instrument of this justice. It is well known that the Inquisition kept meticulous records of its activities, including its "interrogations," and the whole process amounted to a legal system, with investigators, judges, defendants, witnesses, rulings, and naturally sentences.

In fact, during the early days of the Inquisition, perhaps the greatest thinker of Christendom gave his approval to Christian war and violence. Like Augustine, Thomas Aquinas (1225–74), considered a particularly rational Christian, confirmed the theory of Christian just war and just persecution, reasoning that deliberate religious error (holding the wrong beliefs) was perjury, only infinitely worse by giving false testimony about God. Perjury was a crime, and heresy was a much graver crime, so persecution of the heretic was essentially criminal justice: religious nonconformists "by right . . . can be put to death and despoiled of their possessions by the secular [authorities], even if they do not corrupt others, for they are blasphemers against God, because they observe a false faith. Thus they can be justly punished more than those accused of high treason."[43] Religious error was also equivalent to disease, so persecution was equivalent to medicine, a purging of corruption from the spiritual body, a kind of surgery to remove an unhealthy and cancerous body part.

Onward, Christian Soldiers

Neither the official Crusades nor the Inquisition exhausted or quenched the Christian appetite for destruction. As mentioned, crusading shifted its focus to nearby and internal enemies when the Muslims could not be vanquished. Nevertheless, sporadic crusading zeal eyed the Holy Land, as with the so-called Shepherd's Crusade: after a band of French shepherds received an angelic vision to march to Jerusalem in 1320, a mob of ten thousand pillaged its way south, killing Jews and even ransacking churches. Finally the Pope ordered that they be stopped, and the mob was dispersed by force, "fugitives being hung by the score from trees or the local gibbets."[44] In other words, the Church executed its own would-be crusaders.

The crisis of the Turks reached its apex in 1453, when the imperial city of Byzantium or Constantinople was finally captured and renamed Istanbul; subsequently, the Turkish armies reached the very gates of Vienna in the heart of Europe before being repelled, and Islam controlled parts of southeastern Europe into the 1800s. Phillips suggests that the last great crusading battle was the naval encounter at Lepanto in 1571, in which a Christian fleet defeated the Turks.[45] On the other side of the continent, we must not forget the Spanish *Reconquista*, the centuries-long crusade against the Muslim occupiers of the Iberian peninsula, which was only complete in 1492. That this was a crusade is evinced by the fact that the Church "granted the privileges of crusaders to men fighting in expeditions organized by local nobles or town authorities against the Moors" and that the conquest of Granada "seems to have been almost completely financed by the sale of indulgences, and the thought police of the Spanish Inquisition were closely linked with it."[46] Even though the battle had long since been won, the Spanish office of *Comisario general de la cruzada* was not closed until 1851.

But Christendom was never short on enemies and hostilities. After the Waldensians and Cathars were fought and suppressed, as well as John Wycliffe's Lollardy movement in the 1300s, a more dire threat emerged in the form of Jan Hus's followers. The struggles with Waldensians, Albigensians, and Lollards were one-sided affairs, but the Hussites presented an organized military challenge to Church authority. Hussite forces captured towns in 1419 using artillery mounted on wagons. Pope Martin V called for a crusade against these interlopers in 1420, and the Hussites won several engagements with Catholic forces, eventually controlling almost all of Bohemia. By 1426 the Hussite army was twenty-four thousand strong, able to mount a holy war of its own, and since the official Church could not crush it despite repeated attempts, a peaceful settlement was reached in 1436.

The greatest menace was yet to come, for in 1517 Martin Luther launched his protest against certain Church teachings and practices. This "protestant" movement grew and spread quickly, posing a mortal danger to the established Church. War was inevitable, mostly inspired by religion, but not completely: for instance, flexing its political muscles, a French Catholic army invaded Rome in 1527 and, in this Catholic-on-Catholic action, "sacked it amid . . . scenes of violence, murder, rape, looting, and destruction" reminiscent of the Fourth Crusade.[47]

But predictably, most of the belligerence was between Catholics and their Protestant foes, which suited Luther fine, since he opined (rightly) that "where there is no battle for the Gospel it rusts and it finds no cause and no occasion to show its vigor and power. Therefore, nothing better can befall the Gospel than that the world should fight it with force and cunning."[48] And Luther got his wish: intermittent fighting led to a formal concession by the Catholic Church in 1555 called the Peace of Augsburg, which established the principle of *cuius region, eius religio* ("he who rules a territory determines its religion"), giving local kings the power to choose the religion of their subjects, thus forever sundering the unity of Christendom.

But this agreement hardly ended the religious conflict. Persecution of Protestants continued in Spain, and the Huguenots met a terrible fate at the hands of French Catholic society. As early as 1547 King Henri II condemned their heresy and ordered them to be burned at the stake. Twelve hundred Huguenots were massacred at Vassey and Sens in 1562, which ignited a war between the two sects that persisted on and off for more than thirty-five years, with intense fighting from 1562 to 1572. Then on the night of St. Bartholomew's Day, August 24, 1572, Huguenot homes were attacked, leading to days of rioting and three thousand Huguenot casualties. According to Richard Dunn, "When the news reached the pope, he was so delighted that he gave a hundred crowns to the messenger."[49] Conflict dragged on until 1598, when Henri IV proclaimed toleration for the Huguenots in the Edict of Nantes (which was revoked in 1685 by Louis XIV).

The most sustained and deadly confrontation, though, was played out across Central Europe, where the fragile religious coexistence promised by the Peace of Augsburg dissolved in 1618. For thirty years, religion-enthused armies crisscrossed Europe in the aptly named Thirty Years' War, which blended the crusading spirit with political and territorial ambition to produce the "biggest of all the wars of religion."[50] Flaring first in Bohemia, the old battleground of the Hussites (just as much of the Huguenot war had been fought in former Albigensian strongholds), after a few years of religious fervor the conflagration devolved into a succession struggle and political competition, with non-German armies of French, Spanish, and Swedish soldiers tramping through German land. In fact, although the fundamental religious questions were settled by 1622, each side carried along its religion and suppressed rival religions: Catholic King Ferdinand banned Lutheranism and Calvinism, while Protestant King Gustavus Adolphus of Sweden intervened to support the Protestants. It is estimated that seven or eight million Christians lost their lives to fellow Christians during those three decades, some cities depleted of a third of their population. And all for what? The final resolution was the Peace of Westphalia in 1648, which basically restated the Augsburg principle of "to each prince his own religion." That is, Catholics, Lutherans, and Calvinists agreed to respect each other's territorial truths; Anabaptists and other Christian sects—as well as all non-Christians—were still open to persecution.

The era of Christian wars certainly did not end before the Protestant civil war in England in the 1640s. Catholicism had been overthrown a century earlier by Henry VIII, but the Puritans, the Christian fundamentalists of their day, were not satisfied with the anti-Catholicism of the new Anglican church or Church of England. An uprising that cost Charles I, the divine-right king of England his head, placed Puritans in power. What Dunn called "the last and grandest of Europe's age of religious wars"[51] left Oliver Cromwell in charge of republican and Puritan England from 1643 to 1658. He saw his rule as a mandate for "godly men" to renew English society. Among the memorable achievements of the godly government was the invasion of Catholic Ireland, initiating a religious and political competition for that little island that persists to this day.

If the religious conflicts of the Crusades, the Inquisition, and their long list of progeny were almost played out in Europe, they were simultaneously going global. As we will discuss in a later chapter, European exploration and colonization inevitably carried Christianity with it. Not only on the periphery (or in the heart) of Europe would Christianity be a rallying cry and a weapon of domination and legitimation; already by 1500, and for more than four subsequent centuries, peoples around the world would feel the bite of Christian love. Many still feel it today, although other religions have developed a capacity to bite back.

How far Christianity has come from its original assertion of peace and love, even if that assertion was more a matter of necessity than principle (Christians, as a weak minority, valorizing weakness and meekness). As Christianity attained power, it found clever arguments in support of its own vice and violence, perfecting the art of casuistry, the practice of specious or subtle reasoning for the purpose of rationalizing or misleading. To be sure, early Christians had models of "just war" provided by the ancients; all they had to add was specifically Christian justifications. But then, justice is in the eye of the beholder, and even more so, history has shown that "the greater the justice of my cause and the more violating a rule is necessary for my cause to prevail, the greater my justification in violating the rule."[52] Unfortunately, few people find anything more just, and therefore justifying, than their religion.

From Augustine's time to Aquinas' to our own, Judith Salisbury reckons that the first and most obvious basis for just war is its combatants: "If Christians were fighting pagans, for example, God was on the side of Christians, so the battle was just."[53] When Christians opposed other Christians, as they increasingly did, the reasoning had to bend, but each side was no less certain that justice—and God—was with them. But as we have seen, Christians have been able to muster a still more perverse rationale for their violence—*love*. Christian love has explained and supported often white-hot hatred, or perhaps more disturbingly yet, cool dispassionate harm. Psychological research has shown that those do the most, and the most exquisite, damage who feel that they are doing good *or do not feel anything at all*. One can imagine the satisfaction of the Crusader mowing down innocent citizens of Muslim (or Christian) towns, or of the Inquisitor calmly torturing a heretic or witch while patiently transcribing every moan and scream of the victim, and experiencing the pleasure of Church father Tertullian, picturing his adversaries in hell:

> How shall I admire, how laugh, how rejoice, how exult, when I behold so many proud monarchs, and fancied gods, groaning in the lowest abyss of darkness; so many magistrates who persecuted the name of the Lord, liquefying in fiercer fires than they ever kindled against the Christians; so many sage philosophers blushing in red hot flames with their deluded scholars; so many celebrated poets trembling before the tribunal, not of Minos, but of Christ; so many tragedians, more tuneful in the expression of their suffering.[54]

Or perhaps one can imagine the Crusader returning to his barracks, or the Inquisitor returning to his cloister, thinking of nothing more than a day's work done and God's justice and love dispensed. Spare me from such justice and love.

6

THOU SHALT NOT SUFFER A WITCH TO LIVE

The Wicked Christian Witch Hunts

John W. Loftus

It is not without great vexation that it has recently come to Our
hearing that . . . very many persons of both sexes have forgotten
their own salvation and deviated from the Catholic Faith. Committing abuses with incubus and succubus demons, they have no
fear of using their incantations, chants and conjurations and other
unspeakable superstitions and acts of sorcery . . . in order to bring
it about that the offspring of women, the progeny of animals, the
produce of the earth . . . are killed, suffocated, and wiped out. They
also afflict and torture these men, women, work animals, cows,
sheep and animals with terrible pains and torments, both internal and
external, and keep the men from fathering children and the women
from conceiving by impeding their ability to render the conjugal act
to each other. . . . They do this at the instigation of the Enemy of the
Human Race, and the result is that their own souls are endangered,
God's majesty is offended, and a scandalous example is set for many
people.

—The Bull of Pope Innocent VIII, 1484.[1]

The witch mania in Europe was the most persistent and widespread instance of extraordinary social behavior in human history.
Though the myth that sustained it was delusionary to the point of
absurdity, it seemed to those involved to possess sufficient plausibility to authorize appalling perversions of justice and the infliction of horrific cruelties over a period of three centuries. . . . The
European witch mania was all the more extraordinary in that

witchcraft, in the organized form which it was perceived as so
great a menace, simply did not exist. . . . The witch culture against
which the Christian Church took up arms was an artificial construct created by their theologians.

> —Hilary Evans and Robert E. Bartholomew,
> *Outbreak! The Encyclopedia of Extraordinary Social Behavior*[2]

People kill each other due to factors such as fear, ignorance, lust for power, financial gain, the thirst for revenge, and so on. But killing tens of thousands of supposed witches over the course of hundreds of years by Christians (both Catholic and Protestant) is especially egregious for at least three reasons. First, a perfectly good, all-knowing, all-powerful God would surely not allow the Christian Church as an institution to torture and kill so many innocent people for being witches (and they were all innocent). If the Christian God could have done something to stop these killings from happening, and didn't do it, then this makes God's inaction inexcusable to the point where the best explanation is that he doesn't exist.

Second, since people kill others with such guiltless impunity and ruthlessness when they do so believing their God authorized it, a caring, divine, omniscient author of the Bible should have condemned witch killings from the very beginning, before they ever took place. He should have said: "Thou shalt not torture or kill witches or those who worship other gods." But he didn't. In fact, one of the central themes in the Old Testament is the denial of religious freedom and expression.[3] He also failed to provide his people with reasonable rules of evidence to judge criminal cases, as we will see. If God exists, he is worthy of blame for this failure of communication, which caused otherwise good people do horrendous deeds.[4]

Third, no reasonable, scientifically minded person in today's world should believe that the devil (or Satan), who commands a host of demons and empowers witches who cause great harm using their black-magic spells and potions, actually exists. The burden of proof is on Christian believers who say witches *are* so empowered, just as it's on those who believe other claims, such as the existence of fairies, elves, and trolls. There just isn't any objective evidence for such claims.[5] If anyone thinks otherwise, then that person should try to win the James Randi Educational Foundation (JREF) million-dollar prize.[6] The whole concept of a supernatural personal devil originated in the ancient, superstitious, mythical past, and it has no basis in fact.[7] So if we took the Christian religion with its devil and demons out of the mix of factors that cause people to kill each other, then there would be no justification to kill witches for casting black-magic spells, none.[8] With no devil, no demons, and no witches, no one would ever be killed for the crime of witchcraft, ever.

The Biblical Basis for Christian Witch Hunts

The seeds for the barbaric Christian practice of witch hunting were sown in the Bible, believed by Christians to be the word of God. The biblical texts inspired the early-modern European witch hunts (roughly from 1450–1750), the Salem, Massachusetts, witch trials (1692–1693),[9] and the witch beatings and burnings currently taking place in Sub-Saharan Africa (South Africa, Cameroon, Democratic Republic of the Congo, Gambia, Ghana, Kenya, Sierra Leone, Tanzania, and Zambia).[10] Due to space limitations, my focus here is on the European witch hunts. But since witch hunts continue in Sub-Saharan Africa, carried out by Bible-believing Christians, the earlier witch hunts are not merely a historical anomaly. Witch hunts could arise on Christian soil whenever conducive conditions arise.

Between 45,000 and 60,000 people, 75 to 80 percent of them women, were killed as witches during the early-modern witch hunts that took place in Europe. Untold millions of others suffered the shame of false accusations (even if no arrests resulted), arrests (even if no convictions resulted), pornographic body searches for the devil's mark (see Revelation 13:17), sadistic tortures, and living in constant fear. While little could be universally said about all these witch hunts, the common denominator is the Christian belief in the devil and the black witchcraft arts.

Don't think so? Then heed C. S. Lewis, one of the past century's greatest Christian apologists:

> If we really thought there were people going about who had sold themselves
> to the devil and received supernatural powers from him in return and were
> using these powers to kill their neighbours or drive them mad or bring bad
> weather, surely we would all agree that if anyone deserved the death penalty,
> then these filthy quislings [i.e., traitors] did.[11]

There are several Old Testament texts that serve as the justification for witch hunts. In Deuteronomy 18:10–11 we find the most inclusive list of the magical arts in the Old Testament: "Let no one be found among you who sacrifices their son or daughter in the fire, who practices divination or sorcery, interprets omens, engages in witchcraft, or casts spells, or who is a medium or spiritist or who consults the dead." In Exodus 22:18 God is quoted as saying: "Thou shalt not suffer a witch to live" (King James Version). This verse described a woman who practiced one of the above activities, presumably sorcery. The word for "witch" (Hebrew *kashaph*) is feminine, meaning herb user. It's a compound of the words *kash* (herb) and *hapalah* (using). The Septuagint (LXX) translation in Greek renders the same word as *pharmakia* (poison), so it may refer to magic potions. So a biblical witch was a sorceress who used spells or potions that caused harm to others or their property. "Sorceress" might be the most accurate translation of the Hebrew word, although this kind of activity was also done by males. In Leviticus 20:27 we read: "A man also or woman that hath a familiar spirit, or that is a wizard, shall surely be put to death: they shall stone them with stones." The prophet Micah (5:12) said that God "will destroy your witchcraft and you will no longer cast spells." In Malachi 3:5, God said through the prophet: "I will come to put you on trial. I will be quick to testify against sorcerers."[12]

There is also a strong indication in the Bible that witches and sorcerers could actually perform magic. Moses and Aaron could turn their snakes into staffs, but so could the Egyptian magicians (Exodus 7:11–12), just as they could also turn the Nile into blood (Exodus 7:22) and send a swarm of frogs all over the land (Exodus 8:7, but note 8:18). We're told the witch of Endor, who was a medium (or even a necromancer), could actually summon the spirit of the prophet Samuel from the dead (or Samuel himself) at the request of King Saul (1 Samuel 28:3–25). We read in the book of Daniel that magicians actually worked magic and that Daniel was placed as the head over them. He was also an interpreter of dreams.

New Testament texts linked the belief that magic actually worked to the power of the devil, also called Satan, and his demons, who were waging a cosmic war against God. He is pictured as the chief adversary of Christians and the church. He "walks about like a roaring lion, seeking someone he may devour" (1 Peter 5:8). The devil is found tempting Jesus by offering him all the kingdoms of the world (Matthew 4:1–11). He could possess people, like he did the betrayer Judas Iscariot (Luke 22:3), and he had a legion of demons at his disposal who could possess a whole herd of pigs (Mark 5:1–20). These demons joined his rebellion against God (Revelation 12:7–17). To participate in this supernatural war Christians were enlisted as soldiers against Satan and his demons. They were told to "put on the whole armor of God, that you may be able to stand against the wiles of the devil. For we wrestle not against flesh and blood, but against principalities, against powers, against the rulers of the darkness of this world, against spiritual wickedness in high places" (Ephesians 6:11–12). In the end though, the devil and all those who have joined his rebellion against all that is good, including witches, will be cast into "the lake which burns with fire and brimstone" (Revelation 21:8; 22:14–15).

As Brian P. Levack, the foremost historian of witchcraft tells us: "The belief in magic, even harmful magic, exists in almost all cultures, but the belief in the Christian Devil, defined as he was by generations of medieval theologians, is unique to Western civilization and its derivative cultures."[13] The evidence in the Bible for the reality of both the devil and the power of witchcraft is so strong that John Wesley, the cofounder of the Methodist denomination, wrote:

> Giving up of witchcraft is in effect giving up the Bible. With my latest breath I will bear testimony against giving up to infidels one great proof of the invisible world; I mean that of witchcraft and apparitions, confirmed by the testimony of all ages.[14]

Why the European Witch Hunts Took Place

Church historian Brian A. Pavlac informs us that "all four of the major western Christian 'churches' (Roman Catholic, Lutheran, Calvinist, Anglican) persecuted witches to some degree or another" while "Eastern Christian, or Orthodox Churches carried out almost no witch hunting."[15] Why did they happen in the West rather than in the East? Why didn't they take place in the West until roughly the 1400s? There is considerable controversy about this.[16] But one thing seems clear: the towering influence of Thomas Aquinas, the angelic doctor.

Most Christian theologians prior to the tenth century didn't believe in the powers of witchcraft. Augustine (fourth century) had argued that God alone could work miracles in the universe and that neither Satan nor witches had the powers to work magic of any kind. It was the error of superstitious pagans to believe in any other power but God's power.[17] If witches were powerless, then the church didn't need to worry about black-magic spells. The ninth-century *Canon Episcopi* became part of canon law during the High Middle Ages and reaffirmed Augustine's view of the sovereignty of God over magic. However, it did condemn sorcery. Sorcerers and the people deceived by Satan were considered wicked heretics who must be ejected from the church.[18]

In the thirteenth century Thomas Aquinas provided the arguments that inspired the European witch hunts. Contrary to the *Canon Episcopi*, which instructed that heretics were merely to be ejected from the church, Aquinas argued heretics should be killed, a logic that followed from Augustine. Aquinas argued heresy was a "leavening influence" upon the minds of the weak. Since heretical ideas could send people to an eternally conscious torment in hell, it was the greatest crime of them all. So logic demanded that the church must get rid of them.[19] Contrary to both Augustine and the *Canon Episcopi*, where it was asserted that demons were powerless against God's power, Aquinas argued that demons could work miracles,[20] although they could only do so by the permission of God. Aquinas asserted that "magic and sorcery could cause impotence and destroy a marriage."[21] The magical arts were granted to sorcerers as part of a pact they made with an evil higher intelligence—an act that was considered by Aquinas to be nothing short of apostasy from the Christian faith.[22]

All it took for the witch hunts to begin was a sizable number of powerful people who accepted Aquinas's ideas and had the political need to follow through on them. First came an acceptance of his ideas. After Aquinas, theologians came to believe in the powers of witchcraft and that human beings could make a pact with the devil. Why not, if he existed? In making this pact it was believed they had to give him something in return, usually their souls. Stands to reason, doesn't it? In so doing, the witch became not only a heretic and an apostate, but also a devil worshipper, and a rebel against God. Aquinas's ideas came to be embraced by the highest authority, Pope Innocent VIII, when he granted to the famed witch hunter Henrich Kramer complete authority to conduct witch trials in parts of Germany with his Papal Bull in 1484. So influential were Aquinas's writings that they became the main source for Kramer's popular witch-hunting manual *Malleus Maleficarum*, or *The Hammer of Witches* (partially cowritten with James Sprenger) in 1486 after the invention of the printing press.[23] This treatise was "enormously popular between 1486 and 1520, and again between 1580 and 1650."[24] Not coincidentally, these were two of the most intense periods of witch hunting in Europe.

The political need to conduct witch hunts came from several additional beliefs, social/legal factors, and political fears. One such additional belief was the witches' Sabbath. Just like other heretics and apostates it was believed witches secretly congregated together in order to conspire against the Christian (or Catholic) society at night in the witches' Sabbath. Witches therefore came to be regarded as a very serious threat to their society by the elites of that day. Getting rid of them became the task of papal inquisitors and their secular counterparts, who had already been at work against heretics and apostates for a couple hundred years.

The fear that the ruling classes had of rebellion seems to be one of the most important social factors, argues Brian Levack. The witch was "the quintessential rebel." Devil worship was viewed as a political conspiracy by lower classes who were "striving to turn the world upside down, inverting the divinely established hierarchical order of society and rejecting all its moral norms."[25] It was considered treason, the most serious political crime. Levack tells us:

> In order for the intensive hunting of witches to take place, it was necessary for the ruling elite to believe that the crime was of the greatest magnitude and that it was being practiced on a large scale and in a conspiratorial manner. They had to believe not only that individual witches were harming their neighbors by magical means but that large numbers of them were completely rejecting their Christian faith and undermining Christian civilization. They had to believe that magicians belonged to an organized, conspiratorial sect of devil-worshippers.[26]

There were other factors, like the Black Death, which killed around one hundred million people in the known world. In Europe, twenty-five million people died between 1348 and 1350—about one third of the entire population. People in the fourteenth century didn't understand why so many people were dying horrible deaths, and one of the scapegoats was the black-magic spells cast by witches.

Later there was the "heretical" revolt of the Protestant Reformation, which led to the devastating Thirty Years' War (1618–1648), bringing some towns in Germany to rubble. Many superstitious people were forced to come to grips with these types of events, and, more often than not, they believed that God was punishing them or that the Jews, heretics, and/or witches were to blame.

The Rules of Evidence in the Bible

The biggest legal factor of all was the use of torture. The use of torture to extract confessions was highly successful, to say the least. It created the early-modern European witch hunts in countries that allowed it (for the most part England did not). More than anything else, it produced the so-called witch-crazed hysteria, or pandemonium (literally "all demons"), which spread over large swaths of Europe roughly between 1450 and 1750. However, if authorities had adopted better rules of evidence for criminal proceedings, they wouldn't have heard so many confessions under torture, which provided a growing number of accomplices who subsequently also confessed to witch-craft under torture, implicating still others. In turn, the fears of the ruling elite would never have reached the extent they did, so they would not have been so alarmed by the threat of a social upheaval in the first place.

The rules of evidence used to convict people of crimes in the Bible were of no help in the witch trials. Human testimony of two or three eyewitnesses was the standard (Deuteronomy 17:6). One eyewitness was not enough (Deuteronomy 19:15). But this rule could be circumvented by recruiting lying witnesses (1 Kings 21:8–10; Mark 14:56–59). If the judge determined that a supposed eyewitness was falsely accusing someone, then that person would suffer the same penalty intended for the accused (Deuteronomy 19:16–17). If there are no eyewitnesses to a crime, then the accused would be acquitted upon taking an oath of innocence (Exodus 22:10–11).

If judges could not determine whether the accused was guilty, they were to inquire with the priests, who presumably could determine God's verdict (Deuteronomy 17:8–13) by casting lots using the Urim and Thummin. In one case a priest used them to determine whose fault it was that the plunder of the Philistines wasn't greater after a battle. If Saul or his son Jonathan were at fault then God would respond with the Urim, but if the men of Israel were at fault, God would respond with the Thummin. We read: "Jonathan and Saul were taken by lot, and the men were cleared. Saul said, 'Cast the lot between me and Jonathan my son.' And Jonathan was taken." (1 Samuel 14:36–46). In the mythical tale of Jonah, when a storm arose that threatened to kill everyone in the boat that Jonah boarded to escape God's mission to Nineveh, the sea-farers cast lots to determine the guilty party. This was a terrible, superstitious way to determine guilt.

The case of Achan in the Book of Joshua is instructive here. The Israelites failed to conquer the city of Ai. God reportedly told Joshua that their failure was because someone had stolen items from Jericho, a city we're told they had defeated earlier. So to determine the guilty party, Joshua had every tribe come before him one after another. Of them the tribe of Judah was chosen, presumably by lot, the same method used to allocate territories between the tribes when settling in their supposed "Promised Land." Then the clan of Judah came forward, and the Zerahites were chosen, out of which the family of Zimri was chosen. Then each man was presented to Joshua from the family of Zimri, and Achan was chosen, whereupon he confessed and was stoned to death. One can only wonder about the odds of this, since it wouldn't surprise me to learn many of them had stolen things in the frenzy of the plunder.

If a husband suspected his wife of getting pregnant by another man then he could submit her to a trial by ordeal, by drinking water mixed with the dirt of the tabernacle floor that almost certainly had nasty blood pathogens from animal sacrifices in it. If she was guilty she would suffer severe abdominal pains and have a miscarriage. If she survived she was innocent (Numbers 5:11–31). This is horrible. It's not that evidence wasn't sought though. If a husband believed his wife was not a virgin when he married her, she would be required to produce the bed sheet containing the dried blood from her wedding night before the elders at the gate. However, how could she prove this blood was from her wedding night, and what if she lost the bed sheet? If she could not produce it, for whatever reason, she would be stoned to death (Deuteronomy 22:13–21).

King Solomon was known for his wisdom in deciding a case between two harlots who both claimed a particular child was theirs. Solomon settled the matter by ordering that the child be cut in two, with each woman receiving half of the child, then he listened to the women's pleas to determine the real mother (1 Kings 3:16–28). However, it was possible that neither woman was the child's mother. And the real mother might have wanted the child killed rather than have it raised by such a conniving thief. Or, a smarter baby-stealing thief might simply have said the same thing the real mother did, that Solomon should give the child to the other woman, in order to save the child from being killed. What would Solomon do then? We really don't know if the real mother got her child back.

In the trial of Jesus, as told in the Gospel of Mark, he is arrested based on one accuser, Judas. The Sanhedrin was looking for evidence in the form of eyewitnesses, but the eyewitnesses contradicted each other. When they thought they heard a confession from Jesus himself, they sent him away to Pilate (Mark 14:43–64). When Jesus was brought before Pilate, the governor was seeking a confession from Jesus, too, or at least a denial of his accuser's testimony (Mark 1–15). The trials in the other gospels are of the same kind, with the addition in the Gospel of Matthew of the evidence of Pilate's wife, who had a dream indicating Jesus was innocent (Matthew 27:19).

None of these biblical rules of evidence are reasonable ones, except the desire for two or three noncontradicting eyewitnesses, if possible, and the confession of the guilty party (in Achan's case, and in King David's case, see 2 Samuel 12:13). But most crimes are done in secret without any eyewitnesses, and guilty people are not so quick to confess if they know the punishment will be brutal.

If there were a God, he could have averted the witch hunts by simply providing better rules of evidence. Even with just a minimal amount of foresight, any omniscient, perfectly good God worthy of the name would have granted people certain reasonable civil rights. Such a God would have foreseen the need to grant people the right to be presumed innocent until proven guilty. He would have granted people the right to be free from unreasonable search and the seizure. He would have forbidden police entrapment. He would have stipulated the *corpus delicti* principle, whereby a crime must first be shown to have taken place before someone can be convicted of doing it. Just because a cow died unexpectedly or a child got deathly ill does not automatically mean a crime was committed. Such a principle would have disqualified many forced witch confessions, since they admitted to crimes that did not happen or were even impossible for them to have done. An omniscient, perfectly good God would have provided for the use of advocates who could argue on behalf of the accused, trials by a jury of the accused's peers, and a standard of proof beyond a reasonable doubt before an accused person could be convicted of a crime. Most emphatically, such a God would have forbidden accused people from being forced to incriminate themselves or face punishment if they refused to do so. He would have forbidden trials by ordeal. And he certainly would have foreseen the need to condemn torture as a means of extracting a confession. But none of these things are found in the Bible. No legal guidance on these matters can be found from a supposedly omniscient, perfectly good God.

When dealing with this lack of sound divine legal guidance, something I call *the problem of divine miscommunication*, Christian defense lawyers, called apologists, seek only to get their divine client acquitted no matter what the intellectual or moral cost. Rather than face this evidence that shows their God to be nothing more than the product of ancient people, who didn't have a clue about legal matters, these apologists use convoluted legalese to obfuscate and confuse the jury.

Typically they'll say we couldn't possibly know what an omniscient God is thinking, so we have no right to judge him and his ways. However, even if this is the case, it changes nothing. Tens of thousands of people, mostly women, suffered intensely and were killed needlessly because this God didn't do anything to help them. Christians will further object that we don't know if God did anything to help them, to which the obvious answer is that this is my point. If he did something to help them, there isn't any evidence that he did. Such an objection is based on faith, not evidence, the very thing that produced the witch hunts in the first place. God's failure to give sound legal guidance shows an utter lack of care for the very individuals who suffered as supposed witches. No amount of higher divine intelligence could assuage their sufferings or offer any comfort to them as they were being tortured. No amount of future compensation in heaven could justify what this God failed to do either. The human equivalent would be to argue that a person is morally justified in forcibly plucking out a man's eyes so long as the victim is rewarded with a million dollars. If God had some higher purpose or end in sight, then he merely used these people as a means to an end. He did not care for them as individuals. And if God really wants us to believe in him and believe that he loves us, this is a strange way of going about things. For an omniscient God would have known that later generations of intelligent people would find him to be guilty of not doing what decent people would do if they could, and as a result, disbelieve in him and his love.

The best Christian defense lawyers are liberals who admit there are texts in the Bible that, to a great degree, are reflective of an ancient outlook rather than the rigid literalism of conservative believers. In their view, God's revelation is progressive, becoming better as humans grope to understand the divine. In other words, theology evolves. Liberals didn't come by this conclusion easily though. Down through the centuries they came to it as the realities of life and the results of science forced them to accept it. Yet this view is exactly what we would expect to find if there is no truth to their theology. It's what we would expect if there is no divine mind behind the Bible or the church. If there is a God then his so-called progressive revelation is indistinguishable from him not revealing anything at all, and, as such, progressive revelation should be rejected as an unnecessary theological hypothesis unworthy of thinking people. Furthermore, such a view actually undermines their theology, for it leads to theological relativism, since there was no point in the history of the church when any theologian could say that a final, unchanging theology had been attained. So the theology of yesterday was true for Christians of the past, as the present-day theology is true for others, as the theology of tomorrow will be true for still others. Liberals therefore cannot state any theological truth that is true for all time. As far as they can know, the end result of revelation could be the death of God, the conclusion that we don't need God, which would make him effectively dead. As far as liberals can know, atheism may be the future of their theology. The only reason they won't accept the relativism of their theology is that they perceive a need to believe. They are playing a pretend game much like the people in M. Night Shyamalan's movie *The Village*. In my opinion, liberals should just stop pretending.

The bottom line is that the whole notion of progressive revelation is a "heads I win tails you lose" strategy. If their God had revealed the truth from the beginning these Christians would use that as evidence that he exists. Because he didn't, they have introduced progressive revelation, which betrays their desire to believe no matter what the intellectual cost. What they're doing is justifying their God "after the facts," rather than asking "before the facts" what they would expect of their God if he lovingly communicated to human beings.

Let the Tortures Begin

Up until the thirteenth century European criminal trials largely followed the rules of evidence we've just seen in the Bible. It was an accusatory system in which the accuser must prove the accused is guilty before a judge. If he or she couldn't do this, the court would look to some sign from God, not unlike what we find in the Bible. The most common method was trial by ordeal. The accused would carry a very hot iron or be forced to stick one's hand in very hot water, then, after a few days, the accused would be declared innocent if God had healed the hand. Accused people could also be tied up and cast into water. If they sank they were considered innocent (and then pulled up), but if they floated they would be considered guilty. Some innocent people drowned from this, of course. Accused people could also be forced to swallow a big morsel of food in one gulp. If they didn't choke, they were considered innocent. Or, the accuser and the accused would be forced to engage in a duel or challenge of some kind. The winner of the contest would be judged correct in the court case. One way the accused could be declared innocent, when other things failed, was by compurgation, where the accused could swear by oath that he or she was innocent and then gather a few people who would swear by oath that the person would not have committed the crime. If accusers didn't succeed in making their cases, they could suffer the same punishment the accused would have suffered. None of these methods were reasonable. As such, they were not very successful in determining guilt.

In the thirteenth century this system was drastically altered. First, trials by ordeal were largely but not exclusively abandoned after the Fourth Lateran Council of 1215, which prohibited clerics from presiding over them. Second, with the rediscovery of Roman canon law, the accuser no longer had to prove that the accused was guilty. Officers of the courts were to investigate any accusations and prosecute the crimes instead. They would even take the initiative to investigate crimes. It was an inquisitional system, and it took root in some countries quicker than in others. The main effect of this change was that the new inquisitional system eliminated the risk accusers faced if the people they accused were found innocent. This was very important when it came to accusing people of being witches. In effect, it "made individuals vulnerable to frivolous, malicious, politically motivated or otherwise arbitrary prosecutions."[27] Third, Roman law also allowed for torture in order to extract confessions from the accused; torture was not commonly used during most of the Middle Ages.[28] The legal standard adopted from Roman law for capital crimes was the testimony of two eyewitnesses, or the confession of the accused. Nothing else would satisfy the court. Because heresy and witchcraft were capital crimes that typically produced few if any eyewitnesses,

> judges had to rely exclusively on confessions in order to obtain convictions. Confessions, however, were not always forthcoming, and consequently judicial authorities began to allow the use of torture in order to obtain them. The use of torture in heresy, witchcraft and other cases was therefore the direct result of the adoption of inquisitional procedure. The logic of one led to the application of the other.[29]

The day the church as an institution officially authorized inquisitors to use torture against heretics was May 15, 1252, when Pope Innocent IV issued the papal bull titled *Ad extirpanda*. This bull was issued in response to the murder of Peter of Verona, the papal inquisitor of Lombardy. He was killed by a heretical group of Cathar followers. The bull argued that since heretics are "murderers of souls as well as robbers of God's sacraments and of the Christian faith" they are "to be coerced—as are thieves and bandits—into confessing their errors and accusing others."[30]

Using torture to extract confessions from heretics during the Inquisition produced a number of tall tales, such as confessions of human sacrifice, cannibalism, sex orgies, and pacts with the devil. Historian Brian A. Pavlac tells us that from these confessions under torture, "heresy quickly became associated with supernatural, even magical properties."[31] We see this first with the Cathar and Waldensian heretics, but also with the Knights Templar, a group of monk knights who fought in the Crusades. Many later confessed to witchcraft and demonic activity under torture during the trials of 1309. Eventually the concern for heretics in general was largely transferred to the greatest heretics of them all, witches.

Following the procedures developed during the Inquisition, witch hunters would come into a region and preach against witchcraft. Afterward they would ask people to come forward with promises of leniency if they willingly confessed to any dabblings they might have had with witchcraft. They were likewise invited to implicate others of this crime. Sometimes financial rewards were offered to people willing to come forward. Interrogations of the confessors and the accused followed. One of the first things they did, if the witch hunters suspected they were looking into the eyes of a witch, was to have them strip searched. As part of this, all the accused's body hair would be shaved in order to look for the devil's mark. Most any blemish could be considered to be this mark, the one the devil was believed to have branded on them. If the mark was pricked with needles and there was no sign of pain, then that was all they needed to proceed with the tortures. If witch hunters were already convinced that the accused was guilty, it was believed the devil made his mark to be invisible to the naked eye. At this point nothing the accused could say or do would exonerate him or her except the ability to physically withstand any and all tortures. One sixteenth-century accused witch named Maria Hollin, from Mindelburg, Germany, refused to confess to witchcraft, even after having endured fifty-six torture sessions over an eleven-month period, so they were forced to release her.

Bloodless tortures included stretching techniques like the strappado and the rack. The rack could dislocate the knee, hip, elbow, and shoulder joints. A victim could even end up being paralyzed. The strappado was the most common method of torture. A victim's hands would be tied behind the back and hoisted up using a pulley system. The victim would then be left hanging in excruciating pain while being interrogated. Meanwhile, torturers would jerk the ropes on occasion. Sometimes the torturers would hang various weights to the victim's feet to add to the pain. The actual interrogation of an unnamed woman at Eichstätt, Germany, in 1637, reads as follows:

> After being tied to the pulley [i.e., the strappado], and hoisted up a little, she says, that, yes, she could be a witch, yet when released, she announces she is not a witch. Therefore she is pulled up somewhat higher, and then a second and third time, and then released on the admission that she is a witch. But immediately she becomes stubborn and denies she is a witch. Then again she is pulled even more tightly on the ropes. She confesses that fourteen years ago, when she was unmarried, she had become a witch.[32]

There was forced feeding, forced drinking, and forced sleeplessness. Sleep deprivation was one of the most effective bloodless tortures. Keeping victims awake for extended days at a time rendered them open to suggestion by the interrogators, who used leading questions. Sleep deprivation leads to cognitive impairment, memory loss, confusion, and even hallucinations. Under such conditions, confused prisoners were much more likely to confess.

There were tortures that were specifically sexually sadistic in nature. The Judas Cradle was a tall, thin stool with a pointed wooden or metal pyramid on top. The victim would be stripped and suspended above it, then lowered onto it, making the pyramid enter the vagina or anus, or crush the scrotum. Victims could be dropped onto it, and weights could be hung from their legs. There was the Pear of Anguish, which was a pear-shaped device inserted into the vagina for women or the anus for men. It consisted of four metal leaves that spread open from each other as the torturer turned the screw at the bottom. There was the Breast Ripper, a four-clawed device that would usually be heated. The torturer would then use it to tear apart or rip off a woman's breast.

Then there were even more extreme tortures, such as the crushing techniques of the small but mighty thumb screws, head and leg clamps, and iron boots. There was the Iron Maiden (an iron cabinet with a spike-covered interior that was closed on a victim) and the Witch's Chair, which had hundreds of sharp spikes lining the back, seat, and arm and leg rests. The victim would be strapped tightly into it. Usually the chair was heated by a fire below.

The most extreme tortures killed their victims. They were used mostly after the witch was sentenced to death. The Wheel involved tying the victim's limbs to the wheel's spokes, then slowly turning it while the torturer smashed the victim's limbs with an iron hammer, breaking them in many places. Or the victim could be tied to the outer rim of a wheel, which would then be rolled down a rocky hillside or rolled over fire. Sometimes small spikes were added to the wheel, causing pain to come from all directions. Impalement was a method of torture where a sharp pole was pushed up from the vagina or anus though the body of a victim. The ultimate torture was burning the victim at the stake while still alive, although most of the time convicted witches were strangled before being burned.

There were various limits placed on the amount of torture that could be administered, which varied from place to place and over time. For instance

Heinrich Kramer's treatise on witchcraft, *The Hammer of Witches*, specified that torture should be used in order to gain a confession but that the victim should confirm the confession without torture on a following day. That is, a confession under torture was inadmissible in court. The victim must "freely" confess afterward outside the torture chambers. Torture should not be used again unless "new indications came to light," he said. Christopher S. MacKay, who translated Kramer's work, comments as follows: "A person could be tortured only once on the basis of a given set of evidence, and only the discovery of new evidence would justify a 'repetition' of the torture, but it was permissible to 'continue' the 'same' instance of torture over the course of several days. Thus, the distinction between 'continuing' and 'repeating' torture was more theoretical than substantive."[33]

It was believed that witches could withstand greater pain for extended periods of time due to the power of the devil. Jean Bodin (1530–1596), one of the leading intellectuals of his day in France, argued for this in a popular treatise titled "On the Demon-Mania of Witches" (1580). He added that "one accused of being a witch ought never to be folly [i.e., foolishly] acquitted and set free unless the calumny [i.e., libel] of the accuser is clearer than the sun, inasmuch as the proof of such crimes is so obscure and so difficult that not one witch in a million would be accused or punished if the procedure were governed by the ordinary rules."[34] So abuses were common. In some cases the lack of a confession under extreme torture was even considered to be strong evidence that the accused was in fact a witch.

The case of Johannes Junius, the mayor of Bamberg, Germany, in 1628, is indicative of this abuse. After enduring some torture without confessing, his torturer said to him:

> Sir, I beg you, for God's sake confess something, whether it be true or not. Invent something, for you cannot endure the torture which you will be put to; and even if you bear it all, yet you will not escape, not even if you were an Earl, but one torture will follow after another until you say you are a witch.[35]

Junius was subsequently burned at the stake after deciding to confess.

Now, does anyone think that with these and other tortures available to the witch hunters, they couldn't force anyone to confess to anything they desired? After studying many cases of torture Erick Middlefort found that when torture was used, the rate of witchcraft convictions was as high as 95 percent.[36] The ability of accused witches to withstand these tortures depended on their pain tolerance, the methods used, and whether the torturers adhered to civilized rules governing them.

A Jesuit priest named Friedrich von Spee, who had witnessed witch trials in the German City of Würzburg, published a work titled *Cautio Criminalis* (*Precautions for Prosecutors*) in 1631 that exposed the problems with inter-rogations of accused witches. He wrote:

> Now, in Heaven's name, I would like to know . . . how can anybody, no matter how innocent, escape? O unhappy woman, why have you rashly hoped? Why did you not, on first entering prison, admit whatever they wanted? Why, foolish and crazy woman, did you wish to die so many times when you might have died but once? Follow my counsel, and, before under-going all these pains, say you are guilty and die. You will not escape, for this were a catastrophic disgrace to the zeal of Germany.[37]

The case of the Pappenheimer family in Bavaria, Germany, in 1600 is one of the most horrific cases ever recorded. It is indicative of the kind of behavior that otherwise good people can descend to when such behavior is sanctioned by their faith. The Pappenheimers were vagrants who were accused of witchcraft. Under torture they confessed. They said that they had flown on broomsticks to the witches' Sabbath, had sex with the devil, produced magic potions that they used to cause storms, cannibalized corpses, and committed many robberies, arsons, and murders. Brian Pavlac comments: "Any rational accounting of the numbers would have recognized the impossibility of these confessions, but with witchcraft the impossible becomes credible."[38] On July 29, 1600, a crowd of thousands came to witness their executions. The execu-tioners ripped at Paul and Anna's flesh with red hot pincers and cut off both of Anna's breasts. Then they rubbed them in her face and the face of her two oldest sons. At the place of execution the bones of Paul and his two older sons were broken on the Wheel. Paul was subsequently impaled, and they were all tied to stakes and burned alive. The youngest of the three boys was forced to witness this, and several weeks later he was also burned at the stake.[39]

The Devil in the Details

The Witches' Sabbath

When people confessed to being a witch they were asked to give details. There were so many confessions that gave similar details of the witches' Sabbath that Paola Grillandi, a judge in central Italy in the early 1500s, became a believer that witches could really work harmful magic. It was also the most threatening idea to the elite classes, for if true, it meant there was a significant underclass of peasants who congregated together at night and had been given supernatural powers by the devil to overthrow their empires. Witches under torture confessed to being flown by the devil, sometimes as animals or on broomsticks, to these meeting places for orgies of sex. Women had sex with other women as well as with demons, with their cold penises. Witches confessed to kissing the anuses of demons and slaughtering stolen babies to drink their blood and eat their flesh. Of course, after over three hundred years of searching for and never finding any of these meetings taking place, or even signs that they had taken place, this should have been evidence enough to discount the wild confessions of accused witches, despite the similarities in the stories they told about the witches' Sabbath.

The question is where these similar stories about the Sabbath came from. Scott E. Hendrix, in his article "The Pursuit of Witches and the Sexual Discourse of the Sabbat," addresses this question.[40] He argues that

> rather than asking carefully crafted questions designed to protect the rights of the accused, the inquisitor would rely on leading questions in an attempt to trick, force, or cajole an affirmation of what he already assumed to be true. Therefore, in the case of accusations of witchcraft, the inquisitor would ask highly leading questions such as "how frequently did you involve yourself in sexual congress with demons?" or "tell me about the methods you have used to fly by night to sabbats."

The important point Hendrix stresses is that the witch hunter already knew what crimes were committed. Where did he get that information?

He had gotten the details of these crimes from handbooks such as the *Malleus* [i.e., *The Hammer of Witches* by Henrich Kramer] and his questioning was designed to gain confirmation about these details. . . . These ideas then formed the basis of inquisitorial questioning, so any confessions, made under torture or fear of torture, tell us more about the ideas of the inquisitors than practices of European witches.

There is no doubt that these tales were imaginary, that they stemmed from Greek and Roman mythology, and that they were planted in the confessions of accused witches by means of leading questions asked by the witch hunters themselves. Friedrich von Spee had mentioned this, saying the witch hunters themselves "brought to Germany the whole host of witches with their artfully contrived and wisely spread out tortures."[41] Alonso de Salazar, known as "The Witches' Advocate" in Spain during the Inquisition, wrote, "I deduce that . . . there were neither witches nor bewitched until they were talked and written about."[42]

What about Confessions Made without Torture?

There are cases where it was reported that people "freely" confessed without any torture. Some of these confessions were not free ones. Friedrich von Spee wrote that the tortures "start with the first degree, i.e., the less severe torture. Although exceedingly severe, it is light compared to those tortures which follow. Wherefore if she confesses, they say the woman has confessed without torture!"[43] Some of these voluntary confessions were made on the grounds that it was better to confess and die rather than suffer through the tortures and die anyway. Others were made in response to false promises of leniency. Still others might have been the result of some kind of mental problem, such as senility, dreams the accused couldn't distinguish from reality, self-loathing, or even the influence of drugs. Others were legitimate attempts to come clean by people who really thought they had made a pact with the devil and cast spells as a result. One thing we know is that none of these confessions were true, since there is no supernatural reality that lies behind them.[44]

Gendercide?

I find the case that the witch hunts were a form of gendercide to be plausible for some geographical locations and time periods during the European witch hunts,[45] even though, with most scholars, I agree it isn't an explanation for all geographical locations. Scholars such as Deborah Willis found it "clear . . . that women were actively involved in making witchcraft accusations against their female neighbours."[46] Based on these statistics they deny the gendercidal nature of the witch hunts as a whole. However, some women accused other women of witchcraft because they feared that if they didn't do so first, those other women would accuse them first. This unfortunate situation was forced on them by witch hunters themselves. The fact is that most witchcraft treatises were very misogynistic. The title to Henrich Kramer's popular witch treatise in Latin was *Malleus Maleficarum*, which literally meant "hammer of *male-factresses*," or wrongdoing women. It was "arguably the most misogynist of witchcraft treatises, and it became quite well-known," says Merry E. Wiesner-Hanks.[47] The political machinery was also put into place by men who, for the most part, thought very little of women, considering them to be daughters of Eve, the first weak-willed, carnal woman, who had led Adam into rebellion against God. Because of this, women were their primary targets in efforts to rid society of the influence of the devil, even if in some towns it was males who were predominantly accused and executed. In the 1585 witch hunt in Rottenburg, Germany, authorities became concerned that their efforts could kill off all of the women of the town. In that same year, two entire German towns were left with only one woman inhabitant each after the fires had finally burned out.[48] Steven T. Katz tells us:

> The overall evidence makes plain that the growth—the panic—in the witch craze was inseparable from the stigmatization of women. . . . Though there were male witches, when the witch craze accelerated and became a mass phenomenon after 1500 its main targets, its main victims, were female witches. Indeed, one strongly suspects that the development of witch-hunting into a mass hysteria only became possible when directed primarily at women.[49]

Conclusion: The Decline of the European Witch Trials

Just as there are a number of factors for the rise of the European witch hunts there are also a number of them when it came to their cessation. Several theological reasons were offered at the time. With the rise of biblical criticism a few Christians in the late seventeenth century argued that the biblical texts do not demand the execution of witches.[50] Christians also argued God would never grant the devil permission to use a witch to inflict harm on others (even though God supposedly granted him permission to torture Job). Other Christians argued the devil couldn't be trusted when speaking through the mouths of self-confessed witches, who subsequently accused still others of being witches.

One can only wonder why God had to wait while thousands were brutally tortured and killed. Why couldn't God enable Christians to reach these conclusions before the witch hunts even began? Instead, he watched as the Pappenheimer family was brutally tortured and killed. Could he not have clearly and unambiguously condemned the killing of witches? Did he not know that these witch hunts would be written about centuries later to discredit Christianity? Could he not have intervened at the very minimum, in the most egregious cases, by answering the prayers of these victims for an acquittal.

The waning of religious enthusiasm after 1650 was also a major factor in the decline and cessation of the witch hunts. The Peace of Westphalia in 1648, which ended the religious bloodbath between the Catholics and Protestants, produced an era of decline in the desire to establish a sect-specific Christian society that needed to rid itself of all witches. What's strange is that Christians now claim their faith produced the virtue of tolerance and, along with it, the first-amendment rights found in the American Constitution. The fact is they learned tolerance the hard way, by experiencing the pain and suffering of the intolerance of their own faith. This is exhibit A in our case against faith.

Political changes took place that reduced and eventually eliminated the witch hunts. With the rise of stronger, more centralized states that had authority over local affairs, witchcraft accusations came more and more to be seen as expressions of petty grievances between locals. But why didn't Christians see this much earlier?

Judicial changes took place as well. There was a new judicial awareness that the rules of evidence required for criminal convictions needed an overhaul.

This was due to the growing awareness that, since witch accusations could not be disproved, there had been many miscarriages of justice. There was also the fear that no one was safe from the endless cycle of witchcraft accusations, especially when people were tortured to extract these confessions and then tortured again to name accomplices. They should have known torture was not acceptable long before this, had there really been a good God who inspired the Bible and could foresee the need to specify better rules of evidence.

Finally, there were intellectual challenges coming from philosophy and science, which are hard to quantify but probably played some role among the educated elite who controlled the machinery of the legal process for accused witches. While the judges and magistrates who helped end the witch hunts were themselves believers for the most part, "there was a growing tendency in all fields of thought to reject dogma and inherited authority, to question everything, even the most basic principles upon which one's world-view is based . . . within the literate elite and among university-educated men it was a period of profound and pervasive doubt," writes Brian Levack.[51]

Philosophical materialists like Rene Descartes (1596–1650) and Thomas Hobbes (1588-1679) both rejected the idea of incorporeal substances as a contradiction in terms, and in doing so, they "effectively jettisoned demons from the natural world."[52] The Dutch Jewish philosopher Baruch Spinoza (1632–1677) produced an argument against the possibility of miracles that subsequently undercut the idea that witches could perform them. This argument was later articulated best by Scottish philosopher David Hume (1711–1776). These arguments propelled the rise of Deism in England (1690–1740), with its emphasis on the use of reason to judge religious faith claims. As a result, beliefs in demons and the power of witchcraft were eventually rejected as unreasonable.

The rise of modern science, and with it the Enlightenment that originated in the seventeenth century, was probably a factor. With the discovery of the laws of motion, Isaac Newton (1642–1727) could explain the movements of both the planets in the solar system and objects on earth. The universe could thus be understood as a perfectly working clock, a machine, with its gears operating by the laws of physics. The intervention of God or the devil in this machine-like universe was regarded as increasingly unlikely. In the case of God, it was thought that if he had to intervene in the world, then he didn't make a perfect clock in the first place. Keith Thomas tells us in his magisterial book *Religion and the Decline of Magic*, that "talk of miraculous happenings came to appear increasingly implausible. It was this conviction, rather than any new psychological insight, which accounts for the skepticism displayed towards the confessions of old women who said that they had seen the Devil, or flown through the air, or killed men by their secret curses."[53]

Furthermore, as Brian Levack tells us, there was "the growing conviction among educated Europeans that there were natural explanations for mysterious or apparently supernatural phenomena." They were "also beginning to discover that many of the unusual diseases and aberrant forms of behavior that were customarily attributed to witchcraft could be explained without any reference to the supernatural."[54]

This last point is significant. Technically speaking, we cannot conclusively prove that the devil or his demons don't exist, or that witches cannot work their black magic. But with the advancement of science, supernatural explanations for any given event in our lives become unnecessary and superfluous. A devil-empowered witch may have caused a particular illness by her spell. But what best explains why we can usually trace the illness to a natural cause, such as the consumption of undercooked food? And what best explains why the right medicine predictably cures the illness? If an illness were caused by the spell of a witch, there is no reason to think we would find a natural cause for it. Nor is there reason to think the right medicine would always overpower the spell in curing the illness. This kind of science, and the subsequent hope that the elites of this era placed in the idea of progress, had a major effect on ending the witch hunts.[55]

What then can we make of sociologist of religion Rodney Stark's claim that Christians themselves helped end the European witch hunts? [56] If Christians helped to end them they should also be blamed for starting them. After all, atheists weren't doing these things. Perhaps Christians ought to be congratulated for the Peace of Westphalia in 1648, too, which ended the religious bloodbath between the Catholics and Protestants. Stark should also explain why the witch hunts continue today in Sub-Saharan Africa, led by Bible-quoting witch hunters.

Christians did eventually end the European witch hunts, despite what God failed to reveal in the Bible, but should have. They learned their lessons the hard way, without any discernible help from God. It took centuries of torture and killing for those hard lessons to be learned. And they did it with the help of reason rather than faith, with the tools of biblical criticism and natural science, the hallmarks of atheism. All this shows is the willingness of Christians to revise their beliefs due to the changing times and harsh realities of life, just as they have always done, and just as they will continue to do. They'll never give up on faith. They'll never give up on God. They'll just change what they believe.

I for one am utterly and completely unimpressed.

THEY WILL MAKE GOOD SLAVES AND CHRISTIANS

Christianity, Colonialism, and the Destruction of Indigenous People

David Eller

The English Defence League has spoken forcefully (and occasionally acted violently) against the "Islamization" of English culture and society, and citizens of other European countries, along with the United States, have expressed similar alarm at the aggressive expansion of Islam. Of course, Islam is nowhere near invading and occupying England or the United States.

On the other hand, in 1798, seven hundred years after the battles of the First Crusade (see chapter 5 in this volume), Napoleon landed a French army of thirty thousand in Egypt, reinitiating the conquest of the Middle East. Perhaps three thousand Muslims were killed at the Battle of the Pyramids on July 21 and another three thousand during rioting against the French in Cairo. To head off an Ottoman counterattack, Napoleon invaded Palestine and Syria, where he executed thousands of prisoners of war. The Battle of Aboukir on July 25, 1799, cost another four to six thousand Muslim lives. The French were expelled in 1800, not by Muslims but by the rival invading English. A century later, after World War I and the Sykes-Picot Agreement, England and France would finally divide the Middle East between themselves.

Meanwhile, England had used its military might to enforce the importation of opium (grown in the occupied territory of India) into China. Despite the Chinese emperor's ban on opium in 1810, England refused to cease dealing drugs to the country, and when China tried to interdict the trade, England responded with a pair of "opium wars" (1839–1842 and 1856–1860) to defend

133

its right to be a drug pusher. During this shameful episode, the Christian god spoke to one Hong Xiuquan, informing Hong that he was the younger brother of Jesus and commissioning him to liberate China from its devils. The result was the Taiping (Heavenly Kingdom) movement, which left at least twenty million people dead between 1850 and 1864.

Whatever threat Islam presents in the twenty-first century pales by comparison to the rampage of Christianity around the globe over the past five hundred years. Admittedly, Christian Europe and the United States were not the first to fight wars, found colonies, and build empires. However, Christendom did so on a scale previously unknown and likely never to be known again. In the process, populations were decimated, cultures destroyed, and entire societies exterminated; the survivors were usually left in abject conditions, sick, poor, and restricted to marginal areas. All of this conquest was done by Christians, much of it in the name of Christianity.

The present chapter will discuss the relation of Christianity and colonialism to the destruction of indigenous peoples. It is easy to single out Christian missionaries for blame (and they deserve all the blame we can heap upon them), but Christian missionization would have been—and had been for centuries—ineffectual without the economic, demographic, and military weight of Western colonialism. So, while we will recognize the role of missionaries, we must see them in the context of, and complicit with, a more complete Christian-colonial project that appointed itself the civilizing force of the world, a project that involved explorers, traders, soldiers, settlers, administrators, and governments. Not all of these characters acted out of religious motivation, but their shared Christianity certainly did not prevent their rapacious behavior and often enough justified it.

The story of Christian-colonial violence is too extensive and complicated to be covered thoroughly in one short chapter. It spanned five centuries, every continent, almost every society, and many competing Christian sects. For our purposes, we will select four continents—South America, North America, Australia, and Africa—where the Christian-colonial impact was especially noxious, telling only a few of the tales of domination and discrimination. Entire books could be and have been written about this sordid history and other regions, from the Middle East and Asia to the Pacific Islands, where the same script was played out.

The Christian-Colonial Complex

> Colonialism is a form of imperialism based on a divine mandate
> and designed to bring liberation—spiritual, cultural, economic and
> political—by sharing the blessings of the Christ-inspired civiliza-
> tion of the West with a people suffering under satanic oppression,
> ignorance and disease, effected by a combination of political, eco-
> nomic and religious forces that cooperate under a regime seeking
> the benefit of both ruler and ruled.
>
> —Jan H. Boer, Sudan United Mission[1]

While the Qur'an may admonish believers to spread religion by the sword,
no religion has wielded more swords—and muskets and rifles and machine
guns—in the service of conversion than Christianity. The fierce potential of
Christianity was displayed as soon as the faith attained political primacy,
when its wrath was turned on internal heretics, followers of other religions
like Islam, and tribal peoples in Europe who were not yet Christianized. Christian emissaries also traveled far and wide, bringing the message to people in
India, China, Japan, and Africa but with little success until 1492.

Although we tend to emphasize the year 1492, Western-Christian colonialism cannot be dated to any single year, and at first it was a decidedly small-
scale enterprise, a few trading posts on the African coast and eventually in the
East Indies. Over five centuries, colonialism took many different forms, sometimes trade, sometimes robbery, sometimes settlement, and always eventually
conquest and subjugation. It also had many motivations, including "capitalist striving for profit, the colonies as valves for overpopulation, the spirit
of exploration, scientific interest, and religious and ideological impulses."[2]
In the search for power and profit, Western-Christian colonists seized land,
labor, wealth, markets, and political control, never shying away from the most
superb forms of violence and abuse.

But Western Christians also saw themselves engaged in a "civilizing"
mission, and as Ben Jones puts it, colonialism "was as much an ideological
project as an administrative one."[3] This ideology included Western-Christian
cultural, racial, and religious superiority, so much so that Rudyard Kipling
in 1899 could actually celebrate colonialism as "The White Man's Burden,"
opening his poem of praise with the words, "Take up the White Man's burden,

send forth the best ye breed / Go bind your sons to exile, to serve your captives' need." In short, Western Christians were just so darned superior, it was their *obligation* to bring civilization and Christianity to those whom even Kipling recognized as "captives."

The rationalization for colonial conquest and Christian conversion began with "legal fictions" like *terra nullius* and the right of conquest. *Terra nullius*, literally "empty land," maintained that Europeans were free to occupy any territory that was uninhabited or void of "civilized" humans, that is, people who did not recognize private property, farm the land, and believe in God. Once such territory was taken by force, the right of conquest established the authority to rule and settle it.

In the process, native peoples were often simply dispossessed or exterminated. But Western-Christian colonial powers did not want total depopulation, for the natives were a valuable source of labor, taxes, and political cooperation in territories where natives often greatly outnumbered the settlers and administrators. For those who survived the initial onslaught of invasion, their fate was to be "civilized" in the model of Western society, acculturated to its/our practices of life and labor such as "the seven-day week, the special status of the Sabbath, new modes of dress and conduct, the value of literacy and numeracy, and so on."[4]

Few scholars have written more lucidly on the civilizing mission of colonialism than John and Jean Comaroff. Investigating the African colonial scene, they noted that colonialism inevitably involved coerced changes to political, economic, religious, and cultural habits like dress, speech, marriage, gender roles, and especially work practices. Jean Comaroff stressed how colonialism rewrote "the signs and structures of everyday life,"[5] ending in what both Comaroffs called a "revolution in habits," "an epic of the ordinary," "the everyday as epiphany," and "a quest to refurnish the mundane"[6]—to refurnish the natives' world, specifically, to resemble the proper Western-Christian lifestyle.

In this process, missionaries were crucial; few other Western-Christian invaders lived in such close contact with the indigenous people. The missionaries literally and intentionally modeled civilized life for the natives. For instance, the mission garden provided the prototype of "civilized cultivation," which often entailed the undermining of traditional gender roles, in which women did the bulk of horticultural work. The missionary home became the epitome of civilized domestic space, with right angles, specialized rooms for different functions, doors and locks for privacy, and modern furniture. Situated on the broad streets and square blocks, marked by fences, the mission settlement "became a diorama" for "teaching [the natives] to build a world."[7] In this world, women were consigned to the "domestic" sphere, where they could sit and sew and serve like Western-Christian ladies. Savage nakedness was covered with clothing that marked Western-Christian shame as well as class and gender distinctions. And of course the locals were put to work: modern labor and cash transactions were seen as part of a new "moral economy," stigmatizing idleness and "primitive production" and promoting "the kind of upright industry and lifestyle that would dissolve [paganism's] dirt."[8]

This Christian-colonial complex served not only the interests of the missionaries, who felt quite keenly that they were helping the benighted barbarians, but also the interests of settlers, traders, and colonial administrations. Western-Christian colonists wanted a subdued, pacified, and pliant local population—when they wanted a local population at all. Fiona Bateman and Lionel Pilkington, in their introduction to their edited volume on settler colonialism, argue that, when indigenous societies were small and weak, occupation of their land was "founded on a commitment to annihilate native or indigenous peoples" who "were considered inferior, scarcely human—closer to animals than to civilized people"[9] and who could be eradicated with the same love and justice that was applied to heretics and infidels.

For this purpose, every tool at their disposal was used, from war and alcohol to forced labor and forced conversion. This is why more than a few historians have characterized missionaries as "ideological shock troops for colonial invasion whose zealotry blinded them"[10] not only to the evils of colonialism but of Christianity itself. Working side by side with settlers, corporations, soldiers, and governments, Christianity "provided a sacral warrant for the political domination, economic exploitation, territorial containment, and missionizing imposition of alien beliefs, practices, and values on indigenous people,"[11] with missionaries themselves playing "a special role as agent, scribe, and moral alibi"[12] to a half-millennium of heinous treatment (treatment that, by the way, missionaries have neither disowned nor discontinued, as we will see below).

Latin America

> They should be good and intelligent servants, for I see that they
> say very quickly everything that is said to them; and I believe that
> they would become Christians very easily, for it seemed to me that
> they had no religion.
>
> —Columbus' captain's journal, 1492

The first region to feel the righteous fury of colonial Christianity was the Caribbean islands and Central and South America. At the very moment when the crusade against the Moors of Spain was complete, and in the throes of the Spanish Inquisition, the crusading inquisitorial zeal of Spain was thrown at the New World. The Americas were hardly free of their own horrors, including empire and human sacrifice, with priests donning the flayed skins of victims, but the inhabitants of the continent had never seen the likes of the atrocities that were about to befall them.

Christopher Columbus led the assault, for gold, glory, and God. Landing famously on October 12, 1492, it took just three months until the first intercultural bloodshed occurred on January 13, 1493. After capturing a few natives to carry to Europe, Columbus returned in 1493 with a letter from King Ferdinand, granting Spain possession of islands and mainland alike by authority of the Pope, and issuing this warning to the "Indians":

> Should you fail to comply, or delay maliciously in so doing, we assure you
> that with the help of God we shall use force against you, declaring war upon
> you from all sides and with all possible means, and we shall bind you to the
> yoke of the Church and of Their Highnesses; we shall enslave your persons,
> wives and sons, sell you or dispose of you as the King sees fit; we shall
> seize your possessions and harm you as much as we can as disobedient and
> resisting vassals. And we declare you guilty of resulting deaths and injuries,
> exempting Their Highnesses of such guilt as well as ourselves and the gen-
> tlemen who accompany us.[13]

Having duly blamed the indigenous people for their own fate, violence broke out during this voyage, including killing, rape, and enslavement: sixteen hundred prisoners were taken, of whom more than five hundred were shipped off to Spain. Columbus found his colony at Navidad burned and its inhabitants dead, reportedly because the Christians had abused the native's wealth and women. By 1495, Columbus discovered that his men on Hispaniola had been "kidnapping boys for slaves, women for sex, beating and maiming at will, raping, pillaging." Columbus's brother, Fernando, chronicled that they "found the island in a pitiful state, with most of the Christians committing innumerable outrages for which they were mortally hated by the Indians."[14] Bartolomé de las Casas, who would later emerge as a champion of the Indians, likewise wrote that the natives viewed the invaders as "intolerable, terrible, fierce, cruel, and devoid of all reason," voracious of both food and sex, "abhorrent" for "mistreating them and causing them anguish."[15] Rather than repent, a force of two hundred Christians marched on the natives, killing hundreds and capturing hundreds more. The vanquished people were ordered to pay tribute, and by 1498 Indian land was being expropriated and granted to Spanish soldiers, with the native occupants attached as peasants and serfs to that land. Within two decades of first contact (1514), the genocide of indigenous people on Hispaniola (present-day Haiti and Dominican Republic) reduced the population of several hundred thousand to just thirty-two thousand.

Having conveniently received dominion over all lands west of a line decreed by the Pope in the 1494 Treaty of Tordesillas, the conquest of Central and South America proceeded apace. In 1519 an unauthorized party led by Hernán Cortés invaded Mexico, defeating the Aztec Empire within two and a half years. Disobeying orders, Cortés stranded his men on the mainland, giving them no option but to continue their insurgence. Gaining allies among the local societies ruled by the Aztecs, the *conquistadors* marched to the city of Cholula, where after a peaceful reception the Spanish killed many local noblemen and sacked the city. Arriving at the Aztec capital of Tenochtitlan on November 8, 1519, Cortés arrested the emperor, Moctezuma, and held him for ransom until May 1520.

Fighting off a Spanish army sent to punish him for mutiny and treason, one of the most disgraceful incidents occurred on May 20, 1520, known as the Massacre in the Main Temple. During a religious ceremony, the Spanish descended on the celebrants and murdered every last one in an event reminiscent of the fall of Jerusalem to the crusaders; indeed, no doubt the *conquistadors* felt like the crusaders of old. Facing armed resistance from the Aztecs, Cortés besieged Tenochtitlan for eight months, finally taking the city on August 13, 1521. In vengeance, the Spanish tore down the city, building modern-day Mexico City over its blasted foundations.

Defeating the Aztecs hardly meant subduing the entire region. For forty years, from 1550 to 1590, the conquerors were embroiled in a war with the Chichimeca people, resulting in thousands of indigenous deaths. The pacification of the Yucatan peninsula took even longer, succeeding only in 1697.

Meanwhile, the Christians had set upon the other great civilization of the Americas, the Inca Empire in Peru. In 1529 the Spanish Crown gave Francisco Pizarro permission to attack the Incas, and in the 1532 Battle of Cajamarca the *conquistadors* and their native allies caught the emperor Atahualpa in an ambush or massacre of unarmed Indians, resulting in some two thousand native deaths and the loss of only five Spanish soldiers. Like his Aztec counterpart, Atahualpa was held for ransom, but despite receiving a literal king's ransom in gold, on August 29, 1533, his captors christened him against his will and then murdered him.

Like biblical locusts, the invaders poured into South America, discovering the silver mines in the central and southern parts of the continent. The town of Potosí became one of the most infamous mining centers, eventually producing thousands of tons of precious metal for Spain. It was certainly not going to be Spaniards who did the arduous and dangerous work in the mines, though. Instead, the conquerors modified the Incan labor system known as *mita*, conscripting thousands of men. And when neither men nor mules could survive the grueling labor, African slaves were imported to replace both.

Once the peoples of Central and South America were nearly annihilated (only about ten percent of the original population survived) and fully conquered, the problem of how to rule and exploit them remained, and here the missionaries became invaluable. As Adriaan van Oss concluded, "If we had to choose a single, irreducible idea underlying Spanish colonialism in the New World, it would undoubtedly be the propagation of the Catholic faith."[16] For instance, the already-mentioned letter of King Ferdinand led to a standardized document called the *Requerimiento* (requirement or demand), attributed to Juan López de Palacios Rubios in 1513. Like the royal letter, the *Requerimiento* justified conquest on religious grounds: it first restated the Christian belief in God and Catholicism's authority over all humankind; it then "asked and required" that the Americans acknowledge the Church as the Ruler and Superior of the whole world, and the high priest called Pope, and in his name the King and Queen our lords, in his place, as superiors and lords and kings of these islands and this terra firma . . . and that you consent and give place that these religious fathers should declare and preach to you the aforesaid.[17]

The speech then reiterated the kind offer of friendship, backed up with the earlier threat to damage, dispossess, enslave, and kill those who decline.

Across the continent, management of the vanquished Indians was placed in the hands of various Catholic orders, including the once-gentle Franciscans (formed in the thirteenth century), who "became unequivocally committed to Spanish imperialism, condoning the violence and coercion of the Conquest as the only viable method of bringing American natives under the saving rule of Christianity."[18] Another mighty arm of the Church in the Americas was the newly-founded Jesuit Order, or the Society of Jesus. In a recent study, Denis De Lucca noted the militaristic orientation of the early Society of Jesus (quite contrary to the putatively peaceful message of their namesake), born as it was from the sixteenth-century religious wars in Europe between Catholics and Protestants.[19] Jesuit priests actually taught military skills and architecture in their colleges, knowledge that was naturally transferred to the colonial mission in the Americas and elsewhere.

Another familiar tactic of the Catholics in America was the mission settlements or *reducciones*. From 1610, when Spanish emperor Philip III decided that it would require the "sword of the Word" to convert natives into Christians and obedient colonial subjects, the Jesuits began to construct a system of *reducciones* from Bolivia to California. One hundred thousand members of the Guarani tribe, for instance, were consigned to twenty settlements in Paraguay, and the forced movement of thirty thousand Indians in 1629 left more than half dead.

In a scathing study, George Tinker described the notorious *reducciones* led by the Franciscan father Junipero Serra in Spanish California from 1769 to 1782. Tinker asserted that the missionaries "functioned in complete symbiosis with the structures of Spanish civil government, and even as an extension of it," including receiving their salary from the colonial administration.[20] Serra and other missionaries arrived with Spanish troops, and upon supposed conversion, the indigenous inmates "were no longer allowed to leave the mission except for specific purposes and [with] the express permission of the mission-aries."[21] In the concentration missions, natives were forced to labor to support the missionaries and soldiers, and they were subjected to compulsory religious attendance; worse yet, families were separated and children taken from their parents, the better to train and civilize them. Contemporaries like Father Antonio de la Conception Horra reported corporal punishment in the form of whipping, shackling, placing in stocks, and depriving of water, all of which were deemed reasonable to enforce the peaceful gospel on them.[22] Nutrition also suffered, as the previously self-sufficient peoples were reduced to peasants and serfs who fed their masters.

The focus in this chapter is colonialism, but it is essential to remember that these highly rationalized abuses continued uninterrupted after independence. Local white and mestizo elites perpetuated their domination over indigenous peoples, in alliance with the Catholic Church. Independent Latin American governments were also complicit in the kidnapping of Indians for display in European shows and zoos, like the eleven Selk'nam people who were captured from southern Chile in 1888 and displayed as examples of "primitive humans"; all of the captives died in Europe, like many other indigenous individuals, and their remains were only returned after 2009. When liberation theology, a form of Catholicism sympathetic to the plight of indigenous people (and other poor people) emerged in the late twentieth century, it was criticized by many as communism and subsequently squashed.

North America

Since God Almighty hath made this Countrey so large and fruitful, and that the [native] people be such as you have heard them described; It is much more Prudence, and Charity, to Civilize, and make them Christians, then to kill, robbe, and hunt them from place to place, as you would doe a wolfe. By reducing them, God shall be served, his Majesties Empire enlarged by the addition of many thousand Subjects, as well as of large Territories, our Nation honoured, and the Planters themselves enriched by the trafficke and commerce which may be had with them.

—*A Relation of Maryland*, 1635[23]

The only good Indians I ever saw were dead.
                    —attributed to General Philip Sheridan (1831–1888)

The previous section was not meant to imply that the Spanish or the Catholics were alone in their genocidal handling of indigenous peoples; they were merely the first Europeans to crash into native societies, and the Central and South American Indians were the first to taste Western-Christian zeal and steel. As attested by the case of Junipero Serra, Spanish Catholics also penetrated as far north as Florida, Texas, and California, but within a century they were joined in North America by other Christian colonists from France, Holland, and England.

As discussed in the previous chapter on inquisitions and religious wars, France was the scene of vicious struggles between Catholics and Protestants, and French Catholics carried their crusade into Canada and the Great Lakes region. Michael Welton, for instance, described how the French Jesuits, like their Spanish counterparts, brought a warlike spirit to their missionary work, using what Welton called an "attack pedagogy" to undermine the culture and religion of aboriginal Canadians.[24] Ironically, the Christians used new scientific knowledge against the natives, predicting eclipses and tides and otherwise discrediting native religions with facts rather than faith. The Jesuits were also scandalized by the freedom of women and children in native societies and sought to impose Western-Christian gender and family norms. Welton ultimately characterized the Jesuits as "educational warriors and not neutral facilitators. So once they sensed that the traditional lifeworld was eroding, they focused their attacks on the inadequacy of the indigenous meaning system,"[25] never noticing the inadequacy or perversity of their own.

This section will concentrate on the territory that would eventually become the United States, where some new elements were added to the Christian-colonial complex, most notably Protestantism and corporations. The Dutch and the English who arrived in the 1600s were predominantly Protestant, and, contrary to American mythology, most did not make the arduous journey for "religious freedom" but rather for business. Like the British Hudson Bay Company, which virtually governed Canada for decades, corporations like the

Virginia Company and the Plymouth Company transported the first colonists to North American shores. Yet religious motivations and legitimations were never far from the minds of sovereigns, as in the charter granted to the Virginia Company in 1606 by King James I (of "King James version" of the Bible fame), which justified colonialism as noble work "which may, by the Providence of Almighty God, hereafter tend to the Glory of His Divine Majesty, in propagating of Christian Religion to such people, as yet live in darkness, and miserable ignorance of the true knowledge and worship of God."[26] Accordingly, the Jamestown colonists of 1607 "were sure that the Indians needed them and their civilization"[27] and were dismayed when the Indians tried to eradicate the pestilence of English occupation in 1622. Once the natives had risen up in self-defense, a violent reprisal was not only reasonable but righteous, since were the Indians not obstacles to civilization and Christianity, veritable devil worshippers?

The other early colonists, the Protestant extremists known lovingly in American history as Puritans, did not offer Christian kindness to the natives of Massachusetts for long after the mythical "first thanksgiving." As in many lands before and since, disease scourged the native populations, which the loving Christians considered a "wonderful plague": in 1634 John Winthrop could write that the Indians "are neere all dead of the small Poxe, so as the Lord hathe cleared our title to what we possess."[28] Unsatisfied with the reduction of the indigenous population, wars against the Pequots in 1637 and the Wampanoags in 1675 and 1676 freed up more land for Christian use.

Of course, overt violence was not the only tool of Christian conquest in Massachusetts. Among the first and most important missionaries to the Indians was John Eliot (1604–1690), who began ministering in 1634. Like the *reducciones* mentioned above, Eliot saw controlled Indian settlements as the key to converting and civilizing the heathens, so he instituted his initial "praying town" in 1651, to which thirteen more were added by 1674. Tinker also examined this missionary effort, judging that Eliot "was merely a government functionary using religion as a device to subjugate Indian peoples" and to segregate them from English settlers.[29] The indigenous Christians who were incarcerated in these praying towns were as closely managed as the prisoners of the *reducciones*, and like the latter they "became suppliers for the more substantial and stable Puritan economy."[30] Even so, without greater coercive force the project was doomed to failure, and after 1675 most alleged converts "returned to their traditional communities, joined the fight against the English, and finally rejected Christianity."[31]

Accelerating invasion by English and other colonists inevitably led to more conflict. The natives also could not avoid getting caught up in European colonial struggles, like the "French and Indian war" (1756–1763), which was only the American theater of a global battle between the French and the English. Those Indians who sided with the French in that war, or with the English during the American revolutionary war, were treated as enemies and shoved westward off their traditional lands. When the United States bought a huge chunk of territory from France in the so-called "Louisiana Purchase" of 1803—no doubt without the native inhabitants' knowledge or approval—the United States suddenly came into possession of still more indigenous peoples.

While the United States continued the policy of signing treaties with native societies, it also became more covetous of native land. In 1830 President Andrew Jackson signed the Indian Removal Act, authorizing him to displace Indians living inside American territory and transfer them to "Indian territory" west of the Mississippi River. Jackson was already renowned for his gainful Indian wars: he defeated the Creeks in 1814, resulting in the annexation of twenty-two million acres of Creek land, and he participated in nine Indian treaties, wrestling yet more land from native peoples in southern states.

Removal, however, operated on an unprecedented scale. When the Seminoles of Florida refused to move, America fought wars with them (1835–1842 and 1855–1858). The Creeks, already dispossessed of much of their country, were forced to relocate to the west in 1837, and the Chickasaws followed them during the winter of 1837–1838. Perhaps the most molested of southern tribes was the Cherokee, who were by this time a remarkably modernized people. In 1838, the United States deployed seven thousand soldiers to forcibly march the recalcitrant Cherokees from their homes; during the military removal, some four thousand Cherokees died, causing the survivors to dub the event the Trail of Tears. The Cherokee removal is the most infamous, but removal was a common strategy in nineteenth-century America. The Shawnee, Ottawa, Potawatomi, Sauk, and Meskawaki were also transplanted from the Midwest, and in 1864 the Navajo or Diné people were sent on their "Long Walk," which was only one of multiple forced relocations.

Although promised to the Indians in perpetuity, American settlers first trickled and then poured into "Indian country" west of the Mississippi. The result was predictable frontier conflict, and after its Civil War the American army could be unleashed on the western tribes in a series of plains wars. Handed more than a few defeats, most notably the destruction of George Custer's militia in 1876, American forces fought the Comanche from 1868 to 1874, the Chiricahua Apache from 1860 to 1886, Geronimo's Apache hold-outs from 1881 to 1886, the Utes repeatedly from the 1850s to the 1880s (in a disgraceful historical episode recounted in Peter Decker's *The Utes Must Go!*[32]), the Modoc from 1872 to 1873, the Nez Perce in 1877, and the Crow in 1887. The feistiest of opponents were arguably the Lakota (incorrectly known as the Sioux) and their neighbors the Cheyenne, who fought a series of engagements with the United States army between 1854 and 1877. Among these engagements were massacres of peaceful Indians, such as the disreputable Sand Creek Massacre, in which Colonel John Chivington (a Methodist preacher, by the way) led a force of Coloradans against an unarmed encampment of Cheyenne and Arapaho people in 1864. The putative last "battle" of the Plains Indian wars, in 1890, was also a massacre of nonviolent Ghost Dancers at the Pine Ridge reservation.

We have seen two of the key tactics that the United States used to solve "the Indian problem"—forced relocation and military conquest. The third, as with the *reducciones* discussed already and various institutions we will discuss later, was "civilization" through forced education. As early as 1819 the Civilization Fund Act authorized organizations (primarily religious groups) to provide education to Native Americans. Once native peoples were restricted to reservations, the government allowed various sects to manage education, often dividing reservation populations between multiple denominations.

The most recognized achievement in civilizing and Christianizing the indigenous people was the system of boarding schools pioneered by Richard Henry Pratt. An army officer with experience commanding native soldiers as well as overseeing native prisoners, Pratt opened the Carlisle Indian Industrial School on an unused army base in Carlisle, Pennsylvania, in 1879. Taking advantage of the military character of the facility, Pratt ran a school with barracks and even a jail for the Indian students, where native culture and identity was to be completely abandoned in favor of American civilization. Children's hair was cut, their clothes were confiscated and burned, and they were dressed in military uniforms. They were taught the English language, the Christian religion, and gender-appropriate manual skills. They were forbidden to speak their traditional language or practice their traditional religion, on pains of physical punishment; survivors of the system recall being ridiculed and beaten. For his part, Pratt is credited with stating, "A great general has said that the only good Indian is a dead Indian. In a sense, I agree with the sentiment, but only in this: that all the Indian there is in the race should be dead. Kill the Indian in him, and save the man."[33] Explaining his method and philosophy to a Baptist convention in 1883, Pratt proclaimed, "In Indian civilization I am a Baptist, because I believe in immersing the Indians in our civilization and when we get them under holding them there until they are thoroughly soaked"[34]—even if that meant stealing children from their parents, permanently alienating them from their cultures, and scarring them emotionally.

The scars of American colonialism (sometimes called "manifest destiny" from the Eurocentric perspective) remain today. No one knows how many people occupied the continent before contact—estimates range from as few as two million to as many as eighteen million—but by the end of the Plains Indian wars their numbers had been reduced to two hundred fifty thousand. In the 2010 Census, almost three million Americans claimed Native American ancestry, a mere 0.9 percent of the total population. Although not all Native Americans inhabit reservations today, Indian reservations are some of the poorest and most unhealthy parts of the country: the poorest counties, such as Ziebach and Shannon counties in South Dakota, are on or near reservations. A few tribes have exploited their treaty-given exemption from American law to open casinos and other lucrative businesses, but for the most part the burden of Christian colonialism still weighs on America's indigenous people.

Australia

As late as 1935 a prominent member of [Australian] Parliament told me frankly that "The nigger has got to go, and the sooner the better." This man is a respectable citizen, a member of a Christian Church, and a fine man, except in his attitude to the natives.
—Dr. Charles Duguid, 1936[35]

Christian colonialism in Australia has two significant distinctions. First, in addition to being conducted exclusively by the British, Australia was originally a dumping ground for criminals and undesirables. Second, unlike any other continent, Australia was inhabited exclusively by hunter-gatherers, whose small and mostly nonwarlike bands could offer little or no resistance to white incursion. The confluence of these two factors made the island, as Robert Hughes put it in the title of his history of the country, a fatal shore.[36]

Once again, it is impossible to calculate the precise native population before colonization, but experts figure that no fewer than two hundred fifty thousand and as many as seven hundred fifty thousand Aboriginals occupied the island. The first British convict ships arrived on the southeast coast in 1788, which Meredith Lake notes "roughly coincided with the emergence of the Protestant missionary movement."[37] That very year, Richard Johnson joined the colony as its first missionary, and he, like most Europeans and Christians, looked down on the native inhabitants as savages without clothing, private property, or religion. Lake tells that Johnson "adopted" (which could mean kidnapped) an Aboriginal girl named Booron in an experiment to teach her English and Christianity. Predictably, foreign presence on their land inspired resistance, with a native man named Pemulwuy leading raids on British citizens from 1790 until he was shot to death in 1802, his head reportedly cut off and shipped to England.

On no colonial stage was the purported superiority of white Christians played out more purely than in Australia, where the natives' physical and cultural "primitiveness" rendered them "little more than intelligent animals" in the eyes of the invaders.[38] They were not even deemed useful for labor, partly because they would not submit to Western-style work and partly because there was an abundant supply of white convict slave labor. The three hundred to five hundred Aboriginal societies or linguistic groups had no economic value to colonists, and based on the Christian belief that only humans have souls and moral significance, Aboriginals were widely judged not even worth saving: the very idea that they could be converted to Christianity was not officially embraced until 1825.[39]

In one of the most tragic episodes in the asymmetrical relation between invaders and natives, the southern island of Tasmania was penetrated the next year, where a few thousand native Tasmanians, known as Palawa or Parlevar, could hardly stand against the colonizers and their weapons and diseases. Hostilities—in response to which a writer for the *Colonial Times and Tasmanian Advertiser* newspaper on December 1, 1826, opined that "the government must remove the natives—if not, they will be hunted down like wild beasts, and destroyed!"—eventuated in the so-called Black War (1828–1832), which left much of the population dead. By 1833 there were maybe two hundred Palawa alive, and the survivors were removed to places like Flinders Island, where the missionary named George Augustus Robinson oversaw the death of thirty-one of his fifty-one charges. When the last male native Tasmanian (ridiculously named "King Billy" by his captors) died in 1869, his bones were stolen right out of his body from the morgue, and the skeleton of the very last native Tasmanian, a woman named Truganini, who died in 1876, was exhumed and kept for scientific display until 1976.

This sad pattern was reproduced across the continent for many decades. According to Colin Tatz, between 1824 and 1908 some ten thousand Aboriginals were slain in Queensland (the "deep north" of Australia) alone: "Considered to be wild animals, vermin, scarcely human, hideous to humanity, loathsome, and a nuisance, they were fair game to white 'sportsmen.'"[40] However, and arguably because of the Aboriginals' small numbers and the whites' disdain for them, instead of large battles or wars, the confrontation between natives and trespassers consisted of a long string of small skirmishes or massacres. One of the earliest was at Myall Creek in 1838, where, in reprisal for a cattle theft, twenty-eight Aboriginal men, women, and children who were not involved in the crime were tied up and executed, then sliced or mutilated and burned.[41] A very short list of other massacres includes Murrumbidgee-Murray River (1838, fourteen killed), Campaspe Plains (1839, forty killed), Murdering Gully (1839, thirty-five to forty killed), Gippsland (1840–1850, between two hundred fifty and a thousand killed), Warrigal Creek (1843, over one hundred killed), Yeeman (1857, a dozen killed, with as many as three hundred more during the following year), Barrow Creek (1874, up to ninety killed), Battle Mountain (1884, two hundred killed), Forrest River (1926, eleven killed), and most unforgettably Coniston (1928, between thirty and sixty men, women, and children killed). And this is not to mention the destruction done to the Aboriginal environment and economy from the introduction of sheep, cattle, rabbits, and fences to an unsuspecting continent.

As Aboriginals were being casually exterminated, the noose of missionary love also tightened around their necks. Once again, a standard tactic was separation of children from their parents and societies. Barry Patton has described the practice in southeastern Australia, which began as early as 1815 with the Native Institution at Parramatta, founded by a missionary named William Shelley, who "anticipated that Aboriginal adults would impede its civilizing and Christianizing efforts by their example of 'uncivilized' life and that the children should be distanced from them."[42] As in most colonial settings, "Aboriginal adults were considered not only unresponsive to the Europeanizing message but an uncivilizing influence that had to be marginalized."[43] In other words, intelligent and mature people were immune to their proselytizing, so missionaries had to focus on the young.

Ironically, some parents willingly left their children to the boarding schools, since the institutions provided regular meals, and many missionaries were well aware that their only hold on the children was food—what was known as "flour-bag Christianity." Parents often hung around the schools and took children back to the bush on every occasion, so by the 1840s teachers and missionaries plotted to relocate students to boarding schools distant from their home. Even more cleverly, school officials exploited tribal tensions by placing students in schools situated in the territory of hostile tribes, so that if they attempted to escape they would have to traverse enemy country. All of this amounted to what Superintendent Charles La Trobe proudly called "vigorous coercion," since "nothing short of an actual and total separation, from their parents, and natural associates, and Education, at a distance from the haunts and beyond the influence of the habits and example of their tribe would hold out a reasonable hope of their ultimate civilization and Christianization."[44] That is, Christian colonizers knew that the "truth" of their message was inadequate without the power of compulsion.

These measures hardly exhausted the tactics at the disposal of Christianizers. Whites also took control of the marriage system, encouraging or only allowing marriage between Christian Aboriginals. In some instances they actually promoted intermarriage with whites, to literally dilute the racial and cultural identity of Aboriginals. In 1983 Peter Read published a damning report titled *The Stolen Generation: The Removal of Aboriginal Children in New South Wales, 1883 to 1969*, which brought this history to the full attention of Euro-Christian Australia. As the subtitle indicates, the practice of abducting children and holding them in dormitories apart from their families persisted into the middle of the twentieth century. Andrew Markus saw the dormitory system as a natural "extension of the missionary imperative to exercise control over the lives of the children they removed there."[45]

Interestingly, despite the ongoing colonial-style domination of Aboriginals, including the 2007 "emergency intervention" in Aboriginal communities, the white society of Australia has gone further in accepting its culpability than the supposedly morally exceptional United States. In 1997 the Australian government issued its five-hundred-page admission of guilt *Bringing Them Home: The Report of the National Inquiry into the Separation of Aboriginal and Torres Strait Islander Children from their Families*, followed by Prime Minister Kevin Rudd's formal apology to the Aboriginal people in 2008. As far back as 1976 the country passed the Aboriginal Land Rights Act to allow native peoples to claim their land, and in 1993 a legal suit by Eddie Mabo resulted in the Native Title Act, which rejected the colonial doctrine of *terra nullius* and provided a process for re-establishing Aboriginal ownership of land.

Africa

> When the whites came to our country we had the land, and they
> had the Bible; now we have the Bible and they have the land.
> —African proverb

> The horror, the horror.
> —Mr. Kurtz, in Joseph Conrad, *The Heart of Darkness*

Africa has the dubious distinction of being the last continent that Christian colonizers sunk their teeth deeply into. On the positive side, Africa escaped the worst ravages of colonialism until late in the nineteenth century; on the negative side, when Euro-Christians did arrive, they had four hundred years of practice at the colonial project.

Western-Christian ignominy in Africa of course begins with the slave trade, which for many years was the only major contact with the continent, where Europeans maintained at most small coastal trading posts. Africans began to be transported to Spanish and Portuguese Catholic colonies almost immediately upon their founding, with more than thirteen thousand shipped to the Americas by 1525. At the high point of the slave trade, in the years between 1776 and 1800, two million Africans were transported to the Western hemisphere, the largest number destined for Brazil. According to the Trans-Atlantic Slave Trade Database, a total of over ten million Africans arrived at various slave destinations, and many more did not survive the passage; almost five million were brought to Brazil, 1.3 million to Spanish colonies, 2.3 million to the British Caribbean, 1.1 million to the French Caribbean, and nearly four hundred thousand to the North American mainland.[46] Clearly Christian countries had no qualms with slavery, and the United States had to fight a war against the slave-owning Bible Belt to abolish a "peculiar institution" that violated its Constitution but apparently not its religion.

Whereas colonialism began in Latin America with (often rogue) armies (and missionaries), in North America with settlers (and missionaries), and in Australia with convicts (and missionaries), for many years the only white presence in Africa was intrepid individual explorers (and missionaries). Among these early visitors were Mungo Park (1771–1806), the medical missionary and functionary of the London Missionary Society David Livingstone (1813–1873), Henry Morton Stanley (1841–1904), and Pierre Savorgnan de Brazza (1852–1905). Africa was an exceptionally difficult and dangerous place for European travelers, as its interior was almost entirely uncharted, its mostly humid environment hosted numerous diseases hostile to Westerners, and its population contained many large and well-organized societies, able to resist foreign incursions. Many Europeans died trying to explore the Dark Continent.

According to Frank McLynn, the stage of exploration only gave way to the stage of colonialism around 1890,[47] and Western-Christian occupation of the continent followed rather than preceded the official carve up of what King Leopold of Belgium called "the magnificent African cake." At the Congress of Berlin in 1884–1885, Western heads of state met to divide Africa between them; conspicuously absent were any Africans. Once colonial boundaries were set, each European country raced to study and subdue its holdings. Thus, unlike any other part of the world, the "scramble for Africa" left a quilt of colonial holdings by half a dozen different Western-Christian countries (England and France possessing the bulk of the continent, plus Germany, Portugal, Belgium, and Italy). Every inch of Africa was eventually ruled by some Western power, except for Ethiopia and Liberia (and Liberia was created by the United States, through its American Colonization Society, in 1821 as a final stop for freed slaves!). The fragmented map of modern Africa is due to this colonial game.

Always prepared to defend their homelands, African chiefdoms and kingdoms stiffly opposed the Christian colonizers, now turned imperialists, who were no longer content to trade but wanted to own. Bruce Vandervort explained that there were mostly small wars of conquest and resistance before 1900, but from around 1900 the confrontations were larger and more modern in weapons, tactics, and goals: for instance, the British threw 440,000 troops at South Africa during the Second Boer War (1899–1902).[48] Each European power marched its armies across Africa, sometimes more than one in the same region, as with the English and French invasions of Sudan; in the Battle of Omdurman (September 2, 1898), British forces killed ten thousand Africans and wounded five thousand more at the cost of forty-seven British dead and 382 wounded.

A very abbreviated list of wars between Christian imperialists and Africans includes the Ashanti War (1873–1874), the ninth Xhosa War (1877–1878), the Zulu War (1879), the Abushiri Rebellion (1888–1890), the HeHe War (1891–1898), the Mashona War (1896), the Voulet-Chanoine Expedition (1898), the Ashanti "war of the golden stool" (1900), the Herero Wars (1904–1908), the Maji-Maji Revolt (1905–1907), the Libyan War (1911–1912), and so many campaigns against various tribes that they cannot all be counted. German colonial policy is often regarded as particularly brutal, manifested in General Lothar von Trotha's "extermination order" against the Herero in 1904, which stipulated that "any Herero found inside the German frontier, with or without a gun or cattle, will be executed. I shall spare neither women nor children. I shall give the order to drive them away and fire on them." In reality, though, all Christian imperialists treated their African enemies similarly, using cannons, machine guns, and airplanes against virtually defenseless people.

Let us not forget either the recruitment of African soldiers for Europe's First World War. We tend to think of this disaster as French and German troops facing each other across the trenches, but hundreds of thousands of Africans were conscripted on both sides, pitting Africans against Africans on European soil.

Once the job of "pacifying" the local population (which British soldiers called "hammering") was complete, the exploitation of Africa's treasures could commence. And Africa had two riches in abundance—its natural resources and its labor. Europeans extracted valuable goods like exotic woods and of course ivory, devastating the elephant herds; they also practiced trophy hunting of wild animals. As McLynn also asserted, one of the key challenges in the interior of Africa was transportation, and the imperialists solved the problem by commandeering Africans to provide porterage, literally to carry colonial goods—and indeed colonial personnel—in and out of the country. But soon rubber became the most profitable product of central Africa, with calamitous results.

Of all the horrendous tales of Christian colonialism, perhaps none is as horrendous as the tale of the "Congo Free State" or Belgian Congo. Determined to get his slice of the African cake, King Leopold II of Belgium finagled and deceived to get a huge chunk of central Africa, which was allegedly to be a region open to all traders and free of slavery and other such abuses. Instead, as recounted in the book and film *King Leopold's Ghost*, the king ran the colony as his personal property, policed by his Force Publique, characterized by Adam Hochschild as "counterguerrilla troops, an army of occupation, and a corporate labor police force."[49] Outwardly opposed to slavery, Leopold virtually enslaved the entire central African population, compelling the natives to work as porters, rubber tappers, and other laborers. One colonial official remembered the "file of poor devils, chained by the neck, [who] carried my trunks and boxes toward the dock,"[50] while a Belgian politician described the African workers as

> miserable, with only a horribly filthy loin-cloth for clothing . . . most of them sickly, drooping under a burden increased by tiredness and insufficient food . . . beasts of burden with thin monkey legs, with drawn features, eyes fixed and round from preoccupation with keeping their balance and from the daze of exhaustion. They come and go like this by the thousands.[51]

Discipline and control were maintained with the *chicotte* or rawhide whip, and individuals (including women and children) who did not meet their quotas of rubber or such products frequently had a hand cut off (there are many photographs as witness to the punishment). Estimates of the death toll range from five million to ten million, and the suffering toll cannot be counted. No wonder Joseph Conrad modeled his *The Heart of Darkness* after the horror, the horror of the Congo.

Just as economic exploitation was more exquisite in nineteenth-century colonialism, so was missionization. This was partly due to centuries of experience but also to the same strong, integrated African societies that resisted military conquest. F. K. Ekechi found that the Igbos of west Africa, for instance, were particularly immune to the ministrations of Christians: "Believing that their traditional religion was better for them than 'this new religion,' most of the Igbo people listened to missionary propaganda but remained outside the Christian Church."[52] However, as in other times and places, the missionaries did not depend on faith alone but on the leverage they could exercise. Converts were often exempted from certain colonial obligations such as forced labor or taxation, so some locals accepted Christianity for the worldly advantages it offered. Missionaries would also sometimes intervene with colonial administrators or native chiefs on behalf of converts. And then there was the mission school, which was one of the few available sources of education for indigenous people: Ekechi reasoned that it was the desire for education, "rather than the ambition to embrace the new faith, that led to the rapid spread of the Christian churches in Igboland."[53] And the missionaries knew very well that people cared less for religion than for reading and writing, a priest named Father Shanahan confessing that "those who hold the school, hold the country, hold its religion, hold its future,"[54] adding that "if we go from town to town talking only about God, we know from experience that much of our effort brings no result. But no one is opposed to schools."[55]

Nor was anyone opposed to hospitals, the other site of Christian-colonial penetration of indigenous Africa. Shobana Shankar explains how medical facilities, including hospices for leprosy, represented a "peaceful invasion" of Nigeria in the 1930s,[56] a quite useful "means of introducing 'western education and cultural values' to a wide cross-section of their subjects. Modern ideas, here, clearly meant Christian mission culture."[57] Missionaries of course exploited every asset at their disposal, from medicines to money to motor vehicles, not to mention control over employment, housing, and marriage. Ever alert to the political benefits of proselytization, Leopold in 1883 ordered his missionaries "to evangelize, but your evangelization must inspire above all Belgium's interests." Seven years later, Leopold envisioned a system of children's colonies where Africa's youth could be subjected to religious, vocational, and military instruction by Christian clergy.[58]

Mission Not Accomplished

Colonialism in the formal sense has ended (although many critics claim that globalization and neoliberalism constitute a "neo-colonialism"), but its ravages are still present today. Poverty, injustice, and corruption are rife in places where Christian colonialists promised to bring "civilization," and indigenous people remain the most disenfranchised and endangered citizens of the planet.

And yet missionization is hardly a thing of the past. Christians continue to practice, and to praise, mission work, and most have never come to grips with the history of the undertaking. Quite the opposite: Christians look for every opportunity to inject themselves into other people's countries, characteristically confident that they are doing a good thing. Many readers may be aware of the influx of missionaries to Russia after the fall of communism, and the Iraq War was a godsend for God's soldiers. A video called "White Christian Genocidal Crusades (Holy War), Imperialism, and Colonialism in Iraq" depicts Americans from an organization called the Voice of the Martyrs (VOM), who promote "God's aggressive love" in zones where the American army has opened the door like *conquistadors* from another time.[59] Former executive director of VOM Tom White, who admits in the video to using disguises and deception to infiltrate native societies, says directly that "conflict is a natural part of Christianity" and that wherever there is war, Christians arrive in the wake of the conquering forces. Regular members of the Southern Baptist Convention declare that the Iraq War is "a religious war. They don't hate us, they hate our god. They are believing a lie," and their poster boy is General William Boyken, who publicly and in uniform stated that the "war against terror" is a holy war and that his god is a real god, unlike the god of the non-Christians. No doubt colonial missionaries felt exactly the same way.

More offensive to me as an anthropologist is how anthropological knowledge has been misconstrued and misused by contemporary missionaries. There are actually books like *Anthropology for Christian Witness* and *Anthropological Insights for Missionaries*[60] among a burgeoning literature arming "young missionaries with some basic tools for understanding other cultures and for understanding themselves as they enter these cultures."[61] These are only the latest advances in the "cunning pedagogy" mentioned by Welton, a pedagogy that effectively blends the Christian message with political power, cultural knowledge, and that odd brand of Christian love that we discovered in a previous chapter. Whether it is crusades and holy wars, inquisitions and tortures, or colonialism and missionization, Christian love "could take many forms: constraining, compassionate, controlling, unreciprocated, and even on occasion, violent. And, just as the intentions of this love—as for all forms of love—were not always selfless, its outcomes were often far from benign."[62] Christians who fear and hate Islamization should admit the fear and hatred that many indigenous people felt and feel toward Christianization.

8

THE SLAVE IS THE OWNER'S PROPERTY

Christianity and the Savagery of Slavery

John W. Loftus

In this chapter I will focus on American slavery as a test case for slavery in general and its relationship to Christianity. Before I begin I want the reader to know just a little about what needs to be explained, rather than explained away, something Christian apologists (or defenders) of slavery try to minimize or neglect. I think the brutal facts of American slavery are fairly well-known, but just in case, I recommend the critically acclaimed introduction to it by Peter Kolchin, *American Slavery 1619–1877*. In it he reminds us of what we're dealing with:

> Born in violence, slavery survived by the lash. Beginning with the initial slave trade that tore Africans away from everything they knew and sent them in chains to a distant land to toil for strangers, every stage of master-slave relations depended either directly or indirectly on physical coercion. The routine functioning of Southern farms and plantations rested on the authority of the owners and their representatives, supported by the state, to inflict pain on their human property. Plenty of pain was inflicted.
>
> Slave owners directed especially repressive measures against Africans, for newly imported slaves offered pervasive resistance to the conditions under which they found themselves. . . . New slaves, in short, needed to be "broken in," made to accept their status, a goal that required close supervision, routine application of the lash, and willingness to take draconian measures against those who refused to toe the line.
>
> Slaves who transgressed could look forward to a wide range of gruesome punishments including branding; nose slitting; amputation of ears,

toes, and fingers; castration; and burning at the stake . . . slaves were power-less to stop it . . . virtually no whites questioned the moral basis for slavery at the beginning of the [eighteenth] century.[1] [Africans were not the first ones used as slaves in the New World, see note 1]

As an example of this cruelty, in 1846 Samuel Gridley Howe happened to watch as a slave girl was brought to a New Orleans prison by her master to be flogged in a courtyard, surrounded by balconies of prisoners. He said it "chilled me to the marrow of my bones." The executioner tied her naked body down then proceeded to whip her. Howe said:

> Every stroke brought away a strip of skin, which clung to the lash, or fell quivering on the pavement, while the blood followed after it. The poor crea-ture writhed and shrieked. . . . But still fell the horrid lash; still strip after strip peeled off from the skin; gash after gash was cut in her living flesh, until it became a livid and bloody mass of raw and quivering muscle. . . . But think you the poor wretch had committed a heinous offense, and had been convicted thereof, and sentenced to the lash? Not at all. She was brought by her master to be whipped by the common executioner, without trial, judge or jury, just at his beck or nod, for some real or supposed offence, or to gratify his own whim or malice. And he may bring her day after day, without cause assigned, and inflict any number of lashes he pleases, short of twenty-five, provided only he pays the fee.[2]

Henry Bibb (1815–1854), who escaped from slavery and became a leading abolitionist in his day, wrote of his experiences in his book *Narrative of the Life and Adventures of Henry Bibb, an American Slave*. In the final chapter, after recounting the horrors of slavery, he said this:

> I find in several places, where I have spoken out the deep feelings of my soul, in trying to describe the horrid treatment which I have so often received at the hands of slaveholding professors of religion, that I might possibly make a wrong impression on the minds of some northern freemen, who are unac-quainted theoretically or practically with the customs and treatment of Amer-ican slaveholders to their slaves. I hope that it may not be supposed by any, that I have exaggerated in the least, for the purpose of making out the system of slavery worse than it really is, for, *to exaggerate upon the cruelties of this*

system, would be almost impossible; and to write herein the most horrid features of it would not be in good taste for my book.[3]

Frederick Douglass (1818–1895), who also escaped from slavery and became a leading abolitionist in his day, had some harsh things to say about Christian slave owners of the South:

> Were I to be again reduced to the chains of slavery, next to that enslavement, I should regard being the slave of a religious master the greatest calamity that could befall me. For of all slaveholders with whom I have ever met, religious slaveholders are the worst. I have ever found them the meanest and basest, the most cruel and cowardly, of all others.[4]

Douglass continues elsewhere:

> I can see no reason, but the most deceitful one, for calling the religion of this land Christianity. I look upon it as the climax of all misnomers, the boldest of all frauds, and the grossest of all libels. . . . We have men-stealers for ministers, women-whippers for missionaries, and cradle-plunderers for church members. The man who wields the blood-clotted cowskin during the week fills the pulpit on Sunday, and claims to be a minister of the meek and lowly Jesus. The man who robs me of my earnings at the end of the week meets me as a class-leader on Sunday morning, to show me the way of life, and the path of salvation. He who sells my sister, for purposes of prostitution, stands forth as the pious advocate of purity. . . . We see the thief preaching against theft, and the adulterer against adultery. We have men sold to build churches, women sold to support the gospel, and babes sold to purchase Bibles for the poor heathen! All for the glory of God and the good of souls! The slave auctioneer's bell and the church-going bell chime in with each other, and the bitter cries of the heart-broken slave are drowned in the religious shouts of his pious master. Revivals of religion and revivals in the slave-trade go hand in hand together.[5]

American slavery was brutal, inhumane, and worthy of nothing but our disgust, especially in the antebellum (pre–Civil War) South. I don't think there is any disagreement about this among informed people in today's world. America fought a blood-spattered Civil War to end slavery, but that wasn't the end of the story by any means. The dehumanizing racism that helped sustain slavery has survived in American society for a century and a half. After two hundred and fifty years of slavery, African Americans suffered through ninety years of Jim Crow laws, lynchings, the rise of the Ku Klux Klan, thirty-five years of racist housing policies, and continued discrimination across the board in all other areas in varying degrees.

Yet slavery was defended by Christians who found justification in the Bible for this utterly vile American institution. Two questions arise. First, if a perfectly good, omniscient, all-powerful God exists, then why didn't he do something to avert this horrible tragedy? Second, can the Bible legitimately be used to justify what Christians in America did as slaveholders? These two questions are intertwined, since such a God, if he exists, supposedly inspired the Bible.

What I Can Understand and What I Can't

From the outset let me state a couple of things I understand about the issue of slavery. I understand that slavery has been endemic to humanity in practically all cultures throughout history, and it continues to exist in parts of the world today. What I can't understand is how a perfectly good, all-knowing, all-powerful God could have tolerated slavery in the world at all. Religions should be judged based on how they treat the defenseless. Slaves, especially the women and children, are the most defenseless human beings of all. Given the cruelty that slaves experienced throughout most of church history, all civilized people should reject the Christian religion and its God as nothing but the inventions of a barbaric era. The Judeo-Christian religions took the ancient cultural moral standards of their day and elevated them to the highest authoritative status possible. They were directly tied to the very commands of God. It's this fact that legitimized the institution of slavery long after human empathy toward others would have rejected it.

I also understand that people will find reasons to defend that which is perceived as personally or financially beneficial to them. In colonial America there was no other perceived source of labor that could provide industry with raw materials, especially cotton. So Americans who benefited from slave ownership defended it based on their perception of social and/or economic gain.

What I can't understand is why Christian people worthy of their namesake, who are guided by the Holy Spirit to know right from wrong and given the power to act accordingly, should place financial incentives above the most basic human moral concerns. Even evangelical theologian John Stott admits, "Although slavery of different kinds and degrees was universal in the ancient world, it is inexcusable that the *professedly* Christian nations of Europe (Spain and Portugal, Holland, France and Britain) should have used this inhuman practice to meet the labour needs of their New World colonies."[6]

Just keep in mind that professing Christians are the only kind of Christians we ever see, and they did just what Stott's hindsight exegesis now condemns. Hindsight is wonderful isn't it? When today's Christians look into the past nearly all of them believe they would have condemned the Crusades, the Inquisition, the European witch hunts, the wholesale destruction of indigenous peoples, and slavery. They would have embraced the modern values of religious freedom, freedom of speech, and democracy. Just ask them. But the truth is that we are all children of our times. For Christians to say they would object to slavery if they were Caucasian-born believers who were raised in the antebellum South defies the facts. Christopher Hitchens said it this way: "The chance that someone's religious belief would cause him or her to take a stand against slavery and racism was statistically quite small. But the chance that someone's religious belief would cause him or her to uphold slavery and racism was statistically extremely high, and the latter fact helps us to understand why the victory of simple justice took so long to bring about."[7] Christianity simply reflects the spirit of the times down through the centuries. But if there really is a transcendent, providential God governing church history, then we would expect the church to have risen above the moral standards of the times. The fact that it didn't, and does not now, is a clear indicator that there is no transcendent, providential God.

What I am incapable of understanding is why God didn't interfere at some point with American history to stop slavery dead in its tracks. God could have implanted within us an inviolable moral code against enslaving others, or he could have made us suffer from severe nausea at the very thought of enslaving others. God could have also interfered by placing the right people in power; that is, those who condemned slavery from the beginning, so that slavery in the New World would never have been tolerated. But he didn't.

Christians demur when confronted with these suggestions, saying God gave the gift of free will to early Americans, even if they used it to brutally enslave others. In response, let me just propose a dilemma: Can God interfere with any free-willed human choices? Let's first suppose he can. The Bible strongly indicates he can and does (see Exodus 4:21, 9:21; Deuteronomy 2:30; Joshua 11:20; Proverbs 16:1, 16:9, 16:33, 19:21, 21:1; Job 42:2; Isaiah 64:8; Jeremiah 1:4–5, 10:23; Daniel 4:35; Galatians 1:15; Ephesians 1:4–11). If there was ever a time for God to intervene, this was the time to do it. But he didn't. Furthermore, if God did not do the greater deed of interfering with American slavery, then it doesn't seem reasonable to think he does the lesser deeds of interfering in any of our mundane choices either. The greater the need to interfere, the greater the moral responsibility for a perfectly good God to do so. For Christians to object that God knows best, they need to show how the sufferings that the slaves endured had some greater purpose in their individual lives, for surely such a God would not use them to teach the rest of us moral lessons if he truly loves each individual person.

Let's now suppose God cannot interfere with free-willed human choices. If he cannot interfere, then Christians should stop all petitionary prayers whenever free-willed human actions are involved. They should stop praying for safety in their cross-country travels, since reckless drivers have free will, since criminals we may meet at highway rest stops have free will, since bungling mechanics with free will may have worked on our vehicles, and since incompetent factory workers with free will may have made them. At what point in this process could God ever grant prayer requests for safe travels if doing so involves so many free-willed choices? A whole host of other requests could not be granted by God either, like getting a job promotion or an award in an art contest or the lover we so desire. Nor can he change the course of anything else in human history. If instead, as Calvinist Christians believe, God sovereignly decreed all human history, and along with it slavery, then there is no reason to trust him at all. He would be a malevolent deity, one who couldn't be trusted enough for us to accept anything he tells us, which completely undermines any supposed revelation in the Bible.

More to the point, why would a good God give human beings the freedom that we have so badly abused? Two-year-old children should not be given razor blades to play with. If we give them one, then we are to be blamed if they hurt themselves or others. The giver of a gift is to be blamed when he or she gives a gift to a person knowing in advance that person will abuse the gift. We cannot responsibly give twelve year olds accesses to our liquor cabinets, or the keys to our cars. Likewise, if God gave us the freedom to enslave others knowing we would do so, he is to be blamed for what we do. If anything, he should have waited until such time as we were civilized adults in our thinking before giving us such a "gift." But he didn't.

God didn't even minimize the sufferings of the slaves. At the very least God could have created us all with one color of skin so there would be no race-based slavery. But he didn't. If nothing else, had God created us all with the same color skin, it would have been easier for slaves in America to escape from their bondage and then subsequently blend in with their surrounding society. Peter Kolchin tells us, "Whites were assumed to be free, blacks slaves."[8] As it was, slaves could not escape easily at all, to say the least, even with some outside help from the people who mobilized the Underground Railroad network.

Consider the need for slaves in the production of cotton. Peter Kolchin tells us, "It is almost impossible to overemphasize the importance of cotton to the antebellum Southern (and indeed American) economy." He writes that "cotton created a seemingly insatiable demand for slave labor."[9] This demand was the direct result of Eli Whitney's invention of the mechanical cotton gin in 1793, since it made harvesting cotton much more profitable:

Cotton production expanded from 750,000 bales in 1830 to 2.85 million bales in 1850. As a result, the South became even more dependent on plantations and slavery, with plantation agriculture becoming the largest sector of the Southern economy. While it took a single slave about ten hours to separate a single pound of fiber from the seeds, a team of two or three slaves using a cotton gin could produce around fifty pounds of cotton in just one day. The number of slaves rose in concert with the increase in cotton production, increasing from around 700,000 in 1790 to around 3.2 million in 1850. While it was true that the cotton gin reduced the labor of removing seeds, it did not reduce the need for slaves to grow and pick the cotton. In fact, the opposite occurred. Cotton growing became so profitable for the planters that it greatly increased their demand for both land and slave labor.[10]

At the very minimum any God worthy of the name would have kept Eli Whitney from inventing the cotton gin by keeping such a thought out of his head. But he didn't. God could have also inspired Whitney to invent the mechanical cotton picker at the same time as the cotton gin, which is a machine that harvests cotton somewhat like mechanical corn pickers harvest corn. The first mechanical cotton pickers, invented by John D. Rust in 1933, were capable of harvesting one row of cotton at a time. They could have replaced up to forty slave laborers. But God didn't do this either.

On Saving the Christian Faith from Refutation

Christian apologists will argue that an omnipotent God could not do any of the things I've suggested, for various reasons. But why not? These same apologists will turn around and hypocritically invoke God's omnipotence when it comes to supposed miracles that go contrary to all known natural laws, like a virgin birth or Jesus rising up from the dead or his ascension into the sky, by saying, "with God all things are possible." If God's omnipotence can override natural laws when it comes to these miracles then why is it metaphysically impossible for him to work within natural laws in the ways I've just suggested?

I have found Christian apologists to be experts at picking and choosing between God's attributes of omnipotence, omniscience, and omnibenevolence (or perfect goodness), depending on the problem to be solved. When it comes to God's omnipotence in the face of so much intense suffering, apologists conveniently negate it by focusing instead on God's omniscience, saying we cannot understand his ways. God, like a father, knows best, they'll say when it comes to explaining why an omnipotent God allows so much suffering. So in order to save their faith from refutation they must allow God's omnipotence to go only so far, and no farther. This is where his power arbitrarily ends, where the apologist needs it to end to solve a problem for faith. Process theologians like John B. Cobb Jr. and David Ray Griffin have even been forced to deny God's omnipotence in order to solve the problem of suffering. According to them God merely has the power to persuade. He doesn't have coercive power.

When it comes to God's omniscience in the face of so much intense suffering, apologists conveniently negate it by focusing instead on God's omnibenevolence, that God created a perfectly good world despite the fact that doing so meant there was the probability (or real possibility) free creatures would disobey.[11] They will claim God didn't know how to create free-willed creatures who never disobey, or at the minimum don't disobey very often, or in such inhumane ways. So in order to save their faith from refutation they must allow God's omniscience to go only so far, and no farther. This is where his knowledge arbitrarily ends, where the apologist needs it to end to solve a problem for faith. Evangelicals such as the late Clark Pinnock, along with John E. Sanders, Richard Rice, and Gregory Boyd, are even embracing Open Theism, which denies God can foreknow future free-willed human actions.

Christian apologists will even negate God's omnibenevolence if that is what's required to believe. Since there is clear evidence for a great amount of gratuitous suffering in the lives of so many people—suffering that has no ultimate explanation for the individuals who are suffering—evangelicals such as Michael Peterson, the late William Hasker, and Bruce Little deny what is called *meticulous providence*. In their view some of our suffering is because God is not directly involved in our daily lives.[12] According to them, God does not care to be involved in our daily lives, so we suffer as a result. If this isn't their point, then what is? Certainly an omniscient God knows how to intervene. Certainly an omnipotent God has the ability to do so. Shouldn't an omnibenevolent God have the motivation to do so?

It should be easy for God to eliminate the horrendous suffering in our lives. That's not too much to ask of a truly omnipotent, omniscient, omnibenevolent deity, is it? If you name any specific example of horrendous suffering in this world I can easily show how such a God could have eliminated it without adversely affecting anything else, since such a deity would be able to perform what I have previously called *perpetual miracles*. If we accept that God is omnipotent, for instance, and that he created the universe from nothing, then he should be able to perform perpetual miracles. So God could miraculously intervene without us ever knowing that he had done so. He could have stopped the underwater earthquake that caused the Indonesian tsunami of 2004 with the snap of his omnipotent fingers, and a quarter of a million people would not have died. Then, with a perpetual miracle, he could have prevented it from ever occurring in the future. We would never be the wiser if he wanted to remain hidden for some unknown reason, for, from our perspective, it would never have taken place!

The fact is that the more knowledgeable and powerful a person is, the greater that person's moral responsibility to help others who are experiencing horrendous suffering. Just think of that helpless slave girl you read about earlier, who was being whipped by the executioner. A person who didn't know that this was taking place could not have been held morally responsible for not doing anything to stop it. A person who knew it was taking place but had no power to stop it could not have been held morally responsible for not doing anything to stop it. Since God is believed to be both omniscient and omnipotent, he bears the highest possible degree of responsibility to stop it. The best explanation for God not helping that girl, or any of us who intensely suffer, is that God isn't omnibenevolent. So in order to save their faith from refutation, Christian apologists must allow God's omnibenevolence to go only so far, and no farther. This is where his perfect love ends, where the apologist needs it to end to solve a problem for faith.

Christian apologists are also experts in substituting special pleading as if it were apologetics. If you want to be a Christian apologist you must master this art. If you want to be a *good* apologist you must avoid doing so entirely, although, if you were to succeed in avoiding special pleading, you wouldn't be an apologist at all. Apologists look at the world and force their conceptions of God to fit what they see. It is emphatically not the case that they first define their God based on the perfect-being theology derived from Anselm's Ontological Argument to God's existence. The greatest conceivable being than which no greater being can be conceived ends up being the same one that best suits their need for faith. For when it comes to their conceptions of God they conclude he didn't have the power to create a world without naturally caused suffering, that he didn't know how to create a world where there are free creatures who never disobey, and that he doesn't care enough to intervene in our lives on a daily basis. Either their ontological conceptions of the perfect being really mean something, or they don't. Christian apologists cannot arbitrarily negate them when it suits their faith. What they should do instead is take their ontological conceptions of God and ask what kind of world *should* exist if such a God created it, rather than look at the world that presently exists and force their conceptions of God to fit it. Doing what they do is little more than special pleading. They cannot continue this type of intellectual gerrymandering if they want to be taken seriously. To paraphrase John F. Kennedy, ask not what kind of God should exist given this present world. Ask what kind of world should exist if God exists.

The Bible and Slavery

Let's turn now to the Bible itself. The most noteworthy popular apologists for biblical slavery are Rodney Stark,[13] a sociologist of religion who in 2004 accepted an appointment at Baylor University, the world's largest Baptist university, and Paul Copan,[14] the president of the Evangelical Philosophical Society. There are others.[15] Book length responses to their arguments have been written by biblical scholars Hector Avalos[16] and Thom Stark.[17] I reference these works for honest people who are really interested in reading both sides. I do so candidly, since it should be crystal clear that the biblical-slavery proponents in today's world are not only misguided and ignorant, but in some cases in the habit of misrepresenting the facts in order to maintain their Christian faith.

Let me focus on just one of these defenders, Paul Copan, who argues for six points regarding biblical slavery.

> First, slavery during biblical times was different from slavery in the Old South. Second, since slavery was so thoroughly entrenched in the ancient near East, this practice was mitigated, limited, and controlled in the law of Moses instead of abolished. Third, the law of Moses address abuses since, according to the Bible, masters did not have absolute rights over their slaves. Fourth, the Bible affirms that slaves have full personhood, dignity, and rights alongside their masters, a significant advance compared to the surrounding ancient cultures. Fifth, the biblical writers did not speak directly against slavery for the same reasons the Jews did not speak directly against the rule of Rome: social reform was secondary to certain internal, attitudinal transformations. Sixth, one could easily imagine that making the abolition of slavery a plank of early Christian dogma—within the context of Roman rule—might have offered a misguided or false reason for joining the church. Perhaps the early Christian leaders exercised wisdom by not turning Christianity into a social political movement.[18]

If you want to find devastating responses to these claims, read the books by Hector Avalos and Thom Stark. In what follows I will argue that biblical slavery of any kind was always abusive, since it was still utterly barbaric by our moral standards today. What Copan ends up doing is comparing the best-case scenario of biblical slavery, that of Hebrew Israelites enslaving other Hebrew Israelites, with the worst case scenarios from the ancient world. This grossly misrepresents the facts, and it doesn't matter whether biblical practices were an advancement over other legal codes in the ancient Near East (they were not),[19] Furthermore, if Christianity was not invented to directly address social issues like slavery, then it fails as a divine revelation. For if God inspired it, he failed millions of people who were enslaved for far too many centuries.

There is some controversy among Christians themselves about whether the Jesus pictured in the canonical gospels was a social revolutionary. Most scholars think he was, at least when it suits them. When it doesn't suit them, as in the case of slavery, they change their tune. It is quite apparent to anyone who reads the Gospel of Luke that Jesus upheld and defended the disenfranchised, the poor, women, widows, and the so-called sinner class of people. Yet he used parables that illustrated the master-slave relation-ship without batting an eye (Matthew 18:23–35, 20:1–16, 25:14–30; Luke 16:1–8, 17:7–10). Apparently he was not concerned enough about slaves to condemn slavery. Copan says he did so in one case, the case of the Israelites themselves, when he quoted from Isaiah 61:1, which reads, "The Spirit of the Sovereign Lord is on me, because the Lord has anointed me to proclaim good news to the poor. He has sent me to bind up the brokenhearted, to pro-claim freedom for the *captives*, and release from darkness for the prisoners" (see Luke 4:17–21, my emphasis). Neither the Hebrew word for "captives" in Isaiah, the Greek Septuagint (LXX) rendering of the word, nor the Greek word used in Luke's gospel are the words commonly used for slaves though. The words used mean the same thing: prisoners. Even if one can extrapo-late that slaves were in some sense prisoners of the Roman authorities, then Jesus' use of it was still a self-serving one coming from a failed doomsday prophet. For Jesus was predicting the rise of Israel to rule over the world in his day after a divine cataclysmic intervention. It is hardly a call for the release of all slaves. That didn't enter his mind.

So, was slavery during biblical times different from slavery in the Old

South? Copan declares that even though both sides in the Civil War "read from the same Bible and sought divine support to overcome their adversaries,"

> the common association of Israel's servant laws with those of the antebellum South is seriously misguided. We can plainly affirm that if the three clear laws of the Old Testament had been followed in the South—that is, the anti-kidnapping, anti-harm, and anti-slave-return regulations in Exodus 21:16, 20, 26–27 and Deuteronomy 23:15–16 and 24:7—then slavery wouldn't have arisen in America."[20]

The kind of slavery Copan thinks existed in ancient Israel "wasn't much different *experientially* from paid employment in a cash economy like ours."[21] Really? I am utterly dumbfounded by what faith can lead Christian apologists to say. If faith makes otherwise intelligent people say such ignorant things, I want nothing to do with faith at all. Let's consider Copan's case.

First, let's consider the "anti-kidnapping" laws. In Exodus 21:16 we read: "Anyone who kidnaps someone is to be put to death, whether the victim has been sold or is still in the kidnapper's possession" (New International Version). This verse in the original Hebrew is a garbled mess. Is it condemning kidnapping people, selling kidnapped people, holding kidnapped people as slaves, or all three? What we know is that kidnapping foreigners, selling them, and holding them as slaves were all justifiable as the spoils of war (just consider the Midianite virgins in Numbers 31:17–18, 41). We also know that both slaveholding and selling legitimately owned Hebrew slaves were acceptable for other Hebrews, since regulations are given in these texts. By the process of elimination, this means Exodus 21:16 is likely condemning the kidnapping, selling, and/or holding of stolen Hebrew men and women as slaves. Deuteronomy 24:7, another text Copan refers to, tells us this explicitly: "If someone is caught kidnapping a fellow Israelite and treating or selling them as a slave, the kidnapper must die." The Greek Septuagint (LXX) translation of Exodus 21:16 confirms this: "Whoever steals *one of the sons of Israel* [my emphasis], and prevail over him and sell him, and he be found with him, let him certainly die." So Exodus 21:16 does not condemn the kidnapping, selling, and/or holding of non-Hebrews or foreigners at all, which is exactly what the American slave trade did by kidnapping, selling, and holding foreign slaves from Africa.

There was a distinction in Exodus 21 between how Hebrews and non-Hebrew slaves could each be obtained and treated. How do we know? Because of the context. In the first verse of this chapter God is quoted as telling Moses, "These are the laws you are to set before them [i.e., the Israelites, or Hebrews, as a collective whole]: If you buy a Hebrew servant. . . ." This context is also affirmed in that Israelites cannot sell these slaves to foreigners (21:8). The whole chapter deals with laws that apply between Hebrews. It's describing the master-slave relationship between Hebrews and their Hebrew slaves, not the master-slave relationship between Hebrews and non-Hebrews (we'll get to that relationship shortly). It's the best-case scenario of slavery in the Bible. But even at that, it's certainly not like an employer/employee relationship in today's society, as we shall see next.

Second, let's consider the "anti-harm" laws. In Exodus 21:20–21 we read, "When a slaveowner strikes a male or female slave with a rod and the slave dies immediately, the owner shall be punished. But if the slave survives a day or two, there is no punishment; for the slave is the owner's property" (New Revised Standard Version). Hebrew slaves are the Hebrew master's property (literally their "money") because they were bought by him. Hebrew slaves were indentured servants to other Hebrews due to poverty or debts they could not pay back. They were to remain as slaves until their debt was paid, or until they were released by law after seven years (Exodus 21:2–6). The Babylonians, by contrast, released their slaves after three years.[22] As slaves they could be beaten within an inch of their lives for disobedience, so long as they survived for a day or two after the beating. What it means to "survive" for two days isn't clear. What if a slave survived two days and didn't die until the third or fourth day? Then what? Couldn't Pharisaical lawyers get the slave master off the hook? Why not? There wasn't a legal provision for this. What's clear is the barbarism of even the best-case scenario of slavery in the Bible. Moving on, Exodus 21:26–27 reads: "An owner who hits a male or female slave in the eye and destroys it must let the slave go free to compensate for the eye. And an owner who knocks out the tooth of a male or female slave must let the slave go free to compensate for the tooth." Again, this concerns Hebrew ownership of other Hebrews. It's the best kind of slavery in the Bible, which doesn't say much. It doesn't prohibit a master from whipping a Hebrew slave until his or her flesh peels off.

Third, let's consider the "anti-slave-return" law found in Deuteronomy 23:15–16, which reads: "You shall not give up to his master a slave who has escaped from his master to you; he shall dwell with you, in your midst, in the place which he shall choose within one of your towns, where it pleases him best; you shall not oppress him." Copan argues this law applied to all runaway slaves, both Hebrews and foreigners, saying that if slaves could run away from their masters they should be freed. Such a view makes no sense in a slave state or nation. Slavery probably couldn't exist under those conditions, for it would require chaining all slaves up as prisoners while they worked in the fields, lest they run for the hills. And they would all run if this were the law. Thom Stark shows just how wrong Copan is, for the "you" God is speaking to here represents the Israelites as a collective group. All we have to do is once again examine the context that directly precedes these verses. In them God is addressing the Israelites collectively (1–14). So God is telling them what to do when they find fugitive foreign slaves from another land who have sought freedom from their foreign masters. God is saying the Hebrew people should help these foreign fugitive slaves. So this "anti-slave-return" law would not apply to the escaped slaves in America, since they did not escape from foreign African slavery.

Still, is this "anti-slave-return" law an advancement over other ancient legal codes? Perhaps in some sense, but Stark provides the reason behind it: "The reason slave-harboring was prohibited in other cultures was because of international treaties, which excluded extradition treaties. Israel was permitted to have no such treaties with their enemies. By treating runaway slaves with a modicum of dignity, the Israelites were sticking it to their enemies and erstwhile oppressors."[23]

Copan doesn't mention Leviticus 25:39–46 in this context, but he should have. Here we see clearly the difference between how Hebrew slaves and non-Hebrew slaves were acquired and treated. According to Hector Avalos, this text was "certainly one of the most often quoted by pro-slavery advocates to demonstrate that God allowed slavery."[24] It reads:

> And if your brother becomes poor beside you, and sells himself to you, you
> shall not make him serve as a slave: he shall be with you as a hired servant
> and as a sojourner. He shall serve with you until the year of the jubilee; then
> he shall go out from you, he and his children with him, and go back to his

own family, and return to the possession of his fathers. For they are my servants, whom I brought forth out of the land of Egypt; they shall not be sold as slaves. You shall not rule over him with harshness, but shall fear your God. As for your male and female slaves whom you may have: you may buy male and female slaves from among the nations that are round about you. You may also buy from among the strangers who sojourn with you and their families that are with you, who have been born in your land; and they may be your property. You may bequeath them to your sons after you, to inherit as a possession for ever; you may make slaves of them, but over your brethren the people of Israel you shall not rule, one over another, with harshness.

I find it difficult to harmonize this passage with other biblical texts that allow and regulate Hebrews who enslaved other Hebrews, but then that's not my problem, since discrepancies in the Bible are easily found. Copan accepts the view that this passage in Leviticus was an attempt to revise the harsher laws in Exodus 21, which had previously allowed and regulated the enslavement of Hebrews. Leviticus, by contrast, specifically prohibits enslaving Hebrew insiders or "brothers." Slaves are now to be exclusively non-Hebrew outsiders. But even if this is the case, then, as Hector Avalos says, "calling this an 'advance' would be most questionable," since "it bespeaks of a further differentiation between insiders and outsiders that later authorized the enslavement of non-Christians, including Muslims and Africans."[25]

The contrast between Israelite slaves and foreign slaves in Leviticus is a sharp one. In this text Hebrew masters should not rule over their Hebrew slaves harshly. By contrast Hebrew masters could be harsh in their treatment of foreign slaves. That probably meant anything goes. Foreign slaves could be bought with a price. They were considered property. They could be bequeathed as an inheritance. Since these non-Hebrew slaves could be bequeathed as an inheritance, it's clear that they were slaves for life. Does Copan really think *this* describes an employer/employee relationship? Is that why Copan italicized the word "experientially" earlier, since a person can be a piece of property and not experience anything different than an employer/employee relationship? Try imagining an auction block, then, and watching as your family is sold one by one to different slave masters, never to be seen again.

Avalos argues that any attempt to deny the property status of slaves "is clearly contradicted" by this passage in Leviticus, "for it uses the word 'ebed when describing how the Hebrews are allowed to buy slaves. Verse 45 states that an 'ebed 'may be your property' and may be inherited by the slavemaster's children (v. 46). If buying and inheriting an 'ebed does not 'connote ownership of a person,' then what does?'"[26]

Thom Stark summarizes what we've seen so far:

> Non-Hebrew slaves (foreign slaves) were slaves for life, their children were slaves for life. They could be kidnapped, they could be captured in war, they could be purchased, against their will. They could be treated harshly, as "slaves," which means they could be beaten, even beaten to death, so long as they didn't die immediately! This is exactly like slavery in the antebellum South. In the South, you couldn't enslave a U.S. citizen. But you could purchase a kidnapped African. In the same way, in Israel, you couldn't permanently enslave an Israelite, but you could kidnap, capture, or purchase a foreigner against their will.[27]

Turning to the New Testament, Copan attempts to show that it reveals a more progressive and better attitude about slavery, which eventually had "a leavening effect" such that "oppressive institutions like slavery could finally fall away."[28] Not so. Keep in mind that the Apostle Paul authorized slavery (Eph. 6:5; Col. 3:22–25; 1 Tim. 6:1–6; Titus 2:9–10; Philemon; 1 Pet. 2:18–19) even to the point of saying a person was "called" to be a slave (1 Cor. 7:20–22). The author of 1 Peter 2:18–19 even admonished slaves to suffer under a harsh master. Avalos summarizes what we find:

> Attitudes toward slavery are sometimes worse and more inhumane in the New Testament than in the Old Testament. . . . While the Old Testament set term limits for some slaves, New Testament slavery can be indefinite. While the Old Testament railed against enslaving fellow Hebrews, the New Testament allows Christians to own fellow Christians. The Old Testament required the emancipation of some severely injured slaves, but the New Testament advised Christian slaves to be submissive even to cruel masters. So if there is a trajectory from the Old Testament to the New Testament, it is toward an increasing acceptance of slavery and its cruelties.[29]

Copan appeals to Acts 17:26, which reads: "And [God] hath made of one blood all nations of men for to dwell on all the face of the earth, and hath determined the times before appointed, and the bounds of their habitation." This was one of the most widely used abolitionist texts, Avalos tells us, which "supposedly establishes that human beings were all created equal."[30] However, in the same context Paul quotes from Epimenides of Crete along with Aratus's poem "Phainomena" (verse 28), so it wasn't anything new, or Christian, and it certainly doesn't square up with the rest of what we find in the Old or New Testaments. Seneca admonished his readers to "remember that he whom you call your slave sprang from the same stock, is smiled upon by the same skies, and on equal terms with yourself breathes, lives, and dies." Cicero said "men are grouped with Gods on the basis of blood relationship and descent . . . there is a blood relationship between ourselves and the celestial beings; or we may call it a common ancestry or origin." Avalos asks: "So why do Christian apologists credit Christianity for initiating the idea of universal brotherhood when even the New Testament says that the idea already existed in non-Christian cultures?"[31]

Copan also appeals to Galatians 3:26–28, which reads:

> So in Christ Jesus you are all children of God through faith, for all of you who were baptized into Christ have clothed yourselves with Christ. There is neither Jew nor Gentile, neither slave nor free, nor is there male and female, for you are all one in Christ Jesus.

The problem with making this into a sociopolitical egalitarian text should be obvious. Paul is merely saying all Christians, whatever their social differences, have an equal standing before God. Avalos writes:

> Those espousing a non-egalitarian understanding of this text have the advantage, for being considered the offspring of Abraham, regardless of gender, ethnicity, or slave-status, does not mean that differences have been erased in any other sense. That is to say, Paul does not mean that slaves do not exist literally anymore. Thus, "there is no slave or free" cannot mean "there exist no slaves or free people." Otherwise, if slaves do not literally exist anymore, then nor do free people.[32]

That Paul's text does not prevent him from recognizing social differences is clear from what he says in 1 Cor. 7:20–22:

Everyone should remain in the state in which he was called. Were you a slave when called? Never mind. But if you can gain your freedom, avail yourself of the opportunity. For he who was called in the Lord as a slave is a freedman of the Lord. Likewise he who was free when called is a slave of Christ.

Did God Do His Best?

The question I want to raise at this point is a simple one. Supposing God exists, did he do his best in revealing his will to us? If you believe he inspired the canonized Bible, just ask yourself whether he could have done a better job of communicating his perfect loving will. Ask yourself if he could foresee the problems that would surface in our modern era that have triply discredited the Bible as barbaric to civilized, democratic-minded people, superstitious to scientific-minded people, and unhistorical to historians and to an ever growing number of biblical scholars.

This is never seen so clearly as when we consider the Christian debates over slavery. To see how difficult it was for Christians to determine God's moral will on this issue read Willard M. Swartley's book *Slavery, Sabbath, War, and Women: Case Issues in Biblical Interpretation*. In the first chapter on slavery Swartley conducts a mock debate using the actual arguments of slavery proponents and opponents before the Civil War.[33] Read it and ask if God did his best. Come on, be honest with the question. God either sent mixed messages to his people on this basic moral question or, as I've argued, he approved of such a despicably appalling, intolerable, vile institution.

On March 4, 1865, Abraham Lincoln gave his Second Inaugural Address, just one month before the official end of the Civil War. In it he commented on the lack of divine clarity in the Bible regarding slavery. Referring to anti-slaverly Northerners and proslavery Southerners, he said, "Both read the same Bible and pray to the same God and each invokes his aid against the other."[34] So again, did God do his best? I think any serious intellectual reflection on this matter demands a resounding negative answer, no ifs, ands, or buts about it. There is absolutely no reason why a perfectly good God should have accom-modated his revelation to people who thought slavery was acceptable. If a slaveholder was having a slave girl whipped until her back was bloodied with raw tissue, there is no moral justification for merely telling him to limit the number of lashes he doles out to her. That is simply not good enough. Even a good person who had the authority to command obedience would tell the slave master to stop it and never do it again. Why is it that a perfectly good God didn't do this?[35]

Why didn't the Christian God of the Bible unequivocally condemn slavery from the very beginning of humanity, if he exists? He could have consistently said, "Thou shalt not enslave human beings of any race or nationality, nor beat them into servitude." There are no circumstances where a loving God could ever think it was expedient to allow such an utterly vile institution to exist. The monuments, the temples, the walls, and the cities that slaves built could have been built with hired laborers or volunteers. Human ingenuity would take care of the rest. To say God could not have enforced a command against slavery defies the facts, especially since we're told he imposed his will with a flood, threatened to kill off all the Israelites except for Moses, and sent droughts, famines, and wars against his people for disobedience.

Earlier in this book, in chapter one (question number 1), I had argued with David Eller that the lack of empathy toward other people is a very dangerous thing. It also keeps believers from accepting the truth about their faith. If you were a slave, standing naked with your family on the auction block under the threat of the blood-soaked cowskin, and you watched in tears as your family members were bought by different masters never to be seen again, wouldn't *you* wish the Christian God had clearly condemned slavery? God's defenders simply lack empathy for these people. They refuse to feel their pain. They need to feel it if they honestly want to know the truth. But they can't allow it, since they must defend the faith no matter what the cost. Their faith acts like an anesthetic, deadening the pain they might have for these slaves. Faith is the opiate of the masses in this sense, too, following Nietzsche. People on opium don't have clear heads when it comes to the truth.

Why did the Christian God produce a sacred book that is so incompetent, so barbaric, so inconsistent, and so thoroughly a manmade invention that it lacks plausibility? An omniscient God could have done much better, if he exists, and we don't need to be omniscient in order to say this. For if God created us with finite minds, then he should also have given us what our finite minds need in order to believe. The plausibility of the claim that the Bible is God's word is inversely proportional to the amount of work it takes Christian apologists to defend it from objections to the contrary (that is, the more work its defense requires, the less likely the Bible is God's word), and it requires way too much work to suppose that it is.

Consider the 490-page book edited by evangelical scholars Steven B. Cowan and Terry L. Wilder *In Defense of the Bible: A Comprehensive Apologetic for the Authority of Scripture*.[36] It claims to offer a comprehensive apologetic. Does it? Another evangelical, Douglas Groothuis, wrote a 752-page book titled *Christian Apologetics: A Comprehensive Case for Biblical Faith*, claiming the same thing.[37] Can an evangelical accept the authority of scripture (per Cowan and Wilder) without believing in the biblical faith (per Groothuis), or vice versa? I think not. These two books do not cover the same exact material. So now we're up to about 1,242 pages of combined text for a comprehensive apologetic. Even if these authors discussed all of the essential issues (which they don't) the chapters are not long enough for the issues covered. So the authors refer us to additional books. Are we to read those other books, too? If so, we would be required to read a library of them. That's what a comprehensive apologetic requires. The important question left unaddressed by them is why a defense of the Bible (i.e., the biblical faith) requires so many books. Why does the Bible need such a defense at all? The fact that it takes so much work to defend the Bible is a strong indicator, all by itself, that the Bible is not inspired by God.

For instance, when it comes to the topic of this chapter, if the God of the Bible had clearly condemned slavery from the beginning, and if the church as an institution had never allowed her members to enslave others (because God had clearly condemned slavery), then there would be nothing for Christian apologists to defend. But since the God of the Bible did in fact authorize slavery, and because the church as an institution allowed her members to enslave others, based on what God had authorized, Christian apologists are forced to defend their faith against the objections raised by the church's savagery in condoning slavery. This present chapter (and book as a whole) is merely responding to Christian attempts at defending the indefensible.

To conclude, Sam Harris is right when he says, "Nothing in Christian theology remedies the appalling deficiencies of the Bible on what is perhaps the greatest—and the easiest—moral question our society has ever had to face."[38] The basic premise of Hector Avalos's book on slavery "is that if slavery is not regarded as wrong, then little else can be. And if slavery is regarded as inexcusably wrong, then biblical ethics stands or falls on its attitude toward slavery." His book "is a critique of the broader idea that the Bible should be the basis of modern ethics."[39] There is probably no other ethical issue in the Bible that deserves our utter disgust with regard to the faith-based claim of the inspiration of the Bible. On this rock alone Christian ethics and faith die.

A Final Note on the Abolitionist Movement

Given what we've seen in this chapter the abolitionist movement didn't have much biblical support to work with, to say the least. Hector Avalos's thorough research shows "that reliance on biblical authority was instrumental in promoting and maintaining slavery far longer than might have been the case if we had followed many pre-Christian notions of freedom and anti-slavery sentiments."[40] He develops this argument in part 2 of his book, covering ten chapters. Avalos demonstrates "that it was abandoning or marginalizing biblical argumentation, and shifting to secularized economic, humanitarian, legal, and practical arguments, that made a much greater impact on abolition."[41] The biblical stance on slavery, in the end, "posed an enormous, and sometimes insuperable, challenge for abolitionists."[42]

Indeed.

9

CHRISTIANITY AND THE RISE OF AMERICAN DEMOCRACY

Richard Carrier

T he United States Constitution does not even mention Christianity, and even explicitly denies being founded on any religious principles at all. Not only does the First Amendment prohibit the abolition or establishment of any religion, not only does the Preamble conspicuously omit "preserving Christianity" from all the aims and goals of the Constitution, not only does the President's oath of office, spelled out word-for-word in Article 1, Section 2, not even mention God, much less Christ, but Article 6 goes out of its way to explicitly state that, and I quote, "no religious test shall ever be required as a qualification to any office or public trust under the United States." In other words, the Constitution not only doesn't require anyone to be a Christian, it explicitly prohibits requiring it.

Why? Because the history of Christian fascism throughout the world had by then reached such a fevered pitch of pervasive, Naziesque horror that the Founding Fathers wanted to defang Christian power entirely, so Christians could never again use the power of the state to oppress, murder, or maim. The Constitution was written specifically to stop Christian sectarian war and Christian political oppression. To claim that Christianity was responsible for the Constitution is thus a perversion of the actual order of things. Nothing in the Constitution derives from the Bible or Christian religion. Christianity inspired the Constitution in only one terrible sense: by being so horrific something had to be done to stop it. Not by abolishing it, of course. But by taking away its power, and giving people the liberty to follow any sect or religion, or none, without fear or interference. For the first time in history, since its greedy acquisition of the fascist apparatus of the Roman state nearly fifteen hundred years before, Christendom had to compete on a level playing field, and could no longer threaten people with force to get its way or compel their allegiance.

This is the historical context in which the founding of the United States (and all subsequent democratic revolutions) must be understood. The Treaty of Tripoli, the English text of which was written at the behest of George Washington and signed by John Adams in 1797, said right out, "the Government of the United States of America is not, in any sense, founded on the Christian religion." This English text was read on the Senate floor and passed unanimously among all the senators present (only nine senators of the then thirty-two were absent). This text was also printed in several major newspapers and received little complaint. That pretty much kills the notion that the Constitution establishes the United States as a Christian nation. Meanwhile, if it was in any other sense founded on Christian principles, the Founding Fathers evidently went out of their way to conceal this fact at every turn. Which seems unlikely.

John Adams: Reason Trumps Scripture

To try and combat this fact, Christian apologists claim to adduce a quotation of John Adams from a private letter to Thomas Jefferson (of June 28, 1813). A private letter of course is the exact opposite of an official state document agreed to by the entire Senate and read by the voting public. But that kind of distinction is inconvenient for Christians, so they rarely note where the quote comes from. Anyway, the quote, as you will see it repeated everywhere, reads:

> The general principles on which the fathers achieved Independence were . . . the general principles of Christianity . . . [and] I will avow that I then believed, and now believe, that the general principles of Christianity are as eternal and immutable as the existence and attributes of God.[1]

Now, if you see this in print, you'll see that authors are often honest enough to include several ellipses—which should make you wonder, what was left out of the quote? You would be right to be skeptical. I'm going to quote the whole context, because it's fascinating—and not least because it mentions, and praises, atheists.

Adams wrote to Jefferson, when questioned about his personal thoughts (and not any official state position), that he valued liberty above all, and that that had been the goal of the American Revolution. In speaking of that war and its outcome, Adams wrote (my emphasis in bold):

Who composed that army of fine young fellows that was then before my eyes? There were among them Roman Catholics, English Episcopalians, Scotch and American Presbyterians, Methodists, Moravians, Anabaptists, German Lutherans, German Calvinists, Universalists, Arians, Priestleyans, Socinians, Independents, Congregationalists, Horse Protestants, and House Protestants, Deists **and Atheists**, and Protestants *"qui ne croyent rien."* ["who do not believe anything"] Very few, however, of several of these species; nevertheless, all educated in the general principles of Christianity **and** the general principles of English and American liberty.

Could my answer be understood by any candid reader or hearer, to recommend to all the others the general principles, institutions, or systems of education of the Roman Catholics? Or those of the Quakers, or those of the Presbyterians, or those of the Methodists, or those of the Moravians, or those of the Universalists, **or those of the Philosophers**? No. The general principles on which the fathers achieved independence, were the only principles in which that beautiful assembly of young men could unite, and these principles only could be intended by them in their address, or by me in my answer. And what were these general principles? I answer, the general principles of Christianity, in which **all those** *sects* were united *and* the general principles of English and American liberty in which **all those** *young men* united, and which had united all parties in America, in majorities sufficient to assert and maintain her independence.

Now I will avow, **that I** then believed and now believe that those general principles of Christianity are as eternal and immutable as the existence and attributes of God; and that those principles of liberty are as unalterable as human nature and our terrestrial, mundane system. I could, therefore safely say, consistently with all my then and present information, **that I** believed they would never make discoveries in contradiction to these general principles. In favor of these general principles, in philosophy, religion, and government, I could fill sheets of quotations from Frederic of Prussia, from Hume, Gibbon, Bolingbroke, Rousseau, and Voltaire, as well as Newton and Locke; not to mention thousands of divines and philosophers of inferior fame.[2]

Notice what he is actually saying. First, Adams is carefully distinguishing his own personal beliefs from any official state principles. But more importantly, he includes *atheists* in his list of praiseworthy American freedom fighters, and also says even atheist and anti-Christian philosophers (like Voltaire) were, in his view, advocating for the good principles shared by all Christian sects. In other words, Adams is not saying that America was actually founded on Christian principles in the sense usually meant today; rather, Adams is saying America was founded on universal moral principles shared by all good philosophies, even godless philosophies, Christianity included. He then says that it is his own personal opinion that the Christian God has so arranged it. But again, he is careful to say this is his own personal religious belief, not a state doctrine.

It's worth remembering that John Adams (major founder and second president of the United States) was a Unitarian. He did not believe in an eternal hell or the divinity of Christ or even in miracles. Thus, when he says "Christian principles" he does not mean anything we would consider distinctive of Christianity, such as the saving power of Christ's sacrifice; he means simply a basic human morality common to all religions and philosophies. It's worth remembering that for his views he would be kicked out of nearly every conservative or traditional Christian church in America today.

In contrast to Adams's views, which scorned the notion of America becoming a "Christian" nation rather than a nation inclusive of all faiths and philosophies, including atheism, several times Christians have tried to get the Constitution amended to declare this nation to be founded on Christian principles. Such Christian-nation amendments were formally proposed in Congress in 1864, 1874, 1896, 1910, and 1954. Not once did these amendments even reach a floor vote. They were rejected out of hand. But it's worth noting what these amendments proposed, so we can see what kind of American government Congress repeatedly rejected.

The first quite simply asked that the Preamble be changed to read (the proposed addition here in bold):

We, the people of the United States, **humbly acknowledging Almighty God as the source of all authority and power in civil government, the Lord Jesus Christ as the Ruler among the nations, His revealed will as the supreme law of the land, in order to constitute a Christian government, and** in order to form a more perfect union. . . .[3]

This is of course exactly what the Preamble would have said if the Founding Fathers had wanted the United States to be a Christian nation, to establish Christianity in the Constitution, or to demonstrate that it was founded on distinctly Christian principles. Thus, the fact that this is not what the Preamble said, and still does not say after many repeated attempts to get it to say that, pretty much proves this nation was not, and is not, founded on Christianity.

And since Christians today want to misquote John Adams on this point, it's worth looking at what John Adams himself said in his own book on the historical foundations of the Constitution. I mean, honestly. If there is any place you should check first, it would be a book he explicitly wrote on the very subject you want to know his thoughts on. Adams was a historian, and a pretty good one for his day. And among his works in that field he wrote *A Defence of the Constitutions of Government of the United States of America*, in 3 volumes, published in 1794, just a few years before he signed the Treaty of Tripoli, the treaty that declared that the US government was not founded in any sense on the Christian religion.

Needless to say, Christianity gets virtually no mention in these three volumes, and not once does he identify it as having inspired the Constitution. As we just saw, what one meant by "Christianity" or "Christian principles" can be extremely wishy washy even in Adams's own writing. It means almost nothing that isn't already just as true of atheistic humanism. Which is not what people today mean when they insist the United States was founded as a Christian nation. So we need something more explicit. The Christian-nation amendment is perfect in that regard, but that it has repeatedly failed to pass pretty much rules it out. Our nation was clearly in no meaningful way based on Christian principles in that sense. Rather, what is often claimed today is that the Ten Commandments are the basis for the Constitution. Never mind that the Ten Commandments are Jewish, and thus not distinctly Christian. Christians who don't squirm at the notion of owing anything to the Jews will skate around this conundrum by saying instead that this nation and its Constitution were based on Judeo-Christian principles. Other Christians will just gloss over the distinction altogether.

But even if we hypothesized that the United States Constitution establishes, and was founded on, Reform Judaism, we still have to ask if that is even true. It essentially amounts to saying that the principles of law and government established by Moses are the very principles of law and government that undergird and inspired our Constitution.

So when we look at Adams's three-volume treatise on this question, how much does Moses get mentioned there, or the Ten Commandments? Essentially nil. Same for Jesus. Adams was certainly a god-loving Christian (albeit a heretical Unitarian). And he offers much praise in various of his writings for Christian religion (in the Unitarian sense). But that has no bearing on whether Adams conceived or intended the United States to be a Christian nation, much less founded on the Ten Commandments. To the contrary, he held to exactly the opposite principle. Here I quote from that very book (emphasis mine):

> The United States of America have exhibited, perhaps, the first example of governments erected on the simple principles of nature, and if men are now sufficiently enlightened to disabuse themselves of artifice, imposture, hypocrisy, and superstition, they will consider this event as an era in their history. . . . It will never be pretended that any persons employed in that service had any interviews with the gods, or were in any degree under the inspiration of heaven, any more than those at work upon ships or houses, or laboring in merchandise or agriculture. It will forever be acknowledged that these governments were contrived merely by the use of reason and the senses.[4]

That's a direct denouncement of the Law of Moses, which derived from an interview with God and the inspiration of heaven. Adams is saying the Founding Fathers heeded no such things, but discarded them all (and that means the Ten Commandments as well), and derived American government directly from their own reason and observation, from the natural world alone. That's not a foundation on Christian principles. That's a foundation on atheistic naturalism.

Adams does also say that "morality and the Christian religion, without the monkery of priests" has helped to sustain America's success, but he never once credits any specific principle from that religion (like the Ten Commandments) as lying at the foundation of the American Constitution.[5] That idea isn't even considered. Instead, volume 1 is entirely about the example and influence of Greece and Rome (in other words, the advances in government produced by pagans); volume 2 is about that of the secular Italian republics of the Renaissance (in other words, advances in government produced without Christian creeds or dogmas); and volume 3 surveys more of the same, and concludes with the precedent of the British Commonwealth.

In the words of his reviewer in the August 1795 issue of the *American Monthly Review*, the authors Adams considers as most influential in his survey are these (I quote):

> Particularly among the ancients, Plato, Aristotle, Polybius, Dionysius Hali-carnassus, Cicero, and Tacitus; among the moderns, of Machiavelli, Sydney, Montesquieu, Harrington, Locke, Milton, Swift, Hume, Franklin, Price and Nedham.

From this list, Moses is conspicuous for his absence. So is Jesus. By contrast, an extensive section in volume 1 is devoted to the Athenian constitution established by the pagan statesman Solon of Athens. Adams in fact credits the first invention of representative government to yet another pagan, Lycurgus of Sparta, and then credits Solon with its improvement. No mention of Moses. Or Jesus. Throughout all three volumes the Old Testament gets barely three mentions, none in the words of Adams himself, and all on concepts not adopted by the Constitution, but in fact opposed by it: rule by kings and aristocrats, redistribution of wealth by lot, and legislating a religion—each praised only by Sydney and Harrington, not Adams.

Indeed this was the pervading sentiment among the Founding Fathers (see this chapter's concluding bibliography). Though the British philosopher John Locke inspired the founders even more than Classical writers, even he was heavily influenced by ancient pagan thought. In fact, everything of his conception that became effected in the Constitution derives from the pagan Classics, not the Bible. This is not to say that the founders imagined every political concept of the Greeks and Romans to be correct (nor should they have), but that everything that was until then unique to the US Constitution, which we regard as changing history forever (and for the better), was learned and adopted from them, not from the Bible.

Pagan Philosophy vs. the Bible

Christian apologists like to adduce examples of the Founding Fathers citing the Bible for everything under the sun, and argue that therefore the Bible must have inspired their ideas, but this is a non sequitur. I address the same non sequitur in the context of a different argument, that we have Christianity to thank for modern science, in the last chapter of *The Christian Delusion*. There I remarked that "finding in that period Christian or Biblical arguments for embracing new ideas does not confirm Christianity or the Bible was the cause of those ideas, rather than just the marketing strategy required to sell them at the time."

It is the pagan Classics, not the Bible, where we find the language, concepts, and ideals that characterize the political theory manifest in the Constitution.

For example, that protection of private property is a principal function of government is explicitly stated by the pagan Cicero in his treatise *On Duties*, book 2, paragraph 73. You won't find this anywhere in the Bible. Cicero lived half a century before Christ.

Likewise, the notion that "all men are created equal" is originally, and most influentially, a pagan idea, derived from the ancient philosophy of Stoicism, developed centuries before Christ. It was the Stoic belief that all men and women are brothers and sisters of a common family and that all were citizens of the world who share the same natural rights.

The Stoics claimed this could be demonstrated directly from observation and reason, the very method Adams declares the founders employed. By contrast, "searching the scriptures" gets nary a mention as a method ever resorted to, either by Stoic philosophers or by John Adams. The Stoics likewise developed the philosophical concepts of "liberty" and "human rights" and "freedom of speech" and "equality under the law," all words and phrases that feature prominently in their discourses on morality, law, and government.

The link from Stoicism to the founding of our nation is demonstrated by the Declaration of Independence, which says "that all men are created equal, that they are endowed by their Creator with certain unalienable Rights," which plainly tells us the idea of unalienable rights is the foundational concept behind this sentiment. Yet no such concept appears anywhere in the Bible (and certainly not in the Ten Commandments, the gospels, or the epistles). Rather, the idea of "unalienable rights" derives from the Stoics and their subsequent influence on pagan Roman legal theory. So the Founding Fathers did not find this idea in the Bible. They saw the equality of man in the context of Cicero's "rights of man" (which Cicero described with the terms *ius gentium*, "right of people," and *ius naturae*, "natural right").

Even the Apostle Paul's alleged declaration of equality (in Galatians 3:27–28) does not relate to this, despite Christians claiming otherwise. There Paul says:

> For all of you who were baptized into Christ have put on Christ. So there can be neither Jew nor Greek, there can be neither bond nor free, there can be no male and female. For you all are one man in Christ Jesus. And if you are Christ's, then you are Abraham's descendants, heirs according to the promise.

With this declaration Paul was not asserting a political concept, but a very prejudicial theology, where only those who "have been baptized into Christ" are equals (for only they are, as he says, "united in Christ"). And not only that, but they are equals only in the sense that they all share the same "promise" in the afterlife, not in the sense that they share the same legal rights.

The New Testament in fact denies equal rights: Paul himself is made to say (in 1 Corinthians 14:33–35) that women, even baptized Christian women, do not have rights equal to men, and again (in 1 Timothy 2:11–15) he is made to be even more explicit:

> Let a woman learn in silence with full submission. I permit no woman to teach or to have authority over a man; she is to keep silent. For Adam was formed first, then Eve; and Adam was not deceived, but the woman was deceived and became a transgressor. Yet she will be saved through child-bearing, provided she continue in faith and love and holiness, with modesty.

Though these remarks are likely forgeries, they are in the scriptures, the Christian canon, all the same, and remained Christian doctrine for nearly two thousand years. It was Christianity that in all that time fought against giving women the vote or allowing them to hold political office, just as it was Christianity that defended and even fought, under arms, to defend slavery.

Not only do we see here a denial of equal rights, but we see here scriptural reasoning rather than reasoning from natural facts. This is therefore the very kind of reasoning that Adams explicitly condemns: basing anything on scriptures or interviews with gods. Adams says the Constitution was written by men who repudiated that kind of reasoning, and used instead human reason in light of empirical evidence. And Adams praises this as the very feature that makes America unique and great. Not Christianity. But human reason and empiricism, absent any divine inspiration. The New Testament in fact condemns the method Adams praises, and thus is directly hostile to the very principles on which this nation and its Constitution was founded, which is the exact opposite of being the source of them. I have documented elsewhere (in chapter seventeen of *Not the Impossible Faith*) the pervasive condemnation of the use of reason and the senses (as well as critical thinking and debate) to ascertain the truth throughout the New Testament. Christianity thus, at the heart of its very scriptures, was diametrically opposed to precisely the method of establishing a Constitution that John Adams praised.

So we should not be surprised that slavery is uniformly supported even in Paul's letter to Philemon, and everywhere else in the New Testament. Neither Paul nor Jesus, and certainly not Moses, ever condemned slavery or asked that all slaves be freed. But of course, even the Constitution failed to do that. So perhaps there is indeed one explicit Christian principle enshrined in the American Constitution: the endorsement and perpetuation of human slavery. Although I doubt Christians want to draw attention to that fact. And in any case, the pagans legalized slavery, too. So Christians can only escape being blamed for American slavery by admitting the Constitution was based on pagan, and not Christian principles after all.

But with the bad also goes the good. That all peoples, of all faiths, ought to share the same legal rights is a pagan concept, not a Christian one. Like our Founding Fathers, the pagans never fully realized this ideal in practice, but many pagans advocated it. Musonius Rufus, for example, living a generation after Jesus, declared that men should stop relying on the labor of slaves and work for their own keep. A radical notion then, as it was still in 1776. Rufus also said women were as capable and as intelligent as men and should receive the same educations, just one step away from admitting they should be allowed to vote. Something our Founding Fathers also failed to allow. So again, the Constitution's banning women from the vote could be another example of a Christian principle, in this case of not allowing women to "have any authority over a man," as the Christian Bible proclaims; or else it is just another holdover from universal prejudices about the nature of women, which were not based on religious dogma but erroneous reasoning from observed or imagined evidence. So again, the Christian can only escape blame for denying women the vote for 144 years if they admit the Constitution was not based on Christian principles.

But then we also have to admit that centuries before Christ, the Stoic philosopher Zeno originated the idea that "we should regard all people as our fellow-citizens and neighbors, and there should be one way of life and order, like that of a herd grazing together and nurtured by a common law" (as quoted in Plutarch's essay *On the Fortune of Alexander* [329a–b]). The Stoics based this on the pagan idea (which they claimed to adduce from the evidence of reason and the natural world) that we are all created by God and thereby share equally in his nature. (Sound familiar? Remember that quote a while back from the Declaration of Independence?)

Half a century before Christ, Cicero imported these ideas into Roman legal theory, in his treatise on the ideal republic (*The Republic*, book 3, section 33), arguing that:

> There is in fact a true law, from right reason, which is in accordance with nature, applies to all people, and is unchangeable and eternal. By its commands this law summons men to the performance of their duties; by its prohibitions it restrains them from doing wrong. . . . To invalidate this law by human legislation is never morally right nor is it permissible ever to restrict its operation, and to annul it wholly is impossible. . . . For there will be one law, eternal and unchangeable, binding at all times and upon all people. And there will be, as it were, one common master and ruler of men, that is God, who is the author of this law, its interpreter and its sponsor.

By which Cicero means through God's governance of the natural universe—and not through any church mechanism employing men acting as God's representatives (or through promises of heavens and hells, either). At the same time, John Locke's idea of rights and government as a social contract derives from another pagan, Epicurus (you can see what Epicurus says about this in his *Principal Doctrines*, parts 31 to 37, and by quotation in Porphyry's treatise *On Abstinence*, book 1, section 7). Again, Locke did not find this anywhere in the Bible, and certainly not in the words of Moses, Jesus, or Paul. He got it from pagans.

So with that in mind, I quote one of our Founding Fathers whom Christians would prefer we forget:

> Those men, whom Jewish and Christian idolaters have abusively called heathen, had much better and clearer ideas of justice and morality than are to be found in the Old Testament (so far as it is Jewish), or in the New. The answer of Solon [the Athenian] on the question, "Which is the most perfect popular government?" has never been exceeded by any man since his time, as containing a maxim of political morality. "That," says he, "where the least injury done to the meanest individual is considered as an insult on the whole constitution." Solon lived above 500 years before Christ.

Those are the words of Thomas Paine (*The Age of Reason*, volume 2), the political activist who authored *The Rights of Man* and *The American Crisis*, thus playing a crucial role in rallying Americans to the revolution and keeping up morale and unity during the war. Paine knew where our constitutional ideals came from, just as he later declared in *The Rights of Man*. There he wrote: "What Athens was in miniature, America will be in magnitude." What Athens was in miniature, America will be in magnitude. Not what ancient Israel was in miniature. Athens. Not what the first Christian church was in miniature, either, which incidentally was explicitly Marxist: Acts 4:32–36 (indeed, it's implied the first Christians even killed people who did not comply with their Marxist dictates, just like Stalin did: Acts 5:1–11).

In other words, the Constitution was inspired by the pagan Solon, not Moses—nor Jesus.

Solon's constitution for Athens was credited by Adams and Paine and many other Founding Fathers as what most inspired the American Constitution, with the equally pagan constitution of the Roman Republic a close second (regarded as an improvement on the flaws in Solon's original experiment). Solon gave us elections and trials by a jury of our peers, two concepts never found in the Bible, Old Testament, or New Testament. Then it was from this and the Roman system of government that the Founding Fathers learned and enshrined the principle of a division of powers and the concept of checks and balances, including such ideas as elections, legislatures, and the presidential veto. You won't find any of that in the Bible.

But more conspicuous as inspiration is that neither the Roman nor the Athenian constitutions declared themselves as having come from a divine author or inspiration, unlike the laws of Moses and Jesus. They also did not prohibit religious freedom, nor require that anyone adhere to any religious doctrine. They were, in other words, the original secular constitutions. They were not wholly secular, though, in that they did not explicitly prohibit the establishment of religious laws or tests for office. And yet, our Constitution does explicitly prohibit the establishment of religious laws or tests for office. Which means the Founding Fathers made our Constitution even more secular than these pagan constitutions, which sets our Constitution even further away from having any plausible basis in biblical religion.

Thus, while those pagan constitutions could permit outlawing the teaching of atheism, even enact the death penalty for it, as happened to Socrates, our Constitution forbids that. This is exactly contrary to the legal principles credited to Moses. Deuteronomy 12 states, when speaking of the laws handed to Moses by God, which included the Ten Commandments:

> These are the statutes and the judgments which you shall carefully observe in the land which the Lord, the God of your fathers, has given you to possess as long as you live on the earth. . . . Be careful to listen to all these words which I command you, so that it may go well with you and your sons after you forever, for you will be doing what is good and right in the sight of the Lord your God. . . . Whatever I command you, you shall be careful to do; you shall not add to nor take away from it. . . .
>
> If your brother, your mother's son, or your son or daughter, or the wife you cherish, or your friend who is as your own soul, entice you secretly, saying, "Let us go and serve other gods" (whom neither you nor your fathers have known, of the gods of the peoples who are around you, near you or far from you, from one end of the earth to the other end), you shall not yield to him or listen to him; and your eye shall not pity him, nor shall you spare or conceal him. But you shall surely kill him; your hand shall be first against him to put him to death, and afterwards the hand of all the people. So you shall stone him to death because he has sought to seduce you from the Lord your God who brought you out from the land of Egypt. . . .
>
> Then all Israel will hear and be afraid, and will never again do such a

wicked thing among you. If you hear in one of your cities, which the Lord your God is giving you to live in, anyone saying that some worthless men have gone out from among you and have seduced the inhabitants of their city, saying, "Let us go and serve other gods" (whom you have not known), then you shall investigate and search out and inquire thoroughly. If it is true and the matter established that this abomination has been done among you, you shall surely strike the inhabitants of that city with the edge of the sword, utterly destroying it and all that is in it and its cattle [!] with the edge of the sword. Then you shall gather all its booty into the middle of its open square and burn the city and all its booty with fire as a whole burnt offering to the Lord your God; and it shall be a ruin forever. It shall never be rebuilt.

Just read passages like this, and let it never be said again that our Constitution was based on the Bible.

Remember, what I just read is simply an enactment of the first and second of the Ten Commandments, that it shall be illegal to have or worship other gods or their idols. What does "illegal" mean? That you shall be brutally executed by the state for it. How can anyone think this is the basis of our Constitution? To the contrary, our Constitution explicitly contradicts the Bible on this point, by establishing religious freedom, not the brutal, murderous religious oppression that the Bible commands. Our Constitution, in other words, repudiates the Bible, and explicitly condemns its principles (now all the more so that it enshrines full political rights for women and the abolition of slavery).

The Bible also condemns not just freedom of religion, but freedom of speech. In Leviticus 24 we read that

the son of [an] Israelite woman blasphemed the Name [of God] and cursed. So they brought him to Moses. . . . They put him in custody so that the command of the Lord might be made clear to them. Then the Lord spoke to Moses, saying, "Bring the one who has cursed outside the camp, and let all who heard him lay their hands on his head; then let all the congregation stone him. [Then] you shall speak to the sons of Israel, saying, 'If anyone curses his God, then he will bear his sin. Moreover, the one who blasphemes the name of the Lord shall surely be put to death; all the congregation shall certainly stone him. The alien as well as the native, when he blasphemes the Name, shall be put to death.'"

So much for the First Amendment. And yet this just enacts the third of the Ten Commandments, that it shall be illegal to use the Lord's name in vain, in other words, illegal to speak blasphemy. What does "illegal" mean? That you shall be brutally executed by the state for it. Again, how can anyone think this is the basis of our Constitution? To the contrary, our Constitution explicitly and conspicuously repudiates and outlaws these Biblical principles.

Solon the Athenian vs. Moses the Israelite

Yet I keep hearing the chant, variously phrased, that "the Ten Commandments are the foundation of Western morality and the American Constitution and government." In saying this, people are essentially crediting Moses with the invention of ethics, democracy, and civil rights, a claim that is of course absurd. But its absurdity is eclipsed by its injustice, for as we just saw, Solon of Athens is the lawmaker who is far more important to us, whose ideas and actions lie far more at the foundation of American government, and, as it happens, whose own Ten Commandments (he would sooner have called them "guidelines") had been widely distributed and were influencing the greatest civilizations of the West—Greece and Rome—for well over half a millennium before the laws of Moses were anything near a universal social influence.

In fact, by the time the Ten Commandments of Moses had any real chance of being the foundation of anything in Western society, democracy and civil rights had all but died out, never to rise again until the ideals of our true hero, the real man to whom we owe all reverence, were rediscovered and implemented in what we now call "modern democratic principles." Again, that man is Solon the Athenian. Real or legendary, Solon is said to have been born around 638 BCE, and he lived until the year 558. But the date in his life of greatest importance to us is the year he was elected to draft a constitution for Athens, said to have occurred in 594 BCE.

How important is this man? Let's examine what we owe to him, in comparison with the legendary author of the so-called Judeo-Christian Ten Commandments.

Solon is the founder of Western *democracy* and the first man in history to articulate ideas of *equal rights* for all citizens, and though he did not go nearly as far in that direction as we have come today, Moses can claim no connection to either.

Solon was the first man in Western history to publicly record an actual *civil constitution in writing*. No one in Hebrew history did anything of the kind, least of all Moses. The very idea of a constitutional government derives from Solon.

Solon advocated not only the right but even the duty of every citizen to bear arms in the defense of the state—to him we owe the Second Amendment. Nothing about that is to be found in the Ten Commandments of Moses.

Solon set up laws defending the principles and importance of private property, state encouragement of economic trades and crafts, and a strong middle class—the ideals that lie at the heart of American prosperity (and are codified in the Constitution itself: just read Article 1, section 8, and the Third, Fourth, and Fifth Amendments). Yet these, again, cannot be credited at all to Moses.

Solon was the first man in history to eliminate birthright as a basis for government office, and to create democratic assemblies open to all male citizens, such that no law could be passed without the majority vote of all. The notion of affording women full political rights would not arise in any culture until that of modern Europe, but the concept of democracy is altogether absent in the Bible. To the contrary, under Moses and his successors, all supreme offices in church and government were hereditary (or appointed by the inheritors) and instituted by God, not the people. This notion of rulers being picked by God and governing by divine right (and that they are therefore never to be disobeyed) is enshrined even in the New Testament (Romans 13). Conspicuously, this biblical principle is precisely what the American Revolution was fought to overthrow: King George was a hereditary monarch claiming to rule by divine right, in total accord with the Bible's only political philosophy. The Constitution was fought for and written to destroy that philosophy. It was therefore, again, not based on the Bible, but specifically crafted to overthrow it. The defenders of a biblical government, meanwhile, were the ones fighting against democracy.

Solon invented the right of appeal, and trial by jury, whereby an assembly of citizens chosen at random, without regard for office or wealth or birth, gave all legal verdicts. Moses can claim nothing as fundamental as these developments, which are essential to modern society.

Solon invented the separation of the executive, legislative, and judicial branches of government, whereas Moses had them all united under a single aristocratic council (just read the book of Numbers, 11:16–17 and 27:15–23), yet even they were ruled by fiat from a god-appointed sovereign (Moses, then Joshua, later the judges, and then kings like David and his son Solomon). Once again, that was the very idea the American Revolution was fought against, and that our Constitution now repudiates.

The concept of taking a government official to court for malfeasance we also owe to Solon. We read nothing of the kind about Moses.

The idea of allowing foreigners who have mastered a useful trade to immigrate and become citizens is also an original invention of Solon—indeed, the modern concept of citizenship itself is largely indebted to him. There is nothing like this in the Bible.

And like our own George Washington, Solon declined the offer to become a king in his country, giving it a constitution instead—unlike Moses who, in his own legend, gave laws yet continued to reign.

Solon's selfless creation of the Athenian constitution set the course that led to the rise of the first universal democracy in the United States, and as we saw from the remarks of Adams and Paine, it was to Solon's Athens, not the Bible, that our Founding Fathers looked for guidance in constructing a new state. Moses can claim no responsibility for this.

If we had Solon and no Moses, we would very likely still be where we are today. But if we had Moses and no Solon, democracy might never have existed at all.

So much for being the impetus behind our Constitution. The Ten Commandments of Moses have no connection with that, while the constitution of Solon has everything to do with it.

Whether these men were fictional or historical doesn't matter to that conclusion. Someone created the institutions credited to them, someone weaved these tales to communicate the values their stories embody, so their names still stand as symbols of two differing realities. Only one of them actually lies at the foundation of our Constitution. And he's not in the Bible.

Competing Commandments, Competing Values

Let me close by examining two different lists of Ten Commandments, one offered by each of these men, and comparing their worth and significance to Western society. Of course, neither man's list was unique to him—Moses was merely borrowing ideas that had already been chiseled in stone centuries before by Hammurabi, King of Babylon (and unlike the supposed tablets of Moses, the Stone of Hammurabi still exists and is on display in the Louvre). This point is already established in chapters 5, 6, and 8 of *The Christian Delusion*, so if you are interested about learning more, check them out.

Pretty much the only novelties Moses added to the ideas in Hammurabi's code, in fact, were restrictions of religious liberty, exactly the opposite of both the American Constitution and American social mores.

In the same way, Solon's Ten Ethical Rules were a reflection and refinement of wisdom that was already ancient in his day. And in both cases the association of these men with their moral precepts is as likely legend as fact. But the existence and reverence for their sayings in their respective cultures was still real—which means we can still validly ask:

- Which list of Ten Commandments lies more at the heart of modern Western moral ideals?
- Which contains concepts that are more responsible for our current social success and humanity?
- And which is more profound and more fitting for a free society?

The Ten Commandments of Moses (which you'll find twice, in Deuteronomy 5:6–21 and Exodus 20:3–16) run as follows. And note that I am even going out of my way to leave out the blatantly religious language that surrounds them in the original text, as well as the tacit approval of slavery present in the fourth commandment, none of which is even remotely suitable for political endorsement by a free republic. Yet, even with all that expunged, the Ten Commandments of Moses reduce to this:

1. Have no other gods before me (the God of the Jews).
2. Make no images of anything in heaven, earth, or sea, nor bow to them.

3. Do not vainly use the name of your God (the God of the Jews).

4. Do no work on the seventh day of the week.

5. Honor your parents.

6. Do not kill.

7. Do not commit adultery.

8. Do not steal.

9. Do not give false testimony against another.

10. Do not desire another's wife or anything that belongs to another.

Now, we can see at once that our society is entirely opposed to the first four of these, as well as the last of them. The first three are explicitly repudiated by the Constitution: the First Amendment is not only not based on them, it outlaws them, declaring it illegal to compel anyone to enforce them, and defending everyone's right to disobey them. They are further overthrown by Article 6(c). Indeed, our ideals of religious liberty and free speech, essential to any truly civil society, compel us to abhor those commandments. And our Constitution was specifically created to destroy them.

Then just think about the fourth commandment: as a capitalist society, we scoff at the idea of closing our shops on a choice market day, a concept standing against the very principles of economic liberty. Meanwhile the tenth commandment is as un-American as it gets: our very goal in life is to desire— desiring is what drives us toward success and prosperity. The phrase "pursuing the American Dream," which lies at the heart of our social world, has at its heart the very idea of coveting the success of our peers, goading us to match it with our own industry. We owe all our monumental national success to this. And our Constitution's Preamble declares its purpose as to protect everyone's right to "the pursuit of happiness," in other words it does not enshrine but overthrows the tenth commandment.

Thus, already half of Moses's doctrines cannot be the foundation of our modern society—to the contrary, they are anathema to modern ideals, and were effectively opposed and repealed by the American Constitution.

So that leaves just five commandments. Murder, theft, and perjury have been outlawed by all societies and thus are not peculiar to the Bible. No society could function that did not constrain them to some extent. Whereas by contrast, shunning adultery has never contributed to the rise of civil rights and democratic principles (despite much trying, there is no adultery amendment, and neither is it against the law in most of this country). It is often regarded as immoral—but then it always has been, by nearly all societies, before and since the time of Moses, for the simple reason that it, like lying, theft, and murder, can (at least sometimes) harm others, and thus these commandments are as redundant as they are unprofound. There is nothing peculiarly Christian about them. Or Jewish.

Finally, we are left with only one commandment, to honor our parents. This of course has been a basic principle of nearly every society ever since such things as "societies" existed. Yet the greatest advances in civil rights and civic moral consciousness in human history occurred precisely as the result not of obeying, but disobeying this very commandment: the social revolutions of the sixties, still abhorred by conservatives, yet spearheaded by rebellious teen-agers and young adults, nevertheless secured the moral rights of women and minorities—something unprecedented in human history, and nowhere advo-cated by Moses. And by opposing the Vietnam War our children displayed for the first time a massive popular movement in defense of the very pacifism that Christians boast of having introduced into the world, yet are usually the last to actually stand up for. (And they didn't invent pacifism anyway. Muso-nius Rufus, again, was already an ardent advocate of it, and actively preached against all war and violence.) It can even be said that our entire moral ethos is one of thinking for ourselves, of rebellion and moral autonomy, of daring to stand up against even our elders when our conscience compels it.

Thus, it would seem that even the fifth commandment does not lie at the heart of our modern society—it is largely an anachronism, lacking the essen-tial nuances that a more profound ethic promotes. As a result, we have no laws against dishonoring our parents; and in fact no mention of parental privilege is to be found anywhere in the Constitution. To the contrary, the Constitution even repeals the Ten Commandments' corruption of blood clause: compare Article 3, Section 3 with Exodus 20:5. The Constitution thus was established to destroy those commandments, and end their stranglehold on human life.

So much for the Constitution being based on the Ten Commandments.

Only two of the Ten Commandments are realized anywhere in the Amer-ican Constitution. The nearest you'll find is the declaration in the Fifth Amend-ment that no one shall be "deprived of life, liberty, or property, without due process of law," which in effect agrees with the sixth and eighth commandments, against murder and theft. But like I already said, laws against murder and theft long predate the Ten Commandments; they exist in all religions and societies (including Solon's Athens), and are too obviously necessary for any functional society to have required divine inspiration. So those do not in any sense "derive" from the Ten Commandments of Moses.

Which means the Constitution, and American society in general, are not rooted in the Ten Commandments of Moses.

Let us now turn to the Ten Commandments of Solon (which you'll find listed in Diogenes Laertius's *Lives and Opinions of Eminent Philosophers*, book 1, section 60). These were the ten ethical principles pronounced by Solon, not as laws but as morals, a distinction that does not exist in the Old Testament, so, once again, that we distinguish public law from personal morality today is another example of how unbiblical our constitutional society is.

The so-called Ten Commandments of Solon are:

1. Trust good character more than promises.
2. Do not speak falsely.
3. Do good things.
4. Do not be hasty in making friends, but do not abandon them once made.
5. Learn to obey before you command.
6. When giving advice, do not recommend the most pleasing, but the most useful.
7. Make reason your supreme commander.
8. Do not associate with people who do bad things.
9. Honor the gods.
10. Have regard for your parents.

Unlike the commandments of Moses, when suitably interpreted, none of these is outdated or antithetical to modern moral or political thought. Every one could be taken up by anyone today, of any creed, to some extent (all but Wiccans and Hindus might have cringed at only one of them, which I'll get to in a moment).

Indeed, there is something much more profound in these commandments. They are far more useful as precepts for living one's life.

Can society, can government, prevail and prosper if we fail to uphold the First Commandment of Moses? By our own written declaration of religious liberty for all, we have staked our entire national destiny on the belief that we not only *can* get by without the first commandment of Moses, but that *we ought to abolish it entirely*. And history bears that out.

Yet what if we were to fail to uphold Solon's first commandment? (To trust good character more than promises.) If we ignored that, the danger to society would be clear. Indeed, doesn't this commandment speak to the heart of what makes or breaks a democratic society? Isn't it truly fundamental that we not trust the mere promises of politicians and flatterers, but elect our leaders and choose our friends instead by taking the trouble to evaluate the quality of their character? This can be said to be an ideal that is fundamental to modern moral and political thought.

Of course, two of the commandments of Solon are similar to those of Moses: do not speak falsely, and have regard for your parents. Yet Solon does not restrict his first injunction to false accusations or testimony against others, as Moses does. Solon's commandment is more universal and thus more fundamental, and is properly qualified by the other commandments in just the way we believe is appropriate—for Solon's rules allow one to lie if doing so is a good deed. Since his third commandment simply says "do good things." By comparison, no commandment to do good appears in the Ten Commandments of Moses. Think about that.

Likewise, whereas Moses calls us to honor our parents (the word in the Hebrew means "to honor, to glorify"), Solon's choice of words is more appropriate—he only asks us to treat our parents in a respectful way (the Greek means "to show a sense of regard for, to have compassion upon"), which we can do even if we disobey or oppose them, and even if we disapprove of their character and thus have no grounds to actually "honor" or "glorify" them.

Similarly, instead of simply commanding us to follow rules, Solon's commandments involve significant social and political advice: temper our readiness to rebel and to do our own thing by learning first how to follow others. Take care when making friends, and stick by them. Be reasonable. Try to give good advice—don't just say what people want to hear. Shun the company of bad people.

This advice is just the sort of thing we need in order to be successful and secure—as individuals, as communities, and even as a nation. The notion of exactly what is "good" or "bad" does require thought and reflection. But that's as it should be. Even with that, the ideals represented by Solon's commandments clearly do rest at the foundation of modern American morality and society, and would be far more useful for school children to learn, whose greatest dangers are peer pressure, rashness, and naïveté, the very sins Solon's commandments denounce.

There is only one of Solon's commandments that might give a secularist pause (or even a Christian): the commandment to honor the gods (and in the Greek, that means "to honor, to revere, to pay due regard"). Yet when we compare it to the analogous first four commandments of Moses, we see how much more Solon's single religious commandment can be made to suit our society and our civic ideals: it does not restrict religious freedom, for it does not demand that we believe in anyone's god or follow anyone's religious rules, and it does not outlaw other religions than ours. It remains in the appropriate plural.

Solon asks us to give the plethora of gods the regard they are due, and we can honestly now say that some gods are not due much—such as the racist gods and the murderous gods of hellfire. One might at least argue it is good to be respectful of the deserving gods of others, which we can do even if we are criticizing them, even if we disbelieve in them, so long as those gods are respectable. This would remain true to our most prized American ethic of religious liberty and civility, which we enact in the way we respect the rules of a church, mosque, or synagogue when we are a guest in them, and in the way we don't aim to force anyone to stop paying cult and homage to their deities as they see fit—as long as public safety and human rights are not infringed. Indeed, in perfect line with that fact, Solon's commandment forces us to admit that there are many gods, not one—the many that people invent and hope for, people whose freedom to worship we protect rather than condemn. Exactly the opposite of the Ten Commandments of Moses. (It should also be noted that by similarly referencing a generic Creator, the Declaration of Independence was explicitly heretical by most Christian standards of the age: its authors thus included non-Christian conceptions of God, and thereby endorsed a heretically unitarian and deistic theology. Quite the opposite of a distinctly Christian inspiration.)

It is clear then that if anyone's commandments ought to be posted on school and courthouse walls, it should be Solon's. He has more right as the founder of our civic ideals, and as a more profound and almost modern moral thinker. Solon already has more to do with the creation of courts and juries and the separation of powers that all define our courthouses today. But his moral commandments are also more befitting our civil society, more representative of what we really believe and what we cherish in our laws and economy. They are essentially secular.

Is it an accident that when Solon's ideals reigned, there grew democracies and civil rights and ideals we now consider fundamental to modern Western society, yet when the ideals of Moses replaced them, we had a thousand years of oppression, darkness, and tyranny? Is it coincidence that when the ideals of Moses were replaced with those of Solon, when men decided to fight and die not for the Ten Commandments of Moses but for the resurrection of Athenian civil society, we ended up with the great democratic revolutions, the American Constitution, and the social and legal structures that we now take for granted as the height and glory of human achievement and goodness?

I think we owe our thanks to Solon. Moses did nothing for us—his laws were neither original nor significant in comparison. They even stand against our Constitution and its ideals; they are what our Constitution was written to oppose. When people cry for the hanging of the Ten Commandments of Moses on school and court walls, I am astonished. Solon's Ten Commandments have far more right to hang in those places than those of Moses. The great Athenian's commandments are far more noble and profound, and far more appropriate to a free society. Who would have guessed this of a pagan? Well, maybe everyone of sense.

-:-

Principal Sources and Further Reading

- John Adams, *A Defence of the Constitutions of Government of the United States of America*, 3 vols. (1794)
- Bernard Bailyn, *The Ideological Origins of the American Revolution* (1992)

- Gregory Boyd, *The Myth of a Christian Nation: How the Quest for Political Power Is Destroying the Church* (2005)
- Christopher Brooke, *Philosophic Pride: Stoicism and Political Thought from Lipsius to Rousseau* (2012)
- Richard Carrier, "Did Christians Encourage Critical Inquiry?" *Not the Impossible Faith: Why Christianity Didn't Need a Miracle to Succeed* (2009)
- Richard Carrier, "On Musonius Rufus" (1999), http://infidels.org/library/modern/richard_carrier/musonius.html
- Richard Carrier, "Reply to McFall on Jesus as a Philosopher" (subsection "What about Women?") (2004), http://www.richardcarrier.info/McFallRebuttal1.html#s22
- Richard Carrier, "The Will of God: 24 Evil Old Testament Verses" (2010), https://sites.google.com/site/thechristiandelusion/Home/the-will-of-god
- Timothy Ferris, *The Science of Liberty: Democracy, Reason, and the Laws of Nature* (2010)
- Allen Jayne, *Jefferson's Declaration of Independence: Origins, Philosophy, and Theology* (1998)
- Frank Lambert, *The Founding Fathers and the Place of Religion in America* (2003)
- John Loftus, ed., *The Christian Delusion: Why Faith Fails*, chapters 5, 6, 8, 13, and 15 (2010)
- John Loftus, ed., *The End of Christianity* (2011): "The Logic [and] Failure of Christian Morality" (chapter 14, pp. 335–39)
- Carl Richard, *The Founders and the Classics: Greece, Rome, and the American Enlightenment* (1995)
- Chris Rodda, *Debunking David Barton's Jefferson Lies* (2012)
- Chris Rodda, *Liars for Jesus: The Religious Right's Alternate Version of American History* (2006)
- Heinrich Rommen, *The Natural Law: A Study in Legal and Social History and Philosophy* (1936)
- Christopher Rowe and Malcolm Schofield, eds., *The Cambridge History of Greek and Roman Political Thought* (2006)
- Secular Web, "James Madison on Separation of Church and State" http://candst.tripod.com/tnppage/qmadison.htm

- Matthew Stewart, *Nature's God: The Heretical Origins of the American Republic* (2014)
- Farrell Till, "The Christian Nation Myth" (1999) http://infidels.org/library/modern/farrell_till/myth.html
- Katja Maria Vogt, *Law, Reason, and the Cosmic City: Political Philosophy in the Early Stoa* (2008)
- Kerry Walters, *Revolutionary Deists: Early America's Rational Infidels Paperback* (2010)
- David Wright, *Inventing God's Law: How the Covenant Code of the Bible Used and Revised the Laws of Hammurabi* (2009)
- Michael Zuckert, *The Natural Rights Republic: Studies in the Foundation of the American Political Tradition* (1999)

Other references included the United States Constitution; the Treaty of Tripoli (1797); Thomas Paine, *The Age of Reason* (1794–1807), *The Rights of Man* (1791), and *The American Crisis* (1776); the Congressional Record (1864, 1874, 1896, 1910, 1954); Cicero, *On Duties* and *The Republic* (first century BCE); Plutarch, *On the Fortune of Alexander* (first century CE); Epicurus, *Principle Doctrines* (third century BCE); Porphyry, *On Abstinence* (third century CE); Diogenes Laertius, *Lives and Opinions of Eminent Philosophers* (third century CE); and the Bible. For the context that inspired the Constitution's dethroning of Christianity, it is also worth perusing the *Wikipedia* pages on the "European Wars of Religion" and "Religious Persecution," and following up on their various topics and references.

Part Three

SCIENTIFIC HARMS

10

THE DARK AGES

Richard Carrier

Christianity did not cause the fall of the Roman Empire. Rather, that collapse allowed the rise of Christianity into total political and cultural power. The Dark Ages ensued, an era of widespread barbarity during which almost all the best values, technologies, knowledge, and achievements of the Greco-Roman era were forgotten or abandoned and had to be relearned and reinvented all over again many centuries later. In this period Christianity neither corrected what had gone wrong nor reintroduced any striving for the dreams and aspirations of earlier Greek and Roman idealists, but to the contrary, Christianity embraced a partial and sometimes full retreat from them. Christianity did not decisively kill science or the last glimmer of hope for democracy. But it made no effort to rescue and revive their ideals, either, and instead let them drown, with little sign of regret, and in some cases even to praises of their demise. Thus, Christianity was bad for science and democracy. It put a stop to scientific and political progress for a thousand years, and even after that it made their recovery difficult, painful, and slow.

It's not that Christianity "necessarily and uniformly" stomped out science and democracy, only that we cannot claim Christianity "encouraged" science or democracy during its first thousand years, even if some significant Christian factions did later or now do. Christianity threw up a great many obstacles to the recovery of pagan scientific and democratic values during and after its first thousand years, and to a lesser extent is still doing this today. And then, of course, it's not that all Christianity does this now. Rather, it is that Christianity will always generate factions that do, as it always has (and back then, it only did). And the last thing we want is to allow one such faction back in power, as had been the case during Christianity's first thousand years in the saddle. We must not go back to the Dark Ages.

And yet for over a century there has been a trend afoot to deny the Dark Ages ever happened. Sometimes this is just a silly semantic battle. ("Yes, the Dark Ages happened and were immensely awful, but please let's not call them the Dark Ages, but the Happy Enlightened Fun Time!") Sometimes it's a rosy-eyed denialism. ("What Christian-haters keep calling the Dark Ages really was in fact the Happy Enlightened Fun Time, not dark at all but an era of light and good and progress and really awesome things!") Sometimes it's just Christians trying to avoid admitting their religion screwed everything up and is to blame for almost everything that still sucks in the world. ("Look, okay, the Dark Ages were pretty bad, and set us back a thousand years, but it wasn't Christianity's fault, in fact Christianity made it all better!")

It's time Christians stopped this nonsense and just faced up to the fact: the Dark Ages happened, they were a truly dark era in Western history, and Christians, and Christianity, were to blame for it. This is not to say that Christianity inevitably or solely caused the Dark Ages, but they happened when Christians were in charge, and it was the decisions of Christians that brought them about and failed to avert or reverse them, and it was Christianity (as a belief system, in the form it had then taken) that caused those Christians to make the bad decisions that brought the Dark Ages about; and sustained them for centuries; and even fought against attempts to pull the West out of them—because the Renaissance and Enlightenment had many vocal and sometimes powerful enemies within Christendom, from popes all the way down, and their motives were explicitly theological.

So what were the Dark Ages? Why have they been called that (and should still be called that)? And what caused them, and sustained them for five centuries?

Calling It Like We See It

The *Dark Ages* as a term has come to refer to the cultural, political, intellectual, and economic deterioration (or indeed outright collapse) that occurred in Europe between the de facto fall of the Western Roman Empire in the fifth century CE and the beginning of a slow rise in economic and cultural sophistication by the end of the tenth, a period of roughly five hundred years.

In fact, the levels of knowledge and sophistication achieved by the High Roman Empire, from the first century BCE to the dawn of the third century CE, would not be reached again until at least the fifteenth century, but this second five-hundred year period is more commonly referred to as an era of rebirth, the period when, no longer in decline, the West began once again to claw its way back to where it once had been. A slow crawl. It took five more centuries to get all the way back from where the Dark Ages had dropped us. But it was at least a crawl in a consistently upward direction. The latter part of that period is even officially dubbed the Renaissance, the "Rebirth," although, in fact, a rebirthing of interest in once-forgotten pagan values, literature, and thought had already begun in the eleventh and twelfth centuries. It only expanded to all aspects of art and intellectualism (and even politics and industry) in the thirteenth and fourteenth centuries, by then so permeating and driving Western society as to actually be noticed and remarked upon by everyone experiencing it. That Renaissance would then lead to the West finally advancing in every way beyond the achievements of the Greeks and Romans, beginning in the sixteenth century and culminating in the Enlightenment of the seventeenth and eighteenth centuries, which brought us the Scientific and Industrial Revolutions that now define modern society.

The period from the fifth to the tenth century is also poorly (or less reliably) documented relative to the periods before and after it, making reconstructing what actually happened during it a more challenging task. But that is not all that made it dark. It was a dark time in every other way as well. A fall back into a society mired in ignorance and superstition, economically in ruins, politically in chaos, having lost or forgotten most of the scientific and technological advances of the former era, literally cannibalizing itself to live—as everything from bronze artwork to scientific instruments to public clock tower machinery was melted and recycled as coins or kitchenware.[1]

The Eastern Roman Empire did not experience this same collapse and stark decline, but even it failed to make any significant advances in science, technology, logic, philosophy, or mathematics—ever—and just endured a much longer and more gradual decline into ruin. No Renaissance for them. They, too, ended up just cannibalizing away all the past glory they had inherited, then sat on and did nothing with. Just consider the Archimedes Codex: this contained many of the greatest scientific treatises of the pagan scientist

Archimedes, but in the thirteenth century, within the Byzantine Empire, the ink on its pages was scraped off and the whole book reinscribed with hymns to God.[2] That's kind of what the Dark Ages were like in the West. Ditching science and knowledge and curiosity and achievement, and putting in its place constant mindless praying to a nonexistent deity.

In general a dark age is any era in which a considerable amount of knowledge is lost, especially scientific and technical and political knowledge, while the ruling zeitgeist looks backward to a time before more enlightened ways of doing things were embraced (which is why standards of recording history also decline, thus making the period hard to honestly reconstruct). The loss of 99 percent of all literature, and the corresponding historical and scientific and political knowledge it contained, is the signature of a dark age, and is exactly what happened in the Dark Ages. The abandonment of the highest civilized, technological, historical, democratic, and scientific ideals of the early Roman elite, in exchange for more barbarian ways of thinking and doing, made it even darker still.

It is only on top of that that we note far less was recorded during these centuries, and far less accurately, than had been the case in classical times, and only a small fraction of what was recorded before was preserved, and even what survived remained known to astonishingly few, and put to good use by even fewer. At the same time, the greatest aspirations of the pagans, with their struggling ideals of democracy and equality and human rights, just like their empirical ideals and the scientific spirit they inspired, were chucked in favor of more primitive ideas of "god-appointed" kings constantly at war over a feudal society of de facto peasant slaves and subordinated women, dominated by priests wracked with ignorance and superstition. That's just what a Dark Age looks like. And that's what the West endured.

The whole notion of a "Dark Ages" began during the Renaissance. Because it was then so starkly obvious how horrid and backward that era was in comparison. Artists and writers of the Renaissance simply "contrasted the 'rebirth' of the arts and letters" they were experiencing (all of which inspired by their pagan predecessors) "with the preceding period of cultural darkness."[3] It was not even then claimed to be dark because there was no art or literature or records of that era (these were not the "Pitch Black Ages"). It was hailed as a dark time because it was so immensely ignorant and unsophisticated by comparison with the periods before and after it. Historians during the Renaissance thus took up the concept of a "dark age" to reflect a "fairly general agreement that there was a decline of ancient civilization with the decline of Rome and that this decline led to a period of barbaric darkness" compared to the rising tide of Renaissance culture.[4] This was again not imagined as a literal darkness (like a complete loss of access to any information) but a relative darkness, a rise of ignorance and barbarity in place of a more civilized sophistication in the intellectual and political realms.

Indeed, Petrarch, the Renaissance originator of the "Dark Ages" concept, coined the notion because he regarded the intervening period it designated as worthless, just one long desperate attempt to get back to the achievements of the High Roman Empire that were lost with its collapse and were now finally returning. If the Dark Ages were cut out of history, if history had simply proceeded directly from the fourth to the fourteenth century, with no knowledge and sophistication lost, the world and its history would have been the better for it. (And that's actually entirely true.) Hence Petrarch did not want to recount (as he himself put it) "the lamentable story of how things retrograded."[5] It was all just too sad for him to deem it worth the bother.

Others since have stomached the study of the era better than he. And they have tried redubbing the period the "Middle Ages" instead (still implying a holding pattern between antiquity and modernity), the period we now call the Dark Ages being in that scheme the Low or Early Middle Ages, and the Late or High Middle Ages consisting of the eleventh to fifteenth centuries (and thus either including or butting up against the Renaissance). And yet one cannot change what something is by changing what it is called. Nevertheless, the desperate always try. When it is too shameful to admit that the period that fascinates and occupies them was a blot on the history of mankind, many a desperate medievalist has attempted to deride or discard the term "Dark Ages." These are usually (but not always) Christians, who in their cognitive dissonance cannot bring themselves to believe that all they are really doing is documenting a period of rampant decline that the whole world would have been better off without. But let's face it, that is what they are doing. Attempting to hide from this fact by hiding from such an apt description of it as a term like the "Dark Ages" is like all attempts to change what something is by changing what it is called: a fool's errand. It was a dark age in human history. And it deserves to be called such. Indeed, to guard against forgetting the lessons of history, it morally ought to be called such.

Surveying the Damage

I've already covered the case that Christianity wasn't the savior of science but in fact set it back a thousand years.[6] And Christianity did not give us democracy (of any kind, much less in America), but chucked it and actively fought against it for almost fifteen hundred years.[7] The Dark Ages were just the most depressed symptom of those same hostilities.

As I've already summarized, the evidence of the enormous loss and decline earning the Dark Ages their name is embarrassing. "Archaeologists see very substantial simplifications in post-Roman material culture in the fifth to seventh centuries . . . which in some cases . . . is drastic; only a handful of Roman provinces," namely those constituting the Eastern (thus Byzantine) Empire, "did not experience it."[8] Politically and economically as well: "the resources for political players lessened considerably, and the structures in which they acted simplified, often radically." Likewise for industry, trade, agriculture, architectural infrastructure, and everything else. These facts have been extensively and brutally laid out in recent scholarship.[9] The declines in trade and population were enormous. Many cities fell into ruin, countless roads and bridges and aqueducts vanished or were abandoned, access to literacy and education (and peace and justice) plummeted, and even where available, the Bible more typically replaced secular learning in math, history, philosophy, literature, law, and science as objects of study and tools for organizing society, resulting in many a backward walk in the areas of human rights, morals, security, and welfare.

In many regions this decline was so severe as to mark "a period of stark and rapid economic decline" that was "unprecedented in human history," witnessing "massive economic and cultural dislocation and, in terms of material culture and economic complexity, a return to prehistoric levels."[10] But whether that severe or not, everywhere in the West, even the few relatively "lucky" cities, suffered shocking rollbacks of wealth, comfort, and capability. Overall,

the post-Roman centuries saw a dramatic decline in economic sophistication and prosperity, with an impact on the whole of society, from agricultural production to high culture, and from peasants to kings. It is very likely that the population fell dramatically, and certain that the widespread diffusion of well-made goods ceased. Sophisticated cultural tools, like the use of writing, disappeared altogether in some regions, and became very restricted in all others.[11]

Historians should stop pretending that isn't what happened. We should indeed be worried when historians try to deny these facts and hide them from us. Take note:

> It is currently deeply unfashionable to state that anything like a "crisis" or a "decline" occurred at the end of the Roman empire, let alone that a "civilization" collapsed and a "dark age" ensued. The new orthodoxy is that the Roman world, in both East and West, was slowly, and essentially painlessly, "transformed" into a medieval form. However, there is an insuperable problem with this new view: it does not fit the mass of archaeological evidence now available, which shows a startling decline in western standards of living during the fifth to seventh centuries . . . [which] was no mere transformation, [but] a decline on a scale that can reasonably be described as "the end of a civilization." . . .
>
> [T]here is a real danger for the present day in a vision of the past that explicitly sets out to eliminate all crisis and all decline [like this]. The end of the Roman West witnessed horrors and dislocation of a kind I sincerely hope never to have to live through; and it destroyed a complex civilization, throwing the inhabitants of the West back to a standard of living typical of prehistoric times.[12]

That's what we call dark. And it matters that we admit this and stop trying to deny or hide it. Because those who do not remember history are doomed to repeat it. It is thus most disturbing that the apologetic attempts to rose-color the Dark Ages always seem to be linked with such a "religious focus as to be deceptively wrong."[13] Obsessed with a desperate desire to rescue Christianity from blame, or to heap upon it unearned glory, too many historians simply ignore the real, material facts of what the Dark Ages actually meant to the people who lived through them, and to everyone who had to pick up the pieces—and above all, why they weren't avoided, why they weren't stopped, and why they lasted so long and set us back so far.

Apologists for the Dark Ages like to complain, for example, that there were still books being written and preserved from prior eras in these centuries, so they weren't all that dark. But that's disingenuous. What is so devastatingly dark is how much was lost, and how little got written (compared to the centuries just preceding and then following), and how vacuous almost everything written then was. Indeed this defense of the Dark Ages is insultingly comical because the publishing and record keeping (documentary and literary) of the High Roman Empire was wildly more prodigious (including vast quantities of papyrological and epigraphical records as well as books and manuals and dictionaries and encyclopedias), but virtually none of it was preserved by the Christian stewards of the Dark Ages (for lack of both resources and interest, owing to both the cultural and material decline of the era). Which makes it laughably obtuse to claim there is "more" that survives from the end of the Dark Ages (like, perhaps, from the Carolingian period): yes, because the Dark Ages were so dismal they lost almost all the records and literature produced before it, while the last two centuries of it benefitted from its records being kept by the Renaissance cultures following it. It is thus not the Dark Ages that can claim credit for more records of the later centuries surviving, while it is the Dark Ages that are to blame for having lost nearly everything recorded before their advent. Imagine burning 99 percent of the forests in a neighboring country, and then pointing to your one little glade, which in fact someone other than you has been preserving but is now larger than anything left across the border, and claiming you were the better forest keeper. That's what we're talking about here. So that more survived from, say, the Carolingian period is precisely what demonstrates how dark the Dark Ages were.

And yet even when you look at charts of manuscript production, the Dark Ages stand out as shockingly barren by comparison to the Renaissance—which is one reason why we call that the Renaissance, and not the Dark Ages.[14] The difference is prodigious. And such a chart tracking anything else, every possible benchmark, looks much the same, from economic output and industrial capacity, to literary and artistic quality, or scientific and philosophical progress. For example, charts showing evidence (such as archaeological and geological) of industrial and agricultural production, as well as trade activity, show the High Roman Empire (first century BCE to third century CE) reached levels not matched again in Europe until the fifteenth or sixteenth century, yet likewise show an enormous steep dip right where the Dark Ages are, in some cases a difference of almost an order of magnitude. The degree of decline in every instance is astonishing—in fact horrifying, when you think about the tens of millions of lives such a rapid and enormous economic depression must have destroyed or thrown into misery, for a period twice as long as the United States has even existed.[15]

Again, it's not that literary, intellectual, and scientific content vanished in the Dark Ages, but that it suffered enormous simplifications and a tremendous loss of knowledge, understanding, and sophistication. *The Etymologies* of Isidore of Seville (written in the seventh century) exhibits this: compared to the scientific and encyclopedic writings of the High Roman Empire, Seville's treatise looks like it was written by a child. Any educated Roman of the first century would have spent many a drunken night laughing with his compatriots reading the nonsense and twaddle and wanton errors and ignorance exhibited throughout. And yet that was the height of medieval intellectual culture of the time. So much had been lost. So much ignorance had replaced the enlightened knowledge once common among the educated elite. When one adds to that the tremendous rise in lawlessness, injustice, violence, and chaos that attended those same centuries, the decay of political and social institutions right alongside the literal decay of what was once a grand urban and industrial and agricultural and economic infrastructure, one could hardly deny the Dark Ages were the ancient equivalent to the backstory of almost any futuristic apocalyptic saga from *Mad Max II: The Road Warrior* to *The Postman*.

An even more disingenuous apologetic for the Dark Ages is to claim they were an era of tremendous technological progress. That is simply false. By far (and I mean by far) most of what was invented, improved, or preserved in the West after the fall of Rome came to the fore after the twelfth century. The Dark Ages preceded that. And even what was invented between the twelfth and fourteenth centuries was actually, in fact, almost entirely reinvented (most of what medievalists think was invented in the Middle Ages in fact the Romans already had, most of which during the Dark Ages Christians forgot about, from mechanical clocks and computers and large-scale, privately capitalized industrial watermills, to horseshoes and heavy wheeled ploughs).[16] Even what was preserved through to the twelfth century was only barely so, much of it only in a few isolated places, sometimes only in a single manuscript, perhaps two or three, scattered across the world and collecting dust on forgotten shelves, often damaged or surviving only in translation. And by far most of what survived was preserved only in the comparably wealthier Middle East, virtually none surviving the Dark Ages in the West. (And even in the East, essentially nothing was done with any of this knowledge; the Byzantine Empire just gradually declined into oblivion, having contributed virtually nothing of significance to the advancement of human knowledge or political values.)

It will then be claimed that there were little renaissances in these Dark Ages, but that, too, is disingenuous. They were little more than desperate islands of power reproducing the most stripped-down, distorted, and inferior echoes of a lost classical culture. And they all fell into ruin. These events were nothing at all like the Renaissance that finally signaled the Dark Ages were long over. As has long been known,

> it is precisely this notion of a "new time" which distinguishes the Italian Renaissance from all the so-called earlier "Renaissances" in the Carolingian and Ottonian times or [even] in the twelfth century. These times may have experienced a certain revival of classical studies, but the people living in them did not conceive of or wish for a complete break with the traditions of the times immediately preceding. This idea was peculiar to the Italian Renaissance and [that is what] found expression in the condemnation of the medieval epoch as an era of "darkness."[17]

And indeed even those "certain revival[s] of classical studies" were such only in the barest and most rudimentary sense in comparison with the reality of classical studies under the High Roman Empire. Indeed, the Carolingian Renaissance looks like a joke in such comparison. But one thing can be credited to the later renaissances (of the eleventh and twelfth centuries) that led to the great Renaissance: some of their advocates did see a potential to improve their world with the ideas they were renewing their interest in, and they started fighting for recognition of the importance of recovering this lost literature and its methods and values. That they had to fight for that is to Christianity's discredit. That they were nevertheless allowed enough breathing room to carry on that fight without being brutally hunted down and killed for it is only to Christianity's credit in the rather saddening sense that the most we could ever have hoped of medieval Christendom is that it not murder everyone it disagreed with.

Why Did Christianity Do This to Us?

The Western Roman Empire fell apart because of a series of events that began in the third century CE, which Christians cannot be blamed for.[18] Where Christians take responsibility is what they did when they took the helm. A severe political and economic collapse transpired over the course of the third century that was only halted (and that only badly) by instituting an even more fascist apparatus of state than had ever before existed in the West. But when the Christians took power shortly thereafter, they did not dismantle that fascist state, replacing it with democracy and basic freedoms and active support for science and technology (as would have been the only decision that could have stopped the inevitable demise of the Western Empire). No, they delightfully grabbed that fascist system and ran with it, making it even more brutally fascistic than ever before, and depriving people of even more freedoms.

Christians cannot disown this. Before and during the Dark Ages the Catholic Church owned all scriptoria and chose which books to copy and which to toss in the dustbin. The Church controlled all schools and chose what would and would not be taught in them. The Church decided what governments would exist, and what rights the people would have. All Europeans that lived in those thousand years were under the thumb of priests and churchmen who quickly opposed any freedom of thought or speech that they imagined could ever pose a threat, and to that end had the full force and power of governments and social influence at their command. The Church decided what values would be preached to all the masses, and which values would be derided. The Church therefore must take full blame for the observed effect: the abandonment of a shocking amount of scientific and technical knowledge, and democratic values and ideals, and far more than that, the abandonment of the scientific values that had until then produced and improved that knowledge, and could have continued doing so, as well as the democratic values that, under the emperors, at least had some hope of resurgence with every civil war—which hope Christianity all but wholly crushed.

As just one example of what I mean, the Christians are the ones who turned a once free population into de facto slaves by establishing peasants as serfs who could never leave their land or jobs, and could instead be bought and sold along with the land they were bound to by law, and then were compelled by force to support and serve their landlords. In Orwellian fashion these slaves were called free men, but they were in reality just another kind of slave—the freedoms Rome had given them Christianity robbed them of. Yes, such a defining horror of the Middle Ages was a Christian invention. As were such horrid absurdities as the divine right of kings and the privilege of killing, robbing, or exiling anyone who said anything the Church didn't like. Freedom of speech, gone. Freedom of religion, gone. It was all downhill from there. Without a more effective socioeconomic system, the Western Roman Empire could no longer be effectively or competently led or defended. Its economy could not be restored. And nothing could prevent its being torn apart by neighboring marauders who had been successfully held at bay for centuries until the Christians took charge, now with their worthless and backward ideas helpless to stop the inevitable.

And Christians weren't responsible for the Dark Ages merely because they happened on their watch. Christianity itself is responsible for the Dark Ages—not just the causing of them (by failing to avert them) but the sustaining of them as well for five hundred years—by actually causing Christians to devalue and denigrate the values necessary for scientific, political, technological, and economic success: a positive value for progress and its achievability (scientific, technological, social, economic, and political): a passionate endorsement of the pursuit of curiosity (in all endeavors and fields of knowledge), and an unwavering belief in the necessity and superiority of empiricism, the placing of objective evidence above all other authorities. Christianity condemned them all.[19] By driving Christians away from those values, and thus preventing them from making any decisions in line with them, Christianity as an ideological system caused the Christians of that era to make all the wrong decisions, ushering in the final collapse of Western society, and demotivating any decision that would have been capable of turning things around. Only when they reconsidered the restoration of those original pagan values did anything then change.

Conclusion

So Christians, and Christianity, caused the Dark Ages. But one must be fair. When things finally did start to turn around, when truly revolutionary renaissances began, it was Christians who did the turning. But it wasn't Christianity that caused them to do that. Had it been, they would have done it from the start, and not five hundred years too late. Clearly Christianity of itself offered no means to fix this, and thus kept us in that ditch for centuries.

Already as early as the thirteenth or arguably even the eleventh century, interest in pre-Christian—in other words, pagan—knowledge and values started to return. It was then taken up as something that would beneficially change the Christian ideological system inherited from the Dark Ages. Although to succeed at that, against so many other Christians arrayed to fight against it, these changes had to be transformed to be more palatable to superstitious minds. Thus biblical and "Christian" arguments were invented to market them. But that cannot disguise from us the fact that they were in fact pagan values, not Christian. Because there was nothing inherent in Christianity that would ever have tended to inspire them. Which is why, without returning to its original pagan influence, Christianity didn't inspire them.

That's why Christianity alone was wholly incapable of ending the Dark Ages and returning Western society back to its former and future glory. Only when those old-time pagan values were reinjected into the Christian system did it ever find the means to change this dire state of things. We'd have been better off just having the pagan system from the start. Instead, Christianity dragged us down into the sewers of dystopia, and kept us there, and forced us to endure a long crawl back out, setting us back more than a thousand years on nearly every cultural and intellectual measure of human existence.

THE CHRISTIAN ABUSE OF THE SANCTITY OF LIFE

Ronald A. Lindsay

The prohibition on killing is at the core of morality. No society could long survive if its members could kill each other with impunity, as Thomas Hobbes recognized. Every human society has prohibited the unprovoked killing of its members. Of course, who counted as a member in good standing in any particular society has varied over time. The scope of our moral norms was once limited to our tribe or clan. "Barbarians" or other outsiders were fair game, and they could be killed or, alternatively, reduced to slavery. However, at this stage in human history, it is fair to say that we recognize a global human community. All humans have the right not to be killed, absent exceptional circumstances.

Given this background, the phrase "sanctity of life" has a noble ring to it. It appears to reflect our commitment to respect the lives of others. As a metaphor, "sanctity of life" may serve a useful purpose. The problem is many religious individuals, in particular many Christians, interpret "sanctity of life" literally and rigidly. For them, life is "sacred" because God has dominion over human life, and intentionally bringing about the death of a human being usurps God's authority over human life. Thus, individuals do not even have the right to kill themselves because their lives do not belong to them, but to God.

In this essay I will explore two critical problems created by the traditional Christian interpretation of the sanctity of life. One problem is that, as with other rules supposedly based on God's directives, the sanctity-of-life principle is considered a moral absolute. At least in theory, it prohibits intentional killing without exception. (As we will see, in practice there is significant leeway in its interpretation.) From a secular perspective, all rules should be considered presumptive only; that is, a rule, such as the rule against killing, creates a presumption that a killing is wrong. That presumption can be rebutted. Whether the presumption is rebutted depends on whether there are special circumstances that indicate the underlying rationale of the rule does not apply in those circumstances. Absolutism in ethics, including rigid application of the sanctity-of-life principle, does not allow for this type of consequentialist, pragmatic reasoning.

The foregoing problem deals with the content of the sanctity-of-life principle. The other major problem deals with its scope. What counts as a human life? Here, Christians, especially Catholic Christians, have taken a very expansive view of what it means to be a human person. At least arguably, their view is so expansive that it contradicts contemporary scientific understandings of biology and embryonic development.

A Brief History of the Christian Understanding of the Sanctity of Life

One of the myths of Christianity is that the rules laid down by God are unchanging, and that, therefore, Christian moral precepts have remained the same since Jesus walked the earth. Actually, there has been a fair amount of debate within Christianity about the ban on killing, especially in the early centuries of Christianity.

Many early Christian leaders and scholars argued that Christians should refrain from killing in any circumstance, even in war or self-defense. For example, the early Church father Tertullian (c. 160–225 CE) argued that Christians should not serve in the military because taking up the sword even to defend one's country is impermissible.[1] This pacifist viewpoint cannot be said to be unreasonable in light of the various gospel passages where Jesus emphasized the importance of nonviolence.

Beginning around the fourth century CE, Church leaders modified their pacifist stance, allowing Christians to serve in the military. One unstated reason may well have been political: Christianity was growing in numbers, but it could never hope to achieve approval of the state if it opposed military service. It's no coincidence that Constantine came along around the same time Christian leaders decided killing in a just war constituted an exception to the rule against killing. Interestingly, however, although Augustine, the most revered of the early Christian theologians, maintained that those serving the state could kill in a just war, he questioned whether it was morally legitimate for an individual to kill in self-defense.[2]

It wasn't until Thomas Aquinas, the renowned thirteenth-century theologian, that we see clearly formulated a principle that resembles the contemporary Catholic Christian understanding of the sanctity-of-life principle. Aquinas argued that killing in a just war, by way of judicially ordered punishment, and in self-defense were all justified.[3] In making this argument, Aquinas made use of the slippery concept of "intention" in a way that was to influence much later thinking. Killing in an act of self-defense is morally licit *provided* the person defending herself has the intent of preserving her own life, and not the intent to kill the person attacking her. In such circumstances, the killing of the attacker is merely an "accidental" effect of the praiseworthy intent to save one's own life. This was the birth of the notorious doctrine of double effect, which will be discussed further below.

Aquinas also articulated what has become in the Catholic Church the standard explanation for why suicide is wrong: it is an intentional killing of a human, and this intentional killing usurps God's authority over life, harms the community, and violates "natural law," as it goes against the natural inclination of self-love. Finally, Aquinas, in part to help explain the exceptions (such as capital punishment) to the rule against killing, explained that it is "innocent" humans who cannot be deprived of life.[4]

The influence of Aquinas on Christian thought, especially Catholic Christian thought, is evidenced by the late Pope John Paul II's definitive statement of the Church's position on the sanctity of life: "The deliberate decision to deprive an innocent human being of life is always morally evil and can never be licit either as an end in itself or as a means to a good end."[5]

My summary has emphasized the evolution of the sanctity-of-life principle in the Catholic Church for two reasons: one, the history of the Church was, to a significant extent, the history of Christianity until the time of the Reformation, and two, given the diversity of Protestant denominations and their different viewpoints, it would be difficult to summarize concisely Protestant understandings of the sanctity of life. Suffice it to say that some of the more fundamentalist denominations tend to echo the Catholic Church's views, especially when the specific issues under consideration are the morality of abortion or stem cell research. For example, the Southern Baptist Convention has issued a position statement on the sanctity of life that contends that "procreation is a gift from God, a special trust reserved for marriage. At the moment of conception, a new being enters the universe, a human being, a being created in God's image. This human being deserves our protection, whatever the circumstances of conception."[6]

The Effects of the Sanctity-of-Life Principle on End-of-Life Care

Withdrawal of Life-Sustaining Treatment

It may now be difficult to imagine, but just a few decades ago, the right of patients to end life-sustaining medical treatment was still hotly contested. This was especially the case when surrogates had to make the determination on whether to withdraw treatment from an incompetent patient. With respect to this issue, the Catholic Church sent mixed signals. In 1957, Pope Pius XII had stated that physicians were under no obligation to go beyond "ordinary means" to prolong the life of a patient who had no realistic prospect of recovery.[7] "Ordinary means" did not include ventilators (this was the example the Pope used), but it was unclear what other forms of treatment were "extraordinary" or, for that matter, why a ventilator should be considered extraordinary. The distinction between "extraordinary" and "ordinary" was vague, at best. It appeared to many that the Church was trying through casuistry to avoid being accused of forcing treatment on patients while still adhering to the doctrine that no one could intentionally end a human life. The result was confusion among Catholic physicians, patients, and the patients' guardians.

In any event, it was not until the late 1970s that a legal consensus began to emerge in the United States that a patient had the "right-to-die," that is, to stop life-sustaining treatment. The legal case that proved to be the seminal decision was *In Re Quinlan* (1976).[8] Karen Ann Quinlan was a twenty-one-year-old woman who had sustained a serious brain injury. She went into a persistent vegetative state and was kept alive only through a feeding tube, a ventilator, and intensive nursing care. She was receiving this treatment in a Catholic hospital. Her parents, who were Catholic, sought to stop use of the ventilator; the doctors refused, fearing murder charges. Her parents went to court to obtain the right to stop the ventilator, but they faced vigorous opposition from a court-appointed guardian, and the trial court refused to allow the Quinlans to stop treatment. By this point, the case was attracting widespread publicity, with many individual Christians and Christian groups demanding that the Quinlans respect the sanctity of life. For example, C. Everett Koop (later to be appointed President Reagan's surgeon general), wrote at the time that once someone has been placed on life support, "to turn off the life-support mechanism is to deliberately produce death." Such an action "is . . . homicide."[9] Koop contended that patients and their surrogates did *not* have the right to demand cessation of life-sustaining treatment; the "Judeo-Christian concept of the sanctity of human life" had to be respected.[10]

Eventually, on appeal to the New Jersey Supreme Court, the Quinlans won the right to withdraw the ventilator. Interestingly, however, the feeding tube remained because neither Quinlan's parents nor the court considered this "extraordinary" treatment. Anyway, most everyone expected Quinlan to die after removal of the ventilator, but they were in for a surprise. The Catholic nuns who had been taking care of Quinlan had been weaning her from the respirator, and, as a result, she continued to live after its removal. Quinlan lived another nine years.

At the time, Catholic theologians were at pains to point out that the actions of the nuns were not required or even approved by official Church doctrine. But the average Catholic perhaps should not be blamed for not understanding the subtleties of Church doctrine. If the Church constantly hammers home the point that one can never do anything intentionally to bring about another's death, ordinary believers might be excused for not grasping the differences between permissibly stopping certain treatments that will bring about death and bringing about death through other, impermissible means.

Moreover, following the Quinlan decision, there continued to be significant debate both in and out of the courtroom about cessation of "ordinary" treatment, in particular whether cessation of medically administered hydration and nutrition was morally or legally permissible. Gradually, against conservative religious opposition, courts came to recognize that hydration and nutrition were forms of treatment like anything else, and could be stopped at the direction of the patient. The remaining differences among the various jurisdictions in the United States have to do with the standards for determining the patient's wishes when the patient is incompetent, but the principle that patients may refuse treatment of any sort is now well-established.[11]

Physician-Assisted Dying

However, the sanctity-of-life doctrine still wields enormous influence in another policy dispute involving end-of-life care, namely in the dispute over legalization of physician-assisted dying, also known as physician-assisted suicide (hereafter PAD). It is safe to say that although various secular arguments have been made against the legalization of PAD, such as the potential for relatives pressuring patients to hasten their death, the most common and probably the most emotionally appealing argument against legalization is that PAD involves an intentional killing and, therefore, violates the sanctity-of-life principle. Certainly, this is the principal argument made by the Catholic Church and other religious organizations when they campaign against legalization of PAD, as they did successfully in Massachusetts in 2012, where they mounted an expensive advertising blitz to defeat a ballot initiative.[12]

As we will see, the sanctity-of-life principle as applied to the debate over PAD is less a carefully articulated moral view than a hodgepodge of confused and contradictory attitudes, question-begging characterizations, and result-oriented reasoning. In particular, I will show there are three principal flaws in the claim that we cannot permit assistance in dying because it violates the sanctity of life. First, at least in the manner in which PAD is carried out in the United States jurisdictions that have authorized it by statute (Oregon, Washington, and Vermont), PAD cannot plausibly be characterized as a "killing," certainly not if it is the physician who is the alleged killer. Second, it is not possible to draw a distinction between assistance in dying (considered impermissible) and refusals of treatment (considered permissible) on the ground that the former always constitutes an intentional killing, nor does such a distinction make any sense from a policy perspective. Finally, and most important, banning assistance in dying fails to promote the underlying rationale of our norms against killing others. We condemn killing others because almost always such actions are very harmful to the interests of others. Hastening the death of a terminally ill person *who requests that assistance* may not be harmful to that person's interests, however. Rigid application of the sanctity-of-life principle in such a circumstance elevates dogma over the interests of the individual.

Before discussing the flaws in the sanctity-of-life principle, it is important to know precisely what we are considering when we are discussing the legalization of PAD. Here one must distinguish between the United States model and the model that has developed in some European counties, in particular, the Netherlands and Belgium. In those countries, physicians are permitted to perform euthanasia; that is, they can directly bring about a patient's death, typically by an injection. In the United States, it is the patient who must ingest a drug to hasten his or her death. This is not an unimportant difference, and it has special relevance to the issue of whether PAD involves a "killing."

This is a summary of how the law works in Oregon, Washington, and Vermont: Eligibility for assistance in dying is limited to mentally competent patients who have received a diagnosis from their attending physician that they have a terminal illness that will cause their death within six months. The diagnosis must be confirmed by a second, consulting physician. Patients who want assistance in hastening their death must then manifest a durable, verifiable desire for assistance. Specifically, the patient must make two oral requests for assistance, separated by at least fifteen days, and one written request, signed in the presence of two witnesses. Moreover, physicians are required to inform the patient of alternatives to a hastened death, such as comfort care, hospice care, and enhanced pain control. To ensure that the patient's request is informed and truly voluntary, a patient must be referred to counseling if either the treating or the consulting physician believes the patient might be suffering from a psychological disorder that can cause impaired judgment.[13]

If these various procedures and requirements have been complied with, the physician may prescribe a drug, typically a barbiturate, which the patient may then take to accelerate his or her death. Of course, patients need not fill the prescription they receive from their physician, nor must they take the medication once the prescription is filled. The patient maintains control of the process throughout. This is an important point. In Oregon, where PAD has been legal since 1997, roughly one-third of the patients who have requested medication to hasten their death never utilized these drugs.[14] (Because Washington and Vermont legalized PAD only recently, it is more difficult to generalize from their statistics.) These patients found they were able to withstand the suffering accompanying their condition. This does not imply the prescription was unnecessary. To the contrary, one reason the patients may have been able to withstand their suffering was because they had the assurance they could end their suffering if it became intolerable. Human capacity to endure suffering increases when one has the knowledge that one can end this suffering at any time.

In any event, because of the manner in which PAD is implemented in the United States, it is inappropriate to characterize what the physician does as "killing" the patient. What the physician does is provide patients with the means to hasten their death only if and when they choose to do so. And, as indicated, many ultimately decide not to accelerate their death. Under these circumstances, the action by the physician cannot be described as a "deliberate decision to deprive an innocent human being of life," to use Pope John Paul II's words.

Here the proponent of the sanctity-of-life principle will likely maintain that, whatever the physician's role, surely the patients who take the medication are killing themselves, and, therefore, they are committing a grievous moral wrong. However, why then are the patients who insist on cessation of treatment not killing themselves? These patients have their treatment stopped with the knowledge that doing so will almost certainly accelerate their death. Recall that the Catholic Church, along with most other Christian religious bodies, now considers the withdrawal of life-sustaining treatment to be permissible. What's the difference between removing a ventilator to hasten death and taking a pill to hasten death?

The difference supposedly lies in the "intention" of the patient. Neil Gorsuch, arguably the most articulate contemporary defender of the sanctity-of-life principle, has argued that assistance in dying "*always* involves, on the part of the principal, an intent to kill and also requires that the assistant intentionally participate in a scheme to end life,"[15] whereas cessation of life-sustaining treatment need not involve an intent to end life. This argument is based on the observation that patients refusing treatment may simply want to be free of the burdens of medical care or, as Gorsuch puts it, "they are tired of the invasive treatments and tubes and the poking and prodding that have come to characterize much of the modern medical care" and they may wish to maintain their sense of dignity and privacy and die peacefully at home with their loved ones.[16]

Gorsuch acknowledges that the patient who refuses treatment knows he is going to die, but using the doctrine of double effect (DDE)—a doctrine associated with Christian moral teaching—he argues that even though death is foreseen, the cessation of treatment is nonetheless permissible. Stated as succinctly as possible, DDE holds that an action that has a foreseen bad effect, as well as a good effect, may nonetheless be permissible if the action itself is good or morally neutral, the person performing the action intends only the good effect, the bad effect is not a means to the good effect, and the good effect has positive consequences that, in some sense, outweigh the bad effect.[17] For Gorsuch the patient refusing treatment is performing an act that is morally neutral (not undergoing treatment), the patient only wants to be relieved of the burden of treatment, death (the bad effect) is not a means to the good effect of being relieved of burdensome treatment, and under some moral calculations allowing the patient the right to be relieved of burdensome treatment outweighs the bad consequence of the patient's death. As Gorsuch observes, "We all know that death cannot be cheated forever."[18]

To speak plainly, this reasoning is nothing more than casuistry. The key premise in this chain of reasoning is the claim that the person refusing treatment does not intend to die, although death is foreseen. The patient simply wants the treatment to stop and if, by some miracle, the patient would remain alive after the treatment stops, the patient would not be disappointed. But we can describe the actions of the patient who requests and receives assistance in dying in similar terms. The patient requests assistance in dying not because the patient really wants to die but because the patient wants to put an end to the intolerable conditions in which she finds herself. If through some improbable and unanticipated chemical reaction the barbiturate the patient ingests does not result in death but rather in a remission of the cancer or other terminal condition, the patient would be overjoyed, not disappointed—because what the patient intends is an end to the intolerable conditions, not her death.

If we determine intent not by examining the patient's understanding of what is likely to happen, but rather the motivations and desire of the patient, there is nothing to distinguish the terminally ill patient who dies as a result of stopping treatment and the terminally ill patient who dies as a result of ingesting a barbiturate. Both patients are knowingly taking actions that almost certainly will result in their deaths and their motivations and desire may be, and probably are, identical: they want to end their suffering and be free of conditions they find intolerable even if doing so means their death.

The only reason there is even a superficial appeal to the distinction between cessation of treatment and assisted dying based on intention is that those who employ this distinction covertly shift their focus when they move from discussing cessation of treatment to assistance in dying. In discussing cessation of the treatment, they focus *not* on what the patient knows will happen, but rather on the patient's motivations and desire. Then, when discussing assisted dying, the focus switches to what the patient knows will happen and the patient's motivations and desires are ignored. Invoking intention to distinguish cessation of treatment from assistance in dying is nothing more than a shell game— sadly with suffering patients as the victims of this sophistry.

The foregoing argument shows there is no morally significant difference between allowing patients to stop life-sustaining treatment and allowing terminally ill patients to request and receive medication that can hasten their death. If we permit one practice, we should permit the other. But we still have to address the hardline advocate of the sanctity-of-life position, namely someone who opposes *both* cessation of life-sustaining treatment and assisted dying. Such a person cannot be accused of inconsistency. Although this is not the official position of the Catholic Church, and only a minority of Christians hold such a view, we should consider how this position can be refuted.

To begin, we must acknowledge that if the person holds to the sanctity-of-life principle on purely religious grounds—that is, the principle is treated as a matter of faith—then reasoning serves no purpose. One cannot argue with faith, which is both its strength and its weakness. That said, if someone claims God has revealed that a deliberate decision to deprive someone of life is always wrong, one can always claim a contrary revelation. One can even claim that God has whispered a special revelation indicating that in a particular case, assisted dying is permissible. There is Christian precedent for such a claim. The Old Testament relates the story of Samson, informing us that he brought a temple down upon himself and the Philistines who had been tormenting him, asking God both for vengeance and death for himself.[19] Did Samson commit suicide when he brought the temple down? Certainly, the revered Augustine thought so. Nonetheless, Augustine concluded Samson's action was permissible because God had given him a secret command.[20] What can one say about a supposedly exceptionless moral rule that can be ignored based on messages from the spirit world?

To their credit, some contemporary Christian scholars have tried to formulate an argument for the sanctity-of-life principle not based on faith, or the religious claim that our lives belong to God, or disputed assertions about "natural law." In a nutshell, this is the argument:

1. One should never act with the intention of destroying an instance of a basic good of human nature.
2. Human life is a basic good of human nature.
3. One should never act with the intention of destroying an instance of human life.[21]

Although premise 1 is susceptible to criticism, the key premise here is obviously number 2. What does it mean to say that human life is a basic good?

The Christian philosopher Joseph Boyle explains a basic good as follows: First, Boyle maintains we should distinguish between things that are instrumentally good and things that are intrinsically good. Instrumental goods are things that are valued only as a means to an end. Insect repellent is an instrumental good. We do not purchase insect repellents to display in a trophy case nor do we shape our lives to maximize the acquisition of insect repellent; insect repellent can be very valuable, but only as means to protecting our comfort, our skin, and our health.

Second, according to Boyle, life cannot be merely an instrumental good. That is to say that we do not value life only because it is a useful means for obtaining other goods. Moreover, Boyle argues that because it is not an instrumental good, life must be intrinsically valuable. It cannot be an "extrinsic" good because that would imply its value is dependent on its relation to other goods. In other words, preservation of life is justified by the preservation of life and nothing further. We do not value life for the consequences it produces, but rather it is desired for its own sake.[22] Gorsuch similarly observes, "To claim that human life qualifies as a basic good is to claim that its value is not instrumental, not dependent on any other condition or reason, but something intrinsically good in and of itself."[23] In sum, Boyle maintains that goods can be divided into two exhaustive categories, namely instrumental and basic goods, and life must be a basic good with intrinsic value because it clearly is not a merely instrumental good.

The critical flaw in Boyle's argument is that it is sound *only* if we accept that all goods must be divided between intrinsically valuable goods and instrumentally valuable goods. If there is a category of goods that are extrinsically valuable (that is, dependent for their value on other goods), but that can nonetheless serve as an end or goal of human action (that is, they are not valued only as a means to something else), then Boyle's argument collapses.

Human life seems to be such a good; that is, a good whose value is dependent on its relationship to other goods. Admittedly, human life does not seem a mere instrumental good; human life can convincingly be described as something that is valued as an end or goal, not as a means to an end. Nonetheless, the value of human life is arguably dependent on its relations to other goods, for example, rationality, cognition, and sentience, and when these relations are severed, the value of human life is substantially diminished, if not eliminated. Certainly, many people believe that the value of life is explained by reference to other goods. Furthermore, that the value of life is extrinsic, not intrinsic, is decisively supported by the consideration that no one regards living in a persistent vegetative state to be desirable. Yet if we strip away all goods except life itself, all that would remain would be a bare, biological existence, devoid of cognition, emotion, or any experience. Bare, biological life does not appear to be a good desired for its own sake. It does not have "intrinsic" value. Therefore, life's value is dependent on its relationship to other goods.

At the end of the day, Boyle's argument, however sincere, operates as a smokescreen. Boyle never comes to grips with the central issue of whether life is worth preserving when it is no longer possible to pursue other goods. Obviously, the preservation of life is necessary if we are to fall in love, enjoy friendship, obtain knowledge, work on our personal projects, and so forth. However, this does not imply that life is a basic or ultimate good such that we must preserve it when it no longer bears a relation to these other goods; that is, when someone is in such a wretched condition that there is no longer any possibility of working on one's projects, experiencing joy, and so on. Instead of addressing this issue squarely, Boyle, Gorsuch, and others circumvent the issue by constructing a result-oriented classification scheme that allows them to place life in the intrinsically valuable category and then claim that it is wrong

under any circumstance to end a life. Provided one does not accept their classification scheme—and they provide no good reason to accept this scheme—
their argument for the sanctity-of-life principle is wholly unpersuasive.

Boyle, Gorsuch, and others who try to defend the sanctity-of-life principle
in secular terms are not really engaged in an open, philosophical inquiry into
the circumstances under which we should prohibit bringing about a person's
death (including our own death). Instead, whether they acknowledge it or not,
they start from the position that the sanctity-of-life principle *must* be correct
and they work backward, trying to devise arguments to defend that principle.
However, in addressing a divisive moral issue, such as the permissibility of
assisted dying, we should begin by examining the underlying rationale for relevant moral norms to see how that rationale applies to the situation in question.

At the beginning of this chapter, I noted that the prohibition on unprovoked killing is at the core of our morality, and that society would soon dissolve if such a norm were not in place and enforced. Why is that? The answer
may seem obvious, but it's worth stating it expressly: killing someone is
extremely prejudicial to that person's interests. People almost always want
to live. Killing them deprives them of their future, of everything they want to
experience, accomplish, enjoy.

In the case of a suicide, however, the person is indicating that he or she
does not perceive death to be against his or her interests. Even so, based on
human experience, we do not necessarily have to give dispositive weight to
such beliefs. Although neither attempted suicide nor suicide is any longer a
crime in most developed countries, attempted suicide can result in temporary
involuntary confinement in a mental-health facility. This is a good thing. Most
attempted suicides by physically healthy individuals are the result of either
temporary or permanent emotional or mental instability. Such suicides are
almost always tragedies that should be avoided, if at all possible. Accordingly,
it is permissible to restrain such individuals, at least temporarily. Furthermore,
for physically healthy individuals contemplating suicide, no offer of assistance is needed or morally appropriate. Generally speaking, if a healthy, able-
bodied person is too ambivalent to kill himself without assistance, suicide is
for him almost surely the wrong decision.

But terminally ill individuals are in a different category. First, a person's
terminal illness provides us some assurance that the request for assistance in

dying is not the product of some hasty, irrational decision. Unlike the typical healthy suicide, who is overreacting to some temporary setback—perhaps more imagined than real—a person who is dying is confronted with an objectively verifiable condition that will bring about his death in a relatively short time. The choice for the terminally ill who are suffering is whether to hang on for a few more weeks in intolerable conditions or to accelerate their death, so they can have some measure of peace before they die. Second, the terminally ill need assistance if they are going to hasten their death. Given their frailty and immobility, violent means of ending their life are not an option, and the state maintains control over the medications that could end their life quickly and painlessly.

The rationale for the norms against killing or assisting physically healthy persons to kill themselves simply do not apply in the case of hastening death for the terminally ill. What makes bringing about someone's death a moral wrong in normal circumstances is that the death completely deprives the person of the ability to pursue and fulfill her interests. However, one who seeks to be put to death because she wishes to avoid existing in a wretched, intolerable condition will not be deprived of any desired future state. There is no impairment of any interest because she has no interest in remaining alive given the conditions in which she finds herself. For the terminally ill then, we should recognize an exception to the general rule that bringing about someone's death is morally impermissible. To insist otherwise based on the sanctity-of-life principle elevates dogma over reason and compassion, and converts morality from a set of practices that serve human interests into a set of absolute rules that one must blindly follow regardless of the consequences. Those who resist legalization of PAD based on the sanctity-of-life principle are making the terminally ill suffer for the sake of a platitude.

The Sanctity-of-Life Principle and the Status of Zygotes, Embryos, and Fetuses

As noted at the beginning of this chapter, one problem with the sanctity-of-life principle is its dogmatic rigidity. Another problem is its application to entities that are not regarded by many, including most secular individuals, as having the same status as human persons. Specifically, the Catholic Church and several other Christian denominations take the position that a zygote, a fertilized egg, has the same moral status as an adult human. On this view, from the moment of conception forward, it is impermissible to harm or destroy the zygote, embryo, or fetus (an embryo is a zygote that has started cell division; an embryo is classified as a fetus eight weeks after conception).[24] Accordingly, many Christians oppose embryonic stem cell research and abortion at any point in time.

This has not always been the position of the Catholic Church. The early Church fathers did not consider abortion immoral until after ensoulment, and for them, ensoulment did not occur at the moment of conception. Instead, ensoulment occurred only after the body was formed, which was usually understood as three months after conception.[25] Aquinas refined this timeline and threw in a dose of sexism, declaring that abortion was impermissible after "quickening," which for boys was forty days and for girls eighty days.[26] It was not until the nineteenth century that the Catholic Church officially stated that abortion at any point after conception is equivalent to homicide. Although the Catholic Church has justified the clarification of its position by stating that modern science has made the notion of "quickening" as a moral marker obsolete, modern science is actually at odds with the Church's position on the moral status of the zygote and embryo, as we will see.

In what follows, I will provide three arguments against the position that zygotes, embryos, and early-stage fetuses have the same status as adult humans. This will not be a comprehensive set of arguments on the abortion issue, as that lies outside the scope of this essay (among other things, we would need to address a woman's reproductive rights and how they relate to the rights, if any, of the embryo or fetus). However, the arguments will be sufficient to establish that Christian opposition to embryonic stem cell research and early-stage abortions is unwarranted. This opposition is based on religious metaphysics, not science.

The Early Embryo Is Not an Individual

An essential premise of the position that human personhood begins at conception is that even though the zygote and embryo do not currently possess the capacities and properties of human persons, they possess the potential to develop these capacities and properties, and this potential is sufficient to provide these entities with the moral status of a human person. Another essential premise of this position—but one that is not always acknowledged—is that zygotes and embryos are already individuals even at the earliest stages of development. To claim that someone is harmed, there must be "someone" there. Individuality is essential for being a human person and having moral rights. We do not grant moral rights to mere groupings of cells, even if they are genetically unique.

There is a major difficulty with the claim that zygotes and embryos are individual persons. Until about fourteen days after conception, at a point called gastrulation, when the precursor to the spinal cord begins to form, an embryo can divide into two or more parts, each of which, given appropriate conditions, might develop into a separate human being. This is the phenomenon known as "twinning" (although division into three or four separate parts is also possible). The phenomenon of twinning establishes that there is not one determinate individual from the moment of conception; adult humans are *not* numerically identical with a previously existing zygote or embryo. If that were true, then each of a pair of twins would be numerically identical with the *same* embryo. This is a logically incoherent position. If A and B are separate individuals, they cannot both be identical with a previously existing entity, C.

Many of those who contend that embryos are entitled to the same rights as human persons are aware of the twinning phenomenon but they discount its significance. They maintain that this process does not undermine the claim that there was at least one individual from the moment of conception. In the words of the 2002 majority report on human cloning from President Bush's Council on Bioethics: "The fact that where 'John' alone once was there are now both 'John' and 'Jim' does not call into question the presence of 'John' at the outset."[27]

But the consequences of this reasoning are bizarre, and create further problems for the "person from conception" advocate. If twinning does occur, and if "John" was there from the beginning and "Jim" originated later, this implies that at least some twins (and triplets, etc.) have different points of origin. This anomaly creates insuperable difficulties for a view that insists *all* human persons come into existence at the moment of conception. Are some twins not human?

More importantly, the assertion that "John" is present from the outset— that is, there must be at least one individual present from the moment of conception—is nothing more than a dogmatic claim masquerading as scientific fact. There is no scientific evidence to establish the presence of a "John." What the science of embryonic development shows is that the early embryo consists of a grouping of cells with a genetic composition similar to the genetic composition of adult humans and that, after a period of time, under certain conditions, these cells begin to differentiate and to organize themselves into a unified organism. Before gastrulation, there is no certainty that these cells will differentiate and organize, nor is there any certainty that these cells will become one, two, or more individuals. Prior to the controversies surrounding embryonic stem cell research, the National Institutes of Health actually established a panel of experts to study the status of the embryo. In the words of the Human Embryo Research Panel, the cells of an early embryo do not form part "of a coherent, organized, individual."[28] The phenomenon of twinning confirms that the early embryo is not a unified, organized, determinate individual. To insist otherwise is to rely on religious dogma, not science.

A Potential Person Is Not a Person

Those who claim that there is a human person from the moment of conception forward recognize that a zygote or embryo does not possess the capacities of an adult human, or even a human child. Among other capacities, it lacks reason, cognition, and sentience. However, they argue that it is potentially a person with these capacities. Sometimes this argument is bolstered by the claim that the process of becoming a human person is inexorable: left undisturbed, the zygote becomes an embryo, which becomes a fetus, which becomes an infant, and then a child. This argument is conceptually confused and, again, ignores the science regarding embryonic and fetal development.

In arguing for the moral status of the zygote and embryo based on their potential, the proponent of the person-from-conception view is actually making a huge concession. The proponent is conceding that what really matters are the qualities and capacities of what the zygote or embryo might *become*, not their current qualities and capacities. But then the zygote and embryo, as they are now, lack the value we attribute to human persons. As the saying goes, an acorn is not an oak tree, nor for that matter is a lottery ticket an entitlement to a million dollars.

To bridge the gap between potentiality and actuality, the proponent of the person-from-conception view will often argue that the genes in the zygote and embryo drive their inevitable development into a human person. First, as to zygotes and embryos that are not inside a uterus, this is plainly false. They cannot develop on their own. Without the requisite biological and chemical interaction with a mother, which regulates the epigenetic state of the zygote and embryo, these entities have no prospect of developing into a human person. This consideration is especially important in the context of embryonic stem cell research, as the embryos used in the research obviously are not implanted in a uterus.

Moreover, even as to implanted embryos, the path from conception to birth is one marked by uncertainty, not inevitability. One important fact about embryonic development that is often overlooked is that between two-thirds and four-fifths of all embryos that are generated through standard sexual reproduction are spontaneously aborted. [29] So, in fact, the odds are very high that a zygote will not eventually develop into a child. The zygote has significantly less chance of becoming a child than a person has of winning a coin toss. Granted, the rate of miscarriages diminishes significantly after twelve weeks, but at a minimum the high percentage of miscarriages shows that the zygote, embryo, and early fetus do not possess the potentiality often attributed to them.

In Practical Terms, No One Treats Zygotes and Embryos as Human Persons

Imagine there was a virus with a fatality rate of over 50 percent that began sweeping the world. Wouldn't we put aside all other concerns to focus on this dread epidemic? No resource, financial or otherwise, would be spared in trying to end this plague.

But, if you accept the Catholic Church's position, then we are experiencing such a catastrophic event. I just noted that between two-thirds and four-fifths of all embryos "die" before coming to term. Why aren't we spending billions of dollars to find a cure for this problem? The obvious answer is that despite all the dogma drumbeat from the Catholic Church and other Christian organizations that human personhood begins at conception, and that abortion, even in very early stages, is equivalent to murder, we don't really perceive zygotes, embryos, and early-stage fetuses as human persons. This inconsistency between the claimed status of these entities and how much weight is actually given to their supposed interests is stark.

Recall also that the controversy over embryonic stem cell research during the Bush administration focused on whether the federal government would fund this research, not on whether the government would ban the research completely. But if embryos are human persons, how could we possibly allow any such research to take place, whether federally funded or not? We don't allow experimentation on adult humans that poses a risk of serious harm, and we would not allow any research involving human subjects absent informed consent. Yet research on the embryo carries no criminal penalties.

Finally, a hypothetical can serve to crystallize our moral intuitions on this subject. If fire was spreading rapidly through a building and a firefighter had to choose between saving one person in one wing of the building versus saving ten in another, presumably we would all agree that given these limited options, the firefighter should save the maximum number of people and go to the wing with ten persons and rescue them. Now assume the unfortunate building is an IVF clinic and the choice is between saving one person in one wing versus ten embryos in another. I doubt most people would hesitate before saying the firefighter must rescue the one person. But, of course, if embryos are the equivalent of human persons, this is not the proper course of action.

None of these examples refute the Christian dogmatist's position. The dogmatist can avoid inconsistency by saying yes, we should establish a Save the Embryo Foundation to find a cure for miscarriages, we should criminalize embryonic stem cell research, and we should regard preserving an embryo from a fiery fate as the moral equivalent of saving a human person's life. But in doing so the dogmatist exposes the absurdity of his position.

Conclusion

To state the obvious, human life has great value. Our moral norms and our civil and criminal law recognize this value and prohibit the taking of another person's life in almost all circumstances. We all benefit from such prohibitions;

they further our interests. Unfortunately, when religious doctrine intrudes on common sense moral reasoning, moral reasoning becomes confused and veers off course. Dogma prevails over careful consideration of the relevant factual circumstances and the consequences of our actions. In insisting on their understanding of the "sanctity of life," many Christians have taken positions that are actually inimical to human interests. In reviewing how the sanctity-of-life principle has been applied, one conclusion becomes apparent: human life is too valuable to be left in the hands of the theologians.[30]

THE GENDER BINARY AND LGBTI PEOPLE

Religious Myth and Medical Malpractice

Veronica Drantz

Introduction

The religious story most responsible for the persecution of lesbian, gay, bisexual, transgender, and intersex (LGBTI) people is the biblical "Adam and Eve" creation account. This mythical explanation of human origin is the source of the "gender binary" concept having three pertinent, implicit notions: (1) there are only two sexes (male, female), (2) sex and gender are the same (female = woman, male = man), and (3) there is only one kind of sexual attraction (heterosexual).

Everyone in a culture dominated by an Abrahamic religion (Christianity, Judaism, and Islam) is familiar with the Adam and Eve myth and the corresponding gender binary that is imposed on the social order. Currently a third of Americans, including two-thirds of white evangelical Protestants and half of black Protestants, reject the concept of evolution, saying that "humans and other living things have existed in their present form since the beginning of time."[1] Most people are ignorant of the scientific discoveries since the mid-twentieth century about sexual behavior and sexual development and how this evidence explains human sexual diversity and refutes a binary view of sexuality.

LGBTI people are currently engaged in a global struggle for their human rights. This diverse collection of sexually different people shares one feature—they innately defy the gender binary, not clearly fitting into either the "Adam" or the "Eve" categories.

The Medicalization of LGBTI People

Much of the harm done by religion to LGBTI people has been through its influence on the medical profession. Since colonial times in America, intersex people have been medically understood as a problem because "a binary system of sex, the ideal established and authorized by the biblical Adam and Eve, was rigid, and choosing only one for each individual (despite ambiguity and contradictory markers) was mandatory."[2] Until the nineteenth century, references to homosexual behavior in Anglo-American texts as "unnatural" or "a crime against nature" and the resulting persecution of homosexuality were justified by the biblical Sodom and Gomorrah tale[3] and Old Testament law assigning the death penalty for a man who "lies with a male as with a woman."[4]

By the turn of the twentieth century, sexual behavior became the province of medicine, thus removing the responsibility for defining homosexuality from religion. While homosexuality remained sinful to many in the religious realm, in the medical realm homosexuality was now a disorder. This shift to the medical domain was accompanied by an important development, the creation of a category of person—the "homosexual."[5] Homosexuality was no longer just a behavior; it was now a kind of identity—a type of person. Consequently, various pseudoscientific medical and psychoanalytic theories were postulated for the etiology and the "cure" of homosexuality that perpetuated and exacerbated homophobia by placing homosexuality in the realm of pathology.

Designated as disordered rather than just different, LGBTI people have been and continue to be victims of medical malpractice purely because they are neither Adams nor Eves. Psychiatrists, surgeons, endocrinologists, pediatricians, and other medical experts have subjected LGBTI people to bogus and horrific treatments with reckless disregard for patient health and well-being—all the while ignoring the basic tenets of medical ethics and the ever-growing scientific evidence showing LGBTI people to be natural variations. Beyond this, medical stigmatization of LGBTI people has contributed to their oppression in the world at large. This treatise will contrast the scientific evidence with the ongoing medical (mis)treatment of LGBTI people to vividly illustrate the insidious effect of the biblical creation myth.

The Scientific Study of Sexuality

Sexual Behavior

The famous reports by Alfred Kinsey on the sexual behavior of human males[6] in 1948 and of human females[7] in 1953 marked a cultural shift from viewing homosexuality as a form of pathology toward that of viewing it as a natural variant of sexuality. Kinsey criticized scientists' portrayal of homosexuals as "inherently different types of individuals" and devised a scale from zero to six to represent the continuum along which human sexual behavior or fantasy can be classified from "exclusively heterosexual" to "exclusively homosexual." He found that 37 percent of males and 13 percent of females had at least some overt homosexual experience to the point of orgasm while 10 percent of males and 2 to 6 percent of women were more or less exclusively homosexual. Kinsey's work showed that homosexuality was more common than previously thought.

Released in 1951 between the two Kinsey tomes, *Patterns of Sexual Behavior* by C. S. Ford and F. A. Beach was also highly influential in the study of sexual behavior.[8] This classic cross-cultural report integrated information on sexual activity from 191 cultures representing Oceania, Eurasia, Africa, North America, and South America. Significantly, homosexual behavior was accepted in 49 of the 76 cultures for which the relevant data were available. Homosexual behavior in other mammals was reported as well. This work indicated that homosexuality was widespread and natural.

In 1957 Evelyn Hooker published her groundbreaking study exploiting data from several projective tests, including the Rorschach, that many clinicians believed to be the best method of assessing total personality structure and that was employed for the diagnosis of homosexuality at the time.[9] The failure of expert psychologists to distinguish nonpatient homosexuals from nonpatient heterosexuals using these test results showed that homosexuality occurs in persons who demonstrate normal psychological adjustment, seriously challenging the view that homosexuality was always associated with psychopathology.

More recently, homosexual behavior has been found to be widespread in the animal kingdom—from worms, insects, and frogs to mammals and birds.[10] Furthermore, not just gay people but other gender-diverse people also are found all over the world.[11] Worldwide the variety of gender expression is almost limitless, and hundreds of societies have long-established traditions of three, four, five, or even more genders.

The etiology of this sexual diversity is, however, another matter. The questions of how sexual diversity develops and whether core sexuality can be changed would be answered by the physiologists.

Sexual Development

Physiologists call the mechanism of sexual development in mammals the "organization-activation" mechanism.[12] The most important variable in "organization" of the genitalia is the presence or absence of testosterone or other androgenic substances during critical periods of fetal development. It is obvious that our genitalia are "organized" before birth, since we come into the world with them already shaped. But we also know that these genitalia are immature and not working yet. "Activation" happens at puberty when hormones from the gonads cause the genitalia to mature and function.

The first six weeks of embryonic development is termed the "indifferent stage" because during this time the genitalia of typical females and males are identical: one pair of bipotential gonads, two sets of internal genital primordia (one female, one male), and one set of indifferent external genitalia.

Development of the gonads is under direct genetic influence. If the sperm that fertilizes the egg carries an X chromosome a "genetic female" (XX) is produced, and gonads made of such cells become ovaries making their possessor a "gonadal female." If the fertilizing sperm contains a Y chromosome, a "genetic male" (XY) is produced. A special gene on the Y chromosome (SRY gene) codes for a transcription protein that causes the gonads to develop into testes, producing a "gonadal male."

The internal genitalia, the external genitalia, and the brain of typical females develop without any hormonal support, and the ovaries secrete significant amounts of hormones starting only at puberty. In contrast, the testes must secrete two hormones during fetal development in order to produce a typical male.

Internally we start as hermaphrodites with the beginnings of both the male and female systems. In typical females, the primordial male system (Wolffian system) automatically withers away and the future female system (Mullerian ducts) automatically develops—no hormonal support being required. In the male, the testes secrete Mullerian-inhibiting hormone that stifles development of female internal genitalia and testosterone that supports development of the male internal genitalia and the male brain. In the cells of the external genitalia, an enzyme converts testosterone into dihydrotestosterone that then masculinizes the external genitalia as in typical males. Notice that the male must make one hormone for defeminization and another hormone for masculinization.

Externally we start out with only one set of genitalia that then develop as in typical females or typical males or somewhere in between; that is, ambiguous genitalia. At the seventh week the male and female begin to look different because by this time the testes have formed in the male and are secreting testosterone. The original indifferent phallus becomes the clitoris of the female or the penis of the male. The embryonic primordia that become the labia minora in the female become part of the penile shaft in the male, and what become the labia majora in the female becomes the scrotum in the male. By the twelfth week this story is over, and however the genitals look is how they will look at birth.

In order for testosterone or dihydrotestosterone to work, it has to get inside the target cells and bind to a receptor molecule. Think of these hormone molecules as little "keys" and the receptor molecules as "locks." The key fits in the lock and the resulting molecular complex becomes an active transcription factor that interacts with other proteins and the DNA of target cells, causing particular genes to be expressed that produce maleness.

Therefore, somatically, males are altered females. Everybody is a variation of the female somatic theme. Females are default and males are fully altered females. Since hormones have dose-dependent effects, there must be some people around who are partly altered, creating a type of intersex state.

More than Two Sexes

Intersex people are a glaring refutation of the gender binary because they differ physically from "standard" males or females. There are many different kinds of intersex people.[13] Some have an unusual number of sex chromosomes (for example, XXY); most do not. Some kinds of intersex people have ambiguous genitalia. Intersex people demonstrate that the organization-activation mechanism works in humans the same way it works in all other mammals. Two such examples will be discussed here.

One kind of intersex state is androgen insensitivity syndrome (AIS). An AIS individual is a genetic male (with a Y chromosome in every cell), a gonadal male (possessing testes, not ovaries), and a hormonal male (because the testes secrete testosterone—lots of it), with high blood testosterone levels. But the testosterone works only weakly or not at all because AIS individuals have inherited an unusual version of the gene that codes for a poorly working or nonfunctioning testosterone/dihydrotestosterone receptor. This gene is on the X chromosome, and therefore genetic males receive only one copy from their mothers (who are carriers). Certain mutations change the resulting protein's shape so that the "lock" no longer fits the testosterone or dihydrotestosterone "key." Other mutations affect the interaction of the hormone-receptor complex with the DNA to decrease the effect of testosterone and dihydrotestosterone on gene expression and tissue differentiation. Hence the external genitalia of people with complete AIS are female-typical, while those with partial AIS are ambiguous. Internally, male genitalia fail to develop due to the absent/reduced functionality of the testosterone/dihydrotestosterone receptor, and female internal genitalia are absent due to the unimpaired Mullerian-inhibiting hormone activity of the fetal testes.

A mirror condition is the classical form of congenital adrenal hyperplasia (CAH), in which genetic mutations affecting adrenal gland enzyme activity significantly increase androgen hormone production during fetal development of genetic females. Depending on the type of mutation and other genetic factors, the resulting external genitalia will be masculinized, ranging from a clitoris that is enlarged or external genitalia that are very ambiguous to full penis formation. The milder nonclassical form of CAH produces female-typical genitalia at birth, but as with the classical form, high adrenal androgen output and its masculinizing effects persist throughout life.

Gender Identity and Sexual Orientation—Nature or Nurture?

It's very clear that our genitalia are not "chosen" or "learned," and to suggest otherwise would be laughable. But what about sexual orientation? And gender identity? Do we learn our gender identity? Do we choose our sexual orientation?

Research in molecular biology has revealed that not only the development of the embryo's gonads but also early development of the brain is under direct genetic control. Sex-specific differences in expression of genes,[14] including genes on the X and Y chromosomes,[15] occur in embryonic brains before the gonads differentiate and sex hormones are made. Sex hormones subsequently made by the gonads travel in the blood and influence the development of not just the genitalia but all target tissues in the fetus, including the brain.

Four lines of evidence show that in people and other mammals the "organization-activation" mechanism works in the brain as it does in the genitalia: (1) experiments on brains of nonhuman mammals and other vertebrates, (2) the David Reimer story, (3) sexuality of intersex people, and (4) comparisons of human brain anatomy and physiology (transgender versus cisgender, gay versus straight).

The Animal Work

In 1959 the first paper showing the biological origins of sexual behavior reported on the effect of treating female guinea pig fetuses with testosterone only during the later stages of development, after the genitalia have already formed.[16] Upon puberty/activation these guinea pigs, although female, exhibited male-like sexual behavior. This showed that testosterone organized the brain in a male-like fashion and that sexual behavior was affected later in life. Many other kinds of mammals have been studied since then and all the studies point to the "determining influence" of prenatal hormones on sexual behavior.

We also know from the animal work that the hypothalamus is an ancient part of the brain (present in some form in all vertebrates) and that it has a similar structure in all mammals. The hypothalamus is involved in "instinctive drives and behaviors" like hunger, thirst, sleep, body rhythms, and sexual function. When you are hungry, thirsty, sleepy, cold, hot, or "horny"—that is your hypothalamus "talking" to you and driving you to respond both consciously and unconsciously. You are not in charge of your hypothalamus; it is in charge of you!

The hypothalamus controls sexual function largely through its vascular and neural connections with the pituitary gland, which it controls. The hypothalamus and pituitary together function as a "mind-body connection" that via their hormonal secretions govern activity of the gonads and other major glands, thus regulating body-wide physiology. Certain regions of the hypothalamus are involved in sexual behavior rather than gonadal function. One of these regions is the anterior hypothalamus. In this region are sexually dimorphic nuclei with receptors for sex hormones, which indicates that this grey matter functions in sexuality. Lesioning of this anterior hypothalamic region destroys sexual behavior while hormone implants in this brain region restore it. The anterior hypothalamus and related hypothalamic regions are now recognized as nodes of the brain's "social behavior network." This social behavior network is interconnected with the brain's emotional "mesolimbic reward system," and together these two systems serve to control animal behavior, much of which concerns mating and parenting. These brain systems that control animal sexual behavior are so ancient they were already in place at the start of vertebrate evolution.[17] We are gradually realizing what should have been obvious: if animals had to learn their sexuality, there wouldn't be any animals.

The David Reimer Story

In order to explain the evidence from David Reimer's story and that of intersex people, two adversaries must be introduced: John Money and Milton Diamond. John Money was a psychologist who formulated the "psychosexual neutrality-at-birth theory."[18] John Money maintained that we learn our sexuality, that we come into the world with a sexually blank brain, and then we learn our sexual identity and our sexual orientation. This theory evolved into the "optimal gender of rearing policy" that required conventional-appearing genitalia so that the child and the parents wouldn't get confused about what gender the child was supposed to be. And if the patient's genitalia were surgically "normalized" in infancy, then the patient must be lied to because knowing the truth would spoil the optimal-gender rearing.

Milton Diamond was a graduate student in the lab that published the above-mentioned first paper on the biology of sexual behavior. As a biologist, Diamond had an evolutionary view of sexuality based on the animal work. He wrote a great paper challenging Money's theory way back in 1965 when he was still just a graduate student, but nobody paid attention because Diamond was unknown and John Money was already a big shot at Johns Hopkins.[19]

Over the years Milton Diamond has been a leading proponent of the "sexuality-at-birth theory" that is largely explained by the "organization-activation mechanism" of sexual development, including that of the brain.

David Reimer was John Money's most famous patient.[20] His case was known as the John-Joan case in the medical literature. David Reimer was an identical twin boy whose penis was destroyed in a circumcision accident. The distraught parents consulted John Money, who decided to "make him a girl." So they castrated and surgically altered this baby to make him look female, raised him as a girl, told him he was born a girl and other lies. John Money announced to the world that this nature-versus-nurture case was a great success—David was growing up as a happy, well-adjusted girl and young woman.[21] The truth was that this child was miserable and made a lousy girl. At the age of fourteen, David decided to live as a male. At this point, the father broke down and told David the truth. For the first time, David Reimer understood who he was.[22] He subsequently underwent surgery and hormonal treatments and married a woman with children—trying hard to reclaim his life and live it according to his sensibility.

Meanwhile John Money kept telling the world that the John-Joan case was a big success. When David started living in the world as a man, John Money claimed to lose track of him. How convenient! But fortunately, Milton Diamond found David Reimer—living as a man.[23] Until meeting Dr. Diamond, David Reimer had no idea that his case was the famous medical "John-Joan" case and that his misrepresented case had become the model of standard care for a baby born with ambiguous genitalia or a baby boy with a destroyed penis or micropenis. When David Reimer learned that thousands of intersex babies around the world had had their genitalia mutilated and had been lied to and raised in a gender that didn't feel right for them—much like what he had experienced—he decided to come forward and tell his story. Diamond's resulting report was the beginning of the end for John Money's theory.

John Money's theory elevated external genital morphology as the single most important criterion guiding treatment of intersex people. "The decision of which gender to choose would be based, according to Money's philosophy, not on the gonads, hormones, chromosomes, or psychology, but rather on the ease with which the genitals could be surgically shaped."[24] The phall-o-meter was designed by an intersex group to show how John Money's theory plays out in medical practice.[25] If you are a baby boy, your penis can never be too big, but it certainly can be too small. If your penis is smaller than an inch in length, it will be hacked off and you will be raised as a girl. And a clitoris can never be too small, but it certainly can be too big. And if it's too big, we're hacking it off, with its nerve endings, and that will make you an Eve. You have to be an Adam or an Eve. You have to be able to penetrate or be penetrated. You can never be both or neither or in between.

In spite of serious flaws in statistical and research methods,[26] Money's theory took hold in the fifties and prevailed through the subsequent decades until Diamond's discovery of the John-Joan hoax in the mid-nineties. Even now, in spite of the fact that Money's theory is not supported by the evidence, John Money's terrible legacy lives on.

The Sexuality of Intersex People

Ever since John Money's theory has been exposed as bogus, intersex people have been coming forward out of the shadows, out of the secrecy and shame, and now we can learn about their sexuality.

So what about people with complete AIS? What is their gender identity? They feel female, presumably because the testosterone receptor could not work in their brains. What about the people with partial AIS? Their gender identity is unpredictable—some feel like females, others like males, and some feel intersex and adopt this as an identity.[27] Many raised as girls live as men when they get older. Some raised as boys live as women later in life. This is presumably because the testosterone receptor works well enough in the brain to cause a male identity in some individuals but for others it doesn't.

While most females with CAH feel female and are heterosexual, some CAH females exhibit more male-typical play behavior, less satisfaction with female sex of assignment, and less heterosexual interest.[28] CAH females also report more same-sex fantasy.[29] Higher rates of bisexual and homosexual orientation are found not only in women with classical CAH but also in nonclassical CAH women, and they are correlated with the degree of prenatal androgenization.[30] These results are consistent with the organization-activation mechanism.

Individuals with cloacal exstrophy offer compelling evidence for the organization-activation mechanism in human gender identity. Cloacal exstrophy involves malformation of the entire pelvic region, and genitalia are poorly developed. Half of these individuals are genetic males with testes that secrete testosterone in a male-typical fashion during fetal development, but because of Money's policy, such genetically male babies were routinely castrated, subjected to feminizing genitoplasty, lied to, and raised as girls. Even so, many of these individuals, upon growing up, chose to live as men—without knowing that they had been lied to.[31] Clearly something very powerful and very innate is going on here, and it has nothing to do with their upbringing.

Biology of Gender Identity

In the brain, the central subdivision of the bed nucleus of the stria terminalis (BSTc) interconnects with and relays emotional information from the amygdala of the mesolimbic reward system to the sexual hypothalamus of the social behavior network. This region is necessary for sexual behavior in animals. The BSTc is larger in typical men than in typical women—suggesting that this nucleus is important in sexuality of males and that of females. Two studies, the first looking at the presynaptic endings coming from the amygdala,[32] and a second study looking at the postsynaptic cells in the BSTc,[33] found similar results. Gay men have a BSTc structure similar to that of straight men, indicating that this region is not involved in sexual orientation. In contrast, male-to-female transsexual people have a BSTc that is small, resembling that of typical women. The researchers incorporated control patients to show that the size of this nucleus was not affected by fluctuations in circulating hormones of adulthood—the inference being that this brain region is organized before birth. In the second study, one individual with a lifelong female sensibility that was never acted on (no surgery or hormone treatment), upon death at an advanced age showed a BSTc in the typical female range. Moreover, one female-to-male transsexual brain was included in the second study and showed a BSTc right in the middle of the typical male size range. Subsequent comparative brain studies have detected many other trans brain differences. This tells us that trans people are not crazy. They are not lying or imagining their gender identity. What they say about how they feel about themselves is "real." They are telling the truth about their felt gender identities.

Plus, there is evidence for a genetic basis to transsexuality. A high proportion of male-to-female people carry a gene that codes for a longer version of the androgen receptor that weakens the androgen effect.[34] This could explain why their brains were not altered during development to give them a male identity. There is also a high proportion of female-to-male people who carry a gene variant coding for an enzyme that causes a high production of sex steroids before birth that could masculinize the brain and cause them to have a male identity.[35]

Biology of Sexual Orientation

Because the animal work showed that the anterior hypothalamus is required for sexual behavior, Simon LeVay looked at this brain region of gay versus straight men and found one pair of nuclei, the third interstitial nuclei of the anterior hypothalamus, to be very different.[36] Straight men have much bigger nuclei and gay men have nuclei similar in size to those of typical females. LeVay's work was subsequently corroborated in two separate studies.[37] Moreover when scientists compared the brains of rams known to be exclusively gay to those of straight rams, they found the same differences in the anterior hypothalamus that were found in humans.[38] In addition, multiple sex-atypical differences have been found in brains of gays and lesbians that likely contribute to the somewhat different cognitive abilities of gays and lesbians compared to their straight counterparts.[39]

Functionally we know that the anterior hypothalamus is activated by opposite-sex pheromones in straight men and women but by same-sex pheromones in gay men[40] and lesbians.[41] There is also evidence for genetic factors in gayness[42] and lesbianism,[43] and an epigenetic mechanism for homosexuality has also been hypothesized.[44]

Summary of the Science on Core Sexuality

Prominent researchers in the field have concluded that "gender identity and sexual orientation are programmed or organized into our brain structures when we are still in the womb."[45] Addressing the etiology of transsexuality, they say, "since sexual differentiation of the genitals takes place in the first two months of pregnancy and sexual differentiation of the brain starts in the second half of pregnancy, these two processes can be influenced independently, which may result in extreme cases in transsexuality." Thus transsexuality is not the result of faulty learning of gender roles; it is innate. In a statement regarding intersex people, they warn pediatricians against infant genital "normalization" surgeries by saying, "This also means that in the event of ambiguous sex at birth, the degree of masculinization of the genitals may not reflect the degree of masculinization of the brain." In other words, don't think that you can determine the gender identity of the infant by looking at the genitalia. In a humdinger sentence they add, "There is no indication that social environment after birth has an effect on gender identity or sexual orientation." In essence, the evidence supports Milton Diamond's theory. We don't learn our gender identity. We discover it! And we don't learn our sexual orientation. We discover that, too!

Medical Malpractice against LGBTI People

So what have the medical doctors been doing to LGBTI people? They have pathologized and stigmatized LGBTI people, and medical policy historically has been to "fix" them, making them conform to the gender binary.

Medical Malpractice against Gay People

Alan Turing, "father of computer science," who helped win World War II by breaking the Nazi enigma code, was convicted of homosexuality in 1952 and subjected to chemical castration in lieu of a prison sentence.[46] Two years later at the age of forty-one, Turing committed suicide. The medical atrocities imposed on gay people in an attempt to make them straight include castration, sex-hormone administration, negative conditioning to homoerotic stimuli, brain surgery (hypothalamic lesioning), electroshock therapy, and chemical induction of epileptic seizures.[47] None of these treatments have worked—constituting an impressive kind of evidence for the immutability of sexual orientation.

No scientific evidence—only the prevailing religion-based homophobia—was required for psychiatrists to designate gay people as crazy. In 1952 the American Psychiatric Association (APA) published the first edition of its "bible," the *Diagnostic and Statistical Manual of Mental Disorders*,[48] in which homosexuality appeared as "Sociopathic Personality Disturbance." This they did in spite of two aforementioned publications, Kinsey's 1948 volume showing homosexuality to occur in large numbers of men and Ford and Beach's anthropological report of 1951 showing homosexuality to be present in a range of cultures, that should have cautioned these "men of science" to do otherwise. And in spite of two additional aforementioned reports, Kinsey's 1953 volume reporting homosexuality in women and Hooker's 1957 study revealing gay men to have normal psychological adjustment, homosexuality was again listed in the *DSM*'s second edition of 1969 but with a new name, "Sexual Deviation." So deeply embedded was the notion of a sexual binary in psychiatry, and so closeted were the homosexual psychiatrists in their midst, that the scientific evidence against homosexuality being a mental illness generated no professional dispute.

The single most important achievement in the gay-rights struggle has been the removal of homosexuality from the *DSM*. Having successfully challenged police and government authority in the Stonewall riots[49] in New York City in 1969, gay activists then began to challenge psychiatric authority through a clever grassroots political effort that taught the science to the psychiatrists! In 1970 a group of thirty gay activists led by Frank Kameny[50] and Barbara Gittings[51] broke into the American Psychiatric Association meeting in Washington and turned the staid proceedings into chaos, with Kameny shouting: "We are here to denounce your authority to call us sick or mentally disordered!" Continued confrontation, including disruption of the next APA meeting in 1971, led to an agreement that Gittings and Kameny would organize a panel of psychiatrists to discuss homosexuality titled "Psychiatry: Friend or Foe to Homosexuals: A Dialogue" for the 1972 APA meeting. Appearing on the panel was "Dr. Anonymous,"[52] who in heavy disguise and with voice distorted to further protect his identity, described to his colleagues the plight of being a closeted gay doctor practicing in a field that regarded him as mentally ill. Gittings read aloud letters solicited from other gay psychiatrists too afraid to appear even in disguise. This testimony from gay psychiatrists was a transformative event that led to a meeting of the gay activists and the psychiatrists of the APA Task Force on Nomenclature and Statistics. At this meeting the gay activists "presented the scientific evidence to the psychiatrists and convinced the task force to study the issue further."[53] After its research review, the Nomenclature Committee proposed that homosexuality be eliminated from the *DSM*. Homosexuality was removed from the *DSM* in 1973. One headline in a Philadelphia paper read "Twenty Million Homosexuals Gain Instant Cure."[54]

But the psychiatric quackery was not over. When the diagnosis of homosexuality was deleted in 1973, the APA did not initially embrace a normal variant model of homosexuality.[55] Instead, in recognition of the opposition during the revision process of *DSM-II*, the APA made a controversial compromise by replacing "Sexual Deviation" with a new name, "Sexual Orientation Disturbance." Now individuals comfortable with their homosexuality were no longer considered mentally ill; only those who were "in conflict with" their sexual orientation were mentally ill. Those opposing this new pathology pointed out there were no reported cases of unhappy heterosexuals seeking treatment to become homosexual. In response to the opposition still another epithet, "Ego-Dystonic Homosexuality," was invented for the third edition of the *DSM* in 1980 that perpetuated directly or indirectly a mental-illness model of homosexuality. Finally, during the revision process of *DSM-III* in the mid 1980s, openly gay and lesbian members of the APA played a decisive role by arguing that empirical data did not support the diagnosis. They further argued that distress caused by social persecution is normal, and that making patients' subjective experience of their own homosexuality the determining factor of their illness was not an evidence-based approach but instead tantamount to labeling culturally induced homophobia as a mental disorder. The APA committee agreed and "Ego-Dystonic Homosexuality" was removed from the *DSM*'s revised third edition in 1987. It is clear that without political activism, first from gay nonpsychiatrists on the outside and then from gay psychiatrists on the inside, the APA would not have behaved "scientifically" by looking at the evidence objectively in its assessment of homosexuality.

The complete removal of homosexuality from the *DSM* stimulated other mental health organizations to also depathologize homosexuality.[56] The World Health Organization removed homosexuality from the International Classification of Diseases in 1992. In 1998 the APA declared its opposition to any psychiatric treatment based on the assumption that homosexuality is a medical disorder or that patients should change their sexual orientation, including "reparative" or "conversion" therapies. In 2000 the APA recommended that, in the absence of research substantiating reparative therapies, ethical practitioners refrain from attempts to change sexual orientation. In October 2013 the World Medical Association (WMA) condemned conversion or reparative methods in a statement that cited the higher prevalence of depression, anxiety disorders, substance misuse, and suicidal ideations and attempts among adolescents and young adults with a homosexual or bisexual orientation due to stigmatization, discrimination, bullying, and peer rejection. Saying the reparative therapy exacerbates these effects and that no evidence exists for the efficacy of reparative therapy, the WMA asserted that "psychiatric or psychoanalytic treatment must not focus upon homosexuality itself, but rather upon conflicts which arise between homosexuality and religious, social and internalized norms and prejudices."[57] The WMA said that it is "unethical for physicians to participate during any step of such procedures." And in 2014 the World Psychiatric Association became headed by its first openly gay president. Saying that psychiatry should apologize for the harm done to gay and bisexual people, he has vowed to fight reparative therapy and the notion that still prevails throughout much of the world that homosexuality is an illness.[58]

But "reparative therapy" continues—including "shock treatment."[59] Ex-gay ministries such as Evergreen International,[60] PATH,[61] and Witness Ministries[62] parade their religion-based agenda as medical treatment. They shame and traumatize gay youth in vain attempts to turn them straight, while creating a climate that encourages antigay discrimination and prejudice. Among the ex-gay groups is NARTH,[63] a small group of psychologists and analysts that continues to argue that homosexuality is a dysfunction and can be corrected. Although a secular organization, which differentiates it from other ex-gay groups that are primarily religious in nature, NARTH often partners with religious groups such as Courage .[64] Officially endorsed by the Vatican, Courage no longer claims to make a gay person straight. Instead, the organization's goal is to make gay individuals celibate for life—a goal that surely is equally impossible! In 2013 Courage hosted a conference in the Chicago area offering training in reparative therapy by a NARTH member, and Cardinal Francis George celebrated mass for the event. While embarrassing scandals over bogus gay "cures" [65] and apologies from former ex-gay officials[66] have weakened or even shut down some groups such as Exodus International,[67] others like Restored Hope Network[68] and Voice of the Voiceless[69] have sprung up to take their places. Antigay quackery remains legal throughout the United States except in California and in New Jersey, which recently passed legislation banning reparative therapy.[70] Only now is a national ban on reparative therapy being proposed.[71]

Medical Malpractice against Transgender People

The APA has judiciously ignored the growing biological and anthropological evidence showing transgender people to be natural variants, just as they did with LGB people. In 1980 trans people became officially crazy in the revised *DSM-III* with "gender identity disorder" (GID). Many trans people accepted the stigma of being mentally ill in exchange for the diagnosis required by medical insurance for gender transition care. In the successive revisions of the *DSM*, the focus of the "disorder" shifted from distress with one's assigned/birth sex toward a focus on one's gender identity itself being disordered. This conceptualization of gender identity as disordered plus the absence of a formal APA opinion about treatment of a diagnosis of its own creation contributed to an ongoing problem of many healthcare insurers and other third-party payers claiming that hormonal treatment and sex reassignment surgery were "experimental," "elective," or "'not medically necessary," and therefore not reimbursable or covered under most insurance plans. The APA had created a pathology for which trans people could not access treatment!

Then in 2008 for the development of *DSM-V*, the APA appointed to the work group on Sexual and Gender Identity Disorders two of the most transphobic reparative therapists in the field! The selected chair of the committee built a reputation of "curing" gender-nonconforming children via "therapy" (for example, not letting boys play with dolls or girls play with trucks)[72] and has been identified as the leader of an "invisible college" of group-think researchers who use misgendering and pathologizing language in their writing about trans people—more so than authors from other professions.[73] The second therapist, a member of the "invisible college," had published many articles pathologizing gender variance and authored a particularly stigmatizing theory of transgenderism.[74] The appointees remained, even though activists registered their dismay.[75]

In 2009, to address both the social stigma of GID and the lack of access to medical care, GID Reform Now protested at the APA's annual meeting for reform in the *DSM-V*.[76] Holding a poster reading "Difference Is Not Disease" and wearing a T-shirt emblazoned with "Transgender Menace," Kelley Winters requested that the APA: (1) "affirm in public policy statements that gender identity and expression which differ from assigned birth sex do not in themselves constitute mental disorder," (2) release "a statement clarifying the medical necessity of hormonal and surgical transition treatments for those who suffer distress with physical sex characteristics that are incongruent with our gender identities," and (3) "encourage legal and social recognition of all people consistent with our gender identity and expression." Similar demands were made to the APA by nontrans allies solicited via an Internet petition.[77] The World Professional Association for Transgender Health also recommended a narrowing of the diagnostic criteria to those who experience distress associated with gender incongruence and recommended that Gender Identity Disorder be renamed Gender Dysphoria to reflect that the diagnosis applies only to some transgender individuals at those times in their lives when they actually experience clinically significant distress related to incongruence.[78]

The activists' efforts were rewarded in the *DSM-V*, released in May 2013. Gender Identity Disorder has been renamed Gender Dysphoria. Gender nonconformity itself is no longer a mental disorder—just the clinically significant distress associated with the condition. The "gender dysphoria" title is less pathologizing and emphasizes the importance of distress about the incongruity for a diagnosis.[79] The work group claimed that it didn't remove the condition as a psychiatric diagnosis, as many activists had suggested, because to do so would jeopardize access to medical care.[80] There is also an "exit clause" so that individuals who have successfully resolved their incongruence no longer are considered to have a mental disorder—making for a curious situation in which a mental disorder is cured by surgery on genitalia and other nonbrain body parts!

But transgender people are still in the bible of "mental illnesses." Echoing its treatment of LGB people, the APA has pathologized the distress of transgender people. The diagnosis of gender dysphoria promotes a pathologizing view of people's reasonable responses, like "distress" in the face of societal inequities and medical-access barriers, instead of recognizing and challenging the inequities responsible for their distress. In fact, the APA has been a major contributor to this distress. Only in 2012 did the APA release a position statement supporting access to insurance coverage for transition care[81] and another statement opposing discrimination against transgender people.[82] These statements happened probably only because of efforts by the LGB caucus of psychiatrists that wrote them.

The scientific evidence shows trans people are not mentally ill. The ideal solution would be "to remove all psychiatric gender diagnoses from the *DSM* and transfer with no gaps in services to the alternative of getting medical services for gender affirmation available through biomedical pathways."[83]

Medical Malpractice against Intersex People

What is the medical community doing to intersex people? Genital normalization surgeries continue. Clitoral reduction is still a "standard clinical procedure."[84] Curtis Hinkle, founder of Organization Intersex International, says "the basic problems faced by the intersexed are socio-cultural in nature and not medical and are a result of the dogmatic fundamentalism inherent in the current binary construct of sex and gender. Some intersexed individuals are subjected to genital mutilation in childhood as a result of this totalitarian, sexist oppression."[85] Whatever happened to medical ethics: "informed consent" and "first, do no harm?"

In 1996 intersex activists calling themselves "Hermaphrodites with Attitude" took to the streets for the first time in history to confront the American Academy of Pediatrics (AAP) with their pamphlets and flyers.[86] Their message was that "early surgical intervention leads to more than 'just' physical scars and sexual dysfunction" and that lack of education and counseling for intersexuals, their families, and the community at large "does not lead to a blissful, healthy, well-adjusted ignorance. Rather, it too often leads to a life-threatening shroud of silence, secrecy, and self-hatred." The AAP ignored the letter's request that representatives meet with the activists, instead releasing a press statement summarizing their John Money–inspired medical policy for intersex treatment.[87]

Now that Money's theory has been discredited, there have been a few follow-up studies on genital normalization surgeries that reveal appallingly dismal outcomes. In spite of multiple surgeries, high percentages of these patients hate their bodies and have problems with sexual desire and function.[88] The researchers never asked: "What if we had done nothing to these patients? What if we had left the genitalia and the nerve endings intact?" A recent study has found no new evidence for significant improvements in long-term post-operative outcomes.[89]

Milton Diamond attended the AAP conference in 2000 and told the pediatricians that they should declare a moratorium on infant genital normalization surgeries until they could prove that the surgeries produced good outcomes in follow-up studies.[90] The pediatricians declined to support a moratorium, and offered parental distress and prejudice as justification for the continuation of the damaging surgery. Contrary to Dr. Diamond's recommendation, the pediatricians also voted to not inform their former patients of their true intersex status and previous medical treatments. They ignored the wish of intersex activists to be designated as "intersex" and in 2006 devised new pathologizing terminology, "disorders of sexual development (DSD)," instead.[91]

On Human Rights Day 2013, intersex activist Hida Viloria explained to the United Nations that it's very easy to discriminate against intersex people because they are closeted. "That's why even though intersex is 1.7% of the population, as common as having red hair, you don't all know that you know an intersex person. And the stigma against us is so great that right now—everyday, today, in New York, in San Francisco, in the most liberal western cities in the world—we are being cut up. Our bodies are being decimated to remove our traits, and the discrimination is that great that it's considered better to do this to a baby than to let them have an intersex body."[92]

Forces outside the medical profession are pushing the medical world to be more compassionate toward intersex patients. The United Nations recently condemned medically unnecessary normalizing procedures, such as irreversible genital surgeries, saying evidence has shown the procedures may be physically and psychologically harmful, and infants and young individuals cannot consent to them.[93] A historic lawsuit has now been brought against the State of South Carolina on behalf of the adoptive parents of M. C., who was subjected to genital surgery that removed his phallus and potentially sterilized him "without notice or a hearing to determine whether the procedure was in M. C.'s best interest," and who now identifies as a boy.[94] The lawsuit contends that the decision to medically assign M. C. a biological sex amounted to medical malpractice and a violation of M. C.'s constitutional rights. His adoptive mother said, "By performing this needless surgery, the state and the doctors told M. C. that he was not acceptable or loveable the way he was born. They disfigured him because they could not accept him for who he was—not because he needed any surgery."

Other forms of intersex erasure include intimidation of patients by doctors to accept one-size-fits-all treatments, such as testosterone treatment for XXY patients to make them into "Adams"—even for those who don't feel male or who like their bodies the way they are. These treatments often change the patients' bodies in ways they abhor. And now new frontiers of intersex erasure include prenatal intervention and selective abortion to prevent intersex births.[95] Additionally, the new *DSM-V* includes a new form of craziness ("gender dysphoria in DSD") for intersex people who are unhappy with the gender assigned to them at birth!

Common LGBTI Medical Issues

Healthcare providers are poorly educated in the care of LGBTI patients and often harbor negative attitudes toward them.[96] Trans patients have difficulty accessing doctors who respect their gender identity.[97] Many national health systems and insurance companies do not cover the cost of follow-up care or damage repair from earlier surgeries conducted on intersex people.[98] Due to doctors' ignorance, many intersex patients are misdiagnosed.[99] Others are traumatized by their medical experiences and afraid to return for care. To date Germany is the only country to have formulated, at least on paper, ethical guidelines for the medical treatment of intersex people.[100] Ethical guidelines for the medical care of LGBTI patients are sorely needed.[101]

Conclusion

The medical community has neither offered apologies nor made attempts to mitigate the damage it has done to LGBTI people. In David-versus-Goliath fashion, LGBTI people have had to self-educate, mobilize, and protest to have their concerns heard by the medical experts, and any improvements in the medical care of LGBTI people have resulted from the outside pressure LGBTI people brought themselves.

The scientific message that "core sexuality is innate" needs to reach everyone. LGBTI people are natural variations—different, but not disordered! Medical doctors should not be policing sex or gender. The medical profession must have health and happiness as its goal for LGBTI people—not their conversion into "Adams" and "Eves." Healthcare providers must be educated and given sensitivity training about LGBTI people, and ethical guidelines for LGBTI medical care must be established—because medical practice should be based on scientific evidence and ethical principles, *not* religious myth!

CHRISTIANITY CAN BE HAZARDOUS TO YOUR HEALTH

Harriet Hall, MD

Religion will always be a controversial subject, but its impact on health is one area that lends itself to objective investigation. Do religious people live longer? Are they healthier? Prayer, laying on of hands, pilgrimages to Lourdes, faith healing, and exorcism rituals might have a role in providing subjective comfort to some people; but do they have any objective, measurable influence on illness outcomes? Those are questions that science can ask and answer.

According to a 1999 study in the *Lancet*,[1] 79 percent of adults believe that spiritual faith can help people recover from disease and 25 percent use prayer as medical therapy. A poll of doctors attending a 1996 American Academy of Family Physicians meeting showed that 99 percent believed religious beliefs can heal and 75 percent believed the prayers of others can promote a patient's recovery.[2] There has even been talk of tearing down the wall of separation between medicine and religion. But the data don't support those beliefs.

Scientific Studies

Some studies do appear to show reductions in morbidity and mortality associated with religious devotion. Dr. Oz has argued for the health benefits of religion, claiming that attending religious services can protect against age-related memory loss and thinking problems, can cut the risk of high blood pressure by 40 percent, and can reduce the risk of depression. Other sources have reported that people of faith were less likely to commit suicide. On the other hand, religious patients who believe their illness means punishment or abandonment by God have a 19 to 28 percent greater mortality.

But the studies that appear to support those claims are flawed and unconvincing. They find apparent associations, but association doesn't necessarily mean causation. That's the *post hoc ergo propter hoc* fallacy: the idea that if the sun comes up when the rooster crows, that must mean the rooster causes the sun to come up.

One of the problems with this kind of research is the inconsistency in definition of religiosity. Is it defined by church affiliation, by church attendance, by self-report of religious beliefs? What do those actually measure?

Another problem is that most studies have failed to adequately control for other factors that might have been responsible for the results. Church attendance is associated with better health (but only in women—why would this be?). People with poor health and decreased functional capacity are less likely to leave the house, so maybe health determines church attendance rather than the other way around. Some studies show decreased mortality with church attendance; others don't. In studies of prayer, how is prayer defined and how could you control for other people's prayers outside the study protocol?

One study found that Seventh-Day Adventists (SDAs) had lower total cholesterol levels than age-matched healthy controls,[3] but SDAs are vegetarians who avoid alcohol and tobacco. So we might be seeing the effects of lifestyle rather than of religion.

A recent study at Harvard looked at response to treatment for depression and found that belief in God was associated with greater improvement, but those who believed in God also believed in doctors (that is, believed that treatment would be effective).[4] In other words, it appears that some people are simply "faithful." They have a tendency to believe in both doctors and preachers, and their faith is linked to optimism. It appears to be the personality trait of optimism that improves their mental health rather than a belief in God per se.

Most studies have failed to adequately control for confounders, covariates, and multiple endpoints. In a trial of intercessory prayer for patients in a coronary care unit (CCU)[5] Byrd looked at twenty-nine endpoints. Patients who were prayed for did better on six measures, but those six were not independent of each other (for instance, pneumonia is linked to antibiotics and heart failure is linked to newly prescribed diuretics). There was no difference in the other twenty-three variables such as days in the CCU, length of stay in hospital, and number of discharge medications. When a study has that many endpoints, one can expect to find a few positive correlations just by chance. That study has never been replicated.

Sometimes researchers have even resorted to outright deception and fraud. In 2001, a randomized double-blind study published in the *Journal of Reproductive Medicine* reported that intercessory prayer doubled the pregnancy rate in women undergoing *in vitro* fertilization for infertility.[6] The study's design was bewilderingly complicated; it was unethical, with no informed consent and no review by an institutional review board (required to ensure protection of human subjects); and there were other suspicious discrepancies. One of the three listed authors, Rogerio Lobo, didn't even know about the study until six to twelve months after it was completed, when he was asked to provide editorial assistance in writing the report. Another, Kwang Cha, initially failed to respond to inquiries, and later unsuccessfully sued a critic of the study for defamation. The third author, Daniel Wirth, was a parapsychologist with no medical training; he was a con man with a twenty-year history of criminal activities who had been investigated by the FBI and ended up in prison after he pled guilty to fraud. The study data can't be trusted, the findings have never been replicated elsewhere, and even the authors claimed to have been surprised by the unlikely results. It was never retracted by the journal, and it's still widely cited in the medical literature as "proof" of the efficacy of prayer. It isn't proof of anything except the fact that faulty studies sometimes get published.[7]

And then there was Leonard Leibovici's retroactive prayer study in 2001.[8] He identified patients previously treated for blood infections at the Rabin Medical Center, randomized them into two groups, and then had people pray for patients in one of the groups—four to ten years *after* they had been discharged from the hospital! Then he reviewed their hospital records and found that length of hospitalization and duration of fever were significantly lower in the group that was prayed for. He later explained that his experiment was "intended lightheartedly to illustrate the importance of asking research questions that fit with scientific models."[9]

The Catholic Church has long accepted medically unexplained healings as miracles on evidence that is far from compelling to the scientific mind. It has validated sixty-seven miracles at Lourdes. But two hundred million pilgrims have visited Lourdes since its establishment in 1860, so sixty-seven amounts to a success rate of only .0000335 percent or one in three million. Joe Nickell has pointed out that these "medically inexplicable" cases were actually explicable: they were virtually all conditions susceptible to psycho-somatic influences or known to show spontaneous remissions. When Anatole France visited Lourdes and saw all the discarded crutches, he said, "What, what, no wooden legs?" No, there are no reports of amputated legs being inexplicably restored. Now that *would* be a miracle.[10]

After Mother Teresa died, the Catholic Church began the beatification process, a preliminary step to sainthood that requires a documented miracle attributable to the saint's intercession. An Indian woman, Monica Besra, testified that a cancerous tumor in her abdomen had been cured by the application of a locket with Mother Teresa's picture. She reportedly saw a beam of light emanating from the locket. The church believed it had verified her case as a miracle, and it approved Mother Teresa's beatification. The patient's own husband denied it: he said the doctors cured her! One doctor who was involved in her treatment told reporters that she never had cancer, only a cyst and tuberculosis that gradually resolved with anti-tuberculosis drugs over the course of a year. Some Catholic writers rationalized the criticism of her miracle as a "sign of contradiction"—a sign that indicates the presence of the divine when a holy person is subject to extreme opposition.[11]

Dr. Richard Sloan remains unconvinced. As he wrote in the *Lancet*,[12] "Even in the best studies, the evidence of an association between religion, spirituality, and health is weak and inconsistent." He wrote a book, *Blind Faith: The Unholy Alliance of Religion and Medicine*,[13] examining all the published evidence and exposing the questionable research practices of scientists who manipulate scientific data and research results to support their unfounded belief that mystical interventions can heal.

Faith Healing

There is no credible evidence from scientific studies that religion improves health, but there is clear evidence that it can harm. In his book *In the Name of God: The True Story of the Fight to Save Children from Faith-Healing Homicide*,[14] Cameron Stauth reports:

Year after year, hundreds of people—possibly even thousands—were killed, maimed, disabled, and disfigured. Most of the victims were among America's most vulnerable: children, women in childbirth, and the elderly. But it was extremely well hidden.

Christian Scientists believe "there is no life, truth, intelligence, or substance in matter. . . . Therefore, man is not material. He is spiritual."[15] They think illness is an illusion created by incorrect thoughts, so therefore it can be banished by correct thoughts. They not only deny the reality of illness, they deny the reality of the material world. Today they condone medical care in certain circumstances; but originally they didn't accept any form of medical treatment, but only prayer by practitioners, usually in the patient's home. The practitioners charge for their services. There are Christian Science nursing homes staffed with "nurses" who are trained in metaphysics, not in medicine. They provide only comfort care and are not even allowed to use a thermometer. The fees of Christian Science practitioners and nurses are covered by Medicare, Tricare, and many other government programs and private insurance companies. The IRS does not tax the income of practitioners, and their services are deductible as medical expenses. Essentially, nonbelievers are being compelled to subsidize religious beliefs.

Besides Christian Science, there are many other religious groups that prefer prayer and faith healing to medical care, and some that strictly prohibit any form of medical care. Jehovah's Witnesses prohibit blood transfusions. Faith healing is practiced by Pentecostalists, the Church of the First Born, the Followers of Christ, and numerous smaller sects. It typically involves prayer, laying on of hands, anointing with oil, and sometimes exorcisms.

In his book *In the Name of God* Stauth tells horror stories about children dying in agony after prolonged suffering from conditions that could have been easily cured or controlled with proper medical care, such as appendicitis, hernias, infections, tumors, premature birth, and diabetes. He tells of children killed by suffocation or trauma during exorcisms or religion-motivated punishments. He tells about parents who starved a sixteen-month-old to death for refusing to say "Amen" and then carried his body around in a suitcase awaiting his resurrection.

Even those who might consider getting medical care in an emergency let their children die because they are too medically ignorant to recognize an emergency. When an infant went into convulsions, they interpreted it as an improvement because he was "more active." A girl had been in a diabetic coma and was breathing noisily; eventually her body systems started to shut down and her breathing quieted. They thought she was improving because she was breathing more easily, but she died shortly afterward. When a child died of a fever and the authorities arrived to investigate, the corpse still had a temperature of 104 degrees hours after the time of death; one can only imagine how high it must have gone.

Adults are not just influenced but are often coerced by their coreligionists. In most faith-healing sects, wives have no role in medical decisions; they must defer to their husbands' wishes in everything. And men coerce each other, too. In one case an older man with congestive heart failure was forcibly restrained by his two adult sons to keep him from going to the hospital. Semmelweis discovered how to prevent puerperal fever (childbed fever) in 1847, and today it is almost unheard of in the developed world. But a father who believed in faith healing intervened in a home delivery and cut his wife's episiotomy with dirty scissors. She developed a uterine infection and died (and so did the baby).

Baby Justin Barnhart's parents belonged to Faith Tabernacle. They prayed over his abdominal tumor as it gradually grew to the size of a volleyball and killed him at the age of two. It was a type of tumor that was curable with medical treatment in 90 percent of cases. Think of the size of a two-year-old and the size of a volleyball: it's hard to understand how any parent could sit by and watch that happen without doing anything but praying.

Teenagers who refuse medical care are trying to please their parents and may not be competent to make their own decisions. A teen with severe asthma was forced by DHS (Department of Human Services) workers to get treatment against her parents' wishes; she stopped treatment as soon as she turned eighteen, telling her doctor "I'm free now. I don't have to see you anymore. God wants me to suffer." How sad that she accepted suffering that could have so easily been prevented! How pathetic that she believed a "loving" God wanted her to suffer!

Rita Swan, a former Christian Scientist whose infant son died of untreated meningitis in 1977, has dedicated her life to preventing the deaths of other children. She founded the organization Children's Healthcare Is a Legal Duty (CHILD) and has campaigned across the country to abolish laws that exempt people with religious beliefs from prosecution for child abuse, neglect, and murder.

In 1998, she and pediatrician Seth Asser published a study titled "Child Fatalities from Religion-Motivated Medical Neglect" in the journal *Pediatrics*.[16] They identified 172 well-documented cases of children who died between 1975 and 1995 from treatable illnesses with a good prognosis because parents withheld medical care for religious reasons. The cases spanned twenty-three sects in thirty-four states. There were many more cases with incomplete information or that were never reported. At the time, all but five states had religious shield laws to prevent prosecution of parents.

In most states, it is essentially legal to torture and murder a child as long as you believe you are following the precepts of your religion. For years, district attorneys refused to prosecute these cases; and when they did, juries were sympathetic to parents who obviously loved their children and thought they were doing what was best for them. Recently we have started to see convictions and changes in the laws.

Neal Beagley, whose parents were Followers of Christ in Oregon, was born with a congenital defect that caused repeated urinary tract infections. It could very easily have been repaired with surgery, but he was never treated and he suffered from ill health all his life until he died of kidney failure at age sixteen. Before his death, he became too weak to walk to the bathroom; but his father made a joke of it and carried him, refusing to see how sick he was. Neil's parents were convicted of criminally negligent homicide and each served sixteen months, one after the other so their other children would always have a parent at home.[17]

Another Followers of Christ baby, Alayna Wyland, had a hemangioma above her eye that kept enlarging until it was a horrific baseball-sized purple mass that entirely covered her eye and obstructed her vision. Her parents prayed and anointed her with oils, confident that she would be healed. When she was nine months old, the courts removed her from her home, put her in foster care, and ordered medical treatment. Under the care of specialists, the mass largely disappeared and her previously hidden eye became visible again. Her vision in that eye was only 20/1000. They got to her in the nick of time to prevent permanent blindness, but she may still require years of treatment and they are not sure how much her vision will improve. Alayna's parents were sentenced to ninety days in jail and three years of probation.[18]

In Pennsylvania, Herbert and Catherine Schaible, members of the fundamentalist First Century Gospel Church, let their two-year-old son die from untreated bacterial pneumonia. They were convicted of involuntary manslaughter and put on probation for ten years. The court ordered them to get medical insurance and to have a pediatrician care for their other children, but they ignored the terms of their probation and four years later they allowed a second child, their seven-month-old son, to die of exactly the same illness. They reasoned that it was more important to obey the laws of God than the laws of man. Their pastor said the parents lost their sons because of a "spiritual lack" in their lives. They were charged with murder and pleaded "no contest." Their seven other children were put in foster care.[19]

In Oregon, Daryl and Shannon Hickman's baby was delivered at home by an unqualified midwife. He was so premature that his lungs had not finished developing. His breathing seemed all right at first, then it deteriorated rapidly—a sequence that is typical for such a premature baby and would have been predicted and treated if the baby had been under competent medical care. They ignored his labored breathing until he died. They were convicted of second-degree manslaughter.[20]

It's tragic when well-meaning parents go to prison and when the authorities have to take children away from parents who love them. No one wins. The parents are victims, too.

Can you imagine being a parent and watching your child suffer with illnesses like those? What's it like to be immersed in that culture? Here's an enlightening personal account from a woman who prefers to remain anonymous:

> I am a former member of the Followers of Christ. I can only describe the deaths of their children as ritualistic torture. For anyone who is against changing laws to protect children, I ask you to read the coroner's reports of the children who have died. Then think how you would feel if you were restrained for days while you screamed in pain until you were too weak to fight the disease any longer. It is not only the children who are suffering from this abuse. Many adults have begged to be taken to a doctor only to be told no and restrained.
>
> I suffered for years from ear infections that progressed to the point of bleeding eardrums. I went to school with whooping cough. I often wonder

how many kids I infected with contagious illnesses that could have been prevented.

I cannot begin to make people understand how horrific a life like this is. . . . My brother opted for no medical care because he didn't believe in medicine. When his illness caused pain that was intolerable he went to the emergency room. The taxpayers in Idaho are now paying for hundreds of thousands of dollars in medical bills just so his life could be spared for another three years. He passed away earlier this year. Just think of the economical impact this could have on the U.S. . . .

I never wanted to be part of the church even as a child. I have always wondered why we never went to the dentist and eye doctor. Our animals always had vaccines and vet care. When I asked why . . . no one in the church ever gave me an answer. Children were to be seen and not heard. To completely understand where I am coming from you would have to know my whole story. I left the church and my family when I was 16. I chose to get married to escape the abuse at home.

The church members believe that medicine is a temptation from Satan and to go to a doctor is to give into that temptation. To them it shows a weakness in faith.[21]

Vaccine Exemptions

Christian Science, faith healing sects, and many other religious groups reject vaccination. Most states allow religious exemptions for vaccines. This has reduced the herd immunity of the population and has contributed to numerous outbreaks of vaccine-preventable diseases such as measles, pertussis (whooping cough), and *Hemophilus influenza B* infections.

At a Christian Science school (Principia College in Missouri), there was an outbreak of measles in 1985 that affected 15 percent of the student body. It eventually caused 125 confirmed cases and 3 deaths. Public health investigators were thwarted at every turn. Quarantines were not enforced. For three weeks they were unable to get a blood sample to confirm a diagnosis: every time they would talk a child into it, school officials would persuade the child to refuse. They were not even allowed to take a throat swab for viral identification. Finally they succeeded in getting a blood sample from a victim who had caught the disease from her Christian Scientist brother but was not a Christian

Scientist herself. When they interviewed students and asked how long they'd had the rash, they would respond, "What rash?" They even covered up mirrors so they wouldn't accidentally see the rash. They refused to acknowledge it because they believed it was their own fault: any sign of illness meant their mind was not right with God.[22]

Incredibly, measles broke out again in the same school nine years later. There were 247 cases in that one school compared to 934 for the entire country that year.[23]

Smallpox was completely eradicated from the world by means of an aggressive vaccination campaign; the last case occurred in 1977. Like smallpox, measles is a human disease with no animal reservoir; vaccines had completely eliminated it in the United States by 2000. Cases since have occurred only when someone brings the virus in from another country, often unknowingly, since patients are contagious for up to four days before the rash appears. The vaccine is highly effective. 99.7 percent of children are protected after two doses, but that means three in one thousand do not develop immunity. That shouldn't be a problem, because the disease can't spread if there are enough immune people in the community to prevent it from propagating (that's called herd immunity). But the recent increase in vaccine refusals (for religious reasons and from fears created by misinformation) has decreased the herd immunity in many communities to where the disease can spread. In Ashland, Oregon, there is 25 percent noncompliance citywide, and in individual schools the statistics are much worse. In one Waldorf School in California, a whopping 84 percent of kindergarteners were noncompliant. This is an epidemic waiting to happen. All it will take is one child returning by plane from a trip to a country where measles is still occurring.[24]

In its 2008 newsletter,[25] CHILD reported for that year:

- A Washington measles outbreak with nineteen cases, sixteen in children who were unvaccinated because of their parents' religious beliefs.
- In Illinois, there were fifty cases of pertussis compared to one in 2007. The index case had a religious exemption.
- One hundred forty cases of measles in the United States, where it had once been eradicated.
- Pennsylvania had seven cases of *Hemophilus influenza* and three deaths

in an eight-month period, two in denominations strongly opposed to medical treatment. The Hib vaccine, introduced in 1985, had reduced the incidence of this disease by 99 percent and had reduced the deaths to ten a year for the entire country.

• Mississippi, one of only two states that don't allow religious exemptions (the other is West Virginia), was the state with the lowest incidence of pertussis.

The majority of recent outbreaks have been in religious communities. In 2013, a member of a megachurch, Eagle Mountain Church in Newark, Texas, returned from a trip to Indonesia with measles and transmitted it to twenty-one people. Almost all the victims had refused vaccination because the church's founder had spoken out against vaccines and encouraged faith over medicine. The church quickly organized vaccination clinics, but the pastor gave a decidedly unscientific mixed message: "So I'm going to tell you what the facts are, and the facts are the facts, but then we know the truth. That always overcomes facts."[26]

Other Religious Exemptions

The revised 2011 law in Oregon eliminated religious beliefs as a legal defense for crimes against children, but it didn't eliminate religious shields for caregivers of dependent adults. And it didn't eliminate religious exemptions for immunizations, metabolic screening of newborns (for inherited diseases like phenylketonuria or PKU), newborn screening for hearing problems, vitamin K and prophylactic eye drops at birth, and bicycle helmets. Bicycle helmets? When I heard that, I wondered where in the Bible it says "Thou shalt not wear bicycle helmets." I have read the entire Bible and don't remember anything in it that suggests it is sinful to take reasonable precautions to prevent injury. I was relieved to learn that the exemption is probably intended for the benefit of Sikhs, whose religion requires them to wear turbans, and possibly for certain Orthodox Jews who are required to wear special headgear. Apparently wearing symbols of their religion is more important to them than the fact that serious head injury is five times more likely for those wearing a turban than a helmet.

A major public health effort is focused on screening newborns for conditions that may not be otherwise detected until irreversible damage has been done. The number and type of tests depends on the jurisdiction. The first test to be mandated was a blood test for phenylketonuria (PKU), a hereditary metabolic disorder where the inability to process the amino acid phenylalanine causes mental retardation unless the child is put on a phenylalanine-restricted diet early in life. The test is done by putting a drop of blood from a simple heel stick on filter paper. After it dries it can be easily mailed to a lab for analysis.

With time, other blood tests were added for fatty-acid-oxidation disorders, thyroid and adrenal disease, sickle-cell disease, organic acidemias, cystic fibrosis, urea-cycle disorders, and lysosomal-storage disorders. Newborns can also be screened for hearing loss with a bedside test, and for congenital heart defects with pulse oximetry (that's like the little clip they put on your finger in the ER to monitor your blood oxygen level). Other conditions that are also screened for in some locales include severe combined immunodeficiency and Duchenne's muscular dystrophy. And other tests are being considered for future additions to the list.

Four states prohibit parents from opting out of the testing: Nebraska, South Dakota, Michigan, and Montana. That has led to lawsuits arguing that religious exemptions should be allowed. Why would anyone object to screening an infant for these devastating but treatable diseases? Scientologists advocate silent birth (also called quiet birth). No one should speak during the birth process, no one should talk to the baby for the first week of life, and nothing should be done to cause the baby any discomfort (like drawing blood). They believe that words heard during that time or stressful conditions can create "engrams," detailed recordings in the memory that create life problems and psychosomatic illnesses later in life and must be erased by expensive Scientology "auditings" with an E-meter.

Some religions believe that the Bible prohibits any drawing of blood. Sometimes they rely on Bible verses like "Whoever sheds the blood of man, by man shall his blood be shed; for in the image of God has God made man" (Genesis 9:6). And some go by the statement in Leviticus that "the life of the flesh is in the blood," interpreting it to mean that removing blood will shorten life.

Criminal defendant Gregory Michael Zimmerman cited these verses when he refused to give a blood sample to law enforcement for DNA analysis. The United States Court of Appeals confirmed his right to refuse on religious grounds. Authorities managed to get his DNA anyway: they collected a sample by a cheek swab.

Other Medical Harms from Religion

For a long time, the pain of childbirth was seen as women's punishment for Eve's disobedience; and it was considered immoral to do anything to relieve the pain of divine punishment. Queen Victoria set an example by having Dr. John Snow administer chloroform for the delivery of her eighth and ninth babies. The social elite in London soon followed suit, and pain relief for childbirth was gradually accepted as the norm.

A substantial number of Jehovah's Witnesses have died because they refused lifesaving transfusions. One teenage Jehovah's Witness in Portugal refused surgery for a tumor on his lip because he feared it would necessitate transfusions; for thirty-seven years the tumor grew and grew until it was fifteen inches long, weighed twelve pounds, and obscured his face.[27] Often when the courts order transfusions the Jehovah's Witnesses are relieved because they won't have to take responsibility for letting their child die, an outcome that they do not want.

Scientology has been responsible for a number of deaths, especially in its Narconon programs for addicts. Patients have been taken off needed medication and have died when they were denied medical care for illnesses like cancer, a burst appendix, and epilepsy. Lisa McPherson died severely dehydrated, bruised, and underweight from Scientology attempts to treat her psychosis with an abusive "purification rundown." Several other Scientologists with psychiatric illnesses are known to have committed suicide or murder.[28]

The sexual abuse of children by Catholic priests has been prominent in the news, and the church hierarchy has been implicated in covering it up. There is an online database of publicly accused (not necessarily sued or convicted) priests by diocese in the United States.[29] Ninety-one are listed for Portland, Oregon, thirty-four for Seattle, sixty-five for New York City, two hundred forty-five for Boston, two hundred sixty-five for Los Angeles, forty for Miami, and so on. An Oklahoma pastor called for a similar database for the Southern Baptist Convention, but it was rejected as "unfeasible." Clerics of almost every religion have been accused of sexual abuse, including Mormons and Hasidic Jews. An imam in an Iowa mosque was charged with sexual abuse and argued that the charges "violated his religious freedom." Rapists are more religious than average; religious patriarchal attitudes and the sexual repression due to a religious view of sex as sinful have been cited as possible contributing factors to sex crimes.

Homosexuality is considered a sin by many religions. Conversion therapy attempts to change homosexuals into heterosexuals. They try to "pray the gay away." They also use aversive behavioral modification with nausea-inducing drugs and electrical shocks to the genitals. Gays are tortured for a natural trait that they were born with and can't control, and the treatment doesn't work. I read one account of a young man whose abusive parents had brainwashed him into believing that he was the only homosexual in America, and he was amazed when he met another one in college. California and New Jersey recently passed laws prohibiting therapy aimed at changing the sexual orientation of minors. The California law has been legally challenged and was upheld by a federal appeals court.

Religion has a bad attitude about sex in general. Religious parents continue to reject the HPV vaccine for their daughters on the grounds that it will encourage premarital sex, even though we now have evidence that vaccine recipients are not more sexually active. Religious parents have fought sex education in the schools, arguing that it will encourage premarital sex and promiscuity. They have pushed for "abstinence only" education even after it has been proven not to work.

Abortion is considered a sin, the murder of a fetus that has full rights of personhood because God breathes a soul into the embryo at the moment of conception. Monty Python famously lampooned this reasoning by taking it one step further back, with the song "Every Sperm Is Sacred." Religious lobbyists have been responsible for the passage of antiabortion laws. Those laws no more eliminate abortions than Prohibition eliminated alcohol. They only make women resort to illegal back-alley abortions that are often botched and that kill women. The Catholic Church not only prohibits abortion, it prohibits the use of condoms, birth-control pills, or any form of birth control except the rhythm method. There's a name for people who use the rhythm method: parents. It's ironic that 82 percent of American Catholics think birth control is okay and have decided not to follow the dictates of their church. And it's ironic that Christians have disregarded the Golden Rule and the Ten Commandments to the extent of bombing abortion clinics and killing abortion doctors in the name of their religion. What ever happened to "turning the other cheek"?

Catholics prohibit abortions for any reason, including rape and threat to the mother's life. The Catholic policy was the law in Ireland until 2013, when Ireland finally passed a Protection of Life during Pregnancy Law that legalized termination of pregnancy when it threatens the life of the mother. The new law was a response to the 2012 death of Savita Halappanavar, an Indian woman whose death in a Galway hospital was widely publicized. There was an international public outcry, complete with rallies and protests; the United Nations even got involved. Savita was a thirty-one-year-old dentist who was admitted to the hospital because she was miscarrying in the seventeenth week of pregnancy. She requested an abortion. She developed septicemia (blood poisoning); but doctors were required by law to put the temporary welfare of the fetus first, even though they knew its imminent death was inevitable. They were legally required to refuse an abortion. She died in the hospital after a week of suffering. At least something good came out of her tragedy: the new law will prevent others from dying like she did.[30]

In the United States, hospitals that have merged with Catholic hospitals are required to follow Catholic policies. Patients may not be aware of this, and they may not have a choice of hospitals. The ACLU is suing the United States Conference of Catholic Bishops on behalf of Tamesha Means. In 2010, when her waters broke after eighteen weeks of pregnancy, she went to the only hospital in her county, a Catholic hospital. She was told by the hospital staff that there was nothing they could do, and twice they sent her home in severe pain. By her third visit she had developed an infection, yet they tried to send her home again. While discharge paperwork was being filled out, she began to deliver; and then she finally got proper care. The standard of care in a non-Catholic hospital would have required providers to tell her there was virtually no chance the fetus could survive, and that a therapeutic abortion would relieve her pain and protect her health. Catholic hospitals are required to adhere to directives that prohibit termination of pregnancy even when there is no chance the fetus will survive and when the mother's life or health are at risk; in fact, health providers are explicitly prohibited from informing patients about alternative options.[31]

Many Christians consider masturbation a "grave moral disorder." Those who succumb to the temptation are made to feel guilty and fear punishment by God—for indulging in a behavior that is merely a harmless way of relieving sexual tension. Masturbation is not only harmless but is perfectly natural: a large range of animal species have been observed to masturbate and even to use objects as tools to help them do so. Some base their objections on the Bible verse about Onan spilling his seed on the ground. Others object because they believe any kind of sexual activity other than conventional missionary-position intercourse between a man and a woman who are married to each other is wrong. Some even hold that any kind of sexual activity in married couples that is not intended for procreation is wrong.

Mother Teresa opened 517 missions for the poor and sick in more than a hundred countries. Her selfless devotion to the poor was applauded as a model of Christian charity and she is a candidate for sainthood, but recently her accomplishments and motives have come into question. Doctors who visited her missions in Calcutta found that two-thirds of the patients had come hoping to find a doctor to treat them, and patients were dying with only custodial care. There was a lack of hygiene, inadequate food, no medical care, and no painkillers. Mother Teresa was more interested in saving souls by converting patients to Catholicism than in relieving suffering. She saw beauty in resignation and suffering, and she imposed her views on the dying poor. But when she herself required palliative care, she got it in a modern American hospital. She could have done far more for the poor of overpopulated India if she had provided birth control instead of warehouses for the dying.

The Pope has slightly softened his stance on condoms (now he says they are acceptable, but for male prostitutes only, as a first step to becoming more morally responsible). But it's too little, too late: the Catholic Church's anti-condom policy has clearly contributed to the spread of AIDS in Africa and elsewhere. It has also contributed to overpopulation, with all the ills that brings.

Christian activists have interfered with human embryonic stem cell research on the grounds that it destroys a human embryo, made in the image of God and endowed with a soul, and that it encourages abortions. The Jewish approach is less restrictive. Rabbi Levi Yitschak Halperin explained, "As long as it has not been implanted in the womb . . . it does not have the status of an embryo at all and there is no prohibition to destroy it."[32] Anyway, embryonic stem cell research only uses extra embryos that are leftover from the *in vitro* fertilization (IVF) process and were eventually going to be discarded. Wouldn't it be better to use them for research than to throw them in the trash?

Stem cell research has the potential to revolutionize the treatment of disease. Treatments based on stem cells are already prolonging lives and curing some diseases. Bone marrow transplants are curing leukemia, severe aplastic anemia, lymphomas, multiple myeloma, immune deficiency disorders, and some solid-tumor cancers. We may eventually be able to use stem cells to create made-to-order replacements for damaged organs and to test new drugs. Belief-based arguments pale beside the untold good that might come from stem cell research.

Christian Con Artists

Con men have bilked people of millions in the name of religious healing. There is a long tradition of public faith healings in America, depicted in the novel *Elmer Gantry* and epitomized by the modern examples of Peter Popoff, Benny Hinn, and others. These "healers" don't go into hospitals where the sick are found; they typically perform before large paying audiences. They call audience members to the stage, touch them, and claim to heal them by their special ability to invoke the healing power of God. They claim healing miracles and can produce any number of testimonials from grateful patients, and Benny Hinn even claims to have raised a man from the dead during one of his services. But it's more likely that these "faith healers" have never actually healed so much as a scratch.

In the 1970s, Dr. William Nolen searched the world for faith-healing miracles and couldn't find a single one. He discovered that faith healers could harm instead of heal. He attended a service conducted by Kathryn Kuhlman where he saw a woman with cancer of the spine discard her brace and follow Kuhlman's enthusiastic command to run across the stage; the woman's backbone collapsed the following day, and she died after four months of unnecessary pain and disability. Nolen described his fruitless search in the book *Healing: A Doctor in Search of a Miracle*.[33] A more recent comprehensive book on the subject is James Randi's *The Faith Healers*,[34] in which he reveals the use of deception and fraud by evangelical healers.

Benny Hinn is a prototypical faith healer. The workings of his deception have been revealed in detail,[35] shedding light on how faith-healing con artists fool their audiences. Hinn carries out faith-healing crusades mainly to obtain new names for a mailing list; most of his income is from mail-order business in books, tapes, and so on. He solicits monthly donations, bequests, and other contributions. He pretends to have a direct line to God, saying "God told me" and pausing as if to listen to a divine voice and then saying "Yes, okay, thank you, Sir." He speaks in tongues, but it's just an act: the gibberish is unrelated to any known language and linguistic analysis shows that speaking in tongues doesn't have the characteristics expected of an unknown language either.[36]

Faith healers pretend to make people fall down by touching or blowing on them. It is actually a trained response in people who know what is "supposed" to happen; and if they don't cooperate and fall, assistants give them a little push behind the knees or pull them backward to help them fall. They offer celebrity testimonials: Benny Hinn claims to have healed heavyweight champion Evander Holyfield's heart problems, but Holyfield didn't have a heart problem. They hire enablers, actors trained to present themselves as someone who was cured. They provide wheelchairs and invite people to sit in them; and when those people get up out of the wheelchairs and walk, the audience is fooled into assuming they couldn't walk before.

They gather information on audience members in various ways and pretend to have obtained the information from God (W. V. Grant was exposed when his crib sheets were found in the trash). They signal assistants with a code word when a new "revelation" is required. Peter Popoff's wife, backstage, sent him information via a miniature receiver in his ear; the trick was exposed on national television by James Randi, who revealed the scam on *The Tonight Show Starring Johnny Carson*,[37] playing recordings of her transmissions over a video of Popoff's performance. Popoff confessed to trickery and declared bankruptcy in 1987 but quickly was back in business, raking in $23 million dollars a year by 2005.

They can always fall back on cold-reading techniques. Using the "shotgun" technique, they may simply announce that people in the audience are being healed from a certain disease without specifying who. They use carnival tricks like pretending to have made a leg longer through a positioning illusion. They pretend to heal the "blind" in people who actually have limited sight. And when all else fails, they put the blame on the victim, saying he or she didn't have enough faith.

The harm that these criminals do is immeasurable. They interfere with proper treatment, even encouraging people to discard essential medicines by throwing them onto the stage. They deprive poor people of money they need for other things. They offer false hope to the sick and devastating disappointment and guilt for "not being worthy" and "not believing enough" when victims realize they have not really been cured.

A healer in Brazil, John of God, combines Christianity with psychic surgery. He inserts forceps deeply into a patient's nose, amazing the ignorant but reminding those in the know of the "human blockhead" side-show demonstration. It's not even a trick: there is a normal passage straight back through the nose to the nasopharynx. He offers a choice of "visible" or "invisible" surgery, says he is merely an instrument in God's hands, and claims to have absolutely no recollection of anything during the procedures. One unfortunate woman interviewed on a TV documentary had a growing, untreated breast tumor that she knew was killing her, but she said John of God's treatment had "healed" her in the sense that it had helped her come to terms with her fate. That perverts the medical meaning of healing. Had she not travelled to Brazil and had faith in John of God, surgery could have really healed her and kept her alive.

Religious Child Training

Corporal punishment of children is rapidly losing acceptance in modern society. It is illegal in Delaware and in thirty-four foreign countries. Not only is it cruel, but scientific studies have shown that it is ineffective. It results in increased child aggression and antisocial behavior, and the only thing it accomplishes is to force immediate compliance. The issue got public attention recently when a seven-minute video of a Texas judge giving his sixteen-year-old daughter a prolonged beating went viral on the Internet.[38] When interviewed, the judge responded that he had done nothing wrong, and that he had apologized for losing his temper. That incident was not motivated by religion, but it sparked national outrage and prompted a reconsideration of corporal punishment.

Conservative Christians say corporal punishment is called for in the Bible: God wants us to beat our children. A 1994 book, *To Train Up a Child* by Michael and Debi Pearl, has sold over 670,000 copies and is popular among Christian home schoolers and widely praised in Christian publications.[39] The book is given out in churches and sent free to military families. The Pearls' book and related products bring them $1.7 million a year.

They advocate pulling a nursing infant's hair when he bites the breast, using a switch from as early as six months, and using a quarter-inch flexible plastic plumbing tube to spank children because it can be rolled up and carried in a pocket and is too light to damage muscle or bone. They say "a little fasting is good training," and they recommend hosing off children outdoors in cold weather after potty-training accidents, telling the child he's too dirty to be cleaned indoors. They recommend spanking a child as young as three until he is "totally broken":

> If you have to sit on him to spank him, then do not hesitate. And hold him there until he has surrendered. Prove that you are bigger, tougher, more patiently enduring, and are unmoved by his wailing. Hold the resisting child in a helpless position for several minutes, or until he is totally surrendered. Accept no conditions for surrender—no compromise. You are to rule over him as a benevolent sovereign. Your word is final.

At the same time, they say the parents must not act out of anger. I question whether many parents could administer that kind of punishment without being angry.

They advocate training children as if they were dogs. The book is filled with derogatory language toward children, epithets like "spoiled brats" and references to a child's "unbridled lust" and "terrorist tactics." They make it clear that the husband is in command over wife and children. They express paranoia about the New World Order, which wants to make your child "wait his turn in line for condoms, a government funded abortion, sexually transmitted disease treatment, psychological evaluation and a mark on the forehead." They say homeschooling is the only option. Their bias on gender roles is clear:

> Gender role distinction is demeaned in modern education. Don't let a coven of Sodomites and socialists, hiding behind the badge of professional psy-

chologists, reprogram your natural feelings on male and female distinctive-
ness. A boy needs a man's example if he is expected to grow up to be a man.

This is not child training: it's child abuse and systematic torture. One
reviewer said the book should have been titled "How to kill your child or make
them wish they were dead."[40] A *Psychology Today* article suggested using the
Pearls' methods on the parents until they stop attempting to pass off their
destructive torture as good parenting.[41] Some conservative Christian parents
reject the Pearls' teachings and have started a petition asking booksellers not
to stock the book. A Christian bookselling chain in the United Kingdom pulled
the book from its shelves and apologized to a reader for selling it. But the
book is now available for free download on the Internet, and it continues to be
wildly popular in many Christian and homeschooling circles.

The Pearls' book has been blamed for the deaths of at least three children
whose parents carried out its advice with too much enthusiasm.

(1) Larry and Carri Williams, in Sedro-Wooley, Washington, were homeschooling their nine children, two of them adopted from Ethiopia. In 2011 the
mother found the adopted girl, Hana, age thirteen, unconscious in the backyard,
naked, face down, and with mud in her mouth. She called 911 to say Hana was
being "rebellious" and would not cooperate and come back into the house. Hana
was pronounced dead at the hospital an hour later from hypothermia complicated by malnutrition and gastritis. She weighed only seventy-six pounds.

The parents had become increasingly fundamentalist: the father would
give sermons in the backyard and the mother would only wear dresses and
didn't believe women should wear swimsuits or vote. They subscribed wholeheartedly to Pearl's system of childrearing. They had kept Hana in a closet,
deprived her of meals for days at a time, whipped her, shaved her head, and
made her shower outside with a hose. The night she died, they had punished
her by locking her out of the house in rainy, forty-degree weather; they had
watched out the window and laughed at her as she staggered and fell. The other
children, interviewed after her death, said she was possessed by demons and
people like her went to the fires of hell. The parents were convicted of homicide and sentenced, Larry to twenty-eight years and Carri to thirty-seven.[42]

(2) Lydia Schatz, a Liberian adoptee, died at age seven in California. Her
parents followed Pearl's book but ignored its admonition against extended

lashing. They whipped her for hours at a time. They literally beat her to death: she died of severe tissue damage, and her older sister had to be hospitalized. The father was found guilty of second-degree murder and torture; the mother was convicted of voluntary manslaughter and unlawful corporal punishment.[43]

(3) Lynn Paddock was convicted in North Carolina in 2006 for the first-degree murder of her son Sean. He suffocated after being wrapped tightly in a blanket. His siblings testified that they were beaten daily with a plumbing tube.[44]

Conclusion

I have focused on the health effects of Christianity because this is a book about Christianity, but practically every religion has adverse effects on health. Just one recent example from Judaism: eleven infants in New York City contracted herpes from infected mohels who applied oral suction to the penis during an ultra-Orthodox religious circumcision ritual called *metzitzah b'peh*.[45] Two infants died; others suffered brain damage. Christianity may not be more hazardous to your health than other religions, but it certainly isn't less hazardous.

I don't want to leave the impression that all the health effects of Christianity (or religion in general) are harmful. Religion provides comfort, community, and tradition to many people. It can promote healthy lifestyles (Seventh-Day Adventists are vegetarians who avoid alcohol and tobacco; Mormons avoid coffee, tea, alcohol, tobacco, and illegal drugs). Christian missions and charities do a lot to relieve suffering around the world. The abuses I have described are atypical, and perhaps the saddest part of all of this is that the things that are hazardous to health are not an integral requirement of Christianity. There isn't any reason Christianity couldn't coexist with rational healthcare and good science; and in some Protestant denominations it does. But the evidence is clear: Christianity has done (and is still doing) more harm than good to individual and public health because of religious beliefs that are based on faith, not reality.

14

CHRISTIANITY AND THE ENVIRONMENT

William R. Patterson

Christianity has done a lot of harm in the world and continues to do so.[1] War, witch hunts, assassinations of abortion doctors, slavery, the oppression of women, recriminations and violence against gays, the list goes on. Yet often overlooked is the damage that adherence to Christian dogma has had, and continues to have, on the environment. Environmental damage has the potential to severely degrade the quality of human life, and can in fact be life-threatening. Some of this damage may inflict consequences over generations rather than merely in specific instances of time. There are many environmental challenges that Christian dogmas have negatively impacted by preventing or slowing down their remediation. Excessive population growth ("be fruitful and multiply," Gen 1:28) and the loss of biodiversity through animal extinction and deforestation (seen as the natural outcomes of humankind's dominion over the earth) are only a few examples. John Loftus's chapter in this book on Christianity's effect on the treatment of animals powerfully exposes another. As it would be impossible to sufficiently cover in one chapter all of the environmental issues on which Christianity has a negative influence, I will focus here on the most important—global climate change.

Climate change represents one of the greatest challenges currently facing human beings. It has the potential to radically alter the environment and cause irreparable damage to the planet on which we live. Insofar as Christianity impedes dealing appropriately with this issue, it is not hyperbolic to say that the religion represents a great threat not only to the current generation of human beings but to all future generations as well. This chapter will detail how Christianity has hindered a response to this impending catastrophe and does therefore pose such a threat. Though climate change is being focused on, many of the arguments used by Christians regarding this issue are equally applicable to other environmental issues. It will take little imagination to see how the discussion here applies to a broader range of environmental problems.

The Facts about Climate Change

Before getting too far along into the discussion about how Christianity has impacted our response to climate change (also referred to interchangeably as global warming), it is necessary to get a good grasp of the problem. Here I will provide a brief overview of the science of climate change's causes and impacts so as to make clear the full extent of the problem.

The IPCC (Intergovernmental Panel on Climate Change) defines climate change as "a change in the state of the climate that can be identified (e.g. using statistical tests) by changes in the mean and/or the variability of its properties, and that persists for an extended period, typically decades or longer."[2] This is most apparent in the global rise in temperature observed during the past 150 years. In 2007, the IPCC concluded that "warming of the climate system is unequivocal, as is now evident from observations of increases in global average air and ocean temperatures, widespread melting of snow and ice and rising global average sea level."[3] While it has been conclusively established that global temperatures are indeed on the rise, the fact that human beings are the leading cause of it has also been established with increasing levels of certitude.

The IPCC first reached the conclusion that climate change is in considerable part anthropogenic (human caused) in its 1995 report. Since that time, the strength of that conclusion has increased significantly. In its latest report, issued in 2013, the IPCC states that it is 95 percent confident that human beings are the primary cause of global warming.[4] It also states that "it is now *very likely* that human influence has contributed to observed global scale changes in the frequency and intensity of daily temperature extremes since the mid-20th century, and *likely* that human influence has more than doubled the probability of occurrence of heat waves in some locations."[5]

This is the result of the emission of greenhouse gases, such as carbon dioxide (CO_2), nitrous oxide, and methane into the atmosphere. These gases, once released into the atmosphere, remain trapped there and act to reflect heat back toward the earth that otherwise would have been reflected into outer space by the earth's surface. These gases exist naturally and the greenhouse effect is also a natural one. Since the onset of the industrial revolution, however, these gases have been pumped into the atmosphere at an unprecedented rate, thereby resulting in an enhanced greenhouse effect.[6] According to the IPCC, "The atmospheric concentrations of carbon dioxide, methane, and nitrous oxide have increased to levels unprecedented in at least the last 800,000 years. Carbon dioxide concentrations have increased by 40 percent since preindustrial times, primarily from fossil fuel emissions and secondarily from net land use change emissions. The ocean has absorbed about 30 percent of the emitted anthropogenic carbon dioxide, causing ocean acidification."[7] Ocean acidification, a reduction in pH due to the absorption of CO_2, has negative impacts on oceanic ecosystems.

The IPCC, an intergovernmental panel of climate scientists from all over the world, was first instituted in 1988 by the World Meteorological Organization and the United Nations Environment Programme, two subsidiary organizations of the United Nations. The panel does not conduct original research but rather synthesizes the sum total of climate-related research and analyzes it. This allows for the development of a consensus position based upon the best available science as reviewed by the most eminent climatologists from around the globe. Yet it is not only the IPCC that has reached the conclusion that global warming is happening and that it is primarily driven by human beings. All of the most prominent relevant scientific organizations in the United States have reached the same conclusions. These include the US National Academy of Sciences, American Association for the Advancement of Science, American Chemical Society, American Geophysical Union, American Meteorological Society, American Physical Society, and the Geological Society of America. This consensus is also reflected in the peer-reviewed literature. In an analysis of abstracts from 928 articles published in scientific journals between the years 1993 and 2003, researcher Naomi Oreskes found that none of them contradicted the position that global warming is happening and is mostly driven by human activities.[8]

In addition to the fact that global warming is happening, and that human beings are a significant contributor to it, scientists also agree on many of the impacts that climate change has had, is having right now, and will likely have in the future. The global harms brought about by climate change include, but are not limited to: sea level rise; increased strength of extreme weather events such as hurricanes; droughts; increased spread of certain diseases such as malaria, cholera, and yellow fever in vulnerable parts of the world; famines brought about by agricultural disruption and increased food prices; loss of biodiversity as ecosystems are disrupted and extinctions accelerated (it is estimated that a quarter of all plants and animals currently living will either be extinct or in danger of extinction during the next half century due to climate change[9]); increased risk of large forest fires; economic disruption and loss of productivity; and conflict brought about by the increased scarcity of resources, such as potable water.

Some of these outcomes have already begun to occur. The twelve warmest years on record have all occurred in the past fifteen years. The warmest year on record was 2010.[10] The year 2013 was the fourth warmest year on record and the temperature in the month of November of that year was the highest ever recorded for that month.[11] Climate models vary concerning the expected increase in temperature attendant with a doubling of atmospheric CO_2 ranging from 1.5 to 5 degrees Celsius. Recent research published in the journal *Nature*, however, explains this variation as a result of atmospheric convective mixing and sets the lower threshold at 3 degrees.[12] The warming that has already occurred has had noticeable and measurable impacts. A majority of the world's glaciers are melting, the average annual temperature in the Arctic has risen by five degrees Fahrenheit since 1945, the earth's area of permafrost (permanently frozen land) has been reduced by 30 percent over the past century, and even the ranges of migratory plants and animals have shifted toward the poles by an average of 3.7 miles per decade.[13]

Sea ice in the Arctic is melting at such a rate that new shipping lanes and access to seabeds may emerge. This has resulted in disputes between various states (such as Russia and Canada) over rights there.[14] Russia has even taken the step of expanding its military presence in the Arctic to protect its interests and to ensure its ability to exploit newly emerging shipping and mining possibilities. According to the World Meteorological Organization, "Since the beginning of satellite measurements, the decade 2001–2010 has seen the greatest average annual melting of Arctic sea ice on record and all seven of the lowest Arctic sea ice extents have occurred in the last seven years, since 2007. September Arctic sea ice extent is decreasing at an average rate of 13.7 percent per decade."

Sea level rise is another major effect of increased temperature. The IPCC notes that "the rate of sea level rise since the mid-19th century has been larger than the mean rate during the previous two millennia (high confidence). Over the period 1901 to 2010, global mean sea level rose by 0.19m."[15] In some cases this rise in sea level has threatened the very existence of small islands. This increase will continue into the distant future. "It is *virtually certain* that global mean sea level rise will continue beyond 2100, with sea level rise due to thermal expansion to continue for many centuries."[16] This will threaten major coastal areas and ports throughout the world.

Increased frequency and intensity of forest fires is another predicted outcome of global warming. Speaking of the western part of North America, the IPCC foresaw in 2007 that "disturbances from pests, diseases and fire are projected to have increasing impacts on forests, with an extended period of high fire risk and large increases in area burned."[17] Unfortunately this proved prescient, as forest fires of unprecedented size and frequency have since occurred in Colorado, California, and other western states. The Black Forest Fire near Colorado Springs, CO, burned 5,780 hectares of land and destroyed 500 homes in June 2013. This was the most destructive fire in Colorado history, the second most destructive was the Waldo Canyon Fire, which occurred only the year before.

The effects of global warming have been seen by scholars and military professionals alike as posing a national security threat to the United States. Scholar Joshua Busby, writing in the journal *Security Studies*, argues that "climate change likely poses a national security risk for the United States and its overseas interests, particularly from extreme weather events that may directly affect the U.S. homeland and countries of strategic concern."[18] His concerns were recently echoed by Admiral Samuel J. Locklear III, who is in charge of US forces in the Pacific. He said during an interview that "[climate change] is probably the most likely thing that is going to happen . . . that will cripple the security environment, probably more likely than the other scenarios we all often talk about." Coming from a military leader in a region that includes North Korea and China, that is a strong statement indeed. He additionally remarked, "You have the real potential here in the not-too-distant future of nations displaced by rising sea level. Certainly weather patterns are more severe than they have been in the past. We are on super typhoon 27 or 28 this year in the Western Pacific. The average is about 17."[19]

The damage caused by global warming has been and will continue to be substantial, and it is therefore imperative that the United States (the second largest emitter of carbon dioxide in the world, behind only China) takes concrete steps, along with the rest of the world, to reduce emissions. According to the IPCC, "Continued emissions of greenhouse gases will cause further warming and changes in all components of the climate system. Limiting climate change will require substantial and sustained reductions of greenhouse gas emissions."[20] It also points out that once climate change has occurred it is essentially irreversible on a timescale of hundreds of years or possibly even millennia.[21] These facts make addressing the issue an urgent one. Continued emissions will exacerbate the effects brought about by climate change, and those effects that do materialize will have an impact far into the future. Anything that impedes effective action in the face of these impending dangers is itself harmful and is a threat to human and animal well-being. Christianity is doing just that.

Christianity and Climate Change

Despite the massive consensus about climate change that has developed throughout the scientific community, the public, the media, and politicians have been slower to accept it. Public opinion polling consistently shows that a misunderstanding of the issue is widespread among American citizens. This is largely the result of a concerted campaign of denial led primarily by economic-conservative activists and a handful of scientists in their employ, people whom Naomi Oreskes and Erik Conway refer to as "merchants of doubt" in their book by the same name.[22] Though there is more doubt over the issue within the general public than there is in the scientific community, Christians, especially evangelical Christians, are even more unduly skeptical. Several studies bear this out.

A 2007 study conducted by the Barna Group, for example, found that

"51% of born again Christians consider global warming a major problem, as opposed to 62% of those of other faiths and 69% of atheists and agnostics. Only 33% of evangelical Christians see global warming as a major problem, thereby making them the least likely among fifty population groups studied to view the problem as serious. Atheists and agnostics were the most concerned."[23] Another study by the same organization a year later found that the difference had become even more pronounced when it comes to evangelical Christians, with only 27 percent believing firmly that global warming is even happening; 65 percent of evangelicals also believe that the media is overexaggerating the problem and 62 percent believe that climate change, if it's happening, is not caused by human beings.[24] Church-going Christians of almost all types are significantly less likely than is the general public to accept that global warming is happening. Only 36 percent of church-going Catholics, 36 percent of nonmainline Protestants, and 45 percent of mainline Protestants say that they are very sure that climate change is occurring.[25]

Research carried out by N. Smith and A. Leiserowitz found that "compared to non-evangelicals, American evangelicals are less likely to believe global warming is happening, less likely to believe human activity is the cause, less worried about global warming and less likely to believe that most scientists think global warming is happening."[26] Evangelicals are also less likely to believe that global warming will seriously harm them personally or their families. Similarly they are less likely to believe that global warming will harm nonhuman nature, future generations, or people throughout either the developed or developing world.[27] They are also significantly less likely to support political policies designed to mitigate the harmful effects of global warming.[28] In addition to the laity, a high level of doubt is also expressed by Christian leaders. According to an October 2012 survey conducted by LifeWay Research, less than half (43 percent) of Protestant pastors believe that global warming is real and human-made while 54 percent disagree.[29]

The most probable explanation for this divergence between Christians, especially church-going and evangelical Christians, and the rest of American society is Christian dogma itself. There are several aspects of Christianity that allow its followers to discount the importance, or existence, of climate change. One of these is the idea of dominionism. Some Christians interpret the Book of Genesis to mean that God has granted dominion over the earth and all of its

nonhuman inhabitants to humankind. The passage cited in support of this interpretation is Genesis 1:28, which, in the King James translation, reads, "And God
blessed them, and God said unto them, Be fruitful, and multiply, and replenish
the earth, and subdue it: and have dominion over the fish of the sea, and over
the fowl of the air, and over every living thing that moveth upon the earth." The
earth is God's gift to humankind to use as it pleases to meet its own needs and
to prosper; it is to be subdued. As Steven Deaton, who runs the blog *Implanted
Word*, puts it, "It is time for Christians to accept God's truth and teach it to their
children: God has given us this planet and everything in it to use for our benefit
and the exercise of such is not going to harm this world."[30]

Melinda Christian, writing in the Christian magazine *Answers*, gives a
similar view. She writes, "God did not create human beings merely to serve or
'preserve' the earth. Rather, He made us in His image, as His highest creation,
and He gave us the privilege and duty to glorify Him in everything we do,
including managing the earth to make it more beautiful and productive. Just
as God 'planted a garden,' we want to be good gardeners, too."[31] Former US
senator Rick Santorum reflected this sentiment when he said, "We were put
on this Earth as creatures of God to have dominion over the Earth, to use it
wisely and steward it wisely, but for our benefit not for the Earth's benefit."[32]
There seems to be no recognition in his statement that the earth's benefit and
human benefit are related.

Though some Christians view the biblical injunction to act as environmental stewards in a positive way, others, such as Melinda Christian and Rick
Santorum, view modern industry, and its environmental impacts, as "gar-
dening." To those who take this view, climate change is nothing more than
the result of humankind using its God-given authority to transform the earth
for its own purposes. According to scholar Brian McCammack, "Conservative evangelical environmentalists see carbon dioxide emissions as actually
fulfilling both the subdue-and-rule and be-fruitful-and-multiply commands
of dominion, turning wilderness into the garden and transforming previously
unfarmable areas into regions hospitable to plant growth."[33] From this warped
and harmful perspective, global warming is fulfilling God's mandate and is
therefore a positive rather than a negative phenomenon. This is despite the fact
that scientists agree that the negative repercussions of these changes will be
far more severe than any positive side effects.

But this leads us to another reason that Christians can easily dismiss climate change. They believe that widespread negative impacts are impossible in principle because God's creation is perfect. Regardless of the science, then, Christians know, or think they know, a priori that global warming cannot harm us. According to the Cornwall Alliance, a Christian organization at the forefront of denying the need to take action against global warming, "The earth, and with it all the cosmos, reveals its Creator's wisdom and is sustained and governed by His power and lovingkindness."[34] This belief leads the organization to further declare, "We believe Earth and its ecosystems—created by God's intelligent design and infinite power and sustained by His faithful providence—are robust, resilient, self-regulating, and self-correcting, admirably suited for human flourishing, and displaying His glory. Earth's climate system is no exception. Recent global warming is one of many natural cycles of warming and cooling geologic history."[35]

These Christians begin from the assumption that it's simply not *possible* that global warming is deleterious to human welfare. According to an article authored by scholars J. Arjan Wardekker, Arthur C. Petersen, and Jeroen P. van der Sluijs, from one Christian outlook "mankind is viewed as a 'co-creator' and human development and population growth are considered a blessing and mission, rather than a threat. God would not have created nature so fragile that mankind could easily destroy it, and God would not have intended healthy nature and human development to be incompatible."[36]

This is also supported by passages in Ecclesiastes. Deaton points out in his blog that "Solomon said, 'One generation passes away, and another generation comes; but the earth abides forever' (Eccl. 1:4). He then notes the rising and setting of the sun, the circuit of the wind, and the water cycle (Eccl. 1:5–7). His point is that men do not change the way the world works; man's presence on the earth is not a disruption to the earth."[37] Another line of support for this view comes from the story of Noah. Deaton argues, "When Noah left the ark, the Lord said, 'While the earth remains, seedtime and harvest, cold and heat, winter and summer, and day and night shall not cease' (Gen. 8:22). Unless you are willing to deny God's explicit word, you must accept that mankind, no matter what it does, is not going to cause GW/CC [global warming/climate change]. It is not possible."[38] From this perspective, believing that global warming exists and will have harmful effects is blasphemous. Such a claim challenges God's power and makes him a liar.

These are not merely the thoughts of some within the fringe elements. They have been espoused by people of significant influence. Right-wing radio host Rush Limbaugh recently opined, "If you believe in God, then intellectually you cannot believe in man-made global warming. You must be agnostic or atheistic to believe that man controls something he can't create. It's always been one of the reasons for my anti man-made global warming stance."[39] Even worse, these sentiments have been expressed by actual US congressmen. Representative John Shimkus of Illinois, for example, made the following statement, "I believe [the Bible] is the infallible word of God, and that's the way it is going to be for his creation. . . . The earth will end only when God declares its time to be over. Man will not destroy the earth. This earth will not be destroyed by a flood."[40] In support he cited Genesis 8:21: "Never again will I curse the ground because of humans, even though every inclination of the human heart is evil from childhood. And never again will I destroy all living creatures, as I have done."

James Inhofe, senator from Oklahoma and one of the most vociferous opponents of taking action against global warming, said in an interview, "Well actually the Genesis 8:22 that I use in there [referring to his book] is that 'as long as the earth remains there will be seed time and harvest, cold and heat, winter and summer, day and night,' my point is, God's still up there. The arrogance of people to think that we, human beings, would be able to change what He is doing in the climate is to me outrageous."[41]

Inhofe's statement becomes more ominous when one realizes that he is the former chairman of the Senate Committee on Environment and Public Works and therefore has wielded tremendous influence in stopping any attempts to deal with this problem. The extremely radical nature of his position is seen even more clearly in this statement, "With all the hysteria, all the fear, all the phony science, could it be that manmade global warming is the greatest hoax ever perpetrated on the American people? I believe it is. And if we allow these detractors of everything that has made America great, those ranging from the liberal Hollywood elitists to those who are in it for the money, if we allow them to destroy the foundation, the greatness of the most highly industrialized nation in the history of the world, then we don't deserve to live in this one nation under God."[42]

Another congressional chairman, this one the chair of the House Science

Committee, Ralph Hall, has also expressed skepticism about the ability of human beings to alter the climate, saying, "I don't think we can control what God controls."[43] Congressman Joe Barton of Texas has made mention of the Flood in the context of global warming, saying "I would point out that if you're a believer in the Bible, one would have to say the Great Flood is an example of climate change and that certainly wasn't because mankind had overdeveloped hydrocarbon energy."[44]

These members of Congress all show a clear disdain for the science of climate change as it is currently understood by the vast majority of relevant scientists. Instead they cling to their biblical interpretation of the matter. This follows a pattern of science denial by Christians, especially over the issue of evolution. Katherine Wilkinson argues that "with roots in the creation-evolution debate, a culture of general scientific skepticism exists in many evangelical circles and hangs heavy over evangelical discussions of climate change. Distrust of scientists and a 'populist anti-science sentiment' transfer easily from the former issue [evolution] to the latter [climate change]."[45] Many Christians also see science as generally hostile to their religion, and this feeling applies especially strongly to some evangelicals in regard to environmental issues.[46]

This type of skepticism about science is on display in Deaton's blog. He writes, "The people who push GW/CC are humanist. They are God-deniers. Their 'science' is their religion. They have an agenda, which includes elevating man to the master of this world. Their position is built on arrogance and ignorance."[47] Even worse, however, is that this hostility toward science is on view in the US Congress. Representative Paul Broun of Georgia serves on the House Science, Space, and Technology Committee. Yet incredibly he was videotaped at an event saying:

God's word is true. I've come to understand that. All that stuff I was taught about evolution, embryology, Big Bang theory, all that is lies straight from the pit of hell. It's lies to try to keep me and all the folks who are taught that from understanding that they need a savior. There's a lot of scientific data that I found out as a scientist that actually show that this is really a young Earth. I believe that the Earth is about 9,000 years old. I believe that it was created in six days as we know them. That's what the Bible says. And what I've come to learn is that it's the manufacturer's handbook, is what I call it. It teaches us how to run our lives individually. How to run our families, how to run our churches. But it teaches us how to run all our public policy and everything in society. And that's the reason, as your congressman, I hold the Holy Bible as being the major directions to me of how I vote in Washington, D.C., and I'll continue to do that.[48]

Broun is also a strident opponent of climate science. Is it likely that his Christian-inspired resistance to science is not also behind that?

The same antiscience tactics used by creationists who deny evolution are also regularly used by evangelical global-warming skeptics. It is a common tactic of antievolutionists to claim that evolution is only a theory and therefore not established scientific fact. This is to conflate the scientific meaning of *theory* (a well-tested overarching explanation of a variety of disparate facts) with the colloquial notion that a theory is just a hunch. Of course most people unfamiliar with science don't understand this difference in the usage of the term, and many are convinced by this specious argument. We see the same tactic being applied by Roy Spencer of the Interfaith Stewardship Alliance (ISA) when he says, "Manmade global warming is a *theory*, and not a scientific observation. How much of the current or predicted warming a scientist (or anyone else) believes is due to mankind ultimately comes down to how much faith that person has in our present understanding of what drives climate fluctuations, the computer climate models that contain that understanding, and ultimately, in how fragile or resilient is the Earth."[49] Equating scientific knowledge with faith is another flawed but common antievolution tactic.

Congressman Barton made a similar argument in an interview on C-SPAN, in which he said:

I would also point out that CO2, carbon dioxide, is not a pollutant in any normal definition of the term . . . I am creating it as I talk to you. It's in your Coca-Cola, your Dr. Pepper, your Perrier water. It is necessary for human life. It is odorless, colorless, tasteless, does not cause cancer, does not cause asthma.

A lot of the CO2 that is created in the United States is naturally created. You can't regulate God. Not even the Democratic majority in the US Congress can regulate God.

If you think greenhouse gases are bad, life couldn't exist without greenhouse gases. . . . So, there is a, there is a climate theory—and it's a theory, it's not a fact, it's never been proven—that increasing concentrations of CO2 in the upper atmosphere somehow interact to trap more heat than the atmosphere would otherwise.[50]

In addition to dominionism (the idea that God's design is perfect and can't be negatively impacted by human beings) and a general unfounded skepticism of science, Christians, at least of a certain type, have a further reason not to take global warming seriously—the Second Coming and Armageddon. Because they believe that Jesus' return is imminent and that the end of the world is near (many believe that it is bound to happen within their own lifetimes) there is no real need to worry overly much about the future. God's plan is already underway and will eventually be realized, perhaps soon. As Melinda Christian puts it, "God's Word tells us about a 'new heaven and a new earth' that He is planning for His people, free of sin and the Curse. Our current environmental problems are serious and worth further thought and action, but the Bible puts all such issues into proper perspective. While we need to behave wisely in the fleeting moments we have on this earth, a much greater change is coming, one that should modify our behavior—the 'global warming' described in 2 Peter 3:10. 'But the day of the Lord will come as a thief in the night, in which the heavens will pass away with a great noise, and the elements will melt with fervent heat; both the earth and the works that are in it will be burned up.'"[51]

G. Elijah Dann refers to this as a "theological escape-hatch" that absolves believers of having to worry about the future repercussions of climate change, thereby making it impossible for them to take the problem as seriously as the rest of us. In fact, the consequences of global warming may be seen as a good thing, since they can be interpreted as harbingers of the coming judgment and the establishment of the Kingdom of God. "For them, the Book of Revelation is God's playbook to how things will work out for humanity. The increasingly devastating climatic events are 'signs' of inevitable truths, and they demonstrate that Christ's return is imminent. But secondly, eschatology envisions, after Armageddon and God's judgment, God's promised restoration. Everything will be recreated in, as mentioned, the New Heavens and Earth."[52]

The outcome of these beliefs, as they relate to global warming, is measurable in opinion polls. Research by David Barker and David Bearce found that the probability that a respondent would strongly agree that the government should take action concerning global warming was 12 percent lower if the respondent was a believer in the Second Coming. Conversely, such belief increases the probability by 10 percent that the respondent will disagree with government action to reduce global warming.[53] The researchers conclude that "end-times believers might think a little bit like actuaries. But instead of calculating the life expectancy of individuals, they calculate it for the entire planet. And they calculate that the planetary life expectancy will be much shorter than do nonbelievers. To elaborate, while non-end-times believers have little reason to doubt humankind's infinite persistence, all else being equal, end-times believers 'know' that life on Earth has a preordained expiration date, no matter what—and that all Christians will be raptured before the going gets too tough."[54]

Conclusion

When it comes to the important problem of global climate change, Christian dogma matters. Christians, and especially evangelicals, form a powerful voting bloc and are influential in American politics. McCammack points out that "evangelicals have risen to a point of prominence wherein they seem to possess great influence in American politics, making their impact on future climate change policy potentially quite significant. Considered simply as a voting bloc, evangelical Christians are a force to be reckoned with, making up roughly 30 percent of the American population."[55] Evangelicals are influential enough to have successfully impeded an effective response to this global problem through political opposition. One way they've done this is through electing to Congress representatives who share their views on the issue. Congressmen such as James Inhofe, John Shimkus, Paul Braun, Joe Barton, and Ralph Hall have been able to stop the wheel of progress from moving forward on this issue.

It's true that not all Christians take such an archaic view of the problem. Some Christians see the role of human beings as earth's stewards to include the duty to protect it from the ravages of global warming. There is a faction of evangelicals who have begun to take the issue seriously and are urging that action be taken on it.[56] Groups such as the Evangelical Environmental Network (EEN) and the Evangelical Climate Initiative (ECI) have formed to direct evangelical attention to the problem. These groups are small, however, in comparison to the conservative evangelical forces arrayed against doing anything about the problem, which take the view of the late Jerry Falwell that "the alarmism over global warming . . . is Satan's attempt to re-direct the church's primary focus."[57] Paula Posas, among those who believe that religion has a positive role to play in mediating climate change, admits that "various denominations of major Western religions interpret scripture in a way that de-emphasizes the importance of the Earth. A percentage of these denominations interpret scripture to not require a position on climate change."[58]

Still, secular people, and those generally concerned about climate change and its effects, should seek to form alliances with groups such as the EEN and the ECI, and with other Christian believers who accept the science of climate change and are working to ameliorate the harms caused by it. The problem is too weighty to be picky about allies. Eminent scientist and humanist thinker E. O. Wilson, in his book *The Creation*, urges Christians to work together with scientists to solve environmental problems. He advises us all to "forget the differences . . . meet on common ground."[59] This is good and wise advice as far as it goes. We need as many people on board as possible to resolve not only climate change but other environmental crises as well.

It is easy to become disheartened, however, when one reads passages such as this from Christian apologists: "If a scientist believes in billions of years of earth history, he will assume, for example, that polar ice needed hundreds of thousands of years to build up over two miles in depth. Scientists who believe in the biblical account of Noah's Flood, on the other hand, believe the ice must have appeared shortly after the Flood. Depending on their assumptions, equally skilled scientists can reach very different conclusions."[60] Such a warped view of science and reality—to claim that the earth being more than a few thousand years old is a mere assumption—reveals a wilful ignorance so profound as to make meaningful cooperation on scientific issues nearly impossible. This is especially true when compounded by belief in absurdities such as the Second Coming and the doctrine of dominionism.

Furthermore, even those Christians who accept that climate change is a problem and are agitating to do something about it ultimately rest their positions on irrationalism. If they believe that humans should combat climate change because it is their God-given duty as earth's stewards, then their beliefs are based upon faulty reasons. The outcome happens to be positive, but this is only by happenstance. Far better for their reasons to be based upon scientific evidence and a rational cost-benefit analysis concerning the welfare of human beings and the other animals with which we share the planet. Even though secularists should ally with Christians on the issue of climate change where possible, we should continue to point out the futility and danger of basing such decisions on religious decrees and scripture and insist that rationality and reason are the only consistent bases for making such important decisions.

In a previous publication I examined how humanists should approach environmental issues based upon rational values and scientific understanding. Some of the key findings I discussed there were:

1) Human beings are the sole source of ethical values, but not necessarily the sole object of them.
2) Human beings should develop empathy and sympathy for other human beings, both those presently alive and those who will live in the future, and for all sentient beings with the capacity to suffer.
3) Humanists should accept an inclusive anthropocentric approach to nature.
4) Religious dogmas should not play a role in ethical decision-making.
5) Nature should not be elevated to a divine level.
6) Humanists should embrace a "cosmic patriotism" for the world.[61]

I continue to maintain that these are the sorts of rational, human-based values that must guide our decisions about the environment in general and about global warming in particular. Decision-making impacted by religious belief, dogma, or scripture will only be confused and lack rational foundation. When it results in antiscientific stances such as those taken by global-warming deniers ranging from radio personalities such as Rush Limbaugh to members of Congress such as James Inhofe and his ilk, religion is truly dangerous to the environment and to us, who must live in it. It has contributed to the failure of the United States to take meaningful actions related to the issue, like ratification of the Kyoto Protocol or cap-and-trade legislation. Christianity therefore poses a serious threat to the environment and to its inhabitants. It has reduced the public's acceptance and understanding of global warming and its impacts, decreased support for efforts to mitigate the worst effects of global warming, and resulted in the election of powerful political figures who have successfully blocked effective action by the US government. Since the United States is one of the world's largest emitters of greenhouse gases, particularly CO_2, and since its cooperation and leadership is essential to solving this worldwide crisis through concerted international action, Christian intransigence about the problem has global consequences. When it comes to the environment in general, and to global warming in particular, the most pressing environmental problem of our time, Christianity is certainly *not* great.

15

DOTH GOD TAKE
CARE FOR OXEN?

Christianity's Acrimony against Animals

John W. Loftus

In this chapter I'll take a good look at what the Bible says about the treatment of animals. Like most any topic we find in the Bible, from abortion to war, there will be inconsistencies and contradictory emphases within its pages, since the books compiled in the canonical Bible were written and edited by different people at different periods of time. So we shouldn't be surprised to find inconsistencies within the Bible when it comes to the proper treatment of animals as well. And this is what we find. Andrew Linzey and Tom Regan are probably today's most important Christian voices in support of a new, respectful animal theology, having written a number of books on the topic. They admit that "what is clear, and what can be asserted confidently . . . is that . . . there are alternative, initially plausible and yet mutually inconsistent ways of interpreting the holy scriptures, some of which support humanistic interpretations of the values nature holds, others not."[1] Indeed, that is par for the course.

As history has moved on, so also has our sense of morality. With this newer heightened sense of morality Christians have been forced time after time to look for minority voices in the texts of the Bible. But doing so cannot exonerate the Bible from the majority voices that are to blame for the horrendous treatment of animals down through the ages in the Western world. Any religion should be judged by how it treats the defenseless, and animals are the most defenseless of all.

Peter Singer wrote the groundbreaking 1975 book *Animal Liberation*,[2] considered by many to be the instigator of the modern animal-rights movement. He brought to our attention how terribly people in the Christianized Western world treated animals. He sounded the alarm for a more compassionate approach toward them. Out of this concern came the organization People for the Ethical Treatment of Animals (PETA), founded in 1980 by Ingrid Newkirk and fellow animal rights activist Alex Pacheco. On the PETA website we read:

> Every day in countries around the world, animals are fighting for their lives. They are enslaved, beaten, and kept in chains to make them perform for humans' "entertainment"; they are mutilated and confined to tiny cages so that we can kill them and eat them; they are burned, blinded, poisoned, and cut up alive in the name of "science"; they are electrocuted, strangled, and skinned alive so that people can parade around in their coats; and worse.
>
> The abuse that animals suffer at human hands is heartbreaking, sickening, and infuriating. It's even more so when we realize that the everyday choices we make—such as what we eat for lunch and the kind of shampoo we buy—may be directly supporting some of this abuse. But as hard as it is to think about, we can't stop animals' suffering if we simply look the other way and pretend it isn't happening.[3]

Animals suffer greatly as a result of factory farming methods, trapping, animal experimentation, and being used in the entertainment, clothing, and pet-trade industries. Some researchers don't think animals experience pain. In some cases animals have even been nailed to boards and dissected while still very much alive. To silence their screams their vocal chords were cut. These things are being done by Christians who see nothing wrong with treating animals as mere property. Andrew Linzey openly admits that "Christianity has a terrible record on animals."[4] That's an understatement. Yet to his credit he sees no reason to disguise this poor record. Animals are not things. They do not exist for the exclusive purpose of human consumption. They are not mere objects. They are not mere fodder for involuntary laboratory experiments or genetic engineering. They are not to be used as a means to an end. Conclusive research shows that animals with a central nervous system experience pain. Some of them are intelligent and self-aware, and some behave ethically toward others.[5]

As we look at the following biblical texts, I ask why God didn't reveal the truth about the intrinsic worth of animals from the very beginning. Why didn't God tell believers in his book that animals felt pain and that they deserve to be treated with respect and dignity? Why didn't God dictate several laws to the Israelites against animal cruelty? If God exists and has any foresight at all he should have done so. Then there would be no biblical justification for the kind of animal cruelty we have seen in the Christianized Western world. My explanation for this lack of divine guidance is that there is no divine being to be found in the Judeo-Christian religion. It is a man-made, man-centered religion, period. I maintain that the dominant Christian view held throughout the centuries is indefensible in our modern scientific era.

So let's take a good, hard look at the relevant biblical texts, keeping in mind that it would be uncharacteristic of a perfectly good and omniscient God to wait until the publication of Darwin's magisterial *Origin of Species* in the nineteenth century to reveal a proper understanding of the biblical texts. Such a God would have known that his followers could not understand what he really wanted them to think about animals prior to that time. So not revealing the truth before then means that he is at least partially to blame for their mistreatment for centuries.

The Dominion Mandate

In the first chapter of Genesis there are six successive creative days represented. The first three days prepare the earth for the populations that will be created to inhabit it in the last three days. Mankind is created last. After creating the world God declares it all "good." Good for what purpose? Good for whom? Humans alone are said to be made in God's "image," and to humans alone were given what has been called the "Dominion Mandate" over the earth. According to it we humans are commanded to "subdue" and have "dominion over the fish of the sea and over the birds of the air and over every living thing that moves upon the earth" (Genesis 1:28).

It is quite clear from reading this Genesis text that mankind is considered to be the apex, the crown jewel, the pinnacle of creation. J. R. Porter tells us, "It shows human beings as the crown of creation." This is why "humanity receives the divine blessing and is given the role of God's vice-regent . . . to have dominion or control over the future course of the world."[6] The progression of creation in Genesis 1 leads to mankind as the supreme creation, the climactic accomplishment of God. Being placed above all creation, humans are to rule over everything under them: Adam over Eve; Adam and Eve over the rest of creation.

It is argued that other passages say otherwise, such as Psalm 8, Psalm 144:3, and the ending of Job, where man is considered insignificant. But insignificant compared to whom? Human beings are insignificant compared to God alone. This says nothing against the belief that human beings are the apex of God's creation. It's entirely consistent for mankind to be the reason for creation while at the same time God is so above us that the Psalmists can wonder why God even bothers with us at all.

The world was created for men according to the Bible, human beings. It was a "good" world. And God tells us what we are to do with the rest of creation. We are to subdue it and have dominion over it, something reiterated in Genesis 9:1–3 and Psalm 8. When we look at the Hebrew words for "subdue" and "dominion" we see just what God wanted from us. The Hebrew word for "subdue" is a very harsh word, which literally means "to trample on." According to an authoritative lexicon it means to "tread down, beat or make a path, subdue; 1. bring into bondage, 2. (late) subdue, force."[7] We see this word used in Zechariah 9:15 when Israel is trampling on the weapons of her enemies. In Jeremiah 34:11 it's used to refer to slave owners taking back released slaves and subduing them again. The word "subjugate" would be an appropriate translation for what this word means, and doing this demanded force. The same word is used in Esther 7:8 by King Ahasuerus, who was angered at what he considered Haman's attempted sexual assault ("subduing") of Queen Esther. It's also the derivative word for "footstool." What God said was for us to make the rest of creation a footstool for our own purposes. Before I go on, let me put my feet up on one. Ahhhh, that feels good.

The word "dominion" doesn't fare any better. It has a similar meaning to the word "subdue" except that it also includes the idea of chastisement. This is no benign way to rule over nature. It means to "master" someone, especially when he or she refuses to be subdued. It's used of King Solomon's overseers, who forced his slave laborers to build the temple in 1 Kings 9:23. It's used in Isaiah 14:2 to describe a time when the Israelites defeated their oppressors.

One of these words was enough to convey the harshness of this man-given lordship over the earth, but because both words are used together, they are meant to confer upon mankind a dictatorial and domineering rule over nature.

Roderick Nash, a history and environmental studies professor at the University of California, Santa Barbara, sums it up in these words: "The image is that of a conqueror placing his foot on the neck of a defeated enemy, exerting absolute domination. Both Hebrew words are also used to identify the process of enslavement. It follows that the Christian tradition could understand Genesis 1:28 as a divine commandment to conquer every part of nature and make it humankind's slave."[8] Even Bishop John Shelby Spong agrees, claiming the Genesis 1:26–28 text "set the stage for seeing the earth as the enemy of human beings."[9] As such, Spong continues, the Christian attitude that was derived from it is "anti-earth."[10]

In 1967 professor Lynn White Jr. laid the blame for our present ecological crisis upon Christian understandings of the biblical desacralization of nature in an essay titled "The Historical Roots of Our Ecological Crisis."[11] Regarding the Genesis creation account, White argued that Christians believe "God planned all of this explicitly for man's benefit and rule: no item in the physical creation had any purpose save to serve man's purposes." And he charged that "especially in its Western form, Christianity is the most anthropocentric religion the world has seen." He wrote: "Our science and technology have grown out of Christian attitudes toward man's relation to nature. . . . Despite Copernicus, all the cosmos rotates around our little globe. Despite Darwin, we are not, in our hearts, part of the natural process. We are superior to nature, contemptuous of it, willing to use it for our slightest whim."

Several Christian scholars have objected to White's interpretation of the Genesis creation texts. For instance, biblical scholar John C. L. Gibson admits that "dominion" and "subdue" were "autocratic, imperialist verbs," but he goes on to argue that "what professor White is describing, though a very real Christianity, is a debased and adulterated Christianity." Gibson claims that "these verses in Genesis could not possibly have been taken by their first hearers to suggest that 'man' could do what he liked with God's creation." Accordingly, "'Man' is God's representative on earth, his ambassador, and possesses no intrinsic rights or privileges beyond those conferred on him by his divine master, to whom moreover he has to render account."[12] Gordon

Wenham, senior lecturer in religious studies at the College of St. Paul and St. Mary in Cheltenham, England, concurs. He argued that although man rules over the world, he "rules the world on God's behalf," and as such, in this text "mankind is here commissioned to rule nature as a benevolent king, acting as God's representative over them and therefore treating them in the same way as God who created them. This is of course no license for the unbridled exploitation of nature."[13] Richard Bauckham, professor of New Testament studies at the University of St. Andrews, Scotland, documented several responses to Lynn White's thesis. His claim is that these responses "can fairly be said to have refuted it over and again."[14]

I find it puzzling that these Christian scholars dispute what seems quite evident from the Genesis text itself. While we must grant that the dominion mandate cannot mean humans can do anything we want to nature, including animals, the words used are extremely harsh ones when compared to our sensibilities toward animals today. How can someone "trample upon" a slave or a sheep beneficently? Saying this is an oxymoron.

It's said by Christians that our rule on earth must be based upon the model of a loving, kind God. Implicit for them is the benign, loving, beneficent God of Anselm's eleventh-century perfect-being theology modified by centuries of theological gerrymandering. Having come to believe that God is perfect in love, Christian scholars would want us to think of the biblical God's lordship in the same manner, as characterized by a loving, beneficent king. Hence, man's rule over nature must exercise the same moral care as God supposedly does. But in the Bible this is emphatically not what we find about God's rule.

The people in biblical times conceived of God as being like the brutal human rulers to whom they were accustomed. This God could be cruel. He could be kind, too. He would be cruel toward those who do not submit to his rule by obeying his every command. He would be kind to those who do. This God could slam the world with a flood for disobedience, pulverize the Egyptian nation with devastating plagues, send snakes to kill three thousand people for their disobedience, and be pleased when babies are dashed against the rocks (Psalm 137:9; Isaiah 13:18). He could send a drought or famine or plague of locusts, or even another nation to kill every man, woman, child, and animal for being disobedient. This God also threatens us with eternal punishment if we don't believe or obey him. This so-called omnibenevolent God is described as a God of War, a Jealous God, and an Avenging God. This would be the divine model for man's lordship over the earth. Be kind to subjects who are in obedience. But be very harsh toward those subjects who are disobedient. Trample on them. Break them down. It was a patriarchal world. Mankind was to dominate over the world just as God ruled. And so it couldn't have been a pretty world to live in for women, slaves, children, or animals.

We simply do not see God's special providential care for animals in the dominion mandate. This Genesis text predates the supposed fall of Adam and Eve, so it takes precedence over the subsequent troubles caused by the introduction of sin in the world. It therefore sets the stage for interpreting the rest of the biblical texts regarding the treatment of animals. And obedience is not something that comes naturally to lions, tigers, bears, hippopotamuses, eagles, vultures, spiders, scorpions, snakes, skunks, or parasites. We must force them to "obey" if we can. If we cannot, and they get in our way, or they are not useful to us in some way, then according to this mandate we can kill them. We are their masters and they are our slaves, just as God is pictured as our master and we as his slaves.[15]

Even if I'm wrong (I'm not), a new problem surfaces. The problem is no longer an exegetical one but a historical one. The problem becomes not what the Bible says, as reinterpreted by modern Christian scholars, but why God allowed this biblical text to be used by Christians to abuse animals in the first place. If he saw his people abusing animals, couldn't he step in and denounce this abuse at any time during the biblical era or afterward? He could've been much clearer, easily, even if these modern Christian scholars are correct in their present exegesis based on hindsight. So the fact that God wasn't clear is an indictment of a perfectly good God who should've known how human beings would interpret these verses. As the CEO of any company knows, if there is any miscommunication about the goals of that company, the fault is the CEO's. If the company does wrong because it misunderstood the CEO's directives, then it's his or her fault. God could have said, "Thou shalt not mistreat or abuse animals." Then there would be no biblical justification for this abuse and no institutional support for it.[16]

Some Old Testament Passages Both Good and Bad

There are some passages in the Old Testament that could be seen as showing care for animals: The Sabbath day was a rest day for both man and beast (Exodus 23:12; Deuteronomy 5:14). The Israelites were told that if they saw their "brother's ass or his ox fallen down by the way," they were to help get it back on its feet (Deuteronomy 22:4). We also read: "If you chance to come upon a bird's nest, in any tree or on the ground, with young ones or eggs and the mother sitting upon the young or upon the eggs, you shall not take the mother with the young; you shall let the mother go, but the young you may take to yourself; that it may go well with you, and that you may live long" (Deuteronomy 22:6–7). The ox was not to plough with the ass (Deuteronomy 22:10), nor were the Israelites to muzzle the ox when it treads out the grain (Deuteronomy 25:4). In Psalm 36:6 we're told God saves a beast as well as a man. In Psalm 147:9 we're told that God gives beasts their food, and in Psalm 148:7–10 they praise him. In Jonah 4:11 God is concerned for both the Ninevites and their beasts.

Expressed in all these verses is some minimal concern for animals, yes. But one can question why Israelites cared for their animals given the harshness we find in the dominion mandate. There is no evidence they cared for the intrinsic worth and value of animals. It was because they needed them. Animals were part of their domain, their property. There are a few Old Testament laws where animals were said to be owned by their masters, who were deserving of restitution from those responsible for the animal's loss (see Exodus 21:28–35; Leviticus 24:17–21). Caring for them, just like caring for their wives and children and slaves, was important to Israelite men. For by doing so it made life easier for them as the masters of their households. Animals merely had instrumental value, not intrinsic value. If a man became emotionally attached to an animal and provided it special care, which no doubt was done, that was well and good. But it would do little to stop him from butchering it for a future meal or offering it in sacrifice to God. The Israelites were given permission to eat the ox, the sheep, the goat, the hart, the gazelle, the roebuck, the wild goat, the ibex, the antelope, sheep, birds, and fish, what are known as "clean" animals. (Deuteronomy 14:4–20).

Probably the strongest text on behalf of animals in the Old Testament is to be found in Proverbs 12:10, where we read: "A righteous man has regard for the life of his beast, but the mercy of the wicked is cruel." Nonetheless, if someone wants to hang the care for animals on this biblical text then we should be sure to understand something about the genre of Proverbs and wisdom literature as a whole. According to Gordon D. Fee and Douglas Stuart, the book of Proverbs contains "prudential wisdom—that is, rules and regulations people can use to help themselves live responsible, successful lives."[17] If a person wants to be successful then he or she should follow its advice. For readers with this overall context in mind, Proverbs 12:10 is merely saying that if a man wants to be successful he will have regard for the life of his beast, since a righteous man is a successful man, usually. This is why we find in the story of Job, as another book in the wisdom literature, a man who is having a great deal of difficulty defending his righteousness before his critics when disaster has struck him not just once, but twice.

When it comes to animal sacrifices this was done by every Israelite in the Old Testament, especially at festivals and dedication ceremonies, all sanctioned and commanded by God. From the Christian perspective this was a completely unnecessary waste of animal life, and a brutal way to kill them. Even if we admit that animal sacrifices prefigured the sacrifice of Jesus to atone for our sins, according to Christian theology itself, animal sacrifices in the Old Testament did nothing to atone for anyone's sins. In the canonical book of Hebrews (10:1–18) we read that it was "impossible that the blood of bulls and goats should take away sins." So these innumerable animals were brutally butchered for no good reason at all, unless one thinks that using animals in this manner is something a perfectly good God would command. When sacrificed, the animals were tied down, their throats slit, and the blood drained on the altar where they were subsequently skinned and quartered into pieces. Then they were burnt, with the smoke of their flesh rising up to God, who was considered to reside in the sky (i.e., "heaven"), as a sweet smelling aroma (Exodus 29:18, 25; Leviticus 3:16, 23:18; etc.). Depending on the kind of sacrifice offered, some of the meat went to the priests and/or the person making the sacrificial offering.[18]

What we do know is that when God's judgment comes down on people, their animals suffer along with them for their master's sins. This can be seen not only in the Flood story of Noah, but also in the story of God sending the ten plagues upon the Egyptians to free the Israelite slaves in Exodus 7. Water is turned into "blood" and all the fish in the rivers and streams subsequently die. Frogs were made to cover the land and then all but those remaining in the river Nile were destroyed by God. The Egyptian livestock were all killed with a severe pestilence in the fourth plague. All of the Egyptians' horses, donkeys, camels, flocks of goats, and sheep were killed, too. (But then where did they get horses to pull their chariots to chase the Israelites into the Red Sea?) We also see God sending painful boils and a storm of fire and hail on both the Egyptians and their beasts. (Note how many times the Egyptian livestock were punished after they were already killed in the fourth plague!) Then God ends with a scorched-earth policy where an eighth plague of locusts devour every green plant or tree that might have been left to feed animals after the storm of hail. The ninth plague of darkness puts a finishing touch on what God had done to the land, indicating there was nothing left for the Egyptians, their land, or their animals. Here we see a wanton divine disregard for animal life. All of this devastation was supposedly done not because of anything the Egyptian animals did wrong. It was because of the sins of the Egyptians, particularly those of the Pharaoh, who refused to free the Israelites, whose heart was hardened by God so he could do this.

The Prophetic Tradition

When arguing against the so-called New Atheists, John F. Haught, a former chair and professor in the department of theology at Georgetown University, in Washington DC, faulted them for not understanding that the biblical prophetic tradition expresses the moral core of Judaism and Christianity. Describing the moral core of the prophetic tradition, with its emphasis on justice, as "God's preferential option for the poor and disadvantaged," Haught wrote: "To maintain that we can understand modern and contemporary social justice, civil rights, and liberation movements without any reference to Amos, Hosea, Isaiah, Micah, Jesus, and other biblical prophets makes Dawkins's treatment of morality and faith almost unworthy of comment."[19] But conspicuously lacking among the Old Testament prophets are any denunciations of animal cruelty. If the prophets represented God's concern for the disadvantaged and lowly then apparently God was not concerned for animals.

There is a prophetic vision for the future in the book of Isaiah (11:6–9; 65:17–25), which seems to describe a return to the Garden of Eden, or a heavenly reward that animals will experience along with the redeemed. Isaiah 11:6–9 says: "The wolf shall dwell with the lamb, and the leopard shall lie down with the kid, and the calf and the lion and the fatling together, and a little child shall lead them. The cow and the bear shall feed; their young shall lie down together; and the lion shall eat straw like the ox. The sucking child shall play over the hole of the asp, and the weaned child shall put his hand on the adder's den. They shall not hurt or destroy in all my holy mountain; for the earth shall be full of the knowledge of the LORD as the waters cover the sea."

Distinguished New Testament scholar and professor of divinity at Cambridge University, C.F.D. Moule, tells us: "No one with a grain of sense believes that the passage . . . is intended literally, as though the digestive system of a carnivore were going to be transformed into that of a herbivore. What blasphemous injury would be done to great poetry and true mythology by laying such solemnly prosaic hands upon it!"[20] The child will not literally play over the hole of a poisonous asp, and neither will the lion nor the ox eat straw. Evangelical philosopher Paul Copan agrees, pointing out that Christians "must be cautious about literalizing a poetic and highly symbolic text." Right that. In Isaiah 65:20 it says, "No more shall there be in it an infant that lives but a few days, or an old man who does not fill out his days, for the child shall die a hundred years old, and the sinner a hundred years old shall be accursed." If taken literally, Isaiah's vision for the future still involves death.[21] Copan argues: "Surely the text does not urge literalism here! It uses understatement to stress the longevity of life during the Messiah's reign." Copan adds that "the emphasis" in these texts "is not the nature of the lion's diet but his domestication, his being tamed so that he is no longer a threat. To eat straw like an ox is to be tamed and not to be a danger."[22] And in this we find what the dominion mandate is all about, for the best state of affairs is to hope for the domestication of all animals. Nothing in this so-called prophetic wishful thinking undermines that sentiment at all. For domesticating an animal means to train or adapt it to live in a human environment so that it is of use to humans. We've done that to dogs and cats. What are we to do with wolves, leopards, lions, bears and asps? We are to domesticate them all, or else they'll have hell to pay, per God's example.

The prophets did condemn animal sacrifices that did not spring from clean and sincere hearts. The prophetic voice in Psalm 50 typifies this. But it is hardly a text supportive of God's care for animals. Neither is there any care for animals expressed in Isaiah 1:11–17 or Micah 6:6–8 or Amos 6:4–6. All we see is a condemnation of the injustice of those who made "vain" sacrifices to God, or who were merely concerned with their own gluttonous lifestyle. Robert N. Wennberg, Christian professor of philosophy at Westmont College, Santa Barbara, California, sums up the prophetic tradition in these words: "To be sure, prophetic condemnation of animal sacrifices occurred from time to time, but the prophetic objection was not directed against animal sacrifices per se; rather, it was an objection to sacrificial offerings in a context devoid of genuine repentance, devoid of compassion for the needy, devoid of a true commitment to justice. It was any ritual divorced from true spirituality, not only animal sacrifice, that was the object of prophetic condemnation."[23]

There is a prophetic passage in Joel 1:18–20, after a plague of locusts came and devoured the land. In Joel we read these words: "How the beasts groan! The herds of cattle are perplexed because there is no pasture for them; even the flocks of sheep are dismayed. Unto thee, O LORD, I cry. For fire has devoured the pastures of the wilderness, and flame has burned all the trees of the field. Even the wild beasts cry to thee because the water brooks are dried up, and fire has devoured the pastures of the wilderness." But surely this is a prophetic metaphor aimed at the people who had fallen under God's judgment. God was punishing nature, and with it animals, for the sins of man. Again, this is not a text supportive of the care of animals. On the contrary, God punishes animals for the sins of man.

If any of these prophets truly represented the moral core of Judaism and Christianity then there is no concern for animals. None.

New Testament Passages — Jesus and Animals

In the New Testament the treatment of animals gets worse. Robert Wennberg acknowledges this, saying that the New Testament is not "quite the resource for moral concern for animals that the Old Testament is. This has prompted some to view Judaism as a better friend to animals than Christianity."[24] Given elation 22:15). Using "dogs" to represent wicked people who will be eternally condemned to the lake of fire is surely a disgusting image unbecoming of a caring attitude toward them, even if dogs at that time were scavengers. And nothing is said in the final chapter of the book of Revelation about animals being in the new Heavenly Jerusalem either.

The only expressly positive thing about the New Testament with regard to animals is that Christians viewed Jesus' death on the cross as the final sacrifice, so they no longer had any reason to sacrifice animals to their God in worship. Even so, this would be best understood as an unintended consequence of a developing Christian theology. It was not something that Christians ceased doing because of any care they might have had for animals themselves.

A Final Note

Christian philosopher Robert Wennberg candidly speaks about what Christians must do to defend holy writ from the appalling lack of concern for animals found in the Bible. What he says is very interesting, to say the least. He suggests that the defenders of the Bible "are no worse off, possibly better off, than those who in an earlier century turned to Scripture in order to condemn slavery."[34] He openly admits that "Scripture may seem to have been more of an impediment to the Christian community's finally making a decisive break with slavery than it was a help," which I find a major understatement. He admits that "there seems to be considerable textual ammunition for the southern white preacher in the 1850s to rebut attacks on slavery by Christian abolitionists," but that eventually the abolitionists won the debate. Wennberg informs us the Christian abolitionists were not "principally seeking to decide whether slavery is right or wrong." They already knew it was wrong and sought a biblical justification for abolishing it, he claims. What necessitated these attempts "was the independent conviction that slavery is wrong." Hence, just as in the case of slavery, where the goal of explaining these specific texts "is typically an activity that occurs after we have come to see slavery to be an evil, not before," so he challenges the present Christian community to "come to terms with all of Scripture" with the goal of arriving at a "thorough and defensible theological vision of animals and their place in the moral universe."[35]

Such a goal as Wennberg proposes is called *special pleading*, pure and simple. The conclusions have already been reached on other grounds. Now Christians must find reasons for reading those conclusions into the texts of the Bible. Yet the intellectually honest thing to do would be to seek to understand what the Bible actually teaches rather than force it to fit inside the grid of anti-slavery, profeminism, or animal-advocacy concerns. My claim in this chapter is that we do not see much of a concern at all for animals in the Bible. It truly is anthropocentric to the core. As such it's not indicative of what a perfectly good God would reveal to us. If God were truly concerned for the welfare of animals he would've said, "Thou shalt not mistreat or abuse animals," repeating it as often as he needed to while giving details about what it means, without giving any conflicting advice. Then Christian people would be unable to justify the ill treatment of animals down through the centuries. And so there would be nothing to reform, since there wouldn't be such wanton abuse of animals in the Christian world in the first place.

what we've just seen in the Old Testament, this doesn't look good. Peter Singer charged that while the Old Testament "did at least show flickers of concern for their sufferings," the New Testament is "completely lacking in any injunction against cruelty to animals, or any recommendation to consider their interests."[25]

Richard Bauckham tries to remedy this understanding of the New Testament texts in a couple of important chapters dealing with Jesus' teachings and actions in the Gospels.[26] There is some concern shown in the New Testament he argues. In the Gospels we read of God feeding the birds of the air (Matthew 6:26; Luke 12:24, 27) and caring for the smallest of sparrows (Luke 12:6–7). But after each of these sayings we subsequently read that human beings are more important to God than they are: "Are you not of more value than they?" "Of how much more value are you than the birds!" "Fear not; you are of more value than many sparrows." Regarding these passages, Bauckham claims: "Only those who recognize birds as their fellow-creatures can appreciate Jesus' point . . . it is not an argument which sets humans on a different plane of being from animals. On the contrary, it sets humans within the community of God's creatures, all of whom are provided for" by God.[27] When it's said humans are of much "more value" than these particular animals, Bauckham himself admits the best interpretation of the word for "more value" (διαφέρω) is "superior," which refers to "hierarchical superiority."[28] But he falsely suggests that this hierarchical relationship between humans and animals can be compared to human kings who are superior to human subjects. There is nothing here to suggest this. A king is a human being who rules over other human beings. Animals, according to the Bible, are in a different category altogether. They have no intrinsic value of their own.

Jesus is represented as teaching that he could heal on the Sabbath by using examples of animals who could be rescued on that day. Matthew 12:11–12 is typical. Jesus in this passage says to his critics, "What man of you, if he has one sheep and it falls into a pit on the Sabbath, will not lay hold of it and lift it out? Of how much more value is a man than a sheep! So it is lawful to do good on the Sabbath" (see also Luke 14:5 and 13:15–16). Such acts were acts of compassion, Bauckham argues, "intended to prevent animal suffering."[29] But there is nothing here to suggest the reason was to alleviate the sufferings of an animal. It seems evident that the owner's property was in danger of being damaged to some extent, that's all. Surely the desire to keep the sheep from being harmed could be understood as a desire to limit any further loss to the owner. Of course, here is that same Greek word again, expressing the phrase that humans are of much "more value" (διαφέρω) than these animals. It's not that animals have no value at all to God or to man, but the kind of value is different, as I'm arguing. Animals had value precisely because they were a man's property.

In another tale Jesus encountered a man possessed by thousands (i.e., a legion) of demons who feared he would cast them out without providing them another host. So the demons begged him to cast them into a herd of swine, which Jesus did. Upon his command they "came out, and entered the herd of swine, numbering about two thousand, rushed down the steep bank into the sea, and were drowned in the sea" (Mark 5; Matthew 8:24–34; Luke 8:26–39). It was a common myth that demons needed a host to inhabit, and it was also a common myth that if they couldn't find a different host after being exorcised out of one, they would try to return to the one they'd left (Mark 9:25; Matthew 12:43–45). Richard Bauckham tells us that upon being cast into the pigs, the pigs were destroyed by the demons because of "the inherent tendency of the demonic to destroy whatever it possesses."[30] But Bauckham offers no plausible explanation for why Jesus did not just send them back into the abyss from whence they came. Jesus could have imprisoned these demons in a cave in the mountains, sent them into a murderer condemned to die, or a number of other alternatives. He could even have sent them into the pigs and then kept the demons from drowning them. As it stands this shows the wanton disregard of a "miracle working" Jesus toward animal life, which also raises questions about his supposed sinlessness. So Bauckham is forced to admit that the supposed sinless Jesus "permits a lesser evil" here.[31] What exactly is a lesser evil anyway? Isn't it doing something less than the absolute best, given the alternatives? But haven't I just suggested better alternatives? So unless Bauckham can show that my alternatives are not better ones, we must accept that Jesus didn't just do a lesser evil. He sinned by the standard of perfect goodness, the standard God supposedly claims for himself.

A few things are sure about the Jesus portrayed in the Gospels. He was neither vegan nor vegetarian. We read that in contrast to John the Baptist, who came "neither eating nor drinking," Jesus came "eating and drinking" (Matthew 11:18–19). He would eat meat when invited into the homes of some wealthy

Part Four

SOCIAL AND MORAL HARMS

16

THE CHRISTIAN RIGHT
AND THE CULTURE WARS

Ed Brayton

Let us begin by defining our terms. What do I mean by the *Christian right* and what do I mean by the *culture wars*? When writing about the culture wars I'm referring to a range of hot button political and legal controversies that tend to provoke a very emotional response among a particular constituency that is therefore particularly prone to demagoguery. Specifically, issues like separation of church and state; abortion, contraception, and abstinence-only sex education; LGBTI rights; religious exemptions from generally applicable laws; creationism in public schools; and so on. This chapter will briefly explore some of those issues and what I consider the malevolent influence of the Christian right in American culture on all of them.

The Christian right refers to Christian organizations and individuals who are conservative, usually both theologically and politically, and strongly traditionalist. It refers to a large network of ideologically affiliated groups like the American Center for Law and Justice, Liberty Counsel, the Alliance Defending Freedom (originally the Alliance Defense Fund), Focus on the Family, the American Family Association, the Family Research Council, the Traditional Values Coalition, the National Organization for Marriage, and many others.

James Davison Hunter, Labrosse-Levinson Distinguished Professor of Religion, Culture, and Social Theory at the University of Virginia, titled his 1992 book *Culture Wars: The Struggle to Define America*,[1] and the second clause in the title is an apt one. It's a struggle—a series of them, actually—that has been going on since before the founding of America. Those battles were raging at the time the Constitution was written and ratified, they broke out into the bloodiest conflict in our history during the Civil War, and they were at play in tumultuous fights over women's suffrage, prohibition of alcohol, desegregation and civil rights for black Americans, disputes over religion in public schools from the 1940s until today, abortion and reproductive rights, sex education, and today, most obviously, over equality for LGBT (lesbian, gay, bisexual, and transgender) people.

These issues should not be viewed in isolation. In each of them there is a battle between tradition, nearly always justified by reference to the Bible, conservative Christian theology, and social progress. As Professor Hunter put it in an introduction to the book mentioned above, these issues "are not isolated from one another but are, in fact, part of a fabric of conflict which constitutes nothing short of a struggle over the meaning of America."

Let me also make clear that I am not criticizing Christianity in general. On all of these issues there are many Christians who are on the side of justice, equality, and fairness. Baptist ministers were among the staunchest supporters of strict separation of church and state at the time of the nation's founding. Quakers, Unitarians, and others fought for the abolition of slavery. Many of the women who brought about equality in the right to vote were Christians. Most of the prominent leaders of the civil rights movement were Christian clergymen like Reverend Martin Luther King Jr. And in today's battles over gay rights, the Episcopalian Church in this country, among others, has helped lead the way.

But it is my contention that *conservative* Christianity has been the primary impediment to social progress in the United States from its very origins. The Constitution was, in at least two key ways, a radical break with centuries of precedent in the West. The first was that it contained no statement of a covenant with God. Gary North, a Christian Reconstructionist who believes that America should be a theocracy but rejects the idea that the Constitution is a product of a Christian worldview, argues in *Conspiracy in Philadelphia* that the Constitution "was a covenantal break with the Christian civil religion of twelve of the thirteen colonies,"[2] all of which had constitutions or charters that explicitly spelled out their dependence on and official belief in God.

This was very controversial at the time, and conservative Christians tried many times to change that by amending the preamble to the Constitution, first during the ratification conventions and later through the amendment process. During the Civil War, the National Reform Association proposed a constitutional amendment that would have changed the preamble to this:

We, the people of the United States, humbly acknowledging Almighty God as the source of all authority and power in civil government, the Lord Jesus Christ as the Ruler among the nations, His revealed will as the supreme law of the land, in order to constitute a Christian government, and in order to form a more perfect union, establish justice, insure domestic tranquillity, provide for the common defense, promote the general welfare, and secure the blessings of life, liberty, and the pursuit of happiness to ourselves, our posterity, and all the people, do ordain and establish this Constitution for the United States of America.

Though these attempts to add a Christian nation amendment to the Constitution failed both in Congress and in the states, the effort to pass one continued until the 1950s.

The second was the ban on religious tests for office in Article 6. Nearly all the colonies at the time had provisions that required those who ran for public office to be Christians and often even specific types of Christians (Catholics, for instance, were often left out). Prominent ministers and anonymous pamphleteers of that day, seeking to preserve their exclusive access to power, railed against this perceived flaw in the Constitution.

Amos Singletary, a delegate to the Massachusetts ratifying convention, said that "though he hoped to see Christians [in office], yet by the Constitution, a papist, or an infidel was as eligible as they."[3] Henry Abbot, a delegate to the North Carolina convention, warned that because of this ban on religious tests "pagans, deists, and Mahometans [*sic*] might obtain offices among us."[4]

An article opposing the passage of the Constitution that appeared in newspapers in New York, New Hampshire, Connecticut, and Massachusetts warned of the many groups of people who might occupy public office if it were to pass:

> lst. Quakers, who will make the blacks saucy, and at the same time deprive us of the means of defence-2dly. Mahometans, who ridicule the doctrine of the Trinity-3dly. Deists, abominable wretches-4thly. Negroes, the seed of Cain -5thly Beggars, who when set on horseback will ride to the devil-6thly. Jews etc. etc.[5]

So from the very start, many conservative Christians were opposed to the very idea of a secular government and sought to maintain the status quo, with all the extent privileges it granted them to continue their domination of public policy. Losing that early battle did not deter them, however, from continuing to oppose nearly every advance of liberty, equality, and justice in the nation's history. Conservative Christianity was the primary source of opposition to the ending of slavery, to women's' suffrage, to the legalization of contraception, to ending racial segregation and, today, to equality for the LGBT community and much more. This chapter will look at how the Christian right continues to battle against equality and fairness in several areas of public policy.

Reproductive Rights

There are few issues that animate and motivate the Christian right in America more than abortion. After the ruling in *Roe v. Wade* made abortion legal throughout the United States in 1973, it became the central issue around which the Christian right organized politically. For two decades after that ruling, which said that women had a fundamental right to choose to have an abortion in the first two trimesters of pregnancy, abortion was a powerful fundraising tool and rallying cry, however little progress was made in undermining reproductive rights. But in 1992 the Supreme Court handed down a ruling in a case called *Planned Parenthood v. Casey* that formally upheld the right to choose while undermining its enforcement by allowing state restrictions on that right as long as they did not constitute an "undue burden" on a woman's ability to procure an abortion.

With that new ruling in place, the Christian right, operating through the Republican Party that they now largely controlled, began passing laws at the state level containing a whole range of new restrictions on the right to choose. Those restrictions included parental consent laws, waiting periods, and, more recently, mandatory counseling and ultrasound requirements.

The passage of such restrictions really sped up after the 2010 election, when the Republican Party channeled the energy of the Tea Party movement to nearly double the number of state legislatures over which it had full control (from fourteen to twenty-seven) while more than doubling the number of Republican governors (from nine to twenty-one).[6] Though they rode into office promising to focus on "jobs, jobs, jobs," the Republicans in those legislatures immediately got to work passing more restrictions on a woman's right to choose. From January 2011 to the end of 2013, 205 such laws had been passed, more than in the entire previous decade.[7]

Many of those new laws are now called Targeted Regulation of Abortion Provider, or TRAP, laws. The National Abortion Federation defines TRAP laws as laws that "single out abortion providers for medically unnecessary, politically motivated state regulations."[8] They divide such regulations into three distinct types:

- a measure that singles out abortion providers for medically unnecessary regulations, standards, personnel qualifications, building and/or structural requirements;
- a politically motivated provision that needlessly addresses the licensing of abortion clinics and/or charges an exorbitant fee to register a clinic in the state; or
- a measure that unnecessarily regulates where abortions may be provided or designates abortion clinics as ambulatory surgical centers, outpatient care centers, or hospitals without medical justification.

All of these laws are designed to make it prohibitively expensive, often impossible, to keep an abortion clinic open. Proponents argue that such regulations are necessary to protect the health of the patient, despite the fact that only .3 percent of all abortions involve any medical complications.[9] The effect of TRAP laws has been significant and immediate. Bloomberg News reported in late 2013 that as a result of those laws, at least seventy-three clinics that performed abortions have shut down.[10] Robin Marty, coauthor of *Crow after Roe: How "Separate but Equal" Has Become the New Standard in Women's Health and How We Can Change That*, notes that these effects are particularly pronounced in the poorest and most vulnerable populations. "Thanks to their crusade to enforce their own biblical ideology and their stranglehold on a number of legislatures in red states, abortion is becoming legal in name only," Marty said. "Just like the days before *Roe*, those with money, means and connections will always be able to decide when and if to remain pregnant and have children. Those who are poor, especially people of color, will be cut off from that same right, and forced to remain pregnant and give birth simply because they don't have financial ability and resources to obtain an abortion if they want one."[11]

Many of these laws have been challenged in state and federal courts and are working their way up to the US Supreme Court. On January 13, 2014, the Court denied cert in (that is, refused to hear an appeal of) the first major case, *Horne v. Isaacson*, which involved an Arizona state law banning abortion after twenty weeks, leaving in place a 9th Circuit Court of Appeals ruling that struck down the law as unconstitutional. But there are at least two dozen other cases involving other types of abortion regulations passed since 2011 in the courts, and observers agree that the Supreme Court is almost certain to hear at least a few of them.

Whether the Supreme Court will uphold or overturn such laws is not only an open question, the outcome almost certainly relies on the vote of a single man, Justice Anthony Kennedy. Justices Antonin Scalia and Clarence Thomas have long been on the record as wanting to overturn *Roe v. Wade*, while fellow conservatives Justice Samuel Alito and Chief Justice John Roberts have not yet had much opportunity to rule on the issue, but they are presumed to be strongly anti-choice. Likewise on the liberal side of the Court, Justices Steven Breyer and Ruth Bader Ginsburg are solidly pro-choice while the two most recent additions to the Court, Justices Elena Kagan and Sonia Sotomayor, are presumed to be as well. That leaves Justice Kennedy in his usual position as the fifth and deciding vote, and on abortion his track record is mixed, to say the least.

In 1992, the Supreme Court took up a case called *Planned Parenthood v. Casey*, which challenged a set of regulations passed by the State of Pennsylvania, including requirements for parental and spousal notification. In the original conference between the justices, there were five votes to repudiate the central holding of *Roe v. Wade*, the fundamental right to choose an abortion. Justice Kennedy was one of those five votes. But as the opinions began to be written and circulated among the members of the court, Justices David Souter and Sandra Day O'Connor began to work on Justice Kennedy to change his mind.

Their lobbying worked. Despite the fact that Kennedy had joined Chief Justice Rehnquist's opinion three years earlier in *Webster v. Reproductive Health Services* that advocated overturning *Roe v. Wade*, he changed his position in *Casey* and voted to uphold *Roe* while accepting certain types of restrictions and regulations on the right to choose an abortion. It was not until the release of the papers of the late Justice Harry Blackmun, which for the first time made public the exchanges between the justices on the Court in the case, that American women found out just how close they had come to losing their reproductive rights. And when the legal challenges to the most recently passed restrictions on abortion reach the Court, it will almost certainly be Justice Kennedy who will once cast the deciding vote that determines how far the Supreme Court is willing to go in allowing reproductive rights to suffer death by a thousand cuts.

What is at stake in these battles is nothing less than the ability of women to control their own reproduction, which is a vital and necessary precondition for legal equality. Susan Cohen of the Guttmacher Instituted noted in a 2001 report titled "Reproductive Health and Rights: Keys to Development and Democracy at Home and Abroad":

> There is a growing recognition that having fewer children, and at times and in circumstances when they best can be cared for, constitute both an individual and a social good, because doing so takes a lesser toll on the health of the mother, improves the health prospects of her children and makes it easier to ensure that each child thrives. Having the ability to time and space their pregnancies also allows women to become educated, establish themselves in the workforce and at least begin to take their rightful place alongside men in community life. In both developed and developing countries, fertility control and the maintenance of reproductive health are not luxuries; they are essential to women's lives and by extension, to the well-being of their partners and children and to the future of the societies in which they live.[12]

Abstinence-Only Sex Education

Another hot-button issue for the Christian right is sex education in schools. Many conservative Christians oppose sex education in public schools completely (indeed, many of them oppose *having* public schools entirely). Their argument has long been that teaching a child about sex should be the exclusive purview of the parents, not the state, and conservative Christians tend to be very upset when the school teaches things that disagree with their religious views, which they believe demand total abstinence until marriage.

The first federal law to provide funding for abstinence-only sex education was the Adolescent Family Life Act (AFLA), passed by Congress in 1981 and signed into law by President Reagan. The AFLA provided funding for research and demonstration programs for including abstinence in sex-education classes. In 1996, the Temporary Assistance for Needy Families Act (TANF), better known as the welfare reform bill, included a provision that established grants to states for abstinence-only sex education and established eight criteria that all abstinence-only sex-education programs must meet to receive federal funding.

Many of those grants went to Christian right organizations to develop the abstinence-only sex-ed programs. The first criterion was that an abstinence-only program "has as its exclusive purpose teaching the social, psychological, and health gains to be realized by abstaining from sexual activity." Because of that, those programs "may not in any way advocate contraceptive use or discuss contraceptive methods except to emphasize their failure rates."[13] Over the years, those programs have received hundreds of millions of dollars in federal funding, but in June 2009 the funding for those programs expired (funding was renewed in 2010). Many states also provide their own funding for abstinence-only sex education.

The Christian right's advocacy of those programs, unfortunately, has come at the expense of children in our public schools. Study after study has found abstinence-only sex education to be ineffective at best and damaging at worst. A 2011 study from researchers at the University of Georgia, for example, found that states that require abstinence-only sex education "have significantly higher teenage pregnancy and birth rates than states with more comprehensive sex education programs."[14] Kathrin Stanger-Hall, the lead author of the study, said that the result "adds to the overwhelming evidence indicating that abstinence-only education does not reduce teen pregnancy rates."[15]

In 1997, Congress authorized a longitudinal study of more than two thousand students in four different communities, two urban and two rural, to look at the long-term effects of abstinence-only sex ed. The study followed the students through high school and found that there was no significant effect on when they started having sex or how often they used birth control when they did.[16]

The Sexuality Information and Education Council of the United States presents multiple studies that show that abstinence-only programs are ineffective at best and quite dangerous at worst.[17] A study published in the *American Journal of Sociology* in 2001 found that while such programs did help some young people delay their first sexual experience, it also found that they were "one-third less likely to use contraception when they did become sexually active."[18] The result was the same rate of STD infection for those who made virginity pledges (a common part of abstinence-only sex-ed programs) despite having started having sex later, perhaps because those who made the pledge were "less likely to seek medical testing and treatment, thereby increasing the possibility of transmission."[19] Comparisons of communities with high numbers of virginity pledgers showed that "in communities where more than 20% of young adults had taken virginity pledges, STD rates were 8.9% compared to 5.5% in communities with few pledgers."[20]

The Sexuality Information and Education Council also reports on several studies done by states that funded or mandated abstinence-only programs that showed that the programs have virtually no positive effect. A study of such programs in Pennsylvania, for instance, concluded that "taken as a whole, this initiative was largely ineffective in reducing sexual onset and promoting attitudes and skills consistent with sexual abstinence."[21] A Texas study of abstinence-only programs in that state found that there were no "strong indications these programs were having an impact in the direction desired," largely because they "seem to be much more concerned about politics than kids."[22]

One reason for this ineffectiveness may be that such programs often contain inaccurate information. In 2004, a report prepared for Representative Henry Waxman by the minority staff of the House Committee on Government Reform found that eleven of the thirteen programs whose content was examined contained "false, misleading, or distorted information about reproductive health."[23] Those misleading claims included vastly overstating the failure rate of condoms in preventing the spread of HIV and other sexually transmitted diseases. One curriculum taught that "the popular claim that 'condoms help prevent the spread of STDs,' is not supported by the data," while another taught that condoms failed to prevent the spread of HIV during heterosexual sex a staggering 31 percent of the time.[24] The US Centers for Disease Control, however, says that using condoms consistently and correctly is "highly effective in preventing the sexual transmission of HIV infection and reduc[ing] the risk of other STDs."[25] One curriculum also falsely stated that you can contract

HIV through exposure to sweat and tears, while another incorrectly stated the number of chromosomes in the human genome.

Many of the abstinence-only curricula also contained false information about the risks associated with abortion, with one telling students that 5 to 10 percent of women who have an abortion become sterile and that subsequent pregnancies are more likely to result in premature birth. In reality, the Waxman report says, "These risks do not rise after the procedure used in most abortions in the United States."[26]

The executive summary of the report concludes that "serious and pervasive problems with the accuracy of abstinence-only curricula may help explain why these programs have not been shown to protect adolescents from sexually transmitted diseases and why youth who pledge abstinence are significantly less likely to make informed choices about precautions when they do have sex."[27]

Unfortunately, this is not the only issue on which the Christian right has fought both knowledge of and access to contraception. The passage of the Patient Protection and Affordable Care Act (better known as Obamacare) and implementation regulations that require health insurance policies to include birth-control services for women with no copay has resulted in dozens of lawsuits against the federal government over what is now known as the contraception mandate. Few things in recent memory have enraged conservative Christians more than this policy, prompting flights of rhetoric invoking tyranny, the destruction of religious freedom, Hitler's Germany and Stalin's Soviet Union, and calls for President Obama to be removed from office by impeachment or even by military coup.

All of the "pro-family" groups that have ostensibly made stopping abortion their priority for the last few decades are also strongly opposed to teaching young people how to safely and effectively use contraception and to making it more widely and cheaply available to women of all ages, which creates a fairly obvious tension. Studies show that greater access to contraception reduces rates of unintended pregnancy and abortion dramatically.

In January 2013, researchers from Washington University of St. Louis published the results of a study that gave more than nine thousand women, most of them lower income, free contraception. The results were astonishing. The rate of abortion among study participants ranged from 4.4 per 1,000 women to 7.5 per 1,000, compared to a national rate of 19.6 abortions per 1,000 women, a drop of 62 to 78 percent.[28]

Dr. James T. Breeden, president of the American College of Obstetricians and Gynecologists, told Fox News, "I would think if you were against abortions, you would be 100 percent for contraception access."[29] That those who are most stridently against abortion are also those most committed to precisely the opposite suggests to many that the goal of the Christian right is not so much to reduce abortion as to assert control over women's sexual and reproductive lives. As Angi Becker Stevens put it in 2011:

> Historically, abortion—as well as all forms of contraception—was typically seen as an evil not out of concern for the unborn, but rather out of the belief that allowing women to separate sex from child-bearing would lead to a complete collapse of womanly morality, allowing women to have sex willy-nilly for no other reason but pleasure. In other words, contraception and abortion would allow women the same sexual freedom enjoyed by men. There also was a widely accepted view that any woman who wished to avoid motherhood was inherently some kind of deviant; shunning the "natural" role of mother was viewed as a serious gender transgression.[30]

LGBT Equality

But today it appears that no issue is as vital to the Christian right than stopping the progress of greater equality for LGBT people, both in the United States and abroad. The Christian right has long been opposed to any advance in gay rights, but its zeal has risen dramatically since 2003, when two important court rulings kicked off the latest round of battles over equality.

The first came on June 26 of that year when the US Supreme Court ruled in *Lawrence v. Texas* that state laws against sodomy were unconstitutional. As a result, states could no longer arrest and punish anyone for engaging in consensual sex with someone of the same gender. The case overturned an earlier ruling from 1986 in *Bowers v. Hardwick*, which had upheld state sodomy laws. Like every key gay-rights victory since then, the majority opinion was written by Justice Anthony Kennedy, a Reagan appointee.

Contrary to both expectations and the analysis of many critics, Kennedy's ruling was not based on the right to privacy found in *Roe v. Wade* but on a broader "right to liberty." The two men arrested under the Texas sodomy statute, the ruling said, "are entitled to respect for their private lives. The State cannot demean their existence or control their destiny by making private sexual conduct a crime. Their right to liberty under the Due Process Clause gives them the full right to engage in their conduct without intervention of the government."[31]

The Court explicitly overruled its own seventeen-year-old decision in *Bowers*, saying that the previous Court had "fail[ed] to appreciate the extent of the liberty at stake. To say that the issue . . . was simply the right to engage in certain sexual conduct demeans the claim the individual put forward, just as it would demean a married couple were it said that marriage is simply about the right to have sexual intercourse. . . . [Sodomy] statutes . . . seek to control a personal relationship that, whether or not entitled to formal recognition in the law, is within the liberty of persons to choose without being punished as criminals."[32]

The ruling in *Lawrence* prompted a furious reaction from Christian right leaders. The decision was, the US Conference of Catholic Bishops declared, "deplorable."[33] The Family Research Council said the ruling was "a direct attack on the sanctity of marriage" and that "nothing less than the people's right to self-government is at stake"[34] (this is standard conservative rhetoric whenever the courts overturn a law they support; when they overturn a law they don't support, this right to self-government is never mentioned).

Albert Mohler of the Southern Baptist Theological Seminary called the ruling a "tragic turning point in our nation's culture war."[35] Tom Minnery, president of Focus on the Family, said the Court "continues pillaging its way through the moral norms of our country" and accused the justices of endangering "the welfare of the coming generations of children."[36] William Devlin of the Urban Family Council called the ruling "a bad decision for America, a bad decision for children and a bad decision for families. It's bad public policy and it's also against nature."[37] Phyllis Schlafly's Eagle Forum went even further, saying that the ruling "leaves America wide open for a further plunge backward into Sodom and Gomorrah" and "threaten[s] the very existence of our civilization and its basic institutions."[38]

The second was a ruling from the Supreme Judicial Court of Massachusetts in a case called *Goodridge v. Dept. of Public Health*, which concluded that equal recognition of marriages between same-sex couples was mandated by that state's constitution. The lawsuit was filed by gay couples that had been denied a license to marry by the state. The trial court ruled in favor of the state but the Supreme Judicial Court overturned that ruling. In the majority opinion, Chief Justice Margaret Marshall anticipated one of the primary arguments made against same-sex marriage, that it will somehow damage the institution of marriage itself:

> Here, the plaintiffs seek only to be married, not to undermine the institution of civil marriage. They do not want marriage abolished. They do not attack the binary nature of marriage, the consanguinity provisions, or any of the other gate-keeping provisions of the marriage licensing law. Recognizing the right of an individual to marry a person of the same sex will not diminish the validity or dignity of opposite-sex marriage, any more than recognizing the right of an individual to marry a person of a different race devalues the marriage of a person who marries someone of her own race. If anything, extending civil marriage to same-sex couples reinforces the importance of marriage to individuals and communities. That same-sex couples are willing to embrace marriage's solemn obligations of exclusivity, mutual support, and commitment to one another is a testament to the enduring place of marriage in our laws and in the human spirit.[39]

Indeed, the court concluded that none of the arguments advanced for the need to prevent gay couples from marrying were actually advanced by such a ban, saying,

> The marriage ban works a deep and scarring hardship on a very real segment of the community for no rational reason. The absence of any reasonable relationship between, on the one hand, an absolute disqualification of same-sex couples who wish to enter into civil marriage and, on the other, protection of public health, safety, or general welfare, suggests that the marriage restriction is rooted in persistent prejudices against persons who are (or who are believed to be) homosexual. . . . Limiting the protections, benefits, and obligations of civil marriage to opposite-sex couples violates the basic premises of individual liberty and equality under law protected by the Massachusetts Constitution.[40]

Once again, the response from leaders of the Christian right was very strong. The Catholic bishops of Massachusetts issued a series of statements calling the ruling "radical" and "devastating." Bishop George Coleman said that the ruling would lead to the "disappearance of the civil institution of marriage."[41] Focus on the Family said the ruling was an example of "judicial tyranny."[42]

In the wake of those rulings, stopping what they call the "gay agenda" became priority number one for members of the Christian right. Peter Sprigg of the Family Research Council, who has called for recriminalization of homosexuality,[43] said in the wake of *Goodridge*, "There is no issue we care more about."[44]

The Bush White House, which had not commented on the ruling in *Lawrence*, did make several statements in opposition to the state court ruling in *Goodridge*. President Bush himself called the ruling "deeply troubling."[45] Alan Sears of the Alliance Defense Fund (now the Alliance Defending Freedom) wrote that the SJC "has become a tyrannical force, willing and capable of wreaking havoc" and that the country was, as a result, "sliding further down the slippery [slope] of moral degeneracy."[46]

Mat Staver of Liberty Counsel, a Christian-right legal group founded by Jerry Falwell and based at his Liberty University, filed suit in federal court seeking to get the Massachusetts court ruling overturned. That suit made the argument that the state court ruling violated the guarantee in the US Constitution that every state would have a "republican form of government" because the Supreme Judicial Court had overturned state law based on its interpretation of the state constitution. That was an odd argument to make to the federal courts, which are likewise empowered to overturn legislative acts, and the Supreme Court declined to hear the suit without comment.[47]

The political fallout was immediate as these two court rulings encountered furious opposition, particularly from conservative Republicans. Karl Rove, the architect of President Bush's run for the White House in 2000, quickly recognized that this backlash presented a political opportunity. He immediately began encouraging conservatives to put referendums on state ballots to prohibit same-sex marriage, knowing that this hot-button issue would drive conservatives to the polls and that this would benefit Bush's reelection campaign, especially in key swing states like Ohio. Between 2004 and 2008, twenty-two states passed referendums prohibiting same-sex marriage.

In total, thirty-two states have now adopted such amendments, though California's ban was overturned by the Supreme Court on what was essentially a technicality, leaving thirty-one states that still have them. In another landmark decision that came out at the same time as the ruling in the California case, the Supreme Court ruled that the federal government must recognize same-sex marriages legally performed in states that allow them, but it did not overturn the bans on same-sex marriage in the other thirty-one states. Since that ruling, however, lower court judges have used the language of Justice Kennedy's majority opinion, which held that laws against same-sex marriage were motivated only by antigay prejudice, to strike down the bans in Utah and Virginia (both rulings are now on hold pending appeals).

In addition, the 2012 election brought a major setback for the Christian right when voters in three states—Maine, Maryland, and Washington—approved referendums legalizing same-sex marriage, while Minnesota voted to repeal its ban on the practice. After the election, the Minnesota legislature quickly approved a bill legalizing same-sex marriage. The tide, both legislatively and judicially, has clearly turned in favor of equality.

In the wake of those election results, prominent Christian-right leaders have tried to put on a brave face, telling their followers that even though they lost the battle, they're going to win the war. When a bill to recognize same-sex marriages was temporarily delayed in the Illinois state legislature, Tony Perkins of the Family Research Council told his followers that "same-sex 'marriage' is only as inevitable as we make it. If Christians play into the media's hands and adopt this defeatist attitude, then the Left is right: It is helpless. But if believers rediscover the power of the truth, they can do more than stop the dissolution of marriage (like they did in Illinois), they can 'turn the world upside down' (Acts 17:6)."[48] The Illinois bill passed a few months later, but Perkins was still playing the optimist:

> Homosexual activists like to say that momentum is on their side. And until recently, they might have been right. Sixteen U.S. states now recognize a right to same-sex marriage. And unfortunately, the Left's success in places like Hawaii and Illinois have helped feed the lie in America that homosexual marriage is inevitable. But don't believe it, say experts. All we've witnessed lately is the Left taking advantage of easy targets. With the exception of West Virginia, none of the other 34 states are under Democratic control.[49]

Scott Lively, one of the most virulent antigay leaders in the country (he wrote a book claiming that the Nazis were led by "butch" gay men out to destroy their more effeminate compatriots) and now a candidate for governor of Massachusetts, sounded even more optimistic in predicting that 2014 would be the "Year of the Pro-Family Push-Back!"

> The homosexual movement may have built up a formidable army of activists and an enormous war machine over the past forty years, but even at its best it is no match for an awakened Christian church. And for the first time in my 25 years of service as a Christian social activist I believe the church has been awakened. It hasn't buckled on its armor. It's not even standing on its feet yet. But the church of Jesus Christ—the universal body of Bible-believing Christians spanning every denomination and confession—finally has its eyes open and is aware that the enemy has breached the outer walls. . . . At the close of 2013 the Christian church is now wide awake and concerned. The giant is sitting up on the edge of the bed, ready to put on his shoes and go out to deal with this problem.[50]

But the truth is that public opinion has shifted enormously in the nearly eleven years since *Goodridge* and *Lawrence* put LGBT equality front and center. In 2003 and 2004, public opinion polls showed overwhelming opposition to marriage equality for gays and lesbians, with voters nationwide rejecting it by a two-to-one margin, sometimes approaching three to one. Today that has changed enormously, with most recent polls showing that Americans favor equality by about a 55-to-36-percent margin with the rest undecided. And shortly after the Supreme Court's decision involving DOMA in June 2013, polls showed support for federal recognition of same-sex marriages performed in states where they are legal by a 62-to-34-percent margin. This is an extraordinary shift in public opinion in a remarkably short period of time.

Faced with growing support for equality at home, many prominent Christian-right leaders and organizations have started looking to other countries to promote antigay legislation. In the summer of 2013, the Russian Duma passed a harsh law forbidding "propaganda of nontraditional sexual relations,"[51] which is being interpreted broadly enough that people have been arrested merely for wearing clothing or carrying signs with rainbows on them. Protests in favor of gay equality have also been outlawed. Many prominent Christian-right leaders have not only supported that law but played a role in getting it passed, and they are taking credit for helping do so.

In the days leading up to the passage of that law, Brian Brown of the National Organization for Marriage traveled to Russia and testified in favor of the bill before the Duma.[52] Bryan Fischer of the American Family Association said on his radio show that "this is public policy that we've been advocating and here is a nation in the world [Russia] that is actually putting it into practice."[53]

Austin Ruse of the Catholic Family and Human Rights Institute said that you had to "admire some of the things they're doing in Russia against propaganda," but he lamented the fact that "you know it would be impossible to do that here."[54] Peter LaBarbera of Americans for Truth about Homosexuality said, "Russians do not want to follow America's reckless and decadent promotion of gender confusion, sexual perversion, and anti-biblical ideologies to youth."[55]

Scott Lively has repeatedly praised the bill and even taken credit for "indirectly" helping it pass when he toured that country a few years ago, calling it "one of the proudest achievements of my career."[56] His praise for Russian strongman Vladimir Putin has been effusive, calling him a "hero of family values" and "the defender of Christian civilization."[57] In fact, he says, "Russia could become a model pro-family society. If this were to occur, I believe people from the West would begin to emigrate to Russia in the same way that Russians used to emigrate to the United States and Europe."[58]

Lively has also traveled to Uganda, where a new law adds to the penalties for homosexuality, which was already illegal. Under the new law, anyone who is gay faces up to life in prison (it originally included the death penalty, but international outcry moved the Ugandan parliament to "soften" the bill). He implored the Ugandan government to pass the bill and even called himself the "father" of the Ugandan antigay movement.[59] He is now facing a lawsuit in the United States from proequality and human rights groups accusing him of crimes against humanity for his role in spreading antigay hatred in that country and around the world.

Demand for Religious Exemptions

These battles over gay rights, abortion, and contraception have helped create a new demand from the Christian right for exemptions from the laws that apply to everyone else. Some exemptions were already in place; for example, the courts have long recognized a "ministerial exception" to many types of laws because enforcement of them would require the government to involve itself in church doctrine. For instance, laws that forbid discrimination on the basis of religion are not applied to churches because the First Amendment would not allow the government to force a Christian church to hire a Muslim or Jewish minister.

But over the last twenty-five years, and particularly in the last couple years, Christian-right groups have demanded that such exemptions be extended much further. In 1993, Congress passed the Religious Freedom Restoration Act (RFRA), which allows religious individuals and organizations to ask the courts to exempt them from many types of religiously neutral laws. It also requires the courts to apply *strict scrutiny* to such requests, which means that the burden is on the government to show that enforcing the law against the religious plaintiffs is the *least restrictive means* of achieving a *compelling state interest*. Most states followed suit with similar laws of their own and the courts have, for the past two decades, developed a large body of case law regarding what constitutes a compelling state interest and what the limits of these protections are.

In 2000, Congress passed the Religious Land Use and Institutionalized Persons Act (RLUIPA), which provides similar exemptions from local zoning laws and protections for religious practice for those who are incarcerated. The act applies the same strict scrutiny standards as RFRA, and here again the courts have developed a body of case law regarding the limits of those exemptions.

But those two laws, which many legal scholars argue are unconstitutional because they give special benefits to religious people and institutions that are not available to the nonreligious, are still not enough for the Christian right, which is also demanding laws that provide even broader exemptions, such as the right to of parents to remove their children from any teaching in public schools that they disagree with, especially evolution. As of this writing, in early 2014, there are major battles raging in courts and legislatures over whether Christian nonprofits, and even for-profit businesses owned by Christians, have to comply with state and local laws that prohibit discrimination on the basis of sexual orientation (twenty-one states and many municipalities have such protections, but the federal government does not) and also with the aforementioned mandate that all health insurance policies include coverage for contraception and family planning.

The Supreme Court has already ruled in a case brought by the private company Hobby Lobby against the contraception mandate. Hobby Lobby argued that because the company is owned by Christians who object to contraception it is a violation of their religious freedom to require them to provide such coverage in their group insurance policies. The Court ruled in favor of Hobby Lobby. There are also many legal challenges by religious nonprofit organizations, who under the law do not have to include contraception in their health insurance packages (instead, the insurance companies are required to provide such coverage in a separate rider at no charge), but who object to even putting their objections in writing as a violation of their religious liberty.

Hobby Lobby based its case on RFRA, and in February Marci Hamilton, a law professor at Cardozo Law School, unsuccessfully filed a brief in the case on behalf of several organizations urging the Supreme Court not only to reject that argument but to declare RFRA and RLUIPA to be unconstitutional. That brief argued that those laws violate the Establishment Clause of the First Amendment because they allow "religious entities" to "obtain extreme rights to trump constitutional, neutral, generally applicable laws" and because RFRA "carves up every neutral, generally applicable federal law (i.e., those that are constitutional under the Free Exercise Clause) for the benefit solely of religious actors."[60]

Meanwhile, many state legislatures are attempting to pass laws that explicitly allow Christian-owned businesses to discriminate against gay, lesbian, bisexual, and transgender people. The Kansas House of Representatives passed such a bill but it died in the Senate due to concerns that the exemptions were too broadly written. Several other states are considering or have passed similar bills, which vary by state but typically say that it is legal to discriminate as long as it is based on "sincerely held religious beliefs." A restaurant, hotel, or movie theater could refuse service to a person perceived to be gay, for example, or refuse to hire him.

The most radical of these proposals was in Idaho, where a bill was proposed that would allow businesses to discriminate against LGBT people. In addition, the bill says that an "occupational licensing board or government subdivision" cannot "deny, revoke or suspend a person's professional or occupational license" if he or she engage in anti-LGBT discrimination. That means that a doctor or nurse could refuse to treat someone they think is gay without losing their license. Though it seemed likely to pass the state legislature, the sponsor of the bill withdrew it in late February while lamenting the fact that it had been "misconstrued" as being discriminatory.[61]

In all these cases, the Christian right demands nothing less than to be covered by a different set of laws than those enforced against everyone else (curiously, they never argue that non-Christians should be exempted from the laws that forbid discrimination against Christians). They want two Americas, one for Christians and one for everyone else, and they are aided in those efforts by state legislatures and far too often by the courts as well.

Conclusion

The struggle to define America, as James Davison Hunter called the culture wars, continues today as it has since before the nation's founding. Throughout that history, conservative Christians have been the primary opposition to every single advance in equal rights and equal justice. In each such battle—over slavery, women's suffrage, segregation and Jim Crow laws, and so on—once public opinion has turned completely in favor of progress, it is conveniently forgotten where that opposition came from. And the same arguments, based on tradition and religious belief, are then recycled in the next battle.

If we are to define America by its loftiest ideals as a nation where everyone is given equal protection regardless of gender, race, religion, or sexual orientation rather than one defined by Christian privilege to assert dominance over everyone else, it will only be because we have managed to limit the influence of the Christian right over legislatures, the courts, or both.

WOMAN, WHAT HAVE I TO DO WITH THEE?

Christianity's War against Women

Annie Laurie Gaylor

s a young girl growing up in the sixties, I had been lightly exposed to Bible criticism in my nonreligious family, but reading the Bible made a true unbeliever and feminist out of me. I knew, vaguely, that the Bible advanced antiquated teachings about women. Nevertheless, I was truly shocked at what I discovered when I read the Bible cover to cover in my early twenties. "Sexism" is too breezy a term for the pathological sexual hatred to be found within the covers of a book touted as "holy." Like Nietzsche, after reading the Bible I felt the need to wash my hands.

As I read the Bible with increasing incredulity, I realized how little women could be valued in a society whose most valued book utterly devalues women. It is impossible for women to be free and equal in a culture that refers to a violent and demeaning handbook for women's subjugation as "the good book." Among the most common of the biblical epithets for women are "harlot," "whore," "unclean." Biblical women play one of two roles: they are either superfluous (only about 10 percent of the Bible even mentions women) or diabolical. No remnant of worship of woman for her biological usefulness, which existed in earlier ages and cultures, is to be found in the "Holy Bible." Women as the life source is rather an excuse to degrade and scorn them.

In the beginning . . . is actually an egalitarian version of creation ("male and female created he them" [Genesis 1:27]). This passage, in which "God blessed (italic) *them,*" was traditionally ignored, while the degrading spare-rib version (Genesis 3:22) has been preached for centuries from the pulpit. Every child who grows up in cultures adhering to the Abrahamic religions of

Judaism, Christianity, and Islam still imbibes the tall tale of Eve fashioned out of Adam's rib. The second creation version, describing Eve as a mere afterthought, a "help meet" to man, is patriarchal reversal at its most outrageous, perverting nature by crediting man with "giving birth" to woman:

> And the Lord God caused a deep sleep to fall upon Adam, and he slept: and he took one of his ribs, and closed up the flesh instead thereof; And the rib, which the Lord God had taken from man, made he a woman, and brought her unto the man. And Adam said, This is now bone of my bones, and flesh of my flesh: she shall be called Woman, because she was taken out of Man. . . . and they shall be one flesh. (Genesis 2:21–25)

"Eve," as the prototypical woman, is scapegoated as a sin-inciting, disobedient, impulsive, morally inferior seductress who literally led to the downfall of humankind. But Eve was framed. Significantly, in the favored second version of creation, Adam had been directly warned not to eat "of the tree of knowledge of good and evil," while Eve learned of this anti-intellectual injunction only by hearsay. Regardless of how she heard this warning, in this fable it is actually Eve who is laudable, a seeker of knowledge, wishing to learn, wanting to know right from wrong. The serpent told her very truly that once she ate the fruit "your eyes shall be opened, and ye shall be as gods, knowing good and evil." Wasn't it an act of generosity that, when Eve saw that "the tree was good for food, and that it was pleasant to the eyes, and a tree to be desired to make one wise," she offered the fruit to her husband? When they ate the fruit, "the eyes of them both were opened" (Genesis 3:5–7). For her disobedience (the biblical deity seems enraged mainly by the fact that the couple, now realizing they were naked, modestly made aprons to wear), she is cursed by the patriarchal deity:

> I will greatly multiply thy sorrow and thy conception; in sorrow thou shalt bring forth children; and thy desire shall be to thy husband, and he shall rule over thee. (Genesis 3:16)

By the third chapter of Genesis, women have lost their identity, been blamed for bringing sin and death into the world, and have been cursed with bringing forth children in sorrow and being ruled by men. The myth of Adam and Eve wherein she is blamed, is thrown back into women's faces in count-less New Testament rants, exemplified by 1 Timothy 2:11–14:

> Let the woman learn in silence with all subjection. But I suffer not a woman to teach, nor to usurp authority over the man, but to be in silence. For Adam was first formed, then Eve. And Adam was not deceived, but the woman being deceived was in the transgression.

The scriptural hypocrisy and double standard are of biblical proportions. The New Testament specifically mandates a patriarchal master/slave hier-archy that puts God over man and man over woman. This hierarchy is explic-itly spelled out:

> But I would have you know, that the head of every man is Christ; and the head of the woman is the man; and the head of Christ is God. . . . For a man . . . is the image and glory of God: but the woman is the glory of the man. For the man is not of the woman: but the woman of the man. (1 Corinthians 11:3–8)

To paraphrase feminist theologian Mary Daly, as long as God is male, male is God.

Between the books of Genesis, which begins the Bible, and Revelation, which concludes it, there are approximately three hundred Bible verses or stories that explicitly mandate women's inequality, inferiority, or subservience. Bible law, codified as Mosaic law in the Pentateuch (the first five books of the Bible), con-tains not just "ten commandments" but more than six hundred commandments supposedly dictated by Yahweh to Moses. The sinfulness of sex is a Mosaic obses-sion, with the Bible typecasting women as Eves, Delilahs, and Jezebels. One does not need to be a prophet to predict how poorly women fare in the biblical scheme of justice. While we hear about the "Madonna/Whore" dichotomy, madonnas do not fare much better in the New Testament. Jesus arrogantly asks his mother, "Woman, what have I to do with thee?" Mary Magdelene is deemed too "unclean" to approach Jesus before he has ascended. Jesus admonishes her, "Touch me not," yet he invites Thomas to touch him (John 20:17, 27).

The Bible issues edicts over such matters as feminine hygiene, menstrua-tion, pregnancy, and everyday behavior. No detail about women was appar-ently too private or trite, from women's periods, flat chests (see Song of

Solomon), and childbirth confinement to hair styles (no braids, no gold, no pearls, no "costly array"), housewifely duties, and neighborly (i.e., gossipy) ways. These feminine facets are duly noted, often with over-familiarity, even loathing or fear. According to 1 Timothy 2:9, women are to "adorn themselves in modest apparel, with shamefacededness and sobriety." Western civilization's preoccupation with women's dress and hair and sharp gender roles traces to the Bible, which warns in Deuteronomy 22:5 that men and women who wear each other's garments shall be "abominations." Men are to have short hair and women long hair, again harkening back to Eve's shame: "Doth not even nature itself teach you, that, if a man have long hair, it is a shame unto him? But if a woman have long hair, it is a glory to her: for her hair is given her for a covering" (1 Corinthians 3:14–15).

One of the most repellant of the antiwoman biblical themes is its refrain that women are "unclean." Women are depicted as once-a-month outcasts who menace society and must do penance for those natural functions of their bodies that ensure the continuation of the species. Leviticus declares women "unclean," mandates that a menstruous woman is unclean for "seven days," and must be "put apart." Whoever touches her is unclean, the bed is unclean, the furniture is unclean (Leviticus 15:19–23). After their periods are over, women must, absurdly, offer a "sin atonement." (The Bible specifies that a "burnt offering" of two turtles or two young pigeons must be taken to the priest, who begs "an atonement for her before the Lord for the issue of her uncleanness." One presumes turtles and pigeons were delicacies favored by the priests [Leviticus 15:29–30].) If a man has intercourse with a menstruating woman and "her flowers be upon him," he becomes unclean for seven days (Lev. 15:24). Later this same biblical chapter commands that a couple who commit this act will be "cut off" from their people, a frightening threat in a nomadic culture (Leviticus 20:18). Couples marrying in Israel are still handed instructions advising them of this sanction. Prohibitions against menstruating women are not confined to the Pentateuch's various commandments. The Bible's ultimate putdown is to compare disfavored Israelites to menstruating women: "Her filthiness is in her skirts . . . Jerusalem is as a menstruous woman" (Lamentations 1:8–17). The New Testament continues the squeamish theme, describing how, when a "woman with issue" touches Jesus's garb, it cures her—but his "virtue" leaves him (Mark 5:30).

Perhaps more despised even than "menstruous" women is that biblical speciality: a "strange woman" (meaning non-Israelite). Intermarriage with non-Hebrews was considered a major threat to the one truth faith. Israel is described as committing "whoredom with the daughters of Moab," angering the biblical deity so much that he orders Moses, "Take all the heads of the people, and hang them up before the Lord against the sun." (Numbers 25:1–4). When a Midianite princess is brought by an Israelite into a congregation in the sight of Moses, a priest's son takes a javelin and stabs them, "the woman through her belly" (Numbers 25:8). Among the Bible's famous "strange" women are Delilah, Samson's wife, and Jezebel, credited with persuading her husband Ahab to worship another deity. For acting out the proper role of a supportive wife, Jezebel is thrown off a wall and trodden by horses as her executioner, dining and drinking, watches. Then her bits and pieces are given to the dogs (2 Kings 9:23–37). Proverbs takes the revilement of "strange" women to an intemperate pitch: "The mouth of a strange woman is a deep pit" (Proverbs 22:14), "a strange woman is a narrow pit. She also lieth in wait as for a prey, and increaseth the transgressors among men" (Proverbs 23:27–28).

As I was reading this as a young woman I was appalled by the Bible's name-calling of women, its intemperate denunciation of "whores." "Her house is the way to hell, going down to the chambers of death" (Proverbs 7:9–27). "Whoredom," biblical-style, does not require that women take remuneration. Biblical harlotry typically involves the "crime" of seducing men. Biblical law orders that priests can't take "whores" or "profane" women to wed, or even a divorced woman (Leviticus 21:7). If a priest's daughter "profane herself by playing the whore" she must be *burned* (Leviticus 21:9). The biblical deity in one passage authorizes the grotesque mutilation of two "whores," ordering a horde of captains and rulers on horses to cut off the nose and ears of one of the women, strip her, and force her to "pluck off thine own breasts" (Ezekiel 23:11–48). Revelation describes a terrifying specter, "the great whore that sitteth upon many waters" holding a golden cup "full of abominations and filthiness of her fornication," whose flesh is to be eaten and burned (Revelation 17:1–16).

Such excessive warnings about the evil sexual endowments and powers of women not surprisingly led to historical bloodshed and persecution of women. One verse, "Thou shalt not suffer a witch to live" (Exodus 22:18), resulted in the executions of tens of thousands of women during the witch purges. The witch hunts were fueled by the *Malleus Maleficarum*, a handbook issued in 1486 that explained how to detect, torture, and kill witches. It was written by two Dominican Inquisitors and sanctified by Pope (Not So) Innocent VII. The handbook stated: "All witchcraft comes from carnal lust, which is in women insatiable."[1] The seven primary "crimes" witches were accused of were sexual in nature, including arousing passion in men, causing impotence, and using or doling out birth control. It should be no surprise that the Bible, which characterizes all women as innately evil and transgressing, should have inspired this holocaust against women.

Matrimony is fraught with peril. Women who are discovered not to be virgins on their wedding night are to be stoned to death (Deuteronomy 22:13–21), a barbaric Old Testament rule still enforced by Islamist nations. Under biblical double standards, men may have multiple wives and many concubines. "Wise" King Solomon carries this to ridiculous extremes with his seven hundred wives and three hundred concubines (1 Kings 11:3). Old Testament hanky-panky is common, with two esteemed patriarchs—Abraham and Isaac—essentially prostituting their wives, in Abraham's case his wife actually being his half-sister. Although adulterers of either sex are ordered to be executed, this rule was extended to men who had sex with other men's property; that is, with "another man's wife" (Leviticus 20:10). If a "spirit of jealousy" comes upon a husband, he and the priest can make her drink a vile concoction of "bitter water" brewed with tabernacle dirt and dust and the residue of burnt animal sacrifices, and if she apparently vomits, she is "cursed" (Numbers 5:14–31).

New Testament wives are repeatedly ordered to "be in silence," "to submit," and not to speak in church (they "must ask their husbands at home"), and they are "commanded to be under obedience" (1 Corinthians 14:34–25, among many other injunctions).

> Wives, submit yourself unto your own husbands, as unto the Lord. For the husband is the head of the wife, even as Christ is the head of the Church: and he is the savior of the body. Therefore as the church is subject unto Christ, so let the wives be to their own husbands in everything. (Ephesians 5:22–24)

Peter warns that not only must women learn in subjection, but they must be in fear of their husbands (1 Peter 3:1–7). Although this passage also tells husbands to honor these wives "as unto the weaker vessel," such a mandate places women on a pedestal of clay. The double standard continues over divorce. The Old Testament provides for no-fault divorce—for men. A man merely has to hand his wife a "bill of divorcement" and out she goes (Deuteronomy 24:1).

Motherhood is a curse, and new mothers are "unclean." Women who bear sons are unclean seven days, but if a woman has a daughter, it doubles her days of uncleanness and purification. Even sons are contaminated by association: "Who can bring a clean thing out of an unclean? Not one," laments Job (Job 14:1–4). Paul patronizingly promises that a woman "shall be saved in childbearing, if they continue in faith and charity and holiness with sobriety" (1 Timothy 2:15). John 16:21 claims that a travailing woman forgets all her pain "for joy that a man is born into the world." The progeny of an unmarried mother is reviled: "A bastard shall not enter into the congregation of the Lord; even to his tenth generation" (Deuteronomy 23:2). That's around two hundred fifty years—God sure knows how to carry a grudge! When a woman sings his mother's praises, saying, "Blessed is the womb that bare thee, and the paps which thou hast sucked," Jesus rebukes her: "Yea, rather, blessed are they that hear the word of God, and keep it" (Luke 11:27–28).

The Bible defines women as male property, as established by the Ten Commandments, which insultingly lump women with other possessions, such as asses (Deuteronomy 5 version). Wives take second billing to inanimate objects such as "thy neighbor's house" in the Exodus 20 variation. Even male animals own their female peers; the story of Noah's ark refers to animal pairs as "male and his female" (Genesis 7:2). Women are frequently purchased in Bible stories, best exemplified by the "romance" of Ruth, who is purchased by Boaz (Ruth 4:10). In perhaps the most shocking purchase, David buys Michal, the daughter of King Saul, with the foreskins of two hundred Philistines (1 Samuel 18:27). Naturally, since women can be bought, they can be sold. While slavery is approved in the Bible, a male indentured servant might eventually go free, but not the servant's enslaved wife (Exodus 21:2–6). Numerous biblical provisions detail the rules and regulations of bondwomen, who were at the mercy of their masters and could be assigned sexual duties (Exodus 21:7–11). Think of the centuries of acute personal misery and degradation this caused enslaved women in the antebellum United States and colonial America, where slave owners invoked holy scripture to justify slavery.

The most chilling treatment of women as property is human sacrifice. Even the Bible's bloodthirsty deity stays the hand of zealous Abraham as he prepares to show his faithfulness by slitting his son's throat. But no such commutation was made for the nameless daughter of warrior Jephthah, who sacrifices his own female offspring to honor a "deal" he has made with the biblical deity (Judges 11:30–40).

Since biblical women are property, not surprisingly they are also abductable and rapeable. Innumerable cruel and unrelenting biblical passages treat women as war booty. "To every man a damsel or two" (Judges 5:30). The rape of women is not only described in biblical stories, it is also carefully spelled out in laws governing abduction and rape, such as in Deuteronomy 21:11–14. Essentially, Deuteronomy does not even recognize city rape. If a man finds a woman who is engaged and a virgin in the city, and "lies" with her, she shall be stoned to death because, the Bible assumes, she "cried not." He, too, shall be stoned to death for "humbling" his neighbor's wife. If a "betrothed damsel" is found by a man in the field and the man forces her, only the man shall die, because "there was none to save her." But since the Bible defines rape as a crime committed by men against other men's property, if a man rapes an "unbetrothed virgin" and "they are found," he must pay the woman's father fifty shekels of silver (no provision for inflation) and she must marry her criminal assailant. The Bible's charity toward rape victims is to force them to marry their rapists (Deuteronomy 22:23–29).

Among the many unsavory depictions of rape is the famous story of Sodom, wherein men in the village seek (inexplicably) to have their way with two visiting angels and are instead invited to cavalierly go after Lot's two virgin daughters—who are spared due to the angels' intervention (Genesis 19: 1–8). The grisliest biblical story of rape involves a concubine being thrown into the street to an unruly mob to save the woman's companion. "They knew her, and abused her all the night until the morning: and when the day began to spring, they let her go. . . . And her lord rose up in the morning and opened the doors of the house . . . he found her dead." His idea of mourning her was to cut her into twelve pieces, signifying the twelve tribes of Israel, and to start a war (Judges 19:28).

Even the biblical deity is a rapist:

> Moreover the LORD saith, Because the daughters of Zion are haughty, and walk with stretched forth necks and wanton eyes, walking and mincing *as* they go, and making a tinkling with their feet: Therefore the Lord will smite with a scab the crown of the head of the daughters of Zion, and the LORD will discover their secret parts ["Secret parts" is a translation of the Hebrew "poth," which means "hinged opening," or vagina]. (Isaiah 3:16)

The Bible's unhinged sense of family values is betrayed by its treatment of incest. Although sexual assault and incest prohibitions don't rate in the top ten (commandments), unlike adultery, incest is technically prohibited by the Bible. It is a taboo to marry near relations. Although the death penalty is called for as punishment for "lying with" your father's wife or daughter-in-law, the Bible is replete with unpunished, even exalted incest. The infamous story of "righteous" Lot's two virgin daughters seducing their father has undoubtedly suggested, provoked, and excused countless incestuous assaults upon helpless young daughters by fathers or father figures. The story perpetuates the ultimate double-speak libel: that young daughters seduce their fathers (Genesis 19:30–38).

Just as insidious as the overtly degrading biblical teachings are the Bible's lessons of disrespect, petty scorn, and contempt for women's "nature." The Bible is full of putdowns, stereotypes, and unsolicited advice. There are the insults: "In that day shall Egypt be like unto women" (Isaiah 19:16), "send for cunning women" (Jeremiah 9:17–20), and "Woe to the women" (Ezekiel 13:18–20). Ugly imagery predominates: "As a jewel of gold in a swine's snout, so is a fair woman which is without discretion" (Proverbs 11:22), "It is better to dwell in the corner of the housetop, than with a brawling woman and in a wide house" (Proverbs 25:24). Even motherhood brings no cessation of criticism: "A wise son maketh a glad father: but a foolish son is the heaviness of his mother" (Proverbs 22:14).

Proverbs, of course, offers the ultimate putdown: "Who can find a virtuous woman? For her price is far above rubies." The perfect wife is portrayed as an uncomplaining workhorse who "riseth also while it is yet night." It is not explained why fearing the Lord is offered as this "virtuous woman's" highest virtue (Proverbs 31:10–31).

I was not the first to notice, of course, that the Bible is rife with antiwoman teachings. In fact it appeared to have been written with the express purpose of sanctifying female inferiority. Criticism of biblical treatment of women dates to the 1800s. The first feminist critique, *The Godly Women of the Bible* by Ella E. Gibson, a former chaplain turned freethinker, was published circa 1878. Gibson trenchantly wrote of the Bible that "any family which permits such a volume to lie on their parlor-table ought to be ostracized from all respectable society."[2] Helen H. Gardener, a freethinking woman lecturer and friend of the great nineteenth-century agnostic Robert Ingersoll, wrote *Men, Women and Gods, and Other Lectures* in 1885. After summarizing the treatment of women in both testaments, Gardener urged: "Of all human beings a woman should spurn the Bible first."[3] The great Elizabeth Cady Stanton, an agnostic who sparked the woman's movement by calling for the right of women to vote in 1848, wrote the classic two-volume work *The Woman's Bible*, published in 1895 and 1898. The publication of this work resulted in her repudiation by the very woman's movement she had founded. Her eloquence and discernment about the Bible are unmatched: "The Bible and the Church have been the greatest stumbling blocks in the way of woman's emancipation."[4]

Less than two hundred years ago, the curses of Genesis and the exhortations of the New Testament over women's divinely decreed role as doormat and servant to men were the rule of the land. Women were property of fathers and husbands, classed with children and "idiots," with no identity beyond wife or daughter. Not only were they disenfranchised, but they could not sign contracts, sue, or be sued. Husbands could spend their paychecks and inherit their property. They had no custody rights. At the time the brilliant Elizabeth Cady Stanton grew up, virtually all institutions of higher learning were off limits to her as a woman. The term for this is "civil death," but the origins of this social status were strictly biblical. When Stanton and other early suffragists began speaking out in the late 1840s, religion-incited mobs tried to silence them: "In the early days of woman-suffrage agitation, I saw that the greatest obstacle we had to overcome was the Bible. It was hurled at us from every side," Stanton recalled toward the end of her life.[5] Every freedom women fought for and won, small or large, from wearing bloomers, to riding bicycles, to not wearing bonnets in churches and cutting their hair short, to being permitted to attend universities and enter professions, to voting and owning property, was bitterly opposed by the churches.

The Bible and other "holy books" continue to be hurled at women working for their freedom. Just as Stanton and others fought to wear bloomers (most eventually gave up the fight due to intense public opprobrium), more than a century later as a junior high school student, I had to circulate a petition in order to be permitted to wear slacks to school in the late 1960s. Boys and men in the sixties and early seventies were derided for growing out their hair. Dress reform was being fought well into the 1980s in the United States with President Ronald Reagan barring women in pantsuits from the White House. Reform of rape laws and attitudes did not take place until the late 1960s and 1970s, when many states still had statutes harkening back to the biblical "crying out" test. There has been progress in society's understanding of domestic violence, with the opening of battered women shelters, but all too many dutiful wives are still in thrall to the religious sanctification of wifely obedience. Due to the agitation of the women's movement and not at the initiation of various Christian denominations, women have gradually been admitted as ministers in many branches. Commendably, former president Jimmy Carter, who once served as a deacon and Sunday school teacher, and his wife, Rosalyn, quit the Southern Baptist Convention to protest its ban of women from the ministry in 2000. The Roman Catholic Church, the largest denomination in the United States, remains in the Dark Ages, with its unceasing decrees against ordaining women as priests.

The bitter defeat of the Equal Rights Amendment—first proposed in the 1920s—in the 1980s was due to the Roman Catholic, Mormon, and fundamentalist lobbies. Clergy and "men of God" remain the ringleaders of today's terrorism and harassment of abortion clinic personnel and patients. The right to contraception so valiantly fought for by freethinker Margaret Sanger is newly endangered as fundamentalist Protestant denominations jump on the Catholic hierarchy bandwagon in denouncing forms of birth control as abortifacients. A concerted push to redefine religious liberty as the right to force your dogma on others is being made by the Roman Catholic hierarchy, joined by religious-right groups and even fundamentalists at the helm of for-profit corporations such as Hobby Lobby, a large craft store chain. The Roman Catholic Church is openly at war with President Barack Obama's Affordable Care Act, which treats contraception as a right, as preventive medicine that must be covered by health insurance. As I write this, more than sixty lawsuits are in the courts seeking to deny women workers full contraceptive coverage based on religious objections. The religious war against women's rights by the conservative and fundamentalist branches of Christianity continues unabated.

It was fighting religion and its influence on our civil laws that catapulted my mother, Anne Nicol Gaylor, into feminist activism and opened our eyes to the terrible danger women face from religion, and from dogma controlling government. My mother is a second-generation freethinker and I am a third generation freethinker, and while we were fortunate to be allowed to grow up free of indoctrination, no woman truly grows up free from the Christian right's attempts to intrude on personal lives. As a weekly newspaper editor, my mother had been galvanized into activism after writing the first editorial in support of abortion rights in our heavily Catholic state of Wisconsin in 1968. Her editorial created shockwaves. It also brought her to the attention of desperate women seeking to end unwanted pregnancies. After writing that editorial, my mother's phone never stopped ringing. As a young teenager I was privileged to accompany my mother on her campaign to legalize abortion in Wisconsin as founder of the Wisconsin Committee to Legalize Abortion. I saw firsthand that the opposition to abortion rights and women's rights was irrational, emotional, and nearly always couched in Christian terms.

Wisconsin was the last state in the union to legalize contraception for unmarried individuals, with a statute that referred to contraception in Comstockian language as "indecent articles." Suddenly, while we struggled unsuccessfully to overturn that statute, a court decision in Wisconsin in 1970, when I was fourteen years old, struck down Wisconsin's statute criminalizing abortion—prior to *Roe v. Wade*, the Supreme Court's 1973 decision legalizing abortion nationwide. We felt such relief when a legal clinic opened in Madison, Wisconsin's capital city, in February 1971, with a wonderful doctor and humane staff. Then three weeks later our local district attorney, who was Roman Catholic, illegally raided the clinic—bursting into the examining room where a seventeen-year-old patient was in stirrups, taking her, forcibly examining her, and removing all the records. Hundreds of women had made appointments, and as there was no way to reach them, they were traveling to Madison and arriving at the clinic door crying, with no place to turn. My mother, as a feminist volunteer, was called in by the clinic's social worker to help these women. In response, she organized what would eventually become the longest-lived abortion-rights charity in the country, an abortion fund that basically loaned money to women to fly to New York State, where abortion was legal. A social worker later called her, crying, to relate the inevitable, that a seventeen-year-old girl in rural Wisconsin who had had an appointment had become desperate after the clinic raid, had employed a coat hanger, and had died as a result. We still don't know whether there were other deaths. For a woman who is unhappily pregnant, the right to a safe and legal abortion remains a matter of life and death. It was a travesty I will never forget, as panicked and horrified feminists and supporters flooded the Madison City County building. I carried a placard reading: "The Pope Rules Wisconsin." Eventually, the law prevailed and the clinic reopened, and by 1974, another court decision had finally overturned Wisconsin's archaic "indecent object" statute, allowing even unmarried persons to lawfully purchase contraception.

My mother, at eighty-seven, the principal founder of the Freedom from Religion Foundation, is still taking phone calls from indigent girls and women seeking help to pay for abortions. She continues to administer the Women's Medical Fund, which has helped well over twenty thousand Wisconsin-area women without the personal means to pay for abortions. While abortion remains legal, if under constant assault by the religious lobbies, it doesn't mean much if you're too poor to pay for it. Unfortunately, federal assistance for abortions was cut off at the instigation of a Catholic congressman in the 1970s. This means that in most US states safe abortion is still denied to many US women and girls who otherwise qualify for public assistance. The harm, the uncertainty, the panic, the denial of a constitutional right that the Roman Catholic Church and Protestant fundamentalists and their legislative spokespersons have caused women in just this one area of civil rights is incalculable. In 2013, more than sixty-eight individual pieces of legislation hostile to reproductive rights were enacted in various states. These mischief-making laws seeking to deny women control of their own bodies are enacted at the instigation of the religious lobby. Abortion is not yet an established right in other Western nations where Christianity predominates, such as the Republic of Ireland and some of the Slavic nations. Women continue to suffer and needlessly die, such as Indian dentist and mother Savita Halappanavar, who had the misfortune in 2012 of undergoing a life-threatening miscarriage in a country whose hospitals abide by Catholic dogma—which put doomed fetal life above the life of the pregnant woman. Think of the misery, poverty, needless suffering, unwanted pregnancies, social evils, and deaths that can be laid directly at the door of this church's pernicious doctrine that birth control is a sin that must be outlawed.

When I was growing up and accompanying my mother to Wisconsin's state capitol when bills on abortion and contraception were under consideration, the capitol would be filled with nuns and priests and bused-in parochial-school children in uniforms. Their testimony always began, "But the Bible says . . ." or "God says abortion is murder . . ."

Later, as a college student, I read the Bible for myself and wrote a book about it, *Woe to the Women: The Bible Tells Me So* (1981), the findings of which are summarized in the first part of this essay. I learned that the Bible says absolutely nothing at all about abortion. The word "abortion" does not appear in any translation of the Bible. Out of more than six hundred laws of Moses, none comments on abortion. In fact, one passage detailing miscarriage by misadventure—hurting a pregnant woman so that she miscarries—specifically orders the death penalty if the woman dies, but not for the expulsion of the fetus (Exodus 21:22–25). The Bible defines life as beginning at birth or "breath" in several significant passages, including the story of Adam's creation in Genesis 2:7, when God "breathed into his nostrils the breath of life; and man became a living soul." I read with revulsion the lewd descriptions of women, the promiscuous and gratuitous violence that showed no reverence for human life, with mass killings routinely ordered, committed, or approved by the god of the Bible. The injunction against "killing" refers to the murder of already-born Hebrews, most scholars agree, with open season on everyone else, including children and pregnant women (see 2 Kings 15:16, Isa. 13:36, Lam. 2:20, Hosea 13:16, and Ps. 137:9).

While the Bible is neither antiabortion nor prolife, it does provide a biblical basis for the real motivation behind the antiabortion religious crusade: hatred and control of women. The Bible is antiwoman, blaming women for sin, demanding subservience, mandating a master/slave relationship to men, and condemning women to maternal servitude.

The freethinker and feminist Margaret Sanger, whose motto was "No

Gods—No Masters," always pointed out: "No woman can call herself free who does not own and control her body. No woman can call herself free until she can choose consciously whether she will or will not be a mother."[6] That is one of the reasons why curtailing reproductive rights is a religious crusade. Control women's fertility and you control her life.

———————

By the time I was in college, my mother and I had broadened our activism from merely feminist to secular. My mother felt there were many feminist groups working to free women, but none was getting at the root of women's oppression: religious control of our laws and culture. Many years later, in researching and editing an anthology about women freethinkers, *Women without Superstition*, I learned of the major role even in the nineteenth century that women had played in founding and running secular groups. My mother and I are part of a proud secular tradition. Women have played such a crucial role in the latter-day Enlightenment and the rejection of religious dogma because organized religion has been the principal enemy of women's rights. Out of sheer self-defense, women have been among the most impassioned critics of the church, and among the most ardent supporters of secularism and, in the United States, the constitutional principle of separation between state and church.

The great feminist and agnostic Elizabeth Cady Stanton, the first to formally call for women's right to vote, in a speech in 1885 to the National Woman Suffrage Association, said:

> You may go over the world and you will find that every form of religion which has breathed upon this earth has degraded woman. There is not one which has not made her a subject to man. Men may rejoice in them because they make man the head of the woman. I have been traveling the old world during the last few years and have found new food for thought. What power is it that makes the Hindoo woman burn herself on the funeral pyre of her husband? Her religion. What holds the Turkish woman in the harem. Her religion. By what power do the Mormons perpetuate their system of polygamy? By their religion. Man, of himself, could not do this; but when he declares, "Thus saith the lord," of course he can do it. So long as ministers stand up and tell us that as Christ is the head of the church, so is man the head of

the woman how are we to break the chains which have held women down through the ages? We want to help roll off from the soul of woman the terrible superstitions that have so long repressed and crushed her.[7]

It is absolutely vital for women's advancement, for equality, for women's personal safety, and women's right to full ownership of our own bodies, to keep dogma out of law, to secularize government, to divorce state and religion. The United States does a lot wrong, but the framers of our Constitution got it right when they invested sovereignty in the people, not in a deity, and when they adopted an entirely godless and secular Constitution. And it requires constant vigilance—the theocrats, the religious right, are relentless. They never give up, and we can't either. It is not only that organized religion is the principal enemy of women's emancipation, to paraphrase Stanton. It is that secularists are the greatest friends to women's advancement. As one nineteenth-century American freethinker, Susan Wixon, put it: "Freethought has always been the best friend women had—the noblest, truest ally and champion."[8] It has always been the women without superstition, the religious nonconformists, the unorthodox, the heretics, the Anne Hutchinsons, the Sonia Johnsons, the Taslima Nasrins who dared question and confront the religious status quo that has demanded women's silence, subjection, servitude, and unquestioning obedience. It is thanks to freethinking women and their male allies that we have the rights we have won for women.

We do not have or need a mythical god on our side. We have humanity, we have right, we have progress, we have the Enlightenment, we have reason on our side. We don't need to imagine a patriarch in the sky who rains down bribes of an imaginary hereafter or threats of eternal damnation in order to do good. I question whether someone who can only "be good" based on an imposed authority, as opposed to an inner conscience, can truly be considered moral at all.

Matilda Joslyn Gage, an outspoken nineteenth-century critic of religion who worked with E. C. Stanton, wrote a series of resolutions in 1890: "In order to help preserve the very life of the republic, it is imperative that women should unite upon a platform of opposition to the teaching and aim of that ever most unscrupulous enemy of freedom—the Church."[9]

Her resolutions, which remain relevant, called for:

- a purely civil character of the government, keeping church and state forever separate, with no authority by the church but by the consent of the governed;
- resisting efforts to bring religion into politics;
- ensuring that the state govern civil affairs, protecting freedom of conscience and the free exercise of religion;
- condemning the imposition of any religious instruction or ritual whatsoever upon students in our common—public—schools;
- the right of individual conscience to be protected;
- the first duty of every individual to be self-development, that the lessons of self-sacrifice and obedience taught woman by the church have been fatal not only to her own vital interests but the vital interest of the human race;
- considering every church the enemy of liberty and progress and the chief means of enslaving woman's conscience and reason, and therefore as the first and most necessary step toward her emancipation we should free her from the bondage of the church;
- acknowledging that the Christian church of whatever name is based on the theory that women are inferior and brought sin into the world, and that Christianity is false and its foundation a myth, and that morality does not stem from theology but has a basis in the nature of things, the origin of right being in truth and not in authority.

In her 1893 book *Woman, Church and State,* Gage wrote:

The world has seemingly awaited the advent of heroic souls who once again should dare all things for the truth. The woman who possesses love for her sex, for the world, for truth, justice and right, will not hesitate to place herself upon record as opposed to falsehood, no matter under what guise of age or holiness it appears. . . . During the ages, no rebellion has been of like important with that of Woman against the tyranny of Church and State; none has had its far reaching effects. We note its beginning; its progress will overthrow every existing form of these institutions; its end will be a regenerated world.[10]

SECULAR SEXUALITY

A Direct Challenge to Christianity

Darrel W. Ray

I magine no religion—in your sex life. I think John Lennon could have written that song. That is what we will examine in this chapter. What would sex be like in a society without religion? At the same time, I want to examine the subtle and not-so-subtle ways religion infects our sexual ideas and behavior.

How would society be without religious sexual interference? For starters, guilt and shame would be far less common. Most guilt messages come from notions of sin, uncleanliness, original sin, and so forth. Relationships and marriages would not have the notions of Jesus watching and interfering with how you express your sexuality. Then, of course, the whole rationale for denying same-sex relationships and marriage would disappear. There are no secular reasons to deny marriage to same-sex couples. Using scientific approaches to sexuality, rather than religious notions, would take away the rigid concepts around the gender binary. Transsexuals would be as "normal" as hetero- or homosexuals. Pansexuality, bisexuality, and other variations would be seen simply as different expressions of sexuality. Menstruation would be seen simply as part of being human, with no supernatural sanctions or myths about uncleanliness. The same would hold for masturbation as well as sex before, during, or after marriage. Without religion there would be no celibate priests trying to rape little boys and girls, no fundamentalist ministers telling young girls that god wants them to have sex with them, and no Sunday-school teachers to shame girls and boys when they ask questions about sex.

Ethics around sex would center on the idea of consenting adults. Parenting would not include the terror of a child going to eternal damnation for being homosexual or for masturbating. Without religion, no one would be running around looking for a soul mate, since the whole notion of a soul is religious. Finally, the idea of religiously based monogamy "til death do us part" could be eliminated. Few marriages live by this unrealistic standard anyway. While it may be the way some people want to do marriage, there is no secular reason that marriage can't be done in other ways as well.

Much more could be said about sex without religion, but this should give us a good idea of a world without religious sex. There would be no Catholic sexuality, or Mormon, Baptist, Muslim, Buddhist, or Hindu sexuality. There would just be human sexuality. And humans could figure out how that works for them as individuals and within a larger culture of responsibility and accountability to partners. No religion needed.

Sex and Christianity

But let's take a step back and examine the Christian sexuality that surrounds most of us in Western culture. As the saying goes, "The biggest sex organ is the mind." As I explore in my book *Sex and God*,[1] Christians use their ideas about sex to convert people and ensure their faith maintains dominance in our culture. This mind control infects large numbers of people, even those who are not strongly religious.

Christianity may not have invented the idea of a god being involved in your sex lives, but it raised it to new levels of perfection. A key notion in Christianity is that of a god that watches your every thought and behavior. For some Christian sects, the personal god literally lives inside the person. In others, he just seems to read your mind from afar. In any event, it is an incredibly intrusive idea. Once the personal god or mind-reading god idea is installed in a person, a battle begins. It is a battle of the watching and nagging god against the natural biological, social, and developmental processes we experience as humans. The very act of thinking becomes a hazardous endeavor. Engaging in perfectly normal sexual behavior becomes damning.

How does a person learn about his or her own body, how to pleasure, think about, and enjoy him or herself, with a condemning, nagging, and angry god living and watching inside the mind? It is literally a battle of the mind, and there is no escape once infected with the Christian god. Jesus said, "But I say unto you, That whosoever looketh on a woman to lust after her hath committed adultery with her already in his heart" (Matthew 5:28). It is an impossible standard that means, if taken seriously, that a Christian is constantly being harassed with notions of sinfulness, even if no one else is involved. Indeed, the greatest guilt may come when no one else is involved. How does a Christian pleasure him/herself without committing the thought crime of adultery?

The Christian sexual journey begins by teaching shame for one's own body. After eating the so-called forbidden fruit in Genesis, Adam and Eve knew they were naked and decided to put on some clothes. Body shame and sexual shame are among the first lessons in the Bible. From women's uncleanliness for two weeks during menstruation to having sex with harlots or between men, or stoning women for not being virgins on their wedding night, there are many lessons from the Old Testament. But it is not until Jesus and Paul that we get the new and much more intrusive god living inside the mind.

This Christian sexuality surrounds and infects even the nonreligious, and it can be difficult for secular people to understand it and eliminate it from their worldview. From infancy, we are indoctrinated by the religious culture that surrounds us. Even if you were not raised to be religious, the kids in your school, the boys or girls in your locker room, probably were. You probably had religious relatives or neighbors who spouted sexual nonsense within earshot. You didn't have to belong to the Baptist or Catholic Church to learn that playing with yourself is dirty, that it may ruin your marriage, that pornography will destroy your mind, that having sex before marriage is wrong, and that abstinence is the most virtuous path. These ideas are ubiquitous and can penetrate even the most secular mind. Much like a parasite, religious ideas can infect even secular people and dramatically influence behavior and relationships

Biological Parasites

Any parasite must have a set of tools with which to infect the host, disable its defenses, and take behavioral control. The host then does the bidding of the parasite and helps the parasite get to the next host. Biologists have discovered dozens of examples of this in nature. There are undoubtedly many yet to be discovered. The female Sacculina barnacle infects a crab, destroys its sex organs, and takes control of part of its brain. It convinces the host that the parasite is really the crab's own eggs. The host then takes care of the parasite as if it were valuable eggs. Next the parasite invites male Sacculina in, mates, and reproduces, all at the expense of the crab. In biology, these "tricks" are done with hormones and chemicals that mimic those of the host and manipulate the hosts own nervous system to the advantage of the parasite.

For more examples, read Dennett, Ray, or Dawkins.[2] All discuss biological viruses and parasites that can control other organisms.

Mind Parasites

Much like the Sacculina, Christianity has a toolbox designed to use sex for its own ends. Rather than chemicals and hormones, mind parasites use sets of ideas that work together to create a safe place in the brain for the development and propagation of the parasite. Sexuality is only one part of a religious infection, but it is arguably the most potent. If a mind parasite can take control of part of our sexuality, it has a platform from which to control behavior and propagate to the next host. The Christian parasite bears strong similarities to sexually transmitted diseases. As in biology, there are other ways to pass along pathogens, such as sneezing or eating, but sex has proven to be an efficient path for many religions, including Christianity.

When I speak of sex, I am not speaking strictly of the sex act or of the genitalia, but of the mental constructs that are essential to the formation of sexual identity and behavior. Christianity puts a lot of time and energy into shaping individual and group ideas about sex and sexuality. A person's ideas about sex are more powerful than the sex organs they have. Religion has the ability to strongly influence how an individual uses his or her sex organs and how they feel about those sex organs. Since sexuality is a constant force in our lives, it means religious infection has the power to shape our behavior deeply and permanently.

Christianity even has the power to cut us off from our sexuality, creating eunuchs in the service of Jesus. Many a Catholic priest and nun has disavowed sex to better serve Jesus. Many a Protestant has struggled mightily with guilt around sex, ultimately losing interest in sex and instead refocusing that energy on religious endeavors. In my clinical practice, I have encountered many people who told me that the guilt and conflict they experienced around sex was not worth it. Better to be sexless or celibate than have to deal with such disturbing emotions. This is most interesting when coming from the mouths of married persons who cannot even have sex with their spouse because of the guilt they experience.

The presence of behavior and thinking of this kind demonstrates a well-infected person. The Christian parasite has fully integrated itself into the mind of the victim and cut them off from their sexual drive. It is guilt training that emotionally neuters a Christian. This phenomenon is seen throughout Christianity, whether Catholic or evangelical, Jehovah's Witness or Orthodox. Christians of all types find themselves living sexless lives even as they become better Christians. Christian historical literature is full of saints who gave up sex in order to better serve Jesus. Sexual denial is a concept that is in the very DNA of Christianity. That is in contrast to Judaism and Islam, which never codified celibacy and sexual denial as a key part of their religious infection strategies.

From the beginning, the Christian ideal has been to live a sexless life. Paul even admonished people not to marry. If they can't avoid temptation, he advises marriage, but clearly he sees that as an inferior option (1 Corinthians 7). To achieve eternal life, sex must be under control, and the best option is to eliminate sex. The early church fathers, from Tertullian and Origen to Ambrose and Augustine, were adamant that sexual sin is among the worst offenses against God. Yet, as almost any human can attest, thinking about sex is as natural and easy as breathing. Therefore, to ask a person to not even think about sex, let alone do it, is to ask the impossible. Such standards create the titanic struggles that can be found in the writings of Augustine, Luther, Calvin, Billy Graham, James Dobson, and many other stalwarts of Christianity.

Imagine if you were beaten, harassed, or berated in some fashion every day for thinking about eating chocolate, cherry pie, or other similar deserts. It would not take long for you to lose interest in these or gain a strong fear associated with them. In fact, given the right kind of training, a phobia of sweets might even develop. Even the thought of chocolate cake might make you sick to your stomach. Seeing others eat cake or pie could cause serious discomfort, so much so that you might try to persuade others to avoid eating in front of you. Or worse, you may start condemning others for flaunting their love of sweets in front of you.

Christianity performs a similar function. Good Christians are mentally harassed every day by St. Paul or Jesus for their every sexual thought. Guilt and shame are woven throughout their daily Bible readings as well as sermons, religious writings, radio shows, and devotionals. Constant exposure to messages about the sin of sex can produce a similar result to our sweets example.

If the child of Christian parents were beaten or sexually berated by authority figures, parents, aunts, uncles, ministers, priests, Sunday-school teachers, and even gym coaches, sexual self-hate, guilt, and shame would become so deeply embedded as to totally interfere with healthy sexual development. Christianity at its core is sexually abusive to its adherents. Despite anything modern Christian apologists say, there is no avoiding the constant pounding of guilt and shame into young minds. There is no denying the crystal-clear messages in the New Testament, no matter how religious leaders try to spin their scriptures.

Christian sexual shame is ubiquitous in our culture and comes from people who are infected with the Christian mind parasite. Once infected, they not only believe and behave in sexually negative ways, but they also have a strong need to infect others with the parasite. Like a sweets-phobic person might try to keep others from eating chocolate cake, infected Christians feel they must enforce the good news of sexual repression on the rest of the world.

Methods of Christian Infection

In order to rid ourselves of this mind parasite, or the parts that may still live in us, we need to understand something of how it got there in the first place. The mechanisms are at once simple and effective. Keep in mind as we explore these concepts that chemicals and hormones are manipulated by parasites, enabling them to infect and control the host. Ideas may not be hormones or other chemicals, but ideas have the ability to evoke chemical and hormonal responses. All that is needed to facilitate a mind parasite is the ability to control hormones and other chemical responses in the central nervous system. If this seems too abstract, try the following experiment.

Think of a delicious dessert; a piece of chocolate cake, your favorite ice cream, or an apple pie. For most people, you will have an internal, hormonal response to that simple idea. You may find yourself salivating or suddenly feel hungry. That is an idea evoking a hormonal response. Pavlov discovered this a hundred years ago. Now stay with me here, don't start thinking about that chocolate cake or ice cream and leave me here while you satiate your sudden appetite. Don't keep thinking about the pie in the refrigerator or the chocolate cookie in the cookie jar. And don't blame me if you go off your diet today, I was only putting harmless ideas down on a piece of paper.

This is a simple demonstration of the power ideas have to manipulate our hormones and central nervous system. But this experiment may not have worked for you. You may not like chocolate or ice cream. Pie is not your thing. Or maybe your cookie jar is empty. But if I were with you in person, it would not take long for me to find some idea that evokes a hormonal response. Indeed, all you have to do is turn on the TV. Within minutes, Subway or Pepsi will try and manipulate your hormones. Advertisers know how to get you to buy their product using food or sexual ideas. Sexy women in car advertisements, and picture perfect sandwiches all have the potential to move the "buy meter" a little closer to your credit card or bank account.

On the other extreme, ideas can manipulate our negative emotions and create aversive hormonal responses. Imagine for a moment a terrible car wreck with blood, torn limbs, and loud screams. Even writing this, I find myself holding back. I don't want to think about such a thing, and I certainly don't want to experience it. It creates a strong negative response in me, and it probably has some effect on you as well. It didn't take much to create an image in your head of pain and suffering, an image that you want to erase as soon as possible—an image that evoked a biochemical response in you.

If your defenses are down, if there are few if any competing ideas to help you defend yourself, it is not hard to use this simple approach to train a person, especially a child, to accept ideas like heaven, hell, evil, love, and so on. But you are an adult, and chances are, as you read the above examples, you had contrary ideas popping up in your head, ideas that helped prevent you from running to the refrigerator, or helped you avoid the mental horror of the accident. These interfering ideas are important for your sanity and ability to navigate through the world so that people like me can't get you to eat chocolate all the time. But you didn't always have these competing ideas. As a child, you may have been exposed to ideas like eternally burning in hell that scared you. Ideas about seeing grandpa again in heaven that made you feel good after his funeral. The experiences of feeling scared or feeling good are hormonal responses to ideas.

Let's continue to look at this from a child's perspective. Children are surrounded by ideas from adults that are comforting or terrifying. The pattern of responses can program a child to love or fear or hate. Children have no frame of reference. Their survival depends on the adults who care for them. It is an evolutionary imperative that they listen and learn. Survival often depends on it. If the adult says, "That plant is poisonous, don't eat it." The child who listens survives. But that same adult may say, "Satan is alive in you if you masturbate." The child has no way to know which is true and which is not. The result is knowledge that has survival value and other ideas that serve the Christian parasite. If we could test the hormonal responses of a child in this environment, we would see that ideas about poisonous plants and Satan both create biochemical reactions.

Once training is complete, a child can be easily manipulated by these religious ideas. A simple song can induce a feeling of security (maybe releasing the hormone oxytocin). A quote from the Bible can evoke guilt or fear of damnation (adrenaline, norepinephrine). The testimony from a fallen sinner will make the child wary of leaving the fold and encountering the sinful world outside. Up to thirty different hormones can be released when someone experiences a fearful or dangerous situation. Unfortunately for a child, a religiously inspired threat from an adult or adults can seem as dangerous as that of a predatory animal. Done with sufficient power and frequency, such threats create a person who is easily manipulated by fear of hell, fear of god's retribution, fear of isolation from family or community, or fear of losing protection or status within the community.

This is not only the purview of cults and fundamentalist religions. It can be seen among people from mainstream Christianity as well. The gay Presbyterian, Catholic, or Methodist adult who is afraid to come out is responding to childhood fear training. The polyamorous couples that fear being found out by their parents are reacting to the real fear messages learned in childhood. The parents of these same people are victims as well, and they are often terrified of their own gay, bisexual, lesbian, transsexual, or polyamorous children. They have Christian ideas about sexuality that create a strong impact on their endocrine system. They feel hot flashes, experience panic attacks, can't sleep, and can't stop thinking about how they failed in raising their children. They can't help but think they didn't read the Bible frequently enough, or pray hard enough, or take them to church often enough, or send them to a church-run school to prevent them from becoming sexually sinful. Each time they have one of these thoughts, their pituitary gland dumps more stress hormones into their system.

This obviously oversimplifies a complex process, but these are the essential ingredients. Ideas help create internal emotional states that tie you to a particular religion and religious sexuality. This also shows why leaving one's religion can be traumatic. Dr. Marlene Winell has characterized this as Religious Trauma Syndrome (RTS). Her work has demonstrated that RTS bears a strong resemblance to post-traumatic stress disorder (PTSD) in many people.[3] In a large majority of cases, sexuality is the major source of internal and external conflict. Christian sexuality evokes all the responses we just discussed from parents, children, adult children, and the religious community.

Competing Ideas

Now let's move from the biochemical realm to the very ideas that create these biochemical responses. We need to learn something about how to prevent or eliminate Christian sexuality and replace it with a more life-affirming and sex-positive approach.

Your mind is filled with competing ideas. Most ideas are neutral (soap operas are a waste of time, blue carpet is best for my house). Some are beneficial (always prepare your house for winter, wash your hands) and others can be detrimental (I hate people who disagree with me, I must always be right).

Religions try to create a comprehensive set of ideas inside your head that is largely closed to outside influence. If successful, this set of ideas will result in specific behavior. Religious ideas like "tithing" can push you to put money in the offering plate. Ideas like "salvation" can create a sense of security within the group and also horror of being "cast out" into eternal damnation.

Ideas about an omniscient god can lead you to repress sexual thoughts. Ideas about sexual purity create a sense of imperfection and guilt.

This is why religions pay so much attention to what you think. Even a wrong thought is a sin in Christianity. To question the deity, to challenge the minister, to read the wrong book—these are all opportunities for competing ideas to get into your head or into the heads of those around you. Christianity installs a comprehensive set of ideas in your mind that can take control of behavior and provide defenses against competing ideas—much like the Sacculina example discussed earlier. Competing ideas are dangerous to the Christian parasite. Outside ideas can lead to less consistent religious behavior, poorer transmission to the next generation, or a total unraveling of the carefully crafted Christian infection.

Survival Instinct

Your brain is a teeming repository of competing ideas. You take in ideas and try to organize them in ways that allow you to survive in the current environment. The better you are at organizing ideas and using them to analyze data from your environment, the safer you are and the more likely you are to survive and have children and grandchildren.

An important part of the Christian infection strategy is the conflating of three kinds of survival—physical survival, social survival, and eternal survival. Christianity takes advantage of our natural survival instinct. This may not seem rational, but within an eternal-survival context, it is rational. If you want eternal survival, you must follow the prescribed behaviors. You must stay within the fold to gain salvation. If you want to see your children and grandchildren achieve eternal survival and avoid eternal torture and terror, you must infect them properly. In this way, Christianity is able to evoke the same kinds of survival responses to the idea of eternal survival that might be seen in threats to physical survival. If the large majority of people in a community have the Christian parasite installed in their minds, they will see challenges to Christian hegemony as a survival threat. For example, homosexuality is seen as a direct threat to Christianity. Secular ideas about sex before marriage directly undermine Christian sexual indoctrination during adolescence. The proof of this hypothesis can be seen in the frantic and emotional way people react to these outside ideas. Ministers from the pulpit often evoke the language of war, attack, fighting, and survival when discussing secularism.

Today, the Internet has enabled a world where isolation is difficult, if not impossible. Outside ideas are far more accessible and Christianity has a diminishing power base from which to sanction and persecute people. For those who, in the past, had to keep their mouths shut and go along, there are now options. New competing ideas are in the environment, and it is much more difficult for any religion to control the flow of information inside the minds of any person or group. One of those competing ideas is the notion of secular sexuality.

Secular Sexuality

What does it mean to be a secular sexual? How does a person live as a secular sexual? Where do secular sexuals get their ethics or morals? These are questions secular sexuals must explore and decide for themselves. Christianity has a convenient set of ideas, designed to tell you what you can and cannot do to be a good Christian. These ideas are convenient because they require little thinking and are not subject to question. "Same-sex marriage is against God's law." "Homosexuality is an abomination." "Premarital sex violates God's plan." "Just behave like we tell you to and you will get to heaven."

Secular sexuals have no convenient, built-in rules codified in holy books. No rules that say a woman should submit to a man. No notions that a woman is unclean or more sinful than a man. No ideas about virginity or chastity. No dogma about spilling seed.

Instead we have a set of humanistic values that help us make decisions about how best to live our lives. No god tells us we can only have sex within marriage, we have to determine when sex is best for us and how it should be expressed. We start with a positive view of sex as an important part of our biology. We recognize that we only get one life and one body, so we need to respect and take care of our body and those of others. We try to identify sex-negative messages from our culture and eliminate them from our lives. We resist body shaming and cultural notions of ideal bodies. We decide how to negotiate sexual expression and seek to be fully considerate of others, including their desires, limits, and emotional condition. We think that consenting adults can decide how they wish to be sexual. We think that children must be protected from predatory adults and that the power differential between adults and children must never be exploited by an adult for sexual gratification. We think that children should be educated about sex and sexuality in a safe and caring environment, given science-based information, and taught how to make ethical decisions.

These are some of the ideas and behaviors that flow from the notion of secular sexuality. It is a fundamentally positive view of sex, and an acceptance of others and their choices. It values open discussion on issues of concern like "What comprises consensual sex?" "How should we respond to the choices of others?" "How should I view my body, enjoy my desires, and enjoy others with full respect for who they are?" But this is a new ideal, an ideal that does not currently exist for most people. It is a set of values that require reexamination and rethinking of the sexual self. The secular sexual establishes an environment of self-acceptance and openness to others.

The secular sexual lives a life that is respectful of others and their choices but challenges religious culture in ways that encourages discussion and examination. For example, we challenge homophobia in the same way we might challenge racism. A secular sexual does not bend and bow to religious shaming and, where appropriate, is open about his or her sexuality. For example, secular sexuals may be open about being an atheist, but might also let others know that they are bisexual or polyamorous.

A secular sexual is not a Christian and does not need to act like one. We are comfortable with our bodies and sexuality. We are probably more concerned with violence in the media than sex in the media. We are interested in the sexual rights of the LGBT community and the teaching of science-based sex education in the schools.

A secular sexual is less concerned with religiously based ideas around monogamy, chastity, abstinence, pornography, prostitution and more concerned with adults learning how to make informed choices and living fulfilling lives that incorporate responsible and ethical behavior in relationships. We are concerned with teaching and learning communication skills so that relationships are consensual, nonmanipulative, and fulfilling for all concerned.

Disinfecting Yourself

In reality, sex is no more dangerous than driving to work in your car. That is why we have basic rules for safety. Follow a few simple rules, and you have a reasonable expectation of safety. No god is needed to hand down the ten commandments of safe driving. No eternal sanction is threatened if you drive over the speed limit. No angel is watching if you run a yellow light. You may get a ticket or worse, have a wreck or even get killed, but no gods are involved. No shame messages well up from deep inside you when you do a California stop. No crippling guilt overwhelms you when you cut someone off, though I hope you do feel guilt, just not religious guilt. But even when we follow the rules perfectly, there is still danger. That does not mean we should stop driving.

On the other hand, simply thinking a lustful thought can terrify a religiously infected person, arousing fear that the devil is working in them. Getting caught masturbating or having sex with your boyfriend or girlfriend can bring on crippling shame, hours of prayer, public or semipublic repentance and confession. It can also bring shame down on you from your entire community, making you an outcast or worse.

Challenging Religious Sexual Shame

As a reader, you may object, "I never believed" or "I questioned religion from early on" or "I have never felt shame about my sexuality." If this is true, you are among a tiny minority of secular people who were never infected. Just because you never subscribed to a religion does not mean you weren't infected with religious ideas about sexuality. I would suggest that just being raised in this religiously infected culture, you are very likely infected with religious sexual ideas, though you may not know it.

Here are some simple questions that may illuminate both how you may be infected by religious sexual ideas and some alternative ways to think or "disinfect" yourself.

1. Am I ashamed to admit I masturbate?
   Consider this: You have a sexual relationship with yourself. If you are not comfortable with you and your body and giving yourself plea-

sure, it does not bode well for your ability to enjoy someone else's body and develop a healthy relationship with another. Where did you learn to be ashamed of this most natural sex act?

2. Am I afraid to let my children know that I had premarital sex or had many sex partners before I married my spouse?

Consider this: Of course these kinds of discussions should be age appropriate, but if your children are twenty-one years old and you still try to pretend you didn't have other partners, you are definitely suffering from shame. What belief or shame message motivates you to project a false image to your children and even hold them to a standard you could not uphold at their age?

3. Would I be ashamed if someone found out I like porn? Would I condemn my spouse if I found him or her using porn?

Consider this: Porn is everywhere and has been for thousands of years. Religious myths about porn are just that, myths. It is to religion's great advantage to make people ashamed of porn use, since shame brings people back to Jesus. There is much more to write about this subject, but I don't have the time or space here.[4]

4. Am I ashamed to talk to my partner about sexual fantasies or activities I would like to try?

Consider this: If you cannot talk to the person most important to you about something as important as sex, there is probably a lot of shame involved. I am not suggesting that your partner has to participate in any way. All sex should be consensual. But if you cannot even talk about it, that is a problem. What ideas or beliefs sabotage your ability to communicate with the most important person in your life?

5. Am I afraid of rejection by my partner if I am honest about my sexual desires?

Consider this: Partners can be just as influenced by shame as we are. If you sense rejection when sexual topics are brought up, that is a rich area to explore. Chances are, you will both hit deep areas of shame that may feel like a ship hitting a rock. It stops everything and damages the ship. Exploring hidden programming can lead to a rich discussion that promotes growth and deeper, more fulfilling relationships. Learn to eliminate the hesitancy and fear that come from religious shame.

I could suggest many other questions, but this should suffice to help you explore. If you find that exploring these ideas causes problems, you may wish to find a good sex therapist or a well-trained, sex-positive therapist. You can find many excellent secular therapists at www.seculartherapy.org.

The World Is Changing

As we move forward, humanity will be far less concerned with reproduction. With seven billion people on the planet, potentially growing to nine billion, there will inevitably come a time when growth must stop and even contract. That time has already come to many educated, postindustrial nations. Birth rates have plummeted, often below replacement values in countries like Italy, Sweden, Germany, and even the United States. The only thing sustaining growth is immigration. Significant numbers of people are, and will continue, to choose not to have children. Without children, or far fewer children, the focus of relationships will necessarily change.

Sex will continue to be important for bonding and pleasure. We are biologically wired to want close social relationships, including deeply intimate ones. But "deeply intimate" says nothing about how relationships are structured. Many people have deeply intimate, long-term relationships that look nothing like Christian marriage. These relationships are often "under the radar" because they do not fit the standard Christian model. The single woman who has a long-term relationship with a married man; the priest who has a long-term intimate relationship with another man; the married couple that enjoys swinging after the children are raised and gone; the gay choir director who secretly lives with his partner; the young woman who enjoys sex but has no need for marriage, children, or even a permanent partner; the older man or woman who never wants to marry again but has multiple, long-term lovers. There are many relationship combinations that exist, and they are far more common than Christian culture would have us believe.

These relationship styles have been vilified, condemned, and even persecuted by Christianity. Persecution and prosecution tends to make people hide the way they really behave and live. Christian expectations and ideals lead people to believe that they are abnormal or wrong if they do not conform to the standard models of relationships. But the ideal is far from the way most people actually behave, especially Christians. Pretending to follow the Christian ideal leads many Christians to live a life of deception, lying, and unethical behavior. Unfortunately, many secularists also try to act as if they, too, live the model Christian sex life. (For examples, see the shame questions discussed above.)

As secular sexuals, we can challenge the unrealistic ideals and redefine ethical relationships. We can teach and learn how to negotiate expectations and create the kind of relationships that we want. What we choose will be a product of many factors, but not the product of religious dogma or tradition.

As a skeptic, take a look at the programming you received from religious training and do some reprogramming. This is the only life you have. This is the only body you get. Why waste your sexuality on religious-based shame? There is no god watching you. There is no Jesus judging you. As I tell my college audiences, "Sex is fun, so is drinking, do them both responsibly." Learn to talk with your partners about all things sexual. Negotiate safe sex. Share fantasies and ideas. Learn to love the sexual person you are and the person you are with. Their preferences may be different from yours, but that does not mean either of you are wrong. No matter what sexual style you choose—monogamy, polyamory, swinging, or simply enjoying yourself without another—you can live life now with full respect for others and their sexuality, free of all forms of religious shame.[5]

I am a secular sexual. I hope you will join me in creating a safe and accepting world for everyone, regardless of how they identify sexually.

THE CRAZY-MAKING
IN CHRISTIANITY

A Look at Real Psychological Harm

Marlene Winell and Valerie Tarico

> *I am thirty years old and I am struggling to find sanity. Between the Christian schools, homeschooling, the Christian group home (indoctrinating work camp), and different churches in different cities, I am a psychological, emotional, and spiritual mess.*
> —*A former evangelical Christian*[1]

If a former believer says that Christianity made him depressed, obsessive, or post-traumatic, he is likely to be dismissed as an exaggerator. He might describe panic attacks about the rapture, moods that swing from ecstasy about God's overwhelming love to suicidal self-loathing about repeated sins, or an obsession with sexual purity. A symptom like one of these clearly has a religious component, yet many people instinctively blame the victim. They will say that the wounded former believer was prone to anxiety or depression or obsession in the first place—that his Christianity somehow got corrupted by his predisposition to psychological problems. Or they will say that he wasn't a real Christian. If only he had *prayed in faith* or loved God *with all his heart, soul and mind*, if only he had really been saved—then he would have experienced the peace that passes all understanding.

But the reality is far more complex. It is true that symptoms like depression or panic attacks most often strike those of us who are vulnerable, perhaps because of genetics or perhaps because situational stressors have worn us down. But the reality is that Christian beliefs and Christian living can create those stressors, even setting up multigenerational patterns of abuse, trauma, and self-abuse. Also, over time some religious beliefs can create habitual thought patterns that actually alter brain function, making it difficult for people to heal or grow.

Christians like to talk about the benefits of faith. Testimonies are filled with miraculous transformations: drug abusers go sober, compulsive gamblers break their addictions, guilty and lonely people feel flooded with forgiveness and love. So it is hard for many Christians to imagine that the opposite might also be true—that Christianity sometimes traps people in a cycle of self-doubt, self-criticism, and self-punishment that can drive vulnerable children and adults to mental illness or suicide. There are "crazy-making" aspects of this thought system that are quite serious.

> *I've been told that I may suffer from hadephobia (a condition that is the fear of hell) and that I should seek medical advice. What should I do? I worry that people I love will burn in hell. Is this normal?*

The best research available, taken together, shows a modest positive correlation between religious involvement and mental health.[2] That said, this research is correlational, with some studies showing positive associations, some showing negative associations, and some showing none at all. This is likely due to the wide variety of ways in which religious involvement and mental health are measured, but also to the enormous variations in religion itself.

While the born-again experience can provide dramatic and sometimes instantaneous relief from psychological symptoms or addiction, a similar transformation occurs in many religions and secular self-help intensives. Flo Conway and Jim Siegelman explore this process in their now classic book *Snapping: America's Epidemic of Sudden Personality Change.*[3] In fact, people leaving a restrictive religion have described their experience in similar terms—a sudden flood of freedom, joy, and purpose. Some call their deconversion being "born again again." Here is one of them:

> Add me to the list of people whose depression and self-doubt and self-loathing and etc. etc. etc. all got better after the huge weight of religious oppression was lifted. I am now beginning to feel that "peace that passes all understanding" that Christians are always talking about (but never seem to find). Ironic – Xphish

It is common to consider religion a private affair. Yet beliefs are not merely personal when they motivate action that affects other individuals or public policy. Religious beliefs can compel good people to behave horribly— to shun friends, beat their children, or kill gays because in the mental universe created by belief those bad things are lesser evils. Most often though, the harm is psychological and the victims are the believers themselves.

The purveyors of religion insist that their product is so powerful it can transform a life, but somehow, magically, it has no risks. In reality, when a medicine is powerful, it usually has the potential to be toxic, especially in the wrong combination or at the wrong dose. And religion is powerful medicine!

In this chapter we will discuss why Christianity is so powerful and how it causes psychological harm—how it can stunt child development, why females are particularly at risk, what religious trauma looks like, and how former believers can reclaim their lives and health. For the purpose of this discussion we will focus on the variants of Christianity that are based on a literal interpretation of the Bible. These include evangelical and fundamentalist churches, the Church of Latter-Day Saints, and other conservative sects. These groups share the characteristics of requiring conformity for membership, a view that humans need salvation, and a focus on the spiritual world as superior to the natural world. These views are in contrast to liberal, progressive Christian churches with a humanistic viewpoint, a focus on the present, and an interest in social justice.

It is important to understand that Christianity is not just a religion. It is a broad, encompassing lens through which believers experience the world. It also permeates Western civilization. As such, it can be as difficult to examine as the air we breathe, and it's just as important. Christian assumptions based on symbols, laws, and nomenclature are so ubiquitous in our culture as to blind even many nonbelievers to the harm done in the name of God.

Religion Exploits Normal Human Mental Processes

To understand the power of religion, it is helpful to understand a bit about the structure of the human mind. Rationalism, a 350-year-old theory of mind, sees humans as rational beings, guided by conscious thought and intention. Findings in cognitive science say otherwise.

Psychologist Daniel Kahneman won a Nobel Prize in 2002 for his pioneering work on decision making.[4] At the time Kahneman began, scholars
believed that human beings were "rational actors," especially in the economic
sphere, and that most of our own motives and beliefs were available to our
conscious minds. Kahneman and his colleague Amos Tversky showed that
this is far from true. Instead, as it turns out, much of our mental activity has
little to do with rationality and is utterly inaccessible to the conscious mind.

The preferences, intentions, and decisions that shape our lives are in turn
shaped by memories and associations that can be laid down before we even
develop the capacity for rational analysis. Daniel Siegel is a clinical professor
of psychiatry at UCLA who researches and writes about trauma.[5] He explains
that we have both "explicit" and "implicit" memories stored in our brains,
regardless of conscious awareness. The implicit memories go back to birth
and include our attachment experience, which has a lifelong impact.

Cognitive linguist George Lakoff is known for the concept of *frames*,
popularized through a small book called *Don't Think of an Elephant*.[6] "People
use frames—deep-seated mental structures about how the world works—to
understand facts. Frames are in our brains and define our common sense. It
is impossible to think or communicate without activating frames, and which
frame is activated is of crucial importance."[7]

Frames are acquired unconsciously and operate unconsciously, but they
determine the shape of conscious thought. According to cognitive linguistics,
words link to images, memories, and related concepts that are tangled together
via neural networks. As a consequence we make sense of the world through
metaphors that let us evaluate unfamiliar situations based on those that are
more familiar. For example, when political conservatives and liberals envi-
sion a healthy society they both use the family as a model for how government should work. But where conservatives try to replicate a "strict father"
or authoritarian model, liberals incline toward a "nurturing parent" model.
These "deep frames" lead to very different social priorities. An understanding
of frames helps us understand why religious thinking can seem so alien to
outsiders, for people with different deep frames think differently and reach
different conclusions with the same facts.

Aspects of cognition like these determine how we go through life, what
causes us distress, which goals we pursue and which we abandon, how we

respond to failure, how we respond when other people hurt us—and how we respond when we hurt them. Religion derives its power in large part because it shapes these unconscious processes: the frames, metaphors, intuitions, and emotions that operate before we even have a chance at conscious thought.

Some Religious Beliefs and Practices Are More Harmful Than Others

The social sciences offer insight into universal cognitive and social processes that underpin religion broadly, but when it comes to questions of benefit and harm, huge differences emerge. More rigorous research is needed, but mounting case-study data suggest that, when it comes to psychological damage, certain religious beliefs and practices are reliably more toxic than others.

Janet Heimlich is an investigative journalist who has explored religious child maltreatment, which describes abuse and neglect in the service of religious belief. In her book *Breaking Their Will*,[8] Heimlich identifies three characteristics of religious groups that are particularly prone to harming children.[9] Clinical work with *reclaimers*, that is, people who are reclaiming their lives and in recovery from toxic religion,[10] suggests that these same qualities put adults at risk, along with a particular set of manipulations found in fundamentalist Christian churches[11] and biblical literalism.[12]

1) **Authoritarianism,** creates a rigid power hierarchy and demands unquestioning obedience. In major theistic religions, this hierarchy has a god or gods at the top, represented by powerful church leaders who have power over male believers, who in turn have power over females and children. Authoritarian Christian sects often teach that "male headship" is God's will. Parents may go so far as beating or starving their children on the authority of godly leaders. A book titled *To Train Up a Child* by minister Michael Pearl and his wife Debi,[13] has been found in the homes of three Christian adoptive families who have punished their children to death.

2) **Isolation or separatism,** is promoted as a means of maintaining spiritual purity. Evangelical Christians warn against being "unequally yoked" with nonbelievers in marriages and even friendships. New con-

verts often are encouraged to pull away from extended family members and old friends, except when there may be opportunities to convert them. Some churches encourage older members to take in young single adults and house them within a godly context until they find spiritually compatible partners, a process known by cult analysts as "shepherding." Home schoolers and the Christian equivalent of madrassas cut off children from outside sources of information, often teaching rote learning and unquestioning obedience rather than broad curiosity.

3) **Fear** of sin, hell, a looming "end-times" apocalypse, or amoral heathens binds people to the group, which then provides the only safe escape from the horrifying dangers on the outside. In evangelical "hell houses," Halloween is used as an occasion to terrify children and teens about the tortures that await the damned. In the Left Behind book series,[14] the world degenerates into a bloodbath without the stabilizing presence of believers. Since the religious group is the only alternative to these horrors, anything that threatens the group itself—like criticism, taxation, scientific findings, or civil rights regulations—also becomes a target of fear.

Psychologist Margaret Thaler Singer, author of the now classic *Cults in Our Midst*,[15] spent years analyzing the dynamics of groups that systematically manipulate social and psychological influence, including religious sects and some self-help groups. Any former evangelical will readily see their church in her analysis. Like Heimlich, Singer identified authoritarianism and separatism as core dynamics of groups that cause the most harm. Such groups often claim simply to attract "seekers." In reality, they engage in sophisticated recruiting activities, and by doing so they are able to draw in people who are often intelligent, educated, and otherwise psychologically healthy.

While in the group, members may take on what Singer calls a "pseudopersonality." Upon breaking free, former members may experience disorientation, guilt, anxiety, depression, and even panic. But gradually their individuality and their capacity for curiosity and delight re-emerge. Hundreds of testimonials at websites like ExChristian.net bear witness to this process, making it clear that it is not just "cults" or fringe groups that use powerful tactics of mind control. In fact, of the thousands of believers currently leaving mainstream Christian churches,[16] many who seek help with recovery wrestle with the same issues as former "cult" members.

Half a century ago, psychiatrist Robert Lifton[17] studied totalistic political regimes that were engaged in the process of thought reform, in particular the communist regimes of China and North Korea. He identified eight psychological themes associated with destructive mind control. As subsequent scholars have pointed out, many are used by controlling religious sects:

1. *Milieu control* scripts communications among insiders and discourages communication with outsiders.
2. *Loaded language* creates a form of "group-speak" and constricts thinking. It provides soothing mantras and labels for dismissing criticism or doubt.
3. *Demands for purity* mean that thoughts and behavior get measured against an ideological ideal, the One Right Way.
4. *Confession rituals* elicit moral emotions like shame and guilt and create a heightened sense that someone is always watching.
5. *Mystical manipulation* makes people think that new feelings and thoughts have arisen spontaneously. It creates the illusion that members are there by their own choice.
6. *Doctrine over person* means that people see their own personal history through the lens of ideology. Over time, they may become convinced that they were bad, addicted, or mentally ill prior to joining the group despite evidence to the contrary.
7. *Sacred science* is the mechanism by which groups seek to justify and rationalize their belief system by tying it loosely to what is known about the natural world, philosophy, or social science.
8. *Dispensing existence* gives the group the power of life and death—or eternal life. Members typically believe that they are a part of a chosen elite while outsiders are lesser beings.

Each of these psychological mechanisms can be applied for either secular or religious purposes. When coupled with a charismatic authority figure, the legitimizing stamp of an ancient text, and socially sanctioned religious structure, their power cannot be overstated.

Bible Belief Creates an Authoritarian, Isolative, Threat-Based Model of Reality

In Bible-believing Christianity, psychological mind-control mechanisms are coupled with beliefs from the Iron Age, including the belief that women and children are possessions of men, that children who are not hit become spoiled, that each of us is born "utterly depraved," and that God demands unquestioning obedience. In this view, the salvation and righteousness of believers is constantly under threat from outsiders and dark spiritual forces. Consequently, Christians need to separate themselves emotionally, spiritually, and socially from the world. These beliefs are fundamental to the model of reality or "deep frame," as Lakoff would call it. Small wonder then that many Christians emerge wounded.

It is important to remember that this mindset permeates to a deep subconscious level. This is a realm of imagery, symbols, metaphor, emotion, instinct, and primary needs. Nature and nurture merge into a template for viewing the world that then filters every experience. The template selectively allows only the information that confirms the Christian model of reality, creating a subjective sense of its veracity.

On the societal scale, humanity has been going through a massive shift for centuries, transitioning from a supernatural view of a world dominated by forces of good and evil to a natural understanding of the universe. The Bible-based Christian population, however, might be considered a subset of the general population that is still within the old framework, that is, supernaturalism.

Here are some basic assumptions of the supernatural Christian model of reality:

- Humans live in a world of sin and danger dominated by Satan since the Fall of Man.
- Earthly life is taking part in "spiritual warfare," along with real spiritual entities of good and evil.
- There is a timeline for all existence set by God, starting with Creation and ending with the earth's destruction and Final Judgment.
- Values, morals, and all things important are eternal and unchanging, authored by God, who answers to no one.

- Humans are sinful by nature, guilty and needing salvation, but lacking any ability to save themselves except to repent and subject their will to God.
- Human life on earth is unimportant in the cosmic scheme. Pleasure is for the afterlife, and the "flesh" is sinful. Life's purpose is to serve God.
- Ultimately God is in control and will have justice. Humans do not need to understand His mysterious ways, only have faith and not question. Attempts to control are sinful.

This Christian model of reality has built within it mechanisms for its own survival: fear and dependence, circular reasoning, threats for leaving, social supports for staying, and obstructions that prevent outside information from reaching insiders, especially children. Thus, believers not only get hurt, they get stuck.

Children Are Targeted for Indoctrination because the Child Mind Is Uniquely Vulnerable

Nowhere is the contrast of viewpoints more stark than in the secular and religious understandings of childhood.[18] In the biblical view, a child is not a being that is born with amazing capabilities that will emerge with the right conditions like a beautiful flower in a well-attended garden. Rather, a child is born in sin, weak, ignorant, and rebellious, needing discipline to learn obedience. Independent thinking is dangerous pride.

Because the child's mind is uniquely susceptible to religious ideas, religious indoctrination particularly targets vulnerable young children. A child's mind does not process information in the same way as an

Here I am, a fifty-one year old college professor, still smarting from the wounds inflicted by the righteous when I was a child. It is a slow, festering wound, one that smarts every day—in some way or another. . . . I thought I would leave all of that "God loves . . . God hates . . ." stuff behind, but not so. Such deep and confusing fear is not easily forgotten. It pops up in my perfectionism, my melancholy mood, the years of being obsessed with finding the assurance of personal salvation.

adult's because the brain is not fully formed.[19] Cognitive development before age seven lacks abstract reasoning. Thinking is magical and primitive, black and white. Also, young humans are wired to obey authority because they are dependent on their caregivers just for survival. Much of their brain growth and development has to happen *after* birth, which means that children are extremely vulnerable to environmental influences in the first few years when neuronal pathways are formed.

CHILDHOOD RELIGIOUS INDOCTRINATION

CLOSED RELIGIOUS ENVIRONMENT

FAMILY & CHURCH AUTHORITY

TOXIC DOCTRINES TAUGHT

FEAR: Damnation, End Times, Evil

SHAME & GUILT

FANTASY IDEALISM

REPRESSED CRITICAL THINKING

PUNISHMENT

ISOLATION

IMPOSSIBLE EXPECTATIONS

HARMFUL CHILDCARE PRACTICES

DEVELOPMENTAL DELAYS

EMOTIONAL

INTELLECTUAL SEXUAL

SOCIAL

BLOCKAGE FROM OTHER PEOPLE AND WORLDVIEWS

INFORMATION WITHHELD

SCIENCE

SEX

POLITICS

HISTORY

CULTURE

PSYCHOLOGY

The experiences of infancy and early childhood provide the organizing framework for the expression of a child's intelligence, emotions, and personality. Consequently, children who suffer early abuse or deprivation endure repercussions into adolescence and adulthood. When children are exposed to chronic, traumatic stress, their brains overdevelop the fear response and automatically trigger that response later on. This is called *hyperarousal*.[20] Maltreatment may also permanently alter the brain's ability to use serotonin, which helps produce feelings of well-being and emotional stability.[21] The Adverse Childhood Experiences (ACE) study is a large-scale, long-term study that has documented the link between childhood abuse and neglect and later adverse experiences such as physical and mental illness and high-risk behaviors.[22]

Fundamentalist Christianity puts a young child at risk for this kind of damage because:

1. The parents and church community have a view of the child as sinful and will communicate this in verbal and nonverbal ways, producing a degraded sense of self-worth. Coupled with the fear of punishment, this creates an impaired ability to think critically.
2. The parenting style of discipline is Bible based, which means it interprets much of normal child behavior as "willfulness" and "rebellion" and emphasizes obedience. Corporal punishment is an expected part of parenting.
3. Christian doctrines (especially the fear of damnation and hell) are taught so that the child can understand only in the most primitive manner, which produces intense and potentially traumatizing emotion.
4. The child is not exposed to outside information for comparison. Instead, the religion is taught as the only Truth, delivered by powerful authorities with dire consequences for disbelief. Education and science are limited and filtered.
5. The immersion in Christian doctrine and mindset while being separated and deprived of growth opportunities creates serious developmental delays.

By age five a child's brain can understand primitive cause-and-effect logic and picture situations that are not present. Children at this age are credulous, meaning they trust what people in authority tell them. They also have a tenuous grip on reality. They often have imaginary friends; dreams are quite real; and fantasy blurs with the mundane. To a child of this age, it is eminently possible that Santa Claus lives at the North Pole and delivers presents if you are good *and* that two thousand years ago a man died a horrible death because you are naughty. Adam and Eve, Noah's ark, the Rapture, and hell all can be quite real. The problem is that many of these teachings are terrifying.

Developmentally, a child of five or six is just beginning to imagine another person's point of view. This is why the manipulative presentation of Jesus undergoing grossly horrible suffering is such a violation of the child's burgeoning ability to feel for others. Then the child is blamed for making the death necessary, and the child's new ability to connect cause and effect makes the horror complete.

When assaulted with such images and ideas at a young age, a child has no chance of emotional self-defense. Christian teachings that *sound true* when they are embedded in the child's mind at this tender age can *feel true* for a lifetime. Even decades later former believers who intellectually reject these ideas can feel intense fear or shame when their unconscious mind is triggered, as we shall show shortly.

For many years, one conversion technique targeting children and adolescents has been the use of movies about the "End Times." This means a "Rapture" event, when real Christians are taken up to heaven leaving the earth to "Tribulation," a terrifying time when an evil Antichrist will reign and the world will descend into anarchy. Dylan Peterson is a horror film reviewer who was introduced to the genre of horror as a child in church, watching a film called *A Thief in the Night.*[23] He writes:

> The whole congregation was there on a dark, foggy night. . . . Christian horror film night. . . . To an 8 year old, a claymation inter-dimensional monster isn't nearly as frightening as the thought of having your parents swept up by a Jesus in the clouds who is leaving you on a violent and godless earth to fend for yourself until the universe explodes. . . . The film is about 10 percent theology, and 90 percent old-school horror . . . to those who have weak wills, and to children, this film is truth.

Another adult, recalling a scene in which the main character, Patty, is beheaded by guillotine, says she was so young that she remembers it as if it really happened, and to this day she's triggered at the sight of a white van, which in the movie, took people away to be tortured.

Because children so are impressionable, young children are the target of aggressive "child evangelism," including "Good News Clubs" posing as benign after-school programs for children. According to Eric Cernyar, who is part of a group that is alerting the public, over four thousand Good News Clubs in America's public schools teach five- to twelve-year-olds that they are sinful from birth and deserve to die and go to Hell. Children are warned not to become close friends with non-Christian classmates and to avoid thoughts or scientific facts that displease God.[24]

In his book *Authoritarian Conditioning*, Bob Altemeyer describes how Christians groom children to become "authoritarian followers."[25] Cernyar discusses this as part of the Good News Clubs and the damage that can result.

> Over time, this authoritarian conditioning breeds a sense of personal inadequacy and endangerment. The traumatized self becomes angry, hostile, and resentful. However, because the religion that produces, legitimizes, and represses the trauma is beyond question, the traumatized individual remains blind to its causes.[26]

This description parallels psychologist Alice Miller's view of unconscious rage in a multigenerational cycle of abuse.[27] Miller is careful to clarify that by "abuse" she does not only mean physical violence or sexual violation, she is also concerned with psychological abuse perpetrated by one or both parents on their child.

Damage from religious abuse is exacerbated by the nature of the teachings themselves. The self is bad and incapable, independent thinking is sinful, feelings are untrustworthy, and a hierarchy of powerful

Despite the fact that I've intellectually broken from Christianity, however, I cannot seem to let go of my beliefs. Every single day is a nightmare, plagued with mild panic attacks, de-realization, doubt, OCD, etc. Sometimes I think "Oh, but this is exactly what they warned me about, the world can't be trusted, and it doesn't matter what reason says, the fact is that Christianity is true no matter what and even if it flies in the face of all reason, REASON IS UNRELIABLE, AND YOU JUST HAVE TO KEEP BELIEVING." I know this is illogical, but every time I try to convince myself that, my brain just stubbornly insists that I just believe, believe, believe. My life is a living hell.

authority extends all the way up to God. Questioning what one has been taught is dangerous, with threats of abandonment and eternal torture.

Individuals who have suffered abuse of this kind have the grave disadvantage of lacking the critical-thinking skills and self-confidence to examine their indoctrination. The abuse disables the very mechanisms that would empower disengagement and freedom. Thus a person emerging from the fog can feel like a small child in a frightening and bewildering world.

Harms Range from Mild to Catastrophic

One requirement for success as a sincere Christian is to find a way to believe that which would be unbelievable under normal rules of evidence and inquiry. Christianity contains concepts that help to safeguard belief, such as limiting outside information, practicing thought control, and self-denigration; but for some people the emotional numbing and intellectual suicide just isn't enough. In other words, for a significant number of children in Christian families, the religion just doesn't "take." This can trigger guilt, conflict, and ultimately rejection or abandonment.

Others experience the threats and fear too keenly. For them, childhood can be torturous, and they may carry injuries into adulthood.

Still others are able to sincerely devote themselves to the faith as children but confront problems when they mature. They wrestle with factual and moral contradictions in the Bible and the church, or they discover surprising alternatives. This can feel confusing and terrifying—like the whole world is falling apart. As explained in Valerie Tarico's book *Trusting Doubt*,[28] the need to re-examine core values of love and truth is critical because biblical dogma twists these words beyond recognition.

A number of factors affect the degree of impact, including individual dif-

> *I'm so wounded and traumatized from all the empty promises and circular reasoning. Twisting myself into a pretzel to make my life fit into the Christian world. I want freedom from the anxiety and guilt, I want to enjoy the good things that are happening in my life and not feel stained and dirty.*

ferences and variations in family dynamics, churches, and communities. For some people the impact can include significant psychological symptoms and ruptured families. For others, life satisfaction is diminished by the need to struggle with "leftovers" from Christianity such as sexual repression, fear of death, or trouble enjoying this life. For virtually everyone leaving a Bible-based Christian faith, the adjustment brings stress and challenge.

Delayed Development and Life Skills. A person who spends childhood or young adulthood immersed in a fundamentalist version of reality may miss out on skills that allow adults to flourish in the world outside. One example is the ability to think critically and independently. One reclaimer in therapy exclaimed, "I never had an original thought!" Those who have been taught to repress ungodly feelings like anger or sadness may lack practice in identifying, regulating, and expressing emotions.

> *I always felt separated from the rest of humanity and Christianity was telling me that I should. I felt shame and it encouraged that. I was indecisive and this is a virtue because we aren't allowed to think for ourselves. I lost pleasure in things because nothing mattered but Jesus and the kingdom but Christianity didn't fulfill me either.*

Normal sexuality can be problematic when the "flesh" has been considered sinful prior to marriage, including masturbation and fantasy. Children may grow up with negative body images, ignorance about sexuality, or guilt and shame about sexual impulses. Stories abound about sexual problems in adulthood, including tragic wedding nights because there is no switch to turn on the magic of good sex.

Many Christian parents seek to insulate their children from "worldly" influences. In the extreme, this can mean not only home schooling, but cutting off media, not allowing non-Christian friends, avoiding secular activities like plays or clubs, and spending time at church instead. Children miss out on crucial information—science, culture, history, reproductive health, and more. When they grow older and leave such a sheltered environment, adjusting to the secular world can be like immigrating to a new culture. One of the biggest areas of challenge is delayed social development.

Religious Trauma Syndrome. Today, in the field of mental health, the only religious diagnosis in the *Diagnostic and Statistical Manual* is "Religious or Spiritual Problem."[29] This is merely a supplemental code (V Code) to assist in describing an underlying pathology.[30] Unofficially, "scrupulosity" is the term for obsessive-compulsive symptoms centered around religious themes such as blasphemy, unforgivable sin, and damnation.[31] While each of these diagnoses has a place, neither covers the wide range of harms induced by religion.

Religious Trauma Syndrome (RTS)[32] is a new term, coined by Marlene Winell to name a recognizable set of symptoms experienced as a result of prolonged exposure to a toxic religious environment and/or the trauma of leaving the religion. It is akin to Complex PTSD, which is defined as "a psychological injury that results from protracted exposure to prolonged social and/or interpersonal trauma with lack or loss of control, disempowerment, and in the context of either captivity or entrapment, i.e. the lack of a viable escape route for the victim."[33]

> *Suddenly all of my fears about hell and the wrath of God has returned to me. . . . I've been completely nauseated and vomiting and shaking. The fear that the God of the Bible is real, and the fear that the logic that leads me to believe Christianity just isn't right actually comes from the Devil—or at least from my ever sinful nature—has left me totally doubting my perceptions.*

Though related to other kinds of chronic trauma, religious trauma is uniquely mind-twisting. The logic of the religion is circular and blames the victim for problems; the system demands deference to spiritual authorities no matter what they do; and the larger society may not identify a problem or intervene as in cases of physical or sexual abuse, even though the same symptoms of depression and anxiety and panic attacks can occur.

Religious Trauma Syndrome, as a diagnosis, is in early stages of investigation, but it appears to be a useful descriptor beyond the labels used for various symptoms—depression, anxiety, grief, anger, relationship issues, and others. It is our hope that it will lead to more knowledge, training, and treatment. Like the naming of other disorders such as anorexia or Attention Deficit Disorder (ADD), the RTS label can help sufferers feel less alone, confused, and self-blaming.

Leaving the Fold. Breaking out of a restrictive, mind-controlling religion can be liberating: certain problems end, such as trying to twist one's thinking to believe irrational doctrines, and conforming to repressive codes of behavior. However, for many reclaimers making the break is the most disruptive, difficult upheaval they have ever experienced. Individuals who were most sincere, devout, and dedicated often are the ones most traumatized when their religious world crumbles.

Certain areas of trauma research are especially relevant to understanding this experience. One is the shattered assumption framework,[34] or "loss of the assumptive world."[35] According to Beder,[36] "The assumptive world concept refers to the assumptions or beliefs that ground, secure, stabilize, and orient people. They are our core beliefs. In the face of death and trauma, these beliefs are shattered and disorientation and even panic can enter the lives of those affected."

Rejecting a religious model of reality that has been passed on through generations is a major cognitive and emotional disruption. For many reclaimers, it is like a death or divorce. Their "relationship" with God was a central assumption of their lives, and giving it up feels like an enormous loss to be grieved. It can be like losing a lover, a parent, or best friend. As one person put it, "It is like a death in the family as my god Jesus finally died and no amount of belief could resurrect him. It is an absolutely dreadful and frightening experience and dark night of the soul."

> *I was free for the first time in my life to do whatever I wanted, free from a stifling religion. But then I'd wake up in the morning crying because I miss my family.*

On top of shattered assumptions comes the loss of family and friends. For reclaimers rebuilding their lives, dealing with family rupture is easily one of the most agonizing aspects. The dilemma is to achieve personal integrity while keeping intimacy. Living in a congruent manner means "coming out" in one's most important relationships and risking serious loss. In fact, some gay reclaimers have said that atheism has been their harder coming

> *My parents have stopped calling me. My dad told me I'm going to hell. After twenty-one years of marriage my husband feels he cannot accept me since I have left the "church" and is divorcing me.*

out process. Family responses vary, of course, and time helps. Churches also vary, even with official doctrine about rejection. The Mormon Church, for all the intense focus on "family forever," is devastating to leave, and the Jehovah Witnesses require families to shun members who are "disfellowshiped."

The rupture can destroy homes, splitting spouses and alienating parents from children. Holidays can be excruciating.[37] If life was structured around the church community, the loss a reclaimer experiences can encompass his or her entire social circle.[38] Losing friends and family at a crucial time of personal upheaval leaves a person alone in a world they have been taught is cruel and meaningless.

Many reclaimers struggle with the emotional aspects of letting go long after they stop believing intellectually. Coming out of a sheltered, repressed environment, the former believer may lack coping skills. Ordinary setbacks can cause paralysis or panic. Phobia indoctrination makes it difficult to avoid the stabbing thought, even years after leaving, that one has made a terrible mistake. Problems with self-worth and fear of punishment can linger.

> *I am sixty years old and I still feel the guilt of Jesus' death on the cross for my sins and the fact that I was born a lousy sinner. Sadly I have been chronically ill for seven years. Not a day goes by that I am not thinking that I will not get better, because I do not deserve to get better, as a sinner.*

Many former believers feel anger about growing up in a world of lies. They feel robbed of a normal childhood and opportunity to develop and thrive. They have bitterness for being taught they were worthless and in need of salvation. They have anger about terrors of hell, the "rapture," demons, apostasy, unforgivable sins, and an evil world. They resent not being able to ever feel

> *I have a churning cauldron of rage and hatred inside of me. I will not ever forgive what was done to me in the name of God.*

good or safe. Many are angry that the same teachings are still being inflicted on more children. They have rage because they dedicated their lives and gave up everything to serve God. They are angry about losing their families and their friends. They feel enormously betrayed.

Betrayal trauma theory advocates recognizing sociocultural forces at play, not just the pathology of individual trauma survivors. According to researchers

If I had been beaten, sexually abused, traumatized by an act of violence, or raped, I would be heard. However, I am a trauma victim that society does not hear. . . . Christianity took my childhood, filled me with fear, paralyzed me with anxiety, annihilated my Self, robbed my body of feeling, and stole my future. . . . They suggest that I'm over sensitive or making a big deal out of nothing or that I don't understand who Jesus really was or that it couldn't have been all that bad since I turned out to be such a nice person.

DePrince and Freyd, the most damaging traumas are those that are human caused and involve interpersonal violence and violation.[39] They suggest asking questions about who did the betraying, the nature of the betrayal, and the societal response.

DePrince and Freyd say betrayal may also come in the form of the response the survivor receives from others following the event, such as disbelief, minimizing, or otherwise devaluing the individual's experience. This is the experience of many reclaimers.

Sufferers of Religious Trauma Syndrome feel particularly alone because, except in online forums, there is virtually no public discourse in our society about trauma or emotional abuse due to religion. Criticizing religion directly is still taboo.

For Women, Psychological Costs of Belief Include Subjugation and Self-Loathing

Christianity poses a special set of psychological risks for people who, according to the Iron Age hierarchy found in the Bible, are unclean, heathens, or property—and we would like to illustrate this by discussing the plight of women. One woman tells of her sister's wounds:

When Kathy's husband first started showing a pattern of controlling rage, she sought counsel from her Conservative Baptist minister who gave her some biblical advice: pray and stay. After all, the Bible says, "Wives submit to your husbands as unto the LORD" (Ephesians 5:22). After all, "the husband is the head of the wife as Christ is the head of the church" (Ephesians 5:23), and "God will not tempt (aka test) you beyond what you are able to bear" (1 Corinthians 10:13). And didn't Jesus say "a man will leave his father and mother and be united to his wife, and the two will become one flesh" (Matthew 19:5)? So, she stayed and prayed while he threw out the photo albums of her childhood. She stayed and prayed when he became so wildly angry about a pregnancy that she aborted it (despite her belief that this was a terrible sin), which made him even angrier. She stayed and prayed when he ended one argument by cleaning his gun and "accidentally" discharging it. She stayed and prayed while her social support and mental health deteriorated.

In the biblical code, the set of rules that govern a woman's worth and treatment are property laws, not person rights. Like children, slaves, and livestock, women are assets that belong to men. A woman belongs first to her father and then to her husband, and her most valuable and sacred function is to produce offspring of known pedigree. That is why a father can give his daughter in marriage or sell her into slavery. It is why a rapist can be forced to purchase and keep the woman he has violated, but a woman who damages her own worth by having unsanctioned intercourse should be killed. The misogynist practices that most horrify Westerners when they look at Islam are sanctioned in the Bible, including rape, forced marriage, child marriage, honor killings, and trafficking.

Even in the New Testament, which reflects the cultural consensus several centuries after the Leviticus code, no writer ever suggests that a woman's consent is needed or even desired prior to sex. Women are advised to submit to their husbands just as slaves are advised to submit to their masters. A woman who wants to learn should ask her husband questions in the privacy of their own home (1 Corinthians 14:33–36).

Over the centuries, the fathers and leaders of the Christian church have taken the secondary status of women to heart, and vile quotes pepper their writings in every epoch from the New Testament era to the present.[40] Tertullian, the "father of Latin Christianity" waxed eloquent on the subject: "In pain shall you bring forth children, woman, and you shall turn to your husband and he shall rule over you. And do you not know that you are Eve? God's sentence hangs still over all your sex and His punishment weighs down upon you. You are the devil's gateway."

So did Protestant reformer Martin Luther: "The word and works of God is quite clear, that women were made either to be wives or prostitutes." So did the American patriarchs such as Puritan John Dod: "The second duty of the wife is constant obedience and subjection."

And so do modern fundamentalists like megachurch superstar Mark Driscoll: "Women will be saved by going back to that role that God has chosen for them."

In the German society that spawned the Protestant Reformation the role of women became known as *the three k's*: "Kinder, Kuche, Kirche," meaning children, kitchen, church. Some Christians protest that Jesus himself treated women with dignity and equality, but that is far from the truth. The Jesus of the Gospel writers continues to refer to God as male. He says he has come to fulfill the law—without making an exception for its horribly misogynist dictates. His twelve disciples are all male. He never once suggests that sex should be consensual.

Anecdotal evidence suggests that the combination of denigration and subservience takes a psychological toll on women in Christianity, as it does in Islam.[41] Not only do women submit to marital abuse and undesired sexual contact, some tolerate the same toward their children, and men of God sometimes exploit this vulnerability, as in the case of Catholic and Protestant child sexual abuse. But most of the damage is far more subtle: lower self-esteem, less independence and confidence, abandoned dreams and goals. A few years back, a pair of desperate parents wrote to the Military Religious Freedom Foundation. Their smart, strong daughter was at the Air Force Academy and had been on the path to becoming an Air Force pilot. But through a campus ministry called Cadets for Christ she had gotten wooed into a Christian sect and was now on a path to becoming a submissive housewife.[42] They were seeing the "pseudo-personality" described by Margaret Thaler Singer earlier.

Why Harm Goes Unrecognized

What is the sum cost of having millions of people holding to a misogynist, authoritarian, fear-based, supernatural view of the universe? The consequences are far-reaching, even global, but many are hidden, for two reasons.

One is the nature of the trauma itself. Unlike other harm, such as physical beating or sexual abuse, the injury is far from obvious to the victim, who has been taught to self-blame. It's as if a person black and blue from a caning were to think it was self-inflicted.

The second reason that religious harm goes unrecognized is that Christianity is still the cultural backdrop for the indoctrination. While the larger society may not be fundamentalist, references to God and faith abound. The Bible gets used to swear in witnesses and even the US president. Common phrases are "God willing," "God bless," "God helps those that help themselves," "In God we trust," and so forth. These lend credence to theistic authority.

> *I've been in and out of counseling. I've cried out for help to anyone who would listen, only to have my cries fall on deaf ears and turned backs.*

Religious trauma is difficult to see because it is camouflaged by the respectability of religion in culture. To date, parents are afforded the right to teach their own children whatever doctrines they like, no matter how heinous, degrading, or mentally unhealthy. Even helping professionals largely perceive Christianity as benign. This will need to change for treatment methods to be developed and for people to get the help they need.

Recovery Means Learning to Live in a Whole New World

> *Re-examine all you have been told. . . . Dismiss what insults your Soul.*
>
> —Walt Whitman

The personal growth of an individual recovering from fundamentalist Christianity involves a transformation unlike healing from other kinds of trauma. This is because this kind of "deep frame" touches every aspect of reality. For the most devout believers and the most indoctrinated, change can set off emotional breakdown or complete existential crisis. Because social supports often fall away and professionals don't understand, it can be a lonely time as well—a dark night of the soul requiring courage and stamina. That said, the end result when a person weathers the storm is a new construction of identity and framework for living life with meaningful new commitments. In essence, an individual goes through a personal *paradigm shift*.

The concept of paradigm shift was famously developed by philosopher Thomas Kuhn, as a way of understanding scientific progress. According to Kuhn, a paradigm is a "constellation of beliefs shared by a group" in a scientific context.[43] A shift happens when "anomalies" appear, leading to questioning of the paradigm and the development of a broader science. Shifts like this have happened many times in the history of science, such as the Copernican revolution, the Darwinian revolution, or Einstein's Theory of Relativity.

For individuals going through the collapse of their religious model of reality, there are striking similarities. Their initial worldview of Christian faith is, like a paradigm, a tightly knit system of core assumptions. The believer experiences stages of doubt and questioning when "anomalies" challenge what is assumed to be true. Gradually contradictions accumulate and a crisis is reached. To re-establish integrity, the individual must release the old paradigm and embrace a new one.

In the case of individuals leaving Christianity, the personal paradigm shift is embedded within a much larger societal shift underway as science reveals the natural world and erodes a supernatural cause-and-effect framework:

- *The Supernatural Paradigm* from antiquity posits the existence of an unseen spiritual world to explain the material world. The unseen is beyond human understanding but has ultimate power over human destiny. Human response to this condition is generally passive, while seeking guidance and mercy from an external deity and waiting for a better existence.
- *The Natural Paradigm* views the universe as unitary and natural, vast but available for human investigation. Explanations are sought within the natural order. Human agency is the preferred method of improving the world.

This giant change has been going on for hundreds of years, creating enormous conflict. We might call the transition from supernaturalism to naturalism a "meta-paradigm" shift because it is so comprehensive and encompasses many smaller shifts. It is no less than a transformation in the way humans understand the nature of reality.

For Western civilization, the Enlightenment marked a leap from supernatural to natural explanations that substantially diminished the role of religion. The Christian church no longer rules Europe and cannot burn witches for causing epidemics. At least in public, gods and demons are less often used for explaining natural disasters, crop failures, or disease. While Christianity tries to cling to mind-body dualism, secular science has abandoned the split as a more viable viewpoint. However, despite progress, the world is still in the agonizing middle stages of the meta-paradigm shift, a bit stranded in a wasteland where religionists will shout scripture while hard scientists scratch their heads.

Why is this important? For the reclaimer, the individual and the culture are going through painful throes of revolutionary change in tandem. The context of cultural paradigm shift makes personal transformation anything but easy or clear.

Even so, many former believers are forging ahead, reclaiming their lives, constructing naturalistic frameworks for living, and finding support in each other. To do this, new images and metaphors are needed. For example, instead of standing on a "rock of ages," a bird can perch on a branch, not concerned about it breaking because it trusts in its own wings. Over time, the recovering person acquires new information and new skills. Areas of human knowledge can be freely explored, even if they challenge the Bible.

One of the most useful concepts in the new natural paradigm is understanding humans as animals. To be part of the animal kingdom, belonging to the earth, enjoying nature, and living fully in the present, is a new approach to life. Without the concept of sin at the center of everything, the reclaimer can transform his or her view of self and others. This is an exciting discovery. Answers may not be simple, or even forthcoming, but living with questions has its own kind of wonder. Uncertainty implies mystery, and impermanence brings a kaleidoscope of change.

The person without supernatural beliefs seeks to be fully alive in the here and now. As one put it:

> I am a stronger, better person because I am an atheist. I face reality as it is—even the most unpleasant parts of it—and I am good and moral because that's a part of who I am as a person, not because I am trying to please God or because I am living in fear of him. I have discovered how wonderful it is to face life on its own terms, free of religious myths and lies!

Alan Watts once compared life to listening to music. He said we don't sit waiting for the music to end in order to do something better; we enjoy the music while it is playing, remembering to sing and dance while we can.

In working with former Christians, it has been a pleasure to share this most amazing, healing metaphor.

We Need to Understand This Process Better

In the 1980s one could obtain a doctorate in counseling psychology without taking a single course on the psychology of belief or the relationship between religion and mental illness. By 1994, guidelines for psychiatry residencies required some form of training on "religious or spiritual factors that can influence mental health." But even today such training often focuses on the benefits of religion, not its power to harm. Nurses, doctors, and mental-health professionals who want to understand and heal harm done by religion have nowhere to turn for specialized knowledge, training, or certification.

Based on anecdotal evidence, the need may be enormous. That said, we need real research to find out exactly how many people are being harmed by toxic religion and how best to help them.

Getting real numbers is challenging in part because religious teachings can mask the extent of the damage. When conservative Christians develop mental health problems, they often are encouraged to seek pastoral counseling rather than psychological or psychiatric care. Many fundamentalist sects perceive psychotherapy as a threatening alternative to faith. A Christian woman from Texas put it this way:

> Our faith is our connection to God. Once we break that connection, there is no faith. Why do Christians feel a need to seek the advice or help of another person, when Christ should be all that we need? We don't need psychiatrists to fix us or depression medication to relieve us. There is deliverance in the Word of God. There is breakthrough in the Word of God. There is healing in the Word of God. Every situation that we endure, there is a word for us. To seek out these other methods is to not trust God.[44]

Beliefs like these add an extra barrier for those suffering mental illness, whether that illness was caused by religion itself or by the wide variety of situational and biological factors that can leave a person floundering. Fortunately, many Christian denominations now recognize that not all psychological symptoms are spiritual symptoms. Fortunately, too, a host of resources have sprung up both for those who are struggling within faith communities and those who are in the process of leaving their religion.[45] But this work has just begun.

When members of open, enquiring mainline denominations leave their faith, they rarely need a healing community. They seldom are rejected by family and friends, and few find the loss of Jesus to be as they might have imagined, leaving a vast, debilitating well of emptiness. As a consequence, many moderate believers far underestimate the power of religion to leave a life in tatters.

But for more conservative believers, the loss can be devastating. Most of the regular visitors to sites like ExChristian.net come from fundamentalist or "Bible believing" forms of Christianity. They include evangelicals, Baptists, pentecostals, Mormons, and members of smaller, less known sects. Literally thousands of personal stories posted by reclaimers attest to how harmful such teachings can be. That said, they also offer a glimpse into the many and varied roads to recovery. Reclaiming the self from the pseudo-self, rebuilding meaning, purpose, job skills, and community—including a new family—these can be the work of a lifetime, well worth the time, sorrow, and effort it takes to journey free.

20

ABUSIVE PASTORS
AND CHURCHES

Nathan Phelps

It is difficult to get a religious person to read a book titled *Christianity is Not Great*. It is even more difficult to get one to read a chapter that claims Christianity has perpetuated evil. I understand that . . . somewhat. I know that there are hundreds of millions of people who embrace a religious system because it gives them the vehicle to demonstrate and express their love, generosity, and kindness. For such people religion affirms their sense of goodness and righteousness.

The specifics of the religion, the doctrines, are often background noise to the bigger purpose of religion for them. Individuals can easily dismiss the harm others have committed in the name of a God because it wasn't them and they don't condone it. We tend to be binary in our thinking. We are attracted to either/or propositions. If I am good I will embrace the good camp and defy the alternative, the evil camp. But even in the few moments it takes to read this paragraph our rational mind tells us that such a dichotomy must be false. Of course goodness covers innumerable points on a continuum, and it is defined differently in different places. The same goes for evil. It covers innumerable points on a continuum and has many faces, many expressions.

Considering why we are so quick to criticize and dismiss contrary ideas is for another chapter or another book. My objective in raising this point is to perhaps loosen the tension of some readers. It's to challenge you, if you are instinctively opposed to the proposition of this chapter, to pause and consider your emotions and motives. My hope is that you will read the facts that I present and reconsider your binary mindset. Maybe you will have fresh eyes and a critical mind. Perhaps you will be willing to dismantle at least a portion of your mental schema . . . shift a paradigm or two and accept that your religion is responsible for the application and justification of profound physical and psychological abuse to other humans.

But in the end, is it about religion being wrong? I don't think so. Over the twenty plus years I struggled with my father's religious beliefs and those I studied as an adult, I came to realize that there were simply too many versions of absolute truth to accept that there was any single correct version. Even then I didn't see religion as bad in any way. But after 9/11 all that changed. Watching America from within its midst, I marveled that we responded to the religious-tinged violence of that day by insisting we turn to religious-tinged violence.

Don't get me wrong, I was steeped in vengeful thoughts and ideas. I was furious. I was scared for my children and the future. I was deeply sad for the neighboring family that lost their daughter in the second plane that hit the towers. Maybe it was because of the emotional intensity. Maybe it was because I had reached a certain place in my journey to reason. Whatever the case, I came away from 9/11 with a certainty that it was the mechanism of faith that represented the greatest threat from 9/11.

So in the end, it is really faith that underlies the evils of religion. It is faith that not so much causes, but allows evil to flourish. It is faith that gives my father and others like him permission to do harm in God's name. It is also faith that prevents otherwise good people from rising up in outrage when these violations occur. Let us continue now and see if I can make that case.

THE CATHOLIC CHURCH SEX-ABUSE SCANDAL

Though your sins be as scarlet they shall be as white as snow."
—Francis J. Crosby

In 1972 Father Gilbert Gauthe, a priest in Broussard, Louisiana, succumbs to his urges, perhaps not for the first time. When confronted by parents demanding to know if he had "been involved with any of the children," he answered "Yes." He asked for help and the parents paid for a series of psychological exams . . . for Gilbert. Neither church officials nor police are advised. A year later he is confronted by the Rt. Reverend Gerard Frey, Bishop of the Lafayette Diocese. He will eventually testify in a deposition that it was three boys he had sex with. Bishop Frey deals with the matter by transferring him to a parish in New Iberia.[1]

In 1974 the Bishop is confronted by another claim and meets with Gauthe again. This time he admits to "imprudent touches" with a young man but assures the Bishop that it was an isolated case. The Bishop takes no action until a year later when he appoints Gauthe chaplain of the diocesan Boy Scouts. Frey later points out under oath that the job was primarily office work and Gauthe would have little contact with the boys. It appears wishful thinking on the part of Frey when we consider Gauthe's testimony that he managed to molest six boys in the parish without ever being challenged for his actions.[2]

The year 1976 finds Gauthe serving as assistant pastor at St. Mary Magdalene parish in Abbeville. Following complaints by two members of the parish that Gauthe had licked their sons on the cheek, Msgr. Richard Mouton, pastor at Abbeville, insists that he seek treatment. He also requires him to move his bedroom and forbids him to have boys in the rectory. But even then it seemed that there was no sense of urgency or concern by the church. No one ever follows up with the psychiatrist and Gauthe admits that he lied to Mouton as well as the doctor.[3]

Even this early in the story several issues stand out starkly. First, in spite of at least three specific claims of criminal activity no one ever thinks to contact civil authorities. Somehow the church has managed to inculcate the idea that they are separate from, and not subject to, civil law. And this is not just among the leadership of the church. On at least two occasions we see church members bringing their grievances to church leaders and relying on them to fix what amounts to a heinous criminal act on the part of one of theirs. How does that happen? What's going on here?

Second, we are exposed to what will be identified as the typical response when church leaders are presented with priests raping boys. Rather than removing this cancer from their midst, they allow it to metastasize. In fact, they promote it. Instead of isolating and destroying the disease, they deliberately capture it and place it where other healthy cells can be damaged or destroyed.

So far Gauthe's abuse appears to have been limited. You will forgive me for using such calloused terms and suggesting that the harms done to these initial victims are any less horrible. The point is that it will seem insignificant by the time the church and Gauthe are done.

Late 1977. Gauthe is less than a year from his last therapy session when Bishop Frey picks him to become pastor of St. John's Church in Henry, Louisiana. Five years pass with Gauthe alone, unsupervised, before cracks start to appear in the dam. In 1983 several families confront Gauthe and the church when they discover their children have been abused by him. Gauthe is removed and remanded to therapy. Attorneys Paul Hebert of Abbeville and Raul Bencomo of New Orleans contact the church demanding redress for families of Gilbert's victims. Negotiations continue for nearly two years before nine victims receive a settlement of over $4 million dollars. Still no criminal charges are laid. Still, the story is kept from the world.[4]

Several factors contribute to the secrecy of this case. First, although the District Attorney had been notified and met with the victim's families, it was necessary for the grand jury to hear testimony from the victims. It was decided to postpone that process until the young boys had more time to work through their trauma with medical experts. Second, and more to the point of this section, the church was adamant that any settlement remain secret.

Back to the points I made earlier, even at this early stage of the scandal we already see clear evidence that the church lives in a protective cocoon of wealth, power, and ignorance of the real world. When confronted with the initial rumblings of this cataclysmic scandal, the greatest icon of morality and truth in the world quickly devolves to finger pointing, name calling, and outright deceit in a desperate bid to avoid accountability.

As the story finally goes public, Rev. Kenneth Doyle, a spokesman for the United States Catholic Conference in Washington declares: "We don't want to give the impression that it's a rampant problem for the church, because it is not, but even one case is too many."[5] Oh, the irony.

Within weeks of Gauthe's removal, Mouton speaks to the parish at Henry, explaining the dismissal of their pastor. Then, in another quirky example of the church's disconnect from reality, he suggests to one of the victim's parents that the children come and confess their sins. This pattern of self-protective denial and attempts to shift accountability will continue over the coming months and years as the world begins to understand the enormity of this very personal and very private betrayal of God's church on earth.

The next two decades see the same story repeated over and over throughout America. New victims are empowered by those who came before and step into the light to tell their story of violation and sexual abuse. The church scrambles for cover, engaging unique legal arguments to keep its priests out of the hands of the law. Church authorities look for scapegoats around every corner. One day it's the promiscuity of the 1960s and 70s that caused it. When that test balloon fails, they float the argument that it is part of the gay-rights agenda to infiltrate their paradigm of virtue and corrupt it from within. And throughout this drama the church continually beats the drum of divine forgiveness.

Another example of the distorted morality wrought by skewed religious sensitivities is seen in the community's response to the revelations about Gauthe. Faced with the facts that there were as many as seventy young boys victimized by the institution that symbolized goodness, peace, and security, parents of Henry, Louisiana, begin to look elsewhere to place blame. Some point their fingers decisively at the church, especially when they learn that Gauthe had been a suspect at two previous churches. But many in the community, seething with anger, can't bring themselves to direct it at their moral center.

Glenn and Faye Gastal were among the first parents to file suit against the church. Where you might expect the community to come to their aid, the opposite occurs. Neighbors turned against the Gastals for exposing their church to public ridicule and financial risk. After all, the money would ultimately come from the pockets of the local people. Meanwhile, with rampant speculation about which children may have been victimized, the community further victimizes them, as the children sense the mood and protect their secrets. The Gastals eventually lost their business as a result of the community's reaction.[6]

Such a crime committed by a member of the public would have been met with universal condemnation and an easy agreement as to the cause. But add a religious flavor to the mix and people lose their innate moral compass. It is as though they fear challenging their God, fear that they will be separated from him. There is this bizarre idea that when the word *God* is invoked, perhaps we are incapable of making rational decisions for ourselves, perhaps we really don't understand everything like God does. So let's don't be too decisive in the face of our creator. The centuries-long notion that the Catholic Church is the direct connection to absolute morality creates a mental and emotional disconnect in its members. Neurons misfire as the mind acts to protect itself from this massive cognitive dissonance. The internal struggle is profound, as the misaligned hierarchy of loyalties are exposed.

Vermillion Parish, Louisiana, is in turmoil. The stories crisscross the nation, and people respond to them according to their interests and understandings. For some the scarlet red color represented by the term *vermilion* is a stark symbol of the sin arising from that place. Like the morning blood-red sky that strikes fear in the heart of sailors, America and the world wonder about the storm to come.

And come it does. Despite the best efforts of the Catholic Church to protect itself with claims of immunity from civil authority as well as by stonewalling every effort made by civil and criminal authorities, the walls begin to crumble. Throughout, America kept hearing from William Donahue of the Catholic League as he launched one trial balloon after another, trying to find some claim of outward responsibility that would resonate with the public. When the John Jay College issued a study that claimed 80.9 percent of victims were male, Donahue responded, "I maintain it has been a homosexual crisis all along."[7]

Consider this for a moment. Let's assume that he's right. What changes? You still have leaders of the largest Christian organization in the world deliberately abusing young children, and you still have leaders deliberately hiding that fact and placing more children in harm's way. Once you acknowledge that fact, you quickly see the disingenuous nature of Donahue's claim. He imagines that the world will forgive the church and blame all this on those evil gays and their agenda.

The first question that should be asked of Mr. Donahue is, if the Catholic Church finds homosexuality so intolerable, what is it doing filling priest positions with homosexuals? This question puts the accountability right back where it has always belonged, with the individual priests who molested children and the leaders of the Catholic Church who allowed it to happen.

While Catholic leaders cry foul, more and more victims come forth. More and more lawyers press for justice. More and more money flows from the coffers of God's treasury.

In 1994 the diocese of Lincoln, Nebraska, pays $40,000 to one victim. In 1997 the Dallas diocese pays over $31 million to an undisclosed number of abused children. In 2003 the church in Louisville, Kentucky, gives $25.7 million to 240 victims. In 2003 the Boston diocese pays out $85 million to settle claims with over 550 victims. Portland's diocese files chapter 11 bankruptcy to help facilitate the payment of $53 million to over a hundred young victims in July of 2004.[8]

The church in Tucson, Arizona, files bankruptcy after it settles with an undisclosed number of victims for over $22 million. A $48 million settlement is part of the bankruptcy proceedings for the Spokane, Washington, diocese in December of 2004. In January 2005, $100 million dollars is paid to 87 victims in Orange, California, after more than thirty priests, nuns, and others acknowledge their actions.[9]

Davenport, Iowa; Los Angeles, California; Charleston, South Carolina; Phoenix, Arizona; San Diego, California; Fairbanks, Alaska; Sacramento, California; Memphis, Tennessee; Savannah, Georgia. The suits continue over the next ten years. Millions are paid out as church after church is forced to acknowledge the harm done to our most innocent citizens.

And who are these innocent citizens? With all the confusion and grief, even the sheer enormity of this situation, it seems too easy to forget that each of these young people has a name, a face, a lifelong memory, and a burden of shame. What have they endured and how can we possibly understand it, let alone repair it?

Brian Galyean in 2011 is a forty-two-year-old actor and swimmer living in San Francisco. Recently he has been struggling with depression, which is unlike him. Generally he is a source of joy and support to all who know him. His excitement is infectious and his kindness is unmatched. Unable to shake the dark cloud, he decides to return to his home base of Dallas, Texas, to spend a few days with family and friends. This is the place where he gets recharged by the love and support he finds there. Right now he really needs it. Something is terribly wrong and he can't define it.

Back in Dallas he decides to attend a church service where a friend of his serves as minister. After the service he waits patiently in the long line of parishioners as they say their good-byes. A tall man in front of him blocks him from the view of his friend. As the tall man leans down to hug the minister Brian's face comes into view and the minister cries with joy, "Oh my God, Brian Galyean!" They greet each other with a warm hug and his friend insists that Brian stay back until he's done so they can catch up.[10]

As the congregation thins out Brian feels his excitement fading with the dimming lights. What's going on here? His minister friend comes to him and gives him a hug. He invites him up to his office where they can talk. With a growing sense of foreboding Brian follows him up the stairs and down the dark hallway. As the darkness descends he's suddenly aware that his friend is wearing vestments similar to the Catholic priests of his youth. They reach the office door and his friend invites him in. Brian freezes and his eyes fill with tears. He is gently ushered into the office, where he sits for the next two hours, weeping.

The memories come in a rush. The fourteen-year-old boy called to the diocesan's office at St. Monica. He feels confusion and uncertainty at the nakedness and touching. He remembers the odors, the garments on the floor, the fear and shame. When it becomes too much he musters the courage to leave the church, and he finds a new home at St. Rita, another Catholic Church run by Jesuits. It isn't long before one of the priests there marks the newcomer as his own. Brian discovers soon enough that it isn't the location, but rather the institution. This must be normal, but if feels so wrong. So Brian hides it. The fear shuts his mouth and the shame brands his heart. This is 1983. There is nothing in Brian's world that explains this to him. He internalizes the wrong and blames himself. Finally, at the age of seventeen, after a third priest has his way at St. Rita, Brian leaves the church.

When the story of abuse by Catholic priests breaks some years later, Brian's mind has made his experiences disappear from memory. But now, twenty-five years later, they're back with a vengeance and he has no choice but to confront them. Today Brian continues his counseling. In a poignant moment of brutal honesty he tells me that a night rarely goes by that he isn't awakened by the leering face of one of these priests haunting his dreams.

But there are other victims. Many devout Catholics have had their idea of the world, and the afterlife, shaken to its foundation. In his book *Losing My Religion: How I Lost My Faith Reporting on Religion in America and Found Unexpected Peace*, William Lobdell details the painful journey he took as he reported on the Catholic scandal and lost his faith in the process.

This is the human face of these crimes. Told and retold a thousand times. Assumptions of guilt and responsibility haunt and condemn the minds of so many. But somehow this doesn't get the consideration it should. We see church leaders squabble over technicalities. We watch as they move heaven and earth to avoid responsibility, and no one stops to think, what about the terrible harm to these children? Even today very few religious people are able to silence their rhetoric, stop the justification, and quietly contemplate the horrible crimes committed against the innocents. For heaven's sake, what is wrong with us?

In 2002, the accounting firm Arthur Andersen voluntarily surrendered its CPA license after a court found it guilty of criminal charges relating to the failure of Enron. There was no equivocation in the court of public opinion. Arthur Andersen existed to ensure that the financial reality of their clients was reported accurately. When they failed to provide that in the Enron case, they failed to justify their existence. They disappeared, and rightfully so. Tens of thousands of people lost their financial future because Arthur Andersen failed to do what it existed to do.

Let me say it one more time. Members of the general public were overwhelmingly satisfied with the fate of Arthur Andersen. They should have been.

But when we see the exact same failure on the part of the Catholic Church, it is as though our collective brain goes numb. Here again, we have an organization that failed spectacularly to perform the primary function for which it existed: providing an unassailable moral standard in the world. Justice demands that the church surrender its license and go away. But thirty years later here it is. What is wrong with us?

On February 12, 2014, the Roman Catholic diocese in Helena, Montana, filed for chapter 11 bankruptcy protection. It was a legal maneuver to protect the organization long term as it prepared to pay $15 million dollars to hundreds of victims.[11] In twenty-first-century America, this has become the norm. Nearly thirty years after Gilbert Gauthe, we still don't know the extent of the damage.

Two years ago at a Vatican summit Michael Bemi and Pat Neal told the attendees that the cost is incalculable but massive beyond any doubt. Focusing only on the American church, they estimated $2.2 billion has been paid out to as many as one hundred thousand victims. In their presentation they rejected four myths about the crisis. One, that it is exclusively an American problem. Two, that the crisis has been exaggerated by a godless society. Three, that the crisis has been created by greedy lawyers out to make a buck. Four, that there is a homosexual component to this outrage.[12]

How does this end? What is the root cause of this aberrant behavior? Can the church recover? These are some of the questions on our minds. These are the questions on my mind:

1. How can an organization that is the self-proclaimed standard of morality in the world justify its continued existence in the face of this profound immorality?
2. Is there enough money or resources to fix these victims?
3. How can society continue to call religion a force for good in light of this tragedy?
4. When will people open their eyes and understand that faith disconnects us from reality?

GOD HATES FAGS

> Foolishness is bound up in the heart of a child, but the rod of correction will drive it far from him.
>
> —Proverbs 22:15

> He that spareth his rod, hateth his son; but he that loveth him chasteneth him betimes.
>
> —Proverbs 13:24

Presenting the idea that a religion that has stood for two thousand years may be bad for us is a daunting challenge. For every example of bad you will find a hundred examples of good that was motivated by Christianity. Or was it? I was on a plane recently, flying to Cedar Rapids, Iowa, to speak at Northern Iowa University. I chatted with the woman beside me on the short flight. She had been visiting her daughter in Montana and was on her way home to Waterloo, Iowa. I asked her why her husband hadn't gone with her and she told me he was on a missionary trip to Jamaica.

Good for him. At the end of the day, it's not what you say; it's what you do. This man was acting on his beliefs, his ideals. He would say he was responding to God's commandment that humans be kind to one another and help the needy.

I received an e-mail awhile back. A new acquaintance of mine was putting together a Podcast-A-Thon with various leaders of the secular movement. His goal was to raise funds for Foundation beyond Belief, a leading charity for the secular community.

Good for him. At the end of the day, it's not what you say; it's what you do. This man was acting on his beliefs, his ideals. He would say he was responding to his innate nature, which understands the importance of human beings being kind to one another and helping the needy.

The point here is that equivalent actions took place, but the motivation for one of them doesn't impose a disprovable variable in the mix. In the real world we don't see any difference between the faithful and the disbeliever when it comes to the positive attributes assigned exclusively to religion. But we do see a difference when an individual or group wants to justify patently bad behavior. Secularism has no external motivation that demands harm to others. Humanism, in rejecting the God hypothesis, is left with the unadulterated rule of doing good for goodness's sake.

Nowhere in modern times can we find a better example of a group needing religion to justify an evil then the Westboro Baptist Church. Since 1991 the church's God Hates Fags campaign has produced tremendous harm to the national psyche.

In May of 1991 my father and several of my siblings showed up at the corner of Gage Boulevard and 10th Street in Topeka, Kansas. Behind them was Gage Park, a sprawling 160-acre park with large stands of trees, recreation areas, and the city's zoo. It was also a popular meeting place for gay people. They stood for a time with signs warning the good citizens of Topeka that there were fags in them there trees. Their goal was to get the city to be proactive in running them out of the park and keeping it safe for law-abiding citizens.

Surprisingly, in this predominately conservative area, folks took offense to their signs and protest.

Let me give some background. My father, Fred Phelps, was raised in Meridian, Mississippi. He was a good student, a golden-glove boxer, class Valedictorian, and on his way to West Point as a seventeen-year-old high school graduate. Some folks in his hometown acknowledge he has a tendency to deliberately upset people just to get a reaction. But that doesn't mean much. During the summer following his graduation he attends a revival meeting at a local church. There he has "a spiritual experience."

After that, he abandoned the plans his father had spent so much time and effort developing. It took the recommendation of a leading political figure to get Fred into West Point. He decides to go to Bob Jones University instead. Over the next few years, as his zeal for God grows, he is found in Twin Hills, Alberta, Canada, at the Prairie Bible Institute, another extremely conservative Bible college. Then he travels the western United States, narrowly avoiding a brush up with a group of Mormons in Utah and excoriating peyote-influenced Native Americans in Arizona.

His hellfire sermons catch the interest of *Time* magazine in 1951, as his reputation grows as a fearless advocate for an absolute, divine morality. His dance card fills quickly as various churches invite him to speak. Over the next few months he travels the country preaching his version of hellfire and brimstone Calvinism to any church that will have him. One such church is in Phoenix, where he meets a young Bible-college student named Margie Marie Simms in November of 1951. After three weeks of "courting" he proposes. They are married in May of 1952, and by 1955 he has settled in Topeka, Kansas. After a protracted battle with the leaders of the church that helped set him up at Westboro, he wrestled control away from them, freeing himself to present his Bible truth, without restriction, to the good folks of Topeka. Each Sunday he practices his hellfire presentation and rhetoric on the dwindling congregation. After giving advice to a parishioner that he beat his disobedient wife the parishioner ended up in jail. After unilaterally excommunicating a young woman for getting pregnant out of wedlock there was a mass exodus from my father's church, so he found himself preaching to just his wife and two baby boys.

Confident in his righteousness, he refused to compromise his truth. He also had to get a real job. While my mother continued to have babies, my father went through a handful of different careers with marginal success. He finally decided to go back to school for a law degree. The pressure resulted in him becoming addicted to prescription drugs. His addiction resulted in more and more physical and verbal violence toward his wife and young children.

He always justified his behavior using the Bible. When he couldn't, he ignored it. With a law degree he began his career, but he was soon suspended for ethics violations. More Bible-justified violence followed as he developed his reputation as a disenfranchised pugilist for the downtrodden.

As I mentioned, Fred is a Calvinist. Calvinism teaches that everyone born on this earth deserves eternal damnation and suffering, but God picks a small remnant that he decides to save in each generation. Men don't choose to be saved, God decides. The perceived degradation of the one great truth of the Bible has convinced my father and his followers (almost exclusively my siblings and their families) that they are the only people on earth who are favored by God today. God hates the rest of the world, to a person, for a variety of reasons. At the center of humankind's immorality is our growing acceptance of equality for gays.

That isn't the only unusual idea that drives their campaign. There are a number of other doctrines and ideas in Fred's religion that would raise eyebrows today. At Barack Obama's inauguration in January 2009, my sister Shirley declared on camera that the new president was the Antichrist and God would only let him rule for forty-two months before he would suffer a fatal injury. As my father liked to say, they have the Bible for that. When July 20, 2012, came and went, with Obama suffering no ill fate, the silence was deafening from God Central in Topeka.

Another example of the strange world of the Westboro Baptist Church is that its members believe that none of them will die. Death is a judgment from God. The only way around that sticky wicket is to contrive the argument that Christ will return before any of them pass. They will follow in the footsteps of Enoch and Elijah as the only people in the history of the world (according to the good book) to escape death. One can only imagine the danger such a belief would cause society if it became widespread.

The Reverend has been a fighter from the beginning. As a child he was a Golden Glove boxer. As a husband he was quick to beat his wife back into submission if she strayed. As a father he used Proverbs to justify violently beating his children with a mattock handle, confident in God's promise that "if you beat him with a rod he will not die" (Proverbs 23:13). So even when the blood flowed down the child's legs he continued on with godly zeal.

As an attorney, he was quick to do battle in the courtroom as well. If a judge challenged him he would fight back without reservation. When he was forced to confront the consequences of his imprudent actions, he would declare it a satanic assault on God's church. Often he would introduce biblical arguments in his legal battles. Unfortunately, it was an effective tool because the simple folk of Kansas sitting in a jury box certainly didn't want to defy God.

It was all of this history that aided in creating his reputation in the community as a fierce, angry, dangerous man. The first time I stepped off the elevator in the state capitol building and saw the John Steuart Curry mural of John Brown on the wall, the immediate impression was: Fred Phelps. The crazy eyes and unruly hair, the arms spread with a Bible in his hand, and his foot stomping on the head of a dead Civil War soldier. This was my father. Crazy for God.

So you can see why the people of Topeka might respond with anger at their God Hates Fags campaign. They knew what they were dealing with. It wasn't so much the message as the messenger and delivery. People in the know understood this was just his latest iteration of cruelty and abuse.

What does all this have to do with the argument that Christianity is not great? Clearly this man has the wherewithal to be cruel and unkind without God. My point is that God gives him permission. In 1971 police took my brother and I from school to the station. They photographed the mass of bruises on the backsides of our bodies and brought charges of child abuse against my father. Then they sent us home with him. My father defended his actions with Bible verses and insisted the physical damage was justified for the Cs and Ds on our report cards. Throughout the process there was a decided attitude of erring on the side of caution when confronted with God's word in the courtroom. Ultimately the charges were dropped.

Once again we see the powers that be deferring to divine authority, as it exists for that time and place. We see a self-imposed blindness on the part of our leaders, unwilling to look at the world as it is, deferring to an imagined morality dictated in a two-thousand-year-old book. We see our advancement as a society stymied by a bronze-age anchor. Apparently not much has changed. Not long ago a member of the Kansas legislature introduced a bill that would legalize corporal punishment that left marks on a child.[13]

So, you see, everything from the slavish notion that women are inferior, to brutal violence against children, to justifying inequality toward an entire community, all his abuse has the seal of approval of the Christian God and a political system afraid to challenge him.

Would Fred have been violent and cruel anyway? I have no doubt. But the right question is whether we should continue to cling to a belief system that allows for that behavior. It's no argument to suggest that evil will exist anyway, therefore we should let an existing justification for it continue.

ETCETERA

Lest I leave you, dear reader, with the notion that these are extreme though isolated cases of pastoral abuse. Let us take a minute to consider a few more examples where Christian leaders are causing harm to themselves, and their parishioners, in the name of Yahweh.

In February 2014 Kentucky pastor Jamie Coots succumbed to the bite of a rattlesnake and died. It wasn't a chance encounter with a snake though. Pastor Coots was a Pentecostal preacher. He was also a snake handler. Coots pastored the Full Gospel Tabernacle in Jesus Name. His grandfather founded the church. This was the ninth time Coots had been bitten. One of those times he lost a section of a finger that rotted away from the snake venom.[14]

Coots, and those like him, hold to the biblical proclamation: "They shall take up serpents; and . . . it shall not hurt them" (Mark 16:18). Let's hope it didn't hurt when he died.

So where is the abuse in such a scenario? I would argue it goes back to his grandfather, who introduced to the family the notion that exposing yourself to mortal danger is okay if you do it in the name of the Christian god. Now, in the emotion of losing his father too early, Cody Coots takes up the family mantel. But instead of acknowledging the lesson of his father's death, Cody has made it clear that he will never seek medical help if he is bitten by one of the serpents he takes up in the name of God.[15]

And let's consider for a moment one of the most legendary hate groups in the history of America. The Ku Klux Klan formed just after the Civil War ended. It became the unofficial paramilitary arm of southern segregationist governments. Its members used terror and murder to maintain control over the black population of the South. And they did it in the name of God. Today's KKK is a kinder, gentler version, but the message is still there. The purity of the white Christian race must be maintained in the name of the Christian God.

And then there are the countless Christian leaders who use the faith of their flock to fleece them on a daily basis. Christians across America can tune in to numerous televangelists for an exhibition of human gullibility. Tapping into the paradigm of divine power, these Bible thumpers use the faith of their viewers to line their own pockets with gold.

Even the most genuine Christian promotes the legitimacy of faith. This meme permeates our society and captures the more gullible among us in webs of Christian-based deceit. Innocent people are harmed constantly in these scams. Scams committed in the name of Christ. Scams perpetuated by this malignant idea called faith.

CONCLUSION

I hear a version of this argument often: "But the Westboro Baptist Church is a rare exception. Most Christians use the teaching of the Bible to raise their children with love and acceptance." First, let me reiterate that I'm not saying Christianity is all bad. I'm saying as long as this single source of good and morality in the world produces *any* evil, it is suspect. I hear over and over how God is above man and his truth is perfect truth. His justice is perfect justice. If it is true that we are in the presence of some system, some force, that rises above the squalor of human existence, it should consistently be far and above anything man can offer.

I recall as a young child thinking we should have halos and be so much better than the world such that it would be self-evident we were chosen by the God of the universe. There should be perfection in our words and deeds, a perfection that could not be disputed. The sad reality is that no such ideal even comes close to emanating from Christianity or any other religion. In practice, religious folks and nonreligious folks look pretty similar for the most part.

Considering the catastrophic harm of the Catholic Church over the last half-century, there is simply no justification for its continued existence. As the self-proclaimed source of morality, the sole reason it exists, we can easily say it is a failure. Why do millions continue to support an entity that has created and protected such harm to so many? Certainly these words are extreme, but it is not hyperbole to say that the Catholic Church has perpetrated one of the worst evils on humans in modern history. Why does it get a pass? We watched with smug satisfaction when Saddam Hussein was hanged for his crimes. What is the difference?

The second point I would make about the argument that Westboro Baptist Church is the exception is that it's not true. There are hundreds of thousands of people out there who have grown up in a similar situation to mine, their parents demanding perfection and blind obedience in God's name. Young people separated from their family because they were unwilling or unable to profess a faith they do not have. In spite of the best intentions of many religious folks, the cold, hard reality is that many subscribe to cruelty and violence in the name of their God. They may not get their own hands dirty, but they accept doctrines that protect those who do harm in the name of God. They give tacit approval to outdated ideas like physically beating children to keep them safe from hell.

It is not enough to raise the *No True Scotsman* argument to dodge accountability. The ideas exist in the Bible. If you proclaim allegiance to the Bible, you claim responsibility for its content and the injustice it perpetuates in society. There are too many areas where Christianity fails to lead the way today, and it is no longer acceptable to try to define a middle ground that isn't there.

If my family is a rare exception, an organization like Recovering from Religion could not exist today. But it does exist, and the number of people who avail themselves of RfR's resources is growing exponentially. If the violence and emotional damage from Christianity were minimal, there would be no need for RfR's new Hotline Project, which thousands of people call to find support and aid when their Christian family turns its back on them. If my argument were no more than a tempest in a teapot, RfR's Therapy Project wouldn't be adding new therapists by the hundreds across the United States.

Christianity is not great as long as it continues to slough off damaged children and young people. Christianity is not great as long as it remains the driving force behind the brutal, unequal treatment of gay people. Christianity is not great as long as it supports the notion of inequality for women. Christianity is not great as long as it continues to perpetuate the idea that it's okay to believe something without evidence or in spite of opposing evidence. And Christianity is not great as long as it continues to impede the life-affirming, lifesaving, scientific efforts in the world.

Part Five

MORALITY, ATHEISM, AND A GOOD LIFE

21

"TU QUOQUE, ATHEISM?" — OUR RIGHT TO JUDGE

Jonathan MS Pearce

Throughout the chapters in this book you have seen how the authors have woven the threads of argument that have made a patchwork quilt, a tapestry of accusations, to be hung around the body of Christianity, that serves to highlight the harm done under its auspices and in its name.

Christians throw the accusation at atheists that we have no epistemic right to judge the moral dimension of the Christian faith. Take Russian novelist Fyodor Dostoyevsky (who concerned himself with the problem of evil) for example. One of the foremost modern apologists, William Lane Craig, stated in his book *Reasonable Faith* about Dostoyevsky:

> Actually, he sought to carry through a two-pronged defense of theism in the face of the problem of evil. Positively, he argued that innocent suffering may perfect character and bring one into a closer relation with God. Negatively, he tried to show that if the existence of God is denied, then one is landed in complete moral relativism, so that no act, regardless how dreadful or heinous, can be condemned by the atheist. To live consistently with such a view of life is unthinkable and impossible. Hence, atheism is destructive of life and ends logically in suicide.[1]

Oh dear, we atheists are apparently a miserable and evil bunch! And what of Craig himself?

> In a world without God, who is to say which actions are right and which are wrong? Who is to judge that the values of Adolf Hitler are inferior to those of a saint? The concept of morality loses all meaning in a universe without God. . . .

In a world without a divine lawgiver, there can be no objective right and wrong, only our culturally and personally relative, subjective judgments. This means that it is impossible to condemn war, oppression, or crime as evil. Nor can one praise brotherhood, equality, and love as good. For in a universe without God, good and evil do not exist—there is only the bare valueless fact of existence, and there is no one to say that you are right and I am wrong.[2]

You can't get any clearer than that. This, I would argue, is representative of the Christian approach to atheistic morality and to whether atheists have a right to judge others. And it is this view that I will challenge.

Do we nontheists have an epistemic right to judge Christians, to assign moral value to *their* actions? Are we throwing around accusations of harm without having our own foundation upon which to base them, as many Christians claim?

There are three things to say in direct answer to this question. First, it *doesn't matter*. By this, I mean if all the atheists and nonreligious people of this world did not so much as exist, these concepts and ideas and accusations leveled at Christians and Christianity would still have merit. In fact, there are Christians around the world who are critical enough of their own religion and, moreover, of all the other thousands of denominations other than their own, as to make these accusations valid, irrespective of whether they come from atheists. If every author in this book happened, in some bizarre twist, to be a committed (yet critical!) Christian, would these points not still hold? Of course they would.

Consider Thom Stark, a liberal Christian, who took Paul Copan and his book *Is God a Moral Monster?* to task in *Is God a Moral Compromiser?* Stark prefaced his work with these comments:

In critiquing Paul Copan's apologetic defenses of our frequently morally problematic Bible, my aim is not to turn anybody away from the Christian faith. In fact, I am critical of apologetic attempts to sweep the Bible's horror texts under the rug precisely because I believe such efforts are damaging to the church and to Christian theology, not to mention to our moral sensibilities. . . .

But despite [contemporary popular apologists'] very good intentions, *they seem oblivious to the real harm they're doing*. Not only are they giving permission for Christians to be dishonest with the material, they're rein-forcing delusions that disconnect well-meaning Christians from reality, blinding them to the destructive effects many of these horror texts continue to have upon Christian communities and in broader society.[3]

So you can see that Christians themselves (the ones who are critical enough) hold similar views to mine. They see the harm that their own apologists perpetuate through the use of contrived theology whose only purpose serves as self-authenticating validation.

As Bishop John Shelby Spong stated in *The Sins of Scripture: Exposing the Bible's Texts of Hate to Reveal the God of Love*:

> This book [the Bible] has been relentlessly employed by those who say they believe it to be God's Word, to oppress others who have been, according to the believers, defined in the "hallowed" pages of this text as somehow subhuman. Quotations from the Bible have been cited to bless the bloodiest of wars. People committed to the Bible have not refrained from using the cruelest forms of torture on those whom they believe to have been revealed as the enemies of God in these "sacred" scriptures. A museum display that premiered in Florence in 1983, and later traveled to the San Diego Museum of Man in 2003, featured the instruments used on heretics by Christians during the Inquisition. They included stretching machines designed literally to pull a person apart, iron collars with spikes to penetrate the throat, and instruments that were used to impale the victims. The Bible has been quoted throughout Western history to justify the violence done to racial minorities, women, Jews and homosexuals. It might be difficult for some Christians to understand, but it is not difficult to document the terror enacted by believers in the name of the Bible.[4]

These are just two examples of many. Christians are critical enough of themselves to point out the harm their holy book and its adherents have caused. If their points are correct, then so, surely, are ours.

The second thing to say in response is that we are merely testing the hypothesis that God is love. One highly contentious view that almost everyone hears about God is that he is love. God is love. This view is somewhat controversial in the context of much of what you have read in this book. What the authors have established is an evidential problem-of-evil argument against

God. Christianity and Christians have contributed harm to this world; how is this fact coherent with the existence of an all-loving, morally perfect God?

If we can establish, and I think we have quite forcefully done so, that Christianity has created a great deal of harm then Christians are under even more pressure to answer the ubiquitous problem of evil. Seeing *Christianity* as *the* problem of evil has a certain ironic ring to it.

God is love is a truth claim. It is a hypothesis that is being put to the test. We can actually use the dirty linen of the Bible and of Christianity since biblical times to make the bed; and we can see if the Bible lies comfortably in it. We can use the morality of the Bible to be its own judge, jury, and executioner. And let's face it, the Bible won't be averse to meting out the most final of punishments: there is rather a lot of execution therein.

Accordingly, the claim that God is love is problematic on many levels.

The third response is that atheists do have the right to judge. We have an epistemic right to judge that Christianity and Christians have caused this world harm. We do so because morality is a coherent concept in a worldview absent of a god.

To show this, I will start by defining the relevant terms then briefly critiquing the main concepts of Christian ethical systems, with particular reference to the idea that (the Judeo-Christian) God himself appears to be a moral consequentialist. This refutes the claim of his acolytes that he is needed to ground morality. I will show that most philosophers are nontheistic and hold to a variety of nontheistic moral value systems that do not necessitate a god and invariably undermine Christian morality. I will go further to argue that morality indeed *presupposes atheism* in order to make sense.

Defining Our Terms

Before we investigate morality, it is useful to establish what we mean by it. First, and obviously, we must look to find a useable definition as to what *morality* is.

Generally, the study of morality is split into three components: *descriptive morality*, *meta-ethics*, and *normative morality*. Normally philosophers replace the term "morality" with "ethics." Descriptive ethics is concerned with what people empirically believe, morally speaking. Normative ethics (which can be called *prescriptive ethics*) investigates questions of what people *should* believe. Meta-ethics is more philosophical still in attempting to define what moral theories and ethical terms actually refer to. Or,

> What do different cultures actually think is right? (descriptive)
> How should people act, morally speaking? (normative)
> What do *right* and *ought* actually mean? (meta-ethics)

Morality, as the term will be used here, will generally be understood as "normatively to refer to a code of conduct that, given specified conditions, would be put forward by all rational persons."[5]

The second important term to attempt to unravel is *objective*. This is a more difficult term to define than one may think. Usually it means something that is independent of an agent's mind, or mind independent. This is the understanding I will use here for the sake of argument. Thus objective morality refers to facts about what constitutes moral behavior, and these facts lie in the nature of the agent's action, regardless of cultural and individual opinion.

One hugely important question at this point concerns the existence of properties such as "is an abstract idea." This is important because theists end up arguing at only skin depth, at the veneer of philosophy. Whether an atheist has the right to make moral judgments is a question that has as its basis much more fundamental meta-ethical and metaphysical philosophy. What theism and theists rely on is some form of (Platonic) realism such that there is a realm where abstract ideas and forms exist. This is not immediately, or even after some critical analysis, apparent. What are rights, moral laws, or morality actually made of? What is their ontology? What are the properties of these abstract ideas? The conceptualist (a form of nominalism, the position that denies the existence of universal abstract ideas in some way) claims, for example, that abstract ideas like morality are concepts in each individual conceiver's head. Thus *objective morality* is potentially a nonstarter, or it requires a more befitting definition. Now the philosophy gets very in-depth here, but it is actually critically important. It is easy to *say* that atheists have no ground for objective morality and that theists do. It is a lot harder to *show* how objective morality exists in some kind of mind-independent reality. Even God can be argued to be an abstraction (since he apparently has *infinite* qualities, a concept that has no *actual* reality).

This terminology of "objective morality" is ubiquitous in debates with Christian apologists, as we can see with William Lane Craig's Moral Argument, which he uses in every debate:

(Premise 1) If God does not exist, objective moral values do not exist.
(Premise 2) Objective moral values and duties do exist.
(Conclusion) Therefore, God does exist.[6]

There is a philosophical problem here because this might well imply that there must exist some kind of Platonic realm, as mentioned, where these ideas actually exist. Without humans in the world, and the actions that carry such moral values, can we actually say that these ideas exist mind-independently? For example, if one were to posit a moral theory that was universally subjective, such that each rational and knowledgeable person with a sound mind would arrive at the same conclusion in valuing a moral action, would this qualify as "objective"? Or if we were to agree on what would be a self-evidently good state of affairs (human flourishing, lack of pain, increase of pleasure, etc.), then this goal could be achieved or known by a thorough empirical analysis (qua science)—would this qualify as objective?[7] If ideas and concepts exist only conceptually, rather than *out there* in the *ether*, does the concept of "objectivity" even make sense?

This idea of universal subjectivity would explain commonality between people, as well as the differences (taking into account societal influences) much better than morality existing as some Platonic form. Or is it just a fanciful way of smuggling in God? If the idea of objective morality is incoherent, are we left with *any* grounding for moral judgments sans God, and perhaps, even with God?

I have had many conversations with theists who make claims about objective morality without properly defining it and then, upon being pressured, reveal it to mean something like "valid and binding." But this ends up being a circular claim. You cannot have an objective morality without a god, since objective morality means a value system validated by some entity. In other words, you can't have "God-derived morality" without God! Well, indeed.

Nevertheless, let us take this mind-independent concept of *objective* and apply it to morality and see whether it holds up. Interestingly, unless theists also hold to some kind of Platonic form, or actual ontological existence of morality in God (whatever that could possibly mean), they face the same questions.

On Christian Theories of Ethics

I will endeavor to run briefly through two major Christian ethical theories to see if they hold up.

Christian Natural Law Theory

Christians claim that they are more entitled to make moral proclamations than atheists, that they have some more direct conduit to the fount of morality than their heathen counterparts. God is, in some way or another, the benchmark, the objective standard, or the oasis of moral rectitude.

Historically speaking, the Natural Law Theory has been the prevalent system adhered to by Christians from Augustine and Thomas Aquinas through to more recent times and thinkers such as C. S. Lewis (and the Catholic Church, though it is debatable as to whether its leaders and theologians qualify as modern thinkers!). The main idea is that God has designed and actualized the world in such a way that morality is woven into its fabric. Thus morality can be derived from the world around us both in doing the right thing and having the right motive. As Paul said in his letter to the Romans:

> For when Gentiles who do not have the Law do instinctively the things of the Law, these, not having the Law, are a law to themselves, in that they show the work of the Law written in their hearts, their conscience bearing witness and their thoughts alternately accusing or else defending them. (Romans 2:14–15)

Of course, the obvious rejoinder here is that if morality is built into the very world around us (perhaps "written on our hearts"), then Christians have no more privileged access to this morality than non-Christians. As theologian J. Philip Wogaman states in *Christian Ethics: A Historical Introduction*:

> All people are capable of knowing natural law, which is universal, whether
> or not they are Christian. Thus Aristotle and other philosophers, depending
> on the clarity of their thought, are capable of understanding and dependably
> presenting and applying natural law. . . . Human law exists as the specific
> application of natural law to the circumstances of earthly life. Human law is
> the enactment of law by civil authority. . . .
>
> It does not rest upon special Christian revelation.[8]

Natural law is a reflection of divine or eternal law in the same way that
one can differentiate between cardinal and theological virtues. This presents
a problem:

> But how, then, can a philosopher (like Aristotle) with no insight into the
> supernatural end of humankind fully grasp the significance of the natural law
> that finds its true expression as a means to an end? . . . To Thomas [Aquinas],
> the ends of natural law, which can be grasped by natural reason, are still
> divinely appointed means to the more ultimate end even when that in itself
> cannot be grasped by natural reason alone.[9]

Of course, such a theory *sounds* nice, but what does it really mean to
have something written on our hearts? What is the ontology of such morality?
These fundamental philosophical questions remain unsatisfactorily answered.

What is interesting is that a book like Wogaman's, which documents the
historical "evolution" of Christian ethical thought and philosophy, as fascinating and comprehensive as it is, is a testament to the fact that Christians
themselves struggle to agree on a "true" (divine or divinely inspired) ethical
system. It is hard for Christians to take the intellectual high ground with regard
to moral philosophy when they cannot even agree among themselves!

Divine Command Theories

Yes, the title to this section uses the word "theories" not "theory." There is
more disagreement to be found among Christians who claim privileged access
to moral truth.

The basic premise is this: morality does not exist independently of God,
it is instead reflected (or perhaps determined) by God's commands. God com-

manded it; therefore, it is good. Of course, Socrates, in Plato's *Euthryphro*, asked, "Is the pious loved by the gods because it is pious, or is it pious because it is loved by the gods?" Or rather, does God command it because it is good, or is it good solely because God commands it?

There are two ways in which Christians can approach divine commands. First, one obeys such moral commands prudentially, meaning that if one doesn't then the eternal hellfires await. Those hot places are not worth entertaining, thus we follow the "good" path. Such a view is integral to the notion that without God we would all be atheist mass murderers, and analogies to Hitler abound. This, however, is fallacious in being an *argumentum ad baculum*, or an appeal to force.

Theologians tend to favor the idea that we follow God's commands because God is good. The commands reflect his perfectly good nature (remember Craig?). Plato's ruminations, though, leave us with a potential circularity. If God *is* good then we have a sort of tautology and cannot have any independent appreciation of the value of his goodness. But if there is an independent criterion then I have no need of God for a moral judgment. Philosopher Kai Nielsen looks at this tautology with reference to the claim "puppies are young":

> If we had no understanding of the word "young" and if we did not know the criteria for deciding whether a dog was young, we could not know how correctly to apply the word "puppy." Without such a prior understanding of what it is to be young we could not understand the sentence, "Puppies are young."[10]

P. Wesley Edwards, in an excellent essay "Does Morality Depend On God?" shows us the inherent problems with this approach:

> Now for the statement, "God is good," or more generally, "X is good," to even make sense, we need some idea of what "good" means. For example, if I say, "Fred is perfectly zugblub," then you have no idea what I mean unless you have some idea of what "zugblub" means. Suppose after pointing this out to me, I respond, "Fred is the very standard by which zugblub is defined; Zugblub is part of the very essence of Fred. Indeed, Fred actually forms the necessary ground of all zugblub. That is what zugblub means."

This so-called definition of zugblub communicates no information. The problem is that I have not defined zugblub independently of Fred. All my definition amounts to is different ways of saying "Fred is Fred" and "zugblub is zugblub." These are true statements to be sure, but not particularly informative ones. In other words, my definition of zugblub is tautological—an empty truth.[11]

There is simply no way of getting around this circularity. Even appealing to God's nature, as opposed to his commands, gets the theist into the same problem. From the evidence of the Bible itself we can see that God derives his morality from the consequences of his actions, not, it seems, as intrinsically value-laden reflections of his nature (as we shall see).

One of the most fundamental issues with Divine Command Theory is that we don't seem to know clearly what the commands are. Biblical studies revolve around interpretation of one historically compiled text. Theologians disagree on what certain texts mean and what they are in some way commanding. That there are some forty thousand denominations of Christianity suggests that there is a denomination for everyone, no matter your moral preference.[12] Is homosexuality morally evil or good (or neither)? Abortion? Divorce? Eating shellfish? Working on the Sabbath? War? Should we look after our environment or should prosperity rule? There is no clarity. Pragmatically speaking, divine command theories are nothing but impotent abstract ideals.

Of course, one could also object that if God commanded us to torture babies for fun it would be good (or take people as slaves). The theist would counter that God hasn't done this, nor *could* he, since it is not in his nature. The problem here, though, is that we have no idea what it means to say God's nature is good apart from what he does. In fact, if God's nature is good then whatever he does is good. Can he do and say things that would run counter to our conception of his goodness? Based on this divine command theory we discover what it means to say he's good by what he does. So the Christian response is trumping God's omnipotence with his supposed omnibenevolence—yet another example of how the characteristics of God are internally incompatible. Could it be, then, that God knows vastly more about the consequences of any act than we do? Theists enjoy appealing to the omniscience of God, pulling the "God moves in mysterious ways" card. We have to entirely trust, supposedly, in God's providence. Using our God-given reason, which one must assume is reliable, since it is given to us by an all-good God (being made in his image, surely we have access to his good nature and reason), we are, however, left with some rather irrational-looking prospects. The evidence of the Old Testament leaves us questioning such faith in divine omniscience: we read of God changing his mind, deceiving, countenancing slavery and rape, committing genocide or mass murder, punishing people for using free will in a way that he presumably foreknew, and so on. In some cases, good people are rewarded on earth while others, children and old people alike, have to wait for heaven for their rewards, while still others are punished on earth, although other truly bad people get away with it and have to await hell, presumably. Such evidence hardly points to an obvious, divinely inspired morality. As A. C. Grayling states, "We are being asked to accept as sound the following reasoning: 'A loves B and therefore B must do as A requires.' This is an obvious non sequitur."[13]

Whole books fail to exhibit any coherent account of divine command theory or theories. All of these theories are highly problematic.[14]

On Atheist Ethics: What Philosophers Think

Love it or hate it, if we are going to discuss ideas of morality and moral philosophy then we must defer to the experts to some degree. Not, of course, in a fallacious manner of *appealing to authority* or, indeed, an *argumentum ad populum*. Just because a certain number of qualified philosophers think something doesn't make it true. Yes, we know this. However, it is sheer folly to ignore the views of the people who spend their lives investigating moral ideas. I would not build a nuclear power station without having a few chats with well-qualified particle and nuclear physicists while at the same time bending the ears of some proven structural engineers.

So what *do* philosophers think? Luckily, in 2009 the biggest ever survey of professional and graduate philosophers took place—the PhilPapers survey.[15] In this survey we learned some important things. We learned that 27.7 percent of philosophers are moral antirealists. What this means is that roughly a quarter of philosophers deny the objective truth value of moral statements. Further to this, some 25.9 percent of philosophers accept or lean toward moral deontology, 23.6 percent moral consequentialism, and 18.2 percent virtue ethics. Now we are getting into the pertinent detail. These are the three main contenders for moral theory, split roughly equally, with a healthy "other" (isn't there always!).

What we can learn from this is that there are a variety of different moral theories that one can adopt, including the denial of moral theories. But the important result is as follows: 72.8 percent of philosophers are atheists, 14.6 percent being theists. A huge majority of philosophers deny the existence of a god of any kind. And yet we have just learned that some 67.7 percent believe in deontology, consequentialism, or virtue ethics. So, clearly, many philosophers believe that you do not need to believe in a god to coherently hold a moral philosophical worldview. These are, one presumes, the best philosophical minds, who are most qualified to make such pronouncements on morality, so it really is important to garner their opinion.

Now, it's understood that many of these philosophers may have had a specialization in an area that wasn't moral philosophy, but every qualified philosopher will at some point have learned about moral philosophy and, indeed, due to the interconnectedness of philosophical disciplines and due to many concepts deriving from moral philosophy, I cannot envisage any philosopher taking that survey without having a view on moral philosophy. I wager it to be more informed, indeed, than most theists who make far-reaching claims about morality.

Some Moral Theories That Atheists Can and Do Hold

As Sam Harris has said, "Religion gives people bad reasons for acting morally, where good reasons are actually available."[16] In this vein, I will set out some of the more common moral theories to show that atheists have a number of moral foundations upon which to start building a coherent worldview (there are some others).

Virtue Ethics

Virtue ethics is perhaps the best-known coherent atheistic moral value systems. Virtue ethics isn't necessarily a method to use to define whether a particular action is more morally good than another; it is more a way of living (the good life), taking Aristotelian ideas and developing them. Therefore, a virtue ethicist is more concerned about what an action says about the character of the person in *being*, and not so much in *doing*; that is, do such actions allow the agent to flourish as a human being?

Imagine a scenario where someone needs to be saved. A virtue ethicist would see that helping the person would be charitable or benevolent, a reflection of his or her character.

What is pertinent about this theory is that it seems at its core to be a naturalistic theory, not needing a god to justify itself. As Julia Annas confirms in "Virtue Ethics: What Kind of Naturalism?":

> On this issue of the good life most modern forms of virtue ethics are naturalistic, and often take a form called neo-Aristotelian, harking back to the best-known naturalistic theory from antiquity: Aristotle's. When we are investigating what the good life is, these theories hold, and how living virtuously might achieve it, we are aided by investigating our human nature. This in turn we do by seeing how we humans are a part, though a distinctive part, of the world that the sciences tell us about.[17]

Deontological Ethics

Deontology is a moral framework championed best by Immanuel Kant. Deontologists believe that there are things that we categorically should do, things that ought to be done irrespective of the context. In other words, no matter how good the effects of an action might appear, the action might still be bad. Kant, as the deontological flagbearer, argued there were moral laws and prohibitions that ought to be adhered to regardless of the consequences. He argued that people should not be used as means to an end. Imagine again a scenario where someone needs to be saved. A deontologist would act according to a rule such as Kant's Categorical Imperative: "Act only according to that maxim whereby you can, at the same time, will that it should become a universal law."[18] Saving others can be willed as a universal law and we should do it, unconditionally, as an end in itself (of course, I simplify here in recognition of the need to be succinct).

Kant was a sort of Enlightenment deist when it came to God. He thought that morality was wrapped up with the idea of God. However, Kant's core ideals were humanistic, and his arguments for a deontological form of ethics needed no god. It seems that religion, for Kant, was the *reason to be* moral, not the *grounding of* morality. As A. C. Grayling notes in *What Is Good? The Search For The Best Way To Live*:

> Kant was not a personally religious man, and his "postulates" for making external sense of morality shared the notional, deistic character that (for example) Voltaire's views have. The significant fact is that the content of Kant's moral theory is thoroughly humanistic, in arguing, first, that morality's most fundamental presupposition is the autonomy of the will, meaning that will obeys laws it imposes on itself and not those prescribed by an outside source such as a deity or sovereign; and secondly, that the law such a will thus obeys must be shown to be valid on purely formal grounds—as a matter of logic. In this respect Kant's theory is a paradigm of Enlightenment thinking.[19]

Without having to go deeply into ideas of deontology I have shown that it is quite plausible and coherent for atheists and naturalists to adopt deontology. Let's apply deontology, then, to the Bible and Christianity:

1. It is wrong to commit genocide (but God and Yahwists did it, e.g., 1 Samuel 15, Exodus 17).
2. It is wrong to lie (but God did, certainly by proxy, e.g., 1 Kings 22:23, Jeremiah 4:10, 2 Thessalonians 2:11, and others).
3. It is wrong to rape (but God sanctioned it, e.g., Judges 21, Numbers 31, Deuteronomy 20, 21, 22, etc.).
4. It is wrong to own slaves (but God allowed for it, e.g., Leviticus 25, Exodus 21, etc.).

And so on. You get the point.

Consequentialism

Consequentialism is an opposing theory to deontology. This theory claims that the normative moral properties of an action are derived from its consequences. This is a far more complex area than it may at first appear. Different theories or interpretations of consequentialism mean that it is a rich and varied territory. Value can depend on the act itself, the motive or intention, a generalized rule, the total consequences, or those consequences particular to a constrained time and context, and so on. And again, to make matters more complex, the value can be seen not only in terms of maximizing pleasure and minimizing pain, but also in terms of more pluralistic consequences such as promoting freedom and knowledge.

It must be said that "many naturalists, if they are moral realists in their meta-ethics, are consequentialists in their ethics."[20] (Conversely, the more religiously fundamentalist or conservative you are, the more likely you are to be a deontologist.[21])

Thus an action, for a theory such as the consequentialist theory of utilitarianism, would be morally valued for the amount of pleasure or pain it causes. And it seems fairly intuitive that we ought to try to make the world better than it is, which is what underlies the idea of consequentialism. Imagine once again a scenario where someone needs to be saved. A utilitarian would claim that the moral value of the action would be derived from the consequences of doing so, which would maximize well-being.

Utilitarianism, then, is a nonderivative ethics. When I ask deontologists why a certain charitable action was done, they will say, "Because it is the right thing to do." If I keep asking why it's the right thing to do, and if they can give an answer to each "why," then they are deriving the reasons further back. For the utilitarian, the why questions end when "happiness" (that is, holistic happiness) is invoked. Pleasure is self-evidently good or pleasurable, such that when asked why we want to be happy, we end up with an axiom: because it makes us happy. This nonderivative axiom gives a fairly robust foundation to at least some types of consequentialism.

And of course the crucial point to make here is that a god is not necessary, or even remotely useful, for such a concept to be coherent.

Let's apply consequentialism to the Bible and Christianity:

1. It is wrong to commit genocide, as a rule, because it obviously increases pain and decreases pleasure for a huge number of people, including those who survive, and it also damages the mental dispositions of those meting out the punishment (but God and Yahwists did it anyway).

2. It is usually, but not always, wrong to lie because of the negative consequences brought about by lots of people so doing. However, if a murderer came to my house and asked where the children he wanted to kill were hiding (children who happened to be in my attic), it would be right to lie. It is contextual. (And God did it by proxy, anyway.)

3. It is wrong to rape, as a rule (as in rule consequentialism,[22] where rules of thumb are pragmatically put in place to save the disutility of trying to calculate, say, pleasure), and given that the intention for it is wrong based on the consequences of causing harm to others (but God sometimes sanctioned it).

4. It is wrong to enslave people based on the consequences it causes. Owning a slave might give a slave-holding family five units of utility, but it would give the slave more units of disutility (but God sanctioned it).

Now, the simple claims above can involve a huge amount of more complex philosophy, but the broad points are fairly obvious: a god is not necessitated for consequentialist morality to hold, and one can use such a moral system to evaluate the Bible and Christianity.

What does remain to be said is this. Research has shown that people who see themselves as deontologists, such that they propose absolute laws such as "It is wrong to have an abortion," will also use consequentialist ethical reasons to back up their claims. In other words, people often use both forms of moral reasoning, especially considering that most typical, nonphilosophical people (when tested) appear to have consequential intuitions about morality. A paper by Ditto and Liu found that when priming (when exposure to a particular stimulus can have measurable influence on a later stimulus) deontological people with either strong essays for or against a deontological argument (say, abortion), they would adjust their consequentialist arguments to follow their deontological bias.[23]

Of course, this has been a whistle-stop tour around the more prominent of moral theories. There is much more to be said about them. And they need not be mutually exclusive. For example, with some ingenuity a virtue ethicist could also be a deontologist or a consequentialist. But they can be and are embraced by many atheists, and so they provide a good grounding for judging the harms of Christianity.

God Is a Consequentialist

Interestingly, when we look at Paul Copan's *Is God a Moral Monster?* the justifications start out being deontological (on the issue of genocide), but Copan moves toward consequentialist reasons when the deontological ones appear to be weak. A case of having your cake and eating it, too. In the end, God is portrayed as a consequentialist, though Copan would emphatically deny this.

So let us look at how Mark D. Linville sees morality in the hugely influential *Blackwell Companion to Natural Theology*:

> Moral agency is thus what we might call a dignity-conferring property.
>   If such an argument is to succeed at all, one requirement is that morality itself must be of intrinsic rather than instrumental value.[24]

An instrumental moral value is one that is justified by a more basic value (such as happiness). William Lane Craig seems to agree in discussing the views of William Sorley:

> Where, then, does objective moral value reside? Sorley answers: in persons. The only beings that are bearers of intrinsic moral value are persons; non-personal things have merely instrumental value in relation to persons. Only persons have intrinsic value, because meaningful moral behavior requires purpose and will.[25]

But let's look at the evidence. What has God done (or supposedly done)?

- Destroyed humanity, bar eight chosen survivors, and the animal kingdom, bar two (or seven) of each kind (Noah's Flood).
- Sacrificed Jesus of Nazareth to pay for the sins of humanity.

- Demanded, or countenanced, the destruction of entire peoples (e.g., the Amelakites).
- Allowed the 2004 Indonesian tsunami to go apparently unhindered, killing 240,000 people and destroying untold numbers of habitats, organisms, and ecosystems.

And so on and so forth. In fact, it appears that any piece of suffering can only be justified as instrumental to achieving a greater good. It is clear that destroying almost all of life on earth is not an intrinsically morally good action. For a start, it apparently defies God's own absolute commandments. And this is the problem with absolute morality; it renders context and consequences irrelevant. But with the sacrifice of Jesus and the death of human and animal life in the flood, only the consequences could possibly warrant the action.

Theodicies seek to provide answers as to why such suffering exists. Indeed, the job of a theologian in response to all of the examples given in this book is to defend God, and to justify his actions and inactions, with various consequentialist theodicies. If people are being used in service of a greater good then they are being used as a consequentialist means to an end.

All of the suffering described in this book can be morally permissible only if God is a consequentialist. And if he is, then he has no need of himself for his own morality. He can be judged quite easily by an atheist, thank you very much.

So the questions become:

What is this greater good?
Why hasn't God communicated it to the very people who are suffering?

In my book *The Little Book of Unholy Questions* I asked this question to God (as yet unanswered, I hasten to add):

282. If my child was to walk on the flowers in my garden, trampling them, it would be immoral to punish him without telling him what he had done wrong. This would communicate to my child his misdemeanor so that he would not do it again. What have we done wrong to deserve cancer, malaria, the tsunami, the Holocaust, disability, cholera, etc., and is it right that you have not communicated to us why we have had these "punishments"?[26]

There is no clear communication from God as to why this suffering is taking place, why we are being punished, if indeed our intense suffering results from some kind of punishment. If suffering exists for any other reason, God is still not communicating what it is, despite being (so we're told) an all-loving ruler. His subjects are suffering each and every day in a universe where there *could* be no suffering. As the suffering ones, we have every right to know why this is the case. Even if, as theists propose, morality is grounded in God, our moral indignation at his poor design, inexplicable inaction, and lack of communication is merely a reflection of God's own morality. As Paul Copan stated in his book with Craig *Passionate Conviction: Contemporary Discourses on Christian Apologetics*:

> We would not know goodness without God's endowing us with a moral constitution. We have rights, dignity, freedom, and responsibility because God has designed us this way. In this, we reflect God's moral goodness as His image-bearers.[27]

Craig, however, tries to slip out of this bind:

> Moral duties arise in response to imperatives issued by God. Since God does not issue commands to Himself, God has no moral duties. Rather God's acts must simply be consistent with His perfectly good nature. So consequentialism *cannot* apply to God, having as He does no moral duties. His actions, such as permitting some evils in view of overriding goods, must simply be consistent with His being all-loving, punishing evil, etc.[28]

But God can command child sacrifice; genocide; slavery; rape; the killing of adulterers, witches, and homosexuals; the destruction of humanity bar eight; and so on. There really is nothing off limits to God and his commands (Craig claims "God's having no moral duties does not imply that He can do just anything"[29]). If God must be consistent with his own perfectly good nature then why does he have so much wrath and jealousy? His own actions appear to violate his own perfect commands to us, so Craig is not really exonerating God here. The sense of "good" here is somewhat dubious and question begging. Craig's answer to this accusation is muddled at best, and I do not think he remotely succeeds in his defense of the accusation. It raises more questions than it solves (though it actually solves none).

To conclude, it seems apparent that the moral value derived from the actions of God has its basis in the consequences of those actions and not in their intrinsic morality. Either the objective morality claimed by theists does not exist or it is consistently trumped by the consequences of the actions. Whether the consequences are defined with a measure of classical utility (maximizing pleasure/minimizing pain) or something else, such as promoting justice or love, is neither here nor there. What is apparent is that theists might do well to adjust their own moral philosophy or to explain why the moral code of God is different from our own. If God is supposed to be the moral benchmark against which we all act, and whose moral nature is reflected in our own personal moral dignity, then theists need to better explain this disparity.

Morality Presupposes Atheism

Philosopher Stephen Maitzen has argued that there is an interesting case to be put forward in support of an atheistic moral standpoint. Atheism, it appears, actually appears necessary for morality. Maitzen argues that "theism and ordinary morality are incompatible: theism can't accommodate an ordinary and fundamental moral obligation acknowledged by many people, including many theists."[30] Morality, he admits with refreshing honesty (and accuracy) is hard to define sharply, but it does include, for example, "the obligation we at least sometimes have to prevent easily preventable, horrific suffering by an innocent person."[31] Morality, it seems, is at loggerheads with what he declares as "theological individualism," which means that God only permits "undeserved, involuntary human suffering" if it produces a net benefit, a greater good, for the sufferer.[32]

This *seems* to make intuitive sense; the idea is that God creates or permissively allows suffering for a greater good. The suffering cannot be gratuitous because God would then be needlessly allowing suffering, something that an omnibenevolent God would not do.

It is important to note here that compensation in heaven is not a good moral justification for suffering or evil. That a child can be molested by a Catholic priest is never justified merely because the child will get an eternity in a heavenly bliss. Compensation is not a rationally sustainable moral justification; for example, I could not go up to a man in the street and punch him in the face then offer him $10,000 in compensation. That would not justify my violent action (even if the victim actually felt that he came out better for it).[33] I can compensate the victim, but the original action is not morally good or justified. The Christian theist might say, "But hey, since the final outcome for the person hit in the face might be better, using heaven in the same way appears to be consequentially morally good!" If this is the case, one must admit that moral value is ascertained consequentially and that we have no need for God in our moral proclamations. The theist cannot have it both ways, again.

With that in mind, suffering on earth cannot be redressed in heaven in any morally justifiable manner (from the theist's own point of view). This leaves us with all suffering being necessary for a greater good, to put it simplistically. But this puts the theist in an awkward position, as Maitzen argues.[34]

The analogy goes as follows. If there were a necessarily painful vaccine for a disease that was the only way of curing the disease in an individual, we would be morally obliged to allow the painful injection to go ahead. This is obvious. However, Maitzen equates this with human suffering. Our suffering is explained as a necessary suffering for a greater good. Therefore, we are morally obliged to let it happen precisely because God allowed it for a greater good. We are therefore morally obliged to let the suffering of all humans take place.

For example, if a small boy is abused by a priest then, given God's attributes, there must be a net gain for the boy somehow, otherwise God is not all-loving. If there is a net gain, then we are morally obliged to let the abuse happen in the same way that we are morally obliged to allow a vaccination to take place. This is the case even if the child wants us to prevent the molestation, since this would also be the case when a child wants to refuse a vaccination: we would insist it take place.

Jerry Coyne, author of the book *Why Evolution Is True*, shows us that Christians have actually adopted this approach to accepting God's judgment:

> We justify science rather than faith as a way of finding out stuff not on the basis of first principles, but on the basis of *which method actually gives us reliable information about the universe*. And by "reliable," I mean "methods that help us make verified predictions that advance our understanding of the world and produce practical consequences that aren't possible with other methods." Take a disease like smallpox. It was once regarded as manifestations of God's will or displeasure. Indeed, inoculation was once opposed on religious grounds: that

to immunize people was to thwart God's will. You can't cure smallpox with such an attitude, or by praying for its disappearance. The disease was cured by scientific methods—the invention and testing of inoculations—and completely eradicated on this planet by the use of epidemiological methods. Science gets us to the Moon; religion can do no such thing.[35]

God surely judges that the pain caused by smallpox is necessitated for the attainment of a greater good. Who are we to intervene in God's supreme judgment? In exactly the same way, we cannot fault the craziness of the members of the Westboro Baptist Church who are actually being more logically consistent (consistently wrong, I might add) than liberal Christians. When they congregate with placards celebrating the death of US soldiers or carry out some other such intuitively reprehensible outburst, they are merely celebrating God's judgment. Who are we mere ignorant mortals to question God allowing *some* soldiers to die but *not others*?

The problem is that ordinary morality has a common core that appears across cultures, religions, and nonreligious communities. We sometimes have a moral obligation to prevent suffering. This much seems obvious. And these obligations of ours, at least often, don't seem to be commands from the Judeo-Christian God. The argument goes that theological individualism (TI), the existence of God and the existence of intense suffering, together with our obligation to prevent it, are not mutually coherent. Something must go. The theist would try to argue that TI (that God only permits undeserved, involuntary human suffering if it produces a net benefit, a greater good, for the sufferer) must go, but TI must hold if God has the attributes that theists claim.

Therefore, it seems that God must go. And thus morality, not being coherent with God, necessitates atheism. Let me lay out Maitzen's whole argument:

(1) If God exists and TI is true, then, necessarily, all undeserved, involuntary human suffering ultimately produces a net benefit for the sufferer.

(2) If, necessarily, all undeserved, involuntary human suffering ultimately produces a net benefit for the sufferer, then (a) we never have a moral obligation to prevent undeserved, involuntary human suffering or (b) our moral obligation to prevent undeserved, involuntary human suffering derives entirely from God's commands.

(3) We sometimes have a moral obligation to prevent undeserved, involuntary human suffering, an obligation that does not derive entirely from God's commands. Two subconclusions follow from the three premises just established:

(4) So: It isn't the case that, necessarily, all undeserved, involuntary human suffering ultimately produces a net benefit for the sufferer. [From (2), (3)]

(5) So: God does not exist or TI is false. [From (1), (4)]

(6) If not even God may treat human beings merely as means, then TI is true.

(7) Not even God may treat human beings merely as means. It remains, then, only to draw the argument's final two inferences:

(8) So: TI is true. [From (6), (7)]

(9) So: God does not exist. [From (5), (8)][36]

Conclusion

It seems clear to me from various points of view that morality does not necessitate God. And to be clear about this, one must not get confused between the *grounds for moral judgment* and the *repercussions of a moral action* (on the moral agent). That I have a promissory note and I might end up going to heaven or hell at the end of my life (despite the all-knowing god being well aware of what I would do and creating the world with this outcome anyway) affects in no way the morality of an action in this here life. No, atheists have several very good cases for morality, which can themselves take on many guises depending on what properties our reality has. Moreover, it appears that morality and God are not good bedfellows; indeed, morality requires atheism to make sense.

My case, though, did not finish there, for it appears that God himself is a consequentialist from the evidence presented both in the Bible and in the suffering that takes place each and every day since the dawning of complex life. This alone seems to invalidate the numerous different Christian ethical systems that exist, two of which I outlined. And the two I did illustrate here have many problems, which means that Christians should worry more about establishing *their own* moral value systems under God than they do about equating atheists with Hitler.

After all, Hitler killed far fewer people than God (given floods, the creation of diseases, the creation of free will, and so on, presuming he had full knowledge of what these marvelous gifts would lead to). And at least with Hitler we had some idea as to why he did it, and people don't get so defensive when we take him to task, rightly accusing him of being a moral monster.

Do we have grounds to judge? Damned right.

ONLY HUMANS CAN SOLVE THE PROBLEMS OF THE WORLD

James A. Lindsay

If I wanted to be cliché, I would start off by saying, "I've got good news and bad news!" The good news, of course, is that we don't have any good reasons to believe God exists and we have plenty of strong reasons to believe he/she/it does not—a phrase I will summarize henceforth with "God doesn't exist." The "bad news" is that this seems to confer upon us a responsibility: only we humans can solve the problems of the world. This responsibility has not been conferred upon us, though; we have always had it. The news, then, is not bad because now we know we can do better without the hindrance of a belief in a God that doesn't exist.

Throughout this anthology, you have been invited to take a close look at many of the outright harms that religious faith, Christianity in particular, visits upon the world. Here, then, we face the apparently hard question of who will heal these injuries and move humanity forward. The answer is obvious, we will! Humans, and essentially only humans, can solve the world's problems, if they are to be solved at all.

We humans are the only ones who get to pick up from where we are and move forward. This is how it has always been, and now we are ready to do it better by doing it without religion. The future of the world now lies in secularism equipped with neohumanist ethics, with our decisions informed by science and our policies responding to our best understanding of reality. No longer do we need to rely upon outdated guesses enshrined by dogmatism and protected by authority, too often cruelly. No longer should we depend upon the placebo of religion to try to meet our challenges.

God Doesn't Exist

I should, I suppose, give some defense for the claim that God doesn't exist, since it is by far the most obvious reason for my conclusion that only humans can meet the challenges of our world. My case that God doesn't exist is laid out in some detail in the two books that I have written.[1] There are, effectively, four possibilities in which we might not be able to say God doesn't exist. First, there is the possibility that "God" is utterly remote, the Deist's God that has no interaction with the world. Second, there is the possibility that "God" is utterly vague, something like the pantheist God equipped with some kind of epistemic cloaking device. Third, there is also the possibility that "God" is, by definition, utterly unknowable. Finally, there is the possibility that "God" is an abstract notion through which people seek to make sense of the world—in which case it is germane to notice that "God" becomes a human solution to the challenges we face as well.[2]

In the first three possibilities, which I need not deal with individually, what is being called "God" may really exist, but we cannot know it. Thus, anyone who claims to know it is wrong. This is an epistemic roadblock, which I insist in *God Doesn't; We Do* can only be resolved by evidence that would break us out of one of those possibilities.[3] This is precisely the reason why Peter Boghossian correctly notes that faith is identifiable with "pretending to know things you don't know."[4] It is also the reason why John Loftus concludes that "faith is a parasite on the mysterious,"[5] as it leeches its substance not from what we know but rather from what we don't know. On that characterization, incidentally, it is worth noting that many of the mysteries upon which faith depends for its nourishment evaporate entirely if one fails to accept theism.

I will admit that I cannot dispel these three conceptions of "God," nor can I claim to know that they do not exist. Partly this is because they are unfalsifiable, and largely it is because they are irrelevant. Nothing is to be gained by believing in, or lost by failing to believe in, a remote "God," a vague "God," or an unknowable "God." One of the chief harms of Christianity and its brothers,[6] in fact, lies in insisting not only that there is something to be gained but that what is to be gained or lost is the single most important article in the universe. Since these conceptions of God cannot matter (unless an unknowable "God" also happens to be an abomination, as suggested by Christianity and its brothers) and cannot be known to be correct, I do not seek to dispel them but merely to ignore them. Seriously, why not?

Each of these three possibilities can also be seen as an aspect of the fourth: "God" as abstraction. If I feel a pressing need to have an ultimate answer to cosmogenesis then I can invent the Deist's God as an abstraction that satisfies that question. Dreaming of "God" as a vague sense of how the universe works functions likewise. To posit "God" as being unknowable is, in fact, to render it a matter of pure speculation from our perspective. What these and every other notion, of "God" or otherwise, that resists testing on the rock of reality all have in common is being mental constructs by which we seek to understand the world.

I cannot say with the kind of certainty that my detractors would desire that the God represented by any of these ideas doesn't exist. But I don't have to. All I need to say is that no one, not me and not they, can say that they *know* such a God exists. For if they do then they are pretending to know things they don't know. That is enough by far.

The Problem of a Silent God

What I want to focus on here is the possibility that a God actually exists and is not remote, vague, or unknowable. This is the "doing God" that I made my case against in *God Doesn't; We Do*,[7] and this is the God that those of us who do not believe in are right to consider a hypothesis to be tested.[8] This or, to be more accurate, any of these conceptions of God is the one I say doesn't exist.

As a reminder, "God doesn't exist" means specifically that we have absolutely no good reasons to believe such a being exists and plenty of good reasons not to believe it does. The most important reason is what I call the Problem of a Silent God.

And this is a real problem for anyone who would believe. It cannot be skirted so easily as believers tend to think. The nature of this problem is that they have penned themselves into believing in a God that interacts with and influences the world while leaving absolutely no trace of evidence that it has ever done so. Their God is silent. Their belief is that their God interacts in the world in a way that is identical to failing to interact with the world.

They will, of course, object to this characterization because it is both forthright and honest, not presented with the usual detritus used to obscure the plain truth of it, namely divine hiddenness and free will. That's the thing, though; this characterization is a plain-language description of the divine hiddenness argument, which is hinged upon the doctrine of free will. God, many believers insist, must be entirely hidden from us so that we are free to choose to worship it of our own volitions.

And yet still they will object, pointing to the evidences of their scriptures, supposedly corroborated by archeological and historical findings, and to their personal subjective experiences. "God *did* give evidences! God *does* give evidences if asked for in faith!" They must believe this if they value evidence at all.[9] If God did give evidences, though, divine hiddenness is not only nonsense but capricious, and when God is claimed to grant personal subjective experiences, these are indistinguishable from many other phenomena that are taken as proof by people suffering from confirmation bias.

The Problem of a Silent God, of which I consider the Evidential Problem of Evil a major part,[10] is the rock of atheism. To emphasize the problem, we have had countless human challenges, ranging across the entire spectrum of all that could be called by that name, in which some God could easily have revealed itself and saved the day—or even done so in a hidden manner by arranging things so that these challenges never arose. Only by insane appeals to the necessity of all of our suffering and struggle can apologists hope to defend themselves against this problem, raising what I have called the Problem of Apologetics as a subcategory of the Problem of a Silent God.[11] Put simply, if God weren't silent, we would have no need for apologists (or churches or religions, for that matter).

Indeed, these problems directly reflect what may be the best reason to accept that God is best understood as merely an abstraction by which people try to understand the world. When asked for evidence of anything physical, scientists work very hard to uncover physical evidence of the phenomenon in question. Historians work very hard to validate their arguments about matters of historical fact by examining what physical evidence is available and filling in the gaps with the evidence we have concerning how people tend to act in relevant situations. Theologians, though, when pressed for evidence go to philosophy, a field that deals with abstractions. They do this because they *do not have evidence* and don't need it to argue for an abstraction. No one would begin a philosophical argument of any kind if asked to present evidence that dairy cows exist. She would just go to a dairy.

Because I do not accept as real an abstract God via some axiom that declares its existence, I am able to follow in the footsteps of Richard Dawkins[12] and Victor Stenger[13] and consider the existence of God as a hypothesis about the world. On the basis of the Problem of a Silent God, I am confident in concluding that the plausibility of this hypothesis—the confidence with which we can say we think it is likely to be true that God exists—is either negligibly low or almost surely zero.[14] In either of these cases, almost surely zero or negligibly low plausibility for the existence of God, I repeat that I am quite confident that God doesn't exist.

The corollary is obvious. If God doesn't exist then God doesn't solve our problems for us. Thus, only humans can solve the problems of the world.

But There Are Proofs!

Surely the above discussion about a silent God will not quell the objections of believers who insist that God's existence is a philosophical necessity. There are a number of arguments to the necessity of the existence of God and then the necessity of all of the desired properties that the believer wishes to bestow upon that God, and no apologist ever seems satisfied until they have all been gone over in triplicate. These famous arguments, contrary to the hopes of their defenders, help make my case.

I frequently find the language in these arguments to be quite telling to the point that most of the arguments[15] tend to define God in the way that they seek to prove. Take Aquinas's famous *Quinque Viae* (Five Ways) arguments. Each ends with effectively the same phrasing: *et hoc dicimus Deum*, "and this we call God."[16] In all five arguments, then, Aquinas points at some abstract idea meant to settle some debate beyond the reaches of the knowledge of his day—a Prime Mover, a First Cause, a Final Cause, and so on—and then refers to a proposed resolution to that debate as what "all men call God."[17]

These suggestions, all branded by the name "God," are handled by exactly the same dilemma that I mentioned just previously: they are either testable or they are not, in which case they face a second dilemma of being either abstractions or impossible to claim as knowledge. Aquinas's arguments, sophisticated as they may seem, do not solve the riddle for him. That is, he can make the argument, but he cannot know he is right about what he said, although, if I may be so bold, "abstraction" seems to be by far the most compelling possibility. I say this with the caveat that physics has shown since Aquinas's time that, at the least, the Prime Mover and First Cause arguments are obsolete.[18]

There are other arguments of this kind as well, some sillier than others, but perhaps the most compelling and famous one at present is the Kalām Cosmological Argument. It has become so well recognized because it has been so thoroughly championed by evangelical Christian apologist William Lane Craig, who has given a book-length defense of it.[19] It is outside of my purpose to provide yet another refutation of the Kalām argument,[20] and so I will not do so here. Instead, I would simply like to point out that what the argument would manage to do, even if it were sound, would be to define God as the uncaused First Cause—an abstraction designed to explain the existence of the universe.

To go one step further, I point out additionally that the Kalām God is at most the Deist's God, and really it is less. A First Cause need not imply many of the aspects of the Deist's God, as there is no clear point of necessity for this Cause to possess agency, intelligence, or benevolence; nor is it clear that such a Cause has or had any point in mind even if equipped with those attributes. Even granting a purpose in mind, the Kalām argument still leaves a broad gap to what it argues for (Islam, originally, and now Christianity). To see what I mean, one need only imagine a somewhat imperfect Creator who was ordering the universe bit by bit as it saw fit, this cause leading to that, and so on, who then bumbled and accidentally started the whole thing in motion before everything was properly arranged.[21]

The Kalām argument, for all its fame, produces a deity that is either abstract or unknowable, and so, like so many other philosophical arguments for the existence of God, helps make my point. God doesn't exist, almost surely, and thus only humans can solve human challenges.

What about Morals?

Of all of the rebuttals remaining about God's necessary existence, an argument to morality is most deserving of a brief mention. This is not just because it accords generally with my point but because it also ties directly into solving the challenges we face. Of course, in the first place, as I've previously argued, the existence of many of these challenges, in light of the Problem of a Silent God, casts serious doubts upon a moral argument for God's existence.

The moral argument to which I am referring is basically that God is the (only possible) grounding for objective moral values, and since we clearly have moral values in some meaningful sense, God must therefore exist. Take a moment, though, to understand what is being said here: there is some grounding for objective moral values, and this thing is what many believers call "God." Yet again, we see an appeal to an abstraction as a means to define God, and so we have good reasons to suspect that the God being defined this way is itself an abstraction.

To keep from getting repetitive about this matter, I want to shift the attention now to a few points about morals, as they bear significantly upon many, if not all, of the human challenges that we face. There are significant problems with the idea of religious claims to objective moral values—the far more interesting question of scientifically objective moral values being raised by neuroscientist Sam Harris in *The Moral Landscape*.[22] One of the more serious issues is that religious ethics, whatever they claim in objectivity and universality, significantly lack in credibility, at least when viewed from outside the relevant sect. Most Christians do not accept Islamic moral values except when they coincide with Christian ones, which is certainly not always. In fact, many Christians do not even accept the moral codes of *other Christians*, say on divorce, abortion, and homosexuality, to name a few.

The reason for this is not mysterious: God doesn't exist. When religious people wish to ground their moral values in a fiction, no one who sees that fiction for what it is will accept the asserted authority of those moral values. The values themselves will only be agreed upon when they coincide with those of the person hearing about them, something that appears to have been well understood at least back to Plato early in the fourth century BCE, as indicated by his famous Euthyphro dilemma.[23] This reason, though, leads to problems that are likely to be present so long as religions exist.

Fundamentalist believers are not often taken to be sophisticated believers—a comment that is simultaneously largely uncontroversial and indicative that more liberal forms of belief are effectively synonymous with sophisticated forms of belief.[24] Thus, it is not surprising to find fundamentalists holding to narrow moral views that, far from being universal, seem to apply only to a group of like-minded people who reinforce ingroup and outgroup statuses. Indeed, the research appears to bear this out, showing less universality in prosocial behaviors associated with religious fundamentalism and being primed with traditional religious concepts.[25]

Narrow values and prosocial behaviors constitute a major challenge in our currently globalizing world. It may seem very tempting to say that we should simply live and let believe, but how are we to achieve this? We cannot live and let believe if the beliefs cannot agree, and worse if they are driven apart by reminders that they are religious ethics. So problematic are the disagreements, in fact, that this use of the word "live" sometimes has to be interpreted literally. The moral duties perceived in the religious context are always sect-specific, are often based on uninformed speculations about the world, and exhibit a shocking lack of agreement with one another.

If we are to achieve a goal of a sufficiently universal set of ethics, we will have to admit that morality cannot really be religious. It will not do to call "religious" the various sound ethical precepts that happen to appear in the teachings of a religion. The ethics cannot be taken to be the unique province of any sect. The problem is plain: no sect will fully accept another's ethics. In our search for a solution to this challenge, we cannot ignore the operative reason for it, that religions are not believed from the outside (from where they often are not remotely believable). This insight is clearly articulated in what John W. Loftus has called "the Outsider Test for Faith," a silver-bullet argument against the idea that religions can be evaluated fairly from within (which happens to be the only place where they can be believed).[26]

As religion seems to breed fundamentalism in individuals who seem prone to it,[27] rival interpretations will always evolve. This conclusion is reinforced by the fact that theologies, placing their dogmas ahead of observable evidence, lack the sort of rigorous methodology needed to converge in opinion. We are increasingly able to see this clearly now, and so we see why religious ethics are not a good solution to our problems.

We must be fair, though. The fact remains that the religions are human endeavors that seek to meet the challenges of the world, often ethical ones, and they contain some worthy insights. We need not abandon what wisdom lies there as we turn toward secularism, and no one needs to adhere to any absolutes to be informed by ideas claimed by religious traditions. Literature is a beautiful thing for meeting the human mind in profound ways, and the scriptures are all ancient literature. Further, we should welcome all who embraces the secularist cause, regardless of sect or creed, recognizing there is wisdom in their experiences. We still seek to solve our problems, so everyone who commits to effective reasonable paths to those goals is on our team.

We must not deceive ourselves, however, into believing that committing ourselves to any religious sect or creed can be the path to our solutions. Religions are based upon a faulty epistemology called faith that we must leave behind. Humanity, when religious, fractures into sects, so only by walking away from religion to a superior ethical standard—a secular standard—can we have real hope. Where we agree with one another, our ethics is based upon the clear, reasonable, open thinking of secularism, and where we disagree, the problem is religious sect-specific faith itself.

Can the Christianities Solve the Problems of the World?

The plain answer to this question, because God doesn't exist and therefore Christianity is false, has to be *almost surely not*. Still, and for these same reasons, throughout its entire history, Christianity has been a monumental effort for people to meet their challenges. But by turning our consideration to this point, we will be able to see more clearly how unlikely it is that Christianity can be the solution to our problems.

Ultimately, only a few honest questions about the phenomenon of Christianity need to be considered to illustrate that for much of the last twenty centuries it has been one of the world's most significant human efforts to meet the challenges we face. Why, for example, are there so many different sects and denominations within Christianity? Why, in fact, are there any competing and contradictory religious attempts, such as Islam, to solve these same problems?

And how can this diversity be read as purely human attempts at solutions to our various psychological, social, and political problems?

This diversity, of course, suggests at least two things about whether or not religions, or more specifically the Christianities, can solve our problems. First, Christian attempts thus far appear to have been unsuccessful, and second, they are unlikely ever to succeed. At bottom, the reason is because God doesn't exist, and thus, in addition to lacking divine solutions to our problems, we also see that religious attempts are fraught with irreconcilable disagreement that causes many of the worst problems we hope to solve!

The reasons revealed by contemplating these questions are, of course, complex and myriad, so any attempt to provide a single, universal answer will surely be refuted. There is one answer, though, that stands out as being highly plausible: human beings, without divine help, have been attempting to address developing cultural issues and the best explanations for the world in which we live. Certainly, this process has been influenced by historical events, superstitious beliefs, good and bad guesses about the world, a search for universal meaning, and evolving moral frameworks, but at the bottom of it all, human beings are trying to meet these challenges as well as we can.

Through that effort, our understanding of the world changes, and the people who live and work in it change. Religions like Christianity often attempt to set up universal (this being the meaning of the word Catholic, in fact), eternal standards that then clash with these changes, and differences in interpretation lead sects to splinter. This situation can account for much of the Christian diversity in the world.

Take, as one notable example, the birth of the Church of England at the demand of King Henry VIII. It is commonly suggested that Henry broke off from the Catholic Church largely over the matter of divorce. Regardless of whether or not this was Henry's main motivation, divorce is a topic that still leads modern Christian churches to split into new ones five hundred years later.[28] Divorce, though, is but one of many controversial topics with sociocultural significance, and in modern Christianity we see churches and denominations splitting over divergent views on any number of issues.

The reason churches and then denominations split is that each church, sect, and denomination is doing what its leadership thinks is best for meeting the largely psychosocial challenges faced by its members. These challenges are human challenges, and these divergent belief structures are human attempts to solve them. The issue is that the method is focused on beliefs, often relating to moral issues, that cannot be substantiated by salient evidence. Religious leaders proceed by edict, and people seem to gather around edicts they like.

To elaborate, religious attempts at solutions to our challenges were, for a time, decent efforts, but they have always been doomed to fail. Religion proceeds by dogmatically asserting what I have termed "supertruths," propositions held as true regardless of their actual warrant. Religious supertruths are often arrived at by "revelation," which is indistinguishable from someone imagining them to be true. Because of its love affair with absolute truth, religion attempts to maintain acceptance of its supertruths through authority and tradition, and so it does not make itself open to disconfirming evidence. Of course, setting oneself up to fall on the wrong side of evidence is hardly the fingerprint of divine origins.

Here, then, is where a sharp line is drawn between religion and secularism, especially when the latter is reinforced by extended humanist values and scientific inquiry. Secularism does not appeal to religious supertruths to meet our challenges. Instead, it proceeds in ways that make considering the real-world consequences of our attempted solutions a very large part of the effort. Religion may well have had its time and place as a centerpiece of human solutions for human societies, but that time is over, and to be frank, it has been for centuries.

One Human Challenge: The Dawning of a Secular Age

By virtue of looking broadly, from above the various sects and creeds of the world, we can see that secular values are the next stage in approaching humanity's challenges. Those of us who have eliminated personal religion from our lives already see this clearly, as have many who still are religious. For example, there are forward-looking sects within Christianity, the liberal end of the Episcopal Church being one, that embrace most secular values quite deeply. We should note, though, that those sects tending in the right direction hold values progressively informed by the advancement of human societies, which they then interpret through the framework of religion. That is to say that religions progress by adopting secular values, even if they are then reinterpreted as religious ones. Getting outside the sect provides the necessary lens to see this laudable feat.

Secularists know, for instance, that the separation of church and state was a major human advance—because we see from outside and measure the results with a less biased metric. We also see that this is why science must proceed upon an assumption of methodological naturalism, and why it should be allowed to do so without interference from desperate seekers of something beyond nature. We know science works. We prove it millions of times a day by boarding aircraft, allowing surgeons to cut into our bodies, and flipping light switches, to name a few. We know secularism works, too.

Faith-based approaches, as evidenced by sects like the Westboro Baptist Church and Jihadist Islam, do not work because they fail to adopt secularism at their cores. Where religion fails to secularize it carries the potential for unnecessary harm. It is, of course, irrelevant that there are other causes of harm; those do not exonerate faith-based thinking and religion *qua* religion from the harms for which it is responsible. The call, then, must be for secularization and a marginalization of faith.

Time presses because, in fact, we live at a precarious time in human history. The world is profoundly different than it was even a century ago and even more so than it was when the scriptures of the world's biggest religions were written. We now, for the first time in human history, genuinely possess the power to destroy ourselves, either intentionally or accidentally. It is for this reason that religion, particularly evangelical Christianity's newly rekindled fascination with reactionary science denialism, may be flirting with suicide for humanity.

Faith Flirts with Suicide

To elaborate briefly, we now live in a very technology-dependent world. Our global citizenry numbers more than seven billion people and maintains exponential growth. Our environment is heating up, our oceans are acidifying while they rise, and our arable land is becoming desert—all at an alarming rate. We have cause for enormous concern because these facts about our growing population and causes for environmental concern are not mutually compat-ible. People need to eat; indeed they will kill to do so if necessary; and given the current state of affairs, we very well may *need* technology—the fruit of science—to survive. Evangelical Christians' attempts to defend their faith at all costs include undermining public trust in science, thus risking suicide for humanity.

Of course, the primary science that many evangelical Christians want to deny is biological evolution, but the attack gets levied against trust in science more generally. From the philosophical Christians, the denial is less crude than direct attacks on established science. Instead, it is insidious and subtle, attacking the foundations of evidence-based reasoning at its core, always ready to interject God as if this constitutes a legitimate alternative explanation.

Consider apologist William Lane Craig, who has said, "Most of our beliefs cannot be evidentially justified. . . . Many of the things we know are not based on evidence, so why must belief in God be so based?"[29] This view has been echoed by evangelical Christian apologist Randal Rauser, who writes, "Our sensory experience leads us very naturally to believe in the external world. So it is for the Christian's experience of God. . . . My challenge to you is to explain why belief in the external world is properly basic but belief in God cannot be."[30] Subtle these may be, clothed all in careful philosophical termi-nology and tricky arguments, but they are corrosive to whatever trust in science their faith-dependent readership might have. These statements promote "other ways of knowing" that eat away at the hard-earned, well-deserved epistemic respect commanded by the sciences.

Public trust in science is needed now more than ever, and the issue has less to do with our scientific ability than with politics. We need to implement strate-gies on an intelligent, integrated, global scale with surprising rapidity to prevent some serious outcomes that may, indeed, be disastrous. Global climate change, for example, is estimated to be doing more than $1.2 trillion in damages annu-ally,[31] and global food shortages are a growing source of concern. To imple-ment the necessary changes successfully requires enough public trust in science to enable, allow, and fund them. A religious ethic that places maintaining and spreading faith-based beliefs above public trust in science is unlikely to be com-patible with meeting this imminent human challenge.[32]

The issue is obvious. We face some immense technological challenges in our world, and the only hope we have to solve them is to obtain the best information we can and find an effective means of implementing solutions on the required scale. Science is simply the best way we have to come to know things about the world, and it must be compared against faith because faith is among its biggest obstacles at present. We need effective methods to gather knowledge, we need enough trust in those methods to implement that knowledge, and pretending to know what we don't know[33] is just not going to work out for us.

Faith cannot solve many of our most important problems, and though it may seem to solve some smaller ones, like how to find a sense of security in an uncertain world, it creates big ones as well. Actually, religion is practically, and perhaps necessarily, a major hindrance to the human endeavor. As noted author and neuroscientist Sam Harris has pointed out, "We have a choice. We have two options as human beings. We have a choice between conversation and war. That's it. Conversation and violence. And faith is a conversation stopper."[34]

As Harris has similarly remarked, religious faith by its nature is intrinsically divisive, and so it presents a major obstacle to achieving a stable, generally peaceful global society.[35] The answer to this problem, of course, is plainly available in secularism, which presents no such inherent difficulty to us. It could be argued, in fact, that the first secular value is that other cultures and other ways of thinking have a right to exist, and that no group's bald claim on the truth is correct merely because it says it is. This does not commit us to accepting all cultural practices and values on their faces, but it does level the field upon which they are appraised.

Further, our development of evidential evaluation of falsifiable hypotheses—in brief, science—provides us with an effective tool to inform our discussions properly and to remove that which is absurd. The conversation Harris sagely urges can lead us to a true global community, but only once we can agree upon the standards. Secularism, extended humanism,[36] and science offer the most viable set of such standards we have come up with so far, and agreeing upon them is perhaps only difficult because of religious belief.

Our biggest challenge, then, at this cusp in human history, is to repudiate certain bad ways of solving our problems. The list of goals is short and clear, but the implementation will take a sustained effort not yet clearly defined. There must be a push for secularism, extended humanism, and public trust in science, and *we* must do it.

Secularism as the Solution and the Future of Religion

How, though, are we to address the problem of religious resistance to our challenge of promoting secularism and the rise of a stable, peaceful global society? We can do it, perhaps best, by promoting secularism, though this takes constant effort, patience, and time.

The beauty of secularism is that it does not require brutal force or absolute authority to maintain it; instead, it is inherently adaptable to our situations. Under secularism, individuals and groups are given respect and secured the right to do as they will to meet their personal needs, so long as their efforts do not significantly infringe upon the opportunities of others. For this reason, once secular ethics are adopted by a culture, it is considered profoundly regressive to turn away from them. Secularism, while it may not be *the* answer to our wide and complex human psychosocial challenges, is a solution that can be global and that can be achieved without having to engage in the kinds of harmful abuses that appear to be endemic to religion.

So, if we can agree that turning to secularism, embracing extended humanist values, and relying upon scientific inquiry for answers to many of our biggest human challenges is the way we need to go, we need to be stirred to action to get there. Some groups in our world already embrace and champion these values, and others do not. This challenge, then, is yet another one we face. We can neither rely upon God to solve it nor entrust the solution to those claiming a god is on their side. Religious faith is, as we have seen repeatedly throughout this volume, extraordinarily and inherently ill-equipped for the task. We can do better now.

No religion has the truth cornered. In fact, no religion even has a valid method for attempting to ascertain the truth, much less any capital-T variant of it. Instead, religions have an ideological commitment to supertruths, many of which are starkly and demonstrably false, and to ancient scriptures filled with them. Those scriptures are more often barbaric, horrible, and confusing than they are illuminating and comforting, and they are functional mills of unacceptable extremism in certain kinds of believers.

On the other hand, every religion claims, at some level, to have the one Truth, frequently exclusively. That alleged Truth is usually claimed to be contained in the scriptures, which then get elevated far above their proper stations as ancient mythological literature. For these reasons, each religion is not only wrong, but dangerously wrong, its sectarian ethics being necessarily contentious because no other religion can accept them. A permanent feature of religious thought is that from the outside it lacks sufficient justification though from the inside it pretends to need none. A better standard, unfettered by doctrinal creeds, is sorely needed. Secularism offers that standard.

The world religions addressed human challenges in a time now gone. To quote noted polemicist and author Christopher Hitchens, in his book *God Is Not Great*, after which this anthology is titled:

> One must state it plainly. Religion comes from the period of human prehistory where nobody—not even the mighty Democritus who concluded that all matter was made from atoms—had the smallest idea what was going on. It comes from the bawling and fearful infancy of our species, and is a babyish attempt to meet our inescapable demand for knowledge (as well as for comfort, reassurance, and other infantile needs). Today, the least educated of my children knows much more about the natural order than any of the founders of religion, and one would like to think—though the connection is not a fully demonstrable one—that this is why they seem so uninterested in sending fellow humans to hell.[37]

In Conclusion, a Call to Action

In short, we can do better now, and we *must* do better now. Religion in all its forms must change or die. To change means to change radically: the world's religions must embrace secularism, repudiate failed ways to claim knowledge, and completely revise themselves as sets of cultural practices and ethical systems only loosely informed by the scriptures that traditionally defined them. That is their challenge. That is what they must become, under whatever pressure we put upon them from the outside. Religious humans must make their religions fully compatible with secular societies that embrace evidence-based thinking—and they must reorganize to put secular ideals, including science and humanist ethics, before any set of supertruths, however comforting. God, as always, isn't going to do it for them. God doesn't exist.

We have reached a point in our history where the challenges confronting us pose enough of a risk to assert that evidence-based policy is a necessity, and so rational, effective modes of approaching the world need to come to the forefront of human societies. To avoid being irrelevant philosophical musings, religious faith always ends up making claims that encroach upon scientific inquiry—and now it does so just to retain enough salience to engage believers—and because it seeks to protect itself against disconfirmation, it has always worked, and will continue to work, to erode public trust in science. This situation can no longer be tolerated. The faithful must fix this problem, and the rest of us need to stop pandering to them until they do, at least in matters of public policy. We cannot give faith-based suggestions to solve major problems any room at the table.

We who accept that God does not exist are ahead of history and on the right side of evidence, and we have to help bend the social, intellectual, and moral arcs of our cultures toward the best possible future. That future, while uncertain, is one in which we have embraced secularism, recognizing that no sect can have a corner on the truth. It is also one that knows that informed, skeptical investigation with a willingness to be found wrong is the most successful method we have found to actually corner the truth. Also, it is a future in which we apply a salient ethical system based upon real-world flourishing and suffering of human beings and all other sentient beings.

We must continue to speak, write, and act for a future in which we do better at meeting our needs than can religion, burdened by its stubbornness and many harms. We must continue to solve our challenges. There are no credible reasons to believe in any God, so never before has it been so widely recognized that only humans can solve the problems we face in this world. We must all recognize this if we are to gain our best future.

LIVING WITHOUT GOD

Russell Blackford

Introduction

For the purposes of this chapter, I will take it as established that atheism is the most reasonable answer to the God question. That is, someone who has thought carefully and honestly about the existence of gods, including the Christian deity, should end up unconvinced (to say the least!) that such beings exist. There is a vast literature on that subject, and elsewhere I've set out some of my own reasons for rejecting Christianity and any form of orthodox theism.[1] On this occasion, my focus is on what happens next once you're inclined against god-belief. I will, that is, be addressing concerns about living without religious guidance.

Can you live a good life without the concept of God or the dictates of (say) holy books, churches, and priests? Yes, you can. But there are emotional barriers to leaving religion behind. You might be unwilling to walk away from your religious beliefs and religious community if the personal cost is too high. Likewise, you might feel that your religion demands your loyalty if you see it as socially beneficial. And in any event, the prospect of a life without religious guidance might appear daunting.

I'll consider a cluster of related questions. Some arise at the personal and some at the social level. At the personal level, you might wonder whether a life without god-belief, and particularly a life without the answers and reassurances offered by your religion, will lack meaning and purpose, turn out to be depressing, or drift into aimlessness. Where, you might be thinking, will you find guidance if you abandon the rich worldview and the moral norms that your current religion offers? Should you look for a nonreligious alternative?

At the social level, the obvious fears relate to what might happen without religious institutions, doctrines, and practices to bind societies together. Even if you feel confident enough that *you* can flourish without religion, what about other individuals or your society in general? Might a society without religion become fragmented, lonely, angst-ridden, exploitative, possibly even violent or otherwise dangerous, and generally an unpleasant place to live? Might it be populated by alienated, callous individuals who live diminished lives and treat each other badly?

There are difficult issues here, and we must each address them as honestly as we can. I will not claim that it's easy to walk away from religious beliefs and communities. I will not claim that religion offers no benefits at all. Above all, I will not offer you a comprehensive belief system or worldview to replace one that you may be abandoning. Instead, I'll invite you to encounter the complications of life with a particular kind of skepticism and to cultivate virtues that can sometimes be difficult: intellectual honesty; tolerance of differences; openness to evidence and argument; and an appreciation of complexity, ambiguity, and doubt. Above all, I'll commend thinking for yourself about what to believe and how to live.

This is, of course, very different from religious ideas of what is involved in living well. What I propose will not always be comfortable or easy. It will make demands, and it may sometimes lose you friends.

But you just might find it liberating.

Religions and Comprehensive Worldviews

Religions usually come complete with ritual observances and standards of conduct prescribed for believers—and often for others as well—but historically they have been far more than systems of ritual and morality. They tend to be comprehensive worldviews. They make sense of the world and the human condition in terms of a supernatural realm and its workings. Religions, including the various kinds of Christianity, posit a supernatural dimension to human life and well-being, and they describe transformative powers that can change us at a deep level to ensure our attainment of supernatural benefits.[2] Often, though not always, these benefits include some kind of afterlife.

There is much to criticize in Bruce Sheiman's book *An Atheist Defends Religion*—something of a one-sided paean of praise to religion's merits.[3] But Sheiman gets it about right when he describes religion in terms of "belief in and efforts to relate to a Transcendent Spiritual Reality,"[4] which he then defines as incorporating three characteristics:

1. It is a spiritual reality that is not subject to the physical laws and temporal limits of the natural world.
2. It is an objective reality that transcends the material world, is the source or creator of that material world, and is usually conceived of as being *more real* than our material reality.
3. It is the preeminent *good* to which we must properly orient our moral behavior if we are to attain ultimate fulfillment.[5]

In the case of Christianity, there is a strong emphasis on spiritual salvation through the sacrificial atonement of Jesus of Nazareth. According to this central Christian doctrine, Jesus was crucified for the sins of humankind but supernaturally rose from the dead shortly afterward. Supposedly, these events have enormous transformative power. The Christian churches promise their adherents access to a spiritual dimension of existence in this world, followed by a heavenly afterlife in the presence of God.

Beyond this, most religions make claims about humanity's origin and place in the larger scheme of the cosmos. Historically, they have often explained the world and its events by describing the activities of gods, spirits, demons, and other supernatural intelligences. These are frequently associated, as Susan Haack mentions, with dangerous natural phenomena such as fire, floods, and disease.[6] From a religious viewpoint, and certainly from an orthodox Christian one, human beings play a role, perhaps even a central one, in a great cosmic drama.

We should recognize that religion has psychological attractions. However, much has happened, particularly in the past four to five hundred years, to cast doubt on all religions. They stand revealed as premature attempts to understand the world. Religious doctrines and narratives have lost credibility as societies have changed and secular knowledge has advanced.

Reputable textual-historical scholarship now makes sense of foundational religious texts in ways that reject traditional understandings of their origins and historical reliability. For its part, science has offered alternative explanations of many events once assigned to supernatural causes.[7] In response, some religious leaders and organizations have attempted to redefine their doctrines in nonliteral terms, interpreting traditional writings such as holy books as metaphors, or merely as culturally important documents that contain a mix of wisdom and ignorance. However, any such process of reinterpretation is likely to run into problems.

Once a religion begins to thin out its truth claims, perhaps saying less and less about the observable world, it becomes more difficult to refute decisively. Nonetheless, the process has a downside. If a religious organization abandons doctrines that many of its adherents consider central, this can cause alienation and even schism. Perhaps some vague spiritual sentiments can survive the ongoing discrediting of religion, but as it thins out, a once rich and detailed religious worldview may lose much of its power to explain the human condition, and hence much of what made it attractive to adherents in the first place. A church or sect that weakens its claims to avoid conflict with secular knowledge may well find itself losing market share to theologically conservative rivals.

Where does this leave us? The explosion in secular knowledge over the last few hundred years has been impressive, dramatic, and unprecedented, and it goes on with no end in sight. Many scientific findings are now so well evidenced that they are very unlikely to be overturned. No matter how much is discovered, however, scientific discoveries tend to raise new, deeper questions. The humanities expand our knowledge of history and culture, but they are notoriously hampered in producing truly robust findings about such questions as the motivations of historical actors and the meanings of cultural products such as literary or artistic works. These questions inspire passionate, erudite, and useful debates, but all too often they cannot be answered decisively.

Between them, the sciences and humanities have done much to advance our knowledge and understanding, but they do not provide us with an ultimate, finished, or comprehensive picture of the world. Rather, they offer an open-ended adventure in inquiry and learning.

We are at a point in history when the authority and prestige accorded to religion have been reduced by social change and several centuries of intellectual progress. At the same time, there remains a tendency for many human beings to develop, seek out, or promote comprehensive worldviews. These are systems of belief and practice that purport to explain much about the human condition in an integrated, rather stable package, while also providing guidance in how to live (including how we should exercise whatever power we might sometimes have over others). If religious worldviews have been discredited, should you embrace one of the other comprehensive worldviews currently on offer?

First, note that nothing about atheism prevents anybody adopting some kind of comprehensive but nontheistic explanation of the world and the human condition. In itself, atheism is merely a lack of god-belief. It rules out literal belief in a monotheistic or polytheistic religion, but it can be consistent with many other ideas, beliefs, and commitments. Lack of belief in any God or gods does not even rule out all beliefs in entities or forces that would commonly be regarded as supernatural. A view of the world based around magic or astral influences, for example, might count as a religion while technically being atheistic. Such a worldview might include rituals, standards of conduct, and promises of spiritual transformation, thus resembling theistic religions in all important respects.

Thus, I cannot insist that living without God (or gods) necessarily entails the rejection of all systems of religious or supernatural belief. Nonetheless, most thoughtful atheists consider all such systems to be discredited. A more serious option for atheists might involve embracing some kind of comprehensive secular worldview, most likely a political ideology. The intellectual merits of these can vary, and not all stand as straightforwardly discredited. Any thoroughgoing attempt to criticize some version of Marxist thought, for example, will need to engage with it across a wide range of fields of secular learning, including history, economics, and many others. Extensive study might persuade you of the truth of one or another ideological system, and the system might be sufficiently detailed to provide guidance in how to live your life. Nonetheless, let me offer a note of caution.

To date, political ideologies have a poor track record in producing convincing justifications. In the extreme, as with Stalinism and Pol Pot's fanatical brand of agrarian socialism, these ideologies are not only utopian—seeking a more perfect society—but downright apocalyptic. Indeed, many such ideologies have clearly been influenced by religion: the strongly directional theory of history favored by Marxism in its various guises owes much to Christian apocalypticism.

It should also be noted that Nazism was a special case. Though Nazi leaders were suspicious of the Christian churches as rival centers of power, there were close connections between Nazism and Christians beliefs, both orthodox and otherwise. Nazi Germany was never an atheist state, and the roots of the Holocaust owed much to traditional Christian prejudices. Throughout the history of the Christian churches, theological anti-Judaism nourished hostile and even violent forms of anti-Semitism. All this helped form an environment in Europe where the Holocaust was thinkable. Ian S. Markham, an Anglican theologian, acknowledges this in a book that otherwise defends Christianity:

> The history of Christian anti-Jewishness is deep and widespread. Although Hitler was hardly an orthodox Christian, the tragedy of the Holocaust was assisted by the anti-Semitic environment the Church had created.[8]

During the second half of the nineteenth century and the early decades of the twentieth, prior to Hitler's rise to power, there were many claims that Jesus himself was not Jewish and that Judaism posed a violent threat to Christianity.[9] In particular, Houston Stewart Chamberlain's *Foundations of the Nineteenth Century* (1899) and Gustav Frenssen's novel *Hilligenlei* (1905) popularized ideas of a non-Jewish—in fact, German in the case of Frenssen's novel—Jesus. Susannah Heschel observes, "Between the success of Chamberlain's tract and Frenssen's novel, it is unlikely that many literate Germans, on the eve of World War I would have been unaware of the claim that Jesus was not a Jew."[10] These unorthodox ideas played a large role in Nazi attitudes, but the Nazis generally repudiated outright atheism. With the possible exception of Martin Bormann, the leading Nazis embraced variations of theistic belief. Even avowed paganists among the Nazis, such as Alfred Rosenberg, did not support an atheistic worldview.

The idea that Nazism was related in any way to religious thought, and particularly to Christianity, is unthinkable to contemporary religious apologists and many opinion leaders. The example of Bormann suggests that Nazism did not strictly require theistic belief, but many Nazi leaders regarded themselves as Christians and saw Christian teachings as relevant to their political ideology and goals.[11]

Superficially nonreligious worldviews are frequently influenced by religious ways of thinking; apocalyptic political ideologies, in particular, display some of the worst features of monotheist religions. They offer participation in large-scale historical struggles that might seem, for the practical purposes of limited beings like us, almost as grand and inspiring as the cosmic drama described by Christianity. Political ideology can limit inquiry, encourage tribalism and authoritarianism, and even inspire atrocities. In the past, ideologues have attempted to force social and economic transformations at an extraordinary pace, and on an immense scale, with no toleration for dissent. In the upshot, we should approach all comprehensive worldviews with caution, particularly when they display authoritarian and apocalyptic elements.

Indeed, there is a potential problem for any cultural movement, including the beginnings of an identifiable atheist movement that has coalesced in the early decades of the twenty-first century. The atheist movement has helped nonbelievers to organize in opposition to religious excesses and to challenge religion's social and political power. Those are goals that I wholeheartedly support. But there is the possibility for *any* movement to harden into a new ideology, enforcing its own orthodoxy with a "correct" line on a wide range of questions. Self-scrutiny is important, and we all need to be aware of our own possible tendencies to authoritarian thinking.

Living without a Comprehensive Worldview

To sum up at this point, living without God does not rule out embracing some kind of nontheistic comprehensive worldview. Atheism is inconsistent with any theistic system of beliefs, but not with nontheistic systems involving supernatural phenomena or with naturalistic worldviews that may take the form of political ideologies. Nonetheless, all comprehensive worldviews should be seen as discredited or, at best, poorly supported by evidence, and they frequently tend toward dogmatism, tribalism, and authoritarianism. Often they show apocalyptic tendencies that encourage fanaticism and cruelty.

How, then, should we live our lives? It is worth emphasizing that our most robust knowledge from the sciences and humanities leaves us with an incomplete picture of the natural world and of human history and culture. We have enough in the way of well-established findings to reject many traditional belief systems and extraordinary claims, but much still remains to be discovered. This suggests that we ought to live with a certain amount of open-mindedness and a reluctance to embrace truth claims that are not supported by strong evidence.

This might itself be classified as a worldview, since it involves a general understanding of the world in which we find ourselves. For example, we can reasonably predict that no spooky entities or forces will be discovered by the sciences and humanities in their continuing inquiries. Causal mechanisms awaiting discovery by science are unlikely to include, for example, powerful disembodied intelligences such as demons. Likewise, the people who acted in history, shaping societies and cultures, are unlikely to have exercised magical powers or to have received exhortations from gods and angels. In a general sense, then, I propose that we live our lives on the assumption that philosophical naturalism is true: that is, on the assumption that there are no supernatural entities, forces, and so on. For practical purposes, we can discount the possibility that these exist.

But philosophical naturalism as I've briefly described it is not an *apocalyptic* worldview: it offers an ongoing process of naturalistic inquiry rather than a prescription for large-scale and sudden change. Nor is it a *comprehensive* worldview in the sense that I have been discussing. It offers very little in the way of an orthodoxy or in specific advice about how to live our lives. It allows our detailed knowledge of the world and ourselves to be filled out through the processes of scholarship and science, and for this knowledge to accumulate and change over time. It is, moreover, consistent with a kind of skepticism.

There is much that we understand with confidence from everyday experience and from the formal inquiries of scholars and scientists, so I am not advocating skepticism of any radical kind. All the same, one general truth that we should all accept is that in many situations we cannot be justifiably confident about the answers to questions that confront us. This can apply in areas of science where the evidence is incomplete, and it is commonplace in the humanities, where the available facts frequently leave us struggling to answer the most interesting questions. For example, no matter how many documents we discover and translate, no matter how many artifacts and inscriptions we unearth, the full motivations of a political leader from an ancient civilization may remain open to varying interpretations. In many cases, there are practical limits to our ability to obtain truly decisive evidence.

The point applies to much in our own lives and our understanding of contemporary events. If an issue is complex, we can find ourselves seeming to get further from the truth the more earnestly we inquire. We may find that settling the truth of some difficult issue requires first settling the truth of *other* nontrivial issues so that we can know what to rely upon as evidence. Our interpretations of other people's intentions and motives can draw on tacit assumptions that are traceable to our own life histories and may not be correct. We may, for example, be making broad and debatable assumptions about human motivations in general. Again, different people who are caught up in a fast-moving sequence of events often have honestly held yet quite conflicting impressions of what happened around them. This is why eyewitness testimony is notoriously unreliable.

Accordingly, I don't merely suggest skepticism about supernatural claims and comprehensive ideologies. I go further and recommend a moderately skeptical attitude to much of what we read or hear. In some situations, admittedly, we may have no satisfactory option but to act on our largely intuitive assessments of the probabilities. Otherwise, we might be paralyzed when making important life choices. In many other situations, though, there is no pressing reason to do anything but suspend judgment until such time as more compelling evidence becomes available. Even where it is necessary to reach a conclusion one way or another, often we should hold to it with a degree of tentativeness, remaining open to revision of our beliefs if new evidence or more compelling arguments become available. We should, I suggest, adopt a mindset that is open to an element of ambiguity and incompleteness in our understanding of the world around us.

One potential problem with this is that it might lead to quietism: an acceptance of things as they are and an unwillingness to press for change. Surely, you might think, there are some situations where there is an urgent need for personal action or political mobilization. I agree that such situations exist, and sometimes dramatic social evils need to be fought even if there is some uncertainty—for example, about pinning down *exactly* what is wrong with them. Think of such varied injustices as chattel slavery, the Holocaust, the South African system of apartheid, the social and political subordination of women in most known societies, laws forbidding homosexual conduct, and many others in history and current practice.

Where there is much at stake, we may, indeed, need to act forcefully and immediately rather than worry about the finer points. But note, once again, that I have argued for only a moderate kind of skepticism, an open-minded attitude rather than a theory of radical philosophical doubt. In the circumstances of, say, the apartheid system, there was more than adequate reason to be confident that the policy was an evil one. It clearly merited vocal and militant opposition. On the other hand, intellectual honesty and a justified distrust of ideologies will often suggest caution or restraint. On some occasions, perhaps many, they should incline you to skepticism about the latest moral panic or storm of outrage.

Meaning and Purpose

Some will object that a life without religion is one without meaning, purpose, or moral guidance. These complaints are somewhat obscure, but they are made so frequently that they evidently have intuitive appeal for many people. In this section, I'll consider the issue of meaning and purpose.[12] In the next, I'll turn to the supposed problem of moral guidance.

If we look with a skeptical eye at the complaint about a lack of "meaning," it is apparent that this word must be used in some metaphorical sense. Human life, viewed in the abstract, is not the sort of thing that we'd expect to have a literal meaning, and neither is the life of a particular person. They are not linguistic signs, like words, or meaningful combinations of signs, like sentences. They are not like works of art, which might convey messages of some kind. There is no reason to think that a human life exists to communicate any linguistic or artistic message, and there isn't any reason why we should want it to. Likewise, there is no reason to imagine that human life in the abstract, or any particular human life, is an artifact devised for a purpose, much as knives, hammers, motor vehicles, and buildings are designed and constructed to perform certain functions.

It's true, let us suppose, that a being as powerful as God is imagined to be could shape our lives so that they literally communicate meanings. Again, such a powerful being could have created us to serve some prior purpose of his own. But it is not at all clear why either of these should be something we'd *want*. Imagine how you'd feel if you really had been created for some specific purpose, as happens in Aldous Huxley's dystopian novel *Brave New World*. If anything, this sounds rather repugnant. Surely we'd rather *not* discover that we were made to serve a purpose established by somebody else.[13]

Complaints about a lack of meaning or purpose in life can make sense if interpreted as a way of referring to lives that are, for example, repetitive, boring, joyless, alienating, or lacking in commitments, values, and a sense of connection with others. However, there are endless ways to have commitments, values, and connections, and to experience joy, without relying on the existence of supernatural beings or guidance from religious authorities such as holy books and priests. We often speak, without invoking any grandiose metaphysical ideas, about people finding "meaning" and "purpose" in their lives. Some people find meaning and purpose in a life of concern focused on those within a rather limited circle of love.[14] Others may be absorbed in causes, hobbies, or careers. There is no clear limit to the sources of meaning and purpose in this everyday sense, and we have no reason to believe that it has much to do with theistic belief or religion generally.

Moral Guidance

Granting that we can find meaning and purpose in our lives without God or religion, where can we find moral guidance? Consider this claim by Dinesh D'Souza, which puts in stark language what is argued by many theologians and religious apologists:

> If there are moral laws that operate beyond the realm of natural laws, where do these laws come from? Moral laws presume a moral lawgiver. In other words, God is the ultimate standard of good. He is responsible for the distinction between good and evil.[15]

Once expressed so plainly, this conception of morality is hopeless. If we think about the question honestly, without making any controversial theological assumptions, there is simply no good reason to believe in anything as bizarre as "laws that operate beyond the realm of natural laws." D'Souza's views notwithstanding, we can discuss all the relevant issues in entirely naturalistic terms with no reference to an extraordinary being such as God.

Consider the phenomena of law and morality as we actually encounter them. Some social constraints on human behavior are recognized and enforced by political institutions such as courts, while others are left to a mixture of public opinion, admonitions from parents and other interested parties, and personal conscience. The constraints that are enforced by political institutions are those we recognize as "legal" rather than "moral." In modern times, the most important laws are usually enacted by formal lawgiving bodies of some kind, often a parliament consisting of one or more legislative chambers such as the two houses of Congress that make up one branch of the US federal government. Less important laws can take the form of subordinate legislation: rules and regulations made by an office-bearer or agency that has been delegated the necessary power by the legislative chambers. Historically, many laws were developed incrementally by the courts, which have often been prepared to adopt and refine a community's commonsense ideas of justice and to recognize useful practices and customs.

Whatever the formal sources of law, the status of a legal rule or principle will depend on its recognition within a system of institutions, particularly by bodies (such as the courts) with the power to decide what is law and what is not. These bodies will tend to apply more fundamental norms that are recognized in the political system (such as a country's written or unwritten constitution). The political system as a whole, including its fundamental norms, must, in turn, rely for legitimacy on its general acceptance by the citizens. That is likely to depend on whether the laws being recognized and enforced by the established political institutions are actually serving social needs. To some extent, this is a matter of judgment that we all must make. If God were a lawgiver, and if we applied D'Souza's analogy rigorously, we would still need to make decisions as to whether God's decrees served a useful social purpose or were merely arbitrary, perhaps even harmful, restrictions and demands.

To highlight this point, what if God decreed that we should murder, rape, torture, steal, and generally cause each other suffering? We would have every reason to regard him as a monstrous being, repudiate the legitimacy of his laws, and rebel as far possible. Given the limitless power usually ascribed to God, rebellion might be futile; nonetheless, the point is made. We regard murder, rape, and other core crimes as unacceptable because of the suffering and other harm they cause, not because they are decreed to be bad by an infinitely powerful being who could, just as arbitrarily, have declared them to be good and commanded us to engage in them.

Furthermore, there is a problem with comparing moral standards to the standards imposed by law. Indeed, it makes just as much sense to explore the *contrasts* between the two.

As we've seen, formal laws are standards of conduct that are recognized by the courts and related political institutions. Often they are a society's most important standards of conduct, such as those included in the core criminal law, but in modern times they also include many detailed regulations aimed at safety, predictability, and social coordination. Many of the less important laws establish standards that are somewhat arbitrary, but they operate in areas of our increasingly complex social life where *some* authoritative standard is needed for social coordination purposes (such as whether to drive on the right or left side of the road).

The core criminal law is strongly reinforced by moral sentiment. Laws against murder and theft, for example, connect closely with such values as nonviolence and honesty, values that, in turn, are closely related to fears of direct harms to our interests. Any society at all will need laws such as these, even if there is variation in the precise form that they take in different societies. However, the realm of morality—or better, ethics—extends far beyond this. It involves many relatively informal standards for how people should conduct themselves and what sort of character they should display. These standards are not enforced through political institutions, such as the courts, though a less formal kind of "enforcement" often takes place. It can include praise for approved behavior, expressions of hostility toward bad behavior, and even such actions as shaming and ostracism for very bad behavior or persistent evidence of bad character.

Ethical standards are often more vague and more flexible than the formal laws, though the latter also need some flexibility; often, for example, the law requires us to act "reasonably" in certain respects, leaving it to judges or juries to determine just what that means in a particular case. Once again, the demands and restrictions of a society's ethical standards are justified, if at all, by the extent to which they serve various needs. If they fail to do so, but the society insists on them for their own sake, they are arbitrary. We then have good grounds to criticize these standards, to resent social attempts at their enforcement, and perhaps to argue for new ones to take their place. Nothing in this picture requires anything like a central lawgiver, much less a supernatural one.

In passing, I should explain that I prefer to use the term "ethics" rather than "morals," "morality," "moral goodness," or similar expressions, partly for the reason that talk of "morality" and so forth does seem to suggest to many people (D'Souza among them) the false idea of a transcendent "moral law." By contrast, "ethics" has the advantage of suggesting an ancient tradition of thought based upon reason. Within the schools of classical Greek philosophy, ethical questions related to rational consideration of how we should, as individuals, live our lives. The main emphasis was on which dispositions of character would best help us to flourish.

More broadly, ethical questions relate to what sorts of decisions you should make, and hence what sorts of acts you should choose to perform, what sort of character you should aspire to, try to cultivate in yourself, and seek to inculcate in children, what laws you should advocate or oppose (and why), and which social institutions you should support. All of these questions can be approached from a purely naturalistic and rational viewpoint.

Of course, the history of philosophy is full of nontheistic systems of ethics, and one embarrassment for secular ethical philosophy is that no single theory has convinced all comers. Religious apologists can trade on their claim to offer clear-cut moral guidance, whereas secular ethical philosophy involves a continuing process of reasoning and debate. But seen from another point of view, that is a *strength* of the secular ethical tradition: it allows for debate about the genuine difficulties in sorting out which standards best suit our individual and social needs.

Furthermore, it is not as if we have no reliable guidance from the secular tradition. For example, it has been well known since ancient times that there is a paradox in focusing exclusively on our own happiness and self-interest. An individual who calculates in this way is likely to miss out on many valuable experiences and relationships and to end up with an unfulfilling, unpleasant experience of life. At the same time, it may be in an individual's interest to appear trustworthy, kind, and generous if she hopes to be well treated by others in certain ways, and the best way to gain such a reputation is to *be* those things, rather than having to calculate incessantly to maintain a façade.[16] You are much more likely to lead a varied, exciting, and flourishing life if you are concerned about the happiness of other people than if you are focused on getting the better of them. Among a group of people who care about each other's happiness and success, everyone gains.[17]

This suggests that cultivating certain virtuous dispositions of character is a rational thing for the individual while also being socially valuable. There is something of a convergence between our own interests and those of our society—all the more so if the society does not attempt to impose arbitrary restrictions. Not surprisingly, we can observe widespread agreement across human societies that it is better for everyone if we cultivate, teach, and promote such dispositions of character as compassion, honesty (including intellectual honesty), kindness, generosity, courage, and reasonableness (in the sense of being willing to make compromises and to settle disputes as peacefully and amicably as we can).

Atheists have every reason to treat others well, abide by mutually beneficial standards, and cultivate valuable dispositions of character. As I've suggested earlier in this chapter, those dispositions of character should include such things as openness to evidence and appreciation of ambiguity. We can support traditional morality when it condemns violence, dishonesty, or ruthless, selfish competition; but at the same time, we should criticize traditional moral edicts that seem arbitrary and cruel. All of this requires thinking for ourselves, not uncritically accepting what we were taught as children.

The natural corollary of this is a liberal position in relation to the law: "liberal" in the sense of opposing authoritarianism and favoring individual liberty. That is, we should not support legal prohibitions of acts unless they are actually harmful in some way. Some activities will need to be regulated for reasons of safety, predictability, and social coordination, although total prohibition will not be justified. Much more would need to be said to flesh out the detail of political liberalism,[18] but the general direction of our political thinking, once we walk away from religion, should be antiauthoritarian.

What Makes Religion So Attractive?

If a religion such as Christianity is not needed for moral or ethical guidance, or to lead a meaningful, purposeful life, what makes it so attractive to so many people?

I have already mentioned the illusion of being part of a cosmic drama. Related to this, we can add the illusion that the universe (or rather, its all-powerful creator and sovereign) loves and cares about us, the illusion of personal immortality, and the illusion that we can understand reality's deepest workings. Christianity offers all of these, and it may be difficult to admit that they are, in fact, mere illusions. The illusion of deep understanding is particularly interesting. Of course, there is a sense in which we can't really understand the idea of an infinitely powerful and knowing, disembodied being, and one historical current of religious teaching emphasizes God's ultimately mysterious nature. Nonetheless, the idea of an infinitely powerful and benevolent father figure at least *seems* straightforward. No special intelligence or technical knowledge is required to obtain a superficial understanding of the idea, and any paradoxes related to God's properties become apparent only after skeptical probing. Thus the illusion of deep, cosmic understanding is available to almost anyone.

Contrast that with the space-time universe actually revealed by science. In many ways this is far more spectacular, wonderful, and mind-boggling than anything imagined in religious mythologies, but the universe as a whole does not care for us and it offers no plausible hints that we can survive the deaths of our physical bodies. Unfortunately, the scientific picture of the universe is far less intuitive than what we are told by religious texts.

One of Bruce Sheiman's more compelling points is that the knowledge produced by science is no longer accessible to most human minds, and indeed some aspects of science, such as how best to interpret quantum theory, may be clear to almost none of us.[19] Richard Dawkins, an outspoken atheist and exemplary scientist—and one of science's greatest popularizers—makes a similar point: "it may be that nobody really understands quantum theory, possibly because natural selection has shaped our brains to survive in a world of large, slow things, where quantum effects are smothered."[20]

Is religion simply *easier* than science? I suspect that no one really understands such prominent Christian doctrines as the Holy Trinity, the sacrificial atonement, and the extraordinary properties attributed to God. All the same, they have satisfied many people over many centuries and apparently offer at least an illusion of comprehensibility.

Something similar applies to religious claims to provide moral or ethical guidance. Though the important questions can be approached from a naturalistic standpoint, religion offers the illusion of something deeper yet simpler. For many people, it may make little difference that religious justifications for moral teachings are ultimately false or even incoherent. What matters to these people, perhaps, is that they are offered teachings that they can accept as a package without too much hard thinking of their own. Furthermore, regular and frequent involvement with a religious organization will expose an adherent to continual admonitions to do good— however that is understood in the religion concerned. Since a religion such as Christianity often emphasizes compassion, its moral teachings contain at least *something* of value, and repeated exposure to them may produce some good outcomes.

For that reason, David G. Myers is incredulous at the suggestion that religion does no good at all:

> If, indeed, there are strong prosocial norms among religious people (many of whom hear almost weekly admonitions to "love your neighbor as yourself," to support "the least of these," and to practice the Golden Rule, to forgive, to embrace gratitude, and so forth), then—given what we know about the influence of values and attitudes on pertinent behaviours—might we not expect *some* effect of internalized values?[21]

If you take a sufficiently pessimistic view of human nature, you might conclude that religion contains much wisdom, even if you think its supernatural claims are not literally true. In that case, the stifling or authoritarian aspects of religion might seem attractive. Consider Alain de Botton, a philosopher and atheist who persistently expresses his sense of human beings as, in effect, miserable, wayward wretches. In his controversial book *Religion for Atheists*, he describes us as creatures who "all incline in astonishingly personal ways to idiocy and spite."[22] Similar statements occur throughout the book, especially its first half, suggesting that its author views himself and the rest of us as inherently inclined to do evil.

Though de Botton denies belief in any supernatural entities or forces, he is sympathetic to what he sees as a traditional "religious perspective on morality" that "suggests that it is in the end a sign of immaturity to object too strenuously to being treated like a child."[23] Later, he claims that we ought to honor Blaise Pascal and other pessimistic Christian thinkers "for doing us the incalculably great favour of publicly and elegantly rehearsing the facts of our sinful and pitiful state."[24]

Thus, de Botton views human beings as rather pathetic, yet dangerous, creatures who require consolation and paternalistic guidance. This negative view of humanity informs many of his proposals to bend art, architecture, culture more generally, and the processes of education toward a program of indoctrination and control. It is not altogether clear how he aims to achieve this, but at least some of it would require concerted action by the state.

For example, de Botton advocates reorganizing museums for the purposes of overt moral instruction and redesigning the curricula of public educational institutions for similar purposes. At many points, he expresses sympathy for the institutions of medieval Christendom, in which all aspects of public and private life were directed, so far as possible, to reinforce the moral teachings of the Catholic Church. Commenting on the Mishnah, the Jewish legal code, he expresses pleasure rather than revulsion or disdain at its minutely detailed prescriptions for personal conduct, not least for adherents' sexual activities.[25]

We should also note de Botton's complaint that modern states interfere with our conduct only at a late stage, after a harmful act has already been committed, "after we have picked up the gun, stolen the money, lied to the children or pushed our spouse out of the window."[26] He would, it appears, prefer a regime where the law deals with small and subtle wrongs such as acts of rudeness and emotional humiliation. There are dangers in this way of thinking, and its authoritarian tendency is, I hope, obvious. Once the state begins to involve itself in conduct that is remote from the infliction of any serious harm, we might justifiably fear an oppressive micromanagement of our lives.

To be fair, some of de Botton's specific suggestions may be attractive—for example, I find some allure in his proposed Temple to Perspective.[27] He describes this structure rather briefly and vaguely, but it would contain paleontological, geological, and astronomical exhibits, chosen and deployed with an aesthetic rather than straightforwardly scientific objective. In that way, it would differ from a conventional science museum. Its architecture and exhibits would be designed to produce awe at the vastness of space and the incomprehensible depth of time. With the right architects, consultants, and designers, perhaps this could be a masterpiece. By all means, let someone raise the funds and build it.

Nonetheless, there is something claustrophobic or worse about de Botton's wish to create institutions, regulations, and thoroughgoing new approaches to social life designed to produce virtuous citizens. That approach has long been favored by religious thinkers, but it is worrying when we see it advocated by an atheist. Governments may well have a legitimate role in conducting educational campaigns to dissuade their citizens from dangerous behavior, but unless you have a grim view of human nature you might shy away from more forceful, thoroughgoing, and pervasive efforts by the state to mold our personalities and control our conduct.

How Beneficial Is Religion?

Clearly enough, there are aspects of religion that many people find psychologically attractive. Some aspects could even be beneficial to them or to others who are affected by their actions. Might the illusions and admonitions of religion achieve enough good to give us pause when we think of criticizing it?

Like de Botton, Bruce Sheiman is a self-described atheist who argues a case for the merits of religion. One part of his argument draws on a body of published research suggesting that religiosity enhances physical and emotional well-being, as well as prosociality (the tendency or propensity to help others or society as a whole).[28] If we accept Sheiman's analysis, we might conclude that religion is a force for good in the world, one that merits our public support.

There is, alas, considerable murkiness here. In 2012, Luke W. Galen reviewed and analyzed the research supporting the thesis that religion promotes prosociality.[29] Galen's paper is lengthy and his conclusions are complex, but the overall implication is that the appearance of religious prosociality is something of an illusion. Actual involvement in religious communities may have a clearer effect than religious *belief*, but not necessarily any more than involvement in communities of other kinds.

Galen identifies significant and recurrent methodological problems in the published studies that would tend to bias them to favor religion. Importantly, many of the studies compare religious people who are active in their churches or other religious organizations with religious people who are not so active.

Clearly that is very different from what would seem like a fairer comparison. This would compare people of varying degrees of religiosity to others who are committed to nonreligious, perhaps noncomprehensive, worldviews, and who might be active in, say, humanist or skeptic organizations, or closely involved with science or the arts.

Galen's study received scholarly responses from David G. Myers and Vassilis Saroglou, both of whom are far more sympathetic to the idea of religiosity as a promoter of prosociality,[30] and Galen, in turn, replied to these.[31] It appears to be accepted on all sides that there are genuine problems with existing studies, and that whatever effects from religion might be discernible through the haze of methodological difficulties are very mixed. In particular, any positive effects on prosocial behavior are minimal, largely confined to an ingroup, unevenly distributed among different kinds of religiosity, and prompted to some extent by the pressures of self-image and reputation rather than by superior altruism.[32]

There are many confounding factors, including the likelihood that people with certain personality types are highly attracted to religion, whereas others are left cold or even repelled by it.[33] If so, the distribution of personalities could affect distributions of such things as emotional welfare and prosociality. Any differences between very religious, less religious, and explicitly nonreligious demographics might have more to do with who finds religion attractive than any transformational powers that religion possesses. At the same time, the personality traits that could plausibly lead to high religiosity are not entirely admirable from a secular viewpoint: highly religious people appear to be more ascetic, more tribal, more authoritarian, and less universalist in their compassion than the general population.

Though the research is inconclusive, it is consistent with a contrasting picture of explicitly irreligious or antireligious people. The available evidence suggest that atheists may be relatively antiauthoritarian, more open to experience, more inclined than the religious to a universal form of altruism, and more disposed to favor addressing problems of poverty and disadvantage through publicly funded programs (as opposed to individual charitable giving). When we organize to achieve goals, they are likely to be different from those of highly religious people, but that does not make them less socially beneficial. There may, in fact, be great social value in such goals as defending secular government, campaigning against pseudoscience in areas such as medical practice, and promoting education in the sciences.

Much of this book has exposed Christianity's crimes and failures. It is worth acknowledging that these do *not* entail that Christianity (or any other religion) has done no good at all for its individual adherents or their societies. Frequent moral admonitions may have some value, depending on what moral standards are being promoted. The illusions of deep understanding, immortality, and participation in a cosmic drama may combine to give many people a sense of satisfaction, focus, and comfort. Involvement in a community of worshippers may have personal benefits as well as providing one outlet for charitable giving.

Accordingly, there is some prima facie plausibility to the idea that religion, including Christianity, brings benefits. Of course, it does not follow that any religion brings a net balance of benefits over harms. Even if Christianity did so during some periods of history, that may not be the case now. Even if it does in some societies, yours might not be among them.

Conclusion — Living and Speaking without God

Some people do find value in religious beliefs and practices, and I've already acknowledged that there could be drawbacks if you walk away from religion. These could include the loss of a community and even rejection by friends and family. But walking away can have benefits of its own.

One is simply the value of living an authentic life, not protecting ourselves with illusions or claiming to know things that we don't. Notwithstanding Alain de Botton's pessimism, we can reject the poisonous idea, conspicuously prevalent in religious teachings, that we and our fellow human beings are pitiful wretches inclined to foolishness, nastiness, and spite. As atheists, we can be guided by our own reflections on how to live a flourishing life, and not by religious notions of sin, guilt, shame, and penance. We can find happiness in facing the world honestly, exercising our critical faculties, and being open to learning and experience. We can enjoy all the ordinary things that make life good: among them are friendship, love, helping other people, and enjoying the pleasures of the senses in ways that don't harm others.[34]

A society of people who think this way is hardly one of dangerous, callous, alienated nihilists. Certainly there is no evidence that the nations of northern and western Europe, where religiosity has dropped to remarkably low levels in recent decades, have suffered from widespread alienation or unrest caused by their large proportion of atheists and other nonbelievers. Like all countries, these have their particular social problems, but on any reasonable measure of social cohesion, safety, well-being, or personal freedom they compare very favorably with the much more religious United States.

But should we muffle our criticisms of religion so as not to offend or distress believers? At one level, intellectual scrutiny of religious claims is simply inevitable. Religions make extraordinary claims about how the world actually works, and they promise extraordinary benefits to their adherents. It would be helpful to know whether any of this withstands rational scrutiny. At a minimum, philosophers will (and should) always investigate the claims of religions, and indeed those of other worldviews that purport to explain the human condition.

Perhaps the question is better phrased in terms of how of how *urgent* it is to criticize religion. If we assume that religion is largely benign then rational scrutiny of religious claims might be left to a relatively small number of specialists writing relatively obscure books or academic papers. Though these critiques would be available to interested members of the public, there would be no pressing need to write for a popular audience or engage in high-profile, perhaps sometimes acrimonious, debates. Related to this, Sheiman makes a reasonable point when he suggests that we should prioritize advocacy of secularism, the separation of religion from state power, over advocacy of atheism.[35] Though he relentlessly exaggerates the beneficence of religion, he is probably right that its worst harms involve a mingling of religiosity with the power wielded by political institutions.

Doubtless we should defend the idea of secular government; indeed I have devoted an entire book to that topic, and I've presented arguments that should appeal even to many religious people.[36] Let's acknowledge, though, that the arguments will not persuade everyone, even of those who have the time and patience to consider them. All too many religious leaders and thinkers do not distinguish clearly between the roles of religious teaching and state power. Instead, they look and work toward a time when their particular worldviews will prevail over rivals and guide the exercise of political power.

When religion claims moral and political authority, it is natural and unremarkable that we question its source and whether it has a rational basis.

It is also important to stress that secular government includes the idea of state neutrality between religion and nonreligion, and not only state neutrality among religions. Realistically, this cannot be obtained unless the arguments for secular government are supplemented by forthright presentation of the arguments against religion itself. Any idea of governments being neutral between religion and nonreligion will have no traction if atheists are silent in the public sphere.

The theme of this book is that religions, and particularly Christianity, perpetrate much harm along with whatever good they do. Their ability to do so will depend on how much political and social power they wield in particular places at particular times, and Christianity has certainly lost much of the power that it exercised in medieval Europe, where the Catholic Church ensured that Christian doctrine and practice insinuated themselves into all aspects of life. Although that has changed, the church retains pretensions of political authority. Even as it teaches that it and other religious organizations should be free from interference by the state in their internal affairs, it also maintains that the state should enforce (what the church regards as) the moral law, which includes a highly prescriptive and illiberal outlook on sexual interaction and sexual pleasure.

If it comes to that, many Protestants think that secularism has gone too far in tolerating conduct that they regard as immoral. And once we look beyond Christianity, Islam is especially notorious for refusing to draw a boundary between the domains of religion and politics.

I've argued throughout this chapter that we can live good lives without God or religious dogma—and as you do so, please speak up about it. The power of religion is waning, but this is a slow, uneven process with many detours, ups and downs, and local reversals. There is no apocalyptic endpoint or guaranteed outcome. Religious voices from many traditions continue to clamor, often with much success, to shape public policy on a range of issues from education to medical research, from freedom of speech to physician-assisted suicide. They seek, in short, to control how we plan and live our lives, including how we die. In most of these areas, faith-based proposals are authoritarian, damaging, and even cruel.

Given these realities, atheists have little choice but to take an opposing stance. This includes challenging the churches' and sects' fundamental claims to intellectual and moral authority. Let us, then, take a lesson to heart: this is still a good time to expose religion's harms and explain why we choose to reject it.

NOTES

Chapter 1. Religious Violence and the Harms of Christianity

1. Jack David Eller, *Cruel Creeds, Virtuous Violence: Religious Violence across Culture and History* (Amherst, NY: Prometheus Books, 2010). He wrote on this same topic in *Atheism Advanced: Further Thoughts of a Freethinker* (Cranford, NJ: American Atheist Press, 2007), under the name David Eller.

2. Eller, *Atheism Advanced*, p. 164.

3. Ibid., p. 167.

4. Eller, *Cruel Creeds, Virtuous Violence*, pp. 36–37.

5. Ibid., p. 39.

6. Eller, *Atheism Advanced*, p. 170.

7. Eller, *Cruel Creeds, Virtuous Violence*, p. 44.

8. Ibid.

9. Eller, *Atheism Advanced*, p. 171.

10. Eller, *Cruel Creeds, Virtuous Violence*, p. 78.

11. Ibid., p. 328.

12. Ibid.

13. Hector Avalos, *Fighting Words: The Origins of Religious Violence* (Amherst, NY: Prometheus Books, 2005), p. 18.

14. Ibid.

15. Simon Sebag Montefiore, *Jerusalem: The Biography* (New York: Vintage Books, 2012).

16. W. Scott "elenkus," "Murder, Massacre, and Mayhem for Millennia" (review of *Jerusalem: The Biography* by Simon Sebag Montefiore), September 29, 2011, Amazon.com, http://www.amazon.com/review/R1JOH9NFP2YWEL/ref=cm_cr_pr _perm?ie=UTF8&ASIN=B004KA9VCE (accessed June 17, 2014).

17. Avalos, *Fighting Words*, p. 29.

18. Greta Christina, *Why Are You Atheists So Angry? 99 Things That Piss Off the Godless* (Durham, NC: Pitchstone, 2012).

19. Greta Christina, "The Armor of God, or, The Top One Reason Religion Is Harmful," *Greta Christina's Blog*, http://gretachristina.typepad.com/greta_christinas _weblog/2009/11/armor-of-god.html (accessed June 16, 2014).

20. Charles Kimball, *When Religion Becomes Evil* (San Francisco: HarperSanFrancisco, 2002).

21. Ibid., p. 208.

22. Ibid., p. 156.

23. John Shelby Spong, *The Sins of Scripture: Exposing the Bible's Texts of Hate to Reveal the God of Love* (San Francisco: HarperSanFrancisco, 2002), p. 217.

24. Ibid., p. 216.

25. Ibid., p. 217.

26. Bertrand Russell, chapter 10, "Ideas That Have Harmed Mankind," in his *Unpopular Essays* (New York: Simon and Schuster, 1950), pp. 146–65.

27. Peter Boghossian, *A Manual for Creating Atheists* (Durham, NC: Pitchstone, 2013), p. 70.

28. Dinesh D'Souza, *What's So Great about Christianity* (Washington, DC: Regnery, 2007).

29. David Eller, "Christianity Evolving: On the Origin of Christian Species," in John Loftus, ed., *The End of Christianity* (Amherst, NY: Prometheus Books, 2011), pp. 23–51.

30. One shows us there are forty thousand Christian denominations. See the Gordon Conwell Theological Seminary website for "Status of Global Mission, 2013, in the Context of AD 1800–2025," http://www.gordonconwell.edu/resources/documents/statusofglobalmission.pdf (accessed January 15, 2014). My thanks to Jonathan Pearce for alerting me to this source.

31. D'Souza's arguments have been dealt a death blow by the authors in my anthology *The Christian Delusion: Why Faith Fails* (Amherst, NY: Prometheus Books, 2010), especially those included in part 5. See also Richard Carrier's "Christianity and the Rise of American Democracy" in the present volume.

32. Phil Zuckerman, *Society without God: What the Least Religious Nations Can Tell Us about Contentment* (New York: New York University Press, 2010).

33. Quoted in "Why My Focus Is on Debunking Evangelical Christianity," November 11, 2007, *Debunking Christianity*, http://debunkingchristianity.blogspot.com/2007/11/why-my-focus-is-on-debunking.html (accessed June 18, 2014).

34. To see this demonstrated I highly recommend watching Derren Brown's "Fear And Faith—Pt-1," which can be seen on YouTube at https://www.youtube.com/watch?v=hfDlfhHVvTY (accessed June 16, 2014). Perhaps this placebo effect helps explain why there is a debate on whether religious faith helps believers to be better people overall. On this see Luke Galen and Jeremy Beahan, "Research Report: Does Religion Really Make Us Better People?" *Free Inquiry* 33, no. 4, and Luke W. Galen, "Does Religious Belief Promote Prosociality? A Critical Examination," *Psychological Bulletin* 138, no. 5 (September 2012): 876–906.

35. I've made this argument in the tenth chapter of my book *The Outsider Test for Faith: How to Know Which Religion Is True* (Amherst, NY: Prometheus Books, 2013), pp. 207–28.

36. Guy Harrison, *Think: Why You Should Question Everything* (Amherst, NY: Prometheus Books, 2013).

37. Boghossian, *Manual for Creating Atheists*, pp. 31–32.

38. On Secular Humanism see the three Humanist Manifestos at "Humanist Manifesto," *Wikipedia*, http://en.wikipedia.org/wiki/Humanist_Manifesto (accessed June 16, 2014), along with James Lindsay's chapter 22 in the present volume. Richard Carrier has additionally argued that atheists are not less happy, healthy, and sane, and that atheism does not cause suicide, in "Atheism Doesn't Suck: How Science Does Not Prove Atheists Are Less Happy, Healthy, and Sane," Freethoughtblogs .com, http://freethoughtblogs.com/carrier/archives/4291 (accessed June 16, 2014), and "Bad Science: No, Atheism Does Not Cause Suicide," Freethougtblogs.com, http://freethoughtblogs.com/carrier/archives/5181 (accessed June 16, 2014).

39. Richard R. Rubenstein, *When Jesus Became God: The struggle to Define Christianity during the Last Days of Rome* (Orlando, FL: Harcourt, 1999), p. 7. Bart D. Ehrman has an excellent discussion of this as well, in *How Jesus Became God: The Exaltation of a Jewish Preacher from Galilee* (San Francisco: HarperOne, 2014).

40. Ibid., p. 7.

41. Phillip Jenkins, *The Jesus Wars: How Four Patriarchs, Three Queens, and Two Emperors Decided What Christians Would Believe for the Next 1,500 Years* (New York: HarperOne, 2011), pp. xii–xiii.

42. Ibid., p. xiv.

43. Brian Moynahan, *The Faith: A History of Christianity* (New York: Doubleday, 2002), p. 456. William T. Cavanaugh has argued that religious wars were caused by the rise of the state in Europe during the sixteenth and seventeenth centuries, and that Queen Mother Catherine de Medici unleashed the Saint Bartholomew's Day Massacre, which was entirely politically motivated. See Cavanaugh, "A Fire Strong Enough to Consume the House: The Wars of Religion and the Rise of the State," *Modern Theology* 11 (1995): 397–420. But Hector Avalos argues that the church was "deeply involved" in this massacre in chapter 14 of his book *Fighting Words*. The Catholic Church produced the "rhetoric and polices that made such a massacre probable," and the church leadership celebrated this massacre afterward. Avalos writes: "If Catherine de Medici, or any other politician, was able to unleash anything, it is because religious hatred was already there to begin with. Had there been no steady drumbeat of violent anti-Protestant rhetoric and instructions from the Vatican and its allied institutions, there would have been no reason for Catholic populations to behave

the way they did against their neighbors" (p. 341). Avalos concludes that Cavanaugh's analysis is "fatally flawed" and that "the massacre of the Huguenots was mostly the result of religious divisions and tensions" (p. 342).

44. To read about this devastating war, see C. V. Wedgwood, *The Thirty Years' War* (New York: New York Review Books Classics, 2005).

45. Paul Copan, *When God Goes to Starbucks: A Guide to Everyday Apologetics* (Grand Rapids, MI: Baker Books, 2008), p. 192.

46. This violence is due in large part to what I call the *Problem of Divine Miscommunication*, which I wrote about in *The Christian Delusion*, pp. 181–206.

47. Kimball, *When Religion Becomes Evil*, p. 27. For a wide-ranging discussion of religious violence in the different faith traditions see Mark Juergensmeyer, Margo Kitts, and Michael Jerryson, eds., *The Oxford Handbook of Religion and Violence* (Oxford: Oxford University Press, 2013).

Part One: How Faith Fails

Chapter 2. The Failure of the Church and the Triumph of Reason

1. Editor's note. This is a reduced selection from a lengthier piece of Ingersoll's titled "A Thanksgiving Sermon," which can be found on the Ingersoll Times website, http://www.theingersolltimes.com/volume-4/#4-50 (accessed June 16, 2014). I realize Ingersoll's rhetoric is exaggerated in some places and his male-oriented language is a product of his times. Nonetheless, what he said seems to be largely spot on and reflective of the oratory skills of Christopher Hitchens.

Chapter 3. The Folly of Faith: The Incompatibility of Science and Christianity

1. Stephen Jay Gould, *Rocks of Ages: Science and Religion in the Fullness of Life* (New York: Ballantine, 1999).

2. Francis S. Collins, *The Language of God: A Scientist Presents Evidence for Belief* (New York: Free Press, 2006).

3. Editorial, *Nature* 432 (2004): 657.

4. Michael Ruse, *Science and Spirituality: Making Room for Faith in the Age of Science* (Cambridge, New York: Cambridge University Press, 2010), p. 234.

5. Charles Webster, "Puritanism, Separatism, and Science," in David C. Lindberg and Ronald L. Numbers, eds., *God and Nature: Historical Essays on the Encounter between Christianity and Science* (Berkeley: University of California Press, 1986), pp. 192–217.

6. Ian G. Barbour, *Religion and Science: Historical and Contemporary Issues* (San Francisco: HarperSanFrancisco, 1997), p. 27.

7. Sam Harris, *The Moral Landscape: How Science Can Determine Human Values* (New York: Free Press, 2010), p. 10.

8. Victor J. Stenger, *Quantum Gods: Creation, Chaos, and the Search for Cosmic Consciousness* (Amherst, NY: Prometheus Books, 2009).

9. Deepak Chopra, *Ageless Body, Timeless Mind: The Quantum Alternative to Growing Old* (New York: Harmony Books, 1993); Rhonda Byrne, *The Secret* (New York; Hillsboro, OR: Atria Books Beyond Words, 2006).

10. Stenger, *Quantum Gods*.

11. William Grassie, *The New Sciences of Religion: Exploring Spirituality from the Outside In and Bottom Up* (New York: Palgrave Macmillan, 2010).

12. Victor J. Stenger, *God and the Atom: From Democritus to the Higgs Boson* (Amherst, NY: Prometheus Books, 2013).

13. Philip Clayton and P. C. W. Davies, eds., *The Re-Emergence of Emergence: The Emergentist Hypothesis from Science to Religion* (Oxford; New York: Oxford University Press, 2006).

14. Alexander Vilenkin, "Creation of Universes from Nothing," *Physics Letters B* 117, no. 1 (1982): 25–28; André Linde, "Quantum Creation of the Inflationary Universe," *Physics Letters B* 108 (1982): 389–92.

15. Andrei D. Linde, "Eternally Existing Self-Reproducing Chaotic Inflationary Universe," *Physics Letters B* 175, no. 4 (1986): 395–400.

16. Hugh Ross, "Big Bang Model Refined by Fire," in William A. Dembski, ed., *Mere Creation: Science, Faith & Intelligent Design* (Downers Grove, IL: Intervarsity Press, 1998), pp. 363–83.

17. Victor J. Stenger, *The Fallacy of Fine-Tuning: Why the Universe Is Not Designed for Us* (Amherst, NY: Prometheus Books, 2011).

18. Mark Fox, *Religion, Spirituality, and the Near-Death Experience* (London; New York: Routledge, 2003).

19. Michael Shermer, *The Science of Good and Evil: Why People Cheat, Gossip, Care, Share, and Follow the Golden Rule* (New York: Times Books, 2004).

20. Center for the Renewal of Science and Culture, "The Wedge Strategy," 1999, http://www.antievolution.org/features/wedge.pdf (accessed November 21, 2013); Barbara Forrest and Paul R. Gross, *Creationism's Trojan Horse: The Wedge of Intelligent Design* (Oxford; New York: Oxford University Press, 2004).

21. Kevin Phillips, *American Theocracy: The Peril and Politics of Radical Religion, Oil, and Borrowed Money in the 21st Century* (New York: Viking, 2006), p. vii.

22. Michelle Goldberg, *Kingdom Coming: The Rise of Christian Nationalism* (New York: W. W. Norton, 2006).

23. Damon Linker, *The Theocons: Secular America Under Siege* (New York: Doubleday, 2006).

24. Chris Hedges, *American Fascists: The Christian Right and the War on America* (New York: Free Press, 2007), p. 10.

25. Chris Hedges, "The Radical Right and the War on Government," Truthdig, http://www.truthdig.com/report/item/the_radical_christian_right_and_the_war_on _government_20131006/ (accessed November 16, 2013).

26. Jeff Sharlet, *The Family: The Secret Fundamentalism at the Heart of American Power* (New York, NY: Harper Perennial, 2009).

27. Jeff Sharlet, *C Street: The Fundamentalist Threat to American Democracy* (New York: Little, Brown, 2010).

28. Peter Montgomery, "Jesus Hates Taxes: Biblical Capitalism Created Fertile Anti-Union Soil," *Religion Dispatches* (March 14, 2011).

29. Jeff Sharlet, "This Is Not a Religion Column: Biblical Capitalism," *Religion Dispatches*, http://www.religiondispatches.org/archive/politics/562/ (accessed November 21, 2013).

30. William L. Fisher, "Christian Responsibility for Government," in William L. Fisher et al., eds., *Christian Coalition Leadership Manual* (Christian Coalition, 1990), pp. 2.5–2.8.

31. Chris Mooney, *The Republican War on Science* (New York: Basic Books, 2005).

32. Scott Keyes, "Jim Demint's Theory of Relativity: 'The Bigger Government Gets, the Smaller God Gets,'" *Think Progress*, http://thinkprogress.org/2011/03/15/ demint-big-govt/ (accessed November 21, 2013).

33. Pew Forum, "The Tea Party and Religion," http://pewforum.org/Politics -and-Elections/Tea-Party-and-Religion.aspx (accessed November 21, 2013).

34. Robert P. Jones and Daniel Cox, "Religion and the Tea Party in the 2010 Elections: An Analysis of the Third Biennial American Values Survey," *Public Religion Research Institute*, http://www.publicreligion.org/objects/uploads/fck/file/AVS%20 2010%20Report%20FINAL.pdf (accessed November 21, 2013).

35. The author thanks John Crisp, Don McGee, Brent Meeker, Kerry Regier, Jim Wyman, and Bob Zannelli for their help with this essay, which is based on the author's book *God and the Folly of Faith* (Amherst, NY: Prometheus Books, 2012).

Chapter 4. Faith, Epistemology, and Answering Socrates' Question by Translation

1. I explain this in detail in chapter two of my book, *A Manual for Creating Atheists* (Pitchstone Press, 2013). Here, I also address and dissect counterarguments to viewing faith as an epistemology.

Perhaps a simpler, alternative explanation is that some people do not think in terms of knowledge, evidence, rational justification and inference, but instead think in terms of what their parents told them, old habits of thought, fear, prejudice, antipathies and attractions; that is, they think uncritically.

In this alternative conceptualization faith is a form of thought and a general approach to ideas. Under this lens, one does not honestly examine beliefs but instead stays in a state of certainty/doxastic closure/belief immutability. The obvious questions then become, how does one enter such an epistemically debilitating state, and why would one perceive this condition as positive? The answer likely extends well beyond the domain of philosophy and into the realm of cognitive neuroscience.

2. That is, people who genuinely believe that reason and evidence are either unnecessary or that their role should be minimized with regard to justifying faith-based beliefs.

Another way to help conceptualize fideism is through Stephen Jay Gould's idea of non-overlapping magisteria. That is, religion has its domain and science has its domain, and never the two shall meet. For example, science covers the material realm (empirical questions) and religion covers the moral realm (moral questions).

This is a crucial topic that does not get nearly the attention it deserves. To understand why Gould's accommodationist non-overlapping magisteria is a catastrophic error in thinking, I highly recommend Jerry Coyne's body of scholarship: Jerry Coyne, "Seeing and Believing" (reviews of *Saving Darwin: How to Be a Christian and Believe in Evolution*, by Karl W. Giberson, and *Only a Theory: Evolution and the Battle for America's Soul*, by Kenneth R. Miller), *New Republic*, February 4, 2009, pp. 32–41, http://www.tnr.com/article/books/seeing-and-believing?passthru =MmQyMDEzM2UxYTJkMTcxNTM5NWZhN2QwOGJlNWRlNjI (accessed June 16, 2014); Jerry Coyne, "Science, Religion, and Society: The Problem of Evolution in America," *Evolution* 66: 2654–2663, http://onlinelibrary.wiley.com/doi/10.1111/ j.1558-5646.2012.01664.x/pdf (accessed June 16, 2014).

3. Christians frequently cite the definition of faith in Hebrews 11: "Now faith is the substance of things hoped for, the evidence [elenchus] of things not seen." On page 35 of *A Manual for Creating Atheists*, I provide an etymological account of the term *elenchus*. I argue that the meaning of elenchus changed considerably from the

way Socrates used the word—from a rigorous process of argumentation by strict rules of logic, to the Christian sense of conviction or persuasion without argument.

4. Sophisticated Theologians™ is a phrase coined by evolutionary biologist Jerry Coyne, "A Sokal-Style Hoax by an Anti-Religious Philosopher," *Why Evolution Is True*, September 25, 2012, http://whyevolutionistrue.wordpress.com/2012/09/25/a-sokal-style-hoax-by-an-anti-religious-philosopher-2/#comment-289429 (accessed June 16, 2014). It's used to indicate complex, vacuous arguments that sound impressive but are ultimately devoid of substance.

5. Boghossian, *Manual*, p. 29.

6. There's an entire corpus of philosophical literature dedicated to understanding and analyzing knowledge and warranted belief. I recommend the *Stanford Encyclopedia of Philosophy* as an accessible, reputable online reference for readers interested in exploring important texts in this epistemological tradition. See "Knowledge as Justified True Belief," *Stanford Encyclopedia of Philosophy*, http://plato.stanford.edu/entries/epistemology/#JTB (accessed June 16, 2014).

7. Traditionally, philosophers have expressed this as follows:

S knows that P if and only if:

1. P is true
2. S believes that P
3. S is justified in believing that P

My second understanding came when I realized that some people were substituting F for J not as an intellectual exercise, or for academic training, but as a guiding template by which they lived their lives. That is, implicitly or explicitly, people used this alternative formulation of knowledge: Knowledge is Faith True Belief. Additional formulations of this are: F is T (Faith is Truth), where knowledge is removed from the equation altogether, and B is K (Belief is Knowledge), where truth is absent. In other words, faith was being substituted for justification.

Perhaps even more remarkable than my moment of clarity was the fact that I never realized this before. Epistemically, it never occurred to me that people living in the modern age substitute faith for justification, think that's sufficient to convey warrant upon their knowledge claims, and then live accordingly. Politically and socially it was of course obvious—people invoked faith as a justification for every manner of social horror, from abnegating the rights of homosexuals to executing blasphemers. But epistemologically this was so monstrously anti-rational and anti-intellectual that I didn't imagine such an egregious breach of reason would even occur to anyone, much less be given epistemological countenance.

8. Alvin Plantinga, *Warranted Christian Belief* (Oxford: Oxford University Press, 2000).

9. Faith then becomes epistemology by proxy, with internal feeling states grounding one's epistemology. For more on this, see William Lane Craig's "Dealing with Doubt," YouTube, November 18, 2011, http://www.youtube.com/watch?v=S -fDyPU3wlQ (accessed June 16, 2014).

10. See Elizabeth Weise, "Fishy Fakes Common in Restaurants, *USA Today*, February 20, 2013), http://www.usatoday.com/story/news/nation/2013/02/20/fish -seafood-fraud-common-oceana-report/1927065/ (accessed June 16, 2014).

11. For an outstanding explanation of evidence and the criteria of adequacy, see T. Schick and L. Vaughn, *How to Think about Weird Things: Critical Thinking for a New Age*, 5th ed. (McGraw-Hill Higher Education, 2008), pp. 179–89. They cover the following criteria of adequacy: testability (180), fruitfulness (182), scope (185), simplicity (186), and conservatism (189).

12. John Baillie, who is arguing for a kind of Christian knowledge, perfectly captures the flavor of a long line of Christian thinkers. His influential work *Our Knowledge of God*, first published in 1939, begins with the statement, "We reject logical argument of any kind as the first chapter of our theology or as representing the process by which God comes to be known." It has been reprinted by Charles Scribner's Sons, in 1959. The history of philosophy is littered with thinkers for whom logical argument, even if it's ostensibly given lip service, is ultimately relegated to a position subordinate to faith.

Saint Thomas, for example, argued that on some questions it is wrong to apply strict logic or to try to be objective (*Quaestiones disputatae de Veritate*). Kierkegaard held that in some matters truth cannot be objective, but must be subjective (*Concluding Unscientific Postscript to the Philosophical Fragments*). While there is controversy surrounding Tertullian's writings and objectives, many scholars think he ventured even further along this line by holding that some truths should be believed specifically because they are illogical (*De Carne Christi*).

Augustine, Anselm, and many other theologians write about direct, experiential knowledge of God, as does the more recent Hans Kung (Joseph Aloisius Ratzinger's teacher). However, these themes are not specific to Christianity; they are found in Judaism and Islam, and they abound in non-Abrahamic traditions such as Hinduism. For example, in Adi Sankara's position on Vendanta in his work *Atma Bodha*, or self-knowledge, Sankara asserts that if atman is brahman, that is, if the soul equals god, then self-knowledge is god-knowledge and the need for logical argument and justification is obviated.

Bypassing, or more accurately trampling over K as J T B, several faith-based traditions make the fideistic metaphysical turn to the "soul equals god" equation, so that self-knowledge or feeling states become a kind of god-knowledge and thus confer a priori warrant upon beliefs. Vedanta in the Indian tradition is just one such example; the pantheist principle is another (Plotinus is also following a logic like this). Additional examples include aboriginal Australian religious traditions, where entering into dreamtime is a way of escaping this world and emerging into another. In this realm, essentially a kind of traveler's tale from a spirit journey, one allegedly learns things and develops knowledge. Native American religious shamanic traditions—like those in Siberia and Mongolia—also refer to spirit quests in which—sometimes through pain rituals—the shaman reaches another world and gains experiential knowledge (this kind of claim also is a stand-in for revelatory experiences, such as being touched, hearing voices, feelings of "otherness," and the like). See S. Brutus, *Religion, Culture, History: A Philosophical Study of Religion* (Daimonion Press, 2012).

All of these traditions make similar extraordinary knowledge claims, identifying or defining entirely new avenues for knowledge that are somehow incomparable and incompatible to knowledge as J T B. One could accept all of these claims as delusions, hallucinations, schizophrenic states, or other sorts of cognitive/thought disorders. However, these states would probably not be defined as such if the agent made no knowledge claims, but simply called them dreams or fantasies or flights of the imagination. Deriving knowledge claims resulting from subjective experiences is what makes the state a disorder—in exactly the same way that Christians who claim the Holy Spirit lives in them, or that they've received a revelation, are victims of what medical anthropologists call culture-bound syndromes.

13. For an insightful glimpse into the historical use of faith and some of the issues surrounding this term, see part 2 of George H. Smith's *Atheism: The Case against God* (Amherst, NY: Prometheus Books, 1989).

14. Wittgenstein's idea of a language game can help one understand these phenomena. For Wittgenstein, words are part of a form of life and yield meaning through their use in context. While there are many flavors of Christianity, one family resemblance, to borrow a phrase from Wittgenstein, is the normative use of the word *faith*. *Faith* is a term that's not always used in the same way—outside of religious contexts, for example, faith is frequently used as a synonym for hope or trust.

15. G. Longsine and Peter Boghossian, "Indignation Is Not Righteous," *Skeptical Inquirer*, September 27, 2012, http://www.csicop.org/specialarticles/show/indignation_is_not_righteous/ (accessed June 16, 2014).

16. W. Shatner, *Dark Victory* (Pocket Books, 2000).

17. If, to the Christian reader this seems flippant, it's not meant to be. The identical fallacy is at play with astrology. In order to criticize the basic premise of astrology,

does one have to study star charts by famous astrologers or make historical surveys of the intricacies of famous people's beliefs about astrology? No. These are starting conditions of people who've already bought into a system of thought.

Additionally, this points to the core of Foucault's power/knowledge dialectic. These ideas support and justify one another in a continuous loop of self-authorization. More specifically, Sophisticated Theologians™ are coming from a tradition that Christianity is beyond critique, an argument with a long history that was given additional force in the Enlightenment, when Orientalist theories made monotheism the highest expression of religion, and Christianity the highest expression of monotheism. Ideology works best when "the way things are" is simply thought of as "natural reflection of truth" rather than a discursive production.

18. All apologetics start with confirmation bias. One would have to thoroughly examine the superstitions of every tradition before deciding to defend one.

19. Answering this question in the affirmative is one explanation for how different faith traditions can make competing claims that cannot all be correct. They can make competing claims because they've incorrectly valued—or undervalued—the role of evidence in belief formation.

Part Two: Political/Institutional Harms

Chapter 5. Love Your Enemy, Kill Your Enemy: Crusades, Inquisitions, and Centuries of Christian Violence

1. Michael A. Köhler, *Alliances and Treaties between Frankish and Muslim Rulers in the Middle East: Cross-Cultural Diplomacy in the Period of the Crusades*, Peter M. Holt, trans. (Leiden and Boston: Brill, 2013).

2. Jonathan Phillips, "The Call of the Crusades," *History Today* (November 2009): 10.

3. Candida Moss, *The Myth of Persecution: How Early Christians Invented a Story of Martyrdom* (New York: HarperOne, 2013).

4. Roland H. Bainton, *Christian Attitudes toward War and Peace* (New York and Nashville: Abingdon Press, 1960), p. 53.

5. Richard J. Regan, *Just War: Principles and Cases* (Washington, DC: Catholic University Press, 1996), p. 17.

6. Ibid.

7. Quoted in Bainton, *Christian Attitudes*, p. 97.

8. Ibid., p. 98.

9. Quoted in Leonard Levy, *Blasphemy: Verbal Offense against the Sacred, from Moses to Salman Rushdie* (New York: Knopf, 1993), p. 48.

10. Quoted in ibid.

11. Quoted in ibid., p. 49.

12. Quoted in ibid.

13. Michael Gaddis, *There Is No Crime for Those Who Have Christ* (Berkeley: University of California Press, 2005), p. 133.

14. Geoffrey Hindley, *The Crusades: A History of Armed Pilgrimage and Holy War* (New York: Carroll and Graf, 2003), p. 10.

15. Ibid., p. 12.

16. Ibid., pp. 17–18.

17. Köhler, *Alliances and Treaties*, pp. 21–23.

18. Hindley, *Crusades*, p. 3.

19. Köhler, *Alliances and Treaties*, p. 23.

20. Ibid., p. 24.

21. "Crusades," New Advent, http://www.newadvent.org/cathen/04543c.htm (accessed December 29, 2009).

22. Hindley, *Crusades*, p. 20.

23. Ibid., p. 48.

24. René Grousset, *The Epic of the Crusades*, trans. Noel Lindsay (New York: Orion, 1970), p. 31.

25. Köhler, *Alliances and Treaties*, p. 28.

26. Hindley, *Crusades*, p. 68.

27. Köhler, *Alliances and Treaties*, p. 58.

28. Hindley, *Crusades*, p. 127.

29. Ibid., p. 153.

30. "Crusades."

31. Phillips, "Call of the Crusades," p. 11.

32. Ibid.

33. Hindley, *Crusades*, p. 1.

34. Ibid., p. 165.

35. Ibid., p. 210.

36. A. L. Maycock, *The Inquisition from Its Establishment to the Great Schism: An Introductory Study* (New York: Harper and Row, 1969), p. 95.

37. Ibid., p. 115.

38. Ibid., pp. 115–16.

39. Joseph Perez, *The Spanish Inquisition: A History*, trans. Janet Lloyd (New Haven, CT: Yale University Press, 2004), p. 149.

40. Ibid., p. 100.

41. Jaime Contreras and Gustav Henningsen, "Forty-Four Thousand Cases of the Spanish Inquisition (1540–1700): Analysis of a Historical Data Bank," in Gustav Henningsen and John Tedeschi, eds., *The Inquisition in Early Modern Europe* (DeKalb: Northern Illinois University Press, 1986).

42. Maycock, *Inquisition*, p. 140.

43. Quoted in Levy, *Blasphemy* (see note 32), p. 52.

44. Hindley, *Crusades*, p. 218.

45. Phillips, "Call of the Crusades," p. 12.

46. Hindley, *Crusades*, p. 249.

47. G. R. Elton, *Reformation Europe, 1517–1559* (New York: Harper and Row, 1963), p. 83.

48. Martin Luther, Christian Quotes, http://christianquotes.org/author/quotes/32/10 (accessed December 25, 2009).

49. Richard Dunn, *The Age of Religious Wars, 1559–1689* (New York: W. W. Norton, 1970), pp. 26–27.

50. Ibid., p. 47.

51. Ibid., p. 147.

52. Judith Lichtenburg, "Some Central Problems with Just War Theory," in R. Joseph Hoffmann, ed., *The Just War and Jihad: Violence in Judaism, Christianity, and Islam* (Amherst, NY: Prometheus Books, 2006), see note 20, p. 23.

53. Joyce Salisbury, "'In Vain Have I Smitten Your Children': Augustine Defines Just War," in Hoffmann, ed., *The Just War and Jihad*, p. 206.

54. Quoted in Timothy Freke and Peter Gandy, *The Jesus Mysteries: Was the "Original Jesus" a Pagan God?* (New York: Harmony Books, 1999), p. 243.

Chapter 6. Thou Shalt Not Suffer a Witch to Live: The Wicked Christian Witch Hunts

1. The Bull of Pope Innocent VIII, *Summis desiderantes affectibus,* December 5, 1484, pp. 71–72, *Wikipedia*, http://en.wikipedia.org/wiki/Summis_desiderantes_affectibus (accessed June 30, 2014).

2. Hilary Evans and Robert E. Bartholomew, *Outbreak! The Encyclopedia of Extraordinary Social Behavior* (San Antonio, TX: Anomalist Books, 2009), pp. 731–32.

3. On this, see what I wrote in "Christianity Is Wildly Improbable," John Loftus, ed., *The End of Christianity* (Amherst, NY: Prometheus Books, 2011), p. 101.

4. I've made this type of argument elsewhere, calling it the *Problem of Divine Miscommunication* in "What We've Got Here Is a Failure to Communicate," John Loftus, ed., *The Christian Delusion* (Amherst, NY: Prometheus Books, 2010), pp. 181–206.

5. On paranormal claims in general see Carl Sagan, *The Demon-Haunted World: Science as a Candle in the Dark* (New York: Random House, 1996); Guy Harrison, *50 Popular Beliefs That People Think Are True* (Amherst, NY: Prometheus Books, 2012); Joe Nickel, *The Science of Miracles* (Amherst, NY: Prometheus Books, 2013); Michael Shermer, *Why People Believe Weird Things* (New York: Henry Holt, 2002); and especially Theodore Schick and Lewis Vaughn, *How to Think about Weird Things: Critical Thinking for a New Age*, 6th ed. (New York: McGraw-Hill, 2010).

6. The JREF offers a one-million-dollar prize "to anyone who can show, under proper observing conditions, evidence of any paranormal, supernatural, or occult power or event." The rules can be found online at James Randi Educational Foundation, http://www.randi.org/site/index.php/component/content/article/37-static/254-jref-challenge-faq.html (accessed June 26, 2014). Since 1964 when Randi first offered such a challenge, no one has even gotten past the preliminary test.

7. See chapter 22, "The Devil Made Me do it!" in my book *Why I Became an Atheist: A Former Preacher Rejects Christianity*, rev. and exp. ed. (Amherst, NY: Prometheus Books, 2012), pp. 443–46.

8. This type of argument is fleshed out in Hector Avalos, *Fighting Words: The Origins of Religious Violence* (Amherst, NY: Prometheus Books, 2005).

9. See David D. Hall, ed. *Witch-Hunting in Seventeenth-Century New England: A Documentary History 1638–1693*, 2nd ed. (Durham, NC: Duke University Press, 2005), and Brian A. Pavlac, *Witch Hunts in the Western World: Persecution and Punishment from the Inquisition through the Salem Trials* (Lincoln: University of Nebraska Press, 2010), pp. 134–47.

10. Brian P. Levack, *The Witch-Hunt in Early Modern Europe*, 3rd ed. (Harlow, UK: Pearson Education Limited, 2006), pp. 299–305; Philip Jenkins, chapter 5, "Good and Evil," in *The New Faces of Christianity, Believing in the Bible in the Global South* (New York: Oxford University Press, 2006), pp. 98–127. See also "Case Study: The European Witch-Hunts, c. 1450–1750," Gendercide Watch, http://www.gendercide.org/case_witchhunts.html (accessed June 26, 2014).

11. C. S. Lewis, *Mere Christianity* (New York: Macmillan, 1952), chapter 2, p. 12.

12. The Bible is inconsistent about its condemnations of magic, since it embraces

the magical arts in several places. On this see my chapter 13, "The Strange and Super-stitious World of the Bible," in *Why I Became an Atheist*, pp. 255–94.

13. Levack, *Witch-Hunt in Early Modern Europe*, p. 9.

14. N. Curnock, ed., *The Journal of the Revered John Wesley*, vol. 5 (Charles H. Kelly, 1912), p. 265, entry for May 25, 1768.

15. Brian A. Pavlac, "Ten Common Errors and Myths about the Witch Hunts, Corrected and Commented," April 30, 2013, Women's History Resource Site, http://departments.kings.edu/womens_history/witcherrors.html (accessed January 15, 2014). On the topic of the Eastern Orthodox Church consult Charles Stewart, *Demons and the Devil* (Princeton, NJ: Princeton University Press, 1991).

16. Brian A. Pavlac, "Ten General Historical Theories about the Origins and Causes of the Witch Hunts," Women's History Resource Site, April 30, 2013, http://departments.kings.edu/womens_history/witcherrors.html (accessed January 15, 2014).

17. See Alan Charles Kors and Edward Peters. eds., *Witchcraft in Europe, 400–1700: A Documentary History*, 2nd ed. (Philadelphia: University of Pennsylvania Press, 2000) pp. 43–44.

18. Brian P. Levack, ed., *The Witchcraft Sourcebook* (New York: Routledge, 2004), pp. 33–35.

19. *Summa Theologica*, Question 11, Article 3, New Advent, http://www.newadvent.org/summa/1011.htm (accessed June 26, 2014).

20. *Summa Theologica*, Question 114, Article 4, New Advent, http://www.newadvent.org/summa/1114.htm (accessed June 26, 2014).

21. Brian A Pavlac, "List of Important Events for the Witch Hunts," April 30, 2013, Women's History Resource Site, http://departments.kings.edu/womens_history/witch/witchlist.html (accessed January 15, 2014). I find this timeline of Pavlac's time-line to be very helpful.

22. Kors and Peters, *Witchcraft in Europe*, pp. 43–44.

23. Two other sources were Johannes Nider and Nicholas Eymeric. Part 1 of Kramer's work, according to Christopher S. MacKay, "is a demonstration of the reality of sorcery, and . . . it is not surprising that the main source here is Thomas Aquinas." When it comes to Kramer's cited works, "Aquinas was a very widely read man, and the large majority of the many citations in the *Malleus* came from him." Christopher S. Mackay, trans., *The Hammer of Witches: A Complete Translation of the* Malleus Maleficarum *of Henrich Kramer* (Cambridge: Cambridge University Press, 2009), p. 16. Hereafter *Malleus*.

24. Levack, *Witch-Hunt in Early Modern Europe*, p. 206.

25. Ibid., p. 66.

26. Ibid., pp. 31–32.

27. Ibid., p. 77.

28. Edward Peters, *Torture* (New York: Basil Blackwell, 1985), pp. 3–50.

29. Levack, *Witch-Hunt in Early Modern Europe*, pp. 79–80.

30. This Papal Bull can be read online at Living Tradition, http://www.rtforum
.org/lt/lt119.html (accessed June 26, 2014). Augustine had previously argued for the
use of torture. See David Eller's chapter 5 in the present volume.

31. Pavlac, *Witch Hunts in the Western World*, p. 34.

32. Levack, *Witch Sourcebook*, p. 205.

33. *Malleus*, p. 548.

34. From 54, 4, as quoted in George L. Burr, *The Witch Persecutions* (Philadelphia: University of Pennsylvania History Department, 1897), pp. 5–6.

35. Levack, *Witchcraft Sourcebook*, p. 201.

36. H. C. Erick Middlefort, *Witch Hunting in Southwestern Germany, 1562–
1684: The Social and Intellectual Foundations* (Redwood City, CA: Stanford University Press, 1972), p. 149.

37. In *Cautio Criminalis*, Spee answers fifty-two questions; this one is from
question thirty-five, as quoted in Sagan, *Demon-Haunted World*, pp. 410–11.

38. Pavlac, *Witch Hunts in the Western World*, p. 62.

39. To read this account, told in excruciating detail, see Michael Kunze, *High-
road to the Stake: A Tale of Witchcraft* (Chicago: University of Chicago Press, 1987).

40. Scott E. Hendrix, "The Pursuit of Witches and the Sexual Discourse of the
Sabbat,"*Antropologija* 11 (2011). http://www.anthroserbia.org/Content/PDF/Articles/
292d4fb4d9504f0dad86fab257b023ca.pdf (accessed June 26, 2014).

41. Spee, *Cautio Criminalis*, question 23, as quoted in Uta Ranke Heinemann,
Eunuchs for the Kingdom of Heaven: Women, Sexuality, and the Catholic Church,
trans. Peter Heinegg (New York: Penguin Books, 1991), pp. 230–31.

42. Quoted in Henry Kamen, *The Spanish Inquisition: A Historical Revision*
(New Haven: Yale University Press, 1998), pp. 207–208).

43. Spee, *Cautio Criminalis*, question 22, as quoted in Sagan, *Demon-Haunted
World*, p. 409.

44. On this topic see Levack, *Witch-Hunt in Early Modern Europe*, pp. 16–18.

45. This case has been made by Mary Anne Warren in *Gendercide: The Implications of Sex Selection* (Totowa, NJ: Rowman and Allanfield, 1985); Adam Jones
in *Gendercide and Genocide* (Nashville: Vanderbilt University Press, 2004); and at
Gendercide Watch, http://www.gendercide.org/case_witchhunts.html (accessed June
26, 2014).

46. Deborah Wills, *Malevolent Nurture: Witch-Hunting and Maternal Power in
Early Modern England* (Ithaca, NY: Cornell University Press, 1995). See also Robin

Briggs, chapter 7, "Men against Women: The Gendering of Witchcraft," in *Witches and Neighbors: The Social and Cultural Context of European Witchcraft* (New York: Penguin Books, 1996), pp. 257–86.

47. Merry E. Wiesner-Hanks, *Women and Gender in Early Modern Europe*, 3rd ed. (Cambridge: Cambridge University Press, 2008).

48. Middlefort, *Witch Hunting in Southwestern Germany*, p. 192.

49. Steven T. Katz, *The Holocaust in Historical Context*, vol. 1 (Oxford: Oxford University Press, 1994), pp. 433 n. 1, 436.

50. Brian P. Levack, ed. *The Oxford Handbook of Witchcraft in Early Modern Europe and Colonial America* (New York: Oxford University Press, 2013), p. 437.

51. Levack, *Witch-Hunt in Early Modern Europe*, p. 265.

52. Keith Thomas, *Religion and the Decline of Magic: Studies in Popular Beliefs in Sixteenth- and Seventeenth-Century England* (London: Weidenfeld and Nicolson, 1971), p. 682.

53. Ibid., p. 690. For more on the decline of the witch hunts see Robert Thurston, *The Witch Hunts: A History of the Witch Persecutions in Europe and North America* (London: Pearson Education Limited, 2007), pp. 213–62.

54. Levack, *Witch-Hunt in Early Modern Europe*, p. 266.

55. See chapter 22 in Thomas, *Religion and the Decline of Magic*, pp. 767–800, for a detailed and nuanced view of this.

56. Rodney Stark, *For the Glory of God: How Monotheism Led to Reformations, Science, Witch-Hunts, and the End of Slavery* (Princeton, NJ: Princeton University Press, 2003), pp. 224, 277–81.

Chapter 7. They Will Make Good Slaves and Christians: Christianity, Colonialism, and the Destruction of Indigenous People

1. Quoted in Toyin Falola, *Violence in Nigeria: The Crisis of Religious Politics and Secular Ideologies* (Rochester, NY: University of Rochester Press, 2001), p. 33.

2. Benedikt Stuchtey, "Colonialism and Imperialism, 1450–1950," European History Online, January 24, 2011, http://ieg-ego.eu/en/threads/backgrounds/colonialism-and-imperialism/benedikt-stuchtey-colonialism-and-imperialism-1450-1950 (accessed June 27, 2014).

3. Ben Jones, "Colonialism and Civil War: Religion and Violence in East Africa," in Andrew R. Murphy, ed., *The Blackwell Companion to Religion and Violence* (London: Blackwell, 2012), p. 501.

4. Ibid.

5. Jean Comaroff, *Body of Power, Spirit of Resistance: The Culture and History of a South Africa People* (Chicago and London: University of Chicago Press, 1985), p. 80.

6. John L. Comaroff and Jean Comaroff, *Of Revelation and Revolution: The Dialectics of Modernity on a South African Frontier*, vol. 2 (Chicago and London: University of Chicago Press, 1991), p. 9.

7. Ibid., pp. 292–96.

8. Ibid., p. 189.

9. Fiona Bateman and Lionel Pilkington, "Introduction," in Fiona Bateman and Lionel Pilkington, eds., *Studies in Settler Colonialism* (New York: Palgrave Macmillan, 2011), p. 1.

10. David J. Silverman, "Indians, Missionaries, and Religious Translation: Creating Wampanoag Christianity in Seventeenth-Century Martha's Vineyard," *William and Mary Quarterly* 63, no. 2 (April 2005): 144.

11. David Chidester, "Colonialism and Religion," *Critical Research on Religion* 1 (2013): 89.

12. Jean and John Comaroff, *Of Revelation and Revolution: The Dialectics of Modernity on a South African Frontier*, vol. 1 (Chicago and London: University of Chicago Press, 1991), p. 88.

13. "King Ferdinand's Letter to the Taino-Arawak Indians," American History: From Revolution to Reconstruction and Beyond, http://www.let.rug.nl/usa/documents/before-1600/king-ferdinands-letter-to-the-taino-arawak-indians.php (accessed February 10, 2014).

14. "History of Colonization 4: Columbus & the Destruction of the Indies—A Chronology," Featherfolk Notes, http://featherfolk.wordpress.com/2008/10/06/history-of-colonization-4-columbus-the-destruction-of-the-indies-a-chronology (accessed February 10, 2014).

15. Quoted in S. Lyman Tyler, *Two Worlds: The Indian Encounter with the European 1492–1509* (Salt Lake City: University of Utah Press, 1988), pp. 155–56.

16. Adriaan C. van Oss, *Catholic Colonialism: A Parish History of Guatemala, 1524–1821* (Cambridge: Cambridge University Press, 2002), p. xi.

17. Palacios Rubios, *El Requerimiento*, Encyclopedia Virginia, http://www.encyclopediavirginia.org/El_Requerimiento_by_Juan_Lopez_de_Palacios_Rubios_1513 (accessed June 17, 2014).

18. Ralph Bauer, "Millennium's Darker Side: The Missionary Utopias of Franciscan Spain and Puritan New England," in Carla Mulford and David S. Shields, eds., *Finding Colonial Americas: Essays Honoring J. A. Leo Lemay* (Cranbury, NJ, and London: Associated University Presses, 2001), p. 35.

19. Denis De Lucca, *Jesuits and Fortifications: The Contributions of the Jesuits to Military Architecture in the Baroque Age* (Leiden and Boston: Brill, 2012).

20. George E. Tinker, *Missionary Conquest: The Gospel and Native American Cultural Genocide* (Minneapolis: Fortress Press, 1993), p. 43.

21. Ibid., p. 51.

22. Ibid., p. 50.

23. Quoted in Roy Harvey Pearce, *Savagism and Civilization: A Study of the Indian and the American Mind* (Baltimore and London: Johns Hopkins Press, 1965 [1953]), pp. 18–19.

24. Michael Welton, "Cunning Pedagogics: The Encounter between the Jesuit Missionaries and Amerindians in 17th-Century New France," *Adult Education Quarterly* 55, no. 2 (2005): 102.

25. Ibid., p. 109.

26. Quoted in Pearce, *Savagism and Civilization*, p. 6.

27. Ibid., p. 8.

28. Quoted in ibid., p. 19.

29. Tinker, *Missionary Conquest*, p. 27.

30. Ibid., p. 33.

31. Ibid., p. 40.

32. Peter Decker, *The Utes Must Go! American Expansion and the Removal of a People* (Golden, CO: Fulcrum, 2004).

33. Charla Bear, "American Indian Boarding Schools Haunt Many," National Public Radio, May 12, 2008, http://www.npr.org/templates/story/story.php?storyId =16516865 (accessed February 12, 2014).

34. Barbara Landis, "Carlisle Indian Industrial School History," http://home .epix.net/~landis/histry.html (accessed February 12, 2014).

35. Quoted in Andrew Markus, *Governing Savages* (Sydney: Allen and Unwin, 1990), p. x.

36. Robert Hughes, *The Fatal Shore: A History of the Transportation of Convicts to Australia, 1787–1868* (London: Harvill Press, 1986).

37. Meredith Lake, "Salvation and Conciliation: First Missionary Encounters at Sydney Cove," in Amanda Barry, Joanna Cruickshank, Andrew Brown-May, and Patricia Grimshaw, eds., *Evangelists of Empire? Missionaries in Colonial History* (Melbourne: University of Melbourne eScholarship Research Centre, 2008), p. 87.

38. Hughes, *Fatal Shore*, p. 273.

39. Ibid.

40. Colin Tatz, "Confronting Australian Genocide," *Aboriginal History* 25 (2001): 23.

41. Hughes, *Fatal Shore*, p. 277.

42. Barry Patton, "Aboriginal Child Separations and Removals in Early Melbourne and Adelaide," in Amanda Barry, Joanna Cruickshank, Andrew Brown-May, and Patricia Grimshaw, eds., *Evangelists of Empire? Missionaries in Colonial History* (Melbourne: University of Melbourne eScholarship Research Centre, 2008), p. 125.

43. Ibid., p. 127.

44. Ibid., p. 131.

45. "Dormitories and the Destruction of Aboriginal Culture," The Stolen Generations, http://www.stolengenerations.info/index.php?option=com_content&view=article&id=157&Itemid=125 (accessed February 13, 2014).

46. The Trans-Atlantic Slave Trade Database, "Assessing the Slave Trade," http://www.slavevoyages.org/tast/assessment/estimates.faces (accessed February 13, 2014).

47. Frank McLynn, *Hearts of Darkness: The European Exploration of Africa* (New York: Carroll and Graf, 1992), p. 128.

48. Bruce Vandervort, *Wars of Imperial Conquest in Africa 1830–1914* (Bloomington: Indiana University Press, 1998), p. 185.

49. Adam Hochschild, *King Leopold's Ghost: A Story of Greed, Terror, and Heroism in Colonial Africa* (Boston and New York: Houghton Mifflin, 1998), p. 123.

50. Ibid., p. 119.

51. Ibid.

52. F. K. Ekechi, "Colonialism and Christianity in West Africa: The Igbo Case, 1900–1915," *Journal of African History* 12, no. 1 (1971): 103.

53. Ibid., p. 107.

54. Ibid., p. 110.

55. Ibid., p. 113.

56. Shobana Shankar, "Medical Missionaries and Modernizing Emirs in Colonial Hausaland: Leprosy Control and Native Authority in the 1930s," *Journal of African History* 48, no. 1 (2007): 45.

57. Ibid., p. 48.

58. Hochschild, *King Leopold's Ghost*, p. 133.

59. "White Christian Genocidal Crusades (Holy War), Imperialism, and Colonialism in Iraq," YouTube, November 18, 2012, http://www.youtube.com/watch?v=hxpIKFEXJF4 (accessed February 14, 2014).

60. Charles H. Kraft, *Anthropology for Christian Witness* (Maryknoll, NY: Orbis Books, 2009 [1996]); Paul G. Hiebert, *Anthropological Insights for Missionaries* (Grand Rapids, MI: Baker Book House, 1985).

61. Hiebert, *Anthropological Insights*, p. 10.

62. Claire McLisky, "Professions of Christian Love: Letters of Courtship Between Missionaries-To-Be Daniel Matthews and Janet Johnston," in Amanda Barry, Joanna Cruickshank, Andrew Brown-May and Patricia Grimshaw, eds., *Evangelists of Empire? Missionaries in Colonial History* (Melbourne: University of Melbourne eScholarship Research Centre, 2008), p. 175.

Chapter 8. The Slave Is the Owner's Property: Christianity and the Savagery of Slavery

1. Peter Kolchin, *American Slavery 1619–1877*, 2nd ed. (New York: Hill and Wang, 2003), pp. 57–59. Native Americans were first conscripted into service as slaves. Writes Kolchin: "Indians also served as slaves, at first usually victims of military defeat or kidnapping but subsequently also bought and sold on the open market." Kolchin tells us that Columbus complained they refused to work properly because the men considered agricultural work to be "women's work," which they were not accustomed to. They also "used their familiarity with the terrain to escape and conspire against their captors. Because it has historically been difficult to enslave people on their home turf, the English found it convenient to export Indians captured in battle rather than hold them locally." Ultimately, however, "the policy of killing the Indians or driving them away from white settlements proved incompatible with their widespread employment as slaves." Ibid., pp. 7–8.

Irish people were also used and abused as slaves in the New World (my ancestry is Irish, so it is personal with me). In an online commentary concerning the book *White Cargo: The Forgotten History of Britain's White Slaves in America*, written by Don Jordan and Michael Walsh (New York: New York University Press, 2008), John Martin of the Montreal-based Center for Research and Globalization points this fact out:

> The Irish slave trade began when James II sold 30,000 Irish prisoners as slaves to the New World. His Proclamation of 1625 required Irish political prisoners be sent overseas and sold to English settlers in the West Indies. . . . Ireland quickly became the biggest source of human livestock for English merchants. The majority of the early slaves to the New World were actually white. . . . From 1641 to 1652, over 500,000 Irish were killed by the English and another 300,000 were sold as slaves. Ireland's population fell from about 1,500,000 to 600,000 in one single decade. Families were ripped apart as the British did not allow Irish dads to take their wives and children with them across the Atlantic. This led to a helpless population of homeless women and

children. Britain's solution was to auction them off as well. . . . [F]rom the
17th and 18th centuries, Irish slaves were nothing more than human cattle.

See "The Irish Slave Trade—The Forgotten 'White' Slaves," Global research, January
27, 2013, http://www.globalresearch.ca/the-irish-slave-trade-the-forgotten-white
-slaves/31076 (accessed July 2, 2014). Some Europeans came voluntarily as indentured slaves for a period of time as payment for transport. However, writes Kolchin,
"during their indenture, servants were essentially slaves, under the complete authority
of their masters; masters could (and readily did) apply corporal punishment to servants, forbid them to marry, and sell them (for the duration of their terms) to others.
Ibid., p. 9. English convicts were also used as slaves in America.

    2. John Carey, ed., *Eyewitness to History* (Cambridge: Harvard University
Press, 1988), pp. 318–19.

    3. Henry Bibb, *Narrative of the Life and Adventures of Henry Bibb, an Amer-
ican Slave* (Qontro Classic Books, 2010), pp. 107 –11, emphasis mine.

    4. Frederick Douglass, *Narrative of the Life of Frederick Douglass, An Amer-
ican Slave*, in *The Norton Anthology of World Masterpieces*, Vol. 2, 6th ed. (New York:
W. W. Norton and Company, 1992), p. 765.

    5. Douglass, *Narrative*, p. 785.

    6. John Stott, *Decisive Issues Facing Christians Today* (Old Tappan, NJ:
Fleming H. Revel Company, 1990), p. 209. Emphasis mine.

    7. Christopher Hitchens, *God Is Not Great: How Religion Poisons Everything*
(New York: Twelve Books, 2007), p. 180.

    8. Kolchin, *American Slavery*, p. 61.

    9. Ibid., p. 95.

    10. "Cotton Gin" *Wikipedia*, http://en.wikipedia.org/wiki/Cotton_gin (accessed
June 30, 2014).

    11. Alvin C. Plantinga, *God, Freedom, and Evil* (Grand Rapids, MI: Eerdmans,
1974).

    12. Michael Peterson, *Evil and the Christian God* (Grand Rapids, MI: Baker,
1982); Bruce Little, "God and Gratuitous Evil," in Chad Meister and James K. Dew
Jr., eds., *God and Evil: The Case for God in a World Filled with Pain* (Downers Grove,
IL: IVP Books, 2013), pp. 38–49; and William Hasker, *The Triumph of God Over
Evil: Theodicy for a World of Suffering* (Downers Grove, IL: IVP Academic, 2008).
For my critiques of this view see my blog post, "Bruce Little on 'God and Gratuitous
Suffering'" at my blog *Debunking Christianity*, http://debunkingchristianity.blogspot
.com/2013/04/bruce-little-on-god-and-gratuitous-evil.html.

    13. Rodney Stark, chapter 4, "God's Justice: The Sin of Slavery," in *For the*

Glory of God: How Monotheism Led to Reformations, Science, Witch-Hunts and the End of Slavery (Princeton, NJ: Princeton University Press, 2003), pp. 291–365.

14. Paul Copan "Is Yahweh a Moral Monster? The New Atheists and Old Testament Ethics," *Philosophia Christi* 10 (2008): 7–37, http://www.epsociety.org/library/articles.asp?pid=45 (accessed June 30, 2014); Paul Copan, chapter 19, "Doesn't the Bible Condone Slavery," in *That's Just Your Interpretation: Responding to Skeptics Who Challenge Your Faith* (Grand Rapids, MI: Baker Books, 2001), pp. 171–78; Paul Copan, chapters 12–14, "Warrant for Trafficking in Humans as Farm Equipment," parts 1–3, in *Is God a Moral Monster? Making Sense of the Old Testament God* (Grand Rapids, MI: Baker Books, 2011) pp. 124–57.

15. Ben Witherington III, *The Letters to Philemon, the Colossians, and Ephesians: A Socio-Rhetorical Commentary on the Captivity Epistles* (Grand Rapids, MI: Eerdmans, 2007); Ben Witherington III, "Was Paul a Pro-Slavery Chauvinist? Making Sense of Paul's Seemingly Mixed Moral Messages," *Bible Review* 20 (April 2004), pp. 8–44. Richard A. Horsley, *1 Corinthians* (Nashville: Abingdon Press, 1998); Richard A. Horsley, "The Slave Systems of Classical Antiquity and their Reluctant Recognition by Modern Scholars," in Allen D. Callahan, Richard A. Horsley, and Abraham Smith, eds., *Slavery in Text and Interpretation* (*Semeia* 83/84; Atlanta, GA: Scholars Press, 1998), pp. 19–66.

16. Hector Avalos, chapter 8, "Yahweh Is a Moral Monster," in John Loftus, ed., *The Christian Delusion: Why Faith Fails* (Amherst, NY: Prometheus Books, 2010), pp. 209–36; Hector Avalos, "Slavery, Abolitionism, and the Ethics of Biblical Scholarship: Reflections about Ethical Deflections," The Bible and Interpretation, http://www.bibleinterp.com/articles/ava358013.shtml (accessed June 30, 2014); and especially Hector Avalos, *Slavery, Abolitionism, and the Ethics of Biblical Scholarship* (Sheffield, UK: Sheffield Phoenix Press, 2011).

17. Thom Stark, "Is God a Moral Compromiser? A Critical Review of Paul Copan's 'Is God a Moral Monster?'" 2nd edition, Religion at the Margins, http://religionatthemargins.com/2011/07/the-real-second-edition-is-god-a-moral-compromiser-a-critical-review-of-paul-copans-is-god-a-moral-monster/ (accessed June 30, 2014).

18. Paul Copan, chapter 19, "Doesn't the Bible Condone Slavery," in *That's Just Your Interpretation: Responding to Skeptics Who Challenge Your Faith* (Grand Rapids, MI: Baker Books, 2001), pp. 171–78.

19. Hector Avalos (*Slavery, Abolitionism, and the Ethics of Biblical Scholarship*, p. 61) argues, "Once we examine those primary Near Eastern sources, we do not find much that is new in Christianity, and we find many Near Eastern advantages that the Bible did not offer slaves. . . . If Christianity made any advances, it would not be because it was original, but because it reverted to 'pagan' practices that preceded it."

20. Copan, *Is God a Moral Monster?* p. 132.

21. Ibid., p. 125.

22. Stark, "Is God a Moral Compromiser?" p. 171

23. Ibid., p. 173.

24. Avalos, *Slavery, Abolitionism, and the Ethics of Biblical Scholarship*, p. 86.

25. Ibid., pp. 86–87.

26. Ibid., p. 64.

27. Stark, "Is God a Moral Compromiser?" p. 168.

28. Copan, *Is God a Moral Monster?* p. 153.

29. Avalos, *Slavery, Abolitionism, and the Ethics of Biblical Scholarship*, p. 138.

30. Ibid., p. 97.

31. Ibid., p. 98

32. Ibid., p. 110.

33. Willard M. Swartley, chapter 1, "The Bible and Slavery," in *Slavery, Sabbath, War, and Women: Case Issues in Biblical Interpretation* (Scottdale, PA: Herald Press, 1983), pp. 31–64. To read the proslavery arguments first hand, see E. N. Elliott, ed. *Cotton Is King, and Pro-Slavery Arguments Comprising the Writings of Hammond, Harper, Christy, Stringfellow, Hodge, Bledsoe, and Cartrwright on This Important Subject* (1860), online at https://archive.org/details/cottoniskingpros00elli (accessed June 30, 2014). See also Paul Finkelman, ed., *Defending Slavery: Proslavery Thought in the Old South: A Brief History with Documents* (Boston/New York: Bedford/St. Martin's, 2003).

34. This short speech can be read online at Bartleby.com, http://www.bartleby.com/124/pres32.html (accessed June 30, 2014).

35. This is what I have argued before, what I call the *Problem of Divine Miscommunication*. See especially chapter 7, "What We Have Here Is a Failure to Communicate," in John Loftus, ed., *The Christian Delusion: Why Faith Fails* (Amherst, NY: Prometheus Books, 2010), pp. 181–206.

36. Steven B. Cowan and Terry L. Wilder, *In Defense of the Bible: A Comprehensive Apologetic for the Authority of Scripture* (Nashville, TN: B & H Academic, 2013). I have reviewed selected chapters of this book on my blog *Debunking Christianity*, http://debunkingchristianity.blogspot.com/search/label/Defending%20the%20 Bible (accessed June 30, 2014).

37. Douglas Groothuis, *Christian Apologetics: A Comprehensive Case for Biblical Faith* (Downers Grove, IL: IVP Academic, 2011).

38. Sam Harris, *Letter to a Christian Nation* (New York: Alfred A. Knopf, 2006), p. 18.

39. Avalos, *Slavery, Abolitionism, and the Ethics of Biblical Scholarship*, p. 1.

40. Ibid., p. 4.

41. Ibid., p. 19.

42. Ibid., p. 17.

Chapter 9. Christianity and the Rise of American Democracy

1. Letter from John Adams to Thomas Jefferson, June 28, 1813, in Lester J. Cappon, ed., *The Adams-Jefferson Letters: The Complete Correspondence between Thomas Jefferson and Abigail and John Adams* (Chapel Hill: University of North Carolina Press, 1988), pp. 338–40.

2. Ibid.

3. "Christian Amendment," *Wikipedia*, http://www.http://en.wikipedia.org/wiki/Christian_amendment (accessed July 2, 2014).

4. John Adams, *A Defence of the Constitutions of Government of the United States of America*, 3 vols. (London: John Stockdale, 1794), preamble.

5. Ibid.

Part Three: Scientific Harms

Chapter 10. The Dark Ages

1. As a result, almost the only bronze art and equipment we now have from the Roman era we have only because it fell to the bottom of the sea before Christians could get their grubby little hands on it, e.g., Jo Marchant, *Decoding the Heavens: Solving the Mystery of the World's First Computer* (London: William Heinemann, 2008); or they did get their grubby little hands on it, and all we can look at now are the holes left by the looting, e.g., Joseph Noble and Derek de Solla Price, "The Water Clock in the Tower of the Winds," *American Journal of Archaeology* 72, no. 4 (October 1968): 345–55.

2. Reviel Netz, *The Archimedes Codex: How a Medieval Prayer Book Is Revealing the True Genius of Antiquity's Greatest Scientist* (Philadelphia: Da Capo Press, 2007).

3. Theodore Mommsen, "Petrarch's Conception of the 'Dark Ages,'" *Speculum* 17, no. 2 (1942): 226–42. p. 228.

4. Ibid.

5. Ibid.

6. Richard Carrier, "Christianity Was Not Responsible for Modern Science," in John Loftus, ed., *The Christian Delusion: Why Faith Fails* (Amherst, NY: Prometheus Books, 2010), pp. 396–419.

7. Richard Carrier, "Christianity and the Rise of American Democracy," this volume.

8. Chris Wickham, *The Inheritance of Rome: A History of Europe from 400 to 1000* (New York: Viking, 2009), p. 9.

9. Bryan Ward-Perkins, *The Fall of Rome and the End of Civilization* (New York: Oxford University Press, 2005); Michael McCormick, *Origins of the European Economy: Communications and Commerce A.D. 300–900* (New York: Cambridge University Press, 2001), pp. 25–122, and following.

10. Peter Sarris, *Empires of Faith: The Fall of Rome to the Rise of Islam, 500–700* (New York: Oxford University Press, 2011), pp. 75–76 (pp. 73–82 discusses the many evidences of this decline).

11. Ward-Perkins, *Fall of Rome*, p. 183.

12. Ibid., pp. 87, 183 (cf. pp. 87–120 and 182–83).

13. Ibid., p. 183.

14. Eltjo Buringh and Jan Luiten van Zanden, "Charting the 'Rise of the West': Manuscripts and Printed Books in Europe, A Long-Term Perspective from the Sixth through Eighteenth Centuries," *Journal of Economic History* 69, no. 2 (2009): 409–445 (cf. esp. p. 416, table 1).

15. For some analysis of this evidence, see Francois de Callatay, "The Greco-Roman Economy in the Super Long Run: Lead, Copper, and Shipwrecks," *Journal of Roman Archaeology* 18, no. 1 (2005): 361–72, and Paul Erdkamp, *The Grain Market in the Roman Empire: A Social, Political, and Economic Study* (New York: Cambridge University Press, 2005). See the comparative summaries in Simon Hornblower and Antony Spawforth, eds., *The Oxford Classical Dictionary*, 3rd ed. (Oxford: Oxford University Press, 1996), in s.v. "technology" (1478), "agriculture, Roman" (45–47), "aqueducts" (133), etc. On, e.g., the equally sad decline in artistic sophistication, quality, capability, and output: Jas Elsner, *Art and the Roman Viewer: The Transformation of Art from the Pagan World to Christianity* (New York: Cambridge University Press, 1995); similarly for literature, Peter Harrison, *Bible, Protestantism, and the Rise of Natural Science* (New York: Cambridge University Press, 1998).

16. Besides, e.g., Noble and de Solla Price, "The Water Clock in the Tower of the Winds," and Netz, *The Archimedes Codex*, see Ann Hyland, *Equus: The Horse in the Roman World* (New Haven, CT: Yale University Press, 1990); Philippe Leveau,

"The Barbegal Water Mill in Its Environment: Archaeology and the Economic and Social History of Antiquity," *Journal of Roman Archaeology* 9 (1996): 137–53; Pliny the Elder, *Natural History* 18.48.172–173 (heavy-wheeled plough drawn by multiple teams and turning the soil); etc. Medievalists are often incredibly uninformed as to how advanced Greco-Roman technology was before the Dark Ages (and thus how much knowledge was lost): John Oleson, ed., *The Oxford Handbook of Engineering and Technology in the Classical World* (Oxford: Oxford University Press, 2008); Örjan Wikander, ed., *Handbook of Ancient Water Technology* (Leiden: Brill, 2000); Kevin Greene, "Technological Innovation and Economic Progress in the Ancient World," *Economic History Review* 53, no. 1 (February 2000): 29–59; M. J. T. Lewis, *Millstone and Hammer: The Origins of Water Power* (Hull: University of Hull, 1997); Tracey Rihll, *The Catapult: A History* (Yardley, PA: Westholme, 2007); etc. Essential introductory reading on how ignorant medievalists are includes Kevin Greene, "Technology and Innovation in Context: The Roman Background to Mediaeval and Later Developments," *Journal of Roman Archaeology* 7 (1994): 22–33, and "Technological Innovation and Economic Progress in the Ancient World: M. I. Finley Reconsidered," *Economic History Review* 53, no. 1 (February 2000): 29–59, along with Andrew Wilson, "Machines, Power, and the Ancient Economy," *Journal of Roman Studies* 92 (2002): 1–32.

17. Mommsen, "Petrarch's Conception of the 'Dark Ages,'" p. 242.

18. For this and subsequent claims in this paragraph see my summary (and references to the scholarship) in Richard Carrier, *Not the Impossible Faith: Why Christianity Didn't Need a Miracle to Succeed* (Raleigh, NC: Lulu, 2009), pp. 435–40 (w. p. 447 n. 32).

19. Carrier, "Christianity Was Not Responsible for Modern Science," pp. 412–14. That entire chapter documents the fact that these three essential values were all *pagan* values, so Christendom did not merely not conceive of them, it deliberately abandoned them. On the quite contrary Christian epistemic values: Carrier, *Not the Impossible Faith*, pp. 329–68, 385–406. On early Christian hostility to curiosity, dethronement of empiricism, and disinterest in progress generally (and eventual return to these pagan ideas over a thousand years later), see Neil Kenny, *The Uses of Curiosity in Early Modern France and German*y (New York: Oxford University Press, 2004), and *Curiosity in Early Modern Europe* (Wiesbaden: Harrassowitz, 1998); Peter Harrison, *The Bible, Protestantism, and the Rise of Natural Science* (Cambridge: Cambridge University Press, 1998), and "Curiosity: Forbidden Knowledge, and the Reformation of Natural Philosophy in Early Modern England," *Isis* 92, no. 2 (June 2001): 265–90; Lorraine Daston, *Wonders and the Order of Nature, 1150–1750* (New York: Zone Books, 1998); William Eamon, *Science and the Secrets of Nature* (Princeton,

NJ: Princeton University Press, 1996); G. E. R. Lloyd, *Greek Science after Aristotle* (New York: W.W. Norton, 1973), pp. 167–71; and Marshall Clagett, *Greek Science in Antiquity* (Salem, NH: Ayer, 1955), pp. 118–82. More evidence will be summarized in Richard Carrier, *The Scientist in the Early Roman Empire* (forthcoming).

Chapter 11. The Christian Abuse of the Sanctity of Life

1. "De Corona," reprinted in *Ante-Nicene Fathers*, vol. 3, ed. Alexander Roberts, James Donaldson, and A. Cleveland Coxe; trans. S. Thewall (Buffalo, NY: Christian Literature Publishing Co., 1885.) Revised and edited for New Advent website by Kevin Knight, http://www.newadvent.org/fathers/0304.htm (accessed January 12, 2014).

2. Augustine, *On Free Choice of the Will*, trans. Anna S. Benjamin and L. H. Hackstaff (Indianapolis: Bobbs-Merrill,1964), pp. 11–12.

3. Thomas Aquinas, *Summa Theologica*, II-II, Q. 64.

4. Ibid.

5. Pope John Paul II, *The Gospel of Life* (New York: Random House, 1995), p. 102.

6. Southern Baptist Convention, "Position Statement on Sanctity of Life," http://www.sbc.net/aboutus/pssanctity.asp (accessed January 12, 2014).

7. Pope Pius XII, "Address to International Congress of Anesthesiologists," November 24, 1957, http://www.lifeissues.net/writers/doc/doc_31resuscitation.html (accessed February 22, 2014).

8. 70 N.J. 510, 355 A.2d 647 (N.J. 1976).

9. C. Everett Koop, *The Right to Live; The Right to Die* (Wheaton, IL: Tyndale House, 1976), p. 105.

10. Ibid., p. 111.

11. See Alan Meisel, "The Legal Consensus about Forgoing Life-Sustaining Treatment: Its Status and Its Prospects," *Kennedy Institute of Ethics Journal* 2 (1992): 309–45.

12. Sy Mukherjee, "Massachusetts Voters Reject Physician-Assisted Suicide Initiative," November 7, 2012, http://thinkprogress.org/health/2012/11/07/1160171/massachusetts-death-with-dignity/ (accessed January 31, 2014).

13. See *Oregon Death with Dignity Act*, Oregon Revised Statutes (2003) 127.800–995. The Washington and Vermont statutes are patterned on the Oregon statute.

14. Oregon Division of Public Health, *Fifteenth Annual Report on Death with Dignity Act* (2013), p. 1. This report is available at http://public.health.oregon.gov/ProviderPartnerResources/EvaluationResearch/DeathwithDignityAct/Pages/ar-index.aspx (accessed February 22, 2014).

15. Neil M. Gorsuch, *The Future of Assisted Suicide and Euthanasia* (Princeton,

NJ: Princeton University Press, 2006), p. 66. Gorsuch is now a federal appellate judge, having been appointed to the bench by George W. Bush. Note that to give the sanctity-of-life principle a secular coloring, he refers to it as the inviolability-of-life-principle.

16. Ibid.

17. See Tom L. Beauchamp and James F. Childress, *Principles of Biomedical Ethics*, 5th ed. (New York: Oxford University Press, 2001), p. 129.

18. Gorsuch, *Future of Assisted Suicide*, p. 66.

19. Samson's death is described in Judges 16:25–30.

20. Augustine, *City of God* (trans. Henry Bettenson), 1.21.

21. See, for example, Joseph Boyle, "Sanctity of Life and Suicide: Tensions and Developments within Common Morality," in Baruch A. Brody, ed., *Suicide and Euthanasia* (Dordrecht, Netherlands: Kluwer, 1989), pp. 221–50, esp. p. 232.

22. Ibid., pp. 236–38.

23. Gorsuch, *Future of Assisted Suicide*, p. 158.

24. A distinction is sometimes made between a preimplantation embryo and a postimplantation embryo. Similarly, divisions can be made among various stages of fetal development. For our purposes, we can ignore these distinctions.

25. Lisa Sowell Cahill, "Abortion: Religious Traditions, Roman Catholic Perspectives," in Warren T. Reich, ed., *Encyclopedia of Bioethics*(New York: Simon & Schuster Macmillan, 1995), p. 31.

26. Ibid.

27. President's Council on Bioethics, *Human Cloning and Human Dignity* (New York: Public Affairs, 2002), p. 177.

28. Human Embryo Research Panel, National Institutes of Health, *Report of the Human Embryo Research Panel* (Bethesda, MD: NIH, 1994), 1: 9.

29. President's Council on Bioethics, *Monitoring Stem Cell Research* (Washington, DC: President's Council on Bioethics, 2004), p. 88.

30. Some passages in this essay are borrowed from chapters three and seven of my work *Future Bioethics: Overcoming Taboos, Myths, and Dogmas* (Amherst, NY: Prometheus Books, 2008).

Chapter 12. The Gender Binary and LGBTI People: Religious Myth and Medical Malpractice

1. "Public's Views on Human Evolution," Pew Research Religion and Public Life Project, December 30, 2013, http://www.pewforum.org/2013/12/30/publics-views-on-human-evolution/ (accessed December 31, 2013).

2. Elizabeth Reis, *Bodies in Doubt: An American History of Intersex* (Baltimore: Johns Hopkins University Press, 2009), p. 2.

3. Genesis 19:1–8.

4. Leviticus 20:13.

5. LGBT Issues Committee of the Group for the Advancement of Psychiatry (GAP), "The History of Psychiatry and Homosexuality," *LGBT Mental Health Syllabus*, http://www.aglp.org/gap/1_history/#declassification (accessed December 22, 2013).

6. Alfred C .Kinsey, W. B. Pomeroy, and C. E. Martin, *Sexual Behavior in the Human Male* (Philadelphia: W. B. Saunders, 1948).

7. Alfred C. Kinsey et al., *Sexual Behavior in the Human Female* (Philadelphia: W. B. Saunders, 1953).

8. C. S. Ford and F. A. Beach, *Patterns of Sexual Behavior (*New York: Harper and Row, 1951).

9. Evelyn Hooker, "The Adjustment of the Male Overt Homosexual," *Journal of Projective Techniques* 21 (1957): 18–31.

10. Bruce Bagemihl, *Biological Exuberance: Animal Homosexuality and Natural Diversity* (New York: St. Martin's Press, 1999); Nathan Bailey and Marlene Zuk, "Same-Sex Sexual Behavior and Evolution," *Trends in Ecology and Evolution* 24 (2009): 439–46.

11. "A Map of Gender-Diverse Cultures," *Independent Lens*, http://www.pbs.org/independentlens/two-spirits/map.html (accessed December 14, 2013); Meggie Palmer, "Being Transgender in the Tiwi Islands," *SBS*, September 18, 2013, http://www.sbs.com.au/news/article/2013/09/17/being-transgender-tiwi-islands (accessed December 14, 2013).

12. Milton Diamond, "Clinical Implications of the Organizational and Activational Effects of Hormones," *Hormones and Behavior* 55 (2009): 621–32.

13. Veronica Drantz, "Intersex People: What You Should Know and Why You Should Care," *Science and Sexuality: The Biology of Sexual Identity, Sexual Orientation, and Intersexuality*, June 17, 2011, http://drdrantz-sciencesexuality.blogspot.com/2011/06/slideshow-intersex-people-what-you.html (accessed July 7, 2014).

14. P. Dewing et al., "Sexually Dimorphic Gene Expression in Mouse Brain Precedes Gonadal Differentiation," *Molecular Brain Research* 118 (2003): 82–90.

15. Laura L. Carruth, Ingrid Reisert, and Arthur P. Arnold, "Sex Chromosome Genes Directly Affect Brain Sexual Differentiation," *Nature Neuroscience* 5 (2002): 933–34.

16. C. H. Phoenix et al., "Organizing Action of Prenatally Administered Testosterone Propionate on the Tissues Mediating Mating Behavior in the Female Guinea Pig," *Endocrinology* 65 (1959): 369–82.

17. Lauren A. O'Connell and Hans A. Hofmann, "The Vertebrate Mesolimbic Reward System and Social Behavior Network: A Comparative Synthesis," *Journal of Comparative Neurology* 519, no. 18 (2011): 3599–3639; Lauren A. O'Connell and Hans A. Hofmann, "Genes, Hormones, and Circuits: An Integrative Approach to Study the Evolution of Social Behavior," *Frontiers in Neuroendocrinology* 32, no. 3 (2011): 320–35.

18. John Money, "Hermaphroditism, Gender, and Precocity in Hyperadreno-corticism: Psychologic Findings," *Bulletin of the Johns Hopkins Hospital* 96 (1955): 253–64.

19. Milton Diamond, "A Critical Evaluation of the Ontogeny of Human Sexual Behavior," *Quarterly Review of Biology* 40 (1965): 147–75.

20. John Colapinto, *As Nature Made Him—The Boy Who Was Raised As a Girl* (New York: HarperCollins, 2000).

21. John Money, *Man and Woman, Boy and Girl: The Differentiation and Dimorphism of Gender Identity from Conception to Maturity* (Baltimore: Johns Hopkins University Press, 1972).

22. H. G. Beh and M. Diamond, "An Emerging Ethical and Medical Dilemma: Should Physicians Perform Sex Assignment on Infants with Ambiguous Genitalia?" *Michigan Journal of Gender and Law* 7 (2000): 1–63.

23. Milton Diamond and H. Keith Sigmundson, "Sex Reassignment at Birth: A Long Term Review and Clinical Implications," *Archives of Pediatric and Adolescent Medicine* 151 (1997): 298–304.

24. Reis, *Bodies in Doubt*, p. 137.

25. Sharon E. Preves, *Intersex and Identity—The Contested Self* (New Brunswick, NJ: Rutgers University Press, 2003), p. 139.

26. D. Cappon, C. Ezrin, and P. Lynes, "Psychosexual Identification (Psychogender) in the Intersexed," *Canadian Psychiatric Association Journal* 4 (1959): 90–106.

27. Milton Diamond and Linda Ann Watson, "Androgen Insensitivity Syndrome and Klinefelter's Syndrome: Sex and Gender Considerations" *Child and Adolescent Psychiatric Clinics of North America* 13 (2004): 623–40.

28. M. Hines, C. Brook, and G. S. Conway, "Androgen and Psychosexual Development Core Gender Identity, Sexual Orientation, and Recalled Childhood Gender Role Behavior in Women and Men with Congenital Adrenal Hyperplasia (CAH)," *Journal of Sex Research* 41 (2004): 75–81.

29. Rosemary C. Veniegas, "Biological Research on Women's Sexual Orientations: Evaluating the Scientific Evidence," *Journal of Social Issues* (2000).

30. H. F. Meyer-Bahlburg et al., "Sexual Orientation in Women with Classical

or Non-Classical Congenital Adrenal Hyperplasia as a Function of Degree of Prenatal Androgen Excess," *Archives of Sexual Behavior* 1 (2008): 85–99.

31. William G. Reiner and John P. Gearhart, "Discordant Sexual Identity in Some Genetic Males with Cloacal Exstrophy Assigned to Female Sex at Birth," *New England Journal of Medicine* 350 (2004): 333–41.

32. J. N. Zhou et al., "A Sex Difference in the Human Brain and Its Relation to Transsexuality," *Nature* 378 (1995): 68–70.

33. Frank Kruijver et al., "Male-to-Female Transsexuals Have Female Neuron Numbers in a Limbic Nucleus," *Journal of Clinical Endocrinology and Metabolism* 85 (2000): 2034–41.

34. L. Hare et al., "Androgen Receptor Repeat Length Polymorphism Associated with Male-to-Female Transsexualism," *Biological Psychiatry* 65, no. 1 (2009): 93–96.

35. Eva-Katrin Bentz et al., "A Polymorphism of the CYP17 Gene Related to Sex Steroid Metabolism Is Associated with Female-to-Male But Not Male-to-Female Transsexualism," *Obstetrical and Gynecological Survey* 63, no. 12 (2008): 775–77.

36. Simon LeVay, "A Difference in Hypothalamic Structure between Heterosexual and Homosexual Men," *Science* 253 (1991): 1034–37.

37. William Byne et al., "The Interstitial Nuclei of the Human Anterior Hypothalamus: An Investigation of Variation with Sex, Sexual Orientation, and HIV Status," *Hormones and Behavior* 40 (2001): 86–92; Alicia Garcia-Falgueras and Dick F Swaab, "A Sex Difference in the Hypothalamic Uncinate Nucleus: Relationship to Gender Identity," *Brain* 131, no. 12 (2008): 3115–17.

38. C. E. Roselli et al., "The Volume of a Sexually Dimorphic Nucleus in the Ovine Medial Preoptic Area/Anterior Hypothalamus Varies with Sexual Partner Preference," *Endocrinology* 145 (2004): 478–83.

39. I. Savic and P. Lindstrom, "LET and MRI Show Differences in Cerebral Asymmetry and Functional Connectivity between Homo- and Heterosexual Subjects," *Proceedings of the National Academy of Sciences* 105 (2008): 9403–9408.

40. I Savic et al., "Brain Response to Putative Pheromones in Homosexual Men," *Proceedings of the National Academy of Sciences* 102 (2005): 7356–61.

41. H. Berglund, P. Lindström, and I. Savic, "Brain Response to Putative Pheromones in Lesbian Women," *Proceedings of the National Academy of Sciences* 103 (2006): 8269–74.

42. D. H. Hamer et al., "Linkage between DNA Markers on the X Chromosome and Male Sexual Orientation," *Science* 261 (1993): 321–27; S.Hu et al., "Linkage between Sexual Orientation and Chromosome Xq28 in Males but Not in Females," *Nature Genetics* 11 (1995): 248–56.

43. A. M. L. Pattatucci and D. H. Hamer, "Development and Familiality of Sexual

Orientation in Females," *Behavior Genetics* 25 (1995): 407–20; J. M. Bailey and D. S. Benishay, "Familial Aggregation of Female Sexual Orientation," *American Journal of Psychiatry* 150 (1993): 272–77; J. M. Bailey, M. P. Dunne, and N. G. Martin, "Genetic and Environmental Influences on Sexual Orientation and Its Correlates in an Australian Twin Sample," *Journal of Personality and Social Psychology* 78 (2000): 524–36.

44. William R. Rice, Urban Friberg, and Sergey Gavrilets, "Homosexuality as a Consequence of Epigenetically Canalized Sexual Development," *Quarterly Review of Biology* 87, no. 4 (2012): 343–68.

45. A. Garcia-Falgueras and D. F. Swaab, "Sexual Hormones and the Brain: An Essential Alliance for Sexual Identity and Sexual Orientation," *Pediatric Neuroendocrinology* 17 (2010): 22–35.

46. Michael K. Lavers, "Queen Elizabeth Posthumously Pardons Alan Turing," *Washington Blade*, December 26, 2013, http://www.washingtonblade.com/2013/12/26/queen-elizabeth-posthumously-pardons-alan-turing/ (accessed December 31, 2013).

47. Dick F. Swaab and Alicia Garcia-Falgueras, "Sexual Differentiation of the Human Brain in Relation to Gender Identity and Sexual Orientation," *Functional Neurology* (January–March 2009).

48. "Diagnostic and Statistical Manual of Mental Disorders," *Wikipedia* http://en.wikipedia.org/wiki/Diagnostic_and_Statistical_Manual (accessed December 23, 2013).

49. "Stonewall riots," *Wikipedia*, http://en.wikipedia.org/wiki/Stonewall_riots (accessed December 27, 2013).

50. "Frank Kameny," *Wikipedia*, http://en.wikipedia.org/wiki/Frank_Kameny (accessed December 27, 2013).

51. "Barbara Gittings," *Wikipedia*, http://en.wikipedia.org/wiki/Barbara_Gittings (accessed December 27, 2013).

52. "John E. Fryer," *Wikipedia*, http://en.wikipedia.org/wiki/John_E._Fryer (accessed December 27, 2013).

53. "The History of Psychiatry and Homosexuality," *LGBT Mental Health Syllabus*, LGBT Issues Committee of the Group for the Advancement of Psychiatry (GAP), http://www.aglp.org/gap/1_history/#declassification (accessed December 22, 2013).

54. "Barbara Gittings."

55. "History of Psychiatry and Homosexuality."

56. Ibid.

57. World Medical Association, "WMA Statement on Natural Variations of Human Sexuality," adopted by the sixty-fourth General Assembly, Fortaleza, Brazil, October 2013, http://www.wma.net/en/30publications/10policies/s13/ (accessed December 28, 2013).

58. Tris Reid-Smith, "World's Top Psychiatrist Comes Out, Promises Stand

on 'Gay Cures,'" *GayStarNews*, November 27, 2013, http://www.gaystarnews.com/article/worlds-top-psychiatrist-comes-out-promises-stand-gay-cures271113 (accessed December 28, 2013).

59. Carrie Maxwell, "SPLC, Truth Wins Out Hold Meetings on Conversion Therapy," *Windy City Times* 27, no. 26 (April 18, 2012), p. 5.

60. "LDS Resources for Same-Sex Attraction," Evergreen International, http://www.evergreeninternational.org/ (accessed December 28, 2013).

61. P.A.T.H. Positive Alternatives to Homosexuality, http://www.pathinfo.org/ (accessed December 28, 2013).

62. Witness Ministries, http://www.witnessfortheworld.org/ (accessed December 28, 2013).

63. National Association for Research and Therapy of Homosexuality, http://www.narth.com/ (accessed December 28, 2013).

64. Zack Ford, "Catholic Celibacy Conference Will Include Trainings By Ex-Gay Therapists," *ThinkProgress*, July 15, 2013, http://thinkprogress.org/lgbt/2013/07/15/2303331/catholic-courage-ex-gay/ (accessed November 20, 2013).

65. "George Alan Rekers," *Wikipedia*, http://en.wikipedia.org/wiki/George_Alan_Rekers (accessed December 28, 2013).

66. Wayne Besen, "TWO Commends Former Exodus Lobbyist Randy Thomas for Apologizing to the LGBT Community," *Truth Wins Out*, July 23, 2013, http://www.truthwinsout.org/pressrelease/2013/07/36380/ (accessed November 20, 1013); "Randy Thomas, Former VP of Ex-Gay Group Exodus International, Apologizes to LGBT Community," *Huffpost Gay Voices*, July 25, 2013, http://www.huffingtonpost.com/2013/07/25/randy-thomas-exodus-apologizes-lgbt-community_n_3653634.html (accessed December 28, 2013).

67. "Exodus International," *Wikipedia*, http://en.wikipedia.org/wiki/Exodus_International (accessed December 28, 2013).

68. Restored Hope Network, http://www.restoredhopenetwork.com/ (accessed December 28, 2013).

69. Voice of the Voiceless, http://www.voiceofthevoiceless.info/ (accessed December 28, 2013).

70. Stephanie Pappa and Tia Ghose, "Gay Conversion Therapy: What You Should Know," LiveScience.com, August 19, 2013, http://news.yahoo.com/gay-conversion-therapy-know-201649505.html (accessed December 28, 2013).

71. Scott, "USA, California: Congresswoman Proposes National Ban on Reparative Therapy," *Gay Marriage Watch*, December 5, 2013, http://purpleunions.com/blog/2013/12/usa-california-congresswoman-proposes-national-ban-on-reparative-therapy.html (accessed December 6, 2013).

72. "Kenneth J. Zucker on Transsexualism," Transsexual Road Map, http://www.tsroadmap.com/info/kenneth-zucker.html (accessed December 18, 2008).

73. Y. G. Ansara and P. Hegarty, "Cisgenderism in Psychology: Pathologizing and Misgendering Children from 1999 to 2008," *Psychology and Sexuality* 3 (2012): 137–60.

74. Transgender Community, "Objection to DSM-V Committee Members on Gender Identity Disorder," Care2 Petition Site, http://www.thepetitionsite.com/2/objection-to-dsm-v-committee-members-on-gender-identity-disorders/ (accessed December 18, 2008).

75. Jenn Burleton, "DSM-V & Kenneth Zucker," TransActive TransMissions, May 10, 2008, http://transactive.blogspot.com/2008/05/dsm-v-kenneth-zucker.html (accessed December 18, 2008); Rea Carey, "Task Force Questions Critical Appointments to APA's Committee on Sexual and Gender Identity Disorders," *National Gay and Lesbian Task Force*, May 28, 2008, http://www.thetaskforce.org/press/releases/pr_052808 (accessed December 18, 2008).

76. Autumn Sandeen, "GID Reform Now Protest at Annual APA Meeting—Speaker Kelley Winters, Ph.D.," *Pam's House Blend*, May 24, 2009, http://pamshouseblend.firedoglake.com/2009/05/24/gid-reform-now-protest-at-annual-apa-meeting-speaker-kelley-winters-phd/ (accessed June 19, 2009).

77. Kelley Winters, "Request for APA Position Statements in Support of Human Dignity and Medical Care for Trans People," GID Reform Advocates, June 22, 2009, http://www.gidreform.org/200906APAstatementsA.pdf (accessed July 1, 2009).

78. G. De Cuypere, G. Knudson, and W. Bockting, "Response of the World Professional Association for Transgender Health," *International Journal of Transgenderism* 12 (2010): 119–23.

79. W. Parry, "Gender Dysphoria: DSM-5 Reflects Shift in Perspective on Gender Identity," *Huffington Post*, June 4, 2103, http://www.huffingtonpost.com/2013/06/04/gender-dysphoria-dsm-5_n_3385287.html?view=print&comm_ref=false (accessed June 27, 2013).

80. "Gender Dysphoria," American Psychiatric Association, http://www.dsm5.org/Documents/Gender%20Dysphoria%20Fact%20Sheet.pdf (accessed June 27, 2013).

81. J. Drescher and E. Haller, "Position Statement on Access to Care for Transgender and Gender Variant Individuals," *APA Caucus of Lesbian, Gay, and Bisexual Psychiatrists*, May 2012.

82. J. Drescher and E. Haller, "Position Statement on Discrimination against Transgender and Gender Variant Individuals," *APA Caucus of Lesbian, Gay, and Bisexual Psychiatrists*, May 2012.

83. Y. G. Ansara et al., "Response to the Proposed Psychiatric Diagnosis of 'Gender Dysphoria' and the Report of the American Psychiatric Association Task Force on the Treatment of 'Gender Identity Disorder,'" edited version: September 10, 2012. Ansara Online, http://ansaraonline.com/publications/apa_response_letter_2012 (accessed September 25, 2012).

84. M. C. Ristorucci, "Weill Medical College Says Poppa's Surgical Procedure Is Standard," *Transgender News*, October 5, 2010, http://www.cornellsun.com/section/news/content/2010/10/05/weill-medical-college-\says-poppas%E2%80%99-surgical-procedure-standard (accessed October 10, 2010).

85. Curtis E. Hinkle, "Solidarity with the Intersex Community," GoPetition, October 24, 2006, http://www.gopetition.com/petitions/solidarity-with-the-intersex-community.html (accessed July 2, 2008).

86. Max Beck, "Hermaphrodites with Attitude Take to the Streets," Intersex Society of North America, http://www.isna.org/books/chrysalis/beck (accessed January 19, 2014).

87. "News Release: American Academy of Pediatrics Position on Intersexuality," Intersex Society of North America, http://www.isna.org/books/chrysalis/aap (accessed January 19, 2014).

88. C. J. Migeon et al., "Ambiguous Genitalia with Perineoscrotal Hypospadias in 46,XY Individuals: Long-Term Medical, Surgical, and Psychosexual Outcome," *Pediatrics* 110 (2002): e31; B. Kohler et al., "DSD Network Working Group: Satisfaction with Genital Surgery and Sexual Life of Adults with XY Disorders of Sex Development: Results from the German Clinical Evaluation Study," *Journal of Clinical Endocrinology and Metabolism* 97, no. 2 (2012): 577–88.

89. Sarah Creighton et al., "Childhood Surgery for Ambiguous Genitalia: Glimpses of Practice Changes or More of the Same?" *Psychology and Sexuality* 5 (2013): 34–43.

90. P. A. Lee et al., "Consensus Statement on Management of Intersex Disorders," *Pediatrics* 118 (2006): 488–500.

91. Hinkle, "Solidarity with the Intersex Community."

92. "UN Leaders, Sport Stars and Activists Join Forces for Equality" (Video), Free and Equal, United Nations Human Rights Office, https://www.unfe.org/en/actions/human-rights-day-round-up (accessed December 18, 2013).

93. "Report of the Special Rapporteur on Torture and Other Cruel, Inhuman, or Degrading Treatment or Punishment, Juan E. Mendez," United Nations General Assembly Human Rights Council, http://www.ohchr.org/Documents/HRBodies/HRCouncil/RegularSession/Session22/A.HRC.22.53_English.pdf (accessed January 19, 2014).

94. Jessica Mason Pieklo, "Historic Lawsuit Claims Doctors Performed Unnecessary Surgery on Intersex Child," *RH Reality Check*, May 20, 2013, http://rhrealitycheck.org/article/2013/05/20/historic-lawsuit-claims-doctors-performed-unnecessary-surgery-on-intersex-child/ (accessed December 31, 2013).

95. J. Eisfeld, S. Gunther, and D. Shlasko, "The State of Trans* and Intersex Organizing: A Case for Increased Support for Growing but Underfunded Movements for Human Rights," (New York: Global Action for Trans* Equality and American Jewish World Service, 2013), pp. 5–6.

96. Committee on Lesbian, Gay, Bisexual, and Transgender Health Issues and Research Gaps and Opportunities, *The Health of Lesbian, Gay, Bisexual, and Transgender People: Building a Foundation for Better Understanding*, Institute of Medicine of the National Academies (Washington, DC: National Academies Press, 2011) p. 75, http://www.ncbi.nlm.nih.gov/books/NBK64806/pdf/TOC.pdf (accessed July 7, 2014).

97. Eisfeld et al., "State of Trans* and Intersex Organizing," pp. 4–5.

98. Ibid., pp. 5–6.

99. C. L. Minto et al., "XY Females: Revisiting the Diagnosis," *BJOG* 112 (2005): 1407–10.

100. C. Wiesemann et al., "Ethical Principles and Recommendations for the Medical Management of Differences of Sex Development (DSD)/Intersex in Children and Adolescents," *European Journal of Pediatrics* 169 (2010): 671–79.

101. Ruth P. McNair and Kelsey Hegarty, "Guidelines for the Primary Care of Lesbian, Gay, and Bisexual People: A Systematic Review," *Annals of Family Medicine* 8, no. 6 (2010): 533–41.

Chapter 13. Christianity Can Be Hazardous to Your Health

1. Richard Sloan, "Religion, Spirituality, and Medicine," *Lancet* 353, no. 9153 (1999): 664–67.

2. Walter Larrimore, "Providing Basic Spiritual Care for Patients: Should It Be the Exclusive Domain of Pastoral Professionals?" *American Family Physician* 63, no. 1 (2001): 36–41.

3. Richard Walden et al., "Effect of Environment on the Serum Cholesterol-Triglyceride Distribution among Seventh-Day Adventists," *American Journal of Medicine* 36 (1964): 269–76.

4. David Rosmarin et al., "A Test of Faith in God and Treatment: The Relationship of Belief in God to Psychiatric Treatment Outcomes," *Journal of Affective Disorders* 146, no. 3 (2013): 441–46.

5. Randolph Byrd, "Positive Therapeutic Effects of Intercessory Prayer in a Coronary Care Unit Population," *Southern Medical Journal* 81, no. 7 (1988): 826–29.

6. Kwang Cha, Daniel Wirth, and Rogerio Lobo, "Does Prayer Influence the Success of *In Vitro* Fertilization-Embryo Transfer?" *Journal of Reproductive Medicine* 46, no. 9 (2001): 781–87.

7. Bruce Flamm, "The Bizarre Columbia University 'Miracle' Saga Continues," *Skeptical Inquirer* 29, no. 2 (2005), online at http://www.csicop.org/si/show/bizarre _columbia_university_miracle_saga_continues/ (accessed July 9, 2014).

8. Leonard Leibovici, "Effects of Remote, Retroactive Intercessory Prayer on Outcomes in Patients with Bloodstream Infection: Randomized Controlled Trial," *British Medical Journal* 323, no. 7327 (2001): 1450–51.

9. "Studies on Intercessory Prayer," *Wikipedia*, http://en.wikipedia.org/wiki/ Studies_on_intercessory_prayer#Retroactive_intercessory_prayer (accessed July 9, 2014).

10. Statistics from "Lourdes," The Skeptic's Dictionary, http://skepdic.com/ lourdes.html (accessed July 9, 2014); Anatole France, quoted in Joe Nickell, "Examining Miracle Claims," The Secular Web, http://infidels.org/library/modern/joe _nickell/miracles.html (accessed July 9, 2014).

11. "Mother Theresa, *Wikipedia*, http://en.wikipedia.org/wiki/Mother_Teresa (accessed July 9, 2014).

12. Sloan, "Religion, Spirituality, and Medicine."

13. Richard Sloan, *Blind Faith: The Unholy Alliance of Religion and Medicine* (New York: St. Martin's Press, 2006).

14. Cameron Stauth, *In the Name of God: The True Story of the Fight to Save Children from Faith-Healing Homicide* (New York: St. Martin's Press, 2013), p. 56.

15. Mary Baker Eddy, quoted in "The Scientific Statement of Being and Correlative Scripture," Christian Science Quarterly Bible Lessons, http://christianscience .com/bible-lessons/related-information/for-church-services/the-scientific-statement-of -being-and-correlative-scripture (accessed July 9, 2014).

16. Seth Asser and Rita Swan, "Child Fatalities from Religion-Motivated Medical Neglect," *Pediatrics* 101, no. 4 (April 1998): 625–29.

17. Stauth, *In the Name of God.*

18. Ibid.

19. Ibid.

20. Ibid.

21. Private e-mail communication, November/December 2013.

22. Charles Jennings, "Measles among Religiously Exempt Persons" in Mark Dworkin, ed., *Cases in Field Epidemiology* (Burlington, MA: Jones and Bartlett Learning, 2011), pp. 83–89, available online at Google Books, http://books.google

.com/books?id=NmxO66FyRC0C&pg=PA84&lpg=PA84&dq=what+rash?+principia
+college+measles+outbreak&source=bl&ots=BczEdoiDbX&sig=Fay2pNXEkJfwdlS
XNwLhPQIcA3Q&hl=en&sa=X&ei=tCO8U_iYB8WBiwKMtYG4CQ&ved=0CBw
Q6AEwADgK#v=onepage&q=what%20rash%3F%20principia%20college%20
measles%20outbreak&f=false (accessed July 9, 2014).

23. "Measles—United States, 1994," United States Centers for Disease Control,
July 7, 1995, http://www.cdc.gov/mmwr/preview/mmwrhtml/00038118.htm (accessed
July 9, 2014).

24. Statistics for Ashland in Ryan Pfeil, "Ashland's Low Vaccination Rate
May Be Focus of Study," *Medford Mail Tribune*, December 28, 2011, http://www
.mailtribune.com/apps/pbcs.dll/article?AID=/20111228/NEWS/112280317 (accessed
July 9, 2014); statistics for Waldorf school in Hannah Dreier, "More Private Schools
Fall below Threshold for Immunizations," *San Jose Mercury News*, September 10,
2012, http://www.mercurynews.com/ci_21507188/more-private-schools-fall-below
-threshold-immunizations (accessed July 9, 2014).

25. Rita Swan, "Belief Exemptions Lead to Outbreaks of Vaccine-Preventable
Diseases," *Children's Healthcare Is a Legal Duty* 3 (2008): 1–6.

26. Lauren Silverman, "Texas Megachurch at Center of Measles Outbreak,"
September 1, 2013, National Public Radio, http://www.npr.org/2013/09/01/217746942/
texas-megachurch-at-center-of-measles-outbreak (accessed July 9, 2014).

27. Susan Donaldson James, "12-Pound Tumor Swallows Man's Face," ABC
News, http://abcnews.go.com/Health/man-lost-face-tumor-lifesaving-surgery-chicago
-doctor/story?id=12943815 (accessed July 9, 2014).

28. "Suicide and Violence: A to Z," They Should Not Have Died, November
23, 2010, http://theyshouldnothavedied.wordpress.com/ (accessed July 9, 2014);
Lawrence Wright, *Going Clear: Scientology, Hollywood, and the Prison of Belief*
(New York: Alfred A. Knopf, 2013).

29. "Database of Publicly Accused Priests in the United States," Bishop
Accountability.org, http://bishop-accountability.org/priestdb/PriestDBbydiocese.html
(accessed December 6, 2013).

30. "Death of Savita Halappanavar," *Wikipedia*, http://en.wikipedia.org/wiki/
Death_of_Savita_Halappanavar (accessed July 9, 2014).

31. Bob Brenzing, "Muskegon Woman Sues Catholic Bishops after Hospital Fails
to Treat Her Miscarriage," WZZM/*Detroit Free Press*, December 2, 2013, http://www
.wzzm13.com/news/article/274683/2/Muskegon-woman-sues-Catholic-bishops-after
-miscarriage (accessed December 5, 2013).

32. See "Stem Cell Controversy," Stem Cell Freaks, http://www.stemcellsfreak
.com/p/stem-cell-controversy.html (accessed July 9, 2014).

33. William Nolen, *Healing: A Doctor in Search of a Miracle* (New York: Random House, 1975).

34. James Randi, *The Faith Healers* (Amherst, NY: Prometheus Books, 1987).

35. "Benny Hinn: False Prophet!" Jesus-is-Savior.com, http://www.jesus-is -savior.com/False%20Doctrines/benny_hinn.htm (accessed December 5, 2013).

36. Vern Poythress, "Linguistic and Sociological Analyses of Modern Tongues-Speaking," *Westminster Theological Journal* 42, no. 2 (1980): 367–88.

37. James Randi, "Popoff's Still at It," James Randi Educational Foundation, http://www.randi.org/site/index.php/swift-blog/1660-popoffs-still-at-it.html (accessed December 5, 2013).

38. "Judge William Adams Beats Daughter for Using the Internet (update)," YouTube, http://www.youtube.com/watch?v=Wl9y3SIPt7o (accessed December 5, 2013).

39. Michael Pearl and Debi Pearl, *To Train Up a Child: Turning the Hearts of the Fathers to the Children* (Pleasantville, TN: No Greater Joy Ministries, 1994).

40. Customer review of *To Train Up a Child: Turning the Hearts of the Fathers to the Children*, Amazon.com, http://www.amazon.com/To-Train-Up-Child-children -ebook/product-reviews/B0038KA6GC?pageNumber=57 (accessed July 9, 2014).

41. Susan Newman, "Spanking Gone Too Far," *Psychology Today*, http://www .psychologytoday.com/blog/singletons/201111/spanking-gone-too-far (accessed December 5, 2013).

42. Kathryn Joyce, "Hana's Story," *Slate*, November 9, 2013,http://www.slate .com/articles/double_x/doublex/2013/11/hana_williams_the_tragic_death_of_an _ethiopian_adoptee_and_how_it_could.html (accessed July 9, 2014).

43. "Death of Lydia Schatz," *Wikipedia*, http://en.wikipedia.org/wiki/Death_of _Lydia_Schatz (accessed July 9, 2014).

44. Rachel, "Sean Paddock and 6 Siblings," Homeschooling's Invisible Children, May 5, 2013, http://hsinvisiblechildren.org/2013/05/05/sean-paddock-and-6-siblings/ (accessed July 9, 2014).

45. Alexandra Sifferlin, "How Eleven New York City Babies Contracted Herpes through Circumcision," *Time*, June 7, 2012, http://healthland.time.com/2012/06/07/ how-11-new-york-city-babies-contracted-herpes-through-circumcision/(accessed July 9, 2014).

Chapter 14. Christianity and the Environment

1. I'd like to thank Glen Sussman of Old Dominion University for his valuable comments on an early draft of this chapter.

2. IPCC, "Fourth Assessment Report: Climate Change 2007," 2007, available at http://www.ipcc.ch/publications_and_data/ar4/syr/en/mains1.html (accessed July 30, 2014).

3. Ibid.

4. Justin Gillis, "Climate Panel Cites Near Certainty on Warming," *New York Times*, August 19, 2013.

5. IPCC, "Climate Change 2013: The Physical Science Basis: Summary for Policymakers," 2013, p. 17.

6. Harvey Blatt, *America's Environmental Report Card: Are We Making the Grade?* (Cambridge, MA: MIT Press, 2005), p. 130.

7. Ibid., p. 9.

8. Naomi Oreskes, "Beyond the Ivory Tower: The Scientific Consensus on Climate Change," *Science* 306, no. 5702 (December 2004): 1686.

9. E. O. Wilson, *The Creation: An Appeal to Save Life on Earth* (New York: W. W. Norton and Company, 2006), p. 5.

10. World Meteorological Organization, "WMO Provisional Statement on Status of the Climate in 2013," available at http://www.wmo.int/pages/mediacentre/press_releases/documents/ProvisionalStatementStatusClimate2013.pdf (accessed July 31, 2014).

11. National Oceanic and Atmospheric Administration, "Global Analysis—November 2013," available at http://www.ncdc.noaa.gov/sotc/global/2013/11/ (accessed July 31, 2014).

12. Steven C. Sherwood, Sandrine Bony, and Jean-Louis Dufresne, "Spread in Model Climate Sensitivity Traced to Atmospheric Convective Mixing," *Nature* 505 (January 2014): 37–42.

13. Blatt, *America's Environmental Report Card*, p. 127.

14. Steven Chase, "Turf War with Russia Looms over Ottawa's Claim to Arctic Seabed," *Globe and* Mail, December 5, 2013, available at http://www.theglobeandmail.com/news/politics/turf-war-with-russia-looms-over-ottawas-claim-to-arctic-seabed/article15777123/ (accessed July 31, 2014).

15. IPCC, "Summary for Policymakers," in M. L. Perry, O. F. Canziani, J. P. Palutikof, P. J. van der Linden, and C. E. Hanon, eds., *Climate Change 2007: Impacts, Adaptations and Vulnerability. Contribution of Working Group II to the Fourth Assessment Report of the Intergovernmental Panel on Climate Change* (Cambridge: Cambridge University Press, 2007): 7–22, p. 9.

16. IPCC, "Climate Change 2013," p. 26.

17. Ibid., p. 14.

18. Joshua W. Busby, "Who Cares about the Weather? Climate Change and U.S. National Security," *Security Studies* 17, no. 3 (2008): 468–504, pp. 499–500.

19. Admiral Samuel J. Locklear III, quoted in Bryan Bender, "Chief of US Pacific Forces Calls Climate Biggest Worry," *Boston Globe*, March 9, 2013.

20. IPCC, "Climate Change 2013," p. 17.

21. Ibid., p. 26.

22. Naomi Oreskes and Erik M. Conway, *Merchants of Doubt: How a Handful of Scientists Obscured the Truth on Issues from Tobacco Smoke to Global Warming* (New York: Bloomsbury Press, 2010).

23. Barna Group, "Born again Christians Remain Skeptical, Divided about Global Warming," September 17, 2007, available at https://www.barna.org/barna -update/donors-cause/95-born-again-christians-remain-skeptical-divided-about-global -warming#.UswDwtDna00 (accessed July 31, 2014).

24. Barna Group, "Evangelicals Go 'Green' with Caution," September 22, 2008, available at https://www.barna.org/barna-update/culture/23-evangelicals-go-qgreenq -with-caution#.UswF0NDna00 (accessed July 31, 2014).

25. Ibid.

26. N. Smith and A. Leiserowitz, "American Evangelicals and Global Warming," *Global Environmental Change* 23, no. 5 (October 2013): 1009–17, p. 5.

27. Ibid., p. 5.

28. Ibid., p. 6.

29. Russ Rankin, "Majority of Pastors Doubt Global Warming, but Recycle at Church," LifeWay Research, April 15, 2013, available at http://www.lifeway.com/ Article/research-majority-of-pastors-doubt-global-warming-but-recycle-at-church (accessed July 31, 2014).

30. Steven F. Deaton, "Global Warming: A Biblical View," *Implanted Word*, available at http://www.implantedword.com/global-warming-a-biblical-view (accessed July 31, 2014).

31. Melinda Christian, "Global Warming in Perspective," *Answers* (October– December 2008): 84–89, p. 88.

32. Rick Santorum, quoted in Stephen Lacey, "Santorum's Incoherence: Manmade Global Warming Is a 'Hoax' But Using 'Science and Discovery' Makes Us Better Stewards," *Think Progress*, February 7, 2012, available at http://thinkprogress .org/romm/2012/02/07/420181/santorum-manmade-global-warming-hoax-science -stewards/ (accessed July 31, 2014).

33. Brian McCammack, "Hot Damned America: Evangelicalism and the Climate

Change Policy Debate," *American Quarterly* 59, no. 3 (September 2007): 645–68, p. 648.

34. CornwallAlliance,"TheCornwallDeclarationofEnvironmentalStewardship," available at http://www.cornwallalliance.org/2000/05/01/the-cornwall-declaration -on-environmental-stewardship/ (accessed July 31, 2014).

35. Cornwall Alliance, "Evangelical Declaration on Global Warming," available at http://www.cornwallalliance/articles/read/an-evangelical-declaration-on-global -warming (accessed July 31, 2014).

36. J. Arjan Wardekker, Arthur C. Petersen, and Jeroen P. van der Sluijs, "Ethics and Public Perception of Climate Change: Exploring the Christian Voices in the US Public Debate," *Global Environmental Change* 19 (2009): 512–21, p. 516.

37. Deaton, "Global Warming."

38. Ibid.

39. Rush Limbaugh, quoted in J. M. Green, "Belief in God: What's the Harm (Rush Limbaugh Edition)," *Debunking Christianity*, November 20, 2013, available at http://debunkingchristianity.blogspot.com/2013/11/belief-in-god-whats-harm-rush -limbaugh.html (accessed July 31, 2014).

40. Shimkus, quoted in Craig A. James, "Christian Beliefs Disqualify Congressman on Global Warming," *Religion Virus*, November 15, 2010, available at http://religionvirus.blogspot.com/2010/11/christian-beliefs-disqualify.html (accessed January 7, 2014).

41. James Inhofe, quoted in Brian Tashman, "James Inhofe Says the Bible Refutes Climate Change," *Right Wing Watch*, March 8, 2012, available at http://www .rightwingwatch.org/content/james-inhofe-says-bible-refutes-climate-change (accessed July 31, 2014).

42. James Inhofe, quoted in McCammack, "Hot Damned America," p. 655.

43. Ralph Hall, quoted in Matt Pearce, "U.S. Rep. Paul Broun: Evolution a Lie 'From the Pit of Hell,'" *Los Angeles Times*, October 7, 2012.

44. Joe Barton, quoted in Andrew Kaczynski, "Republican Congressman Cites Biblical Great Flood to Say Climate Change Isn't Man-Made," Buzzfeed, available at http://www.buzzfeed.com/andrewkaczynski/republican-congressman-cites-biblical -great-flood-to-say-cim (accessed July 31, 2014).

45. Katherine K. Wilkinson, "Climate's Salvation? Why and How American Evangelicals are Engaging with Climate Change," *Environment* 52 (2010): 47–57, p. 53.

46. John Copeland Nagle, "The Evangelical Debate over Climate Change," *University of St. Thomas Law Journal* 5, no. 1 (2008): 53–86, p. 72.

47. Deaton, "Global Warming."

48. Paul Broun, quoted in Pearce, "U.S. Rep. Paul Broun."

49. Roy Spencer, quoted in McCammack, "Hot Damned America," p. 654.

50. Joe Barton, quoted in Ali Frick, "Barton: We Shouldn't Regulate CO2 Because 'It's in Your Coca-Cola' and 'You Can't Regulate God,'" *Think Progress*, available at http://thinkprogress.org/2009/05/19/barton-carbon-god/ (accessed July 31, 2014).

51. Christian, "Global Warming in Perspective," p. 89.

52. G. Elijah Dann, "Why Christians Can't Take Climate Change Seriously—Even When They Say They Do," *Huff Post Religion*, July 31, 2013, available at http://www.huffingtonpost.com/g-ellijah-dann/christians-climate-change_b_3668179.html (accessed January 7, 2014).

53. David C. Barker and David H. Bearce, "End-Times Theology, the Shadow of the Future, and Public Resistance to Addressing Global Climate Change," *Political Research Quarterly* 66, no. 2 (2013): 267–79, p. 272.

54. Ibid., p. 269.

55. McCammack, "Hot Damned America," p. 646.

56. Ibid., p. 645.

57. Jerry Falwell, quoted in Nagle, "Evangelical Debate over Climate Change."

58. Paula J. Posas, "Roles of Religion and Ethics in Addressing Climate Change," *Ethics in Science and Environmental Politics* (2007): 31–49, p. 41.

59. Wilson, *Creation*, p. 167.

60. Christian, "Global Warming in Perspective," p. 85.

61. William R. Patterson, "Ecohumanism: Principles and Practice," *Essays in the Philosophy of Humanism* 16, no. 2 (Fall–Winter 2008): 71–87, pp. 77–78.

Chapter 15. Doth God Take Care for Oxen?: Christianity's Acrimony against Animals

1. Andrew Linzey and Tom Regan, eds., *Animals and Christianity: A Book of Readings* (New York: Crossroad, 1988), pp. xii–xiii.

2. Peter Singer, *Animal Liberation* (New York: Avon Books, 1990).

3. People for the Ethical Treatment of Animals (PETA) "The Issues," http://www.peta.org/issues/ (accessed August 1, 2014).

4. Andrew Linzey, *Animal Theology* (Urbana and Chicago: University of Illinois Press, 1995), p. 149.

5. One can watch a really good take down of William Lane Craig's view that animals don't suffer much pain in two online videos on my blog *Debunking*

Christianity: "Stephen Law on the Apologist Claim that Animals Don't Feel Pain," *Debunking Christianity*, http://debunkingchristianity.blogspot.com/2012/10/stephen-law-on-apologist-claim-that.html (accessed August 5, 2014), and "William Lane Craig's Views on Animal Suffering Debunked Further," *Debunking Christianity*, http://debunkingchristianity.blogspot.com/2013/02/william-lane-craigs-views-on-animal.html (accessed August 5, 2014). See also the important work of Frans de Waal. Frans de Waal, ed., *Tree of Origin: What Primate Behavior Can Tell Us about Human Social Evolution* (Cambridge, MA: Harvard University Press, 2002); Frans de Waal, *Primates and Philosophers: How Morality Evolved* (Princeton, NJ: Princeton University Press, 2009); Frans de Waal, *The Age of Empathy: Nature's Lessons for a Kinder Society* (New York: Broadway Books, 2010); and Frans de Waal, *Evolved Morality: The Biology and Philosophy of Human Conscience* (New York: Brill Academic, 2014).

6. J. R. Porter, "Creation" in Bruce M. Metzger and Michael Coogan, eds., *The Oxford Companion to the Bible* (New York: Oxford University Press, 1993), p. 140.

7. See Francis Brown, S. R. Driver, and Charles A. Briggs, *The Brown-Driver-Briggs Hebrew and English Lexicon* (Peabody, MA: Hendrickson, 1996)

8. Roderick Nash, *The Rights of Nature: A History of Environmental Ethics* (Madison: University of Wisconsin Press, 1989), p. 90.

9. John Shelby Spong, *The Sins of the Scripture: Exposing the Bible's Texts of Hate to Reveal the God of Love* (New York: HarperCollins, 2005), p. 49.

10. Ibid., p. 55.

11. Lynn White Jr., *Science* 155 (March 10, 1967): 1203–1207.

12. John C. L. Gibson, *Genesis* (Philadelphia: Westminster Press, 1981), pp. 79–81.

13. Gordon Wenham, *Genesis 1–15* (Dallas, TX: Word books, 1987), p. 33.

14. Richard Bauckham, "Human Authority in Creation," chapter 7 in *God and the Crisis of Freedom: Biblical and Contemporary Perspectives* (Philadelphia: Westminster John Knox Press, 2002), p. 131.

15. Hector Avalos shows us this with regard to Christ in the New Testament. He is our slave master and we work in God's plantation. See chapter 6 in Hector Avalos, *Slavery, Abolitionism, and the Ethics of Biblical Scholarship* (Sheffield: Sheffield Phoenix Press, 2011), pp. 139–56.

16. I've made this argument, which I call the "Problem of Divine Miscommunication," in my chapter "What We've Got Here Is a Failure to Communicate," in John W. Loftus, ed., *The Christian Delusion: Why Faith Fails* (Amherst, NY: Prometheus Books, 2010).

17. Gordon D. Fee and Douglas Stuart, *How to Read the Bible For All Its Worth* (Grand Rapids, MI: Zondervan, 1982), pp. 195–203.

18. For more on the biblical depictions of this sacrificial system see Roland de Vaux's classic work *Ancient Israel: Religious Institutions*, vol. 2 (New York: McGraw-Hill, 1965), pp. 415–56.

19. John F. Haught, *God and the New Atheists: A Critical Response to Dawkins, Harris, and Hitchens* (Louisville, KY: Westminster John Knox Press, 2008), p. 68.

20. C. F. D. Moule, *Man and Nature in the New Testament* (Philadelphia: Fortress Press, 1964), p. 11.

21. There was animal predation before the fall in the supposed Garden of Eden, as I've shown in chapter 9 "The Darwinian Problem of Evil" in *The Christian Delusion*. See also evangelical author Ronald E. Olson's book, *Death before the Fall: Biblical Literalism and the Problem of Animal Suffering* (Downers Grove, IL: IVP Academic, 2014).

22. Paul Copan *That's Just Your Interpretation* (Grand Rapids, MI: Baker Books, 2001), p. 229, n. 34.

23. Robert N. Wennberg, *God, Humans, and Animals* (Grand Rapids, MI: Eerdmans, 2003), p. 296.

24. Ibid., p. 291.

25. Peter Singer, *Animal Liberation* (New York: Avon Books, 1990), p. 191.

26. Richard Bauckham, "Jesus and Animals I: What Did He Teach?" and "Jesus and Animals II: What Did He Practice?" in Andrew Linzey and Dorothy Yamamoto, eds., *Animals on the Agenda: Questions about Animals for Theology and Ethics* (Urbana and Chicago: University of Illinois Press, 1998) , pp. 33–60.

27. Ibid., p. 41.

28. Ibid., pp. 45–46.

29. Ibid., pp. 37–38.

30. Ibid., p. 47.

31. Ibid., p. 48.

32. Wennberg, *God, Humans, and Animals*, p. 298.

33. F. F. Bruce, *New Century Bible: First and Second Corinthians* (London: Oliphants, 1971), pp. 84–85.

34. Wennberg, *God, Humans, and Animals*, pp. 299–302.

35. Ibid., p. 308.

Part Four: Social and Moral Harms

Chapter 16. The Christian Right and the Culture Wars

1. James Davison Hunter, *Culture Wars: The Struggle to Define America* (New York: Basic Books, 1992).

2. Gary North, *Conspiracy in Philadelphia: The Broken Covenant of the U.S. Constitution* (NiceneCouncil.com, 2011), preface.

3. Isaac Kramnick and R. Laurence Moore, *The Godless Constitution: A Moral Defense of the Secular State* (New York: W. W. Norton & Company, 2005), p. 32.

4. Kramnick and Moore, *Godless Constitution*, p. 32.

5. Kramnick and Moore, *Godless Constitution*, p. 33.

6. "The GOP Takeover in the States," *Washington Post*, November 13, 2010, http://www.washingtonpost.com/wp-dyn/content/article/2010/11/13/AR20101113023 89.html (accessed August 5, 2014).

7. "More State Abortion Restrictions Were Enacted in 2011–2013 Than in the Entire Previous Decade," Guttmacher Institute, January 12, 2014, http://www .guttmacher.org/media/inthenews/2014/01/02/index.html (accessed August 5, 2014).

8. "The TRAP: Targeted Regulation of Abortion Providers," National Abortion Federation, http://www.prochoice.org/about_abortion/facts/trap_laws.html (accessed August 5, 2014).

9. Ibid.

10. Esmé E. Deprez, "The Vanishing Abortion Clinic," *Bloomberg Business Week*, November 27, 2013, http://www.businessweek.com/articles/2013-11-27/abortion -clinics-face-shutdown-spiral-as-republicans-push-restrictions (accessed August 6, 2014).

11. Robin Marty, e-mail to author, January 9, 2014.

12. Susan A, Cohen, "Reproductive Health and Rights: Keys to Development and Democracy at Home and Abroad," *Guttmacher Report on Public Policy* 4, no. 6 (December 2001), https://www.guttmacher.org/pubs/tgr/04/6/gr040601.html (accessed August 6, 2014).

13. "A History of Federal Funding for Abstinence-Only-Until-Marriage Programs," Sexuality Information and Education Council of the United States, http:// www.siecus.org/index.cfm?fuseaction=page.viewpage&pageid=1340&nodeid=1 (accessed August 6, 2014).

14. Chelsea Toledo, "Abstinence-Only Education Does Not Lead to Abstinent Behavior, UGA Researchers Find," *UGA Today*, November 29, 2011, http://news.uga

.edu/releases/article/abstinence-only-education-does-not-lead-to-abstinent-behavior/ (accessed August 6, 2014).

15. Ibid.

16. Laura Sessions Stepp, "Study Casts Doubt on Abstinence-Only Programs, *Washington Post*, April 14, 2007, http://www.washingtonpost.com/wp-dyn/content/ article/2007/04/13/AR2007041301003.html (accessed August 6, 2014).

17. "What the Research Says . . . Abstinence-Only-until-Marriage Programs," Sexuality Information and Education Council of the United States, http://www.siecus.org/ index.cfm?fuseaction=Page.ViewPage&PageID=1195#_edn5 (accessed August 6, 2014).

18. Ibid.

19. Ibid.

20. Ibid.

21. Ibid.

22. Ibid.

23. United States House of Representatives Committee on Government Reform—Minority Staff Special Investigations Division, "The Content of Federally Funded Abstinence-Only Education Programs, Prepared for Rep. Henry A. Waxman, December 2004, http://www.apha.org/apha/PDFs/HIV/The_Waxman_Report.pdf (accessed August 13, 2014). Hereafter "Waxman Report."

24. Ibid.

25. "Condoms and STDs: Fact Sheet for Public Health Personnel," Centers for Disease Control and Prevention, http://www.cdc.gov/condomeffectiveness/latex.htm (accessed August 6, 2014).

26. "Waxman Report," p. i.

27. Ibid., p. ii.

28. "Access to Free Birth Control Reduces Abortion Rates," Washington University School of Medicine in St. Louis, October 12, 2012, http://medschool.wustl.edu/ news/patient_care/Contraceptive_Choice (accessed August 6, 2014).

29. "Study: Free Birth Control Leads to Fewer Abortions," Fox News, October 5, 2012, http://www.foxnews.com/health/2012/10/05/study-free-birth-control-leads -to-fewer-abortions/ (accessed August 6, 2014).

30. Angi Becker Stevens, "Anti-Choicers Still Just Want to Control Women's Sex Lives," Alternet, November 6, 2011, http://www.alternet.org/story/152986/anti -choicers_still_just_want_to_control_women's_sex_lives (accessed August 6, 2014).

31. *Lawrence v. Texas*, 539 U.S. 558 (2003).

32. Ibid.

33. "*Lawrence v. Texas*," *Wikipedia*, http://en.wikipedia.org/wiki/Lawrence_v _texas (accessed August 6, 2014).

34. Ted Olsen and Todd Hertz, "Does Lawrence v. Texas Signal the End of the American Family?" *Christianity Today*, June 1, 2003, http://www.christianitytoday .com/ct/2003/juneweb-only/6-30-11.0.html (accessed August 6, 2014).

35. Ibid.

36. Ibid.

37. Donald E. Wilkes Jr., "*Lawrence v. Texas*: An Historic Human Rights Victory," *Flagpole*, October 15, 2003, available at http://www.law.uga.edu/dwilkes _more/47lawrence.html (accessed August 6, 2014).

38. Ibid.

39. *Hillary Goodridge & Others v. Dept. of Public Health & Another*, 440 Mass. 309 (2003). See Google Scholar, http://scholar.google.com/scholar_case?case =16499869016395834644&q=Goodridge+v.+Dept.+of+Public+Health&hl=en&as_sdt =800006&as_vis=1 (accessed August 13, 2014).

40. Ibid.

41. "Responses of Roman Catholic Bishops in Massachusetts to Goodridge Decision," Massachusetts Catholic Conference, http://www.macatholic.org/sites/ma catholic.org/files/assets/Responses%20of%20Roman%20Catholic%20Bishops%20in %20Massachusetts%20to%20Goodridge%20Decision.pdf (accessed August 6, 2014).

42. "DOMA Ruling an Example of Judicial Tyranny," Family Council, https:// familycouncil.org/?p=5312 (accessed August 13, 2014).

43. Kyle Mantyla, "FRC's Sprigg Wants to See Homosexuality Criminal-ized," Right Wing Watch, February 3, 2010, http://www.rightwingwatch.org/content/ frcs-sprigg-wants-see-homosexuality-criminalized (accessed August 6, 2014).

44. Rachel Clarke, "Gay Marriage Ruling "Threatens US Soul," BBC News, November 18, 2003, http://news.bbc.co.uk/2/hi/americas/3281527.stm (accessed August 6, 2014).

45. Rose Arce, "Massachusetts Court Upholds Same-Sex Marriage," CNN, Feb-ruary 6, 2004, http://www.cnn.com/2004/LAW/02/04/gay.marriage/ (accessed August 6, 2014).

46. Alan Sears, "Massachusetts Courts Plunge down Slippery Slope of Own Cre-ation," WND, November 26, 2003, http://www.wnd.com/2003/11/22009/ (accessed August 6, 2014).

47. "U.S. Supreme Court Won't Block Same-Sex Marriages," WND, May 14, 2004, http://www.wnd.com/2004/05/24646/ (accessed August 14, 2014).

48. Brian Tashman, "Perkins: Tide Turning against Marriage Equality," Right Wing Watch, December 5, 2013, http://www.rightwingwatch.org/content/perkins -tide-turning-against-marriage-equality (accessed August 6, 2014).

49. Ibid.

50. Scott Lively, "Time for Pro-Family Pushback in 2014!" Pro-Family Resource Center, http://www.defendthefamily.com/pfrc/newsarchives.php?id=4962679 (accessed August 6, 2014).

51. Innokenty Grekov, "Russia's Anti-Gay Law Spelled out in Plain English," Policy Mic, August 8, 2013, http://mic.com/articles/58649/russia-s-anti-gay-law-spelled-out-in-plain-english (accessed August 6, 2014).

52. Zack Ford, "NOM's Brian Brown Helped Export Homophobia to Russia," Think Progress, http://thinkprogress.org/lgbt/2013/10/04/2734421/noms-brian-brown-helped-export-homophobia-to-russia/ (accessed August 6, 2014).

53. Kyle Mantyla, "Fischer: Russia's Anti-Gay Law Is Exactly the Sort of "Public Policy That We've Been Advocating," Right Wing Watch, August 26, 2013, http://www.rightwingwatch.org/content/fischer-russias-anti-gay-law-exactly-sort-public-policy-weve-been-advocating (accessed August 6, 2014).

54. David Crary, "Some US Conservatives Laud Russia's Anti-Gay Bill," Associated Press, http://bigstory.ap.org/article/some-us-conservatives-laud-russias-anti-gay-bill (accessed August 6, 2014).

55. Ibid

56. Kyle Mantyla, "Lively: Russia's Anti-Gay Law Is 'One of the Proudest Achievements of My Career," Right Wing Watch, August 24, 2013, http://www.rightwingwatch.org/content/lively-russias-anti-gay-law-one-proudest-achievements-my-career (accessed August 6, 2014).

57. Scott Lively, "Praise for Putin," Scott Lively Ministries, September 3, 2013, http://www.scottlively.net/2013/09/03/praise-for-putin/ (accessed August 6, 2014).

58. Crary, "Some US Conservatives Laud Russia's Anti-Gay Bill."

59. Tony Dokoupil, "'The Rainbow Belongs to God': Anti-Gay US Pastor Sets Sights on Sochi Olympics," NBC News, September 18, 2013, http://www.nbcnews.com/news/us-news/rainbow-belongs-god-anti-gay-us-pastor-sets-sights-sochi-v20546485 (accessed August 6, 2014).

60. *Burwell v. Hobby Lobby Stores, Inc.*, No. 13-354, http://sblog.s3.amazonaws.com/wp-content/uploads/2014/01/Hamilton-brief-Hobby-Lobby.pdf (accessed August 13, 2014).

61. Mark Joseph Stern, "Idaho's New Anti-Gay Bill: Doctors and Teachers Can Turn Away Gays," *Slate*, http://www.slate.com/blogs/outward/2014/02/19/idaho_anti_gay_segregation_discrimination_against_gays_will_be_legal.html (accessed August 6, 2014).

Chapter 17. Woman, What Have I to Do with Thee?: Christianity's War against Women

1. Montague Summers, trans. *The Malleus Maleficarum of Heinrich Kramer and James Sprenger* (New York: Dover, 1971), Part 1, Question VI, p. 47. In a new translation of this work by Christopher S. MacKay titled *The Hammer of Witches: A Complete Translation of the Malleus Maleficarum* (Cambridge: Cambridge University Press, 2009), the text is translated, "Conclusion: Everything is governed by carnal lusting, which is insatiable in them [i.e., women]." It goes on to read, "Hence, and consequently, it should be called the Heresy not of Sorcerers but of Sorceresses, to name it after the predominant element. Blessed be the Highest One, Who has, down to the present day, preserved the male kind from such disgraceful behavior" (p. 170).

2. Ella E. Gibson, *The Godly Women of the Bible* (New York: Truth Seeker, 1881).

3. Helen H. Gardener, *Men, Women and Gods, and Other Lectures* (New York: Belford, Clark, and Co., 1885).

4. Elizabeth Cady Stanton, in *Free Thought Magazine* 14 (1896).

5. Elizabeth Cady Stanton, in an interview for the *Chicago Record* (1897). Reprinted in Annie Laurie Gaylor, ed., *Women without Superstition: No Gods—No Masters* (Madison, WI: Freedom from Religion Foundation, 1997), p. 172.

6. Margaret Sanger, "A Parents' Problem or Women's?" Birth Control Review (March 1919): 6–7.

7. Elizabeth Cady Stanton, "Remarks at the 1885 National Woman Suffrage Association Convention," in Susan B. Anthony and Ida Husted Harper, eds., *History of Woman Suffrage*, vol. 4 (Indianapolis, IN: Hollenbeck Press, 1902), pp, 60–61.

8. Susan Wixon, "Woman: Four Centuries of Progress," speech delivered at the Freethinkers' International Congress, Chicago, Illinois, October 1893. Published as a pamphlet in December 1892 by the Truth Seeker Company. Reprinted in Gaylor, *Women without Superstition*, pp. 285–91.

9. Matilda Joslyn Gage, speech at Woman's National Liberal Union Convention for Organization, February 24–25, 1890, Washington, DC, convened by Matilda Joslyn Gage. Reprinted in full in Gaylor, *Women without Superstition*, pp. 220–24.

10. Matilda Joslyn Gage, *Woman, Church, and State: A Historical Account of the Status of Women through the Christian Ages—With Reminiscences of the Matriarchate*, 2nd ed. (New York: Truth Seeker Company,1893), chapter 10, "Past, Present, Future." Available online at Sacred Text, http://www.sacred-texts.com/wmn/wcs/index.htm (accessed August 12, 2014).

Chapter 18. Secular Sexuality: A Direct Challenge to Christianity

1. Darrel Ray, *Sex and God: How Religion Distorts Sexuality* (Bonner Spring, KS: IPC Press, 2012).

2. Daniel Dennett, *Breaking the Spell* (New York: Penguin, 2007); Darrel Ray, *The God Virus* (Bonner Spring, KS: IPC Press, 2009), Richard Dawkins, *The God Delusion* (New York: Houghton Mifflin Harcourt, 2006).

3. Marlene Winell, *Leaving the Fold* (Berkeley, CA: Apocryphile Press, 2013). See her chapter with Valerie Tarico in the present anthology. Also visit the Journey Free website at http://journeyfree.org/rts/ for a full discussion of RTS.

4. For much more on this topic read Dr. Marty Klein's book *America's War on Sex*, 2nd ed. (Santa Barbara, CA: Praeger, 2012) and my book *Sex and God*, or read an interesting blog post by Greta Christina on why porn is important (see Greta Christina, "Why Porn Matters," *Greta Christina's Blog*, http://gretachristina.typepad.com/greta_christinas_weblog/2010/08/why-porn-matters.html [accessed August 8, 2014]).

5. Other resources to help you challenge your sexual programming: Albert Ellis, *Sex without Guilt* (Fort Lee, NJ: Barricade Books, 2004), Dossie Easton and Janet Hardy, *The Ethical Slut*, 2nd ed. (Emeryville, CA: Celestial Arts, 2011), Christopher Ryan and Cacilda Jetha, *Sex at Dawn: How We Mate, Why We Stray, and What It Means for Modern Relationships* (New York: Harper Perennial, 2012).

Chapter 19. The Crazy-Making in Christianity: A Look at Real Psychological Harm

1. All quotations from former believers unaccompanied by a note number and citation, including those enclosed in text boxes, are from personal and confidential communications with Doctors Winell or Tarico.

2. Charles H. Hackney and Glenn S. Sanders, "Religiosity and Mental Health: A Meta-Analysis of Recent Studies," *Journal for the Scientific Study of Religion* 42, no. 1 (March 2003): 43–55; Gene G. Ano and Erin B. Vasconcelles, "Religious Coping and Psychological Adjustment to Stress: A Meta-Analysis," *Journal of Clinical Psychology* 61, no 4 (April 2005): 461–80.

3. Flo Conway and Jim Siegelman, *Snapping: America's Epidemic of Sudden Personality Change*, 2nd ed. (New York: Stillpoint Press, 1995).

4. Daniel Kahneman, *Thinking Fast and Slow* (New York: Farrar, Straus and Giroux, 2011).

5. Daniel Siegel, *The Developing Mind: How Relationships and the Brain Interact to Shape Who We Are*, 2nd ed. (New York: Guilford Press, 2012).

6. George Lakoff, *Don't Think of an Elephant! Know Your Values and Frame the Debate—The Essential Guide for Progressives* (White River Junction, VT: Chelsea Green Publishing, 2004).

7. George Lakoff, *Thinking Points: Communicating Our American Values and Vision* (New York: Farrar, Straus and Giroux, 2006), p. 10.

8. Janet Heimlich, *Breaking Their Will: Shedding Light on Religious Child Maltreatment* (Amherst, NY: Prometheus Books, 2011).

9. Janet Heimlich, interviewed by Valerie Tarico, "The Fragile Boundary between Religion and Child Abuse," *Away Point* (May 8, 2011), http://awaypoint .wordpress.com/2011/05/08/the-fragile-boundary-between-religion-and-child-abuse/ (accessed August 11, 2014).

10. Marlene Winell, "Reclaimers," Exchristian.net, July 7, 2012, http://new .exchristian.net/2012/07/reclaimers.html?utm_source=Exchristiandotnet-Encouraging Ex-christians&utm_medium=Exchristiandotnet-EncouragingEx-christians&utm _campaign=ExChristian.Net+—+encouraging+exChristians&utm_content=Ex Christian.Net+—+encouraging+ex-Christians#.Uv66BPbMe8x (accessed August 11, 2014).

11. Marlene Winell, *Leaving the Fold: A Guide for Former Fundamentalists and Others Leaving Their Religion* (Berkeley, CA: Apocryphile Press, 1993, 2007).

12. Edmund D. Cohen, *The Mind of the Bible-Believer* (Amherst, NY: Prometheus Books, 1988).

13. Michael Pearl and Debi Pearl, *To Train Up a Child: Turning the Hearts of the Fathers to the Children* (Pleasantville, TN: No Greater Joy Ministries, 2011).

14. Tim Lahaye and Jerry B. Jenkins, Left Behind, a series of twelve adult books and forty young-adult books (Carol Stream, IL, Tyndale House Publishers, 1995–2004).

15. Margaret Thaler Singer, *Cults in Our Midst: The Continuing Fight against Their Hidden Menace* (Hoboken, NJ: Jossey-Bass, 2003).

16. "'Nones' on the Rise," Pew Research Religion and Public Life Project, October 9, 2012, http://www.pewforum.org/Unaffiliated/nones-on-the-rise.aspx (accessed August 11, 2014).

17. Robert Lifton, *Thought Reform and the Psychology of Totalism: A Study of "Brainwashing" in China* (Chapel Hill, University of North Carolina Press, 1989), pp. 419–25.

18. Valerie Tarico, "Why Bible Believers Have Such a Hard Time Getting Child Protection Right," *Away Point*, October 21, 2013, http://awaypoint.wordpress .com/2013/10/21/why-bible-believers-have-such-a-hard-time-getting-child-protection -right/ (accessed August 11, 2014).

19. Jean Piaget, Howard E. Gruber, Jean Jacques Voneche, eds., *The Essential Piaget* (New York: Basic Books, 1977).

20. Bruce Duncan Perry, "The Neurodevelopmental Impact of Violence in Childhood," in Diane Schetky and Elissa Benedek, eds., *Textbook of Child and Adolescent Forensic Psychiatry* (Washington, DC: American Psychiatric Press, 2001), pp. 221–38.

21. Jane Healy, *Your Child's Growing Mind: Brain Development and Learning from Birth to Adolescence* (New York: Broadway Books, 2004).

22. Centers for Disease Control and Prevention, *Adverse Childhood Experiences Study*, retrieved from http://www.cdc.gov/nccdphp/ACE/ (accessed August 2009).

23. Dylan Peterson, "A Thief in the Night Keeps Me Awake" (movie review), *Total Darkness vs. Blinding Light*, April 30, 2009, http://dylanclub.blogspot.com/2009/04/thief-in-night-keeps-me-awake.html (accessed August 11, 2014).

24. Eric Cernyar, "The Good News Club: Not Safe for Children," retrieved from Intrinsic Dignity, http://www.intrinsicdignity.com.

25. Bob Altemeyer, *The Authoritarians* (Ramona Hill, CA: Cherry Hill, 2008). The book can be read online at http://members.shaw.ca/jeanaltemeyer/drbob/The Authoritarians.pdf (accessed August 11, 2014).

26. Cernyar, "Good News Club."

27. Alice Miller, *For Your Own Good: Hidden Cruelty in Child-Rearing and the Roots of Violence*, 3rd ed. (New York: Farrar, Straus and Giroux, 2002).

28. Valerie Tarico, *Trusting Doubt: A Former Evangelical Looks at Old Beliefs in a New Light* (Independence, VA: Oracle Institute Press, 2010).

29. The DSM V diagnosis, V62.89, for Religious or Spiritual Problem reads: "Examples include distressing experiences that involve loss or questioning of faith, problems associated with conversion to a new faith, or questioning of spiritual values that may not necessarily be related to an organized church or religious institution." This diagnosis has been part of a discussion in developing the recent edition of the DSM manual to consider spirituality a part of culture. The V-Codes have been framed as "diagnoses in the context of life markers and socio-cultural conditions."

30. James W. Ellor, "Religion and Spirituality among Older Adults in Light of DSM-5," *Social Work and Christianity* 40, no. 4 (2013): 372–83.

31. Steven J. Seay, "Scrupulosity" Steven J. Seay, Ph.D., Licensed Psychologist, February 8, 2012, http://www.steveseay.com/scrupulosity/ (accessed August 11, 2014).

32. Marlene Winell, "Religious Trauma Syndrome: It's Time to Recognize It" (published as a series in 3 issues of *Cognitive Behavioural Therapy Today* (2011), also available online at BABCP, http://www.babcp.com/rts (accessed August 11, 2014).

33. "Complex Post-Traumatic Stress Disorder" *Wikipedia*, http://en.wikipedia. org/wiki/Complex post-traumatic stress disorder (accessed August 11, 2014).

34. Ronnie Janoff-Bulman, *Shattered Assumptions: Towards a New Psychology of Trauma* (New York: Free Press, 1992).

35. Jeffrey Kauffman, "Safety and the Assumptive World," in Jeffrey Kauffman. ed., *Loss of the Assumptive World* (New York: Brunner-Routledge, 2002), pp. 205–11.

36. Joan Beder, "Loss of the Assumptive World—How We Deal With Death and Loss," *Omega* 50, no. 4 (2004–2005): 255–65.

37. Marlene Winell and Valerie Tarico, *Heretic Holidays: Tips from Two Religious Renegades* (Amazon Digital Services, 2012).

38. See "Religious Trauma Syndrome, Tony Beck, Marlene Winell, Part 1," YouTube, December 13, 2010, http://www.youtube.com/watch?v=Id70RLR4GeE (accessed August 11, 2014), a recording from the Texas Freethought Convention of October 2010, when Marlene Winell first presented Religious Trauma Syndrome.

39. Anne P. DePrince and Jennifer Freyd, "The Harm of Trauma: Pathological Fear, Shattered Assumptions, or Betrayal?" in Jeffrey Kauffman, ed., *Loss of the Assumptive World* (New York: Brunner-Routledge, 2002), pp. 71–82.

40. Valerie Tarico, "Fifteen Bible Texts Reveal Why God's Own Party Is at War with Women," *Away Point*, March 9, 2012, http://awaypoint.wordpress.com/2012/03/09/15 -bible-texts-reveal-why-gods-own-party-is-at-war-with-women/ (accessed August 11, 2014); Valerie Tarico, "Twenty Vile Quotes against Women by Church Leaders from Augustine to Pat Robertson," *Away Point*, July 1, 2013, http://awaypoint.wordpress .com/2013/07/01/mysogynistquoteschurchfathers/ (accessed August 11, 2014).

41. Leisa Crawley, "Physical and Mental Health of Muslim Women across the World: Does Culture and Religion Affect the Health of Muslim Women?" Yahoo Voices, September 29, 2010, http://98.139.236.92/search/srpcache?ei=UTF -8&p=http%3A%2F%2Fvoices.yahoo.com%2Fphysical-mental-health-muslim -women-across-6872652.html&pvid=nAqn7Tk4LjEpPwLZU.TTRBCUMTIuM1Po _mn_vcHo&type=YHS_SF_1700&param1=iyzTqxyuayxkXZEXjiqI44sgEHSDUpk 0h_rpo-8PiH65K_KXLgHg4gTduo1eLFNAtJNrXt5c_72Z0nVc3p8vunNZdd-LiWTz 7-8978noQ2Za7xQIo52omNNX688aOKZY&hsimp=yhs-SF01&hspart=Lkry&u =http://cc.bingj.com/cache.aspx?q=http%3a%2f%2fvoices.yahoo.com%2fphysical -mental-health-muslim-women-across-6872652.html&d=5033148907588869&mkt =en-US&setlang=en-US&w=AmsQUywkTbDwz9AcJghQx4wJNV4fXUh2&icp=1& .intl=us&sig=ZTIc2nM0l4fP95cIhEhPYA-- (accessed August 11, 2014).

42. Chris Rodda, "Cadets for Christ: Women, Evangelicals, and the Air Force Academy," *Huffington Post*, December 26, 2010, http://www.huffingtonpost.com/ chris-rodda/cadets-for-christ-solicit_b_800382.html (accessed August 11, 2014).

43. Thomas Kuhn, *The Structure of Scientific Revolutions* (Chicago: University of Chicago Press, 1962).

44. Diana Bridget "Christianity and Mental Health: Have We Lost Our Faith?" *Christian Post*, January 14, 2013, http://www.christianpost.com/news/christianity -and-mental-health-have-we-lost-our-faith-88270/ (accessed August 11, 2014).

45. Resources include Journey Free: Resources for recovery from harmful religion (journeyfree.org), *Away Point*: Articles by Valerie Tarico (AwayPoint.wordpress. com), and ExChristian: Encouraging de-converting and former Christians (Exchristian.net).

Part Five: Morality, Atheism, and a Good Life

Chapter 20. Abusive Pastors and Churches

1. Jason Berry, "The Tragedy of Gilbert Gauthe, Part I," *Times of Acadiana*, May 23, 1985. Available online at BishopAccountability.org, http://www.bishop -accountability.org/news/1985_05_23_Berry_TheTragedy.htm (accessed August 15, 2014); Jason Berry, "The Tragedy of Gilbert Gauthe, Part II," *Times of Acadiana*, May 23, 1985. Available online at BishopAccountability.org, http://www.bishop -accountability.org/news/1985_05_30_Berry_TheTragedy.htm (accessed August 15, 2014).

2. Ibid.

3. Ibid.

4. Ibid.

5. James Gill, "Boy Scouts and Catholic Church Were Inclined to Silence on Abuse," *New Orleans Times-Picayune*, October 24, 2012. Available online at *Eassurvey's Weblog*, http://eassurvey.wordpress.com/category/gilbert-gauthe/ (accessed August 15, 2014).

6. Berry, "The Tragedy of Gilbert Gauthe, Part I"; Berry, "The Tragedy of Gilbert Gauthe, Part II."

7. "John Jay Report," *Wikipedia*, http://en.wikipedia.org/wiki/John_Jay_Report (accessed August 15, 2014); William A. Donahue, "John Jay 2011 Study on Sexual Abuse: A Critical Analysis," Catholic League, http://www.catholicleague.org/wp -content/uploads/2011/05/John-Jay-Report-1-27-12-Update.pdf (accessed August 15, 2014).

8. "Settlements and Bankruptcies in Catholic Sex Abuse Cases," Wikipedia,

http://en.wikipedia.org/wiki/Settlements_and_bankruptcies_in_Catholic_sex_abuse _cases (accessed August 15, 2014).

9. Ibid.

10. I personally interviewed Brian Galyean, and he reviewed and confirmed the accuracy of this section prior to publication.

11. Laura Zuckerman, Montana Catholic Diocese File for Bankruptcy in Abuse Settlement," Reuters, January 31, 2014, http://www.reuters.com/article/2014/01/31/ us-usa-montana-diocese-idUSBREA0U1ZY20140131 (accessed August 15, 2014).

12. John L. Allen Jr., "Vatican Abuse Summit: $2.2 Billion and 100,000 Victims in U.S. Alone," *NCR Today*, February 8, 2012. Available online at the Foundation to Abolish Sex Abuse, http://abolishsexabuse.org/index.php?option=com_content &view=article&id=1524:vatican-abuse-summit-22-billion-and-100000-victims-in-us -alone&catid=71:world-news&itemid=181 (accessed August 15, 2014).

13. Adrienne Lu, "Is Harsher Corporal Punishment for Children Coming to Kansas," PEW Charitable Trusts, February 19, 2014, http://www.pewtrusts.org/en/ research-and-analysis/blogs/stateline/2014/02/19/is-harsher-corporal-punishment-for -children-coming-to-kansas (accessed August 15, 2014).

14. Joel Christie, "Reality TV Snake Pastor Died of Snake Bite after Refusing Treatment Because 'It Was God's Plan,'" *Mail* Online, February 18, 2014, http://www .dailymail.co.uk/news/article-2560727/Kentucky-Pastor-famous-practicing-rare -Christian-snake-handling-tradition-KILLED-bitten-rattlesnake-refusing-treatment -Gods-plan.html (accessed August 15, 2014).

15. Ibid.

Chapter 21. "Tu Quoque, Atheism?"—Our Right to Judge

1. William Lane Craig, *A Reasonable Faith*, 3rd ed. (Wheaton, IL: Crossway Books, 2008), p. 69.

2. Ibid., p.75.

3. Thom Stark, *Is God a Moral Compromiser? A Critical Review of Paul Copan's "Is God a Moral Monster?"* 2nd ed., Thom Stark, http://thomstark.net/copan/ stark_copan-review.pdf (accessed July 20, 2013), p. 1, my emphasis.

4. John Shelby Spong, *The Sins of Scripture: Exposing the Bible's Texts of Hate to Reveal the God of Love* (New York: HarperCollins, 2005), pp. 4–5.

5. Bernard Gert, "The Definition of Morality," *The Stanford Encyclopedia of Philosophy*, http://plato.stanford.edu/entries/morality-definition/ (accessed July 20, 2013).

6. See, for example, William Lane Craig, "Morality and Does God Exist?" *Reasonable Faith with William Lane Craig*, http://www.reasonablefaith.org/morality-and -does-god-exist (accessed July 20, 2013).

7. Here we could use a goal-oriented approach such that if we wanted *a* (e.g., human flourishing), then would need to do *x* (some action to achieve *a*). This conditional has an *apodosis* (then . . .), which follows factually from the *protasis* (if . . .), something which could be established using an empirical method. The matter-of-fact aspect of this conditional statement can make such a hypothetical moral approach objective or factual, though it then becomes important to establish the goal as being self-evident or factual in some such way.

8. Philip J. Wogaman, *Christian Ethics: A Historical Introduction* (Louisville, KY: Westminster/John Knox Press, 1993), pp. 88–89.

9. Ibid., p. 90.

10. Kai Nielsen, *Ethics without God* (Amherst, NY: Prometheus Books, 1990), p. 59.

11. P. Wesley Edwards, "Does Morality Depend On God?" *Freethought Debater*, December 30, 2011, http://www.freethoughtdebater.org/2011/12/30/does-morality -depend-on-god/ (accessed August 12, 2014).

12. As according to "Status of Global Mission, 2013, in the Context of AD 1800–2025," Gordon Conwell Theological Seminary, http://www.gordonconwell.edu/ resources/documents/statusofglobalmission.pdf (accessed January 11, 2014).

13. A. C. Grayling, *What Is Good? The Search for the Best Way to Live* (London: Weidenfeld & Nicolson, 2003),p. 63.

14. For example, Richard Carrier, in rebutting theist Matthew Flannagan's attempt to defend DCT (who attacked Sinnott-Armstrong's defense of naturalistic ethics), showed that "any defense of DCT is fallaciously circular and empirically untestable, whereas neither is the case for ethical naturalism." See Richard Carrier, "On the Facts as We Know Them, Ethical Naturalism Is All There Is: A Reply to Matthew Flannagan," *Philo* 15, no. 2 (Fall-Winter 2012): 200–211.

15. D. Bourget and D. Chalmers, "The PhilPapers Surveys: Preliminary Survey Results," 2009, PhilPapers, http://philpapers.org/surveys/results.pl (accessed July 20, 2014).

16. Sam Harris, "Do We Really Need Bad Reasons to Be Good?" *Sam Harris*, http://www.samharris.org/site/full_text/do-we-really-need-bad-reasons-to-be-good/ (accessed July 20, 2013). This approach is robustly defended by Richard Carrier in *The End of Christianity*, the previous volume edited by John W. Loftus. The chapter is an excellent description of how science can eliminate the *is-ought* problem with regard to morality and moral facts. See Richard Carrier, "Moral Facts Naturally Exist (and Science Could Find Them)," in John W. Loftus, ed., *The End of Christianity* (Amherst,

NY: Prometheus Books, 2011), pp. 333–64, 420–29. In fact, in the first of Loftus's edited volumes, *The Christian Delusion*, David Eller supports the main thrust of this section on secular morality from an anthropological point of view. For this excellent account, see David Eller, "Christianity Does Not Provide the Basis for Morality," in John W. Loftus, ed., *The Christian Delusion* (Amherst, NY: Prometheus Books, 2010), pp. 347–67.

17. Julia Annas, "Virtue Ethics: What Kind of Naturalism?" in Stephen M. Gardiner, ed., *Virtue Ethics Old And New* (Ithaca, NY: Cornell University Press, 2005), p. 11.

18. Immanuel Kant, *Grounding for the Metaphysics of Morals*, 3rd ed., trans., James W. Ellington (Indianapolis, IN: Hackett, 1993), p. 30.

19. A. C. Grayling, *What Is Good? The Search for the Best Way to Live* (London: Weidenfeld & Nicolson, 2003), pp. 139–40.

20. Alexander and Moore, "Deontological Ethics," *The Stanford Encyclopedia of Philosophy*, http://plato.stanford.edu/entries/ethics-deontological/ (accessed August 12, 2014).

21. O. A. Young et al, "Thou Shalt Not Kill: Religious Fundamentalism, Conservatism, and Rule-Based Moral Processing," *Psychology of Religion and Spirituality* 5 (2013): 110–15; Jared Piazza, "If You Love Me Keep My Commandments: Religiosity Increases Preference for Rule-Based Moral Arguments," *International Journal for the Psychology of Religion* 22 (2012): 285–302.

22. Rule consequentialism, such as rule utilitarianism, is a complex area. In fact, there are many strains of consequentialism (qua utilitarianism), all of which I necessarily give scant explanation due to constraints of space. I advise reading the entry in the *Stanford Encyclopedia of Philosophy* for "Consequentialism," in which there is a further link for rule consequentialism. Walter Sinnott-Armstrong, "Consequentialism," *The Stanford Encyclopedia of Philosophy*, http://plato.stanford.edu/entries/consequentialism/ (accessed July 20, 2013).

23. P. H. Ditto and B. S. Liu, "What Dilemma? Moral Evaluation Shapes Factual Belief," *Social Psychological and Personality Science* 4, no. 3 (May 2013): 316–23.

24. Mark D. Linville, "The Moral Argument," in William Lane Craig and J. P. Moreland, eds., *The Blackwell Companion to Natural Theology* (Hoboken, NJ: Wiley-Blackwell, 2009), p. 439.

25. Craig, *Reasonable Faith*, p. 105.

26. Jonathan MS Pearce, *The Little Books of Unholy Questions* (Fareham, UK: Ginger Prince Publications, 2011), p. 114.

27. Paul Copan and William Lane Craig, *Passionate Conviction: Contemporary Discourses on Christian Apologetics* (Nashville, TN: B & H Publishing Group, 2007), p. 91.

28. William Lane Craig, "Is God a Consequentialist?" *Reasonable Faith with William Lane Craig*, http://www.reasonablefaith.org/is-god-a-consequentialist (accessed August 12, 2014); Harris, "Do We Really Need Bad Reasons to Be Good?"

29. Craig, "Is God a Consequentialist?"

30. Stephen Maitzen, "Ordinary Morality Implies Atheism," *European Journal for Philosophy of Religion* 2 (2009): pp. 107–26, p. 107.

31. Ibid., p. 108.

32. Maitzen states that you can ignore the qualifier of unreservedness, if you do not believe in retributive punishment.

33. This can be a complex issue, though it seems like such an action could be morally good under consequentialism given consenting adults, even on hindsight after being punched.

34. Maitzen, "Ordinary Morality Implies Atheism," pp. 110–11.

35. Jerry Coyne, "How Can We Justify Science? Sokal and Lynch Debate Epistemology," *Why Evolution Is True*, http://whyevolutionistrue.wordpress.com/2012/03/14/how-can-we-justify-science-sokal-and-lynch-debate-epistemology/ (accessed July 15, 2013).

36. Ibid., adapted from the whole paper.

Chapter 22. Only Humans Can Solve the Problems of the World

1. James A. Lindsay, *God Doesn't; We Do: Only Humans Can Solve Human Challenges* (CreateSpace, 2012), and *Dot, Dot, Dot: Infinity Plus God Equals Folly* (Fareham, UK: Onus Books, 2013).

2. The fourth chapter of *God Doesn't; We Do* is dedicated to exploring this topic in far more detail. There, I use the term "soft" definition of God for these kinds of conceptions to contrast against more specific "hard" definitions that either rely upon claims to worldly evidence or very specific descriptions. Abstract conceptions of God are offered as a separate consideration that offers to resolve the definitional issue of the term "God."

3. Lindsay, *God Doesn't; We Do*, chapter 5.

4. Peter Boghossian, *A Manual for Creating Atheists* (Durham, NC: Pitchstone, 2013), p. 24.

5. John W. Loftus, *The Outsider Test for Faith: How to Know Which Religion Is True* (Amherst, NY: Prometheus Books, 2013), p. 219.

6. The "brothers" of Christianity are other religions that have significant conse-

quences for failure to believe or act correctly. Most obvious is its true brother, Islam, and its father, Judaism, but through the doctrines of karma and reincarnation, Hinduism and religious Buddhism can easily be added to the list, rather as cousins in an extended family of bad ideas. This is true of many other smaller religions, too, of course. To note, I have chosen "brothers" in place of "sisters" here specifically because the overt misogyny that is so central to most portrayals of these religions leads me to conclude that if given a gender, it must be the male gender.

7. Lindsay, *God Doesn't; We Do*, chapter 4.

8. James A. Lindsay, "When Is God a Hypothesis?" *God Doesn't; We Do* (blog), 19, 2014, http://goddoesnt.blogspot.com/2014/01/when-is-god-hypothesis.html (accessed January 19, 2014).

9. In this regard, some Christians, at least, do not. These accept varying amounts of fideism and thus openly admit that they don't know their beliefs are true but believe them anyway. Jesuit priest and retired head of the Vatican Observatory George Coyne would be a noteworthy example.

10. Lindsay, *God Doesn't; We Do*, chapter 7.

11. Ibid.

12. See Richard Dawkins, *The God Delusion* (New York: Houghton Mifflin, 2006), chapter 2.

13. Victor Stenger, *God: The Failed Hypothesis—How Science Shows That God Does Not Exist* (Amherst, NY: Prometheus Books, 2007).

14. "Almost surely zero" is a technical mathematical term that suggests that the plausibility in question is mathematically zero while remaining open to being a possibility. It is slightly stronger than "negligibly low" and weaker than absolutely, or exactly, zero. The fifth chapter of my first book *God Doesn't; We Do*, and the twelfth and thirteenth chapters of my second book *Dot, Dot, Dot*, elaborate upon my case for that conclusion.

15. Theologians often offer the word "proofs" here, but as I think there is no such thing as a false or incorrect proof, I will shy away from that term.

16. Thomas Aquinas, *Summa Theologica*, presented by Kevin Knight on *New Advent*, 2008, http://www.newadvent.org/summa/1002.htm#article3 (accessed January 19, 2014).

17. Ibid.

18. The Prime Mover argument could be accounted for by little more than gravity together with any, even random, inhomogeneity in the energy density of the universe at any point in its history, a possibility strengthened by the other fundamental forces of nature. The First Cause argument suffers from a lack of knowledge that such a thing is required.

19. William Lane Craig, *The* Kalām *Cosmological Argument* (Eugene, OR: Wipf and Stock, 2000).

20. Refutations of the Kalām argument are so widespread now that it hardly makes sense to cite one. My own contribution to this unnecessarily growing body of thought can be found in *God Doesn't; We Do*, pp. 145–49.

21. Bryan Higel (@BryanHigel) suggested something very similar to this to me on Twitter, using the metaphor of the Creator setting up the dominoes that would be its intended creation and then accidentally knocking over the first (the First Cause) before it was ready.

22. Sam Harris, *The Moral Landscape: How Science Can Determine Human Values* (New York: Free Press, 2010).

23. The Euthyphro dilemma appears in Plato's dialogue *Euthyphro* and asks, "Is the pious loved by the gods because it is pious, or is it pious because it is loved by the gods?"

24. This point is made frequently and well by John W. Loftus. See, for instance, "What's the Difference between Fundamentalism and Evangelicism?" on his blog *Debunking Christianity*, January 12, 2014, http://debunkingchristianity.blogspot.com/2013/10/whats-difference-between-fundamentalism.html (accessed January 19, 2014).

25. Wade C. Rowatt, Tom Carpenter, and Megan Haggard, "Religion, Prejudice, and Intergroup Relations," in Vassilis Saroglou, ed., *Religion, Personality, and Social Behavior* (New York: Psychology Press, 2013), pp. 170–92.

26. Loftus, *Outsider Test for Faith*.

27. Ibid., p. 172.

28. I personally witnessed a friend's Pentecostal church split over exactly this issue in the early 2000s. The pastor had said something too strictly condemnatory about divorce, quoting Jesus, as it turns out, which upset those on the church board, many of whom had been divorced and remarried. The board fired the pastor, and when he left, a large minority of the congregation went with him and formed a new church not far from the original.

29. William Lane Craig, "The Witness of the Holy Spirit," *Reasonable Faith*, http://www.reasonablefaith.org/the-witness-of-the-holy-spirit (accessed July 20, 2013).

30. Randal Rauser, *The Swedish Atheist, the Scuba Diver, and Other Apologetic Rabbit Trails* (Downers Grove, IL: InterVarsity Press, 2012), p. 49.

31. Fiona Harvey, "Climate Change Is Already Damaging Global Economy, Report Finds," *Guardian*, September 25, 2012, http://www.guardian.co.uk/environment/2012/sep/26/climate-change-damaging-global-economy (accessed July 23, 2013).

32. On this topic, see William Patterson's chapter on the environment in this anthology.

33. This alludes to Peter Boghossian's analysis of the word "faith" from his *Manual for Creating Atheists* (2013).

34. This quote is widely attributed to Sam Harris, including on Goodreads, where it appears without citation. While I recognize that it may be spurious or, more likely, modified, it is similar enough to a remark Harris made that conveys his attitude with fidelity. I include it over the other for its quality in reading. The reference to Goodreads can be found at http://www.goodreads.com/quotes/302665-we-have-a-choice-we-have-two-options-as-human (accessed January 3, 2014). A similar statement can be found in "A View from the End of the World" (December 9, 2005), transcript by DotSub, at http://dotsub.com/view/4b07c2fa-2f4b-4fe2-a3c3-2228778de747/view Transcript/eng (accessed January 3, 2014).

35. Sam Harris, *The End of Faith: Religion, Terror, and the Future of Reason* (New York: Norton, 2004), pp. 25–27.

36. By the phrase "extended humanism" I mean the general sentiment of humanism extended to all of sentience, as is appropriate.

37. Christopher Hitchens, *God Is Not Great: How Religion Poisons Everything* (New York: Twelve, 2007), p. 64.

Chapter 23. Living without God

1. Russell Blackford, "Unbelievable!" in Russell Blackford and Udo Schüklenk, eds., *50 Voices of Disbelief: Why We Are Atheists* (Malden, MA: Wiley-Blackwell, 2009), pp. 5–9; Russell Blackford and Udo Schüklenk, *50 Great Myths about Atheism* (Malden, MA: Wiley-Blackwell, 2013), pp. 185–235.

2. See Charles Taylor, *A Secular Age* (Cambridge, MA: Harvard University Press, 2007), pp. 15–20.

3. See, for example, Sheiman's weak discussion of "scientism" in atheist thought: Bruce Sheiman, *An Atheist Defends Religion: Why Humanity Is Better off with Religion than without It* (New York: Alpha Books, 2009), pp. 152–54. For a corrective to such rumblings about the vice of scientism, compare Blackford and Schüklenk, *50 Great Myths about Atheism*, pp. 153–57.

4. Sheiman, *Atheist Defends Religion*, pp. 143.

5. Ibid., pp. 143–44.

6. Susan Haack, *Defending Science—within Reason: Between Scientism and Cynicism* (Amherst, NY: Prometheus Books, 2007), p. 268.

7. Ibid., pp. 268–72.

8. Ian S. Markham, *Against Atheism: Why Dawkins, Hitchens, and Harris Are Fundamentally Wrong* (Malden, MA: Wiley-Blackwell, 2010), p. 19.

9. Susannah Heschel, *The Aryan Jesus: Christian Theologians and the Bible in Nazi Germany* (Princeton, NJ: Princeton University Press, 2008), pp. 26–66.

10. Ibid., pp. 43–44.

11. Richard Steigmann-Gall, *The Holy Reich: Nazi Conceptions of Christianity, 1919–1945* (Cambridge: Cambridge University Press, 2003), pp. 266–67. While much of Steigmann-Gall's detailed thesis is controversial, there should be no controversy about the general point that many Nazis were sincere Christians and thought they were doing God's will.

12. Blackford and Schüklenk, *50 Great Myths about Atheism*, pp. 34–42.

13. Julian Baggini, *Atheism: A Very Short Introduction* (Oxford: Oxford University Press, 2003), p. 59.

14. James R. Flynn, *How to Defend Humane Ideals: Substitutes for Objectivity* (Lincoln: University of Nebraska Press, 2000), pp. 10–11.

15. Dinesh D'Souza, *What's So Great about Christianity* (Washington, DC: Regnery, 2007), p. 233.

16. Gilbert Harman, *The Nature of Morality: An Introduction to Ethics* (New York: Oxford University Press, 1977), pp. 148–49.

17. Ibid., p. 149.

18. Throughout *Freedom of Religion and the Secular State* (Malden, MA: Wiley-Blackwell, 2012), I explore various conceptions of liberalism. This is, of course, a topic that involves long traditions of thought and an ever-expanding body of literature.

19. Sheiman, *Atheist Defends Religion*, pp. 13–19.

20. Richard Dawkins, *Unweaving the Rainbow: Science, Delusion and the Appetite for Wonder* (London: Allen Lane, 1998), p. 50.

21. David G. Myers, "Reflections on Religious Belief and Prosociality: Comment on Galen (2012)," *Psychological Bulletin* 138 (2012): 913–17, p. 914.

22. Alain de Botton, *Religion for Atheists* (London: Hamish-Hamilton, 2012), p. 83.

23. Ibid., p. 95.

24. Ibid., p. 181.

25. Ibid., pp. 71, 84.

26. Ibid., p. 84.

27. Ibid., pp. 259–63.

28. Sheiman summarizes much of the literature in *An Atheist Defends Religion*, pp. 24–31, 69–83.

29. See generally Luke W. Galen, "Does Religious Belief Promote Prosociality? A Critical Examination," *Psychological Bulletin* 138, no. 5 (2012): 876–906.

30. Myers, "Reflections on Religious Belief and Prosociality"; Vassilis Saroglou,

"Is Religion Not Prosocial at All? Comment on Galen (2012)," *Psychological Bulletin* 138 (2012): 907–912.

31. Luke W. Galen, "The Complex and Elusive Nature of Religious Prosociality: Reply to Myers (2012) and Saroglou (2012)." *Psychological Bulletin* 138 (2012): 918–23.

32. Saroglou, "Is Religion Not Prosocial at All?" p. 907.

33. Compare Saroglou, "Is Religion Not Prosocial at All?" p. 911.

34. For a similar list, see A. C. Grayling, *What Is Good? The Search for the Best Way to Live* (London: Phoenix, 2004), p. 230.

35. Sheiman, *Atheist Defends Religion*, pp. 131–32.

36. Blackford, *Freedom of Religion and the Secular State*, pp. 41–54.

ABOUT THE CONTRIBUTORS

Dr. Russell Blackford is conjoint lecturer in the School of Humanities and Social Science at the University of Newcastle, Australia. He is a prolific essayist and author whose works include *Freedom of Religion and the Secular State* (2012), *50 Great Myths about Atheism*, coauthored with Udo Schüklenk (2013), and *Humanity Enhanced: Genetic Choice and the Challenge for Liberal Democracies* (2014).

Dr. Peter Boghossian is a full time faculty member in the philosophy department at Portland State University. He has an extensive publication record across multiple domains of thought. His book *A Manual for Creating Atheists* (2013) teaches readers how to talk people out of faith and into reason. His twitter account is @peterboghossian.

Ed Brayton is the media relations coordinator for the Foundation beyond Belief, cofounder and past president of Michigan Citizens for Science, and a member of the advisory board of the Center for Inquiry—Michigan. His forthcoming book is to be titled *By Their Love: Violence in Defense of Christian Privilege*.

Dr. Richard Carrier has a doctorate in ancient history from Columbia University and is the author of many books including *Sense and Goodness without God* (2005), *Proving History* (2012), and *On the Historicity of Jesus* (2014), along with many other chapters and essays. Visit him online at www.richard-carrier.info.

Dr. Veronica Drantz earned a doctorate in animal physiology and has taught science to medical professionals most of her life. She founded and directed Chicago's first college degree program in electroneurodiagnostic technology. Currently she is on the faculty of a doctoral anesthesia program in which she has taught physiology and related sciences for forty years.

Dr. David Eller earned a doctorate from Boston University in anthropology and teaches anthropology in Denver, Colorado. He has written two textbooks titled *Violence and Culture: A Cross-Cultural and Interdisciplinary Approach* (2005) and *Introducing Anthropology of Religion: Culture to the Ultimate* (2007). He has published two books on atheism, *Natural Atheism* (2004) and *Atheism Advanced* (2008). His most recent work represents the culmination of twenty years of research on religion and violence: *Cruel Creeds, Virtuous Violence: Religious Violence across Culture and History* (2010).

Annie Laurie Gaylor is the cofounder and copresident of the Freedom from Religion Foundation. She founded, edited, and published the *Feminist Connection*, a monthly advocacy newspaper, from 1980 to1985. She has written two books, *Woe To The Women: The Bible Tells Me So* (1981) and *Betrayal of Trust: Clergy Abuse of Children* (1988). Her anthology *Women without Superstition: No Gods, No Masters* (1997) is the first collection of the writings of historic and contemporary women freethinkers.

Dr. Harriet Hall, also known as "The SkepDoc," earned a doctorate from the University of Washington School of Medicine, served twenty years in the US Air Force, and retired as a full colonel. She wrote about her experiences as a woman in three male-dominated fields (medicine, aviation, and the military) in a memoir titled *Women Aren't Supposed to Fly* (2008). She writes about "complementary and alternative medicine," science, quackery, and critical thinking. She is a contributing editor to both *Skeptic* and *Skeptical Inquirer* magazines, and is a member of the Executive Council for the Committee for Skeptical Inquiry. She is coauthor of the textbook *Consumer Health: A Guide to Intelligent Decisions* (2012).

Robert Green Ingersoll (1833–1899) was the foremost orator and political speechmaker of late nineteenth-century America. He bitterly opposed the religious right of his day. He was an early popularizer of Charles Darwin and a tireless advocate of science and reason. He argued for the rights of women and African Americans. For more, see Susan Jacoby, *The Great Agnostic: Robert Ingersoll and American Freethought* (New Haven, CT: Yale University Press, 2013). The Ingersoll Times is an indexed website containing his speeches and writings (http://www.theingersolltimes.com/).

Dr. James A. Lindsay earned a doctorate in mathematics and a degree in physics. He is the author of *God Doesn't; We Do: Only Humans Can Solve Human Challenges* (2012) and *Dot, Dot, Dot: Infinity Plus God Equals Folly* (2013).

Dr. Ronald A. Lindsay has a law degree from the University of Virginia and earned a doctorate (in bioethics) from Georgetown University. Since 2008 he is the president and CEO of the Center for Inquiry and its affiliates the Council for Secular Humanism and the Committee for Skeptical Inquiry. He has written widely on bioethics issues and is the author of *Future Bioethics: Overcoming Taboos, Myths, and Dogmas* (2008), and *The Necessity of Secularism* (Pitchstone, 2014).

John W. Loftus earned M.A., M.Div., and Th.M. degrees in Philosophy, Theology, and the Philosophy of Religion, the last of which was under William Lane Craig. He also studied in a Ph.D. program at Marquette University for a year and a half in the area of Theology and Ethics. He is the author of *Why I Became an Atheist: A Former Preacher Rejects Christianity* (rev. ed., 2012) and *The Outsider Test for Faith: How to Know Which Religion Is True* (2013). He edited *The Christian Delusion: Why Faith Fails* (2010) and *The End of Christianity* (2011). He has also coauthored, with Dr. Randal Rauser, *God or Godless? One Atheist. One Christian. Twenty Controversial Questions* (2013).

Dr. William R. Patterson earned a doctorate in the International Studies program at Old Dominion University. He has published numerous articles in academic journals on a variety of subjects, including ecohumanism, atheism, and the philosophy of social Darwinism.

Jonathan MS Pearce earned a degree from the University of Leeds, a PGCE from the University of St Mary's, Twickenham, and a Masters in Philosophy from the University of Wales, Trinity St. David. Pearce has written *Free Will? An Investigation into Whether We Have Free Will or Whether He Was Always Going to Write This Book* (2010), *The Little Book of Unholy Questions* (2011), and *The Nativity: A Critical Examination* (2012). Working as a publisher and teacher, he lives in Hampshire, UK, with his partner and twin boys.

Nathan Phelps is the son of Pastor Fred Phelps of the Westboro Baptist Church, who gained infamy from the church's protests at soldiers' funerals around the United States. He was taught his father's extreme version of Calvinism from an early age, accompanied by extreme physical punishments and abuse. Today he lives in Calgary, Alberta, and works as the executive director of the Center for Inquiry. He serves on the board of Recovering from Religion, is a vocal LGBT advocate, and speaks out against the dangers of religion and child abuse.

Dr. Darrel Ray is the founder and chairman of the board of Recovering from Religion, an international organization that assists individuals struggling with the consequences of leaving religion. He is author of the bestselling book *The God Virus: How Religion Infects Our Lives and Culture* (2009) and also *Sex and God: How Religion Distorts Sexuality* (2012). He is director of the Secular Therapy Project, a registry of therapists who are committed to secular methods for people in the secular community.

Dr. Victor J. Stenger is adjunct professor of philosophy at the University of Colorado and emeritus professor of physics at the University of Hawaii. He is a prolific author with twelve critically acclaimed books that interface between physics, cosmology, philosophy, religion, and pseudoscience. His 2007 book *God: The Failed Hypothesis—How Science Shows That God Does Not Exist* was a New York Times bestseller. His latest book, *God and the Atom*, came out in 2013.

Dr. Valerie Tarico earned a doctorate in counseling psychology from the University of Iowa and completed postdoctoral studies at the University of Washington. She is the author of the book *Trusting Doubt: A Former Evangelical Looks at Old Beliefs in a New Light* (2010) and chapters in *The Christian Delusion: Why Faith Fails* (2010) and *The End of Christianity* (2011), both edited by John W. Loftus. She founded WisdomCommons.org and writes regularly for online news and opinion sites including AlterNet and *The Huffington Post*. Her articles can be found at AwayPoint.Wordpress.com.

Dr. Marlene Winell holds a doctorate in human development and family studies from Pennsylvania State University. She was raised in a missionary family and was an avid part of the Jesus Movement before deconverting. Marlene is the author of *Leaving the Fold: A Guide for Former Fundamentalists and Others Leaving Their Religion* (2006). Her services related to recovery from religion and her work on Religious Trauma Syndrome can be found at www.journeyfree.org.